The Traveler

The Traveler

One Man's Quest for Humanity from the South Seas to Revolutionary Paris

ANDREA WULF

Alfred A. Knopf
New York
2026

A BORZOI BOOK
FIRST HARDCOVER EDITION PUBLISHED BY ALFRED A. KNOPF 2026

Originally published by Alfred A. Knopf, a division of
Penguin Random House LLC, 1745 Broadway, New York, NY 10019.

Knopf, Borzoi Books, and the colophon are registered trademarks of
Penguin Random House LLC.

Library of Congress Control Number: 2026937240
ISBN: 978-0-593-80340-0 (hardcover)
ISBN: 978-0-593-80341-7 (ebook)

penguinrandomhouse.com | aaknopf.com

Printed in the United States of America
1st Printing

The authorized representative in the EU for product safety and compliance is
Penguin Random House Ireland, Morrison Chambers, 32 Nassau Street,
Dublin D02 YH68, Ireland, https://eu-contact.penguin.ie.

To Reiner

Man is neither good nor evil by nature; but the circumstances into which fate places him, from his very earliest beginnings, can make anything of him.

George Forster

Contents

PART III
Ambitions

PART IV
Revolutions

Route of Reinhold and George Forster's
Russian Expedition, 1765
N
0 100 200 300 Miles
0 100 200 300 400 500 Kms
NORWAY
SWEDEN
Baltic Sea
St Petersburg
Gdansk
Nassenhuben-
Hochzeit
Königsberg
(Kaliningrad)
Vilnius
Moscow
Volga
RUSSIAN EMPIRE
POLAND
Saratov
Yeruslan
Don
Lake
Elton
Volgograd
Ryn Desert
Volga
HABSBURG
POSSESSIONS
Kalmyk
Steppe
Danube
Black Sea
Caspian Sea
OTTOMAN
EMPIRE

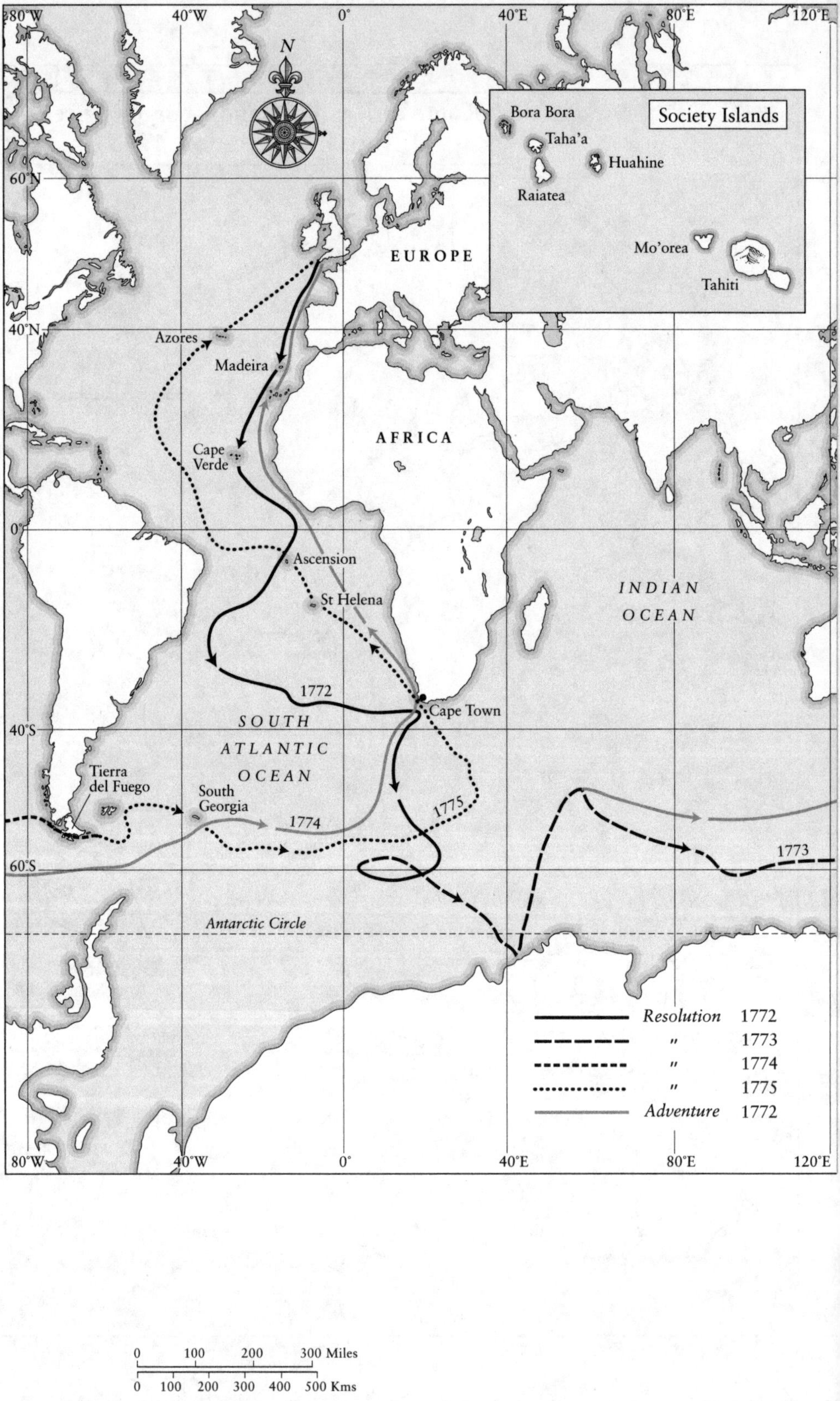

80°W
40°W
0°
40°E
80°E
120°E
N
60°N
40°N
0°
40°S
60°S
Society Islands
Bora Bora
Taha'a
Huahine
Raiatea
Mo'orea
Tahiti
EUROPE
AFRICA
Azores
Madeira
Cape Verde
Ascension
St Helena
INDIAN OCEAN
1772
Cape Town
SOUTH ATLANTIC OCEAN
Tierra del Fuego
South Georgia
1774
1775
1773
Antarctic Circle
Resolution 1772
" 1773
" 1774
" 1775
Adventure 1772
0 100 200 300 Miles
0 100 200 300 400 500 Kms

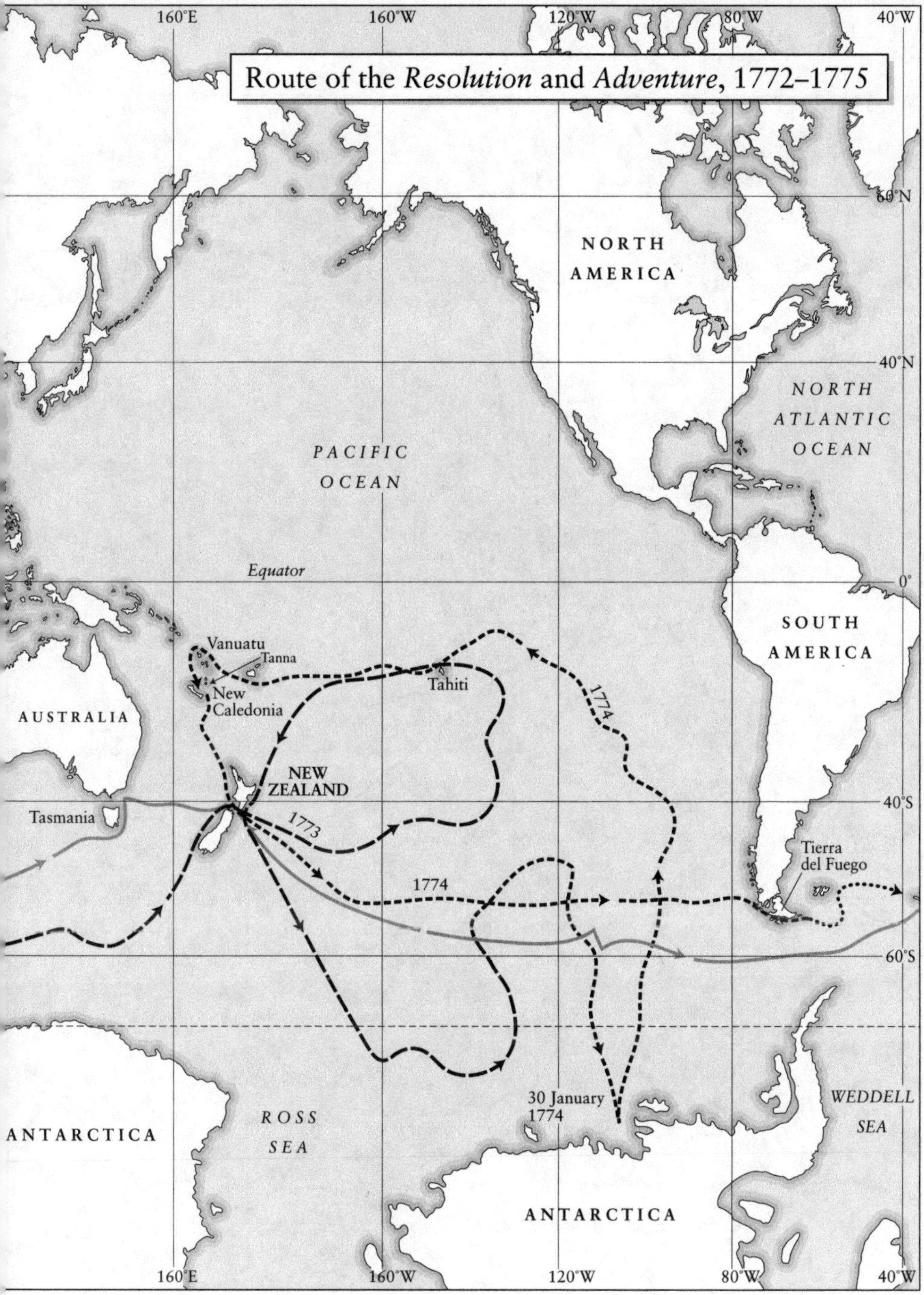

Route of the *Resolution* and *Adventure*, 1772–1775
160°E
160°W
120°W
80°W
40°W
60°N
40°N
0°
40°S
60°S
NORTH AMERICA
NORTH ATLANTIC OCEAN
PACIFIC OCEAN
Equator
SOUTH AMERICA
Vanuatu
Tanna
New Caledonia
Tahiti
AUSTRALIA
NEW ZEALAND
Tasmania
1773
1774
1774
Tierra del Fuego
30 January 1774
ANTARCTICA
ROSS SEA
WEDDELL SEA
ANTARCTICA

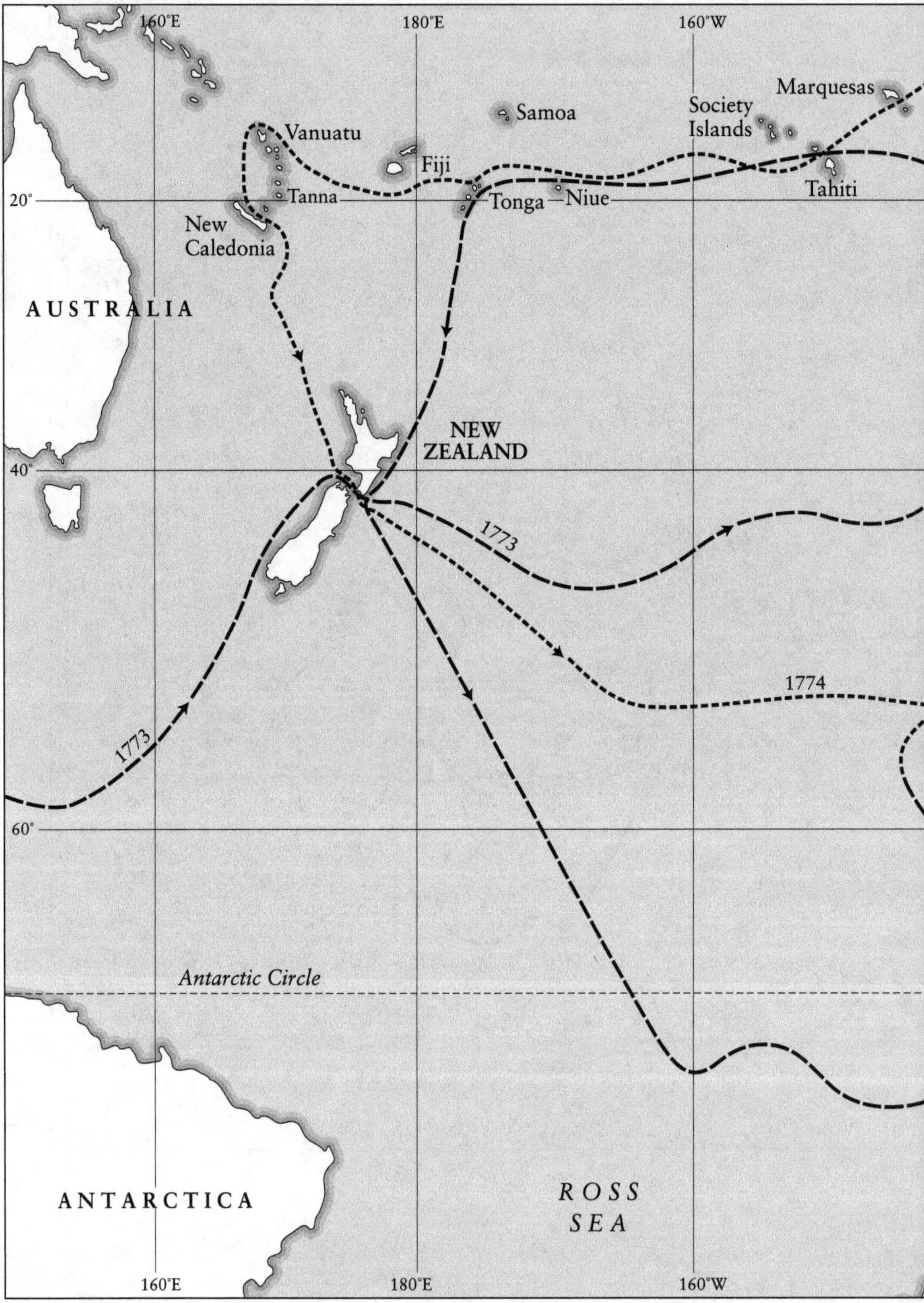
160°E
180°E
160°W
Marquesas
Society Islands
Samoa
Vanuatu
Fiji
Tahiti
20°
Tanna
Tonga
Niue
New Caledonia
AUSTRALIA
NEW ZEALAND
40°
1773
1774
1773
60°
Antarctic Circle
ANTARCTICA
ROSS SEA
160°E
180°E
160°W

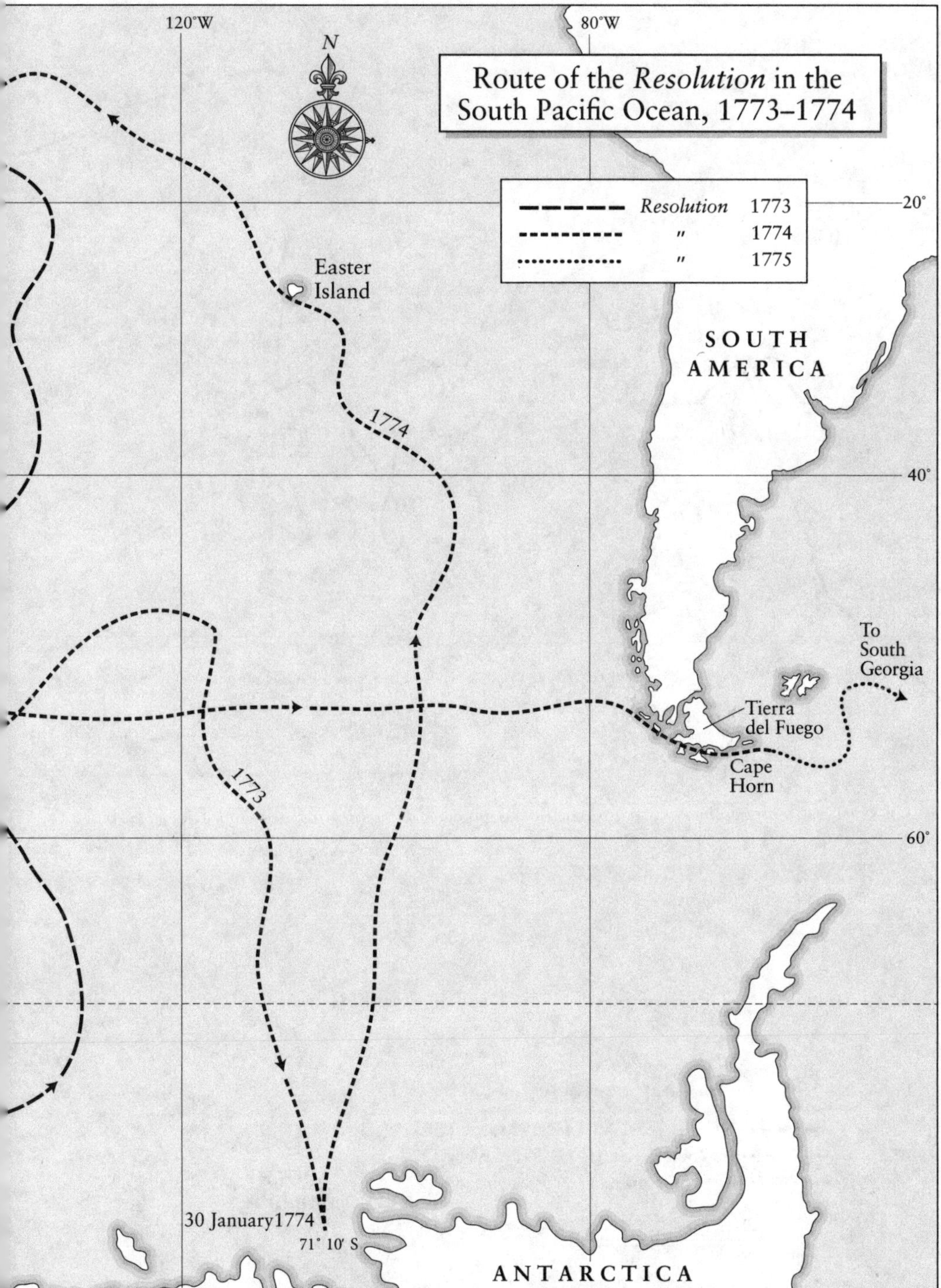
Route of the *Resolution* in the South Pacific Ocean, 1773–1774
Resolution 1773
" 1774
" 1775
N
120°W
80°W
20°
40°
60°
Easter Island
SOUTH AMERICA
1774
1773
To South Georgia
Tierra del Fuego
Cape Horn
30 January 1774
71° 10′ S
ANTARCTICA
120°W
80°W

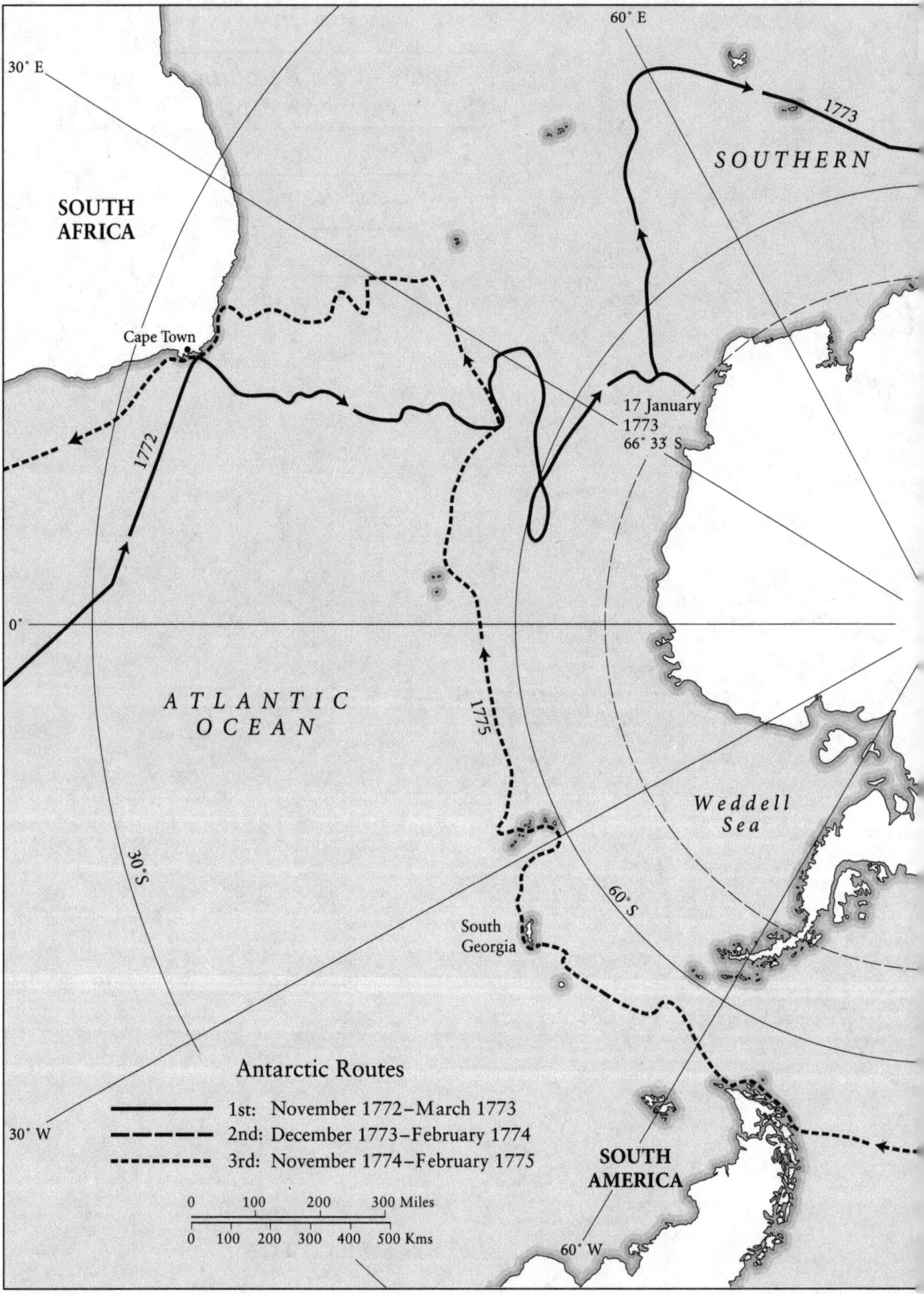
60° E
30° E
1773
SOUTHERN
SOUTH
AFRICA
Cape Town
1772
17 January
1773
66° 33′ S
0°
ATLANTIC
OCEAN
1775
Weddell
Sea
30°S
60°S
South
Georgia
Antarctic Routes
1st: November 1772–March 1773
2nd: December 1773–February 1774
3rd: November 1774–February 1775
30° W
SOUTH
AMERICA
0 100 200 300 Miles
0 100 200 300 400 500 Kms
60° W

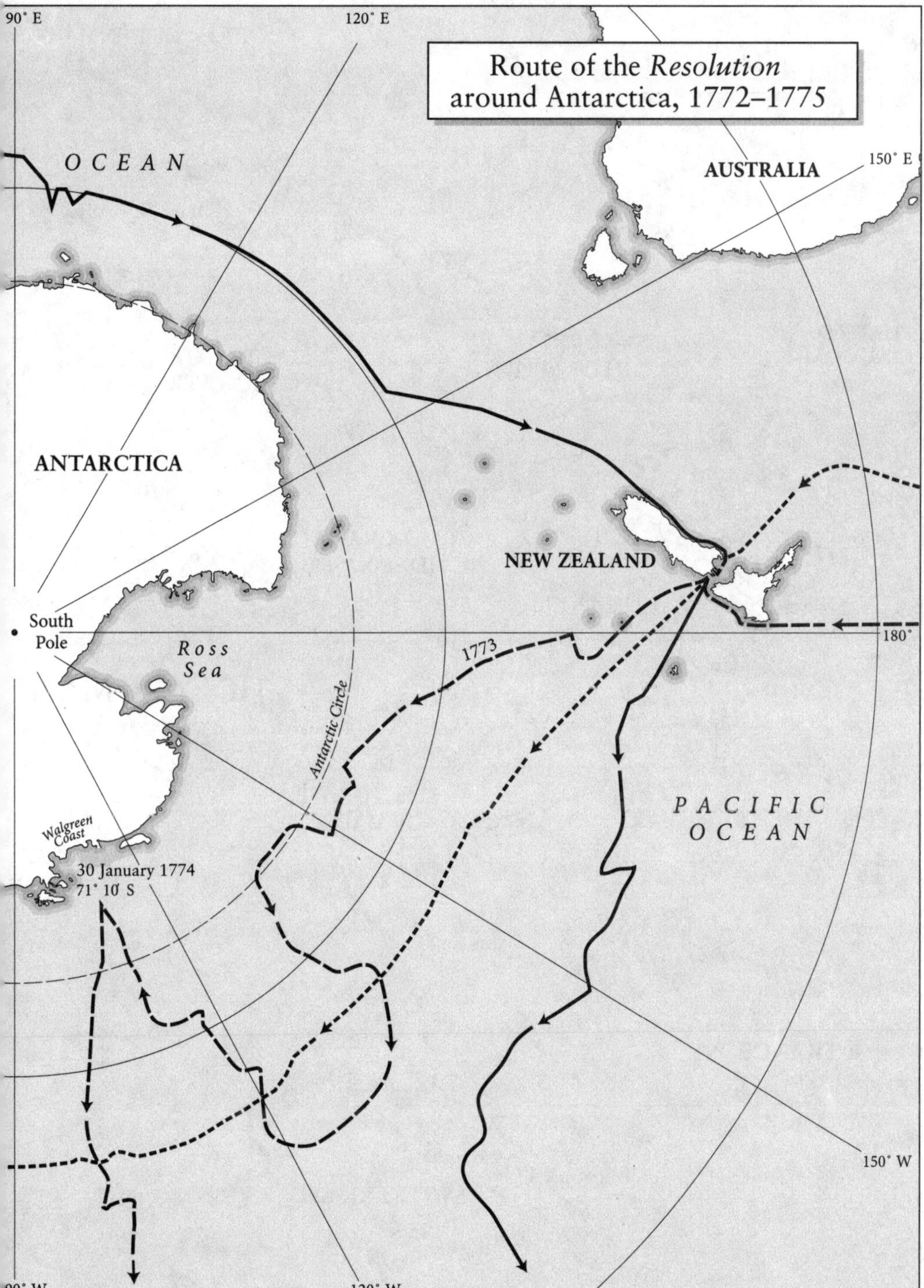

Route of the *Resolution* around Antarctica, 1772–1775
90° E
120° E
150° E
180°
150° W
120° W
90° W
OCEAN
AUSTRALIA
ANTARCTICA
NEW ZEALAND
South Pole
Ross Sea
Antarctic Circle
1773
PACIFIC OCEAN
Walgreen Coast
30 January 1774
71° 10′ S

Europe in the 1780s
N
NORTH SEA
KINGDOM OF DENMARK
HOLSTEIN
Hamburg
Elbe
UNITED KINGDOM
DUTCH REPUBLIC
Amsterdam
The Hague
Rotterdam
ELECTORATE OF HANOVER
Hanover
Weser
Dunkirk
Antwerp
AUSTRIAN NETHERLANDS
Lille
Brussels
Liège
LANDGRAVIATE HESSE-KASSEL
Düsseldorf
Cologne
Bonn
Rhine
Koblenz
Göttingen
Kassel
Fulda
Halle
Weimar
HOLY ROMAN EMPIRE
Frankfurt
Main
Mainz
ELECTORATE OF MAINZ
Meuse
Seine
Paris
Strasbourg
Stuttgart
Rhine
Munich
FRANCE
Neuchâtel
Pontalier
Travers
SWITZERLAND

BALTIC
SEA
Königsberg
(Kaliningrad)
To
Vilnius
Gdansk
Nassenhuben-
Hochzeit
WEST PRUSSIA
KINGDOM OF PRUSSIA
Oder
Vistula
Berlin
Wörlitz
ELECTORATE
OF SAXONY
Leipzig
Freiberg
Dresden
Prague
BOHEMIA
Danube
Vienna
AUSTRIA

Author's Note

Today, George Forster's name is often spelled 'Georg', following German convention – but in this book he is 'George', as this was how his family predominantly wrote his name, along with many of his contemporaries. He was baptized George, and in his father's letters he was consistently called George. Until he left England in 1778, that was also how George himself spelled his name. After that, he used both variations. His wife, Therese, used both as well, as did Alexander von Humboldt and his publisher Karl Spener. He appeared as 'George Forster' on the cover of *A Voyage Round the World* – in both the English and the German editions.

For ease of understanding and consistency, all distances at sea are given in land miles rather than nautical miles (with apologies to my readers who are sailors).

George Forster lived at a time when many of his contemporaries held what we now regard as deeply racist views. To demonstrate how differently he thought, I have quoted their writings because the words themselves reveal how notions of racial hierarchy and prejudice were normalized in Enlightenment thought. George Forster occasionally used the term 'negro' – then the common descriptive term – and it appears in this book within quotations in that historical sense. Its preservation here serves to maintain historical accuracy and illuminate past attitudes, never to endorse them.

Prologue

A gunshot pierced the calm.

Then there was silence, followed by sounds of a commotion. A man came running towards them, but turned and hid in a bush as soon as he saw George Forster and his companion. Other islanders they passed looked at them with disgust. A woman trembled in fear. George couldn't understand what was happening, but as they hurried on, several men waved their arms, urging them on towards the beach. When they finally stepped out of the jungle, they found two islanders on the ground, cradling a third man in their arms. There was blood everywhere. George saw the gunshot wound just under the ribs. '*Marokee*', the two men cried out and it was obvious that it meant 'he is killed'.

An hour earlier, George had walked through the tropical forest, daydreaming. He had thought of the previous two weeks and the many hours he had spent with the islanders. They had shared meals of roasted yams and delicious coconut pies with a crust of baked bananas. They had taught each other words, exchanged names, and tried to communicate by pointing and guessing. Young boys, some no older than five or six, showed off their marksmanship by throwing reeds like spears with perfect accuracy, and the men demonstrated their precision with bow and arrow. In the early evenings just before sunset, the islanders lit fires and the women began to cook. To entertain them, George sang German and English songs and they returned the favour by singing harmonious solemn melodies and playing a flute made of eight reeds. It had been, he said, as if they were all 'members of one great family'.

He had been at peace with the world. It was a warm day but a gentle breeze had tempered the heat as George had meandered across the island. Once in a while the dense vegetation of entangled trees, branches, foliage, climbers and epiphytes had opened up, and he had caught a glimpse of a wide valley surrounded by low hills and numerous

View of Tanna when the *Resolution* anchored there in August 1774

plantations. Open thatched huts with roofs that ran down to the ground on two sides were scattered about and thin columns of smoke rose from cooking fires. One islander hummed as he worked a small field. Some villagers sat in the shade of towering fig trees, while others planted yams or dug the soil with tree branches. Banana trees loaded with golden fruit grew under the dappled light of large palms and straight stalks of sugar cane stood upright in small patches of cultivated ground.

It was 19 August 1774 and this was Tanna, a tropical island in the Vanuatu archipelago in the South Pacific, over 1,000 miles north of New Zealand. Nineteen-year-old George Forster was the assistant naturalist and draughtsman on Captain James Cook's *Resolution*. Two years after leaving England and sailing tens of thousands of miles to the Antarctic Circle, New Zealand, Tahiti, Tonga and other South Pacific islands, they had arrived at Tanna at the beginning of August – the first Europeans to visit the island.

And then the gunshot.

Rushing out onto the beach, George struggled to comprehend what had happened. It was difficult to make sense of the different stories that the *Resolution* crew told him, but apparently the dead man had ignored the warnings of a marine who was guarding the beach. When the *Resolution* had arrived at Tanna, Cook had followed his usual practice and drawn two lines in the sand to mark out an area which the crew would use for landing their dinghies. This line, Cook had tried to explain to the islanders, was a boundary they were not allowed to cross. So when one man had walked towards the line, the marine on guard had pushed him back. Undeterred, the islander had moved forward again, only to be pushed back even harder. He then stumbled but steadied himself and nocked an arrow on his bow. But before he could draw, the marine had pulled the trigger.

George was horrified. 'Instead of making amends at this place for the many rash acts which we had perpetrated at almost every island in our course,' he lamented, 'we had wantonly made it the scene of the greatest cruelty.' Why kill an innocent man for crossing an arbitrary line in the sand? The islander had simply refused to be controlled by a stranger on his own island. But George wasn't surprised, having witnessed how the *Resolution*'s crew treated the indigenous people they had encountered in the previous two years. They used their muskets to intimidate them and several islanders had been killed. Many more had been wounded. The Europeans brought death and disease, George later wrote, and he could only hope that 'the intercourse which has lately subsisted between Europeans and the natives of the South Sea islands may be broken off in time'.

Few Europeans approached indigenous people with such an open mind – most explorers viewed them through a lens of arrogance at best, and with brutal disgust at worst. Across the world they had been enslaved, exploited and murdered. In an era when most Europeans regarded indigenous people as lesser beings – even sometimes as beasts – George Forster's attitude shines out in the darkness of colonial history.

At the time, racism was so deeply ingrained in Western society that even Immanuel Kant, the most famous philosopher of his age, published articles in which he declared Black people to be an inferior race who 'have by nature no feeling that rises above the ridiculous'. George Forster, by contrast, believed all humans equal, and due equal respect. There was good and evil in all societies. The world was neither black and white, he explained, nor clearly divided into virtuous and immoral, but instead was a complex tapestry woven from the many shades of human lives.

A liberal thinker far ahead of his time, he was one of the first to talk about what we now call human rights and believed in the importance of our shared humanity – irrespective of colour, culture or gender. He wrote to his closest friend, Samuel Thomas Soemmerring, 'what is tolerance, of which we are such ardent advocates, if not the coexistence of differing opinions?'

By the time he was in his early twenties, George Forster was celebrated across Europe. Kings, poets, scientists and revolutionaries wanted to meet him and sought his advice. I became curious about him when I was researching and writing *Magnificent Rebels* and the *Invention of Nature*. He was a trusted friend of Caroline Michaelis-Böhmer-Schlegel-Schelling (a protagonist of the former book) and a mentor to Alexander von Humboldt (the subject of the latter). 'I have spent half a century, wherever a restless, eventful life has taken me, telling myself and others what I owe to my teacher and friend Georg Forster,' Humboldt said at the age of eighty-eight in 1858. Any man who was admired by the brilliant Humboldt and the formidable Caroline was worth investigating, but it was George Forster's own voice that pulled me into this story. His description of the murder on the beach in Tanna, for example, made me wonder how someone who was brought up in a society pervaded by racism was able to accept other cultures with such an unbiased mind. And in his letters to his wife, he reveals himself to be more progressive than many men today. 'So many men seem to be under the delusion that nothing is common sense but their own intuitions,' he wrote during their courtship, 'I don't know this unfair difference between the sexes.' Today he would be called a feminist and I wanted to understand how he had been able to transcend the conventions of his times in this respect also.

George Forster's letters portray a man who was honest with himself and the wider world around him. He was a compassionate man who found joy and inspiration in others. 'I thank God that there is such a delicious thing as human love in this world,' he said, 'it lifts us up; it chains us to each other, no matter how distant we are; it is the most comforting, happiest feeling in the world!' There is an immediacy and a directness to his words that I have rarely encountered in any previous research. He despised hypocrisy and was vocal about his opinions – 'nothing is so irresistible as the truth'. Unlike most men of his age, he was open about his emotions, admitting to sadness and weakness – 'aching feelings of my loneliness', 'I also feel voids in my heart' – his emotions raw on the page. Who was this eighteenth-century man who seemed too modern for his time?

I began my search for George Forster in libraries and archives through many thousands of letters, pages and words in order to uncover his thoughts, ideas and daily life – but because he was a traveller, I also packed my bags and followed his footsteps through Europe and the South Pacific. I explored European cities with old maps and engravings, trying to work out where he had walked, lived and worked – but I also ventured further afield.

At one point, I found myself sailing towards the crushing surf of Tahiti's reef in a small outrigger sailing canoe – far too close for my comfort but it felt entirely appropriate because the *Resolution* was almost shipwrecked here. I hiked for several days along Queen Charlotte Sound at the northern part of New Zealand's South Island to absorb the natural world and experience the place where George Forster had walked in 1773. I was unprepared for the mesmerizing otherworldliness of the forests and it made me realize just how strange it must have been for him 250 years ago. I spent five magical days in Dusky Sound at the southern tip of New Zealand's South Island – a place so wild and remote that the landscape is essentially unchanged since he stayed there. It was cold, wet and magnificent. I saw the stumps of the trees that the *Resolution* crew had felled to set up their observatory tent, and at the small natural harbour where they had anchored I found the actual tree that they had used as their gangway – still leaning almost horizontally over the water, just as William Hodges, the expedition artist, had painted it. Unbelievable, really, that it still exists. During these moments time and space collided for me.

Everything in *The Traveler* is based on George Forster's works, diaries and letters, and those of his contemporaries – friends, family and foes. Nothing is invented or imagined, but travelling to the places which shaped George's early life helped me to understand him. It also reminded me how much of a nomad he was, never truly at home anywhere, but one of the reasons why he so willingly accepted the 'otherness' of others.

He was a traveller – in body and mind – a crosser of borders, a dreamer of worlds, a breaker of boundaries, a seeker of truth, a painter of words and a believer in humanity. He was a traveller without roots to anchor him to a place, to his clod of earth – a lack of belonging that enabled him to think more expansively and be more tolerant than most of his contemporaries. He subscribed to no particular philosophical school or ideology, nor did he feel that he belonged to a nation. Unbound by place, people or establishment, he was able to unfetter himself from prejudice. All he wanted, he said, was 'to throw more light upon the nature of the human mind'.

The observations he made as a young man on the *Resolution* voyage painted a portrait of the world as one of connections rather than divisions – and at the heart of *The Traveler* is George Forster's quest to find what holds us together rather than what sets us apart. There was unity, he said, behind this 'beautiful manifestation of the variety' of peoples and cultures. He didn't write from the lofty heights of an ivory tower but as an explorer and with a deep love for humankind, grounding his ideas in observation and experience but also in feelings. He challenged some of the greatest thinkers of his age – Rousseau, Kant and the Comte du Buffon – and was feted across Europe. He embraced the ideals of the French Revolution wholeheartedly and became one of Germany's leading revolutionaries. 'One is either for absolute freedom or for absolute tyranny,' he declared, 'there is nothing in between.' His dream was nothing less than a new reality, a hopeful future free of despotism, ruled by equality and liberty, rather than kings and queens.

Some 250 years ago, George Forster began his search for our common humanity, urging that we – as a species – share the right to equality and freedom. No matter who he encountered – whether Māori, Russian, Tahitian, French, Tongan, English, German or Easter Islander – he was aware 'of the rights which I possess in common with every individual among them'. People might look different, or have different cultures and value systems, but in essence we're all the same.

The variety and unity of humankind is like music, George Forster wrote, and our vast diversity 'brings all individual chords to a harmonious composition'. It is our morality – how we treat others – that makes us human. The pursuit of happiness alone was not enough, he said, for 'the real guide to how we should live is *human dignity*.'

This is his story.

PART I

Setting Out

I

'My little travelling companion'

Childhood and Russia: 1754–1766

George Forster was ten when he went on his first expedition.

He was a slender boy, small for his age, but what he lacked in physical strength he made up for in tenacity during the five months that he and his father travelled through Russia. In charge of collecting and identifying plants, the ten-year-old would wander off alone, eyes wide open, searching for new discoveries – sometimes climbing trees, at others keeping his head near the ground to study the vegetation with a magnifying glass. When he returned to the tent with full bags, he would press the samples he had found between paper, carefully arranging blossoms and leaves so that he could classify them later. Soon his collection had risen to 700 specimens.

While other children sat on hard benches in orderly rows at school, learning by rod and rote, George found himself galloping on small Kalmyk horses across the Russian steppes and wading through marshes on the banks of the Volga river. He watched a violent wildfire race across the vast grasslands to the east, its ravenous flames consuming everything in its path. He remembered the terror he felt that day for the rest of his life. Instead of studying arithmetic or conjugating Latin verbs, he observed flocks of black herons, wild boars and wolves, and huge Bactrian camels used by the nomadic Kalmyks as pack animals, which evoked the stories of the *Arabian Nights* and Ali Baba. He met Muslim Tatar traders along the Volga, fierce Cossack warriors from the open steppes to the east who wore sheepskin hats, baggy trousers and colourful caftans, and German settlers so destitute that they lived in earth dugouts in the ground. Near today's Russian border with

Kazakhstan, he marvelled at Lake Elton, a huge shallow salt lake with a shoreline encrusted in a thick white layer like snow, against water which algae had turned blood red. And in the Ryn Desert just north of the Caspian Sea, he felt piercing winds whip across the dunes, as wild as the land itself.

Russia was on a different scale from the flat gentle countryside where George had been raised near Gdansk, in today's Poland. Everything here was vaster and emptier. The skies, lakes and land were bigger, the distances immense, and the weather extreme. He feasted his eyes and tasted new foods. He ate wild asparagus, drank fermented mare's milk – 'of a nauseous or disagreeable Taste' – and enjoyed the refreshing juice of bog cranberries mixed with water and honey after the long dusty days on horseback.

This was not like learning from the books he loved. He could see, smell and feel that he had entered another world. The food had a different flavour, the languages were unfamiliar, and the people looked nothing like those at home. In Russia, he absorbed a new and very foreign country for the first time. At the age of ten, he became a traveller.

He was born on 27 November 1754 in a hamlet in Hochzeit-Nassenhuben – today's Mokry Dwór in Poland – a parish some six miles south-east of Gdansk in a region that would soon become part

View of the Volga, note the camels in the foreground

of the Kingdom of Prussia.* A sickly baby, George had been fed bread and diluted milk but gained little weight during the first months of his life. He had remained small and prone to illness, and his parents feared for his life. At some point during those early childhood years, he contracted smallpox and his face was scarred for the rest of his life – but he survived and grew up to be a shy, curious child. The first of seven children, he was more content alone in the meadows and forests, or with his nose in books, than with people. His family home was a simple single-storey building with damp and cramped rooms surrounded by large trees in the garden. There were no hills or valleys, just fields and a wide horizon – a flat landscape with a river that flooded regularly.

In the early evenings, while the family ate dinner, young George would wander around the room, looking at the book spines on his father's shelves. Gold letters shone against the dark leather and George would run his fingers along them, asking how to pronounce the German, Latin and French titles. It wasn't long before he learned to read. Home schooled by his father Johann Reinhold Forster, a Lutheran pastor, George absorbed the world around him and everything his

Nassenhuben, the parish in which the Forster family lived

* Until the First Partition of Poland in 1772, Hochzeit-Nassenhuben belonged to Royal Prussia – a semi-autonomous region under the Polish Crown that preserved its own local customs, with German as the predominant language in urban areas. After the partition, it was incorporated into the newly established province of West Prussia, governed by the Kingdom of Prussia.

father taught. He was forever scrutinizing and probing, but it was never enough. He wanted to know the names of the beetles crawling in the grass and to understand the songs of the birds in the trees. He pestered his family with so many questions about plants, insects, birds and fish that his father bought natural-history books so that he could explain the Linnean classification system to the boy.

His father often took the classroom outside. Armed with fishing rods, guns, bags for plants and nets to catch insects, they explored the countryside on long walks around their hamlet and Gdansk. Despite the siblings who followed him, George seemed to be the only child who interested his father. But Reinhold Forster was an unpredictable man. Kind and loving one moment, he was also easily provoked, teaching one day with patience and another with the whip. He was proud of his son but also expected him to be better and cleverer than others. Above all he demanded obedience.

'I had no say in what I would have liked to do, to choose the circumstances of how I would appear in the world,' George recalled. 'I was born, raised, and entirely unnoticed and through no fault of my own, my thinking was given a direction; and behold! Now I'm thinking like this and not differently . . . I couldn't and wasn't allowed to change these circumstances and so I bowed my head to fate.' And although he only

Reinhold Forster

attended formal school for a few months in St Petersburg at the age of eleven, his father's love of knowledge and adventure gave George a better education than most boys would ever receive. At the same time, Reinhold's volatility and quarrelsome personality affected his son. A pattern was set. Observing how his father fought, shouted and fell out with friends and strangers alike, George learned to be happy by making others happy.

Reinhold's own life had been overshadowed by a demanding father. He had never wanted to be a pastor. As a young man, he had longed to study natural history and ancient languages, and if not those at least medicine, but he had been forced into theology by his father. In early 1754, at the age of twenty-four, Reinhold had married his cousin Justina Elisabeth and exactly nine months later to the day, George was born. When his isolation in the backwaters of Prussia became too painful, Reinhold reached out to the world with his pen, forging connections with scholars in Germany and across Europe. Distracted by his fascination for science and antiquity, he often neglected his parish duties and left preparing his sermons to the last minute. As he worked through Saturday nights, fuelled by coffee, Reinhold would finish in the early hours and then often fall asleep at the pulpit while his congregation sang hymns. Justina Elisabeth had quickly learned that her husband had ambitions extending far beyond their life in Hochzeit-Nassenhuben. While she bore seven children in nine years (one died in infancy),* trying to feed and clothe them on Reinhold's modest salary, he spent his small inheritance after his father's death on books, accumulating a library of 2,500 fine volumes. George grew up with a father who believed that science, art, and a scholarly exchange with other learned men was more important than the daily practicalities of home life.

George Forster was born into a world electrified by ideas – a period we now call the Enlightenment, or *Aufklärung* in German – and a time when philosophers, scientists and writers believed that reason illuminated the

* George's siblings were Carl, or Charles (16 February 1756), Virginia (10 July 1757), Antonia (19 September 1758), Wilhelmina (12 February 1760), Wilhelm, or William (12 December 1763) and later, while George and his father were travelling, his youngest sister Justina (22 June 1765) was born. Given the gap of more than three years between Wilhelmina and Wilhelm, it's likely that the baby that died was born in 1761 or 1762

path towards human progress. Knowledge was no longer the privilege of a few cloistered scholars or the guarded secrets of the Church, but instead had become a shared pursuit for those who dared to ask questions. The intellectual landscape of this new age had been shaped by the Scientific Revolution of the previous century, when Isaac Newton applied mathematics to the natural world, revealing a universe governed by discoverable natural laws. The authority of demonstrable knowledge was proclaimed and his work inspired generations to apply reason and observation not just to the heavens, but to every aspect of human life.

Across Europe, thinkers were stirred by a sense of possibility, advocating self-determination and independent enquiry. At the close of the seventeenth century, the English philosopher John Locke urged that we 'made use of our own Thoughts'. Instead of blindly following doctrine, tradition or the opinions of others, he encouraged people to observe the world and come to their own conclusions. Those who didn't question accepted truths and norms, he argued, could be more easily manipulated and were not in control of their own destiny. Sixty years later, in 1751, the Scottish philosopher David Hume explained that truth didn't reside in abstract theories. As an empiricist, he believed that no preconceived concepts or innate ideas existed in our mind but that all knowledge came from experience. It was the beginning of a revolution of the mind. Writers, scholars and scientists opened their eyes to the world around them, seeking understanding through systematic investigation, rational thought and empirical evidence.

In France, Diderot and D'Alembert were compiling their monumental *Encyclopédie*, in which they defined a philosopher as someone not bound by religion, tradition or authority, but one brave enough to think for himself. 'Reason determines the philosopher,' they wrote. Also in France, Montesquieu's *The Spirit of the Laws* dissected the anatomy of power and exposed its dangers. This wry observer of men and institutions understood the fragility of liberty and introduced a radical new idea: the separation of powers. The legislative, executive and judicial branches, each acting independently, would check one another to prevent tyranny. Montesquieu imagined a nation not in the hands of a single sovereign but a republic governed by laws, a careful choreography of checks and balances – an idea that would influence the revolutions in America and France.

But the Enlightenment wasn't confined to books and lofty theories. It spilled over into streets and coffee houses, into the drawing rooms of salons and reading societies – vibrant centres of discussions where the latest books, pamphlets and newspapers were read and debated. Literacy rates rose, the book trade expanded, and despite censorship, ideas began to circulate more freely. Inventions from telescopes to lightning rods and new agricultural implements gave people the conviction that they could control nature, fuelling the confidence of the age. In 1753, a year before George's birth, the Swedish botanist Carl Linnaeus introduced a standardized system for naming plants, and two years later Samuel Johnson finished his groundbreaking *Dictionary of the English Language.* Language, knowledge and nature were ordered into neat categories based on what could be observed. It was a time brimming with optimism and curiosity, when people thought that they could grasp the workings of the universe and improve the human condition. Soon, the German philosopher Immanuel Kant would encapsulate the spirit of the time in a single phrase: '*Sapere aude* – Dare to know!' In his influential essay 'An Answer to the Question: What is Enlightenment?', Kant declared that the courage to think for oneself was the very essence of Enlightenment philosophy.

This was the world that George entered, guided by his father. They spoke German at home but 'Germany' as a unified nation did not yet exist. Instead, the German territories were part of the sprawling Holy Roman Empire, made up of more than 1,500 individual states, ranging from tiny principalities to powerful nations such as Prussia and Austria, which competed for influence, territory and dominance. It was a region of political fragmentation set within an age of global rivalry, as Europe's great powers expanded their overseas empires, carving up the world for profit, and in the process annihilating ancient cultures and peoples. Explorations and the transatlantic slave trade fuelled Europe's economies as Africans were enslaved and shipped to the Americas to work on plantations and in mines. As gold, silver, tobacco, sugar, coffee and spices were transported across the oceans,

Europeans maintained that they were repaying the world by bringing civilization to it.

But there was also upheaval in Europe. In November 1755, exactly one year after George's birth, a violent earthquake, followed by a tsunami and fire, almost completely destroyed Lisbon, one of Europe's largest and wealthiest cities – shaking Enlightenment belief in a world governed by reason and the benevolence of God. No matter how much scientists and thinkers understood, or how many inventions had made life more efficient, nature could not be mastered. 'Come, ye philosophers, who cry, "All's well", And contemplate the ruin of a world,' the French philosopher Voltaire lamented in his *Poème sur le désastre de Lisbonne*. Six months later, the even more destructive Seven Years' War began, the first truly global conflict with its origins in familiar divisions between Prussia and Austria, and the gathering imperial contest between Britain and France.

Britain and Prussia were allied on one side, and France, Russia, Austria and Sweden on the other. Political power was at stake but so too were Europe's commercial ventures abroad: the colonies in North America, sugar production in the West Indies, the slave trade in West Africa, and the possession of India. Battles were fought as far apart as the forests of Saxony, the wild Ohio River Valley in North America and the Rio Negro in South America, as well as in India, the Caribbean and Manila. In November 1758, just as George turned four, the war even reached the rural seclusion of Hochzeit-Nassenhuben, when Russian troops allied to Austria against Prussia set up camp around Gdansk.

By the end of the war in 1763, maps had been redrawn. Overtaken by Great Britain as a major colonial power, France was no longer Europe's most dominant force. The French lost their foothold in North America when they had to cede the Louisiana Territory to the Spanish and their colony in Canada to the British.* France kept its sugar islands in Guadeloupe and Martinique but had to retreat from India. Spain lost Florida

* In 1763 the French relinquished the Louisiana Territory to Spain but received it back in 1800. Three years later, the United States purchased the vast tract – more than 800,000 square miles that stretched west from the Mississippi to the Rocky Mountains and from Canada in the north to the Gulf of Mexico in the south – from France for $15,000,000.

to England and Prussia's strength grew, challenging Austria's influence in Europe. Around one million people had died during the war and hunger stalked the continent. Fields and harvests had been destroyed, cities bombarded, and punitive taxes raised to pay for troops and for the war damage.

That was why thousands of war-weary Germans decided to avoid starvation by accepting Catherine the Great's invitation to settle along the sparsely populated banks of the Volga river in the Russian Empire. In early 1765, Reinhold Forster learned from the Russian representative in Gdansk that Catherine the Great was looking for a German-speaking inspector to investigate the settlements. Marooned in the rural hinterland of Gdansk and with dreams too big for the constraints of a pastor's life, Reinhold wanted to travel and applied immediately. Though he often offended and upset others, he was also charismatic. Well-read and curious, he could be charming when he chose to – his deep warm voice adding to the illusion of a kind and earnest man. The Russians were soon convinced and by early March 1765, Reinhold had received his expenses and prepared his departure. He had also decided to take the opportunity to collect botanical specimens and make natural-history observations both at the Volga and the steppes hundreds of miles to the east, aiming to win the approval of European scholars. Determined to make a mark, Reinhold never doubted his abilities – nor those of his eldest son.

Ten-year-old George, he resolved, would be 'my little travelling companion', responsible for the botanical work. George had no choice in the matter but was swept up in his father's excitement. They were going on an expedition – an adventure far from the small world in Hochzeit-Nassenhuben. George's mother, Justina Elisabeth, was left behind, pregnant and in charge of five young children under the age of nine.

Father and son set out on 5 March 1765, travelling more than 1,600 miles via St Petersburg and Moscow to Saratov, a garrison town on the western banks of the Volga which was the administrative centre for the Germans who had settled along the river to the south. Shortly after Catherine the Great had ascended the throne, the German-born empress had advertised her offer to settlers in newspapers and sent recruiting agents across the German states. In a bid to increase agricultural production, she wanted to attract hard-working German farmers and peasants to wrest fields from the wilderness along the Volga. She had promised free land, no taxes for ten years, a cottage for each household, fertile soils, freedom of religion, interest-free loans, local self-government and no military service. The first settlers had arrived in 1764 and quickly realized that life by the Volga was not as golden as her pledges. To silence the discouraging rumours, Catherine wanted a detailed report from Reinhold on the living conditions in the settlements.

In Saratov, Reinhold and George were given an escort of four Cossacks and a soldier – probably for surveillance as much as for protection. The local governor was not keen to have a prying foreigner moving freely through his region. At the end of May, they began their journey south, some 250 miles along the mountainous western bank of the Volga to Tsaritsyn (later Stalingrad, today Volgograd), visiting six newly established colonies en route. This was frontier land, previously home only to small groups of Cossacks and Kalmycks. Brown bears and wolves roamed through the settlements and few provisions had been made for the German colonists. It soon became obvious to the Forsters that the rumours had not been false or malicious but an accurate portrait of the settlers' day-to-day lives.

Over the next few weeks, as George and his father slowly made their way south, they saw just how tough the settlers' existence really was. Conditions were abysmal, with people starving and dying from fevers. It didn't help that the region was overseen by a corrupt governor who ruled arbitrarily, imposing taxes that had never been agreed with the central authorities and fabricating reports for the government in St Petersburg. When the first settlers had arrived the previous year, they discovered that there weren't even houses or timber as Catherine's advertisement had announced. Not only had the promised houses, seeds, ploughs and cattle never materialized, but Russian officials and soldiers intimidated the settlers into not reporting their grievances to St Petersburg. Finding themselves in the wilderness with few tools and no shelter, the Germans had resorted to digging large holes in the ground which they covered with branches, brushwood and soil. More trench than habitation, 'these graves of the living', as they called their new homes, were windowless hovels in which they couldn't even stand. The soils may have been fertile but the climate here was hellish with long freezing winters, torrential spring floods, and brutally hot summers. 'So this is the paradise,' one settler said, 'that the Russian recruiters promised us.'

While Reinhold interviewed the Germans, taking notes about the lack of basic necessities and complaints about the governor's ruthless rule, George watched and listened. It was impossible for the impressionable young boy not to be moved by the stories they heard from hungry children and emaciated parents. Along the banks of the Volga, George saw the harsh reality of inequality and despotism – themes that would obsess him throughout his life. This was the beginning of – as he once described it – 'my inclination to observe people's hearts'. The abject poverty of the German settlements along the Volga made such an impression that, twenty years later, he would tell his wife of his disgust for the governor of Saratov – 'a wicked, despotic and selfish man', George said, 'who kept the colonies in servile dependence to plunder them and fill his own coffers'.

The past shapes the present and future, George would say, for 'everything that happens is determined by what came before and is connected to what follows'. The seeds of the beliefs that shaped George Forster's life were planted in Russia.

He never returned home. Almost eight months after they had set out from Hochzeit-Nassenhuben, George and his father arrived in St Petersburg, at the end of October 1765, to present their findings. They had travelled more than 3,800 miles. From the settlements on the Volga's left bank, they had crossed and covered hundreds of miles east across the vast steppes to the blood-red waters of Lake Elton, and beyond to the sand dunes of the Ryn Desert, to collect plants and observe animals. At Lake Elton they had even discovered a new species of bird, a coal-black lark (*Melanocorypha yeltoniensis*) that sang in a series of drawn-out whistles – 'very fat in autumn and of an exquisite Taste,' Reinhold wrote without a trace of irony. They had seen otters swimming in the rivers, bought coins and ancient manuscripts from the local Tatar merchants, and learned that the most delicious caviar came from the Beluga sturgeon in the Volga and the Caspian Sea. By the end of their journey, they had described and classified more than two hundred plants (although five hundred of George's carefully collected specimens were destroyed during a river crossing), twenty-three mammals and sixty-four birds, as well as numerous reptiles, insects and fish.

This was also the first time that George had been away from his mother and siblings, alone with his father's terrible temper. Reinhold was never going to be an easy travelling companion, but matters became serious when at one point he turned against their Cossack escorts. All his life George had seen how his father criticized, blamed and complained about others. But this was different because there was no patient wife here to calm Reinhold's outbursts. There is no record what sparked his anger – a disagreement, an offensive word or exhaustion – whatever it was, he was so furious that he aimed his loaded rifle at the heavily armed men. George could do nothing but watch the drama unfold, caught between the terror of Reinhold's spiralling aggression and the looming danger of the Cossacks' retaliation. Then there was a sharp bang. Reinhold had fired the gun, wounding the interpreter. The Cossacks could have shot Reinhold but they held back. Perhaps the injury wasn't serious, or more likely Reinhold's commission from Catherine the Great protected him. Nonetheless the confrontation had put father and son in grave danger. They were lucky there were no further consequences.

But trouble was waiting for them in St Petersburg. The Chancellery for the Guardianship of Foreigners, the government department that dealt with the settlers, was not pleased with Reinhold Forster's critical report about the living conditions along the Volga and the accusations he had levelled against the governor of Saratov. Unfortunately for Reinhold, a cousin of the governor worked at the Chancellery. He soon discredited the entire report and the Russian government refused to pay Reinhold's fee. For Reinhold this was clearly an anxious moment, but for his part George went for the first time in his life to school, learning Latin, French, Russian, maths, geography, history and penmanship. Instead of being taught by his impulsive father, he was now in a classroom with boys his own age – children from merchants and professors – at the German Petrischool for Languages, the Arts and Sciences.

His father was growing increasingly frustrated. When the Russians finally offered half of what Reinhold had expected as his fee, he was insulted and rejected the lower payment, threatening to publish a letter about the settlers' dismal conditions in foreign newspapers which would discourage any prospective candidates. He never had a chance against Catherine the Great's government. In August 1766, after months of fighting and with neither side willing to compromise, Reinhold decided to move to London – without receiving any renumeration at all, because he stubbornly continued to turn down the smaller fee.

Why London? Why England? 'We are almost Englishmen,' Reinhold claimed, citing the Forster family's descent from an ancient Scottish family and particularly from an ancestor named George Forster, a Yorkshire Royalist who had fled to Prussia in the 1640s during the First English Civil War. Proud of his British roots, Reinhold had therefore baptized his son 'George', rather than 'Georg' as is common in German. He had always felt a connection to the country that many Germans regarded as the birthplace of the Enlightenment and free thought. 'So I went to the land of freedom, where work is rewarded,' Reinhold later told a friend.

Since 1689, following the Glorious Revolution of 1688, England had been a constitutional monarchy with a powerful Parliament. Across Europe it was regarded as a seat of liberty. The English prided themselves on their freedom of religion and press (at least compared to other countries) as well as a justice system based on the law of *habeas corpus*, which ensured that a person couldn't be imprisoned without trial or explanation. With most of Europe still in the firm hand of absolutism, England's constitutional monarchy and celebration of liberty was so strikingly different that one German visitor had felt 'himself transported to another planet'. Numerous German artists, scientists and musicians, the composer Georg Friedrich Händel and astronomer William Herschel among them, had made their home in England.

Reinhold Forster wrote to inform his wife that he was taking George to London. Justina Elisabeth and the now six other children were to remain in Hochzeit-Nassenhuben. Soon after, the church authorities lost patience and installed a new parish priest, ordering Justina Elisabeth and the children to leave the rectory. With neither money nor support, she was forced to move the family in with relatives in Gdansk and began selling her husband's books to buy food.

2

'We are almost Englishmen'

Early Years in England: 1766–1772

When they stepped off the ship in London on 4 October 1766, father and son had only 3½ guineas – just enough to pay for a month's lodging, no food included. Britain's wealth taunted them. As they walked the narrow streets, eleven-year-old George would have seen hats, gaudy ribbons, glittering jewellery and framed maps in the large shop windows. Hundreds of candles illuminated clocks, bolts of shiny silk and polished silverware. Inside the shops impeccably dressed gentlemen and elegant ladies with corseted waists and rustling petticoats emptied their purses at the counters.

Three years earlier, at the end of 1763, Britain had risen from the ashes of the devasting Seven Years' War as the most powerful empire in Europe, eclipsing Spain and France. Fuelled by the colonies' riches, London was the heart of one of the world's largest economies. The Thames was congested with ships that brought tea and silk from China, sugar and coffee from the West Indies, spices from the East Indies and corn, cotton and tobacco from the American colonies. In the numerous coffee houses, merchants conducted their business and customers read the many newspapers published in England. The coffee may have been served weak – 'an atrocious mess of brown water', as one tourist observed – but liquors were enjoyed strong.

Their first few days were busy. They immediately went to Carl Gottfried Woide, an old classmate from Reinhold's school days in Berlin and now a pastor at the German Reformed Church in London. Woide generously organized lodgings for them in the house he was renting in Denmark Street in Soho, enquired at the British Museum if there was a

View of London and the Thames

vacant position for Reinhold (there wasn't), lent him money, and introduced him to friends and scholars.

George's new home town was boisterous, frenzied and dirty. One million people lived in the British metropolis and every time he stepped outside, the boy was confronted with carriages, chaises and carts that clogged the streets. Porters delivering goods and carrying luggage manoeuvred through the crowds, pushing and crying, 'By your leave', and moving so fast that they regularly knocked pedestrians to the ground. Fiddlers played at street corners and watchmen called out the hour of the day. Pickpockets his own age wove through the teeming streets, trying to steal a few coins, and young girls sold flowers. One German tourist was astonished by the many beautiful women who offered their services on the street. 'Indeed one can have it gratis,' he wrote home, 'all pell-mell at any hour of the day in any street, got up in any way you like, dressed, bound up, hitched up, tight-laced, loose, painted, done up or raw, scented, in silk or wool, with or without sugar.' There were cockfights, drunken brawls and prostitutes, but also bejewelled hands on gilded carriage doors and fashionable men in embroidered silk coats. Butchers threw out entrails and bones, the contents of chamber pots were flung out of windows, dead rats putrefied in puddles, and maids dumped garbage into the streets. Mud, horse manure, straw, human faeces, dog shit and household rubbish . . . the perfume of prosperity.

By contrast to the vast, clear skies that George had seen over Russia's steppes, in London the many coal fires that heated the homes made the air so hazy that even in the autumn, when the days were still long, the lanterns outside the houses were lit at four in the afternoon. London's parks provided much-needed space and air. In St James's Park, about a twenty-minute walk from the Forsters' lodgings, cows grazed and customers could buy fresh milk at the stalls, while hundreds of people promenaded along shaded paths – artists, maids, merchants, ladies and dukes alike.

George lived in his father's adult world. Barring the few months in St Petersburg, he had never attended school. In London he became his father's 'keen-eyed assistant', forced to translate texts to earn some money. A polyglot even at a young age, George had picked up English from the sailors during their long sea journey from Russia. Already fluent, he was immediately set to work by his father to translate and abridge a history of Russia by the esteemed polymath Mikhail Lomonosov from Russian into English.

Soon, Reinhold paraded his wunderkind to scholars in London. On 21 May 1767, George found himself presenting a copy of his Lomonosov book to the learned men of the Society of Antiquaries. Was he proud, nervous or terrified? Small for his age, he would have looked even younger – an earnest boy with thick brown curls wearing his best clothes among all the studious men in their powdered wigs. Exactly two years earlier, George and his father had mounted their horses and had begun their travels through Russia. Instead of neatly dressed and coiffed scholars who studied ruins and ancient artefacts, George had been in the company of rough Cossacks, Russian peasants and impoverished German settlers. He had already seen more of the world than many of the men in the room. But his childhood was over.

While Reinhold was trying to find a job in London, they lived off the proceeds from the Tatarian coins, Kalmyk manuscripts, fossils and idols which they had brought from Russia. But by late May 1767, eight months after their arrival in London, they had run out of money. When

Reinhold had sold everything, he accepted a teaching position at the Warrington Academy in northern England. At £60 a year, the salary was modest but it was at least a regular income. Situated in a small town midway between Manchester and Liverpool, the Academy had been founded ten years before to teach the religious dissenters who at that time were not allowed to study at Oxford or Cambridge universities (then the only two in England). Unlike Oxford and Cambridge with their focus on the Classics and theology, these new schools had a much broader curriculum. Prioritising experimental science, modern languages, history and economics, they provided a more practical education and fostered critical thinking. Assured by several letters of recommendation from London friends that Reinhold Forster was 'agreeable and easy', the trustees of the Academy were pleased that this 'learned foreigner' had agreed to join.*

It was at this point, more than two years after he had last seen the long-suffering Justina Elisabeth, that Reinhold wrote to Gdansk, instructing his wife to pack their belongings and come to England with their six other children. He had also decided that it was time for his eldest son to learn a trade. So in late June 1767, when Reinhold travelled to Warrington, he left George behind as an apprentice to a merchant who traded with Russia. The twelve-year-old boy found himself alone in London. By now fluent in German, French, English and Russian, he had to copy letters and invoices, and deliver parcels to the merchant's clients in London. It was a hot summer. As George ran through the busy streets, pushing through the crowds and forever worried that he would be late, his health began to suffer. Abandoned by his father and overworked by his employer, he lost weight and became exhausted. It would be three long months before his mother, brothers and sisters arrived.

Since her husband's departure, in March 1765, Justina Elisabeth Forster had given birth to another child and managed the family's move to Gdansk. Now she organized the journey to England, barely

* Reinhold replaced Joseph Priestley who had taught at Warrington for the previous five years and who experimented with electricity, later becoming famous – among many other things – for discovering oxygen. A progressive and liberal thinker, Priestley would also became an outspoken supporter of the American and French Revolutions.

surviving on what little money Reinhold had sent her. Physically, she was slender and delicate, but her determination was steely and her patience almost super-human. When she and the six children finally arrived in London in early September, George hadn't seen them for two and a half years, almost a lifetime at his age. This was also the first time he met his youngest sister, Justina, who hadn't been born when he had left for Russia.

After two nights in London, George took his mother and siblings on the journey north in the stagecoach. It took several days to travel the 200 miles to Warrington, and as only George was able to speak English he handled everything, securing seats and managing the cumbersome daily loading and unloading of their luggage. There were bags, trunks, hats, coats, food and his six siblings aged between two and eleven. The children had to be fed and entertained during the long bumpy drive. Whenever they stopped for the night, George had to negotiate food orders and sleeping arrangements in the notoriously overcrowded inns along the stagecoach routes, where travellers often had to share bedbug-infested straw mattresses. It was difficult enough for adult travellers to deal with the greedy landlords and harried waiters, but George was a twelve-year-old boy in charge of seven other people. His three-month apprenticeship had taken its toll and when the family finally arrived in Warrington, Reinhold was troubled to see how thin and emaciated George had become. Instead of sending him back to London, he decided to let him stay.

At last, the family was together again. They moved into a house near the Academy, the rooms noisy with the chatter of seven children as well as six young students who boarded with them to provide a much needed additional income. For a while George even attended lessons in mathematics, physics, history, religion and drawing as well as his father's classes. To supplement his meagre salary, Reinhold began moonlighting at two other schools alongside the Warrington Academy. To fulfil his weekly commitments, he enlisted George as a French, German and geography tutor. 'I intend to come only one time a week,' he told a friend, '& send my Son George twice.' George had to follow his father's orders. By now thirteen and still shy, he found himself in a classroom, instructing boys a head taller than him.

The arrangement didn't last. Almost inevitably, Reinhold had soon managed to upset his colleagues and employers – 'this worthless set of people' – and creditors were knocking on the door. He also hated teaching, telling a friend that he resented being 'confined to a wretched School & the Follies & Tricks of Young Monkeys'. His pupils were unruly and difficult to control, often playing practical jokes on their teacher who spoke English with a heavy German accent. Whatever Reinhold's letters of recommendation had stated, the trustees quickly realized that he was the opposite of 'agreeable and easy'.

In spring 1769, less than two years after his arrival in Warrington, Reinhold was sacked and George found himself translating German and French travel books into English to contribute to the family income. At a time when the vast majority of people rarely ventured beyond the villages and towns they lived in, let alone their countries or continents, travel books had become a hugely popular literary genre. Reinhold saw a business opportunity and mustered his eldest son's linguistic talents. George's grasp of the language was phenomenal, a friend wrote, 'no foreigner has ever been able to write English as he did'. George was not consulted. 'I was yoked too early,' he later said. 'I had to work when I should have been learning.'

The skill of translating was much more than a mechanical word-by-word formulation of sentences. Not only did George have to immerse himself in these other worlds in order to capture them in English, but he had also to adapt his own voice to that of the author – in a strange way, the original text demanded the same obedience that his father expected from him. But at the same time, it also allowed him to travel the globe and escape reality, away from the family's constant need for money and the demands of his irascible father.

Stuck inside the noisy house in Warrington surrounded by siblings, students, papers and books, George now sailed to the shores of Java and encountered jungles filled with tigers and crocodiles in Pehr Osbeck's *A Voyage to China and the East Indies*. All his life he had been driven by curiosity – he wanted to observe, investigate and understand, always thirsty for knowledge. The translations involved long hours at his desk, yet they also fired his imagination. His daily life might have been miserable, but these books transported him to a thrilling unknown world. He walked through the wild forests of the American colonies when he worked on *Travels in North America*, a lively account by a Finnish-Swedish botanist named Pehr Kalm. Carefully considering each word of Kalm's three volumes, George's mind filled with the roaring white curtain of the Niagara Falls and lofty trees. He paddled along rapid crystal-clear rivers and travelled by horseback along rocky paths. But it wasn't just nature. Kalm also wrote about the harsh frontier life of colonial settlers as well as about the Iroquois (or Haudenosaunee as they call themselves) and other Native Americans he had encountered, providing portraits of their customs, society and agricultural practices.

George also translated Captain Louis-Antoine de Bougainville's *A Voyage Round the World* – a rapturous portrait of beautiful islanders in Tahiti, turquoise waters and nature that provided plenty. As his pen filled the pages, he sailed through dangerous storms and accompanied Bougainville to Tahiti, Vanuatu and the Great Barrier Reef. Working on these books, George later said, enabled him 'to travel with them in thought'. We can only imagine how the adolescent boy felt when he translated Bougainville's descriptions of seemingly lascivious Tahitian women or sailors contracting venereal diseases. One woman, Bougainville wrote, excited the crew when she 'carelessly dropt a cloth, which covered her, and appeared to the eyes of all beholders, such as Venus shewed herself to the Phrygian shepherd, having, indeed, the celestial form of that goddess'.

At the end of 1770, the Forsters moved back to London, taking lodgings next to Reinhold's old school friend Woide, who had moved to Somerset House Stable Yard near the Thames. On 13 December, three days after their arrival, father and son went to the Royal Society, the nexus of British scientific enquiry where, since its foundation in the 1660s, fellows met to learn about new scientistic discoveries and exchange ideas with like-minded men. Reinhold Forster knew the Royal Society well, having attended the weekly meetings during their first stay in London. But now he wanted to introduce his son and present George's translations (though Reinhold's name was on their covers). So they made their way to Crane Court, a short fifteen-minute walk from their lodgings in a little cul-de-sac off Fleet Street, where the fellows met every Thursday. The president directed the meetings from a large armchair at one end of a long table, with a bust of the Society's first royal patron, King

Royal Society at Crane Court

Charles II, behind him, while the fellows sat on green-upholstered benches around the table.

At only sixteen George now found himself in the same room with some of the greatest minds in England. Almost every Thursday he accompanied his father to the Royal Society, where he sat under the watchful eyes of the portraits of illustrious previous fellows: the periwigged former president and mathematician Isaac Newton; the philosopher Francis Bacon in a lace ruff and embroidered velvet coat; and the architect Christopher Wren, who rebuilt London after the Great Fire of 1666. At these meetings George heard scholars talk about the physics of light, rare birds in the East Indies, new comets, the latest telescopes, tumours in pregnant women and subterranean geological formations. He saw animals preserved in spirits, pinned insects, a stuffed sea lion and a 24-foot snake, as well as the skeletons of a crocodile and an ostrich. He was receiving instructions unlike any other sixteen-year-old. As father and son attended the weekly meetings and published translations, their names soon spread across the scholarly world. Then, in February 1772, a little more than a year after their return to London, Reinhold was elected a fellow of the Royal Society and became officially part of the British scientific establishment.

George continued to work, translating eight volumes in total, while his father wrote and published numerous essays on botany, insects, zoology, antiquities, geography and mineralogy. 'If I didn't have a son of seventeen who helped me with translating,' Reinhold admitted, 'I couldn't possibly do all this work.' George began to feel like a 'translation-machine', but the reviews were glowing. 'He writes our language,' the *Critical Review* applauded (praising Reinhold, since only he was credited), 'with propriety; always with perspicuity, the great requisite in the communication of scientific learning'. Another critic even declared George's translation of Bougainville's *A Voyage Round the World* 'superior to the original'.

Money remained tight, and George remained at his desk. But on 26 May 1772, eighteen months after their move from Warrington back to London, a knock on the door changed his life. Acting 'in a very mysterious manner', as Reinhold recorded in his journal that night, Charles Irving, a Royal Navy surgeon and inventor, arrived in the late evening to talk to Reinhold. Irving asked if he might be interested in joining Captain James Cook's second circumnavigation of the globe. The Admiralty, according to Irving, was in urgent need of a naturalist because Joseph Banks, the botanist on the *Endeavour* voyage – Cook's first expedition around the world – had pulled out at the last moment.

A wealthy aristocrat, Banks had paid £10,000 for his passage on the *Endeavour* in 1768, embarking with a team of nine that included servants, artists and the botanist Daniel Solander. During the three years of the *Endeavour*'s journey, Banks had lived in a tiny cabin without a porthole, a space no bigger than a modern king-size bed. This time he had planned to travel in style. His team had risen to sixteen men, including four artists and two French horn players, all paid for by Banks. To accommodate them all, he had convinced the Admiralty to alter the *Resolution*, Captain Cook's new expedition ship, by installing a new deck crowned with a 'round house'. But when the building work was done and Cook took the *Resolution* on a test run in the Thames in May 1772, the ship almost capsized because it had become so top-heavy. It was too dangerous to sail, and Cook ordered the additions dismantled. Banks was furious. 'He swore & stamp'd upon the Wharfe, like a Mad Man,' reported one of the midshipmen. In the end, Banks had all his belongings removed and withdrew from the expedition.

Reinhold Forster immediately agreed – on the condition that his seventeen-year-old son accompany him as his assistant and draughtsman. George wasn't asked. The Royal Society's council also lobbied the Admiralty on Reinhold's behalf. Over the past years Reinhold had proven his scientific credentials and impressed patrons and supporters. He was capable, knowledgeable and willing. With Cook planning to leave in less than a month, time was pressing, but after some frantic back and forth Reinhold and George Forster were officially appointed on 11 June, only two weeks after Irving's first visit. Reinhold Forster received £4,000 for his services and equipment – a huge sum compared to the meagre £60 annual salary he had earned at the Warrington Academy. But they had less than two weeks to prepare, buy supplies and pack before the *Resolution* and her consort ship, the *Adventure*, sailed from Plymouth on England's south-western coast.

They needed natural-history books, paper and paints, but also scientific instruments such as a botanical microscope, bottles and spirit in which to preserve fish. But what was essential and what unnecessary? Who better to ask than Joseph Banks. But when Reinhold knocked on Banks' door, he quickly realized how naïve he had been. Banks promised to give him information, but demanded that Reinhold would have to ask precise questions. How would he be able to ask something he didn't know, Reinhold explained to Banks, for he was 'unacquainted with the peculiar & unforeseen particulars'. Clearly annoyed that the Forsters were going instead of him, Banks also refused to show Reinhold any of the plant specimens he had collected during the *Endeavour* voyage. Reinhold and George would have to prepare without his advice.

On 26 June 1772, father and son bade farewell to their family, who remained in London under care of the trusted Woide. He had also agreed to be the children's guardian in case anything happened to Justina Elisabeth.* Reinhold made provisions for dowries for his

* Woide took his responsibilities seriously. Three days after Reinhold and George had departed, he went to Lambeth to find new lodgings for Justina Elisabeth. Reinhold must have insisted that his wife and six children should stay in less central and therefore cheaper accommodations. In the end Woide found a place in Paddington, which was still a village to the west of London. He also helped with the education of the children.

daughters 'provided they shall marry with the Consent of their mother', and money for his sons, 'if they shall behave themselves to the Satisfaction of their mother'. There is no record how George felt when he embraced his mother before leaving. Was he scared? Excited? And what of his siblings? He had two brothers and four sisters, the youngest of whom had turned seven just four days earlier. Did Justina, his little sister, understand what was happening? And what of his mother? After almost two decades of marriage to Reinhold, Justina Elisabeth knew her husband's impulsiveness all too well, but this was different. She might never see them again.

PART II

Discoveries

3

Resolution Voyage

Antarctica: 13 July 1772–February 1773

On 13 July 1772, barely a month after the Forsters' appointment, the *Resolution* and her consort ship the *Adventure* sailed from Plymouth. There were 201 men heading into the unknown, uncertain if they would ever return. At only seventeen, George Forster was not even the youngest on board. Among the sailors and midshipmen were several boys as young as thirteen and fourteen – more than ten were under the age of sixteen.

The British Admiralty had dispatched the ships to find the mythical Southern Continent – *Terra Australis Incognita** – that scientists believed had to exist to counterbalance the landmasses in the northern hemisphere. Scientific curiosity played a role, but more alluring was that this elusive territory could be the source of immense wealth – spices, precious metals and other treasures. Already in 1605 the Spanish had sent the Portuguese navigator Pedro Fernández de Quirós, followed by the Dutchman Abel Tasman in 1642, in search of it. More recently, the French and the British had entered the race. In the previous decade, the French had commissioned Louis-Antoine de Bougainville and the British had organized several expeditions. The *Resolution* voyage was to be the fourth English expedition to sail to the South Pacific – the *Dolphin* went in 1764 and again in 1766, and the third had been Cook's first voyage on the *Endeavour* from 1768 to 1771. The continuing rivalry

* *Terra Australis Incognita* – 'Australis' means 'southern' in Latin – was a hypothetical continent and not to be confused with today's Australia. In the eighteenth century, Australia was known as 'New Holland' and only received its current name in the early nineteenth century. The southern continent was officially named Antarctica in the 1890s.

between Britain and France also played its part. France was trying to make up for its losses in North America and India during the Seven Years' War by claiming new lands in the South Pacific – which Britain was determined to prevent.

The expedition was equipped for many months at sea. The *Resolution* and the *Adventure* were sturdy colliers, originally designed to carry coal. While they were not the fastest ships, they had extensive storage capacity. At 110 feet long and with space for 118 men, the *Resolution* was larger than the *Adventure* at 97 feet and with 83 crew. Filled to the brim, the *Resolution* alone carried almost 60,000 pounds of ship's biscuit, over 17,000 pounds of flour, almost 22,000 pieces of salt meat, 2,000 pounds of sugar, more than 3,100 pounds of raisins, 210 gallons of olive oil, 19 tons of beer, 642 gallons of wine and 1,397 gallons of spirits. Cook had also ordered 3,000 pounds of portable meat soup, 31 barrels of concentrated grain mash to brew beer, plus dried peas, butter, cheese, oatmeal, and 259 gallons of vinegar for cleaning the ship.

There were goats, poultry, sheep, cats (to catch mice and rats) and dogs (as pets on the long journey), as well as twelve four-pounder cannons, twelve swivel guns, muskets, an apparatus for distilling water, the newest scientific instruments to calculate exact geographical positions, an observatory tent with a telescope and other equipment, fishing gear, tools, a forge and plenty of trade goods, including beads, nails, hatchets, combs, looking glasses, sheets, cloths and much more. And as he had requested, Reinhold Forster had also been supplied with four 80-gallon barrels of spirit for preserving animal specimens. The deck itself was crowded with five more vessels for exploring rivers and inlets – ranging in size from a small dinghy to a larger sailing boat, as well as an array of different anchors.

At the back of the upper deck, stretching across the ship's entire width, was the Great Cabin, a light and airy space illuminated by seven large windows at the stern. This was the captain's realm, where he ate and entertained his officers – with his bed in a small cabin next to it. Besides the usual crew of officers, quartermasters, gunners, armourers, a surgeon and two mates, a barber, carpenters, coopers, sailmakers, sailors, servants, a butcher and a cook, the *Resolution* also had a cartographer, a tailor and twenty-two marines,* as well as an astronomer (and his servant), an artist and the Forsters, who had also brought a servant. Seventeen members of the crew – three officers, one marine and thirteen seamen – had previously travelled with Cook on the *Endeavour*.

The lodgings of the officers, scientists and artist were cramped but at least they had cabins. The common sailors slept in the dark and airless lower decks, their hammocks strung from the beams, exactly 21 inches apart. Here the ceiling was so low that no grown man could stand straight. The floor was crowded with the sailors' canvas bags which held their few belongings. With no portholes, the only ventilation came through the hatch – which had to be closed during bad weather. It was dark and damp, and there was no space for the sailors to dry their wet clothes. The sweat and stench of hard-working men would soon be absorbed into the timbers.

George's cabin was tiny. At only six by six feet, it was so small that he could barely move and he had to duck in the doorway to enter. But somehow it contained a narrow bed, a trunk filled with his clothes and other personal effects, a narrow mahogany drop-leaf desk with five drawers and two brass handles on the side so it could be easily lifted, as well as a folding chair. Though small, it was his own space and he didn't have to share it with his father or any of the other men. Reinhold's cabin was identical, and like George's located at the hatch near the main mast. While the captain and some of the officers had portholes which provided light and air, the scuttles in the Forsters' cabins were largely obstructed by the large chainplates that fastened the rigging to the hull. Both cabins were already crowded, but they also had to find space for plant presses, paper, paints and brushes as well as scientific instruments. Reinhold's extensive natural-history library which they needed to identify plants and animals was removed into storage.

Reinhold's and George's cabins had been so hastily and poorly constructed after the demolition of Banks' alterations that there were cracks

* These twenty-two Royal Marines were dressed in red uniforms, equipped with muskets, and served under the Royal Navy to maintain discipline among the sailors, provide security, and act as a military force both at sea and on land.

in the bulkheads and ceilings. They would all too soon find out that whenever the deck above was scrubbed, or if it rained or high waves rolled over the ship, their bedding became drenched. 'Floods of saltwater rushing down upon my head', Reinhold would note in his journal a few weeks later. After inspecting the other officers' cabins, he even offered money to swap but no one accepted. At least, thought Reinhold, they would be rich and famous. Banks had been lionized when he came back from Cook's *Endeavour* voyage. The tales about free love in Tahiti, tattooed Māori warriors, and a perilous escape from the coral claws of the Great Barrier Reef had fuelled the public imagination. As George and Reinhold well knew, travel accounts were enormously popular with readers: ever since Christopher Columbus returned from the Americas at the end of the fifteenth century, European audiences had been keen to travel the world from the safety of their parlours.

Explorers had arrived back in Europe with stories of wild oceans and distant countries filled with treasures. The main reason for those early voyages had been exploitation and wealth – gold, silver, tobacco and rare spices. In the early 1520s, when Ferdinand Magellan's expedition had become the first to circumnavigate the globe, it had returned without Magellan and most of the crew but with a hull filled with precious cloves (worth more than their weight in gold) and other spices. Fifty years later, Francis Drake had commanded the first successful English circumnavigation, and when he sailed back into Plymouth harbour after almost three years, he too brought back a huge cargo of spices and gold – despite having lost two-thirds of his men and four ships. The value of Queen Elizabeth I's share alone exceeded the rest of the Crown's income that year. Valuable spices were also the reason why the Portuguese arrived in Indonesia in the early sixteenth century, later to be overtaken by the Dutch. All these nations – the Spanish, Portuguese, Dutch, French and English – had sent ships across the globe to plunder and make a fortune.

Even expeditions with serious scientific components retained strong imperial undercurrents. When Cook had first set out with the *Endeavour* in 1768, he had done so with the objective of observing a Transit of Venus from Tahiti on 3 June 1769 – a rare astronomical event (the last until 1874) when Venus appeared as a perfect black spot slowly moving over the burning face of the sun, and one which scientists across the world used to calculate the distance between the sun and Earth. Ostensibly gazetted as an astronomical mission, the *Endeavour* had then sailed on from Tahiti to Australia, bringing back reports on crops, soils, geography and climate which would eventually lead to the establishment of a penal colony.

No one had found the southern land, but Cook had studied charts of earlier Pacific voyages – including his own from the *Endeavour* expedition – and was ready for another attempt. His plan was to circumnavigate the globe at a high latitude – the higher the figure, the closer to the South Pole at 90°S (with the Equator at 0°). One look at a map of the northern hemisphere showed that huge tracts of lands were situated in the higher latitudes above 60°N, including large parts of Russia, northern North America, Greenland and Scandinavia – the reason why many scientists were convinced that there should be an equivalent landmass in the South. Cook knew that Cape Horn, the most southern headland of South America, was at 56°S and the southern tip of New Zealand's South Island was at around 47°S, but he didn't know whether there was any land in between as he had crossed the South Pacific closer to the Equator. If he could complete a full circle between 45°S and 60°S in the *Resolution*, he thought the chances of finding land – should there indeed be a Southern Continent – were high.

He had explained to the Admiralty that, failing to discover land, he would sail to New Zealand to obtain provisions – which he knew well enough from his *Endeavour* voyage – before trying again. The Dutch navigator Abel Tasman and his crew had sighted the South Island in December 1642, but Cook and his men had been the first Europeans to set foot on New Zealand (as well as mapping the coast line). Cook hoped to spend the winter months in Tahiti – 'in the more Hospitable Latitudes', he said. But no one knew what to expect so close to the South Pole. The Admiralty had also given Cook secret instructions to bring back seeds, plants, minerals, and reports about climate and soils, as well as 'to observe the Genius, Temper, Disposition and

Number of the Natives or Inhabitants' with a view to claiming territory for Britain.

For the first part of their voyage they moved along the usual trade routes to Cape Town in South Africa. They stopped at Madeira, an island around 300 miles north of the Canaries, where Cook replenished their supplies with fresh meat, fruit and vegetables, as well as 400 gallons of Madeira wine.* As the *Resolution* sailed on to Cape Verde, an archipelago in the Atlantic some 400 miles off the coast of West Africa, and then towards Cape Town, the Forsters quickly fell into a routine of casting their nets and hooks to fish, George drawing and Reinhold describing their catch. Sometimes the ship's officers shot birds which the Forsters dissected. Once the sailors hooked a shark but failed to catch one of the many bonitos that shot past the ship. If the sea was calm, the crew lowered one of the ship's dinghies into the water so that the Forsters could fish, while also measuring the ocean temperature and the direction of currents. The crew nicknamed them the '*Experimental Gentlemen*'.

Just past Madeira the ship was accompanied by porpoises, and at night phosphorescence lit up the sea. George stood hypnotized at the railing and stared into the water. 'The sea appeared luminous,' he wrote, 'particularly the tops of the waves and part of the ship's wake, which were illuminated by a mass of pure light.' Near Cape Town, the spectacle became even more astonishing when the 'whole ocean seem to be in a blaze', although young Midshipman John Elliott was concerned by this 'alarming appearance'. With the waves' crests alight, they could even see the gleaming shapes of large fish swimming beside the ship. George was enchanted. 'Great bodies of light moved in the water along our side, sometimes slower, sometimes quicker; now in the same direction with our course, now flying off from it.' He also wanted to understand why the sea lit up and pulled a bucket of water onto the deck. Swirling,

* The British Consul in Madeira told Cook and the Forsters that a few days earlier a certain Mr Burnett had enquired after the *Resolution* because Joseph Banks had commissioned him to be his assistant botanist. To the great amusement of everybody, it soon became obvious that Burnett was a woman dressed up as a man – 'every part of Mr Burnetts behaviour and every action tended to proof that he was a Woman,' Cook said – apparently Banks had invited his mistress for the voyage. When she heard that Banks had not joined the *Resolution*, she left Madeira.

touching, observing it, George made the water light up again and again. When a little spark became attached to his finger, he investigated it with a magnifying glass and discovered a gelatinous tube with an orifice and intestines. He speculated that they could an early-stage form of jellyfish or maybe even an entirely new species. Whatever they were, he thought that even nature's most minute creatures were awe-inspiring.

As they approached the tropics and the equator, it became so humid that the air seemed to thicken. Reinhold and George's books, journals and instruments became mouldy. These long days at sea with no land in sight were often monotonous, patterned only by the half-hourly sound of the bell announcing time for those on watch. The Forsters quickly adapted to life on board. Everything had to be fastened down or tied into place – mugs, plates and their equipment. George learned to write, draw and even shave as the *Resolution* pitched up and down, adjusting his gait to walk with slightly bent knees and outwardly spread feet 'waddling along like ducks'. Breakfast was at 8 a.m. followed by a frugal lunch of pea soup and sauerkraut at noon – four times a week with salted meat – and a dinner of ship's biscuit and leftovers at 8 p.m.

As days became weeks, George settled into this new rhythm of life, observing the sailors as he did the sea. Above him, the ship's crew clambered up the swaying shrouds, balancing high on the horizonal beams from where they unfurled or reefed the sails, no matter how steep the pitch of the waves. Calloused hands grabbed tarred ropes, their voices shouting and swearing. It was dangerous work and the men's bodies bore the scars of accidents. When they were not working the sails, the sailors cleaned and repaired. There was always something to do. They were caulking, scraping, tarring and painting timbers. Sails could tear, tackle broke and jammed, rigging became tangled, and water coming in from leaks had to be pumped.

George spent hours on deck, watching the bonitos and dolphins chase huge shoals of flying fish. As the winged creatures leaped out of the water, some were eaten by their pursuers or by birds, others landed by accident on the deck of the *Resolution*. 'What empire is not like a tumultuous ocean,' he wondered as he looked at them, 'where the great in all the magnificence and pomp of power, continually persecute and contrive the destruction of the defenceless?'

For a while, he enjoyed the company of a swallow that had followed the *Resolution* from the Cape Verde islands and was soon too far from land to leave them. Drenched by a heavy shower, the bird became so wet that it couldn't fly, but George nursed and dried it under his shirt, and set it free again. But it returned through the open porthole into his cabin, happily feeding on the many flies there. It came in and out during the days but roosted somewhere outside. Early in the morning, 'our swallow returned into the cabin once more, and took its breakfast of flies,' George noted, but then it disappeared for good. He discovered that a sailor had fed it to one of the ship's cats.

During those first weeks and months, George got to know the crew. There was Second Lieutenant Charles Clerke, who was thirty-one and clearly a man addicted to adventures – this was already his third circumnavigation. He had started his naval career at thirteen and had been so keen to join the *Resolution* that he had told Banks 'by God, I'll go to Sea in a Grog Tub if desir'd'. His first time had been on the *Dolphin* under the command of Captain John Byron* from 1764 to 1766 and two years later with Cook on the *Endeavour.* Clerke liked liquor and women, and was popular with the crew for his cheerful personality. He also enjoyed practical jokes. After returning from his first voyage, he had tricked the venerable scientists of the Royal Society into believing that he had seen giants over eight feet tall in Patagonia – his report had been so convincing that they had even printed it in their *Philosophical Transactions*. 'Clerke is a brave officer and drinks and whores,' George would later say, but he was also a steadfast and reliable member of the crew – much trusted by Cook.

Also on board was twenty-three-year-old Richard Pickersgill, the Third Lieutenant who like Clerke was on his third voyage, having sailed around the world on the *Dolphin* with Captain Samuel Wallis from 1766 to 1768 and then on the *Endeavour*. He was a talented surveyor but also liked to drink – 'a good officer and astronomer, but liking ye Grog'. Where Clerke was jovial, Pickersgill was more serious and sometimes gloomy, but he too was dependable and honoured to sail with the *Resolution*. 'The glory inseparable from arduous enterprises,' Pickersgill wrote in his journal, 'is a powerful incentive which raises the mind above itself.'

* This was the future grandfather of the poet Lord Byron.

Then there was thirteen-year-old John Elliott, a midshipman who was proud to be part of the expedition, saying that it was 'quite a great feather, in a young man's Cap, to go with Captain Cook' – his uncle had pulled strings to get him the *Resolution* commission. During the voyage, Cook taught the young midshipmen, who were essentially trainee officers. They had to perform the same duties as common sailors – clambering up the yards to reef the sails, for example – but they also learned how to shoot a musket and steer the vessel. They were instructed in astronomical observations and learned to draw survey coastlines. After their shifts outside, Elliott and the other young midshipmen copied charts for Cook in the Great Cabin and artist William Hodges tutored them in drawing.

George liked twenty-seven-year-old Hodges, a landscape painter from London. He was a mild-mannered and hard-working man with a large aquiline nose and full lips, more at ease with his paintbrushes than with words. This was his first expedition and over the next two and half years he would often accompany the Forsters on their excursions, sketching the scenery and the islanders they encountered in the South Pacific. During the voyage, Hodges also taught George how to complete his botanical and zoological drawings with landscapes in the background.

The crew quickly learned how their captain ran his ship. Cook ruled with a humane but strict hand. Born in 1728 in Yorkshire the

James Cook, captain of the *Resolution*

son of a farm labourer, James Cook's rise from humble beginnings had been unusual. He had joined the Navy, fought in the Seven Years' War, and charted Newfoundland before embarking on his first circumnavigation in 1768. A skilled cartographer, astronomer and marine surveyor, as well as an able mathematician and experienced navigator, Cook had proven himself a successful leader. Now in his mid-forties, he was a tall man with the weathered skin and rough hands of a sailor. More than two decades at sea had honed his eyes to perfection. When Cook stepped on deck and took a look at the rigging which to George seemed a tangled mess, the captain immediately saw if a rope had been tightened too much or too little. Cook's estimates of distances whenever they spotted land, George wrote in admiration, were always the most precise.

Cook was a quiet and private man, innately cautious, but still willing to take calculated risks when necessary. He was meticulous and had been involved in every aspect of the voyage's preparations, from the alterations of the *Resolution* to its provisioning. Knowing that the success of this expedition depended on the health of his crew, he had ordered huge amounts of sauerkraut (19,337 pounds for the *Resolution* alone), along with thirty gallons of so-called carrot marmalade (made according to a new recipe from Germany) and concentrated juice of oranges and lemons to prevent scurvy – as well as introducing a rigorous regime of cleanliness and diet. At a time when often half the crew died of scurvy on long expeditions, Cook's methods proved hugely successful.* Whenever the weather permitted, the men had to scrub the *Resolution* with vinegar and air the hammocks. He made them regularly wash their clothes and punished dirty hands by withholding their daily allowance of liquor. While drunkenness or disobedience was sometimes disciplined with whipping, Cook's methods were unusually mild by comparison with the Royal Navy's tradition of brutal and violent punishment. Unlike more tyrannical commanders, he genuinely cared about the conditions below

* In the 1750s ship surgeon James Lind had proved that scurvy could be treated by eating citrus fruit, but his ideas were only slowly being adopted. Cook didn't know that vitamin C deficiency was the reason for scurvy (that was only discovered in 1930s), but his experience had taught him his men recovered quickly when eating fresh greens, vegetables and fruit.

decks and over the next three years his men came to respect Cook's calm yet uncompromising rule.

On 30 October 1772, two months after departing from Madeira, the ships arrived in Cape Town, where Cook filled their stores. Here, the Forsters met Anders Sparrman, an adventurous twenty-four-year-old Swedish botanist who had trained under the influential Linnaeus in Uppsala and had already travelled to China. Eager to see more of the world, he wanted to join the *Resolution*. They struck a deal. Reinhold was certain that they were going to find so many plants that he would need a second assistant and three weeks later, when the *Resolution* prepared to leave, Sparrman moved his few possessions into the cramped steerage on the lower deck.

They weighed anchor in Cape Town on 22 November 1772 and Cook turned directly south towards the Antarctic Circle in search of the Southern Continent. As the *Resolution* sailed on, temperatures dropped rapidly and the weather became rough. Cook issued jackets and trousers made of heavy woollen cloth for the crew, but the sailors quickly discovered that the Admiralty's sub-contractors had increased their profits by making the legs and sleeves too short. Their footwear was also so shoddily produced, the gunner's mate complained, that 'one might wring the shoes like a piece of flannel', as every drop of water seeped through the soles. The men were always cold and wet.

Five days later, on 27 November, George Forster celebrated his eighteenth birthday in the middle of the South Atlantic Ocean, at 40°4′S. At 4 a.m. the next morning, his father was jolted awake by icy water flooding in through the ceiling – his cabin 'a scene of desolation, not one place being dry'. As they continued south, the weather grew worse and the waves higher. Chairs flew through cabins, dishes fell off tables, wine bottles broke, and there wasn't a dry place on the vessel. Two weeks later, on 10 December, the air thick with snowflakes, they spotted a long chalky cliff coastline rising from the sea. But when they came closer, the men realized this was not land. At least twice as high as the mast of the *Resolution*, the iceberg was about 2,000 feet long with steep straight sides and a flat table top. The next day, they entered an icy labyrinth. The sea here was wild, with violent waves breaking over the tops of icebergs, tossing the *Resolution* around like a dinghy. Soon, one of the crew members noted in his journal, they were 'entangled among the ice'.

Floating pack ice and icebergs made dangerous travelling companions. As a sailing ship cannot reverse, the lookouts had to anticipate and shout a change in direction in advance. Each day, the *Resolution* narrowly avoided being crushed by icebergs or becoming stuck in the ice, while storms, sleet, hail and snow constantly battered it. The wind roared, timbers creaked, and rigging banged against the mast. Although the noise was unbearable and everything wet, George marvelled at this icy world. Tinged in the most brilliant sapphire blues, the icebergs were anything but white, he wrote, relishing the way the setting sun drew their outlines in gold and then turned them purple. At night, he observed the southern lights (*aurora australis*), columns of white light that swirled and radiated across the sky. Nature here was magical, with huge whales diving under the ships and shearwaters gliding low on still wings. Petrels accompanied the *Resolution* and the *Adventure*, and albatrosses rode the winds with barely a flap of their huge wings, dipping down to the water surface only to effortlessly rise again. One evening George counted eighty-six penguins floating by, standing upright on sheets of ice. Penguins waddled in such precise formations, the sailors joked, that they might have been British soldiers doing drills. Another day, thousands of penguins swam beside them so fast that they easily overtook the ship.

When the sea had calmed, the ship's astronomer, William Wales, and Reinhold decided to take one of the small boats out to measure the current and water temperature. Almost forty, the sturdily built Wales was one of the oldest men on board. Serious, diligent and driven by a sense of duty, he set high standards for himself and others. He could also be petty and judgemental, and would eventually fall out with the Forsters. He had arrived with excellent credentials – he had been the assistant astronomer at the Royal Observatory in Greenwich and had measured the Transit of Venus in Hudson Bay on the edge of the Arctic frontier in the northern part of North America in 1769. But he hated the cold. Already during his interview at the Royal Society for the Transit of Venus expedition, he had declared that he was 'preferring a Voyage to a warm climate'. Every morning at Hudson Bay his bedding had been frozen to the headboard of his bed and a half-pint tumbler filled with brandy had turned to ice within minutes. Four years later, he was again in a world of ice. Disciplined and meticulous, Wales focused on his observations.

And so he found himself with Reinhold dropping a thermometer into the icy ocean. Measuring and taking notes, the two men realized too late that the *Resolution* and the *Adventure* had disappeared into thick fog. When they cried out for help, their shouts were swallowed by an eerie silence. Two men with a thermometer, a notebook, no food, no sail and two oars in an open boat surrounded by icebergs. They continued to shout, paddling a few metres in one direction and then back again. What was their most likely death, they wondered. Drowning, freezing, thirst or starvation? Finally, after what seemed an eternity, they heard the metal sound of a bell – 'heavenly music to their ears'. Following the continuous jingling, Reinhold and Wales paddled as fast as they could and reached the ship. That night, their damp beds felt like the most luxurious comfort.

A month later, on 17 January 1773, they crossed the Antarctic Circle at 66°33′S – so far south that Cook was certain they were 'undoubtably the first and only Ship that ever cross'd that line'. Their drinking water froze in the barrel and the rigging turned into 'compleat christal ropes', with icicles dangling like stiff tassels from ropes and railings. The running tackle snapped, the sailors' hands bled and cracked, and

The *Resolution* among icebergs with the crew collecting ice to melt for drinking water

everybody was wretchedly cold. Assistant botanist Sparrman, who loved to eat and saw food where there was none, compared the icy crusts to the 'candied cinnamon of our confectioners'.

When the sea was calm, they hoisted down the small boats and collected floating ice blocks to melt for drinking water. The sailors had to plunge their bare hands and arms repeatedly into the freezing ocean to heave out huge heavy blocks until they were so numb that they couldn't feel their fingers and limbs. The goats and sheep were brought below deck and stabled next to Reinhold's cabin to keep them alive. Separated only by a thin wall with many cracks, the smell was unbearable. The animals 'shit & pissed' against the partition, Reinhold grumbled, and when the ship rolled their urine sloshed into his cabin. After six months on the *Resolution*, his patience, never long held, was running out.

On 8 February 1773, three weeks after first crossing the Antarctic Circle, the ships were enveloped by such thick fog that the *Resolution* lost contact with the *Adventure*. For two days the crew fired guns every half an hour without receiving an answer – the *Adventure* and the eighty-three men aboard her had vanished. For weeks, the *Resolution* sailed on, shrouded in blinding white fog and surrounded by creaking icebergs – 'they made a continual noise a good deal resembling the firing of Musquets', as Second Lieutenant Clerke noted – and despite Cook's efforts, the lack of vegetables and fresh food over the past weeks showed its terrible effects. The men now began to suffer from infected gums, skin irritations, painful limbs and green filaments in their urine – all symptoms of scurvy. While many were complaining about their rations of hard salt beef, one of the midshipmen had developed a taste for the fresh meat of rats. He had a cat, Sparrman observed, who caught and shared the rodents with her master – 'he divided the prey so that the cat had the fore part, and the back part was cleaned, roasted, and peppered for himself.'

Cook was aware that his crew was miserable. 'They had no inclination to proceed any farther,' he noted in his logbook on 13 February, 'I however was resolved to get as far to the South as I conveniently could' – but even he had little hope of finding land. The swell was high, and waves crashed over the deck of the *Resolution*, but he still kept up his regime of cleanliness. When he noticed that the men's clothes looked tattered, he instructed they be given needle and thread, demanding that they repaired tears and fastened buttons. Every Saturday was washday so that there was no excuse to look dirty or scruffy.

They had not seen land since leaving Cape Town three months previously. Cooped up on the small ship, the men became fractious, Reinhold Forster especially so. 'A clever, but a litigious, quaralsom, fellow,' recalled young Elliott, 'olde Mr Forster (tho clever) was very hot, and petulent in argument.' George once again watched how his father made life uncomfortable for himself and those around him. Increasingly unpopular with the crew, Reinhold had fights with sailors and officers alike, and even managed to spark conflict with the usually unflappable Cook. Permanently wet and cold, with goats and sheep next to his cabin and, with the *Resolution* at sea rather than at shore, few opportunities for making discoveries in natural history, Reinhold grew frustrated. Even if someone offered him twice the money, he now fumed, he would decline to join the expedition. 'After having circumnavigated very near half the globe, we saw nothing, but water, Ice & sky,' he wrote in his journal on 15 March 1773.

Never one to hold back, Reinhold's anger was now easily ignited – his cabin was too cold, too smelly, too wet, the crew were too drunk or too loud, and he couldn't concentrate when the sailors sang. He shouted and argued so uncontrollably that on occasion Cook had him thrown out of the Great Cabin. At other times, Reinhold threatened to complain to the king and to have officers or sailors removed from their service,

Caricature of Reinhold Forster – with George, his mother, Elisabeth Justina, and siblings next to the donkey.

grossly exaggerating his connections or influence. His thick German accent amused the sailors and soon they were joking whenever someone had done something wrong that they would tell the king. Years later a cartoon was published in England, depicting Reinhold sitting backwards on a donkey, shouting 'I vil tel de Kinck of you'.

Unlike his father, George was respected and liked. The sailors and officers saw a quiet young man with a mop of brown wavy hair, his skin scarred by smallpox. He didn't talk much but his gentle eyes and friendly smile encouraged trust. Elliott thought him 'a clever good young man'. Studious and polite, George might have looked like a bookish adolescent who spent his days at a desk reading and writing, but over the next two and a half years he was always the first to volunteer to explore wherever they anchored. Instead of physical strength and muscle, he would bring wit, endurance and patience to the voyage. Nothing rattled him. Unlike his father, he never complained, shouted or swore. To George Forster everything was new and exciting.

4

Resolution Voyage

New Zealand (Aotearoa): 17 March–7 June 1773

They had been sailing east along the southern high latitudes for weeks. Finally, on 17 March 1773, Cook turned the *Resolution* north towards New Zealand (Aotearoa)* where he planned to replenish their empty stores. A week later the sailor in the lookout, high on the main mast, shouted 'land ho'. Soon, the southern tip of New Zealand's South Island (Te Waipounamu) appeared at the horizon. A few hours later, they saw the wide entrance of Dusky Sound (Tamatea). Almost exactly three years to the day earlier, on a late stormy afternoon, the *Endeavour* had passed here too – but because it had been getting dark and the wind had proved too strong, Cook hadn't risked sailing into these uncharted waters. This time the weather was in their favour and at noon they entered the almost thirty-mile-long fjord which was dotted with numerous forested islands. The *Resolution* was dwarfed by the mountains that dropped steeply into the water. Silhouettes of peaks and slopes in different shades of greens and greys were layered upon each other, their outlines softened by the distance – a palimpsest of shadow, mist, rock and foliage. It was a majestic sight.

After their four months at sea, New Zealand seemed like paradise and George's descriptions sang with joy – the birds, the light air, the sun, the luscious vegetation and the plentiful fish. 'The weather was

* In the eighteenth century the Māori didn't have a name for the entire archipelago. Aotearoa referred to the North Island and is often translated as the 'land of the long white cloud.' According to some Māori tradition it refers to the clouds that led the legendary Polynesian navigator Kupe to the North Island. Today Aotearoa is a name used for the whole of New Zealand.

delightfully fair, and genially warm, when compared to what we had lately experienced,' he wrote on 26 March 1773, 'we glided along ... wafted by light airs, past numerous rocky islands, each of which was covered with wood and shrubberies, where numerous evergreens were sweetly contrasted and mingled with the various shades of autumnal yellow. Flocks of aquatic birds enlivened the rocky shores, and the whole country resounded with the wild notes of the feathered tribe.' The moment the anchor was dropped, the crew cast their fishing lines, their haul so plentiful that the deck was soon covered with buckets of fish. The meal they cooked from that catch, George said, was 'the most delicious we had ever made in our lives'.

Their anchorage was a little natural harbour surrounded by mountains and encircled by tall shady trees and shrubs arranged like an amphitheatre.* One tree leaned almost horizontally over the water, so far that they used it as a gangway to the *Resolution*, allowing easy access to the shore without needing dinghies. The forests echoed with an orchestra of birds – trills, cawing, chatter, hoots, chirping, screeches, whistling and cooing they had never heard before. The beautiful Yellowhead, a small songbird with a bright yellow head and breast, was abundant and most birds were so unafraid of the newcomers that they fluttered close enough to touch – to the great excitement of the ship's cats. The Forsters caught and described many, George drawing dozens of them: the small fidgety South Island Fantail, for example, which seemed to enjoy showing off its large fan-shaped feathered tail – *pīwakawaka* for the Māori, who regarded it as a harbinger from the spirit world. And the flightless *weka* with its brown mottled plumage, a bird about the size of a chicken – 'both new', as Reinhold noted, because a species that was unknown to European scientists was for him the most important aspect of the haul. There was the *kōtare*, the sacred kingfisher with an iridescent green-blue back and cap, calling its staccato *kek-kek-kek*, as well as the large and colourful wood pigeon – *kererū* for the Māori – an almost regal bird that symbolized peace and fertility. Anders Sparrman enthused about the *tūī*, a medium-sized bird with lustrous blackish plumage and a

* Cook named it Pickersgill Harbour after Third Lieutenant Richard Pickersgill who had found it.

tuft of perfectly white curled feathers under its throat. They were beautiful and had a wonderfully varied song, but, never neglecting his culinary interests, Sparrman also noted that they were quite plump and 'made many delicious pasties and dishes for our meals'.

Two days after their arrival, a small canoe appeared in the distance with seven or eight Māori, staring at the sailors and officers who were shouting and waving a white cloth as a sign of peace. After studying the *Resolution* for half an hour, the men paddled away. Over the next few days, the Māori would have heard the sounds of gunshots across the bay as the Europeans killed hundreds of birds. What did they make of these strangers? Early accounts indicate that they at first thought the Europeans supernatural beings. Three and a half years earlier, in October 1769, when Cook had first arrived in New Zealand with the *Endeavour*, some of the Māori had wondered if the ship might be a sacred island. 'It is an island, an island floating from afar,' they said, 'Aha, ha! The sails of this travelling island are like clouds in the sky!' Some had thought the *Endeavour* was a great bird, others that the Europeans were *atua* – spirits or gods. 'When our old men saw the ship,' a Māori man recalled many years later, 'they said it was an atua, and the people on board were tupua, strange beings or "goblins".' Whatever their initial thoughts, the Māori had quickly realized that the visitors were humans who ignored their gods, trampled over sacred sites, and killed their people. The very first encounter with the *Endeavour* crew had been hostile and ended with one of the Māori shot dead. The skirmishes had continued and the Māori had challenged the *Endeavour* crew with spears and their fierce war dances. Cook respected their courage – 'a brave, warlike people, with sentiments void of treachery' – but was cautious.

In the Māori origin story, sky father Ranginui and earth mother Papatūānuku held each other in such a tight embrace that there was no light. There was no sun, no moon, no stars, no clouds, no winds – nothing but silence and stillness. Rangi covered Papa's nakedness with plants and forests, and made creatures such as insects and crabs. Finally they created their sons, the gods. But Rangi held Papa so tight that their children lived confined and in darkness – crouching, stooping, crawling like lizards, kneeling and lying on their backs. When their son Tāne, the god of forests and birds, pried them apart, a cosmos emerged of twelve layered heavens above the earth and several layered regions below.

The gods spread out. Tāne climbed to the highest of the twelve heavens and returned to earth with the three baskets of knowledge.* One son was god of the sea and another ruled the winds. The last son, however, was never born and still lives inside his mother's womb – when he kicks, the earth shakes, for he is the god of earthquakes and volcanoes. According to Māori tradition, Rangi and Papa still grieve over their separation. Her sighs rise up as mist and his tears fall onto her as dewdrops, signs of their love.

In the Māori universe everybody and everything is descended from Rangi and Papa and their children – birds, trees, rivers, water, insects and winds – and all life is interconnected. The Māori felt a deep kinship with their gods and communicated with them through chants, priests and nature. *Mana* was their sacred ancestral power – and everything could possess it: people, plants, animals, rocks and so on. Places and things where these spirits were present were considered sacrosanct and governed by strict prohibitions to protect them. They were *tapu* – a Polynesian concept that Cook's crew would also encounter in Tahiti and Tonga – which later gave rise to the English word 'taboo'.

When the Māori and the Europeans first met, two opposing world views collided. On one side was the European mechanistic model of nature, where scientific instruments turned mountains, trees and rivers into charts, numbers and long lists. Europeans believed that the world could be collected, preserved, painted, sorted, utilized and brought home. Nature could be pressed into grids and measurements – an understanding based on the idea of classification by which everything belonged within its neat and clearly defined category. In the Enlightenment, nature became to be viewed from a supposedly objective perspective – something to be systematically studied. The Māori cosmos by contrast was defined by its interconnectedness and fluid

* There are several interpretations of what the baskets contained, but according to one Māori tradition one basket (*te kete-aronui*) contained knowledge beneficial to humankind such as love, kindness and the arts; one (*te kete-tuauri*) contained spiritual knowledge, including rituals and chants; and one (*te kete-tuatea*), knowledge associated with black magic, harm and destructive power.

boundaries. Ancestral spirits could transcend space and time, coexisting with their human descendants. Everything – literally everything, from plants and animals to landscape features – was animated by spirits and ancestor gods. Even if the Māori and Europeans had spoken the same language, their completely differing world views would still have required translation.

At Dusky Sound, Cook's crew established a camp on shore, felling a large area of trees for fuel and planks but also to make space for a forge and an observatory in which William Wales took the measurements they needed to calculate their precise geographical position. The sound of hammers and saws echoed through the forest. They cleaned the ship, replaced damaged timbers, stitched sails, filled barrels with fresh water and collected plants, birds, fish and insects. The men washed their clothes and hung them to dry in the trees. They brewed beer from the leaves and branches of the tea tree – *mānuka* – and tall rimu with its dangling foliage. Watching this hive of activity, George Forster initially saw it through the prism of Enlightenment thinking. 'The superiority of a state of civilization over that of barbarism could not be more clearly stated, than by the alterations and improvements we had made in this place,' he wrote, 'all around us we perceived the rise of arts, and the dawn of science, in a country which had hitherto lain plunged in one long night of ignorance and barbarism!'

While the crew repaired the *Resolution*, George and his father tried to find plants. But it rained heavily, and in the dense forests they found themselves battling through dense brushwood, stumbling over a slippery latticework of roots and soil. They had to climb over large rotting tree trunks and wade through mud, slipping on moss and sinking knee-deep into decaying foliage. They also realized that it was too late in the season for collecting most plants. If they were to identify them accurately using the Linnean classification system – which relied on counting stamens and pistils – they needed blossoms. But the New Zealand summer was already over, leaving only leaves and bark to puzzle over. 'We were,' George wrote, 'greatly tantalized by the appearance of numerous trees and shrubs, which had already lost their flowers and fruits, and only served to give us an idea of the great profusion of new vegetables in this country.' The woods were breathtakingly strange – ancient trees covered in hanging moss and so many small ferns that miniature forests grew upon the branches – entire ecosystems suspended in air. Everything was green, cushioned, lush and fecund, dripping with water and life. Fallen trunks, softened by decay, had become mounds of crumbling timber and accumulated humus upon which new growth settled in the eternal rhythm of nature.

George revelled in the beauty – a sunset mirrored in the smooth water, tall mountains embraced by low hanging clouds, foaming cascades that rushed from high perpendicular cliffs and the cacophony of birds. 'The smoothness of the water', he wrote in his journal on 1 April, 'illumined by the setting sun, the different degrees of verdure, and the various notes of birds which resounded throughout the whole cove during this calm evening, greatly softened the rude, uncultivated outlines of this landscape.'

Ten days after they had sailed into Dusky Sound, George volunteered to join Cook and a few men on an exploration of the area. As they paddled along the fjord, they suddenly saw an old man on a rocky outcrop, waving a club and shouting. About sixty years old, the man was six feet tall and had his black hair tied on the top of his head. As the *Resolution* men drew closer, they greeted him and Cook, remembering his previous encounters with the Māori during the *Endeavour* voyage, waved a white handkerchief. The old man, George wrote, 'did not, however, stir from his post, but held a long speech, at certain intervals pronouncing it with great earnestness and vehemence, swinging round his club, on which he leaned at other times'. When they landed, the man at first trembled but then allowed Cook to embrace him and rub his nose against his as a sign of greeting. Cook was often the first to approach the people they met. 'He was brave, uncommonly Cool, Humane, and Patient,' young Elliott wrote in his journal, 'he would land alone unarmed, or lay aside his Arms.' The old man beckoned two women over and Māori and Europeans tried to have a conversation. Cook drily noted, 'we spent about half an hour in chitchat which was little understood on either side.'*

* Despite the communication problems, the Māori later told George that the South Island was called 'Tavai-poe-namoo', the first recording of Te Waipounamu, the Māori name.

Māori at Dusky Sound, after a drawing by William Hodges

When William Hodges sketched them, the Māori seemed pleased with the result. George and some of the officers visited the family many times over the weeks that followed. One day they arrived at the hut to find the Māori dressed in their best finery. 'Their hair was combed, tied on the crown on the head, and anointed with some oil or grease,' George noted, 'white feathers were stuck in at the top; some had fillets of white feathers all round the head, and others wore pieces of albatross skin, with its fine white down in their ears.' Communication remained difficult but George believed that they had dressed up to impress the *Resolution* crew.

A few days later the Māori came on board the *Resolution*. As they entered, the man recited what George thought to be some kind of prayer – 'which seemed to have regular cadences, and to be metrically arranged as a poem' – a *karakia*, an incantation for protection which drove away the spirits. The Māori were as fascinated by the Europeans as George was by them. They wanted to know where the crew slept and what they ate, and as they walked around the *Resolution*, they investigated chairs, hammocks and clothing, and touched the soft fur of the ship's cat.

During those days at Dusky Sound it rained so much that the plants they had managed to collect turned damp and mouldy. Nonetheless,

George continued sketching, and within their first week he had already drawn nineteen birds, three fish and a seal – after a month he had finished seventy drawings. Some days the weather was so miserable that they were stuck on the ship where the darkness forced them to light their candles at noon. Reinhold kept grumbling about his cabin which was filling up with dead birds, fish, shells and plants. It was cramped, dirty and damp, and the smell was repugnant. To make matters worse, their cabins were located next to the hatchway that sailors sometimes used as a temporary storage place, which meant that father and son couldn't leave or enter.

At least their diet improved. After the long weeks on the Antarctic ocean, the men enjoyed a varied menu of roasted, baked, broiled and stewed fish, and a kind of crayfish that was larger than a lobster. They devoured fish pies and soups, pigeon, duck and cormorant accompanied by wild vegetables. Whenever the sun broke through, they explored. One day Cook and Reinhold discovered dozens of seals lazing on a huge rock with thousands of Broad-billed Prions – small seabirds, part of the petrel family – gliding in the sky, showing off their dark M-shaped marking across their wings and back. They shot indiscriminately into the group of seals for three hours, killing fourteen and wounding so many that the water turned red. Back at the *Resolution*, the seals were served for dinner and Cook ordered their fat to be boiled out to be used as lamp oil.

Another day George and a few others paddled to a nearby cove where a large waterfall tempted them to climb the steep mountain from which it tumbled. Mist filled the air and the sun painted a perfect rainbow. The rocks, almost vertical, were fringed with overhanging shrubs and trees, and every hard surface was cushioned with soft mosses, verdant ferns and grasses. The noise of the roaring water reverberated from the cliffs so loudly that it drowned out the men's voices. From here George saw parts of the fjord dotted with little islands beyond which snow-capped mountains rose on one side, their summits enveloped in clouds, and the immense ocean stretched on the other. 'The grandeur of this scene was such,' he said, 'that the powers of description fall short of the force and beauty of nature.'

During those weeks at Dusky Sound, George always volunteered to go on expeditions. They rowed into the many inlets and coves and climbed up mountains. The long days made the men hungry. At night, they cooked a simple meal of fried fish or duck. 'One of the boat's gang-boards, washed clean, answered the several purposes of a table, of dishes, and plates,' George wrote, 'and our fingers and teeth did yeoman's service, instead of knives and forks.' Huddled around the fire, he enjoyed the sailors' stories and adventures from previous voyages – 'intermixed with hearty curses, oaths, and indecent expressions, but seldom without real humour'. Occasionally they met small groups of Māori who called out, sometimes waving branches or white bird skin. 'I could not help admiring,' George said, 'that almost all nations on our globe have tacitly agreed upon the white colour, or upon green branches, as tokens of a peaceable disposition.' Presents were exchanged and George admired the Māori's bravery. Outnumbered by the *Resolution* men, they still often initiated the contact – 'the courage of this people has something singular in it, for it should seem, that in spight of their inferiority of force, they cannot brook the thought of hiding themselves.'

It was time to find their lost consort ship which they had last seen almost three months previously, in early February, in the icy Southern Ocean. In the event that they were separated, Cook had arranged with Tobias Furneaux, captain of the *Adventure*, to meet at Queen Charlotte Sound (Tōtaranui) at the northern tip of New Zealand's South Island. Cook knew the precise geographical location having anchored there during the *Endeavour* voyage in January 1770.* So, with all the ship's repairs completed, at the end of April 1773 the *Resolution* left the little harbour which had been their home for the past month. Contrary winds hampered their progress: for several days they tried to sail into the open ocean but failed, and when Cook fell ill with a fever and stomach cramps, he decided to wait until he was better.

George made use of the extra time and went on an excursion with his father, Pickersgill and a few sailors. Paddling into a long inlet, they were entranced by the many waterfalls tumbling from steep

* It was during the *Endeavour* voyage that Cook had named the sound after the queen of Great Britain, the wife of George III.

rocky cliffs on both sides. The men stayed the night at a little beach, sitting around a fire, frying fish, talking and drinking, until late. They made their beds of layers of fern fronds under a tarpaulin tied to trees, wrapped themselves in their boat cloaks with their gun bags as pillows and fell asleep. The next morning they continued exploring until they found a small cove where they shot birds before it was time to return to the *Resolution*. Just as they were setting out, the weather turned. Strong winds blew across the inlet and whipped up the surface. Taking shifts at the oars and sharing their last rum 'by way of encouragement', they were soon exhausted without making any progress. Wind and waves threw them backwards and they decided to sit out the storm onshore.

Soaked by the rain, freezing cold and hungry, they tried but failed to make a fire. They lay on the damp ground, wrapped in wet cloaks, watching the wild sky. The storm had metamorphosed into a hurricane and the roar of the waves was only interrupted by explosive thunderclaps and huge trees crashing down. Lightning illuminated the broiling water surface. 'We saw the billows foaming, and furiously rolled above each other in livid mountains; in a word, it seemed as if all nature was hastening to a general catastrophe,' George wrote, 'our hearts sunk with apprehension lest the ship might be destroyed by the tempest or its concomitant ætherial fires, and ourselves left to perish in an unfrequented part of the world.'

He remembered it as the longest night of his life. But in the early morning, the winds abated and the exhausted group paddled out to the *Resolution*. They named the inlet Wet Jacket Arm.

Two days later, on 11 May 1773, Cook finally steered the ship out of Dusky Sound. Astronomer Wales was glad to depart, noting that 'we are now (thank God) leaving this dirty, and, on that Account, disagreeable Place.' Where George had seen grandeur, Wales found misery – 'the Country a heap of Mountains piled upon another'. But Cook was pleased with their stay here and wrote long descriptions of the trees that could be used for masts and other repairs, and of wild greens to prevent scurvy, as well as his beer recipe and an extensive list of edible fish and birds – 'better flavoured than I have any where tasted'. Unlike George who wrote evocatively and poetically, Cook provided practical information for future navigators. He gave the exact geographical position and advice on how to approach a bay, as well as descriptions of significant rock formations, peaks and islands that would help them to find it. Precise as always, he also added a warning to avoid a sunken rock near Pickersgill Harbour where they had anchored.

The New Zealand winter was approaching, the air cold and sharp. When George looked back at the coast, he saw mountains already covered in snow almost halfway to the water. But after six weeks in Dusky Sound, the crew had recovered. They had eaten well, the ship was repaired and cleaned. Now they only needed to reconnect with the *Adventure*.

After losing sight of the *Resolution* among the Antarctic icebergs, Captain Furneaux had sailed the *Adventure* to Tasmania, a large island about 150 miles south of Australia which the Dutch explorer Abel Tasman had sighted and visited in 1642. The French had landed there in 1772, but the *Adventure* was the first British ship to anchor. For a few days they charted parts of the eastern coast, stopping briefly to fill up their water stores. They saw some abandoned huts and overgrown pathways but didn't encounter any inhabitants. From there the *Adventure* sailed east to New Zealand's Queen Charlotte Sound, where they arrived in early April 1773, two months after their separation from the *Resolution*.

Like a vast river estuary, the opening of Queen Charlotte Sound was eight miles wide but narrowed as it stretched inland. Sheltered by mountains, the waters within were calm. Steep ravines, rocky headlands and densely forested ridges serrated the coastline where some of the mountains dropped in perpendicular cliffs into the sound, and others sloped down towards long beaches. The water was dark with thin azure bands along the shallow edges. When the *Adventure* reached the rendezvous point at Ship Cove, a natural harbour with a wide sandy beach and a freshwater stream, they discovered trees carved with the names of the *Endeavour*'s crew but no sign of the *Resolution*. Over the next six weeks, Furneaux's men repaired their ship, took on supplies, and also met a great number of Māori who lived in nearby settlements.

The Māori had carefully approached the *Adventure* in canoes. '*Tobia Tobia*,' they called out, using their name for Tupaia – the high priest and navigator from Raiatea, an island near Tahiti – who had joined Cook on his previous voyage and travelled with the *Endeavour* to New Zealand in 1770. As Māori and Tahitian were related languages, Tupaia had not only assisted Cook with his navigation but also acted as the *Endeavour*'s translator. In Māori tradition, Raiatea was also their ancestral homeland so they felt a reverence for Tupaia. Having seen him work as interpreter, guide and navigator, most of the Māori had regarded Tupaia as the Europeans' leader. In the intervening three years, stories about Tupaia, and the *Endeavour*'s thundering cannons and her pale-skinned crew, had been recounted by the Māori across New Zealand. And so they asked the *Adventure* crew – some of whom understood a few Māori words because they had been part of Cook's first expedition – about Tupaia and were saddened to hear that he had died during the *Endeavour* voyage.

Meanwhile, the *Resolution* was approaching the notoriously dangerous and unpredictable waters of the Cook Strait,* the passage that divided New Zealand's North and South Islands, and the entrance to Queen Charlotte Sound. In the afternoon of 17 May, George stood on deck watching the horizon. With no wind, the sea was quiet and the sails hung motionless from the yards. Suddenly, at about three miles distance, he saw a whitish spot appear on the water surface from which a column of moisture was rising, while another descended towards it from the clouds above. When the two wild whirling columns met, they became one, reaching high into the sky. Soon, more of these waterspouts appeared and zigzagged across the water surface, coming closer. These spiralling, dancing giants seemed to suck the sea water up into towering vortexes of water and wind. It was frightening. 'A phænomenon which carried so much terrific majesty in it, and connected as it were the sea with the clouds,' George later wrote, '[it] made our oldest mariners uneasy and at a loss how to behave.' George and the other men watched transfixed as one of the tornadoes raced towards the *Resolution*. As lightning flashed and hailstones pelted the deck, the waterspout was now so close that they could feel the spray of the water hurtling upwards into the spiral. But they were lucky. Just before it hit the ship, the waterspout abruptly changed direction and disappeared.

* The Cook Strait received its name after the *Endeavour* voyage.

The next morning, at 5 a.m., the *Resolution* turned into Queen Charlotte Sound. Once past the entrance Cook fired a cannon and to their delight another answered. A few hours later, they saw the *Adventure* in Ship Cove. That evening the two ships anchored next to each other and the men celebrated their reunion.

Queen Charlotte Sound, at the centre of the Aotearoa archipelago, had been home to numerous different groups of Māori over the past centuries. And as news spread that there were now two large ships, more and more Māori arrived from different parts of the sound, establishing camps at beaches nearby.

George was a gifted linguist, quick to learn Māori names and words as he pointed at plants, animals, clothing, weapons and jewellery, asking to be told what they were called and keen to understand the Māori way of life. He noted the striking tattoos – 'strongly carved with spirals in the face' – and their clothing and hairstyles. Some of the women wore caps made of brown feathers, while others had tattooed lips with several rows of blue punctures on their chin. There were young men with 'amazing bushy hair, which hung wildly over their faces', and others who tied it back and often decorated it with white feathers or carved bone combs. George described their canoes and clothing – 'an apron, made of their

A portrait of a Māori by William Hodges

close-wrought cloth, covered with red feathers, faced with white dog-skin, and ornamented with pieces of the ear-shell' – and watched them dance 'alternately extending their arms, and stamping with their feet in a violent and almost frantic manner'.

Equally fascinated by nature, George recorded black oystercatchers with bright red bills and feet strutting along the beach, and the long-necked shags, part of the cormorant species, roosting on rocky outcrops. Falcons with brown- and cream-flecked plumage glided above him, and the noisy *ka-hek-ka-hek-ka-hek* call of the Fluttering Shearwater echoed across the water. He shot birds and caught fish which he painted, and collected plants to press. One evening, he and his father caught a small tawny-brown spotted owl with beautiful golden-yellow eyes as they scrambled through the dense forest, and a few days later the now extinct slate-grey South Island *kōkako*, a bird slightly smaller than a pigeon with prominent orange wattle flaps under its beak.

The forests were thick and lush, an entangled web of evergreen trees and ferns that seemed prehistoric. Ancient rimus soared high – with dangling spiky foliage which almost looked like Spanish moss from a distance. There were giant pukatea that stood firm with their huge buttress roots and cabbage trees with dense tufts of long sword-like leaves at the tip of their branches, which the Māori used for weaving, the roots an important food source. Tree ferns laced the sky – ponga with crowns of large fronds with a silvery underside that glowed in the moonlight and the even taller mamaku which grew up to 60 feet high.

A lively trade was soon established between the Europeans and the Māori. Glass bottles, nails, hatchets and European clothes were exchanged for carved fishing hooks, tools, jewellery, weapons, cloaks – and sex. The Māori were particularly keen on glass bottles and European shirts, George observed, admiring how 'they were not inclined however to make disadvantageous bargains, and demanded the best price for every little trifle which they offered for sale'.

But when the Māori men presented their women to the sailors, George was appalled. The women were reluctant but, no matter how much they cried, the Māori men decided whether or not they had sex with the Europeans. Like Cook (who worried that his men would introduce vice and disease), George blamed the crew for having started this sex trade. He doubted whether the Māori 'ever debased themselves so much as to make a trade of their women, before we created new wants by shewing them iron-tools'. Nothing could excuse the crew's behaviour. Who was worse, George wondered, the Māori men who forced their women to have sex, or the Europeans who partook?

There were misunderstandings, some offensive, others painful. A Māori woman took a jacket from one of the crew and gave it to a young local man called Koa. When the sailor took it back, Koa punched him. The sailor then tried to step into their canoe but was pelted with stones, and he retaliated by giving Koa a black eye and bloody nose. There were also fights between the Māori – possibly triggered by tensions over exchanges with the Europeans who flooded the local economy with iron goods and other objects – and disputes among the sailors.

'I fear that hitherto our intercourse has been wholly disadvantageous to the nations of the South Seas; and that those communities have been the least injured, who have always kept aloof from us,' George now wrote. Less than two months after praising how the *Resolution* crew had shown the Māori at Dusky Sound the advantages of European improvements – tree felling, repairing, painting – George's attitude had drastically changed. It was an extraordinary statement for the time. More typical was young John Elliott, who was convinced that the Māori were 'ferocious Cannibals' who 'work themselves into a frenzey, foaming at the mouth', and Anders Sparrman, who declared that they had a 'desire to tear their enemies' limbs apart with their teeth'.

George still used the derogatory but then common terms 'barbarians' and 'savages', which for him were simply descriptive terms. Originally 'barbarian', for example, had referred to a non-Roman, non-Greek or non-Christian – or to a foreigner who spoke a different language and who had different customs. George employed it simply to mean 'strange' or 'foreign' – he didn't regard the Māori as inferior human beings. Despite being faced with firearms, two large ships and 200 men, the Māori didn't hide, George noted, struck by their courage. Yet, as he began to think about Māori life, he also quickly realized how difficult it was to learn anything about their beliefs, social structures and moral system – 'the little progress we could make in their language, rendered it impossible to gain intelligence from them.'

George Forster observed with both his mind and his heart, determined to 'banish all rash hypotheses back into their small closet'. The emphasis he placed on feeling rather than reason and objectivity stood in contrast to many (but not all) Enlightenment thinkers who valued rational enquiry, repeatable experiments and empirical observation over emotions and subjectivity.* Almost twenty years later George published an essay in which he dismissed what he called the reliance on reason alone – these 'aberrations of the mind'. He believed that 'in the sharply defined forms of abstraction, all that is good, noble and great . . . is irretrievably lost'.

On 4 June, just as the crew were getting ready to celebrate King George III's birthday on the *Resolution* that day, a large carved double canoe about 50 feet long with twenty-eight men arrived. George saw two elegantly dressed Māori standing in the canoe – the older man wearing a beautiful black dog-skin cloak and the younger, taller man a black cloak ornamented with white patches of dog skin. The younger man gave a long speech – 'from the various tones in which he spoke, and a few gestures with which he accompanied his words, he appeared by turns to question, to boast, to threaten, to challenge, and to persuade us'. His name was Te Ratu, he explained, and enquired after Tupaia.

Te Ratu looked so striking and spoke with such authority that George assumed he was one of the chiefs. The other men in the canoe were also more richly clothed than the Māori they had met so far. Their cloaks were made of flax, dog skin and feathers, decorated with white and red patterns at the borders and fastened at the neck with greenstone or whalebone pins. Even their tools, richly carved and intricately ornamented, spoke of a greater affluence. Some wore their oiled hair tied at the crown of their head and decorated with feathers and combs as those at Dusky Sound, and many had spiral facial tattoos. Cook

* Given the extent of his father's library, it's very possible that George had read David Hume's *A Treatise of Human Nature*, in which the philosopher had declared that 'reason is, and ought only to be the slave of the passions.' Hume didn't mean that people were ruled by irrational passions but that emotions (such as sympathy, love, hate, pride and so on) drove human behaviour, while reason helped them to navigate the world. Hume's moral and political essays were part of George's book collection when it was auctioned in Mainz in 1797.

A Māori warrior wearing a dog fur cloak

invited them on board and they exchanged gifts before the Māori set off again.

Despite the obvious difficulties of communication, George tried to understand the Māori's social and political structures. Observing Te Ratu, he speculated that Māori chiefs always seemed to be strong young men in their prime, although they also respected the old. Perhaps they were elected – men of courage, strength and military prowess – important qualities in time of war and conflict. 'It must be evident to them that the qualifications of a chief are not to be inherited, or propagated from father to son; and it is likewise probable, that these free people may have had opportunities of making the obvious reflection, that hereditary government has a natural tendency towards despotism.'* It would have been surprising had he not also been thinking about rulers in Europe. As George travelled the world over the next two years, his political views would sharpen and focus.

*

* George Forster wasn't wrong. Māori leadership combined inherited and acquired status. Ancestors bestowed sacred power, but it had to be enhanced with personal achievements and bravery in battle. Although a high-born person without abilities or accomplishments might still be respected, he might not wield real power.

On 7 June 1773, three days after the encounter with Te Ratu, the *Resolution* and the *Adventure* weighed anchor and sailed out of Ship Cove for Tahiti. They had been in New Zealand for two and a half months and winter was fast approaching. Cook decided that it was time to leave and to spend the coming months in a warmer climate before returning to New Zealand for another attempt to find the Southern Continent. But rather than taking the direct north-easterly course to Tahiti, he turned east in search of new lands, avoiding the route he had taken with the *Endeavour*. This wasn't a small detour – instead of 2,700 miles as the crow flies, they sailed 6,000.

On a good day they would cover more than 110 miles, sometimes – rarely – more than 150 miles, but there were also days on which they sailed as few as ten or twenty miles. Little or no wind slowed them down, of course, but so did gales and storms when they were forced to reef the sails. On their circuitous voyage to Tahiti they averaged around eighty-five miles in twenty-four hours. The long weeks at sea across the South Pacific were tedious and mostly uneventful. On 7 July, William Wales was sent to the *Adventure* to compare the watches, two days later one of their goats fell overboard and drowned, and four days after that, Reinhold marked the first anniversary of their departure from England with an entry in his journal: 'May providence continue to guard us against Misfortunes & Accidents, & procure me opportunities to describe & discover many useful things in these Seas & the Lands therein, for the benefit of mankind in general ... & may I be enabled afterwards to pass the remainder of my Days in peace & retirement.'

But there was trouble on the *Adventure*. Their cook died of scurvy and twenty other men were also ill. Cook was dismayed by the news as the *Resolution* crew was healthy and he sent instructions to Furneaux on how to stop the disease – lemon juice, marmalade of carrots, New Zealand spruce beer and more sauerkraut. He was certain that it was Furneaux's fault – 'to introduce any New article of food among Seamen, let it be ever so much for their good, requires both the example and Authority of a Commander'. The mood was dark. William Bayly, the astronomer on the *Adventure*, wrote in his journal, 'last night Mr Scott: the Lieut[t] of Marines seemed to be out of his mind, as he ran about Almost Naked talking a great deal of Incoherent stuff'. From his rantings, Bayly could make out that Scott was convinced the surgeon's mate was poisoning his tea.

It was time to change course and reach land. As they sailed north towards Tahiti, it was finally getting warmer and the men packed away their winter clothes – for the first time since leaving the coast of South Africa at the end of 1772. 'The spirits of all our people were much exhilarated in proportion as we approached to the tropics,' George noted, and 'the setting sun illumined the clouds with the most brilliant tints of gold, which confirmed us in the opinion that the colours of the sky are no where so rich and beautiful as between or near the tropics.'

Then, finally, on 7 August, almost exactly two months after leaving Ship Cove, they fell in with the long-awaited tropical breezes which blew near the equator. 'The Trade wind paid us a visit,' Second Lieutenant Clerke wrote in his journal, 'never was there a more welcome Guest.'

5

Resolution Voyage

Society Islands: 16 August–17 September 1773

'It was one of those beautiful mornings which the poets of all nations have attempted to describe, when we saw the isle of O-Taheite, within two miles before us,' George wrote on 16 August 1773, as the *Resolution* approached Tahiti. Before them, an island lifted from the emerald sea, revealing its volcanic origins in the high mountains and black sands. George drank in its splendour:

> The east-wind which had carried us so far, was entirely vanished, and a faint breeze only wafted a delicious perfume from the land, and curled the surface of the sea. The mountains, clothed with forests, rose majestic in various spiry forms, on which we already perceived the light of the rising sun: nearer to the eye a lower range of hills, easier of ascent, appeared, wooded like the former, and coloured with several pleasing hues of green, soberly mixed with autumnal browns. At their foot lay the plain, crowned with its fertile bread-fruit trees, over which rose innumerable palms, the princes of the grove. Here every thing seemed as yet asleep, the morning scarce dawned, and a peaceful shade still rested on the landscape.

The *Resolution* was soon surrounded by a hundred canoes, and trading began. George conducted business out of his small cabin porthole, bartering for new species of birds and fish as ropes were thrown down and baskets pulled up. The *Resolution* and the *Adventure* were the fifth European expedition to come to Tahiti in only six years. The first had been the British vessel *Dolphin* under the command of Captain Samuel Wallis. They had arrived in June 1767, followed by the French captain

Tahiti after a drawing by William Hodges

Louis de Bougainville in April 1768, then Cook's *Endeavour* a year later in April 1769, and finally in November 1772 the Spanish *Áquila* from Peru under Domingo de Boenechea. With each new arrival, European goods had become part of the Tahitian economy. Nails, knives and iron tools eased carving and cutting, clothes were sought after for their vibrant colours, and white cotton bedsheets were particularly valued as production of the local barkcloth was labour-intensive. Other items such as jackets, mirrors and beads became status symbols of wealth and alliances. The Tahitians were eager to trade.

In all the excitement, the crew hadn't noticed that the *Resolution* was drifting towards the reef. Suddenly, an abrupt jolt shuddered the vessel and it became all too clear that they had struck the rocks. With every wave another shock went through the ship's timbers. Now everybody was shouting. The smaller boats were hoisted down and the crew rowed frantically to pull the *Resolution* away from the reef. Even the usually calm Cook barked and swore. It was hot and the men soon became exhausted. As Cook yelled orders, his voice grew hoarse. The Tahitians helped but even so it took almost two hours to free the ship – luckily without any serious damage.

The *Dolphin*'s arrival in June 1767 had long been predicted by the Tahitian gods. In ancient times, the Polynesian deity Maui had foreseen the coming of a long canoe without the usual outrigger.* Later, a Tahitian prophet had warned that a canoe manned by a crew covered from head to toe in cloth would make landfall and change their way of life. 'There will come a new king,' he had said, 'and new manners will be adopted in this land.' At much the same time Vaita, a priest on the nearby island of Raiatea, had fallen into a trance when invaders from neighbouring Bora Bora cut down a sacred tree at Taputapuatea *marae*, the great sacred site of the war god 'Oro. When Vaita roused himself to speak, his prophecy announced the arrival of a new people who would destroy their lands:

> The glorious offspring of Te Tumu
> Will come and see this forest at Taputapuatea.
> Their body is different, our body is different
> We are one species only from Te Tumu.
> And this land will be taken by them
> The old rules will be destroyed
> And sacred birds of the land and the sea
> Will also arrive here, will come and lament
> Over that which this lopped tree has to teach
> They are coming up on a canoe without an outrigger.

Vaita's dark vision had spread across the cluster of neighbouring islands of the South Pacific archipelago, which included Raiatea, Tahiti, Taha'a, Huahine and Bora Bora. So in June 1767, when the *Dolphin* indeed appeared, the Tahitians remembered Vaita's words. Worried about the destruction of their world, they had packed fruits and plantain leaves as peace offerings and paddled in more than a hundred canoes towards the ship. The *Dolphin* was larger than any of their own splendid war canoes, and as they came closer the Tahitians could see that the people on board were, as Vaita had prophesized, unlike any they had encountered.

The *Dolphin* had left England in 1766, and Captain Wallis's men (including Richard Pickersgill now on the *Resolution* and Tobias Furneaux aboard the *Adventure*) were hungry, exhausted, and suffering

* Polynesian outrigger canoes and sailing boats had support floats on the side which were fastened to the vessel to balance it.

from scurvy. Over the next few days they tried to communicate, barter and exchange presents, but disputes soon broke out. The Europeans fired guns and cannons, killing several islanders. Hostilities simmered and a week after the *Dolphin*'s arrival, the ship was approached by a huge Tahitian armada of 300 canoes, carrying around 2,000 people with several thousand more at the shore. Against a backdrop of beating drums and the haunting sound of hundreds of conch-shell horns being blown, stones had been hurled onto the *Dolphin*. The ship's officers were terrified and ordered the crew to retaliate with a shattering broadside; when they did so, more than 300 Tahitians were killed. Over the following days there were more skirmishes. One day, women in canoes exposed their genitals – a sight that brought all sailors on deck – but for the Tahitians it was an act to channel the power of their gods against the enemy.

When this didn't help, they changed their strategy. Maybe the pale strangers were allied with their war god 'Oro. Thunder and lightning were 'Oro's signs of power – and smoke, loud noises and flashes of fire were coming from the ship. Red was 'Oro's colour and the marines on the *Dolphin* wore red coats, just like the Tahitian priests wore red feathers. And so the Tahitians switched tactics and brokered peace by bringing offerings of pigs, chickens and fruits. With explicit sexual gestures they also presented women and girls as young as eleven and twelve to the sailors. Friendly relations soon resumed.

When the French had arrived a year later, in April 1768, under the command of Captain Bougainville, they didn't know about the brutal encounters between the English and the Tahitians. They thought they had reached paradise, and named it New Cythera after the island which in Greek mythology was the home of Aphrodite, the goddess of love. 'These people breathe only rest and sensual pleasures,' Bougainville wrote in his journal, 'Venus is the goddess they worship.'

A year later, Cook's *Endeavour* spent three months on Tahiti to observe the Transit of Venus, and the British crew, like the French, also enjoyed sexual encounters with Tahitian women. Seen through their male, European gaze, they interpreted the girls' behaviour as sexual freedom and local custom, ignoring that they were often very young and had been forced by the male adults. After their return to Europe, sailors and officers claimed that the girls were as 'Eve before her sin' and free 'to offer their favours', a portrait of Tahiti that persisted in the Western world until the twentieth century.

When the *Resolution* and the *Adventure* anchored in Tahiti in August 1773, it had been only four years since the *Endeavour* had left and many islanders remembered Cook's first visit. Several crew members had learned a smattering of Tahitian during the *Dolphin* and *Endeavour* voyages, and Reinhold Forster had also brought a Tahitian vocabulary compiled by previous explorers. He had a published list from Bougainville of 600 words and several handwritten ones by those who had travelled on the *Endeavour*.*

The islanders also told them that shortly after the *Endeavour* had left, war had broken out which had continued for many months. Closely knit tribal coalitions collapsed when two rival chiefs had assembled large fleets. One of the warring chiefs was Tutaha, who had been Cook's friend during his stay in 1769 and one of the principal leaders in the northern part of Tahiti. Possibly feeling empowered by the gifts he had received from the Europeans – 'being greatly enriched by the presents he had obtained', George said – Tutaha had fought against a fierce warrior called Vehiatua, who ruled in the south. There had been several battles, but during one particularly ferocious encounter so many men had died that the ocean had turned red with their blood. It became known as *'Te-tamai-i-te-tai-'ute 'ute'*, the battle of the red sea. But eventually Vehiatua had killed his opponent Tutaha and assumed power.

As for why this had all happened, Cook was unsure – 'I never could learn the cause of the late War or who got the better in the conflict' – but by the time the *Resolution* and the *Adventure* arrived, Vehiatua's son had inherited his father's title, becoming Vehiatua II. Apprehensive that Cook might avenge the death of his friend Tutaha, Vehiatua II initially avoided contact. Only after Cook threatened to sail to the northern part of the island to trade there did the new chief agree to meet. When Cook, the Forsters, and some of the officers arrived at the

* Reinhold was underwhelmed by Bougainville's list, which transcribed Polynesian words in French spelling. Another anonymously published list, he said, was 'excessively ill spelt and had many r's inserted where none were wanted.'

beach, they found Vehiatua II surrounded by a crowd of 500 people. He was dressed in a white cloth around his waist, and his hair was light brown with reddish tips. A gentle, mild-mannered and shy youth of around eighteen, he seemed the opposite of his father. Cook offered him presents and it was Vehiatua II who told them that another European ship had anchored in Tahiti only a few months previously.* Seeing Cook's pocket watch, he became fascinated and asked why it was ticking. 'With a great deal of difficulty we made him conceive that it measured the day, similar to the sun,' George said, delighted when the young chief declared the watch 'a little sun, to shew us that he perfectly understood our meaning'.

Despite these friendly encounters, the Tahitians were reluctant to part with their pigs. The next breadfruit harvest was months away, and the islanders had only just enough food themselves. With the *Resolution* crew deprived of provisions, firewood and water, the Tahitians controlled the exchanges by determining the prices in nails, hatchets and other ironware. And indeed some things were not for sale at all. When George asked to buy a breastplate ornamented with glossy blueish-green feathers and shark's teeth laid out in three semicircles, he was politely rebuffed.

While Cook was busy trying to barter for food, George and his father went on long plant-hunting excursions. As they walked through forests and up the steep mountain slopes, George stopped every few metres to pick flowers and blossoms, filling his bag. The air was warm but not too warm, he thought, just perfect. Reinhold Forster was not as pleased, perpetually worried that they were not finding enough 'new' plants. The more new species he brought back, the greater his contribution would be to the ever-increasing pool of European knowledge and advance his position as an important scientist.

Joseph Banks and his botanist Daniel Solander had spent three months on Tahiti during the *Endeavour* voyage, giving them plenty of time to collect a great number of specimens. When George, Anders Sparrman or others enjoyed invitations to local homes or gentle strolls along meandering paths, Reinhold was forever hurrying them along.

* This had been the Spanish *Áquila*.

Up a hill, down a track, through a forest, into the next bay, he was determined not to waste the few days they had ashore. A circumnavigation was difficult for a naturalist as far more time was spent at sea than on land. It was the wrong season, Reinhold grumbled, the wrong place. 'I have been indefatigable in my several Excursions,' he wrote, 'so as to tire out all my younger Companions' – and still he didn't find enough plants. Nonetheless, he rushed back to the *Resolution* and to his notebooks every time to 'hurl hurriedly on to the paper' his impressions so that nothing was lost. The crew laughed about him – he was one of the 'Experimental Men' who 'pretend[s] to know What Was Never known. Nor Yet Never Will be Known.'

Unlike his father, George didn't mind the lack of new plants because it gave him more time to explore the island, rather than having to draw specimens in his stuffy cabin. Instead, he wanted to 'pick up various circumstances which might serve to throw a light on the character, manners, and present state of the inhabitants'. Wherever he went, he found small groves and gardens planted with bananas and coconut-bearing palms, along with tall breadfruit trees with their glossy jagged leaves and fruits the size of a small pineapple, covered in pebbled skin. There were also plants from the arum family with huge shiny leaves, and the paper mulberry trees which the indigenous people stripped of their bark to make cloth. Winding around trees and shrubs were purple yams, cultivated for their nourishing tubers. Near the houses grew exquisite *Gardenia taitensis*, a sweet-smelling evergreen shrub with a perfectly shaped white flower which is today the national emblem of French Polynesia.

One day, when George and Sparrman ventured up a steep mountain, they found themselves in the clouds, drenched in mist. When the sun burned off the clouds, the two naturalists were mesmerized by the expansive views. They felt like birds flying high in the sky. In the valleys below they saw huts with plantations of breadfruit, banana and yams appearing 'in miniature', Sparrman later wrote, 'and among them the inhabitants moved about like puppets'. Below them, anchored in the bay, which was ribboned by a black beach, they saw the *Resolution* and the *Adventure* – just two dots from that distance – as well as dozens of Tahitian canoes. The island was embraced by a reef that drew a turquoise line in the dark water. Seeing the tiny *Resolution* and *Adventure* in the vastness of the ocean, they were amazed that they had made it here through raging seas and storms. 'It astonished us,' Sparrman wrote, 'to think that we had voyaged so far on board that little vessel.'

With every excursion they made, the island became more enchanting. Passing settlements, the naturalists were often invited to join meals. After long weeks of eating vermin-infested dry biscuit, George relished the delicious tropical fruits, coconuts full of refreshing cool liquid, and roast pork which he found juicier and more tender than anything back home. He also liked the taste of breadfruits, *uru* in Tahitian. Their hard scaly skin turns from green to yellow as they ripen and the flesh inside is white and has a floury fibrous texture. Breadfruits could be harvested for eight months a year and was a staple food for the islanders. The whole fruit was baked on hot stones to be eaten like a loaf of bread with blackened crust outside and a soft tender inside – the reason why earlier explorers had called it 'breadfruit'. Another way of preparation was to peel and place breadfruits in dug-out pits for several weeks so that the pulp fermented into a paste which could be kneaded and baked like bread dough. George's descriptions of food reveal his joy: breadfruits were 'infinitely superior' to European food and the roast pork was 'beyond comparison'.

The islanders' hospitality was warm and affectionate. Sometimes George would feel a hand take and hold his as he sat beside his hosts. Other Tahitians placed their heads on his shoulder – a simple gesture that expressed more kindness than anything they could ever have said with the few Tahitian words he could understand. They embraced George, and more than once opened his shirt to touch his pale skin – 'as if to convince themselves that we were made like them'. When one of the chiefs saw that the Europeans tied their hair back in a ponytail, he took to doing the same. There was affection in these interactions, and George enjoyed being known as 'Teoree', a loose transliteration of his name. They all received names from the Tahitians: Cook had been 'Toote' since the *Endeavour* voyage, Hodges was 'Oreo', Sparrman was 'Pamanee' and Reinhold was 'Matara'. As one of two Forsters, George was the only one who had his first name rather than surname turned into Tahitian. He loved their language – 'every harsh and sibilant consonant being banished from it, and almost every word ending in a vowel' – and the islanders were pleased when he pronounced their words correctly.

As he pushed his nose into beautiful flowers and enjoyed his time with the Tahitians, George became convinced that their attack on the *Dolphin* must have been provoked, or an act of self-defence. 'Surely from all appearances these people had a right to look on our men as a set of invaders,' he wrote, 'to be apprehensive that even their liberty was at stake.' It was only natural, he noted, that occasionally some of the Tahitians were hesitant to interact with the men of the *Resolution* and the *Adventure* because it had only been five years since the Europeans had displayed their destructive power here. Others disagreed. The astronomer William Wales, who liked to expound his views in a broad Yorkshire accent, insisted that it was 'totally impossible for the Europeans to have committed any *outrage* whatever'.

Officially, George had been engaged as a draughtsman and naturalist, but unlike earlier explorers, who often resorted to clichés or oversimplifications, he was an intuitive ethnographer. For Christopher Columbus the main characteristic of the indigenous people he had encountered was 'naked', a term he used to signify a lack of civilization. By contrast, George described what he saw – 'a high forehead, arched eyebrows, large black eyes, sparkling with expression, and a well-proportioned nose'. He also paid particular attention to Tahitian dress, to the materials they used, how they draped cloth, and embellishments such as jewellery, tattoos or headgear. 'The punctuation, which the natives call tattow, consisted of the most singular square blotches on his arms, and of large black stripes across the breast, belly, and back,' he wrote, or how 'a fine white cloth like a muslin, was passed over this in various elegant turns round the body, a little below the breast, forming a kind of tunic, of which one turn sometimes fell gracefully across the shoulder'. On another occasion he described 'a kind of turban, about eight inches high, made of several skains of plaited human hair which they call tamòw', detailing how its front was decorated in rows with dozens of white, sweet-scented, star-shaped flowers which 'had as elegant an effect on the jetty black hair as if it had been set out with pearls'.

Hairstyles in Tahiti, Huahine and Raiatea

He was captivated by the dramatic and expressive dances which the Tahitians performed for their visitors and noted that 'the movement of their arms is certainly very graceful and the continual gesticulation of their fingers has something extremely elegant'. The islanders even incorporated their encounters with the Europeans into their routine. 'Three men performed something of a pantomime drama,' George described, 'which represented travellers asleep, and thieves dextrously conveying away their goods' – and they wore costumes made of blue English cloth.

George filled his notebooks. He described how the Tahitians played a flute with their nostrils – 'a kind of drowsy hum' – and often commented on how perceptive the local people were – 'with a lively intelligent countenance' and 'a very intelligent man'. One day, after walking for miles, he came across a glade in which he saw a *marae*, a ceremonial site made of three rectangular ascending levels of stones, like steps, covered with grasses and small shrubs and a wooden

Death house with corpse, and the chief mourner in his resplendent costume on the left

construction on which a corpse had been laid – a death house or a *fare tupapa'u*. 'On a kind of stage about breast high, a body of a woman was placed, covered with a white piece of cloth, which hung down in various folds,' George recorded, 'young coco-trees and bananas were springing up, and dragon-trees blossoming around it. Near this we saw another hut, where a quantity of eatables lay for the divinity *(eatua)*, and a pole was stuck in the ground, on which we saw a dead bird wrapped in a piece of a mat.' He also noted that the islanders always uncovered their shoulders when they passed one of their sacred sites – 'which is a mark of respect indiscriminately paid at the maraï by all ranks of people, and seems to annex a particular idea of sanctity to these places'.

George was equally beguiled by Tahiti's birds, by its waterfalls, tropical palm trees, and the sumptuous green of banana plants. His descriptions sing off the page: 'the evening-sun illuminating the landscape with the richest golden tints,' he wrote, or the moon 'silvered over the polished surface of the sea'. He was enraptured but he didn't idealize. Four years earlier, Banks had concluded that love was the main activity of the Tahitians, but George also saw ugliness, illness and a society caught up in war with island neighbours. A man who got 'dead drunk' on the local intoxicating kava, for example, was not the finest example of his people – 'his face was inflamed, and his eyes swelled out of his head'. Only eighteen years old, George was empathetic and perceptive, and his ability to capture foreign cultures was unusual. By contrast, when George asked an officer to recount a marriage ceremony he had witnessed during the *Endeavour*'s stay, the man replied that he could not do so. The rituals had been so peculiar, he said, that he 'did not know how to relate them'.

The curiosity was mutual. The Tahitians examined every part of the *Resolution* and the *Adventure*, investigated weapons and clothing, and were thrilled by a Scottish sailor playing the bagpipes (a sound George heartily disliked). While the Europeans claimed to have 'discovered' them, the islanders in turn 'discovered' their visitors, asking their names, where they came from, and wondered why they hadn't brought their wives. One chief asked George about their gods and 'when we told him, that we acknowledged a Divinity, who had made every thing, and was invisible, and that we also were accustomed to address our petitions to him, he seemed to be highly pleased'.

We have no record of what the Tahitians thought about the Europeans' appearance, but we do know how particular they were about cleanliness, and how they despised hairiness, for they were always plucking and shaving their facial hair. It doesn't take much to picture how the hairy, sweaty, bearded and lice-infested Englishmen suffering from infected gums and stinking breath would have been perceived.

Tahitian culture left its mark, quite literally, on the *Resolution* and *Adventure* men. Many of the sailors got tattoos. Their skin was cut with a sharp instrument made of bone, shell or shark teeth, and then a black paste made of smoked and ground nuts was rubbed into the incision. Painful as it was, the men asked for patterns or their initials, and a few had a small star incised on the left side of their chest, calling themselves the 'Knights of Otaheite'.

Over the next four weeks the *Resolution* and the *Adventure* moved around the cluster of islands that Cook had called 'Society Islands' on his first visit in 1769 – 'as they lay contiguous to one another', so close in fact that they were only a day's sail apart. Tahiti is shaped like the number 8 – the larger circle in the north-west called Tahiti Nui and the smaller

The island of Huahine

southern part Tahiti Iti. The *Resolution* and the *Adventure* first stayed on Tahiti Iti and sailed from there on 25 August 1773 to Matavai Bay at the northern coast of Tahiti Nui. On 1 September they left Tahiti and the next day arrived at the nearby island of Huahine, from where they could see Bora Bora, Taha'a and Raiatea in the distance. From 8 September, they stayed for ten days at Raiatea.

Wherever the *Resolution* and the *Adventure* stopped during those four weeks, Cook tried to meet the chiefs. On Tahiti, at Matavai Bay, they were invited by Tu, who would soon become the most powerful man on the island. At six foot three inches, he was the tallest man they met during their time there. Strong, muscular, and with a headful of curly hair, he exuded power. When Tu visited the *Resolution*, he was accompanied by so many dignitaries and attendants that there was hardly space to move. Tu first sent his brother to inspect the quarterdeck before he himself entered the Great Cabin. The guests swaddled Cook in Tahitian cloths – a ceremonial gesture to contain his sacred power, his *mana* – more presents were exchanged and the Scottish sailor again played the bagpipes, which the islanders always adored.

The Europeans tried to make sense of the fluctuating powers on the islands. Purea, for example, who had been a formidable chieftainess in the northern part of Tahiti when Captain Wallis had arrived on the *Dolphin*, had retreated into the hinterland and was according to her own report 'now entirely deprived of that greatness'. Or in Raiatea George was surprised to meet a corpulent chief – his waist apparently measured fifty-four inches – who was a native of Bora Bora. How did he achieve authority on an island that wasn't his by birth and why did the islanders wage war? 'We were at a loss to conceive the motives which could have induced a native of one of these islands to become a conqueror,' George wrote, because according to their own accounts Bora Bora was as fertile as the rest of the Society Islands. 'Therefore nothing but a spirit of ambition could have stimulated them,' he concluded, 'and it gave us pain to be convinced, that great imperfections cannot be excluded from the best of human societies.' The kinship structures, political relationships and conflicts between tribes and islands were complicated to understand, but it was clear that the islands were not the peaceful Arcadian paradise that Bougainville had described in his account (which George had translated into English in 1771) but were experiencing a turbulent time of bloody battles and shifting alliances.

The men were warmly welcomed on the different islands but that didn't mean that they understood each other. Where the Europeans separated the spiritual and physical world, the people of the Society Islands, like the Māori, were convinced that the worlds of the dead (the *pō*) and the living (the *ao*) were porous, with spirits moving easily between the two. Moments such as birth and death made the boundaries even more permeable and had to be managed respectfully with the help of plants and animals. Landscape features told stories, and the flight and song of birds could carry messages from the gods, as could waves, clouds and other animals. Like the Māori and other Pacific islanders, the Tahitians believed that rocks, birds, insects, sharks and trees were often occupied by gods, spirits or their ancestors – some dangerous, others not – all of which had to be treated with care.

Winds could be agents of spirits, the war god 'Oro was manifested in a red-feathered duck, and a great spotted octopus was inhabited by the god 'who held the sky down to earth in the dark period'. The god of medicine was in a centipede that when dropped into a wound could heal it immediately, dolphins were possessed with the spirits of people who had died at sea, and *'ope'a*, a beautiful swallow with a purplish-black plumage, was the shadow of the goddess of air. The islanders brought gifts to their sacred sites – the *marae* – as offerings to the gods and used certain plants or branches to appease them. So, when George and Reinhold shot white-bellied kingfishers and charcoal-grey herons for their collections, they were warned that they were *atua* – spirits and 'shadows of the gods'. The islanders, George noted, 'annexed an idea of holiness to these birds, and called them eatooas, which is the same name by which they design God'.

For the most part the encounters were peaceful and George Forster was moved by the people's 'peculiar gentleness of disposition'. They were intelligent, hospitable and good-humoured people, whose artisanry and skills he held in high regard. But there were also clashes. One day in Huahine, for example, Anders Sparrman returned from a plant-collecting excursion with bleeding wounds on his head and shoulder – half-naked, wrapped in a piece of barkcloth, and with only one shoe. Two men had offered to guide him, he explained, but as soon as he had entered the forest they had attacked him. One snatched his hunting knife, while the other tried to strangle him. They slammed the knife handle on his head, 'which made me see stars, and felled me to the ground'. The Tahitians grabbed his belt and yanked off his black silk waistcoat while punching him in the belly. Sparrman felt the waistcoat tear in the middle. They stripped him of his shirt and tried to pull down his trousers. In the tussle one of his shoes broke and his assailants ran off with his clothes, knife and microscope. 'Red with anger', Sparrman reported the incident to Cook, who reprimanded him for venturing out on his own. Though annoyed with Sparrman, Cook asked one of the chiefs to help recover the items. In the evening the chief returned with the knife and a quarter of the waistcoat.

In Raiatea, it was George who became the cause of trouble when he tried to convince a local man to take him back to the *Resolution* in a canoe. When they argued over the price, George called him a scoundrel and the man grabbed his gun. Hearing the scuffle, Reinhold turned around, lifted his gun and shot at the man. Reinhold had decided to take the response on this occasion into his own hands, because he considered Cook too lenient with the indigenous people. 'Mr Sparrmans robbery in Huahine was not at all vindicated,' he fumed, but he would fight 'to the last drop of my blood in defence of my property'. Luckily, the shot only grazed the man's skin, but Cook was furious when he heard about the incident. He confronted the troublesome naturalist, asserting his authority, but Reinhold noisily rebuffed the captain and reminded him of 'my Independency of him'.

Working himself up into a rage, Reinhold began to shout. When the dispute escalated, he challenged the captain to a duel – a demand Cook wisely chose to ignore but he had the shouting and kicking naturalist removed from the Great Cabin. Had Reinhold been an officer or a sailor, this outburst would have been treated as mutiny, but as a civilian he was outside Cook's jurisdiction. Reinhold stormed off and stayed on shore. It took four days, much pleading from George, and a visit from Captain Furneaux before Reinhold would even consider talking to Cook. In the end, the two men shook hands and a truce was agreed.

It can't have been easy for George to watch his father attack Cook. Since they had left England, George had seen how Cook treated the crew. He admired the captain's 'gentle, paternal discipline', he later said, and his dedication to teaching the young officers everything from longitudinal calculations to the making of charts. Cook cared for the health of his men and seemed to possess a strong sense of what was fair and just. He was the complete opposite of Reinhold.

But there was also much joy. The people of Raiatea entertained their guests with dances and invited them to a feast. A whole pig was placed in a hole in the ground filled with hot stones and leaves – 'called Barbecuing', as Midshipman Elliott noted. They ate tropical fruits but also dog – Cook tried everything that the islanders served in order to gain their confidence and friendship. One of the locals gave them the names of nine nearby islands, all but two of which had also been noted on the map drawn by Tupaia, the Polynesian navigator. Realizing that Reinhold was only satisfied when he found plants with flowers, some of the islanders brought him a fern into which they artfully stuck a blossom. Thrilled about this rare specimen, Reinhold showed it to everyone. It was only after carefully examining it that he noticed what had happened.

It was also in Raiatea that Hitihiti,* an adolescent of around seventeen years, approached George, asking if he could join the expedition. Hitihiti was five foot eight, handsome with large eyes and full lips,

* Hitihiti, or Oedidee as the Europeans called him, was also known as Maheine because he had exchanged names with a chief from a neighbouring island. For the sake of clarity, he remains Hitihiti throughout the book.

Hitihiti, after a drawing by William Hodges

well-dressed, and a relative of a high chief in Bora Bora (possibly from the same family as Tupaia). George couldn't understand why Hitihiti would want to leave. Why 'forsake the easy way of life'? Even when he warned Hitihiti about the hardship, harsh climate and terrible food on board the *Resolution*, the young man didn't waver. George introduced him to Cook, who had no objections. 'He may be of use to us if we should fall in with and touch at any isles in our rout,' Cook wrote in his logbook. After all, Tupaia had been a great asset on the *Endeavour*, assisting with navigation and communication with other islanders. That same day, Hitihiti boarded the *Resolution* with a servant and plenty of provisions.

European explorers had long been interested in commercial exploitation. They wanted gold, silver, spices and other useful plants. In pursuit of them, they had kidnapped, killed and plundered. On his historic voyage in 1492, Columbus wrote in his diary that the people of the Bahamas 'ought to make good slaves for they are of quick intelligence'. The Venetian scholar Antonio Pigafetta, who joined Magellan's voyage around the world, questioned the inhabitants of the Moluccas in Indonesia in the early 1520s not because he was interested in them as people but because he wanted to find gold. The indigenous people, he said, were more like 'irrational animals' than human. Later, in the 1570s, during an English expedition to find the Northwest Passage between the Atlantic and the Pacific oceans in the far north, several Inuit people were killed in Alaska – one of the crew members simply declared that they were 'altogether void of humanity'. It was easier to kill and enslave lesser beings than fellow humans – and Europeans had a long tradition of dehumanizing indigenous people, describing them as vermin and 'brute beasts'. Europeans considered themselves intellectually, physically and morally superior to the rest of the world.

Almost two millennia previously Aristotle, whose influence continued well into the eighteenth century, had written of individuals who were 'slaves by nature', defining them as those lacking the capacity for rational thought or deliberation. In his *Politics* he claimed that they were 'as different from others as body is from soul or beast from human', thereby offering a philosophical justification for their subjugation. Although Aristotle was not referring to different races from across the world, his ideas were later used to argue that Black people and others were naturally inferior and could therefore rightfully be enslaved.

These voyages fuelled the engines of empires and explorers filled their own pockets – the planet and its inhabitants were a resource to be exploited. Others sailed across the world to proselytize, but spreading Christianity didn't make them kinder. When Pedro Fernández de Quirós arrived in Vanuatu in 1606, his men seized the indigenous people, chained and padlocked them, shaved their beards and heads, and dressed them in colourful silks and hats with large plumes. Those were the 'lucky' ones, compared to one man whose head and feet were cut off and displayed on a tree.

Some voyagers took captives to Europe as curiosities and paraded them in palaces and at fairs. Early travellers had been fascinated by the strange and phantasmagorical – dwarfs who lived under the ground or magical creatures that could fly. In the name of science, the English philosopher Francis Bacon had written in the early seventeenth century, 'a compilation, or particular natural history, must be made of all monsters and prodigious births of nature'. Since then the focus had shifted. Instead of the bizarre and weird, explorers began to take a more serious interest in other cultures. Already during the *Endeavour* voyage Cook and Banks had tried to understand the indigenous people they encountered and their way of life. Cook, in particular, was careful not to upset their religious beliefs. 'I who had no intention to offend either them or their gods, did not so much as touch them,' he noted in his journal, when he saw what he thought might be carved wooden idols.

George went further. He found kinship where others saw inferiority. Remarkably unaffected by the prevailing attitudes of his time, he criticized European reactions. The Tahitians, for example, climbed up the anchor chains and into the *Resolution* through the portholes to steal everything they could find – bed linen, iron tools, handkerchiefs and clothing. 'I was so exasperated at his behaviour,' Cook wrote after one of the Tahitians had taken a knife and spoon from his cabin, 'that after he had got a good distance from the Ship I fired two Musquet balls over his head.' Where Cook was annoyed, George tried to understand. 'Virtue and vice are relative concepts,' he insisted, and 'no one should judge a people without considering the moral principles that guide them . . . This way we avoid any accusations of imposing our values upon a foreign nation.' Taking things didn't seem to be regarded as theft in Tahiti. Their houses were open and without doors, which he believed was proof of their lack of greed and that everybody felt safe.

There were other examples. The Europeans didn't grasp the true meaning of the Polynesian word *taio*, which they simply understood as 'friend' though it implied a ritual binding together or sharing of identity that included the free exchange of material possessions. Instinctively, George realized that the Tahitian concept of property must be different. 'The blame then lies in a great measure upon us, for bringing temptations in their way too powerful to be withstood,' he wrote, 'they seem indeed not to think their transgressions of great signification, perhaps from a reflection that they do not materially injure us by any little larceny.' In this, George was at odds with his father and the crew, who thought Cook was too indulgent when the Tahitians stole from them. This forbearance, Reinhold assumed, would 'encourage the Natives to all manner of acts of Violence'. Convinced it would compromise the security of future visits to the island, Reinhold was certain that 'too much lenity is absolutely dangerous'.

His son disagreed. George still distinguished between 'savage' and 'civilized' nations, but his comparisons did not always favour the Europeans. Quite the opposite. 'We have met with the most generous and exalted sentiments among them, that do honour to the human race in general,' he observed when in the Society Islands. 'Vicious characters are to be met with in all societies of men,' he argued, 'but for one villain in these isles, we can shew at least fifty in England, or any civilized country.' When he encountered bad behaviour, he blamed it on human nature in general, not on a specific group or nation. Good and evil could be found in all cultures.

As in New Zealand, George remained disturbed that the sailors and officers had sex with the local girls and women. After one particularly debauched night, George wrote that it was 'as if we had lain at Spithead instead of O-Taheitee', referring to the brothels that served ships arriving at the anchorage near the southern British port of Portsmouth. But he never blamed the women. The awful consequence was that venereal diseases had spread since the arrival of the *Dolphin*. As the *Resolution* and *Adventure* crews sailed from one island to the next, the infections travelled with them.* Most of the crew held the women responsible rather than themselves – the sailors and officers, gunner's mate John Marra wrote, 'had been injured by their mistresses at Otaheite'. They simply regarded the women – and often very young girls – as amorous creatures who had been 'bred to the practice of sensual delights', as Marra said.

As appalled as George was about these frequent sexual encounters, his reflections were also part of his attempt to make sense of Tahitian society. While there were chiefs, priests, and some kind of class system, the barriers seemed minimal, he thought – 'the simplicity of their whole life contributes to soften these distinctions'. Chiefs, for example, paddled their own canoes, as everybody did. 'The lowest man in the nation speaks as freely with his king as with his equal,' George noted, and 'they consider themselves as one family'. Unlike Europe, where class boundaries defined society, Tahiti's hierarchy appeared less

* European vessels brought syphilis and other diseases to Tahiti, and as a result its population shrank from around 40,000 in 1769 to 9,000 only sixty years later.

rigid – though priests and chiefs seemed to inherit their position, there was no despotism. 'There is not,' George said, 'that disparity between the highest and the meanest man, which subsists in England between a reputable tradesman and a labourer.' No one needed to starve here because 'all the necessaries of life are within the reach of every individual'. There was little sign of greed and envy.

Despite his open-mindedness and engagement with the local people, George didn't understand their social structure in all its complexity – 'here and in many other circumstances relative to civil, political, and religious institutions, we are entirely at a loss'. The islanders lived together in small groups based on family ties that shared a garden and huts. These different groups lived under the rule of an *ari'i* – a chief who lived separately and who could be male or female. Descended from the gods, the *ari'i* sacred power – their *mana* – was hereditary. Within the society there were were also priests who communicated with the gods, besides high-ranking landowners, respected warriors, specialized craftspeople, fishermen and commoners for more menial works. George identified three classes – *ari'i* (chiefs), *mánahune* (commoners) and *teuteu* (hereditary servants to the *ari'i*) – but he believed that the distinctions were far more porous than in the European feudal system.*

Although George tried to be unbiased, there were moments when he still viewed the world through the prism of European societies. When he saw an overweight Tahitian man stretched out on a mat and being fed by a woman, he was disappointed – 'we saw a luxurious individual spending his life in the most sluggish inactivity, and without one benefit to society, like the privileged parasites of more civilized climates, fattening on the superfluous produce of the soil, of which he robbed the labouring multitude.' Maybe it was everywhere the same, 'like in Europe the fattened idler in O-Taheiti is merely a miscarriage of the type of government.' If some exploited others, George thought,

* George didn't list *ra'atira*, who were independent landowners (or 'nobles'). In any case, these designations were problematic as they imposed European feudal hierarchies on Polynesian society. The definitions were ambiguous – *manahune* have also been described as gentry or commoners who owned land and *teuteu* have also been referred to as commoners without land.

the oppressed would eventually rise and bring on a revolution – even in Tahiti. What he didn't know was that Tahitian taboo rules didn't allow that man to touch food. There were limits to what a European could understand of this culture, even for an empathetic observer like himself.

6

Resolution Voyage

Tonga: 18 September–29 October 1773

On 18 September 1773, after a month in the Society Islands, the *Resolution* and the *Adventure* sailed west. The crew were sad to leave. Fourteen-year-old Midshipman John Elliott, so dismissive of the Māori in New Zealand, had thought Tahiti a paradise – 'the Men being all fine', he wrote in his journal, and 'the Women beautiful, compaired with all those that we had seen, of the Middle Size, zingy, suple figures, fine teeth and Eyes, and the finest formed Hands, fingers, and Arms that I ever saw'. The stores were filled with fresh fruit, vegetables and water, and on Huahine they had bought plenty of livestock. The *Resolution* left with 209 pigs, thirty dogs, and fifty fowls on board, and so many bananas that the deck looked like a tropical orchard. The men felt rested and healthy – except those suffering from venereal diseases.

They also had two new crew members: Hitihiti, who had boarded the *Resolution* on Raiatea, and Mai on the *Adventure*. Mai was in his mid-twenties, a tall and slim man with long black hair and small hands ornamented with tattoos. Originally from Raiatea, Mai had fled to Tahiti as a boy after invaders from Bora Bora had overthrown the Raiateans. A few years later, in 1767, he had been wounded during the bloody battle between the Tahitians and the *Dolphin* crew – the jagged scar below his ribs a lifelong reminder of the encounter. He then returned to Raiatea, but he was captured and taken to Bora Bora, from where he escaped to the island of Huahine. By his own account, he had assisted one of the high priests and travelled between the islands, but mostly he was burning to avenge Raiatea against Bora Bora. During the *Dolphin* attack he had seen and painfully felt the violent power of European

Mai, after a drawing by William Hodges

guns. So when the *Resolution* and the *Adventure* arrived at Huahine, Mai had asked if he could travel to England to procure firearms in order to fight against the Bora Borans.

Mai was affectionate and full of energy, quickly becoming popular with the *Adventure* crew who nicknamed him Jack. They were especially impressed by his fishing skills and couldn't believe how much more he was able to catch compared to them. James Burney, the Second Lieutenant on the *Adventure*, believed that Mai's curiosity and strength made him perfectly suited for an expedition. George also thought him intelligent, if sometimes too hot-tempered. He preferred the company of seventeen-year-old Hitihiti, who was also liked by the rest of the crew. Elliott was struck by his handsome looks, declaring him 'in every respect a very superior sample of this Country than Omai'.* Mai and Hitihiti were not particularly fond of each other – presumably because Hitihiti was originally from Bora Bora, which had invaded Mai's Raiatea – and they engaged with each other as little as possible.

Both islanders had to adjust to their strange new lives. Cooped up below deck in the airless space where the sailors slept, his hammock

* Mai has often and wrongly been called Omai – because Europeans ignored the fact that the 'O' simply stands for 'it is.' 'O-Mai' means 'it is Mai.'

swaying to the rhythm of the *Resolution*'s pitch, Hitihiti became seasick. How different it was to sail on this cavernous ship compared with a Polynesian outrigger canoe. He only felt better when he ate some pieces of raw dolphin, which he dipped into a bowl of seawater, and some of the fermented breadfruit balls which he had brought on board. On the *Adventure*, Mai was homesick and then terrified when he saw most of the crew assembling on deck the day after he had come on board. The captain's solemn voice, the men lacing their fingers in prayer and tracing a cross from forehead to their shoulders, convinced him that this was some kind of ritual and that they were going to offer him as a human sacrifice. It took a while, Burney said, to understand why Mai was so scared and to convince him that this was just the ship's normal Sunday service.

Despite the initial difficulties, over the next weeks the two islanders became part of the crew, respected and valued. On the *Adventure*, Burney, who had been at sea since the age of ten, looked after Mai. Burney enjoyed Mai's tales from the Society Islands even if he was exaggerating – 'he is a Small matter addicted to romancing.' On the *Resolution*, George and Hitihiti struck up a friendship. Roughly the same age, they talked and taught each other side by side at a table, George's wavy dark-brown hair tied into a ponytail next to Hitihiti's tight black curls. Hitihiti helped George to review his vocabulary from the Society Islands and George in turn taught Hitihiti English. They learned from each other.

Europeans such as Captain Cook and George Forster were not the only explorers who sailed to distant countries. Mai and Hitihiti did so too, risking their lives and not knowing if they would ever return. They left their homes and families, crossed oceans and faced dangerous adventures, driven by curiosity – and in Mai's case also by political and military motives. Like the rest of the crew, Hitihiti traded and bartered wherever they stopped, eager to bring rarities home. Over the next few months he would buy red feathers at Tonga and drums at the Marquesas Islands. At Takaroa, an island around 400 miles north-east of Tahiti, he acquired several dogs with the fine long white fur which the Tahitians used to decorate breast-plates. Mai was equally curious, Burney said, and 'takes great notice of everything he sees'.

Like Cook and the Forsters, Mai and Hitihiti each kept a sort of a journal. Mai counted the days with chips of wood, and whenever they visited a new island Hitihiti added a slender twig to a growing bundle with each stick representing another place. Similarly, Tupaia had recorded his experiences in a series of drawings – a skill he had learned from one of the artists on board the *Endeavour*.

From the Society Islands, the *Resolution* and the *Adventure* sailed over 1,500 miles west and arrived at the Tonga archipelago two weeks later, averaging a swift 110 miles per day. Two Dutch expeditions – Jacob Le Maire in 1616 and Abel Tasman in 1643 – had visited Tonga already in the previous century, but the *Resolution* and the *Adventure* were the first European ships to arrive since that time. It was a testimony to Cook's navigational skills that he found the islands in the vast South Pacific despite the notoriously imprecise geographical locations in the records of previous expeditions.

The *Resolution* travelled with the latest scientific instruments to calculate longitude – a computation which until then had been extremely difficult during long sea voyages. To determine longitude – measuring the east–west position of a ship – the navigator had to compare the exact time of their home port with the local time of their current position. If it was one hour earlier than at home, Cook knew that the distance from the home port was 15° to the west; if it was two hours earlier, they had travelled 30° towards the west; and if it was one hour later, they had sailed 15° towards the east, and so on. The local time was easily set at noon when the sun reached its highest point, but in order to know the time of the home port Cook needed a precise clock that kept time throughout the journey.*

For most of the eighteenth century the only available timepieces had been pendulum clocks, which were completely useless

* Another option to calculate the time at the home port was to observe celestial events – the movement and position of the moon against a background of fixed stars, eclipses of Jupiter's satellites or of the moon, for example, that were predicted to occur at a specific time at home and then to compare it with the local time. The problem was that such astronomical events were too rare to be of real practical use during a sea voyage.

on a pitching boat. In addition fluctuating temperatures thinned or thickened lubricating oils and expanded or contracted the metal parts of the clock, with corrosive saltwater doing its part. In 1714 the British government formed the Board of Longitude and set aside the enormous sum of £20,000 (200 times the yearly salary of the Astronomer Royal) for the discovery of a method to determine longitude during sea voyages. For several decades the British clockmaker John Harrison worked on different timepieces until he perfected his design in 1759 with his subsequently legendary H4, which looked like an oversized pocket watch and had kept its time during two trials at sea. Despite this success, the Board of Longitude refused to award Harrison the full prize money. Cook didn't travel with Harrison's expensive chronometer on the *Endeavour* but received a cheaper copy of the valuable H4 (made in 1770 by the watchmaker Larcum Kendall) to test during the voyage of the *Resolution*. The watch was so precise that Cook could find remote islands and make the most accurate charts of them.

Locked in a box to protect it, the watch was wound daily, and every time they were on land, astronomer Wales checked its accuracy with the help of lengthy lunar calculations and celestial events such as lunar or solar eclipses. But even at sea, Cook sometimes hoisted a boat into the water from the *Resolution* to send Wales to the *Adventure* to compare the timepieces. Already in Cape Town, Cook had written in his logbook that 'Mr Kendalls Watch thus far has been found to answer beyond all expectation'.

Cook had also brought a library of travel accounts ranging from sixteenth-century voyages to the most recent ones to aid him in his search for land, but sometimes the books perplexed him rather than clarified matters because it was unclear which island was which, as explorers from different countries had named them differently. Eua and Tongatapu, for example, the two islands where the *Resolution* and the *Adventure* stopped in the Tongan archipelago, had been named Middleburgh and Amsterdam by Abel Tasman in 1643. 'Had all the former Navigators taken the prudent Step to inquire the Natives, for the Names of the Islands they saw,' Reinhold wrote in his journal, 'we might be able to ascertain with certainty, what are new discoveries &

what not.'* This was why the Forsters always tried to discover and document the local terms because, as George commented, 'the indigenous name of a country is always permanent'.

When they landed at Eua and Tongatapu – or 'Ea-Oowhe' and 'Tonga-Tabboo' as George recorded the names after asking the islanders – the Tongans received them so warmly that Cook named the archipelago the 'Friendly Islands'. The islanders were kind and open, inviting the strangers into their houses, sharing food and other provisions. Even Reinhold, never easily pleased, was won over. His praise was characteristically given with an assumption of condescension. 'Though they are strangers to the high refined civilization among us,' he noted, 'the people are pretty well mannered & I may say civilized.' He recounted his delight that they were willing to carry him through the crashing surf, described how they fanned him with leaves in the midday heat, and compared them to the 'best Spaniels' when they fetched the ducks he had shot.

George almost always avoided language of this kind. 'There is not a trace of intolerance in my nature,' he later explained, adding that 'neither attachment nor aversion to particular nations have influenced my praise or censure'. He was moved by the Tongans' generosity and cheerfulness. He thought them handsome and liked their melodic music – 'they beat time to it by snapping the second finger and thumb, and holding the three remaining fingers upright. Their voices were very sweet and mellow.' He also found their intricately carved clubs remarkable – 'as if our best workmen had made them with the best instruments' – and marvelled at their sturdily constructed houses with internal partitions and immaculately maintained gardens surrounded by sweet-smelling trees.

George tried to see the islanders in the context of their culture and

* It became particularly bewildering when they tried to identify the different islands in the Marquesas archipelago in April 1774, which had been visited by a Spanish expedition in 1595 under the command of Álvaro de Mandaña. There was a lot of guessing on the *Resolution* when the islands appeared on the horizon – 'the Land we see seems to be the Isle of St Pedro,' 'perhaps Magdalena,' 'the Island next to us seems to be what Mendaña called S. Dominico,' or another 'which probably is St Christina,' and so on. They found it difficult, Reinhold noted, to 'reconcile these Sights with Mendaña's account.'

Tongan houses and gardens, after a drawing by William Hodges

environment, and in relation to other South Pacific people. He noted the similarities in language, food preparation, appearance and culture between the people of Tonga and the Society Islands, concluding 'that the customs and language of these islanders have a great affinity with those of the Taheitians'. After adjusting their pronunciation and modifying some words, Mai and Hitihiti were able to communicate and George rightly inferred that the islanders 'must have had one common origin'. Tongan and Tahitian also seemed similar to the Māori language but 'from such little *data*,' he wrote, 'we can only guess at the probable route by which a country, so far to the south as New Zeeland, has been peopled'. With incisive prescience, George noted these connections and would eventually develop a theory of Polynesian migration two centuries before it was proven.

They discovered an owl at Tongatapu they had never seen before and Hitihiti informed them that it was also found on Tubuai, an island some 400 miles south of Tahiti. When Reinhold shot a kingfisher (once again ignoring that they were *atua* – spirits), a concerned Hitihiti tried to make amends with the gods, but Mai ridiculed him, saying that his *atua* 'was eaten by the Men of *Bretànny*'. Excited about Tongan ornaments made of red feathers, Hitihiti purchased them, assuring the crew of their great value on Tahiti because they were signs of divinity, for the founding gods had worn them as they entered the world. A little piece of 'feathered-work' – about two or three fingers' width – Hitihiti explained, would be enough to purchase the largest pig back at the Society Islands. The men went on a shopping spree – bartering so much that the Tongans made fun of them. One islander even attached some human faeces to a stick and offered it as a bargain.

George and Reinhold traded too: an apron made of coconut fibre and decorated with red feathers and shell beads, a flute, a large round breastplate made of whalebone – 'white and polished like ivory' – bark-cloth, wooden neck rests, adzes, panpipes and much more. They bought patterned baskets made of coconut fibres in two colours and decorated with coconut and shell beads – 'elegant in the highest degree' – and mats 'which for workmanship and variety excelled even those of Taheitee'. Even more stunning were the Tongan woodworking skills, with surfaces delicately carved and polished by using tools made of corals and rasps of sting-ray skin. Reinhold and George traded more in Tonga than in any other region during the entire voyage. They even managed to buy a parrot (*Prosopeia tabuensis*) – a beautiful bird with a dark-red head and body, its bright green wings edged in dazzling blue and the source of the coveted red feathers.

George continued to enquire and interpret. He was intrigued to see that most islanders had at least one of their little fingers missing. It reminded him of what he had read about funeral customs in Africa and Paraguay and 'we immediately conjectured that the death of a near relation or friend might require these strange mutilations.' His assumption was later confirmed when an islander pointed at the stump of his amputated finger and then to a place where a relative was buried. George also wondered why the unmarried women slept with the sailors and speculated whether the Tongans believed that 'they will make better wives, than the innocent and the chaste?' When he noticed that the Tongans treated their chiefs with submission and obedience, he inferred there to be a robust hierarchical structure and a stronger central power than in the Society Islands. Their government, George wrote, 'though perhaps not perfectly despotic, is yet far from being democratical'. Similarly, he noticed a vast amount of weaponry which 'corresponded very ill with the pacific disposition, which had strongly shone through their whole behaviour towards us' – for him evidence that they waged some kind of war. He was not wrong. Unlike the people of the Society Islands, who confined their warfare to their archipelago, the Tongans were much more ambitious, and had at times extended their power across thousands of miles to Fiji and Samoa.

For George, the prodigious number of weapons in Tonga contradicted Jean-Jacques Rousseau's popular idealization of the 'Savage man', as did the armed conflicts and raids in the Society Islands that Mai and Hitihiti talked about. Both Tongans and Tahitians were clearly involved in wars. In 1754, the year George was born, Rousseau had written *Discourse on the Origin and Foundations of Inequality among Man*, an essay in which he explained that humans who lived in the state of nature were happy because they were uncorrupted by the vice of civilization. It was widely read and discussed during the decades after its publication and, given its prominence, would have found a place in Reinhold's extensive library.

This 'Savage man', Rousseau wrote, lived in 'that original condition in which he would pass tranquil and innocent days' – there was 'nothing so gentle as man in his primitive state'. There had been no inequality or oppression, he argued, but when people had come together in groups, small communities and then larger societies, they began to compare each other – who was stronger, more handsome or more eloquent. This gave rise to jealousy, vanity, contempt and shame, which according to Rousseau was the first move towards inequality. When the first man had fenced off a plot of land and declared it to be his property, it might have been the first step of civilization but also 'toward the decrepitude of the species'. In his section about modern society Rousseau talked about ambition, avarice, rivalry, slavery and 'a perpetual conflict which ended only in fights and murder'. The price for agriculture, industry, knowledge, science, art, food security and private property was greed, envy, inequality and wars.

When Bougainville had returned to Europe in 1769, his account of Tahiti – translated by George, of course – as an Arcadian paradise of abundance and free love seemed to turn Rousseau's fictional image of the noble savage into reality. Finally, here was tangible proof. Beautiful men and women, seemingly untouched by civilization, joyously living on tropical islands where sweet fruits dangled from trees and the sea was full of fish – a land of plenty where everybody was well-fed and peaceful. This, so many Europeans believed, was Rousseau's imagined society in a natural original state – people who were compassionate and content. George disagreed. 'The happiness of the *tame slave* is just as fictitious as the happiness of the *free savage*,' he would later write, and 'the state of nature, as the philosopher from Geneva [Rousseau] presented it to us, was, as we know, only ever a product of his imagination.' It was certainly not a reflection of what George observed in the South Pacific.

The *Resolution* and the *Adventure* spent less than a week in Tonga before setting out again to sail 1,500 miles to New Zealand. From there Cook wanted to turn south to the high latitudes for a second attempt to find the elusive Southern Continent. Three weeks after leaving Tonga, however, they were caught in a furious storm as they approached New Zealand's Cook Strait. It was now late October 1773, with the southern spring giving way to summer, but huge waves rolled over the decks, drenching bedding and clothing and throwing furniture around in the cabins beneath. Above, as sails ripped and ropes broke free, sailors had to climb into the rigging where they stood on foot ropes fixed to the high horizontal yards, fighting to reef the sails as they seesawed up and down towards the raging sea with each passing wave. At night, they couldn't even see where they were stepping, their feet remembering every inch of the timbers and their hands having to grab ropes instinctively. The storm metamorphosed into a hurricane and the sea was so violently agitated that the wind dissolved the crowns of the waves into vapour, blown like smoke over the ocean. 'The tremendous roar of the waves, the creaking of the timbers, and the rolling motion deprived us of all hopes of repose,' George wrote, 'to complete this catalogue of horrors, we heard the voices of sailors from time to time louder than the blustering winds or the raging ocean itself, uttering horrible vollies of curses and oaths.' No one could sleep.

On the *Adventure*, Mai was terrified, having never seen anything like this, while on the *Resolution*, Reinhold clung to his cot with both hands, regretting that he had ever agreed to come on the voyage. Eighteen-year-old George sought relief out on deck – soaking wet, freezing cold, but mesmerized. The wild ocean 'was at once magnificent and terrific', he wrote, 'now on the summit of a broad and heavy billow, we over-looked an unmeasurable expanse of sea, furrowed into numberless deep channels; now on a sudden the wave broke under us, and we plunged into a deep and dreary valley, whilst a fresh mountain rose to windward with a foaming crest, and threatened to overwhelm us.'

Then, on the evening of 29 October, the fifth day of the storm, the tumultuous seas separated the *Resolution* and the *Adventure*. Cook and the crew on the *Resolution* fought on for four more days before they finally sailed once more into Queen Charlotte Sound, and into Ship Cove, at the northern tip of the South Island of New Zealand.

7

Resolution Voyage

New Zealand (Aotearoa) and Antarctica: 3 November 1773–end of February 1774

When the *Resolution* dropped anchor in Ship Cove on 3 November 1773, the men could see large shoals of fish swimming beside the ship and white-bellied albatrosses floating above them, their enormous black-tipped wings spanning nine to ten feet. Cook had assumed that the *Adventure* would seek out the small harbour at the entrance of the mountain-hugged Queen Charlotte Sound where they had stayed five months before, but their consort ship was nowhere to be seen.

When the locals canoed out, George recognized some of them, calling their names. They included Te Ratu, one of the men he had believed to be a chief during their first stay. George was puzzled to see him dressed in what looked like old clothes rather than his elegant cloak – 'in short, from being the orator and leader of a troop of warriors, he seemed to be degraded to a simple fishmonger' – but he couldn't find out what had happened. The Māori welcomed the exhausted men with fresh fish and water. The *Resolution* crew began their preparations for the second journey south, establishing workshops on shore for their carpenters, coopers and sailmakers. Over the next three weeks they repaired sails, replaced ropes, caulked the hull, scrubbed the decks, stocked up on food and fresh water, and scraped off the mould from their store of ship's biscuit and baked them again.

George and Hitihiti scoured the surrounding forests, mountains and islands for plants and animals. Even as summer was approaching, it was still cold with fog in the mornings and strong winds. George sketched

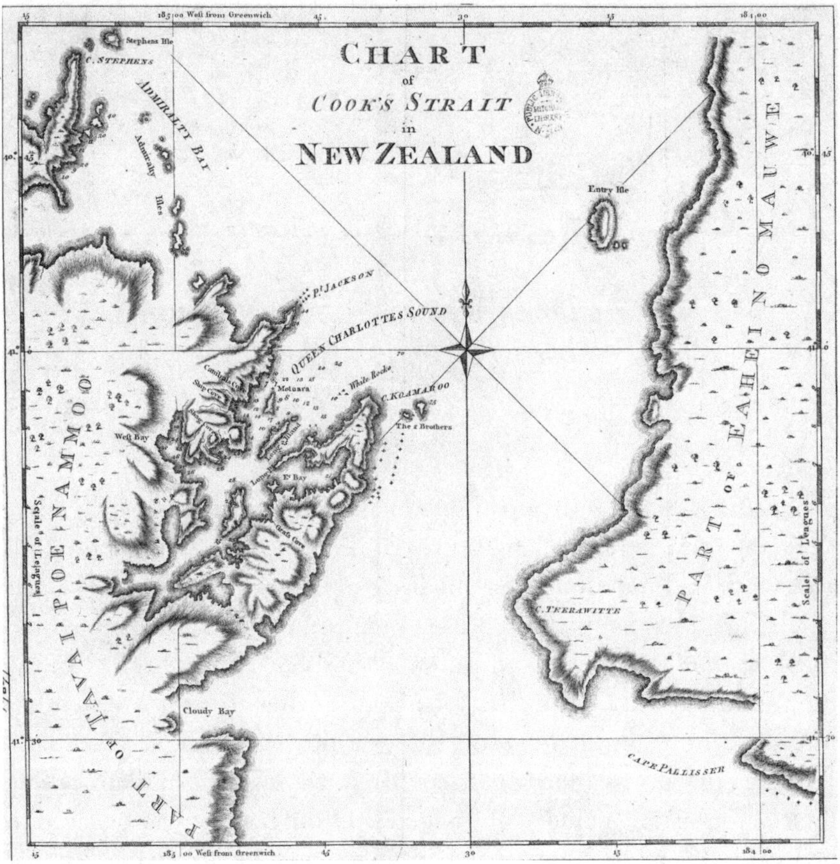

Chart of Cook Strait and Queen Charlotte Sound

his finds, among them a Shining Cuckoo with its metallic coppery-green wings and zebra-striped belly and face, and a small reddish fish that would later carry his name, *Forsterygion varium.* On an island opposite the *Resolution*'s anchorage, George was intrigued to discover that petrels nested in burrows in the ground – the small seabirds 'croaking like frogs and cackling like hens'. When Hitihiti used George's musket to shoot a bird, he hit the target on the first attempt. George was impressed by his friend's marksmanship – Hitihiti's eyes were much sharper than those of the Europeans.

Like Tupaia a few years previously, Hitihiti's language skills proved useful over the next three weeks. Less fluent than Tupaia, his grasp of

Māori was still good enough to communicate and he was certainly better than any of the men on the *Resolution*. Like the rest of the crew, Hitihiti considered the Māori inferior, living a wretched existence compared to life in the tropical Society Islands. 'He also frequently expressed his pity,' George noted, 'whilst he enumerated to us a variety of articles of which they were ignorant.' None of this stopped Hitihiti from sleeping with the Māori women – to George's disapproval.

On 15 November, two weeks after their arrival, the Forsters, Hitihiti and Cook scrambled up a high hill in the hope of spotting the *Adventure* along the coast, but conditions were hazy and there was no sign of the ship. Time was against them, for they would soon have to leave if they were to benefit from the milder temperatures of the Antarctic summer.

A week later, on 21 November, a group of Māori women paddled out and told the *Resolution* crew that they were worried. Their men, the crew learned, had left to attack their enemies. Who those opponents were remained unclear, but the next morning dozens of Māori warriors, their cheeks painted red, arrived in a flotilla of eight canoes packed with cloaks, weapons and greenstone objects to trade with the *Resolution*. Suspecting that the warriors must have raided a neighbouring settlement to sell their goods to the Europeans, George wrote, 'I am much afraid

A Māori village

that their unhappy differences with other tribes, were revived on our account'.

In any event, it was time for the *Resolution* to leave and the next morning Cook took a few men to a neighbouring island to collect sea celery, wild spinach and other greens as provisions for the long journey.* Some officers rowed to a nearby cove to trade. When they pushed their boat ashore, they saw the Māori warriors from the previous day, and also something round and red impaled on a stick, possibly an organ, maybe a heart. As they looked around, they found more organs and intestines scattered on the ground – and to their horror a human head from which the lower jawbone was missing. The skull had clearly been fractured by something blunt, perhaps a club. The victim seemed to have been an adolescent boy. As the officers stared at the bloody heap, the Māori skewered the lung and showed them more body parts. When the officers asked what had happened, the warriors told them that there had been a fight with their enemies. With words and gestures, they explained that they had killed the boy and eaten parts of him, but they too had lost men, pointing at some weeping women nearby who were cutting their foreheads with sharp stones as they lamented the dead.

For Europeans, cannibalism seemed inconceivable. 'In accordance with human nature,' said Immanuel Kant, Germany's most respected philosopher, 'there cannot be many [man-eaters], or, more likely, perhaps none at all.' As explorers had returned from South America and the South Pacific in previous centuries, there had been rumours and the occasional suspicious body parts but no one had ever actually observed the practice. In January 1770, during the *Endeavour* voyage, the Māori had confirmed that they did indeed eat people by picking up a human bone and pretending to bite into it. They 'shew us that they had eat the flesh they bit a[nd] naw'd the bone and draw'd it thro' their mouth and this in such a manner as plainly shew'd that the flesh to them was a dainty bit', Cook had recorded in his logbook. The graphic demonstration had been enough to convince the crew. Richard Pickersgill, who had also travelled on the *Endeavour*, had noted that the 'Barbarrous

* They collected sea celery (*Apium prostratum* or *Tutae Koau* in Māori), New Zealand spinach (*Tetragonia tetragonoides* or *Kōkihi* in Māori) and Cook's scurvy grass (*Lepidium oleraceum* or *nau* and *ngau* in Māori).

cruelty these savages is guilty of which ought to make them to abhord by all who may have occasion to tutch at these Islands'. This didn't stop him from trying to purchase the half-eaten head now, so that he could take it to London to show his friends. He offered a nail and a bargain was struck.

When the men returned to the *Resolution*, Pickersgill placed his grisly purchase on a railing and soon everybody on board had gathered to examine it. Another group of Māori had come to the *Resolution* to trade and they now asked for the head so that they could eat it, but the new owner refused. Second Lieutenant Charles Clerke, who was known and liked for his practical jokes – 'a genal favorite', as young Elliott said – proposed an experiment. Taking a sharp knife, he cut off one cheek and handed it to the Māori, but they gestured that they only consumed cooked flesh. After debating what to do, Clerke put the cheek on a gridiron and grilled it over the fire in the galley kitchen.

Transfixed the crew of the *Resolution* watched the Māori eat the cheek. Some goaded them, and others were revolted. Some even seemed tempted to try a bite themselves. A little later, when Cook returned from gathering wild vegetables, he demanded that the spectacle be repeated. He wanted to prove the rumours once and for all. 'Being desireous of being an eye wittness to a fact which many people had their doubts about', Cook wrote in his logbook, 'I concealed my indignation and ordered a piece of the flesh to be broiled and brought on the quarter-deck where one of these Canibals ate it with a seeming good relish.' Describing the scene as calmly as a scientific experiment at the Royal Society in London, Cook concluded 'that the New Zealanders are Canibals can now no longer be doubted'.

Hitihiti was appalled and 'Metamorphosed into the Statue of Horror'. Crying inconsolably, he hid in a cabin and it took George several hours to calm his friend. George was also shocked but refused to regard the Māori as heartless barbarians, determined to understand their motivation. It couldn't be hunger, given the abundance of fish in Queen Charlotte Sound and the Māori's productive vegetable gardens. Perhaps, then, the motive was revenge. Weighing up the arguments, he noted: 'The New Zealanders never eat their adversaries, unless they are killed in battle; they never kill their relations for the purpose of eating them; they do not even eat them if they die of a natural death, and they take no prisoners with a view to fatten them for their repast.' Although he might never know their exact reasons, 'the action of eating human flesh, whatever our education may teach us to the contrary, is certainly neither unnatural nor criminal in itself.'

Others thought differently. Their only motivation 'was the liking which they have for this kind of food', William Wales believed, the Māori relished the taste and ate human flesh 'in cool Blood'. George disagreed. No matter how gruesome, Europeans had no right to judge something they didn't understand. They couldn't condemn the Māori for what seemed to be an integral part of their culture and heritage. Europeans were brutal too. They might believe themselves far too civilized to be cannibals, he argued, but 'we do not find it unnaturally and savagely cruel . . . to cut one another's throats by thousands, without a single motive, besides the ambition of a prince, or the caprice of his mistress!' Given his wide reading, he may well have known Montaigne's essay *Of Cannibals* in which the French philosopher had made a similar argument, insisting that Europeans 'exceed them in all kinde of barbarisme'.*

On 24 November 1773, the day after watching the Māori eat the cheek, Cook put a message for the *Adventure* into a bottle under a tree in which they inscribed the words 'LOOK UNDERNEATH'. The next day he ordered his men back on board and turned the *Resolution* south towards Antarctica.

Less than a week later, when the *Adventure* sailed into Queen Charlotte Sound, on 30 November 1773, Captain Furneaux was disappointed not to find the *Resolution*. After being separated in the storm a month earlier, the *Adventure* had tried to fight the violent seas of Cook Strait. After five long days, Furneaux had eventually given up because his men were exhausted and their water casks almost empty. He had turned the ship north and sailed to Tolago Bay on the east coast of the North Island where Cook had stopped during the *Endeavour* voyage. After a week

* George owned Montaigne's *Essays* when his library was auctioned off in 1797.

there, during which the crew collected water and made some emergency repairs, Furneaux had set out again on 16 November. It took them two weeks to reach Ship Cove, battling strong gales, high seas and rain which tore their rigging and sails. The *Adventure* crew were glad to set foot on shore. It was Mai who found the inscription on the tree and brought Cook's bottle to Furneaux. Reading the date '24 November 1773', Furneaux couldn't believe that they had missed the *Resolution* by less than a week. The message was brief. As he had 'not the least hopes of meeting with Captn Furneaux', Cook had written, 'he will not take upon him to name any place for a Rendezvous'. As for the *Resolution,* Cook had finished his note by saying he wasn't sure where they would sail after attempting to find the Southern Continent – maybe Easter Island, maybe Tahiti – 'but this will depend so much on the Circumstances, that nothing with any degree of certainty can be determined upon'.

There was not much that Furneaux could do about Cook's decision but he could sail south without the *Resolution*. He ordered his men to get the *Adventure* ready for the cold Southern Ocean. At shore they set up tents as workshops, but soon thefts turned the cordial relationships with the Māori dark. During the night of 14 December, the Māori stole valuable instruments, linen and other items from the tent of the astronomer William Bayly. In his rage, Bayly lifted his gun and wounded one of the Māori. Furneaux thought it wise to leave. Before doing so, he sent ten men in their cutter – a small sailing boat – to collect greens and wild celery for their stores.

When his men didn't return that evening, the captain sent out a search party the next morning. Keeping close to the shore, they looked into every creek and bay they passed. Nothing. There was no sign of their friends. All day they paddled from one bay to the next. There were some Māori settlements where they questioned the locals but couldn't get any answers. Finally, at five o'clock in the afternoon, they saw a large double canoe hauled up at a small beach and a group of Māori who fled on seeing the white men approach. Within the canoe, the men from the *Adventure* found some of their cutter's iron parts and a pair of shoes. Looking around, they saw some twenty baskets in which they discovered fern roots and roasted meat, still warm from the fire. At first they believed it was dog meat, but then found more shoes at the beach and a human hand inscribed with 'T.H'. They immediately knew that it belonged to Thomas Hill, one of the sailors who had been tattooed on Tahiti a few months previously.

Smoke was rising from a nearby hill and they returned to the boat to paddle into the next bay – Grass Cove. As they came closer, they saw several canoes and a great number of Māori at the beach, and a blazing fire beyond the forest. 'The place was throngd like a Fair,' noted Burney, the search party's leader, before ordering the men to lift their muskets and fire into the crowd from the safety of their boat. The Māori fled up the hill and Burney and his men landed. As they searched the beach, they saw dogs chewing discarded entrails and the remains of their friends – hands, hearts, lungs, livers and the severed head of Furneaux's servant – roasting on the fire. More hands and limbs were scattered about. It was 'such a shocking scene of Carnage & Barbarity', Burney reported, 'as can never be mentioned or thought of, but with horror'. All ten men had been killed.

Silently, the men collected body parts and organs. The sun set just before nine o'clock, and as night crept in they finished their gruesome task and paddled back in darkness. Suddenly Burney heard a voice in the distance. Putting down their oars, the crew listened as their boat quietly glided through the water. Nothing. Calling out several times, they waited for an answer, but there was no reply. They must have imagined it. Just before midnight they reached the *Adventure*. They brought their grim haul on deck for the ship's surgeon to examine – but he couldn't work out which body part belonged to which man. In the end, everything was put into a hammock with cannon balls as ballast and given a sea burial. That night every man aboard the *Adventure* slept armed with knives or muskets, fearful that the Māori might attack.

Early the next morning, they hurriedly left Queen Charlotte Sound. The *Adventure* sailed south in search of the Southern Continent but only encountered more icebergs and thick fogs. The waves were so high that they constantly breached the ship and the crew was despondent. When Furneaux discovered that the dried peas and flour were not edible any more, he turned the vessel around. His men were sick and he was certain that there was no land among the ice. On 3 March 1774 he changed the route and headed east to Cape Horn and across the Atlantic to Cape

Town and from there to England, where they arrived on 14 July. They never reconnected with the *Resolution*.

Meanwhile the *Resolution* was sailing south, following Cook's plan to complete a 360° circuit at a high latitude to prove or disprove the existence of land. During their first attempt they had covered almost half of that circle, beginning at 18°E longitude (roughly the same as Cape Town) all the way to 166°E, the longitude of New Zealand's Dusky Sound. No one was looking forward to what George Forster called these 'chilling horrors'. The past seventeen months had been a voyage of extremes. In the tropics, the lower deck and cabins had been hot, humid and airless. Now, as they crossed the Antarctic circle for the second time, it was freezing again. During these long stretches at sea, when there was no other distraction, George took out his watercolours and paintbrushes, working his quick pencil sketches up into detailed images in colour. Reinhold and George's two small cabins had been cramped even on their departure from England, but now they also contained stacks of drawings, along with their collections of dried plant specimens, animals preserved in alcohol in bottles, birds, shells and more. Reinhold continued his complaints: 'My & my Sons accommodations were the worst in the whole Ship', for 'every thing I touch is moist & mouldy & looks more like a subterraneous mansion for the dead than a habitation for the living', and 'my Cabin cold & open to the piercing winds'.

The strong winds and lashing rain persisted. 'Excessive cold and raw', 'squalls with hail', 'a stiff gale', 'a great fall of snow', and 'intolerably cold', noted Marra, the gunner's mate, in his journal as they passed huge icebergs. Snowflakes the size of goose feathers fell thick on the deck of the *Resolution*. Where George had seen beauty, Marra described the icebergs as 'grotesques forms of monsters'. They heard penguins braying as if to outdo the eerie songs of icebergs grinding against each other, adding 'horror to the scene', Marra noted. Sometimes they sailed in fog so dense that they couldn't even see anything, in constant danger of colliding. In mid-December there were so many thick ice floes all around them that the ocean seemed more like a heaving mass than water. Despite Cook's careful handling, the *Resolution* scraped them and shocks shuddered through the timbers. One day they came so close to an iceberg twice as high as their main mast that everyone was convinced it was their end. Cook ordered the men to keep spars ready to push the ship away from it, but all they could do was watch how they inched closer. 'To describe the horror depicted in every person's face at the awful situation in which we stood is impossible,' Elliott recalled, but luckily just as the *Resolution* was about to ram into the iceberg, she turned slightly, just enough to avoid it – 'certainly never men had a more narrow escape from the jaws of death'.

By now, the rigging was so thickly covered in ice that the sailors could barely grasp it, the running tackle was frozen, and Marra recorded that some of the men had icicles an inch long and more dangling from their noses. 'Our ropes were like wire,' Cook wrote in his logbook on Christmas Eve, and 'Sails like board or plates of Metal'. The temperature in George's cabin was only two and a half degrees warmer than on deck.

For exercise, George and Hitihiti walked the quarterdeck. Twelve steps in one direction, and twelve steps back. Up and down, and then again and again and again. Dressed in the same warm woollen trousers and jacket as the rest of the crew, from a distance Hitihiti almost looked like one of them. The two young men tried to get warm by huddling together in front of the stove in Cook's Great Cabin, but even this usually light, airy room was uncomfortable. The air was filled with smoke from the stove, damp sails had been laid out to dry, and everybody was farting from the sauerkraut and dried peas they were eating to avoid scurvy. The two young friends continued their language lessons and Hitihiti distracted himself by sorting the red feathers he had bought in Tonga. Some of the crew began to grumble that the young islander received preferential treatment while they struggled outside. 'He is still indulged in the captain's cabin,' Marra complained.

It was now so cold that the birds they had brought from New Zealand, Tonga and Tahiti died. One day Elliott climbed up to the mast and counted 300 icebergs amid all the floating ice. The 'whole scene looked like the wrecks of a shattered worlds', George wrote at Christmas, 'the ocean about us had a furious aspect, and seemed incensed at the presumption of a few intruding mortals'. The South Pacific Ocean 'had no *pacific* aspect', his father laconically remarked.

Used to a more tropical climate, Hitihiti felt the cold more acutely than the others but he was just as amazed by this icy world – 'white land, or *whennua tèatèa*' as he named it – and the southern lights as George had been a year previously. He was bewildered by hailstones – 'white stones' he called them – which melted in his hand, and by the short Antarctic nights which lasted but a few minutes. He was 'struck with the greatest astonishment', George noted, but also despaired that he could ever make his people believe in the 'wonders of petrified rain, and of perpetual days'.

When Cook doggedly continued to direct the *Resolution* through freezing waters instead of sailing to Cape Horn and then to England, the mood turned dark. Stuck on a small damp ship with diminishing provisions, and surrounded by icebergs that creaked so loudly 'as if the whole earth was cleaving asunder', the men began to quarrel. They were cold, hungry and bored – all the tales and stories from the past had been told so many times that no one wanted to hear them any more. When two drunken midshipmen had a knife fight which almost ended fatally, Cook punished them with twelve lashes each. Most of the men wanted to return home. They had no more fresh food and the salted pork and ship's biscuit was now one and a half years old. The biscuits were swarming with so many little beetles and weevils that swallowing the creatures was inevitable – *Curculio granarius* and *Dermestes paniceus* as Sparrman diligently noted in his journal. Their pea soup was full of larvae and maggots 'as if they had been strewed over our plates on purpose'. It was revolting and the men dreaded mealtimes.

It didn't help that Cook refused to reveal his plans. Whenever he was asked, the captain only smiled and didn't say anything, Elliott observed, 'for he was close and secret in his intentions at all times'. Not even his officers knew how long he intended to keep on going. 'Nothing,' George said, 'could be more dejecting than the entire ignorance of our future destination.'

By the end of December 1773, Reinhold Forster couldn't bear it any more. This was the very idea of hell, he moaned, surrounded by a desolate frozen world and by 'drunken Sailors hollowing & hurraing about us, & peeling our Ears continually with Oaths & Execrations, curses & Dam's'. To the crew's undoubted relief, he stayed in his cabin for most of January 1774. Holed up with the freezing water sometimes rising ankle deep, struggling with fevers, rheumatic pain and headaches, Reinhold had plenty of time to worry about his future. How was he supposed to discover plants and animals in this forsaken icy seascape? While he was sailing back and forth between New Zealand and the icebergs, Joseph Banks and Daniel Solander would be publishing their results from the *Endeavour* voyage in London. Finding an island or land so far away from Britain in such an inhabitable world seemed pointless. As Reinhold filled the pages of his journal, he spiralled into a deep depression. On 15 January, when a huge wave crashed over the deck and through a skylight, all the candles went out. The Great Cabin and Reinhold's cabin were flooded. Water came in from all sides and everything was soaking wet. The water could be bailed out, but bedding and clothing didn't dry in the cold.

Finally, more than two months after leaving New Zealand, they reached 71°10′ south, on 30 January 1774. Ahead, a huge icefield stretched as far as they could see. It was impossible to get through – 'we could not proceed one Inch farther South', Cook had to admit. They couldn't know that they were only 120 miles from Antarctica.* No one had ever been this close. When the captain ordered the *Resolution* to turn north to the warmer latitudes, there was enormous relief. But Cook had no intentions of returning home.

A few days later, he wrote a long entry in his logbook in which he laid out his plans. He was going to search for Easter Island – 'the situation of which is so variously laid down'. From there he would sail all the way to the archipelago which the Portuguese navigator Pedro Fernández de Quirós had called La Australia del Espíritu Santo in 1606 (today's Vanuatu which was more than 5,000 miles west of Easter Island). Quirós had claimed that the island group was very large (he thought it was the Southern Continent), a description which Bougainville, who had stopped there in 1768, had neither confirmed nor refuted – 'I think it a point well worth clearing up,' Cook noted. From there he planned to head south again and then east along the 60°S latitude all the way to Cape Horn at the southern tip of South America – another 7,000 miles.

* This was the Walgreen Coast of Mary Byrd Land of Antarctica.

Even if there wasn't a Southern Continent, 'there remained nevertheless room for very large Islands in places wholy unexplored and many of those which were formerly discovered, are but imperfectly explored and there Situation as imperfectly known'. Prudently, Cook kept his plans quiet.

By now, the crew were ill and emaciated – and despite their sauerkraut rations so weakened by scurvy that many couldn't work or even walk. George was particularly badly affected – his legs were so swollen that he could hardly move, his infected gums bleeding, and his body covered with livid blotches. For the rest of his life, George would struggle with ill health, suffering from stomach cramps and rheumatism. He would always maintain that scurvy and the long cold and damp months among icebergs had wrecked his body – 'my poor stomach has been ruined by salt pork and rotten ship's biscuits'. But despite the excruciating pain, he now and again forced himself out of bed to crawl on hands and knees across the deck. His father had a terrible toothache, a sore throat and rheumatism. 'All things look gloomy & dismall,' Reinhold wrote in his diary, 'I do not live, not even vegetate, I wither, I dwindle away.' Everybody looked pale and had lost their appetite. Regardless, Cook continued his strict cleaning regime – whenever the weather allowed, the ship was scrubbed and the hammocks were brought out to air. But even Cook became sick, suffering from such painful stomach cramps and constipation that the ship's surgeon feared for his life. When purged, given enemas and administered opium, he then suffered a hiccup attack that lasted over twenty-four hours. They were all desperately miserable.

8

Resolution Voyage

Easter Island (Rapa Nui) and Society Islands: 11 March–4 June 1774

As January turned into February, the *Resolution* sailed north through the empty waters of the South Pacific, leaving the icy high latitudes behind. The further north they moved, the milder the weather became and by the beginning of March 1774 the first tropical birds accompanied them. They urgently needed to find an island where they could recover from the hardships of the previous months and restock supplies. Then, on 11 March 1774, the exhausted men sighted Easter Island (Rapa Nui) in the distance, the first land they had seen since leaving New Zealand 103 days earlier. Some 4,400 miles from New Zealand, the remote island had been named by the Dutch navigator Jacob Roggeveen, who had landed there on Easter Sunday 1722. Since then, only the Spanish had stopped here, for five days in 1770.

Everybody on board the *Resolution* was anxious to reach the island, but with contrary winds the ship didn't seem to move towards it at all. The next morning, when George picked up his spyglass, he saw dark-grey cliffs dropping perpendicular into the sea. The little vegetation he could make out looked parched, and their hopes for fresh food sank. It took two more days to reach the island.

Once they dropped their anchors, George saw two men in a canoe paddling towards them. When the islanders reached the *Resolution*, they pointed at a rope which George threw down for them to tie to it a bunch of sweet ripe bananas. 'The sudden emotions of joy in every countenance, at the sight of this fruit, are scarcely to be described,' George wrote, 'they

A scene sketched by William Hodges of Easter Island (Rapa Nui) with the moai – the stone sculptures.

can only be felt in their full extent by people in the same wretched situation with ourselves at that time.' Still in agony from his swollen legs, George forced himself ashore. It was a bleak landscape, desolate and devoid of trees. The sun was brutally hot, and the men burned their faces so badly that their skin blistered and peeled.

Perplexed by the huge stone statues they found here – human figures with extremely large heads and no legs, several metres high – George suspected that they were held in veneration. They asked the islanders 'and from what we could understand, we concluded that they were monuments erected to the memory of some of their areekees, or kings'* – *ariki* was the Polynesian word for chief (or *ari'i* in Tahitian). Usually able to adjust his viewpoint, these statues seemed just too baffling to George to appreciate. 'The workmanship of this figure was rude,' he wrote, 'a European artist would have been ashamed of them.' Where he had thought Tongan woodcarvers the equals of England's best craftsmen, these statues showed 'the arts in their infancy'.

* Today it is believed that the statues were carved between AD 1250 and 1500 as representations of ancestors and sacred spirits. Historians and archaeologists have speculated that the introduction of Polynesian rats and deforestation led to conflict, war, starvation and the societal collapse on Rapa Nui.

George noted that the islanders here looked similar to the Tahitians except for their very elongated and pierced earlobes which almost reached their shoulders – 'in order to bring it to this size, they wore a leaf of a sugar cane, which is very elastic, rolled up in it like a scroll; by which means it was always on the stretch.' They also had barkcloth, favoured red as a colour, had tattoos, and prepared their food not unlike those islanders the *Resolution* crew had met across the South Pacific islands. Their vocabulary revealed a common root with Māori and Tahitian words, he realized, and Hitihiti was delighted to be able to converse with them. Despite being thousands of miles away from New Zealand and Tahiti, George was certain that the islanders had 'one common origin'.

Their faces were painted brown with streaks of white shell lime and some men wore large bushy caps made of brown gull feathers – almost 'as large as the full bottomed wigs of European lawyers'. Some were dressed in tattered blue jackets and European hats, which they had traded with the Spanish explorers who had stopped here four years previously – 'indubitable testimonies of the visit which the Spaniards had made to this island'. Headdresses were regarded as sacred in Polynesia and the islanders snatched Hitihiti's black cap as well as Hodges' hat while he was sketching the statues. On another occasion, an islander grabbed Reinhold's plant bag, and one of the marines shot and wounded

A man from Easter Island with elongated earlobes

him. Though Reinhold mentioned the incident briefly in his journal, George wrote about the moral implications – it was tragic 'that Europeans too often assume the power of inflicting punishments on people who are utterly unacquainted with their laws'.

Trading proved difficult. Not only had the marine injured a man but the islanders had few provisions to spare. When the crew tried to bargain, the islanders tricked them by selling baskets of potatoes in which the bottom layers had been filled with stones. The islanders had no interest in beads or nails, but were keen on coconut shells and Tahitian bark-cloth. Hitihiti once again advised the men to buy red feathers to barter with when they returned to Tahiti and purchased himself as many feather caps as he could find. The *Resolution* remained on Easter Island only three days because there was not enough food for them to stay any longer. Hitihiti added another stick to his journal bundle and 'remembered Easter Island with this observation, *tàta maïtaï, whennùa èeno*, that the people were good, but the island very bad'.

From Easter Island the *Resolution* headed north-west towards the Marquesas Islands, in urgent need of fresh vegetables and meat. For three weeks they sailed almost 2,500 miles through the vastness of the South Pacific. The water was deep blue and the ship was accompanied by flying fish, dolphins and sharks, but many of the crew remained ill, weakened from the long weeks in the ice. They only made a brief stop at the Marquesas because Cook wanted to get as quickly as possible to Tahiti, almost 900 miles to the south-west, so that everybody could recuperate.

When Tahiti's high mountains appeared on the horizon on 21 April 1774, ten days after they had left the Marquesas, George forced himself out of bed. 'I crawled on deck,' he wrote, 'and fixed my eyes with great eagerness upon it, as upon a place where I hoped my pains would cease.' The men were glad to return. Most eager of all was Hitihiti who had never been to Tahiti but had friends and relatives there. He had collected valuable goods and acquired new knowledge, and like European explorers he returned with stories of strange countries. All this 'would give him weight among his countrymen', George believed.

In the early morning of 22 April, they sailed into Tahiti's Matavai Bay, hemmed in by a black beach and palm trees. Seven months had passed since they had left the Society Islands and it seemed even more beautiful and lush. The *Resolution* was immediately surrounded by canoes heaped with breadfruit, bananas, coconuts and fish. Hitihiti was welcomed like a hero. Having travelled further than any living Tahitian, he brought tales from a freezing 'white land' and man-eating Māori, and he was loaded with gifts. 'He was courted and looked upon as a prodigy by all the Tahitians who saw him,' George wrote, 'he was feasted with their choiciest meats, he received several changes of dress, and revelled among the nymphs of the land.'

One day Hitihiti brought a group of Tahitians on board the *Resolution* to show them the half-eaten Māori head that Pickersgill had preserved in spirit. Disgusted, the Tahitians pointed at the head and exclaimed 'te Tae-aï' – *Taehae* which meant 'a savage man' or 'beast'. There were times when the Tahitians refused to believe Hitihiti and came to the crew for confirmation: rain that became stones? Mountains that the sailors melted into fresh water? Days that never ended? 'His stories,' George noted, 'were too wonderful sometimes to find ready belief among his audience.'

Hitihiti had also been right about their trade goods. The red feathers they had brought from other islands, as well as beautifully woven baskets and mats, carved clubs and painted cloths from Tonga and the feathered headdresses from Easter Island and the Marquesas, were of much greater value than European nails, mirrors and beads. One small piece of cloth ornamented with red feathers caused such ecstatic responses, George noted, that it was as if the 'diamond of the Great Mogol' had been brought to Europe. Suddenly all the items they had been unable to purchase during the *Resolution*'s first visit were available. Pigs, which had been almost impossible to buy, now arrived in large numbers. The ship's deck became so crowded with squeaking animals that the sailors had to build a temporary pigsty at the beach. George worried that they had unbalanced the local economy.

George and Reinhold added a valuable warrior's breast ornament which was decorated with feathers, mother-of-pearl, dog fur and shark teeth to their collection. The Tahitians even sold several spectacular mourners' costumes made of barkcloth, plaited coconut fibre, feathers, mother-of-pearl and coconut shell. Worn by the 'mourner' at the funerals of chiefs and other important people, these elaborate outfits consisted of several layers of barkcloth to drape around the body. Over this a chest plate was worn, covered in several rows of around one thousand perfectly cut tiny rectangular pieces of mother-of-pearl. The mourner's face was hidden under a shell mask, which was itself topped with a half-circular crest of long white feathers.

A few days after their arrival the Forsters, Sparrman, Cook and a few others went to visit Tu, the chief they had met during their first visit. To their great astonishment, they arrived to find Tu's war armada of 159 great double canoes assembled at the beach, preparing to leave to help a related chief in a complicated dynastic struggle on Mo'orea, a small island just over ten miles west of Tahiti.

Seeing all the canoes, George was astounded – 'one of the most magnificent sights which it is possible to be entertained with in the South Sea'. Some of the twin-hulled canoes were ninety feet long with tall upright bows and sterns that looked like gigantic beaks rising twenty feet out of the water. The largest had room for 144 rowers, eight men to steer, and fifteen to twenty warriors who stood on a large raised fighting stage. Dressed in different layers of white, red and brown cloth, they wore wicker breast-shields covered in feathers and sharks' teeth. On their heads some balanced towering helmets that were almost five foot high. Also made of wicker, these helmets were covered in glossy bluish green feathers with a border of white plumes and crested with long bright

Tu's war armada in Tahiti, note the warrior in the canoe with the enormous helmet

tail feathers which gave the impression of an iridescent halo – 'resembling that glory of light with which our painters commonly ornament the heads of angels'. There was an almost breathless exhilaration in George's descriptions. The canoes were filled with stones, clubs, spears and other weapons. Accompanying the war flotilla were another seventy canoes, and George calculated around 1,500 warriors and 4,000 rowers. Nothing could have been further from Rousseau's idea of the gentle savage 'whose heart is at peace'.

Meanwhile, Hitihiti was immersing himself in his new life in Tahiti and returned one day to the *Resolution* with a wife. Having been offered land, house and servants, he told Cook that he wanted to stay on the island. The crew tried to persuade him to remain on the *Resolution*, telling him 'what great things he wou'd see and return with immence riches'. Reinhold took him aside. Once the *Resolution* left Tahiti, he warned, Hitihiti would have no protection any more and the chiefs would take away his clothes, shirts, red feathers and everything else. His family in Raiatea would probably think that the Europeans had killed him, never believing the *Resolution* crew that he had remained in Tahiti. Hitihiti changed his mind a few days later and decided to continue with the *Resolution* to Raiatea to see his friends and relatives.

Other islanders now wanted to join the expedition. Several officers applied to take a Tahitian servant to England – Reinhold among them because his servant was often too ill to be of real use – and chief Tu tried to persuade Cook to let one or two of his people join so that they could collect red feathers from Tonga even if the captain couldn't promise their return. Cook refused all requests. The *Resolution* was an expedition ship, not a transport vessel. Reinhold was furious. 'There is no arguing against people, who have no Idea of obliging others,' he said, especially those who 'come to power from nothing' – a barb at Cook's humble background as the son of a farm labourer from the Yorkshire moors.

After three weeks in Tahiti, Cook decided to sail to the other islands in the Society Island archipelago and in mid-May the *Resolution* crew prepared their departure with a heavy heart. John Marra, the gunner's mate, tried to escape the ship to remain on the island. George understood. A common sailor was risking life and limb for his country for little reward – and Marra had chosen to live free of cares under the tropical sky instead of enduring the expedition's hardships. When Marra was spotted swimming from the *Resolution* to the shore, Cook immediately sent a boat after him, only for the deserter to jump back into the sea and then to be apprehended again. Back on the ship, Marra was put in irons for twelve days.

After a brief stop at nearby Huahine, they arrived the next day in Raiatea. The islands were so close that wherever they stopped, the locals asked for a ride. Four of Hitihiti's friends, for example, had travelled with them from Tahiti to Huahine, where an envoy of one of the chiefs embarked, carrying a message for a chief in Bora Bora. His name was 'Hurree-hurree', which, George quipped, 'in its English acceptation, seemed to be remarkably well chosen for a messenger'. The *Resolution* crew also found a stowaway – a woman who had eloped with her lover from Raiatea to Tahiti a few years earlier, but who now longed to see her parents again.

At Raiatea, George sat down with Tutavai, one of the chiefs, to learn about the religious beliefs throughout the Society Islands, noting origin stories and the names of all the gods from the different islands as well as offerings, functions of priests, spirits and cosmology. It was obvious that the Society Islands had 'a system of polytheism as ever was invented', but George also misunderstood what Tutavai explained. George's interpretation that 'the sun, which was created by O-Maùwee, a powerful god, who causes earthquakes' was not quite accurate, as according to Polynesian tradition the demigod Maui had slowed down the sun and discovered fire.

Hitihiti was still trying to decide whether he should stay on the *Resolution* or disembark at Raiatea. He was excited by the thought of seeing Europe, but Cook couldn't promise his return. During these weeks in Tahiti, Huahine and Raiatea, Hitihiti often took Cook aside, trying to find out what the captain's plans were. Was he coming back? Hadn't Cook been to Tahiti a few years previously and returned? Why couldn't he promise to do it again? But Cook couldn't and wouldn't. Even if he preferred the high-born Hitihiti to Mai (whom Cook described as 'dark, ugly and a downright blackguard'), he was unwilling to shoulder the responsibility of bringing him home.

Cook might have been kind to Hitihiti, but just as they were bringing back plants and animals, Europeans also 'collected' indigenous people. When Tupaia had joined the *Endeavour* in 1769, his navigational knowledge, language skills and high status within Polynesian culture had been essential for the success of Cook's first voyage, but Banks had summed up the European attitude when he wrote that he wanted to 'keep him as a curiosity as well as some of my neighbours [have] lions and tygers'. Had he been able to take Hitihiti back to Britain, Cook wrote in his journal, the young Polynesian 'would have been [a] better Specimen of the Nation in every respect than the one on board the Adventure'.

Reluctantly, Hitihiti decided to remain in Raiatea. Cook gave him a letter for Captain Furneaux in case the missing *Adventure* stopped at the Society Islands. There was an emotional goodbye. Hitihiti ran from one cabin to the next, weeping, embracing his friends and unable to utter a word. His heart, George said, 'seemed torn to pieces'. Finally, he climbed into a canoe and looking up at the *Resolution*, again burst into tears. As the ship sailed, George saw him standing in the canoe, a lonely figure waving his arms. 'Our civilized education,' George noted, 'tends to stifle the emotions of our heart; for as we are too often taught to be ashamed of them, we unhappily conquer them'. He would miss his friend. Scanning the diminishing figure, George could see that Hitihiti was still standing, but his arms had dropped and his shoulders were slumped. He had hidden his head under his shirt as if to avoid the sight of the *Resolution* disappearing on the horizon.*

From Raiatea the *Resolution* sailed a westerly course towards the Tongan archipelago. From there Cook wanted to sail back to New Zealand and then south again for his third attempt to find the Southern Continent. Once again, he revealed none of these plans to his men who were desperate to return home after two years at sea.

Over the past months, tensions on board had been growing. Many of the sailors and officers were on edge and increasingly ready to use their

* Hitihiti would travel from Raiatea back to Tahiti and Cook met him again in August 1777 when he returned to the island during his third voyage. Captain William Bligh spoke with Hitihiti in November 1788 when he came to Tahiti to load his ship with breadfruit tree saplings just before the mutiny on the *Bounty*.

muskets when they encountered islanders. The longer they travelled, the more trigger-happy they seemed. Two years cooped up on a small ship and far away from their families and homes had strained the men's health and temper. Firearms were used liberally during encounters with the native populations. 'The best method in my opinion to preserve a good understanding with such people', Cook noted in his logbook, 'is first to shew them the use of fire arms and to convince them of the Superiority they give you over them'. George would never get used to it. Again and again, he described the crew's callousness. They had, he wrote 'a detestable eagerness to try their skill in shooting at men, rather than at a mark!'

At the Marquesas Islands, one of the officers had shot and killed an islander for stealing. It was not the first time. During their first visit to Tonga, one theft had been punished particularly violently when an islander had taken books and a sword from one officer's cabin. As he paddled away, the *Resolution* crew pursued him in their dinghy, firing at the same time. When they came closer, the man jumped into the sea and they seized him with the boat hook – 'catching him under the ribs, dragged him into the boat', George wrote, horrified, but Cook didn't mention the crew's cruel reaction in his journal. The islander had escaped wounded and bloodied, and swam to shore. George had been astounded that the Tongans had remained kind and friendly despite this brutal attack. 'Though they are members of a civilized society', George wrote of the *Resolution* crew, 'they may in some measure be looked upon as a body of uncivilized men, rough, passionate, revengeful.'

Cook tried to be a bit more even-handed. When the Māori in Queen Charlotte Sound had complained that one of the *Resolution* men had stolen some items from their hut, Cook had ordered the sailor to receive twelve lashes. 'It has ever been a maxim with me,' he explained, 'to punish the least crimes any of my people have committed against these uncivilised Nations.' That the islanders absconded with items didn't mean that the crew could too. Reinhold had different opinions and his anger rose with every theft. In Tonga, he had hit and injured an islander with a club for taking a single nail, and on Raiatea he had shot at a man. Quick to anger, Reinhold was as happy to have a fist fight as an intellectual argument. He had punished George with a whip as a child and during their Russian expedition in 1765 had turned his fury and his rifle against the Cossacks who escorted them. All his life George had seen how his father lashed out at others.

Where George realized that the concept of property and making gifts might not be the same in different cultures, Reinhold saw injustice against himself and a threat to European authority. With each incident his thirst for revenge grew. 'None is punished for his Audaciousness & Robbing,' Reinhold objected, and 'they grow bolder every day for this reason.' Every time an islander was killed, George was horrified, but his father now demanded the execution of any person who stole from them. 'In case one were shot dead, the rest would be so alarmed, that no thefts would be more committed,' Reinhold insisted, 'it would cause more honesty among them & greater Security for Europeans.'

Sometimes the islanders fought back. In June 1774, on Niue, a small raised coral atoll some 1,200 miles west of the Society Islands, armed warriors attacked the crew of the *Resolution*. Realizing that without bloodshed nothing could be achieved, Cook ordered his men to retreat. 'The Conduct and aspect of these Islanders occasioned my giving it the name of *Savage Island*,' he wrote in his logbook that evening – but the islanders had succeeded in defending their home.

From Niue, they sailed to Tonga for a three-day visit, where Cook

Fighting on Erromango

shot and wounded an islander for refusing to return some stolen items – 'the shot had torn the flesh very much, and made the wound very painful to the poor man,' George wrote. From Tonga they continued to an island group that Cook called New Hebrides – today the island nation of Vanuatu, some 1,000 miles west of Tonga. On Erromango, one of the islands in the archipelago, there was a fraught encounter with several hundred islanders armed with bows and arrows, long spears, clubs and stones. When the islanders grabbed several oars and seized the cutter in which the crew had come ashore, Cook pointed his musket at them but it misfired. Seeing him aim, the islanders lifted their bows and a volley of arrows rained on Cook and his men. A sailor was wounded in the cheek and the marines began to fire, killing several warriors and wounding others. George was certain that the *Resolution* men were to blame. 'For my own part, I cannot entirely persuade myself that these people had any hostile intentions in detaining our boat,' George said, and not for the first time 'it is much to be lamented that the voyages of Europeans cannot be performed without being fatal to the nations whom they visit.'

9

Resolution Voyage

Tanna: 5–20 August 1774

The day after they left Erromango, the crew noticed a large column of smoke rising in the distance. As the *Resolution* came closer, they heard the rumble of an active volcano. When they tacked into a bay of turquoise water on 5 August 1774, they saw a narrow beach with coconut palms and a tropical jungle with high forested mountains beyond.

An old man watched the *Resolution* sail into the narrow entrance of the inlet that formed a natural harbour at the south-east of the island which the crew soon would call Tanna. When two owls flew over the ship, it was a sign that the spirits were stirring. In the old man's culture the world was sealed where the sky touched the horizon. Beyond were the spirits, and beneath the sea was another sacred world which was the home of their ancestors. Maybe the large ship had come from this sacred world, from beyond the horizon, and the strangers were ghosts of their ancestors. But spirits had to be approached carefully, so the old man and two hundred other islanders paddled out to the *Resolution* with two coconuts and a yam as offerings. They remained cautious and had their bows and arrows drawn. Suddenly, a noise as deafening as the loudest thunder reverberated across the bay – Cook had ordered the cannon to be fired as a display of power. The terrified men leapt into the water.

In the commotion, George saw how one young islander had remained standing in his canoe. A handsome man with a friendly face, he seemed unworried, more perplexed at the fright of his fellow islanders than fearful of the strangers. While the others recovered from the shock, one of the men tried to steal the *Resolution*'s buoy. To deter him, Cook fired a shot. Another man came forward, trying to untie the buoy.

Landing at Tanna, after a painting by William Hodges

Cook ordered that the ship's cannon be fired again. No one was hurt, but the islanders retreated to shore. Reinhold feared that the islanders would 'be troublesome to us, & force us to kill some of them in our defence'.

The island's volcano was only a few miles from their anchorage. That night it set the dark sky ablaze. Every five minutes, explosions fired flames and smoke into the air and soon everything was covered in black ash. The spirits were indeed stirring. The next morning, a few islanders came out in canoes, each bringing a coconut or two and a few bananas as further offerings. When Cook believed that a deal was agreed – a piece of Tahitian cloth for one of the islander's beautifully polished clubs – he lowered down his part of the exchange but the man in the canoe refused to hand over his. Cook gave a sign and a musket charged with small shot was fired into the man's face. He didn't die but he was badly injured.

By now over a thousand islanders were assembling in two divisions at each side of the beach, armed with bows, arrows, slingshots, spears and clubs. As they stood guard, the old man, who had watched their arrival the previous day, paddled out to the *Resolution* and presented some coconuts. In return, Cook gave him a beautiful red barkcloth, but also confiscated his clubs. The old man remained calm. When he returned to the shore, Cook and a contingent of heavily armed crew from the *Resolution* followed him in two dinghies and their cutter. 'I had not forgot the trap I had like to have been caught in at the last isle,' Cook said, 'and this looked some thing like it.' The crew remained in their boats near the shoreline, while the old man paddled ashore where he walked to the centre of the beach between the two warrior divisions. He and two other elders placed a few plantains and a yam on the sand as an offering. Watching from the cutter, Cook gestured at the islanders to lay down their weapons.

When they refused, the captain ordered a musket fired over the warriors' heads. The islanders flinched but stood their ground. George was amazed. Cook had no right to command the islanders to disarm, and there was no reason for them to comply. They outnumbered the *Resolution* men by at least ten to one and probably thought it 'absurd and unjust that a few strangers should prescribe laws to them on their own ground'. They clearly had no intention of giving up their island. 'They looked upon us as invaders,' George wrote, 'and resolved to defend it.' It was then that one of the islanders turned his back to the Europeans and clapped his naked buttocks – a gesture understood in any culture.

Cook had had enough, signalling from the cutter to the *Resolution*. Moments later, most of the ship's artillery – five four-pounder cannons, two swivel guns and four musketoons – was fired at the warriors on the beach. Cannon balls and musket shots whistled over the water. As the palm trees on the beach shattered, the islanders ran, but no one was wounded. Only the old man remained, watching how the crew of the *Resolution* finally brought their boats ashore. He told them his name was Pavegn – 'shark' in his language. The marines drew two lines in the sand sixty yards apart, marking them with wooden poles and ropes to outline the ship's landing patch. By claiming a temporary stake in the islanders' land, Cook tried to impose his power and control.

Over the next two weeks the islanders remained cautious but friendly. They quickly realized that the visitors were not ancestral spirits. Hungry and tired, the Europeans were just other men. One day, when Reinhold Forster's servant went into a bush to relieve himself, a few locals followed and on seeing his genitals shouted 'It's a Man! It's a Man!' They kept their women away but shared water and food. Whenever the Europeans gave them beads or nails, the islanders wrapped these gifts in leaves – probably to protect their own spiritual powers or to avoid being bewitched by the foreigners. George was intrigued but could only guess if this was done 'owing to some superstitious notions, or to a

A man, woman and child from Tanna

fancied idea of cleanliness, or of civility'. If only he could understand their language, he longed for an 'intercourse with human creatures'.

George and his father tried to communicate with them. When Reinhold asked the island's name by pointing to the ground, the men replied '*Tanna*', which meant 'earth' in their language – a misunderstanding that led to the island being known by that name. The *Resolution* had already stopped at a few other islands in the Vanuatu archipelago and people everywhere spoke languages unlike any George had heard over the past two years. They also looked very different to the other Pacific Islanders previously encountered. Their skin was darker, their black hair more tightly curled, and their noses broader. The sailors regarded them as 'poor mean despicable looking wretches' and compared them to a 'Monkey race' when they watched the ease with which they climbed the ship's rigging. Sparrman described them as having a 'grimace of an ape' and Reinhold said they were an 'ill-favoured set of being; that of all men I ever saw, border the nearest upon the tribe of monkies'. Cook called them 'this Apish Nation' – adding that the people were 'the most Ugly and ill-proportioned of any I ever saw'.

George also thought most of them unattractive but was struck by their keen understanding and perceptiveness – 'the features of these people, though remarkably irregular and ugly, yet are full of great sprightliness, and express a quick comprehension.' He questioned these 'ill-natured comparisons between them and monkeys'. 'We should be sorry,' he wrote in his published account of the voyage, 'to supply Rousseau, or the superficial philosophers who re-echo his maxims, with the shadow of an argument in favour of the Orang-outang system'. This 'Orang-outang system' was a new theory that defined orangutans as barbarian humans who had not yet learned speech* – conveniently allowing Europeans to classify indigenous people as ape-like savages along a spectrum from orangutan to civilized cultures. It was absurd, George said, and in any case, they were the 'most intelligent people we had ever met with in the South Seas'.

At Malakula, another island in the archipelago, George and the islanders had begun to teach each other their languages. George, dressed in breeches, shirt and waistcoat, his skin peeling from the constant exposure to the sun, had sat on a tree stump next to the Malakulans, who had painted their faces black. Pointing at objects – a plant, an arm, the sky, a bird, a tool and so on – George and the islanders repeated words to each other, again and again. Seeing the white man with his head bent over his notebook, pen in hand, writing down every word, the islanders became intrigued by the idea of preserving sound on paper. They were as keen to learn new words as George was and their pronunciation was pitch perfect. George was so impressed that he tried out complicated words in other European languages and when they mastered those easily, he moved on to Russian which they also pronounced without difficulty. He tested numbers, counting with his fingers, which they repeated immediately. Their acuteness of understanding was striking, he said, and they were certainly as human as the Europeans – 'we had reason to admire their extensive faculties and quick apprehension'.

George continued his observations on Tanna. One day he met the handsome young man who had remained standing in his canoe when the cannon had been fired on the day of their arrival. He was called

* It was proposed by the Scottish thinker Lord Monboddo in 1773 in his book *Of the Origin and Progress of Language* – inspired by Rousseau, who had written about the possibility that orangutans might be early humans. George Forster read Monboddo's book when he returned to London and incorporated his critique in his own *A Voyage Round the World.*

Fannòkko, he explained, and gave them the names of neighbouring islands and in return learned some English words. He was tall, with large lively eyes, and again George was impressed by his quick grasp of language. Eating together, George found his table manners impeccable – until Fannòkko took a stick out of his oiled hair and used it to scratch his scalp and then as a fork.

George, Reinhold and Sparrman went on small excursions but every time they tried to venture into the forest or towards the volcano, the islanders stopped them. The volcano was a sacred place, the home of spirits, ancestors and divine powers. Some of the islanders threatened to kill and eat the Forsters and Sparrman if they went further – 'they bit their own arms, to express more clearly that they eat human flesh' – while others pointed out paths which they pretended would lead to the desired destination. As a result, George and the others often walked for several miles in circles, only to find themselves back where they had started. But he almost respected their artful deception. When the locals continued to block the approach to the volcano, George accepted that there was no point in pursuing knowledge if it could not be obtained 'without bloodshed and injustice'.

His father was less respectful. When Reinhold shot a bird, he found it clutching what looked like a nutmeg in its feet – one of the most valuable spices which had fuelled the economy of the Dutch Empire since the seventeenth century. He asked a local to show him the tree where it came from but when they didn't find any nuts left, Reinhold asked his guide for the name of the tree by pointing at it. Thinking he meant the birds who had eaten the nuts, the islander replied 'yawinatuan', which was the local name of a pigeon. Reinhold collected some leaves and showed them to another group of people, who now told him the name of the tree. While Reinhold was adamant that it was 'yawinatuan', everybody was confused. Rather than realizing that something had been lost in translation, Reinhold felt cheated, kicking his guide and spitting in his face. As so often before, George watched his father explode. The islander had deceived him, Reinhold shouted.

When Second Lieutenant Charles Clerke told him to stop attacking the man, Reinhold lashed out at him too. He was a free man and could do what he liked, and Clerke had no authority over him, he yelled. Clerke threatened to order the marines to shoot him. Reinhold dragged the lieutenant to Cook, who tried to keep out of the dispute. But Reinhold wouldn't let go, demanding that the captain intervene. When he refused, Reinhold stormed off. By now his outbursts were a regular occurrence. Reinhold Forster, Wales later said, 'never passed a week on board the Resolution without a dispute with one person or other'.

They stayed two weeks on Tanna, enough time to find new birds, fish and plants. The forest stirred and shimmered with song and colour. Dazzlingly coloured parakeets flickered through the canopy, appearing in sudden bursts of red, yellow and blue against the green leaves. There was a Cardinal Honeyeater – no larger than a clenched fist, its body cloaked in silk-black feathers, its head and back in crimson red – a greedy drinker who sipped nectar from perfumed flowers with his curved beak. Hopping from branch to branch was an even smaller bird – perfectly green with a vibrantly yellow belly and a striking white ring around its eye – hence its common name: the Vanuatu White-eye.

When the flowers or fruits which the Forsters needed to classify the plants were too high up in the canopy, they tried throwing stones, shooting off branches, and if all failed they sometimes felled the tree. Describing fish could also be difficult because the moment they were caught, the sailors cut, salted and fried them. In the evening, when they returned to the ship, George drew whatever specimens they had collected. When they anchored at an island, he usually only had time for quick pencil drawings, but he added colour descriptions so that he wouldn't forget. A sketch of a bird, for example, was annotated in one corner: 'Head dark pearly grey, gradually & very softly vanishing in to a fine clear white', iris brown, white under the eyelid, pale greyish feet and so on. Sometimes he would colour just a single leaf or flower, to remind himself later when he returned to the sketch during the long days at sea.

The Forsters bartered, buying mostly clubs, spears and arrows, but failed to acquire other objects such as utensils, cloths or jewellery. No matter how much they begged, these items were not on offer. It was often like this. During their first visit in Tahiti, the islanders had not been willing

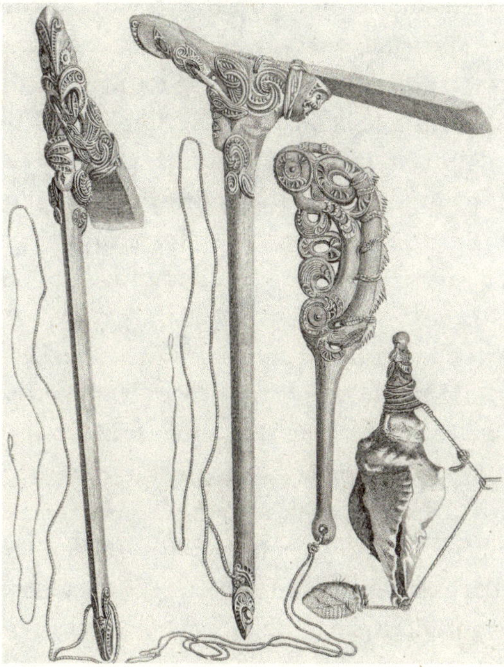

Māori carving

to sell their magnificent breastplates and mourning costumes, only relenting when the Europeans returned to the island with the valuable red feathers. Similarly, in New Zealand, the Māori had at first been reluctant to trade weapons and ornaments made of nephrite, a prized jade-like stone. These were only used by their high chiefs, and carved examples were particularly revered.

The significance of Māori carving can be traced back to their origin stories when the son of chief Rua offended Tangaroa, the god of the sea. As punishment Tangaroa dragged the young boy into the depth of the ocean and turned him into a carved figure on the gable of his underwater house. When Rua searched for his son in the ocean, he heard the carved figures at the gable of Tangaroa's house talking to each other. They told him that one of them was his son and Rua took him and a few others. He brought them ashore but because the wooden figures couldn't speak in the human world, they had to communicate their knowledge visually through the figures, symbols and designs of their carvings – and with that the art of carving became a sacred act and spiritual practice because it connected the Māori to their ancestors and gods. So it wasn't surprising that the Māori were initially unwilling to sell their carved objects. When they eventually did, they deliberately traded their least precious examples as the Forster collections in museums today prove. The green stone blades that the Forsters had bought in New Zealand, for example, show imperfections, abrasions and chips and are made of the darker and less valued nephrite stone.

But why didn't the people of Tanna sell their food utensils, baskets, carved figures, clothing, jewellery, combs, barkcloth and musical instruments? One reason might have been that they took a long time to make, another that some of the objects were considered sacred or animated by ancestor spirits. What may have seemed a useful domestic item to George and Reinhold could have been much more than an object of daily use. The European distinction between practical use and ritual potency was meaningless. Fishhooks, woven containers and cloth on Tanna were often imbued with divine power.

So too the beautifully woven baskets with triangular patterns from Tonga which were usually only carried by chiefs. What George didn't

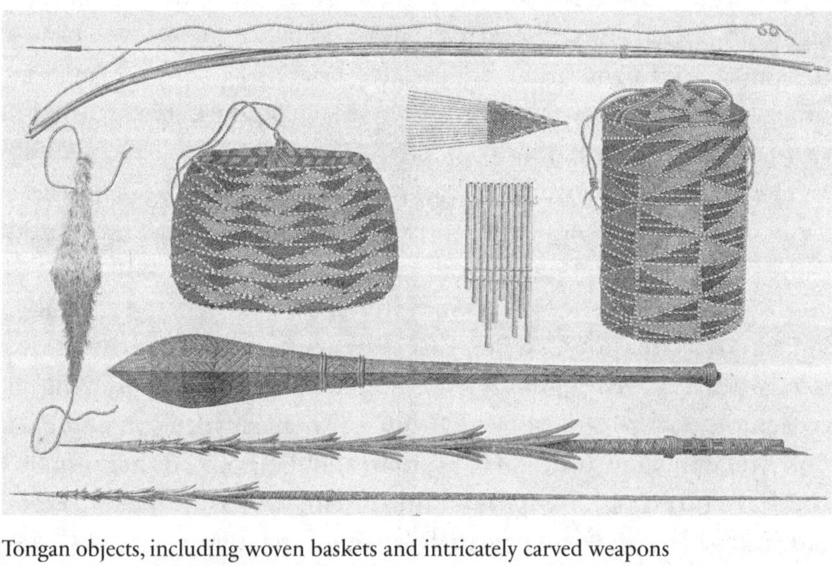

Tongan objects, including woven baskets and intricately carved weapons

know was that the point where the triangles meet was called *manulua*, representing two birds flying together – *manu* meaning bird and *lua* two – and was a metaphor for a chief who could trace his lineage through two high-ranking maternal and paternal lines. Even the Tongans, who had willingly sold many objects, had kept some of their most sacred back. The bark-cloth mats they used for ceremonies were often old and had holes – but were exceptionally valuable and powerful to the Tongans by association with those who had touched them in the past, and there are none in the Forster or Cook collections.

Perhaps, George speculated, the islanders on Tanna didn't want to trade because they were not as affluent as the Tahitians, or they were cautious because of war and skirmishes with neighbouring islands and tribes. It would not be until the twentieth century that the spiritual significance of the objects the Forsters saw was properly understood.

Despite the inauspicious beginnings, trust slowly took root. One day, George and Sparrman were invited to join a family at their home. Exchanging names, they sat down on a tree trunk in front of the hut. As they shared roasted yam roots and taught each other words, George hummed a quiet tune. The islanders wanted more, so he sang a few German and English songs which they liked. But when Sparrman performed Swedish folk songs from his youth, the islanders declared those their favourites.

Then it was their turn. 'We desired them in return to give us an opportunity of admiring their talents,' George said, and they sang a simple tune and played a flute made of reeds. Their music was harmonious and, as far as he could judge, superior to that on other islands – more rhythmic and employing a greater range of notes. When more visits followed over the next days, George began to feel at ease. He played with a little girl who 'peeped at us between the heads of the people who were seated on the ground' and felt her father's 'fondness which sparkled in his eyes'. He enjoyed the food and admired the men's accurate marksmanship with their bows and arrows.

But this peaceful atmosphere came to a sudden end on 19 August, exactly two weeks after they had landed in Tanna. George had gone for a walk through the tropical forest, when after a few hours he ran into

Sparrman. The two men carried on together, chatting happily, until a gunshot ripped through the stillness of the late morning. When they stepped out from the forest onto the beach, moving from shade to bright sunlight, they saw two islanders sitting on the ground, holding a dead man in their arms.

There were lots of people on the beach. Everyone seemed to be talking at once – marines in red uniforms, sailors in loose shirts and trousers, officers in blue jackets and white breeches, and the almost naked islanders. When George enquired what had happened, he was told that the islander had walked into the marked-off area between the two lines that Cook had drawn in the sand. William Wedgeborough, one of the marines who had been on duty at the beach, had waved his bayonet in front of the islander's face and shoved him back. After more pushing and jostling, the islander had aimed his arrow at Wedgeborough, who had then pulled the trigger at close range. The islander fell instantly, blood streaming from a wound under his ribs.

Cook ordered Wedgeborough to be shackled and flogged, while trying to appease the islanders. 'I who was present,' Cook wrote that evening in his journal, 'was astonished beyond Measure at the inhumanity of the act.' There had been no reason to shoot the islander. George too was mortified. Another innocent man had been killed by the *Resolution* crew. The islander had 'refused to be controuled on his own island by a stranger', George said, and had crossed Cook's arbitrary line, 'perhaps with no other motive at present than that of asserting his liberty of walking where he pleased'.

For his part, Wedgeborough protested his innocence, adamant that the islander would have killed him. Cook countered that whenever the crew had lifted their muskets in the past two weeks, the islanders had also raised their weapons, but only 'to let us see they were as ready as us' – they had not used them after the initial fight at the beach. But the *Resolution*'s officers were outraged at Wedgeborough's harsh punishment, lobbying Cook for leniency. 'The question was,' Midshipman Elliott said, 'whether the Sentry was to receive a Poisoned Arrow into him (for he was sure to be hit) or to save himself he was to shoot the Man'. The islanders, he claimed, had been particularly insolent that day. When Cook stood firm insisting that Wedgeborough was to blame, the crew disagreed. 'I ask,' astronomer Wales said, 'whether the world would not think him [Wedgeborough] a wretched fool to stand with a loaded musket in his hand, and suffer himself to be shot with it?'

There was also discussion about how much of the brutal encounter Cook had actually witnessed. One officer claimed that the captain 'saw only a small part of it', and that the choice had been to fire at the islander or to be killed. 'The officer's right to dispose of the lives of the natives remained uncontroverted,' another marine said, and that 'the man was entitled to believe he was not posted there simply to provide a target for arrows.'

Elliott believed that Cook had 'lost sight of both justice and Humanity'. The injustice was not the killing of the islander but the captain's punishment of the offender. Wales agreed – 'no person', he said, 'but the centinel himself can, or ought to be a judge of what was to be done in these circumstances'. Cook prided himself on his sense of justice – he was as willing to discipline indigenous people as his own men. In New Zealand, for example, he had ordered twelve lashes to be given to a sailor for stealing from the Māori, and during the *Endeavour* voyage he had publicly flogged the expedition's butcher for being rude to the wife of a Tahitian chief. Wedgeborough had to be punished for the murder, no matter what the crew's opinions, and after deliberation Cook spared him the flogging but kept him confined for two months.

Sparrman thought the incident must have proven to the people of Tanna that the Europeans were no cannibals as they had not eaten the dead man, although he 'was better fed and plumper than any of his thin comrades'. Reinhold, who would happily write dozens of pages in his journal about his own frustrations or worries, described the murder in just a few lines. In his account, the islander was only 'gently drove back by the Sentry' and overreacted by immediately raising his arrow – placing the blame on the victim rather the perpetrator.

George, by contrast, shifted the perspective to the islander – 'he, to vindicate his right, laid an arrow on his bow.' The islander had been provoked. The people of Tanna had every right to avenge the murder, he believed, because 'we had wantonly made it the scene of the greatest cruelty'. For George, the incident was yet another proof that Europeans brought death and disease. Every time they stepped onto an island, they exacted a price in wounds and death.

10

Resolution Voyage

New Caledonia, New Zealand (Aotearoa), Tierra del Fuego and Cape Town: 4 September 1774–27 April 1775

After the murder on the beach in Tanna on 19 August 1774, the *Resolution* left in a hurry and for the next eleven days charted the coastlines of some of the other islands in the Vanuatu archipelago. On 31 August the ship turned south towards New Zealand from where Cook wanted to embark on 'another Southern Cruse'. Four days later, on 4 September 1774, they saw a large landmass on the horizon which they couldn't find on any of their maps: it was part of a group of islands around 300 miles south-west of Tanna and 800 miles east of Australia. Cook named the island New Caledonia after the Latin name for Scotland.* As they approached the northern end of the island, George saw mountains with only a few scattered trees – to his eyes it looked rather barren, more like Easter Island than Tanna or Tahiti. But when he saw smoke rising, he knew that the island was settled and he 'could not wait the moment which should bring us acquainted with the inhabitants of this land'.

They spent the next week here but there was not much food – the plantations yielded little produce and George missed the variety of delicious tropical fruits he had enjoyed on some of the other islands. But he was struck by the friendliness and hospitality of the people who inhabited the islands. 'When we consider how easy it is to provoke

* Today the island is called Grande Terre, while New Caledonia is the name of the entire island group.

A man from New Caledonia

the mariner to sport with the lives of Indians,' George said, 'we must acknowledge that it required an uncommon degree of good temper, not to draw upon themselves a single act of brutality.' The men were naked except for a penis wrapper – which might look indecent to the *Resolution* crew, George said, but the bulging codpieces made of leather and metal in breeches and suits of armour in sixteenth-century Europe had been equally so.

Where George tried to put what he saw into a global perspective, Second Lieutenant Clerke amused himself by playing jokes on the islanders:

> They were totally naked to the Penis, which was wrapt up in leaves, and whatever you gave them, or they by any means obtained, was immediately apply'd there; nor wou'd they care one farthing for any article or trifle that could not in some form be made to contribute to the decorating of that favourable part . . . I gave one of them one day a stocking – he very deliberately pulled it on there – then gave him a string of beads, with which he tied the stocking up – I then presented him with a medal which he immediately hung to it – in short let that noble part be well decorated and fine they be perfectly happy and totally indifferent about the state of all the rest of the Body.

Reinhold, for once, was content. As the first Europeans ever to arrive in New Caledonia, they could finally collect new species of plants and animals. The vegetation was not as lush and tropical as on the other South Pacific islands, but George found a new passionflower – the first passionflower species, he proudly wrote, that didn't come from the Americas. The birds were just as thrilling. There was a striking small bird with an orange belly and a curious marking across its face that divides the head into a soft grey crown and a white throat. It was later named the New Caledonian Whistler. In the early hours, before the first light of dawn, a shrill *tchoo-tchoo-tchoo* pierced the stillness – the noisy Grey-eared Honeyeater, another bird unknown to European scientists. But it was a parakeet that excited George the most – 'entirely new to zoologists', he noted. Its outrageously green body was offset by blue-edged wings and tail, a flare of yellow around the neck, a black face, and a red crown with two dainty 'horns' of fine black feathers – hence its name, Horned Parakeet. One of the most beautiful, Reinhold thought, was the Red-throated Parrotfinch, 'not bigger than a hummingbird' – a tiny dazzling creature, a glint of bright green, its head and tail fluorescent red, dashing through the low growth. Its song was a delicate high-pitched trill that was easily missed in the forest's cacophony.

Yet, as always, it was the people who interested George the most – 'the character of the inhabitants, and their friendly, inoffensive behaviour towards us, gave us greater pleasure than all the rest'. But just when everything was going well, their luck turned. First, the ship's butcher fell down the hatchway and fractured his skull so badly that he died, and then they ate a fish which almost killed them. It looked ugly, like a pufferfish with a large head. Knowing that many pufferfish were poisonous, Reinhold was apprehensive, but Cook reassured them that he had eaten a similar fish during the *Endeavour* voyage. They had to eat something. Before they handed it over to the cook, Reinhold dissected and George sketched it. When dinner was served – Reinhold was still invited to eat with the captain despite his previous combative behaviour – they all tried a little bit of the fish and felt fine. But at 3 a.m. Reinhold woke feeling dizzy, with completely numb hands and feet. 'I reeled like a drunken Man & could neither walk nor stand,' he said, and called for his servant. Cook, who lay awake with the same symptoms, heard Reinhold complain and tried to get up but he too couldn't feel his limbs. Hearing the commotion, George crawled out of his cabin, unable to walk. The ship's surgeon administered emetics to make them vomit, yet they continued to feel sick. They were lucky to have eaten only a small amount as this was an extremely poisonous toadfish (*Lagocephalus sceleratus*). Two days later Reinhold and George tried to collect plants but returned early, even more sick than before. When they weighed anchor five days after eating the fish, they still felt ill, suffering from headaches, 'spasmodic pains over the body', blistered lips and general weakness.

They left New Caledonia on 13 September, but before they sailed Cook ordered the carpenter's mate to carve the words 'His Britannick Majesties Ship Resolution Sept. 1774' into a tree.

Five weeks later, on 18 October 1774, the *Resolution* sailed for the third time into New Zealand's Queen Charlotte Sound, from where Cook planned to complete his circuit of the high Antarctic latitudes. During their first and second attempts, they had covered about three-quarters of the circuit, but Cook wanted 'to leave not the least room for the Possibility of there being a continent unless near the Pole and out of the reach of Navigation', as he wrote in his log book.

First, they had to replenish their supplies. This time, no Māori welcomed them when they anchored at Ship Cove. Looking around, the crew noticed that some trees had been felled since their last visit, almost a year before, and that the bottle with Cook's message was gone. That the trees bore the marks of iron saws meant that the crew of the *Adventure* must have cut them down.

They lit fires as signs for the Māori but it took five days until the first canoe appeared. On seeing the *Resolution*, the Māori turned around immediately and paddled off. Unusually guarded and reserved, when they finally talked a few days later they referred to a conflict between Europeans and a Māori group who 'came up & killed & devoured them all', as Reinhold recounted in his journal. Everybody was worried. Surely they were talking about the *Adventure.* With the help of a sketch of Queen Charlotte Sound and two pieces of paper to represent the *Resolution* and the *Adventure*, which they moved in and out of the sound to represent their arrivals and departures over the past two years, Cook asked the Māori when the *Adventure* had left. The Māori pointed at the piece of paper and showed them ten fingers – meaning that it had been ten months since their consort ship had departed. The crew was relieved and with the men rested and their stores filled, the *Resolution* left three weeks later, on 10 November 1774.

Strong winds swiftly carried the *Resolution* some 5,000 miles across the ocean towards the southern tip of South America. On 27 November they sailed 210 miles in twenty-four hours, more miles in one day than on any other during the voyage. The day also marked George's third birthday during the voyage and his second celebrated at sea. He was twenty now and had already seen more of the world than most people ever would.

On 18 December, only thirty-eight days after leaving New Zealand, they reached Tierra del Fuego on the south-western coast of South America. This 'Land of Fire' was named by Ferdinand Magellan for the settlement fires he had seen when searching for a passage to the Pacific in 1520. It was a wild landscape shaped of islands and serrated coastlines with high mountain tops hidden in fog and black rocks that dropped into the water. It was bitterly cold and windy. 'This is the most desolate coast I ever saw,' Cook noted in his logbook, 'it seems to be intirely composed of Rocky Mountains without the least appearance of Vegetation, these Mountains terminate in horroable precipices whose craggy summits spire up to a vast height.' That a Spanish explorer had called it the 'Coast of Desolation' in the late sixteenth century, George thought, proved to be a perfectly appropriate name.

Over the next days, as they sailed south and stopped along the coast, George began to see beauty in the bleakness. 'Barren as these rocks appeared,' he wrote, 'yet almost every plant which we gathered on them was new to us, and some species were remarkable for the beauty of their flowers, or their smell.' They dined lavishly on large delicious mussels and marvelled that this harsh landscape held such wonders. Two days later, on 24 December, George, his father, Sparrman, Cook and one of the midshipmen took their small sailing boat to explore the coast, chancing upon a cove filled with thousands of geese. Christmas dinner was more than provided for when they returned with sixty-three geese and Sparrman was overjoyed when the cook served them boiled, roasted and in patties.

Cook called their anchorage in Tierra del Fuego, Christmas Sound

The next day – on Christmas Day itself – four canoes with several adults and children approached the *Resolution*, but when Cook invited them on board George was taken aback at how emaciated and filthy they were.* Around their necks they had tied leather bands strung with shells, and they wore 'a kind of bonnet, consisting of a few white quill feathers of geese' on their heads. Their hair was dishevelled, their noses were runny, and they stank. All they wore was a small piece of seal skin that covered their shoulders, and George wondered how they could survive such a fierce climate almost naked. The children were shivering, huddled over a small fire in the canoes. He felt sorry for them. 'I cannot figure to myself a more unhappy human being,' he said, 'than one who seems to be so far deprived of reason, as not to defend himself against the injuries of weather, whilst he severely feels its effects.' For more than two years George had approached every culture with an open mind, but on seeing these almost naked Fuegians in a landscape of barren rocks and icy winds he thought their lack of adaptation almost incomprehensible. 'It was the most loathsome picture of misery,' he wrote, wondering if they might have been 'outcasts of some neighbouring tribe, which enjoys a more comfortable life'.

For George, the Fuegians were more proof against Rousseau's portrait

* Like his contemporaries, George called them 'Fuegians' – they were most likely Yahgan (Yämana), who lived along the western coast of Tierra del Fuego.

A man from Tierra del Fuego, after a drawing by William Hodges

of the happy savage. Here, in Tierra del Fuego, living in a state of nature did not equate with contentment. The civilized society which Rousseau so despised, George was certain, undoubtably offered greater happiness than these miserable, shivering lives. Rousseau seemed to believe that 'it was incomparably better to be naked and eat acorns in the forest, than to expatiate dressed in nightgown and cap next to the stove'. Thinkers who preferred the state of nature had clearly never left their warm studies.

Meanwhile the sailors had begun to celebrate Christmas with copious amounts of liquor and roasted goose. For two days and nights they drank, sang, fought and ate, becoming so intoxicated that William Wedgeborough, the marine who had killed the islander on Tanna, fell overboard and drowned. At this point Cook lost his patience and ordered most of the men to be dropped off at the shore to sober up. On 28 December 1774, once all the sailors had slept off their hangovers, it was time to leave and round Cape Horn, South America's southernmost headland.

The seas here are notoriously dangerous, with the warmer water and weather fronts of the tropics colliding with the cold southern seas. Where the Atlantic and Pacific oceans meet, gale force winds whip across the water, and with no landmass in the southern seas to block them, waves can build for hundreds of miles, growing in strength and height until they reach Drake's Passage, the narrowest point between South America and Antarctica. Cook knew what to expect from these angry seas where hundred-foot waves were not uncommon. Vessels disappeared or were shipwrecked here: lost in fog and hurricanes, crushed by icebergs, swallowed by waves, or smashed against rocky cliffs.

Unlike many other ships, the *Resolution* was lucky, and at 6 a.m. on 29 December 1774, she passed Cape Horn without incident. To George's delight thirty humpback whales and several hundred seals played in the waves nearby. The whales came so close that when they spouted, the *Resolution* was enveloped by the reeking stench of half-digested krill. George watched mesmerized as the giant animals breached, leaping out of the water and then twisting onto their backs, landing with such force that the sounds their bodies made were like explosions. Repeatedly slapping their tails and fins against the surface, the whales made the water boil.

On 3 January 1775 they left the South American coast and turned east to cross the southern Atlantic towards Cape Town. Two weeks later, they spotted an island on the horizon and made their way towards it. Mountainous with craggy steep cliffs, it was icy and windswept. Its only inhabitants seemed to be large flocks of seabirds – albatrosses, petrels and shags among them – along with seals and penguins. Larger than any of the penguins George had seen so far, these were also tame. He measured them, recording that they were 39 inches tall, with black heads and yellow ear patches. He identified them as King Penguins, but ornithologists suggested later that this might be an altogether new species: the Emperor Penguin – *Aptenodytes forsteri*, named after the Forsters.*

Cook named the island South Georgia, after George III, and hoisted the Union Jack, taking possession for the king and his heirs while the marines fired their muskets into the air 'to give greater weight to this assertion', George wrote drily, 'to the utter amazement of the seals and pinguins, the inhabitants of these newly discovered dominions'. Then,

* Several other species which they found during the *Resolution* voyage were named after the Forsters, including the New Zealand fur seal (*Arctocephalus forsteri*), the Yellow-eyed Mullet (*Aldrichetta forsteri*) and the genus *Forsterygion* – a small fish from coastal New Zealand. Other species named after them are a hawkfish (*Paracirrhites forsteri*) and a North American tern (*Sterna forsteri*).

instead of turning north-east on a straight line towards South Africa, Cook stayed on an easterly course, skirting along the higher latitudes, still in search of the Southern Continent.

During those long weeks at sea, George worked on his drawings. In the previous two and a half years, he had become an accomplished draughtsman. His skills had sharpened and his drawings became more assured. A penguin drawn during their first tour in Antarctic waters, early in 1773, stands rigid and seemingly off-balance on the ice, whereas a spotted eagle ray caught during the second visit to Tahiti in May 1774 exhibits a fierce energy and a realistic three-dimensionality in its muscular wings. Similarly, a South Island Robin which George sketched two days after they had made landfall at Dusky Sound in March 1773 clings awkwardly to a branch, looking as if it is about to fall off, whereas a blue petrel drawn the following year is depicted diving into the waves, its wings wide open, showing a beautiful band of black feathers.

With a few broad brushstrokes George was able to capture the slick body of a dolphin, while he also painstakingly and beautifully drew every tiny feather of the New Zealand *kākā*, a parrot that is a symbol of power and authority in Māori culture. Falcons, owls, colourful parrots, tiny kingfishers perching on branches, herons, geese, ducks, penguins, plenty of petrels, several albatrosses, and dozens of other species filled his portfolio.

George's early sketch of a South Island Robin

George's drawing of a dolphin from late 1774

Nor was it just the showy species – he painted the New Zealand Pipit, an unassuming bird with greyish brown feathers, with the same attention to detail as a kaleidoscopically coloured parrot from Tonga.

His botanical drawings express also growing proficiency. Whereas the grasses he had painted during their first stay in New Zealand stand stiffly on the page, those drawn more than a year later on Tanna seem alive. A tree that he had found on Tahiti – 'one of the most beautiful trees in the world, which we called *Barringtonia*' (after a London patron) – depicts leaves curling as if ruffled by the wind and sculptural blooms so realistic that they look as if they could be plucked off the page. He also shaded his drawing of an evergreen from the Marquesas Islands in black like an engraving, adding texture, volume and movement line by line.

At the end of January, two weeks after leaving South Georgia, the *Resolution* reached 60°04'S latitude and was once again surrounded by icebergs and large ice floats. Sleet, snow and lack of visibility made for hazardous sailing and Cook wrote in his logbook, 'I was now tired of these high Southern Latitudes where nothing can be found but ice and thick fogs'. But he still did not give up. He continued east to finish their circuit until they crossed 19°E at the end of February 1775, almost exactly the same longitude at which they had started their icy explorations at the end of 1772. Only then did he turn north towards Cape Town. 'I had now made the circuit of the Southern Ocean in a high Latitude,' he recorded on 21 February, and 'the intention of the Voyage has in every respect been fully Answered, the Southern Hemisphere sufficiently explored and a final end put to the searching after a Southern Continent.' There might be land near the South Pole at even higher latitudes than they had reached, he admitted, but if so it was buried in snow and ice and therefore utterly inaccessible – 'whoever has resolution and perseverance to clear up this point by proceding farther than I have done, I shall not envy him the honour of the discovery but I will be bold to say that the world will not be benefited by it.'

Less than a month later, on 16 March 1775, near the coast of Africa, they suddenly saw two European ships on the horizon. For two days they raced towards them until they were close enough to hoist down one of their small boats to sail over to what turned out to be Dutch vessels. Since they had left Cape Town almost two and a half years earlier, at the end of November 1772, they had had no news of what had occurred in the rest of the world or how their families were. 'I am however every moment more & more apprehensive & in proportion as we come nearer,' Reinhold Forster wrote in his journal, 'for I don't know, what news I shall have there from my Wife & Children, from my Friends & Patrons', the first mention of Justina Elisabeth and his two other sons and four daughters in almost three years, as if he had only suddenly remembered them.

'I'm as great a stranger to all matters in England,' Lieutenant Clerke declared, 'as tho' I had been these 3 Years underground.' The crew of the *Resolution* would have to wait until they arrived in Cape Town for letters from their families, but the Dutch captain would at least be able to give them other news. Which nations were at war? What had happened during their absence? Which monarch had died? When Cook and the officers returned after a few hours, they brought news of peace in Europe. The next day they encountered an English ship returning from China and when Reinhold and some of the officers rowed over, the captain invited them for lunch – 'delicate roast goose and plump quails', Sparrman noted in envy after their return. Three days later they arrived at Cape Town and found a harbour bustling with ships from across the world.

Before they had left England, it had been decided that the *Resolution* would return via Cape Town – which was why friends and families had sent letters there to wait for the crew on their arrival. The men devoured fresh food and letters and news. They read piles of old newspapers to catch up. 'Sweden delivered from the yoke of aristocratical tyranny', George was glad to learn. In the so-called Swedish Revolution, the young king Gustav III had been the mastermind in a coup d'état which had ended the stronghold that the nobility had exercised over the monarchy. He was not intending to take away freedom, the king had said, but wanted to stop aristocratic despotism and establish 'a right kind of Liberty that only can make you, my dear subjects, happy'. Like other enlightened rulers at the time, he had then begun to reform the justice system and economy, as well as instituting limited religious freedom.

France had a new king: at the age of nineteen, Louis XVI had succeeded his grandfather in May 1774 during the second visit of the *Resolution* to Tahiti. Poland had lost vast swathes of land when Russia, Prussia and Austria had divided around a third of the country between them. Having added a huge territory to Prussia in the Polish partition, the Prussian king was, George noted, 'resting from his triumphs'. George also read that Russia and the Ottoman Empire had signed a peace treaty in July 1774, ending the war that had begun in 1768. With Russia gaining land and the right to protect Christians in the Muslim realm, the treaty marked the beginning of the decline of the once powerful Ottoman Empire, which for long had controlled large parts of south-east Europe and the Middle East. George was optimistic. After the long years of war in Europe, peace seemed finally possible. Everything 'promised general happiness to the human race'.

But trouble was brewing in the British colonies in North America. In December 1773 a group of colonists had dumped more than 300 chests of tea – the entire shipment of three East India Company vessels – into Boston harbour in protest against Britain's new tax regulations on tea. A month later the rebels had tarred and feathered a British customs collector. On 5 September 1774, just as the *Resolution* had landed in New Caledonia, the colonists had convened the First Continental Congress in Philadelphia – a congress of elected colonial delegates – to discuss how best to respond to British rule in North America. Frustrated by the lack of parliamentary representation and economic restrictions, the delegates called for a boycott of British goods and recommended that each colony establish its own militia.

There was also news from the *Adventure*, which had stopped in Cape

Town on her way to England exactly a year earlier, in March 1774. The men of the *Resolution* were horrified to learn that ten crew members had been killed and eaten by the Māori, but Cook refused to pass judgement until the news had been confirmed. He had always found the Māori to be brave and open-minded, 'but they are a people that will never put up with an insult if they have an opportunity to resent it'. George agreed. John Rowe, one of the officers who had been cannibalized, had always shown a brutal disregard for indigenous people and 'been exceeding desirous of firing upon them'. The Māori must have been provoked. 'The whole tenour of their behaviour to Europeans, seems to acquit them of treachery and cruel malevolence,' George wrote, 'it is therefore greatly to be suspected that they took umbrage at some affront, perhaps unwittingly committed by the strangers, and revenged it.'

During the five weeks in Cape Town, the crew repaired and painted their battered ship and replaced the rigging, and on 27 April the *Resolution* finally set sail for Europe. In mid-May they briefly stopped in St Helena, an island 1,200 miles from Africa and 1,800 miles from South America, in the midst of the South Atlantic. Controlled by the East India Company, the island was firmly in British hands and its inhabitants couldn't wait to celebrate Cook and his officers. The *Resolution* was saluted with cannons and the governor and his friends organized the festivities. 'I was very agreeably surprised with the great beauty and elegance displayed in a numerous circle of ladies,' George wrote, 'I thought myself suddenly transported to the most brilliant capital of Europe.' A week later they anchored for three days at Ascension Island, an isolated volcanic rock in the Atlantic which George thought was as dreary as Tierra del Fuego. Their last stop was at the Portuguese Azores in mid-July, where George was moved to meet the mother of one of the sailors who had been killed and eaten by the Māori. She ran a small boarding house and when she realized that George was part of the *Resolution* crew she burst into tears – because 'our arrival put her in mind of the cruel death of one of her sons'. The encounter made George think of his mother, Justina Elisabeth, and of 'how many mothers in Europe, and in the South Seas, have had reason to wail the loss of their sons, and to execrate the enterprizing spirit of mankind'.

It was time to go home. On 19 July 1775 the *Resolution* left the Azores and began the last leg of their journey.

PART III
Ambitions

11

'Great Expectations'

Return to England: 1775–1777

The letters they had written in Cape Town, and dispatched with regular merchant ships to friends and families, arrived in England before the crew did. On 24 June 1775, when the *Resolution* was still in the middle of the Atlantic Ocean some 1,300 miles west of the coast of Senegal, Carl Gottfried Woide received a letter from Reinhold Forster. Having looked after the Forster family in London during the voyage, Reinhold's old friend immediately set out to Paddington where Justina Elisabeth and the children lived. Her feelings of relief that her husband and son had survived the dangerous voyage can only be guessed, but there was little time to celebrate. Reinhold had instructed her to find new lodgings – larger, closer to the city, and grander. They were going to be famous. Four days later the loyal Woide and Justina Elisabeth began house hunting.

Daniel Solander, the botanist who had travelled on Cook's *Endeavour* voyage, also received post from Reinhold. On 28 June, Solander dispatched a rushed report to Joseph Banks: '260 New Plants, 200 New Animals – 71°10' – farthest Sth – no continent – Many Islands, some 80 Leagues long,' he summarized, 'Glorious Voyage – No man Lost by sickness.'

A month later, on 30 July 1775, almost exactly a year after the return of the *Adventure,* the *Resolution* arrived at Spithead on England's southern coast. In the three years they had been away, Cook calculated, they had sailed some 75,000 miles, roughly the same distance as if they had gone three times around the Equator. They had lost only four men – one had died of an illness he had already had before, the butcher had fallen down the hatchway in New Caledonia, and two men had drowned. Not a single man had died of scurvy, thanks to Cook's stocks of sauerkraut. Such a low death count was unheard of for such long sea voyages.

'Thus, after escaping innumerable dangers, and suffering a long series of hardships, we happily completed a voyage, which had lasted three years and sixteen days,'* George ended his travel account. That same day the Forsters left the ship, which would continue to Deptford just a few miles from London, and together with Cook, Hodges and Wales they boarded a stagecoach in Portsmouth. They wanted to reach the capital as soon as possible.

News of the *Resolution*'s return spread quickly. Solander immediately went to see Cook, whereupon he wrote to Banks that 'he rather looks better than when he left England'. Second Lieutenant Clerke dispatched a hurried note to Banks (whom he knew from the *Endeavour* expedition), joking about the stained paper on which he had to write – 'I assure you, but the Cockroaches have piss'd upon it' – but he promised to visit as soon as possible. Two weeks later, when the *Resolution* arrived in Deptford, Solander and several others went to the docks to inspect the vessel. They talked to the crew and looked at the curiosities that the men had brought back. 'Pickersgill made the Ladies sick,' Solander reported to Banks, 'by shewing them the New Zealand head of which 2 or 3 slices were boiled and eat on board of the Ship – It is preserved in Spirits.'

On their arrival in London, Reinhold and George immediately went to see Justina Elisabeth and the rest of the family. There are no accounts of the reunion, but the siblings' excitement on seeing their older brother is easy to imagine. George had changed. He had left as an adolescent but returned a man. His body had endured the greatest deprivations but his mind had expanded, nourished by the colours, smells, sounds and people of distant lands.

There was no time to rest. Father and son had to sort their collections and write letters to other naturalists, reporting their findings.

* In the German edition of *A Voyage Round the World*, George corrected himself to 'three years and eighteen days' (they had also gained a day by sailing eastwards).

Banks received some plant specimens, as did Carl Linnaeus in Sweden. Visitors were knocking on their door. Solander held off for two days but then couldn't bear to wait any more. A week later the Forsters moved from Paddington Green into their new home on Percy Street, a fine three-storey building to reflect their new status as great explorers. It was newly built, finished five years previously, with a large front room on the ground floor where the Forsters could welcome their guests. Tall sash windows flooded the rooms with light and the ceilings were ornamented with elegant plasterwork. Number 16 Percy Street is today in London's bustling centre, just off busy Tottenham Court Road, but in 1775 it was on the city's northern outskirts near the British Museum. George liked it – from his windows he could see the fields and meadows that stretched north towards the distant hills of Hampstead and Highgate.

But just as they were moving their belongings, thieves broke into the family's old lodgings. It was distressing enough that the burglars had taken linen, clothing and other valuables – including the remaining £700 of the £4,000 Reinhold had received at the start of the expedition. But far worse was the realization that all their manuscripts had vanished too. This was a catastrophe. For three years, father and son had kept meticulous journals, recording everything they observed. Now it was all gone. So were their carefully compiled list of vocabularies, painstakingly documented through the many months with the islanders. Hundreds of pages of ethnographical notes had disappeared. They had climbed mountains, battled through seemingly impenetrable forests and faced warriors to collect botanical specimens. George's beautiful drawings of birds, fish and plants had also vanished. All those weeks when he had been stuck in his tiny airless cabin sketching and colouring had been wasted.

The emotional toll was immediate. Justina Elisabeth was shaken by the burglary and collapsed, becoming ill enough that a doctor had to be summoned. Reinhold and George were devastated. The loss was so grave that newspapers reported it – the *Gentleman's Magazine* adding that 'great expectations are formed from the discoveries of this eminent naturalist'. Without their records from the voyage, they would not be able to fulfil these ambitions. Then, just as the severity of the theft sank in, someone found the manuscripts not far from the house. The thieves, it seemed, had only been interested in the valuables – and tossed aside the papers, oblivious to their worth. Around the corner, among rubbish, lay the future of the Forsters' scientific legacy. Their work – and their hope – had been saved.

The first few months in London were a whirlwind tour of visits and meetings. Two weeks after their return, they even had an audience with King George III who was known for his love of the sciences, agriculture and botany. Since returning from the *Endeavour* voyage five years previously, Banks had become the king's close advisor, encouraging him to finance plant-collecting expeditions for what would become the Royal Botanic Gardens at Kew. Newspapers announced the audience and it must have gone well because three days later, on a Saturday, father and son went to Kew to meet Queen Charlotte, the king's wife, and then again on Monday when they presented some South African animals for the king's menagerie – a small antelope, a mongoose, two eagles and other birds which Reinhold had purchased in Cape Town to give to George III.

Reinhold was also keen to share the results of the voyage with the fellows of the Royal Society. Frustratingly, there were no summer meetings, so he would have to wait until early November, when the fellows reconvened. Fortunately the Royal Society Club, a weekly dining circle, kept going a little longer. This was the most exclusive of the Royal Society's gatherings. Reinhold and George had never been invited to these intimate and informal meals, held in the nearby Mitre Tavern. On 10 August 1775, less than two weeks after their arrival, father and son went to the tavern in the company of Solander, their host. The tables were loaded with food – fresh salmon, roast beef, calf's head, tongue and brain, beans and bacon, rabbit stew, venison haunch and pasties, artichokes, French beans and currant jelly. There were tarts for dessert, as well as cheese and butter, and wine was poured plentifully.

This was a feast by any standards, but after three years of deprivation it must have been almost unreal for the Forsters. It hadn't been long ago that their dinner consisted of vermin-infested ship's biscuits and broiled penguin. Now they were eating juicy roasts dripping with fat and vegetables swimming in butter. Among the scientists who dined with them were none other than Sir John Pringle, the president of the Royal Society, and the Astronomer Royal, Nevil Maskelyne. Reinhold couldn't wait to report his findings.

There was also a reunion in London with Mai, the young Raiatean who had travelled on the *Adventure*. It had been almost two years since George had seen him last in Tonga before the *Resolution* and the *Adventure* had become separated off the coast of New Zealand. Joseph Banks had taken Mai under his protection when the *Adventure* had arrived the previous summer, presenting the Raiatean to the king, inviting him to fashionable parties and the opera, as well as regularly taking him to the Royal Society Club. Mai was inoculated against smallpox, stayed at great country houses, attended the opening of Parliament, dressed in velvet suits and satin breeches, and, according to George, played chess with great proficiency. Enraptured by classical music, Mai also enjoyed hunting, and he swam in the North Sea at Scarborough where he relished the freedom of waves and wind. He spoke some English now, but had never adapted to the climate. 'Cold, cold,' he always said, when he was asked about the weather.

As the first Polynesian in Britain, Mai had caused such a sensation that artists lined up to paint him, including Joshua Reynolds, the president of the Royal Academy of Arts and Britain's most prominent portrait painter. Mai became the incarnation of the 'noble savage' for London's high society, the subject of poems and even a play. Newspapers followed his every move but there were also plenty of racist comments, including reports about 'Omiah, the senseless stupid native of Othaheite' and pamphlets that imagined Mai with 'nymphs' who were 'ripe for amorous sport' on the floors of the royal palace. Like the Forsters, Mai also collected 'curiosities' and when he departed for the Society Islands, one year later on Cook's third voyage, he packed among other trophies a barrel organ, a jack-in-a-box, drums and a full suit of armour. He was also given cooking utensils, tools, a wheelbarrow, clothes, seeds, a compass and maps – but only a few guns.

It was busy at 16 Percy Street. One of the first visitors was the young ruler of a small German duchy who was in London at the time. Prince Leopold Friedrich Franz of Anhalt-Dessau arrived with his wife, Princess Luise, when the Forsters were still unpacking. For several hours father and son showed them their collections and George's drawings,

Reinhold and George Forster

entertaining them with anecdotes over a glass of the wine that Reinhold had bought in Cape Town. In the hope of gaining some kind of patronage, Reinhold gave them several objects that he and his son had collected during the voyage, including a map on which George had drawn the *Resolution*'s route.

Everybody wanted to meet them. People enjoyed tales from the voyage, and marvelled at the artefacts and natural-history specimens which father and son were always eager to show. Among their visitors was Georg Christoph Lichtenberg, a witty, hunch-backed professor and scientist from Göttingen with a great love of everything English. He was twelve years older than George and the two men would soon become friends. In awe of the *Resolution*'s expedition, Lichtenberg also went to Deptford to see the now legendary vessel and paid a bribe for a chip of timber as a souvenir. His letters home abounded with descriptions of huge icebergs, tropical islands, southern lights, poisonous fish and South Pacific islanders. George Forster's drawings brought alive the plants and animals, Lichtenberg said, because he was an 'excellent draughtsman', but it was the father who led the storytelling, presenting himself as a dashing adventurer. Reinhold Forster 'is a man of extraordinary passion,' Lichtenberg told a friend, 'I believe he would sail around Jupiter if he could'. Where George was modest, Reinhold boasted. Had he been the captain, Reinhold told Lichtenberg, 'we would now know three times as much.' The Forsters talked as casually about Tahiti and New Zealand, Lichtenberg joked, as if they were little market towns in Germany.

Still only twenty, George had hoped to enrol at Oxford University. Barring a few months in St Petersburg and in Warrington, he had never received any kind of formal education and the prospect of studying was tempting. But his father had other ideas and set his son to work on a book about their botanical discoveries. Reinhold was in charge of naming the plants and he didn't forget his English patrons. The stunning *Barringtonia* from Tahiti had been named for Daines Barrington, the former vice president of the Royal Society who had played an important role in his appointment on the *Resolution*; *Banksia* for Joseph Banks; and *Pennantia* for Reinhold's loyal supporter, the Welsh naturalist Thomas Pennant.* George worked fast, and when *Characteres Genera Plantarum* was published on 1 November 1775, only four months after their return, his name was for the first time also on the cover. But once again George was forced to earn the family's income. He resented the responsibility. 'It was never my lot to be my own master while in England,' he recalled years later to Banks.

Whenever George found time, he went to the theatre to distract himself and devoured all the new books that had been published during his three years away. His favourite was Goethe's bestselling *The Sorrows of Young Werther*, which he read three times, crying for hours (as he admitted to a friend) and embracing the *Sturm und Drang* – the era of 'Storm and Stress' – with its emphasis above all on feeling. His letters show a young man who wrote as fast as he thought. Sentences poured onto the page, going back and forth – no, he couldn't send auricula seeds, he wrote to a German friend who was a keen gardener, only to correct himself in the next sentence: 'Stop, that's not true', he could send them, but it would be too late to sow them.

Eager for fame and fortune, Reinhold decided to write an account of the voyage. With Europe's hunger for adventure and expeditions, the

* Reinhold had met Thomas Pennant through his Warrington contacts in 1768. Part of the landed gentry in Wales, Pennant was a well-connected scientist and fellow of the Royal Society who introduced Reinhold to other scientists and wealthy patrons (including Barrington), as well as regularly lending him money.

book was a guaranteed bestseller, but the problem was that he needed the Admiralty's permission. 'I think the Public, who have contributed largely to your expences during your voyage, have a property in such observations as you have made during the time of your being in their service,' the Earl of Sandwich, first Lord of the Admiralty, told Reinhold a few months after their return. After some back and forth, Sandwich decided that a formal agreement was needed. This contract stated that Captain Cook should write the main narrative, focusing on nautical and ethnographical observations, while Reinhold Forster would only be allowed to write about natural history. Sandwich also requested a sample chapter, which, once submitted, he promptly rejected. Forster had delivered a narrative, Sandwich said, not the 'philosophical remarks' that had been agreed – but the Admiralty could provide an editor to improve the manuscript. Reinhold was furious, unwilling to have his work edited and to 'submit to that Indignity to have my performance treated like a theme of a School-boy'. As George later told his publisher, his father hated being corrected, believing 'every word he had written to be the Gospel'.

Reinhold resolved to defy the Admiralty. With shrewd legal agility, he realized that George, unlike himself, had never signed an agreement with the Admiralty. He approached Benjamin White, a publisher specializing in natural-history books who had already printed their *Characteres Genera Plantarum* and who was open to another collaboration. So in late summer 1776, a year after their return to England, George found himself sitting down at the small mahogany desk which had accompanied him around the world and writing for the next few months – racing to finish *A Voyage Round the World* before Cook published his own account. That August, however, when money became tight, his father took George's vivid watercolours and sketches from the voyage and sold them to Joseph Banks for £420. In one stroke, 301 botanical and 271 zoological drawings – of exotic birds, penguins, dolphins, flying fish and sculptural blooms – were gone. As always, George had not been consulted.

He wrote and wrote and wrote. His health deteriorated and he felt miserable. The deprivations from the voyage, including the constant lack of fresh food, freezing temperatures, permanently wet clothes and a damp cabin, had taken their toll on his body. For the rest of his life he suffered from indigestion followed by diarrhoea, cramps, rheumatism, headaches and colds. 'Life!' he wrote to a friend in Germany, 'this is no life; such emptiness is worse than – yes, maybe even death.' But his father was relentless. As George finished each chapter, Reinhold pulled the pages out of his hands. There was no time to edit – 'what is written is written'. Once in a while George escaped to the little courtyard behind their house in Percy Street. There, in the shade of a lime tree, he paced up and down. In his letters to friends, he revealed his frustrations, but he sealed them quickly before his father could read them. As before, he was the breadwinner for the entire family.

With his drawings sold, George had to paint with words – or *Wortgemählden* as he later called it – conjuring his readers into forests garlanded with resplendent blossoms and populated by wondrous birds. He wrote of gigantic waves crashing over the *Resolution* and intricate Māori tattoos, segueing from descriptions of fish dissections to howling storms. Where earlier explorers such as Christopher Columbus had struggled to describe South America's landscape as anything more than green, George Forster turned even the icy world of Antarctica into shades of sapphire, purple and green.

In the small Tahitian harbour where they had anchored in August 1773 the water 'was as smooth as the finest mirrour, and the sea broke with a snowy foam around us upon the outer reef'. Here 'tall coco-palms nodded to each other, and rose over the rest of the trees; the bananas displayed their beautiful leaves' and rivers 'murmured over a bed of pebbles'. It was so magical, he wrote, that 'no poet could paint it so beautifully'. At Dusky Bay his language sings with the birds: 'The noise of the cascade is so loud, and so repeatedly reverberated from the echoing rocks, that it drowns almost every other sound; the birds seemed to retire from it to a little distance, where the shrill notes of thrushes, the graver pipe of wattle-birds, and the enchanting melody of various creepers resounded on all sides, and completed the beauty of this wild and romantic spot.'

Not only did George have an excellent memory, as the son of one of his father's former colleagues in Warrington said, but his imagination was vivid and poetic – a perfect combination for a travel account. He was a natural storyteller and seemed to instinctively play with contrast, rhythm and pace. Of Tanna – where the islander had been killed for crossing Cook's line in the sand – George painted a gorgeous portrait of peaceful nature and contented people, only to set it dramatically against the brutal shooting at the beach. Or at Tierra del Fuego, he described a small cove bathed in sunshine but surrounded by high snow-capped mountains – summer and winter present at once:

> We found a most beautiful cove on this coast, which formed a circular bason, where the water was smooth and transparent as a mirror. All the lower parts were fringed with trees . . . a prodigious number of small birds sat on every branch, and twittered around us in the sunshine . . . Abundance of mosses, ferns, and climbers grew up between the trees, and were no small impediment to us in walking. Various flowers enlivened these woods, and encreased our collection with new species. Here then there was the appearance of summer; but if we looked up to the monstrous cloud-capt mountains which formed almost perpendicular walls on all sides of the harbour, and beheld them covered with snow and ice, which had sometimes a blue, and sometimes a yellowish tinge, we thought ourselves transported to the Glaciers of Switzerland.

George believed that you had to *see* the world in order to understand it. There was no point in trying to make sense of everything in your study, he explained, 'because in the end, one has nothing else than what comes through these two small openings in your eyes and sets the vibrations of the brain in motion!' Individual experience was indispensable. 'Two travellers,' he wrote, 'seldom saw the same object in the same manner, and each reported the fact differently, according to his sensations, and his peculiar mode of thinking.' He followed his heart and his feelings, he explained in the preface to *A Voyage Round the World*, and he was part of the story – an unusual approach at a time when Enlightenment thinkers championed the eradication of emotion and subjectivity in science and observation.

Unlike most of his contemporaries, George believed that reason alone was not enough to understand the world. That didn't mean that he diminished the value of observation, but he had no interest in simply collecting data – being 'a mere compiler . . . that I cannot do'. Those thinkers who worshipped cold evidence alone 'had their wish; facts were collected in all parts of the world, and yet knowledge was not increased'. Years later he would explain that 'the first point from which all knowledge is gained is based on *Empfindung*' – a German term that can be translated as 'sensations', though it is more nuanced as it not only refers to the physical senses but also implies a capacity to feel and an awareness of a subjective experience of the world. 'Never before has there been a greater danger of elevating cold reason into a universally worshipped idol at the expense of feeling,' he said.

To compose his narrative, he used his own notes and his father's daily journal. But where Reinhold described, George expanded, making seventy pages out of ten in his father's journal. His father's account of getting lost in the fog with astronomer William Wales in the Antarctic ocean, for example, was a terse description of facts in a couple of short sentences, but George rendered it with suspense and drama. Or a day on Tahiti which involved visiting one of the sacred *marae*, seeing a death house where the body of a woman was laid out, and then having dinner with Tahitians, took up less than two handwritten pages in Reinhold's journal (just over 1,000 words). In George's telling it became an exquisite 5,000-word entry that ranges from animated descriptions of nature, nose-flute playing, local eating habits, and Tupaia's map of islands to detailed observations of the *marae*, the *fare tupapa'u* – the house of the corpse – and George's reflection that the arrival of Europeans was harmful for South Pacific societies. Even on the rare occasions when George extracted entire scenes from his father's journal – adding quotation marks to indicate that these were first-hand accounts by Reinhold – he rewrote them substantially, adding, changing, deleting and polishing the language.

He roamed from description to interpretation, from recounting dialogues with the islanders to ethical discourses, from animals to attempts to grasp religious concepts. Underlying everything was his focus on comparison and connection. The smallest detail of a hairstyle or a cooking implement fascinated him, but he also tried to see its broader perspective. One moment, he looked at a particular plant or individual on one island, but he was also a master in expanding his focus to a panoramic view that included climate, soils and history.

The result was a book built around a deep love for nature and humankind. In chapter after chapter, George brought the people they had met to life. Page after page, he provided detailed portraits of the people of the South Pacific. 'The forehead in general was high, the nose broad and flat at the root, and the eyes rather small,' he observed in New Caledonia, 'their cheek-bones were very prominent, and the cheeks commonly plump'. Eye colours, height, length of hair, nose shapes, tattoos, jewellery or hygiene – 'beard shaven or rather clipt by means of a couple of sharp muscle shells' – nothing escaped his attention.

He documented the different weapons on each island – in Tanna, for example, 'they have likewise arrows with three points, but these are chiefly intended to kill birds and fish', clubs that were 'four feet long, strait, cylindrical, highly polished, and knobbed at each end', spears which were nine to ten feet long and which 'they throw with great accuracy, at a short distance', as well as slings 'made of coco-nut fibres, and worn round the arm or waist'. He described tattoos at the Marquesas – 'these punctures were disposed with the utmost regularity; so that the marks on each leg, arm, and cheek, and on the corresponding muscles, were exactly similar. They never assumed the determinate form of an animal or plant, but consisted of a variety of blotches, spirals, bars, chequers, and lines', and in New Caledonia he peeped into the huts 'desirous to see their method of cooking'. He was as intrigued by the elaborate carvings on Tongan clubs as he was by a girl's dexterity in juggling five gourds. All these descriptions remain an important source for what is known about South Pacific culture before the arrival of Europeans.

Yet there was also ugliness and illness: in Tonga he encountered a man with a back covered in oozing ulcers and a woman who only had a hole where her nose used to be and eyes that 'seemed ready to fall out of her head'. At Dusky Sound, he recalled how one Māori woman was 'remarkably ugly, and had a prodigious excrescence on her upper lip' and in New Caledonia he saw people with 'prodigious thick legs and arms, which seemed to be affected by a kind of leprosy'.

He could be funny, too. He joked that one of the sailors didn't bring his Māori 'wife' on board the *Resolution*, 'foreseeing that it would be highly inconvenient to lodge the numerous retinue which crawled in her garments and weighed down the hair of her head'. Or when he saw some Tongans with white, blue and orange powdered hair, he wrote wryly that there was an 'admirable similarity in follies, the modes of the former inhabitants of Europe are in full force among modern antipodes'. In Raiatea, he had also observed how one of the chiefs changed the subject he didn't want to talk about 'with all the art of an European politician'. He used humour to underline how arrogant the European viewpoint sometimes was – judging Tahitians' morals by what they had seen during their brief time with them, he wrote, would be as absurd as if Mai 'were to report to his countrymen, that chastity is not known in England' because he had met the prostitutes of Covent Garden.

George could also be critical about the indigenous people. In New Zealand, he had seen a Māori brutally beat his wife when she attempted to punish their son, who had thrown a stone at her head because he wanted a piece of broiled penguin. The Māori, George wrote, used their women as 'mere drudges'. He also observed the sailors on the *Resolution* like an ethnographer. Used to the harsh life at sea, he wrote, they breathed nothing but war. Having watched them for three years, he admired their strength and bravery, but criticized their easily triggered violence and lack of compassion for the indigenous people. 'By force of habit even killing is become so much their passion,' George wrote, 'we have seen many instances during our voyage, where they have expressed a horrid eagerness to fire upon the natives on the slightest pretences.'

Never shy of condemning the way Europeans treated local people, he again and again described how they shot and killed islanders across the South Pacific. Despite calling Tonga the Friendly Islands the crew injured several islanders by gunshots during their first visit, on 6 October 1773, and then again during their second in June 1774. Others were wounded on Niue, Easter Island and Malakula among other places. One man was killed on the Marquesas, several murdered on Erromango, and one man shot on Tanna in August 1774. The list was shockingly long. Firearms brought death, but George presciently also predicted the lethal effect of new diseases. 'Europeans, above all, should be extremely cautious of communicating any contagious disorder to the people whom they visit in the South Seas,' he wrote, 'such a disease as the small pox, for example, would undoubtedly make dreadful havock.'

Astonishingly, he also wrote about 'the general rights of mankind' – or 'Rechte der Menschheit' in the German edition – a much closer approximation to the later phrase 'human rights' than the recently proclaimed American *Declaration of Independence*. Both the Americans and, thirteen years later, the French revolutionaries mostly excluded women, slaves and non-Europeans. While the 'rights of man' would be widely discussed after 1789, George had already expanded the concept to encompass all humankind as early as 1777.

Yet, he was still inevitably influenced by the attitudes of his age. No matter how much he tried there were certain beliefs – such as the conviction in the primacy of European agriculture – that were deeply rooted in his thinking. He had been incensed when the crew discovered that the three European pigs they had left behind on their first visit to New Zealand had been taken to different parts of Queen Charlotte Sound.* 'By separating the animals, and dividing them as a spoil, these barbarians effectually destroy the possibility of propagating the species,' he wrote, 'too much occupied with the wants of the present moment, they overlook the only means of securing a certain livelihood to themselves, and reject every attempt to civilize them.'

Sometimes, too, he still thought like a colonizer. As the *Resolution* had passed between the islands of the Vanuatu archipelago, George had seen fields of such a rich yellow colour that he was reminded of England's golden cornfields. This island, he wrote, 'seemed to be well situated for the purpose of an European settlement' and the people 'would readily receive the improvements of civilization'. Similarly, he mused that one stretch of land in New Zealand, near today's Wellington, would make a good location for settlers from Europe. Perhaps in the future, if England lost its American colonies, he wrote shortly after the Americans had declared independence on 4 July 1776, the British government could send settlers there. But, he added, only 'if it were ever possible for Europeans to have humanity enough to acknowledge the indigenous tribes of the South Sea as their brethren'.

* Cook had already released several pigs in different parts of New Zealand during the *Endeavour* voyage. The descendants of the European pigs became wild and are now called Captain Cookers.

By the end of 1776, less than four months after he had written the first word, the manuscript of *A Voyage Round the World* arrived at the printer. Publication was eagerly awaited – the naturalist Gilbert White (who was the publisher's brother) excitedly informed friends and family at the end of January 1777 that publication was imminent. George felt no sense of relief because he had to begin the German translation immediately.

Reinhold had signed a contract with a German publisher who had travelled from Berlin to London in the previous summer. Karl Spener was an ambitious young man who had taken over his father's firm at the age of twenty-three and who had met the Forsters already before the *Resolution* voyage when he visited England in 1771. Spener was only five years older than George and would become a trusted friend. George, Reinhold decided, would translate his own book, a daunting prospect given the many years in which George had spoken only English – he didn't even converse in German with his family (and for the rest of his life, his father would speak and write to him in English). George's letters to friends and acquaintances in Germany were always peppered with English words and his written German had become erratic. 'I just have to ask one thing,' he wrote to Spener with apprehension, 'can the Berlin printers spell correctly?' Someone would need to correct the final manuscript.

George was ill, exhausted, and had lost so much weight that even Reinhold Forster had to admit his son might need some assistance. It arrived in the form of Rudolf Erich Raspe, a brilliant eccentric who had fled the German state of Hesse-Kassel after it was discovered that he had been stealing and selling ancient coins from the collections of his employer, Landgrave Friedrich II. With news travelling slowly, Raspe wangled himself onto the guest list of the Royal Society but was soon expelled. He would later write the hugely successful *Baron Munchausen's Narrative of his Marvellous Travels and Campaigns in Russia* – a whimsical satire in which the eponymous protagonist performs such feats as riding on a cannonball, shooting a stag with cherry stones (the stag subsequently grows a cherry tree between his antlers) and visiting the moon.

For the moment, Raspe was to work with George on the German translation of *A Voyage Round the World*. Progress was woefully slow and

Raspe was often ill. Like his fictional character Munchausen, he also had a tendency to exaggerate and lie, coming up with excuses for his failure to deliver and reasons to borrow money from the Forsters. George spent a lot of time merging the voices of two translations into one and the collaboration ended in anger. Raspe, George told Spener, liked only himself and believed that others existed entirely to serve him.

The English edition of *A Voyage Round the World* was published on 17 March 1777.* Six weeks later, Captain Cook's own *Voyage Towards the South Pole* appeared, printed in a larger format and illustrated with more than sixty engravings after the drawings by William Hodges, the expedition artist – but the images of animals and plants were copied from George's drawings which Banks had bought. It was one thing that George hadn't been allowed to use Hodges' evocative landscapes and depictions of indigenous people (as his father believed had been initially agreed with the Admiralty), but quite another that he couldn't use his own drawings after Reinhold had sold them. But to see them published in Cook's book now was a terrible blow.

Thankfully, the reviews of George's *A Voyage Round the World* were mostly positive, with several writers commenting that they felt as if they were actually travelling on the *Resolution*. George was delighted. Samuel Johnson, one of the great literary figures of the age and the author of *A Dictionary of the English Language*, called the book 'a great affection of fine writing'. Johnson's friend and biographer James Boswell declared that 'he carries you along with him'. Those who compared the two books favoured George's *A Voyage Round the World*. 'Captain Cook's own narrative is a mere sailor's journal,' wrote one reviewer, but he was disappointed by the lack of illustrations in George's account. 'Every page of it abounds with life and character,' raved the reviewer for *The Town and Country Magazine*, 'painted with all the force of language.' More than a dozen reviews were published in England, several with long extracts.

Rather than wait for the German translation, many German reviewers also read the English edition. Most admired the book, describing it as 'ravishing' and 'admirable', but there were also critical voices. One took

* The German translation was finished on 2 September 1777 and published in two volumes in 1778 and 1780.

offence at George's description of the Dutch East India Company as 'cruel and ambitious spice merchants', and another disliked the favourable depiction of indigenous people, complaining about his 'acerbic allusions to the cruelty, harshness and vices of the Europeans'. Confident about his arguments and portrait of the islanders, George sent a public reply to one of Germany's leading newspapers, asking: 'Why not deliver eulogies on virtues? They may appear anywhere – in a beggar's hut or a palace, in Europe or Tahiti.' He had no interest in repeating tedious prejudices against the indigenous people – 'I therefore show real virtues among savages, where in similar cases vices prevail among civilized people.'

The most glowing German review came from Christoph Martin Wieland, a distinguished writer who declared George nothing less than a poet. In an extensive commentary, published over three issues of the *Teutsche Merkur*, one of Germany's most important journals, Wieland pronounced *A Voyage Round the World* a thrilling book. The descriptions were painterly and humanistic, executed with intensity and enthusiasm. It was a masterpiece. As always, Reinhold attempted to take the credit, insisting that he had shaped his son. 'I alone was his leader, his teacher,' he later said to Wieland, 'who awakened the dormant spark of divinity in him.'

Within six months, pirated French and Swedish translations were available, followed by Spanish and Russian editions, and then even more French editions. None were authorized. Soon the book was declared a classic but it didn't sell enough copies to support Reinhold's spending habits, and of course they never received any money from the pirated translations. People loved pictures, George admitted, and at two guineas *A Voyage Round the World* cost the same as Cook's generously illustrated and Admiralty-subsidized account. Father and son would have to find other ways to finance their life in London.

12

'A magnificent young man'

Trials and Tribulations: 1777–1779

George Forster drank in his freedom. The carriage jostled along bad roads through the French countryside from Dieppe in Normandy, where his ship had landed, to Paris. The twenty-two-year-old was in France in the hope of selling some of the objects he and his father had collected in the South Pacific and to find an official French publisher for *A Voyage Round the World*. As he stopped in towns and villages to change horses, eat or sleep, he visited churches, walked through gardens, and ordered delicious meals in taverns. 'Supped gloriously, sumptuously,' he wrote, savouring French food as much as he did the French sense of fashion. Everybody seemed to dress however they liked here and he wondered why people in London were 'uniformly clothed in coats precisely of the same make and shape'. He observed the French just as he had the South Pacific islanders. His diary was filled with joy and for the first time an admiration for women: 'one very pretty, but with the air of an arrant coquette', 'the womens short petticoats barely covering the knee', 'a woman one can't help being pleased with' – all in one short paragraph.

When he reached Paris on 6 October 1777, he crossed the Seine at the Pont de Neuilly, a fine large stone bridge with five arches. The carriage went along the royal hunting forest of the Bois de Boulogne all the way to the Louvre – 'really a fine piece of architecture' – to George's lodgings near the Palais Royal. The coachman drove so fast that George feared not only for his own life but also for the pedestrians.

'The cries of Paris are as unintelligible as those of London,' he noted, as he watched the vendors hawking their wares from stalls and shouting at potential customers. Tooth-pullers, quacks, cobblers and knife-grinders offered their services. The city divided its visitors. Some hated Paris – the 'ugliest, beastly town in the universe,' said the English writer Horace Walpole – while others, like Benjamin Franklin, adored it. Franklin, who had arrived the previous year as the ambassador of the newly independent United States, described Paris as 'a prodigious Mixture of Magnificence and Negligence'.

By the time George came to Paris, France had been ruled by Louis XVI for a little over three years. At the age of fifteen he had married Marie Antoinette, the fourteen-year-old daughter of the Holy Roman Emperor, but it would take seven years for the couple to consummate their marriage. Now twenty-three, he was a young and inexperienced king, known to be cautious and indecisive. His ministers convinced him to support the American rebels in their fight for independence and France had secretly dispatched military supplies to the British colonies. Benjamin Franklin had been given the task of negotiating a formal alliance between France and the thirteen colonies.

On his first day in Paris, George began his round through the city. 'I drove furiously about Paris,' he noted in his diary. He spent two days with Jean-Baptiste Le Roy, director of the French Academy of Science and one of the most prolific contributors to Diderot and D'Alembert's *Encyclopédie*, and an evening with Comte de Buffon, the most revered naturalist of the time. At seventy, Buffon's body showed his age but his mind was still razor-sharp, continuing to add to his life's work, the *Histoire naturelle,* which would eventually run to forty-four volumes. That evening George noted in his diary: 'he is old, and wrinkled, and a thin man, but has vivacity and sprightliness, and is fond of making puns in his own language.' Everyone interested in the natural world studied Buffon's work, but now it was he who had questions for George about South Pacific plants and animals.

George visited the Louvre, walked through the Tuileries Garden which was open to the public, and attended the theatre. French women continued to fascinate him. 'They have small feet, rich bosoms, and pretty small features, and often delicate shapes,' he wrote excitedly in his diary. When he went to a fair, he marvelled at the goods for sale, but even more so at the 'large and beautiful Eyes of the Syrens who vend them'. He was promptly seduced – 'I fell into the snare and

The Tuileries Garden next to the Louvre

bought several things which I did not absolutely want.' Exploring the city, he saw the washerwomen by the Seine, beating the clothes and linen with broad flat spatulas – 'so that the impurities and the constituent parts of our Shirts are destroyed together' – and almost got lost in the labyrinth of shops at the Palais Royal. He was moved by an orphanage he visited. There were babies in cradles, some boys were knitting, the girls were running around – 'attended by welllooking wholesome Nurses'. The hospital next door seemed less well organized: the courtyard was too small for those who could walk to enjoy some fresh air, and four to six people shared a bed, often lying next to dead bodies.

George went shopping – black silk breeches and matching stockings – because he enjoyed nice clothes and was always immaculately dressed. He didn't care that he was spending too much money. 'I value my feelings more than all the wealth of the Indies,' he wrote in his diary, and 'whenever I can purchase an agreeable Sensation to my mind, for two Shillings, I'll do it.' In this at least, he was his father's son.

Also like his father, who had already joined the freemasons in Russia and London, George entered a Parisian lodge – his name in the members list would soon be followed by those of Voltaire and Franklin. Priding themselves on their democratic ideals, many members of the lodge supported the American Revolution. They had pledged 'to come rushing to help humanity' and several notable Enlightenment thinkers had joined.* All distinctions of birth and wealth were abolished here and the members were bound to tolerance and equality – all qualities that George greatly valued. It didn't hurt that the freemasons provided an instant network of invaluable contacts in Paris (one of the reasons why he would often join lodges in other cities when he travelled).

Benjamin Franklin, renowned for his experiments with electricity and esteemed as a man of science, also invited George to his home. He had previously met the Forsters at the Royal Society meetings before the *Resolution* voyage. On 9 October 1777, three days after his arrival, George, accompanied by Le Roy, went to Passy – a small village on the outskirts of Paris – where Franklin lived on the estate of a French aristocrat, three miles along the Seine from the Louvre. It was a beautiful spot. Situated on a hill and surrounded by large grounds and gardens with pavilions and formal terraces, the château overlooked Paris and the winding Seine. Seven-course dinners were served in the early afternoon and the wine cellar contained more than a thousand bottles.

Although living in the most fashion-conscious place in Europe, Franklin purposefully dressed down, deliberately playing the role of an American backwoodsman to convey an image of republican virtue and simplicity in contrast to opulent European courts. Just a plain grey suit, George noted, spectacles perched on his nose and his long silver hair open and unpowdered, often topped with a fur cap. Parisian women adored him and wore fur hats in his honour – 'coiffure à la Franklin'. When he had arrived in Paris at the end of December 1776, just nine months before George's visit, people had lined the streets to catch a

* Besides Franklin and Voltaire many other influential Enlightenment figures were associated with the *Les Neuf Soeurs* lodge in Paris, including Jean-Baptiste le Rond d'Alembert, co-editor of the epochal *Encyclopédie*; also, the hot-air balloon pioneer Jacques Montgolfier and astronomer Jérôme Lalande, one of the founders of the lodge. There were several men who would become French revolutionaries, such as the Marquis de Lafayette, who also fought with the Americans in the War of Independence against the British; Jean-Pierre Brissot, writer, abolitionist and leader of the Girondins; and Nicolas de Condorcet, philosopher and mathematician who advocated equal rights for women.

Benjamin Franklin with his fur cap

glimpse of Franklin, and his image was depicted on snuffboxes, medallions and signet rings. Now in his early seventies, he was still flirtatious and was said to have played chess with Madame Brillon – an accomplished musician and composer who also lived in Passy – while she was in her bathtub.

His house was often filled with visitors and George was thrilled to be there. Over dinner they talked about the American Revolution, freedom and equality. After the meal, Franklin took a nap while George stayed on with the other guests. Wine and liquor were poured generously and George relished the company – here was a group who shared many of his beliefs. 'I was as happy as could be,' he wrote in his diary, 'because I was at my ease, and just as if I were at home.' When more guests arrived, 'Papa', as Franklin was called by his friends, returned and the lively conversations continued.

Everybody asked George about his voyage. One woman in particular, 'who seem'd to be an female Philosopher', bombarded him with questions about Tahiti, sexual encounters and venereal disease. At first embarrassed by her frankness, George quickly recovered. 'Everything is allowed to a Philosopher!' he noted, no matter their gender.

Over the next three weeks he saw Franklin – 'the *venerable philosopher of the Western World*' as he called him – several more times. When he returned to London, at the end of November 1777, George hung Franklin's portrait in his room in Percy Street.

George had every reason to be happy. At the age of twenty-two he had been made a fellow of the Royal Society – the greatest honour the scientific world in England could bestow – and he was so highly regarded that doors opened to him all over Paris. *A Voyage Round the World* had been published to great acclaim, even if it hadn't sold to the degree he had hoped. And George had evolved as a thinker. Confident of his analytical skills and deductive capacity, he challenged accepted ideas and eminent scholars as well as his father (at least intellectually). Given his unusual upbringing and experience on the *Resolution*, George did not feel bound to the scientific establishment or the prevailing ideas of the era's most influential thinkers.

Already in *A Voyage Round the World* he had criticized Rousseau and would continue to do so in numerous essays and articles. The French philosopher's admiration for humankind in the original state of nature was as absurd to him as it was removed from reality. 'The traveller wanders through all four continents,' George wrote, 'and nowhere finds the endearing tribe that was promised to him in every forest and every wilderness.' Rousseau's contrast – contradiction, even – between nature and culture was a false dichotomy. George's riposte was to argue that societies advanced towards civilization instead of being degraded by it. He believed in the perfectibility of humankind – it was 'almost certain that humankind will one day become better, more perfect, and thus happier'. But the difference from many other thinkers was that George didn't believe this progress was automatically linked to being morally better. 'I wanted to put a stop to the unjust prejudice,' he explained in 1778, 'by which we in Europe claim virtue for ourselves alone and attribute nothing but wicked deeds and evil nature to the savages.'

Years later, in his essay 'Primer to a Future History of Humanity', George likened the developmental stages of societies to those of humans. It was an advance from baby (which he compared to societies concerned only with self-preservation) to sexualized adolescent (when societies have abundant sources of subsistence, 'the time of their reproduction arrives'), and then adulthood (societies driven by war and despotism), and finally old age (a civilization ruled by reason and sensitivity). The 'baby' stage was a so-called 'primitive' society, whereas 'old age' was comparable to 'civilized' Europe. To the modern mind, this argument feels deeply flawed, but George didn't equate society's final stage with inevitable greatness – nor, as Rousseau had, with decline and oppression.

'Great imperfections cannot be excluded from the best of human societies,' he had already written in *A Voyage Round the World*. There was no evidence that certain nations, people or societies were intrinsically benevolent or bad, noble or depraved – vice and virtue were present in every society. 'The bold attempt to trace all the people of the world to either a good or evil principle lacks only – proof,' he wrote. But this idea of a people or race that was superior or inferior, was, of course, exactly the argument on which racism was based.

Racist sentiments permeated European societies and were expressed by many Enlightenment thinkers. In an essay published the same year as *A Voyage Round the World*, Immanuel Kant had written that 'all Negroes stink' and that they were 'lazy, soft and dallying'. Carl Linnaeus had thought to bring order to nature by imposing a classification system not only on plants and animals but also on humans – subdividing *Homo sapiens* into four categories or variations which were not only distinguished by colour but also by racist judgements. Accordingly, *Americanus* was red, cheerful and irascible, *Asiaticus* was melancholic, haughty and greedy, *Africanus* was black, phlegmatic and lazy, and *Europaeus* was sanguine, wise and muscular. Reinhold Forster, who was finally writing a book about his natural-history observations during the *Resolution* voyage (the only aspect he was permitted to publish), included a chapter on the 'Varieties of the Human Species' across the globe. His opening paragraph assigned 'the small size, the tawny colour, the mistrustful temper' to the Inuits, whereas 'a majestic size, red hair, a blue languishing eye, a remarkably fair complexion, and a warlike, intrepid, but open and generous temper distinguish the Teutonic tribes of the North of Europe'.

In France, Buffon argued that every human was either a perfected or degenerated version of an original prototype. Their state of progress depended on the climate they lived in, Buffon wrote, and Europe's mild climate had conveniently produced 'the most beautiful and well-formed people'. Climate and the environment were the main determining factors on how humans developed, affecting both appearance and character. Since antiquity, thinkers had believed that harsher, more extreme climates made people stronger but also less civilized, lacking the mental capacities of those who lived in milder ones.

Reinhold also subscribed to this popular 'climate' theory of human development but gave it his own twist by arguing that humankind had migrated from the tropical regions near the equator to the frigid zones closer to the poles. 'I believe,' he wrote, 'that the nations inhabiting the frozen extremities of our globe to be degenerated and debased from that original happiness, which the tropical nations more or less enjoy.' The cold, he wrote, 'causes sluggishness, indolence and stupidity of mind', and 'they [savage nations] become incapable of any attachment, affection or endearment'.*

George disagreed and never used the word 'degenerated' in *A Voyage Round the World*. He also disputed the sole influence of climate. The people of New Caledonia, for example, were proof that a harsh environment did not produce brutal barbarians. They were peaceful, civilized and friendly, although they had to work hard to produce food on soil far less fertile than elsewhere in the South Pacific. 'The philosophers who are of opinion that the temper, the manners, and genius of a people, depend entirely upon the climate,' George had written in *A Voyage Round the World*, 'will be at a loss to account for the peaceful character of the inhabitants of New Caledonia'. There were other reasons that explained the differences between people from across the world – 'I am far from being convinced of this general and powerful influence of climates'.

George emphasized that every culture had to be understood in its particular context. All humans had the same predispositions – reason, imagination, feelings – but they were shaped by their environment, culture and education. 'And so humans have become nowhere everything,' he believed, 'but something different everywhere.' During the voyage George had observed a great variety between the peoples he had met, yet

* When George translated his father's *Observations Made During a Voyage Round the World* a few years later, he added footnotes and changed the text. He deleted entire paragraphs (like those quoted above) and the sections in which Reinhold explained that humankind had migrated from tropical to cold climates. 'I skipped entire pages of the original,' George told his publisher Spener.

he saw unity in that diversity. Unlike most Europeans who believed in a hierarchical system of humankind with white people at the pinnacle, George was certain 'that men in a similar state of civilization resemble each other more than we are aware of, even in the most opposite extremes of the world'. As his perspective had shifted during the voyage, he tried to see himself as a foreigner, while simultaneously regarding the locals not as 'exotic' or 'savage' but human. 'All the various tribes of men,' he was adamant, were 'entitled to an equal share of my good will.' Underpinning everything was his belief in unity – 'the passions and innate qualities of human nature are much the same in every climate.'

Where did George Forster's open-mindedness come from? Was it because he had been exposed to different cultures from the age of ten when he had travelled through Russia? Was it because he didn't even know to which country he belonged? To Prussia? To England? Was it his limited conventional schooling? Although he sometimes complained about it, this lack of academic education gave him a certain freedom to think, he told a friend many years later, and allowed him to 'philosophize in an unphilosophical manner'. Words and books were useful, but it was 'precisely this systematic knowledge which prevents an otherwise capable mind from grasping good ideas'. Or was his tolerance a reaction against his narcissistic father whom he had watched shout at friends, colleagues and strangers throughout his life? George had always counterbalanced his father's unpredictable outbursts with kindness and patience. Reinhold's disregard and disrespect for others seemed to have provoked the opposite in George.

Since their return to England after the *Resolution* voyage, George had emerged as an independent thinker – yet his life was still controlled and overshadowed by his father. Reinhold had been spending lavishly on fashionable clothes and their house, as well as buying hundreds of books – so many that he ran out of space in Percy Street. People began to talk. 'They have no manner of economy,' wrote the naturalist Gilbert White. When George shared their financial worries with Anders Sparrman, who had returned to Sweden, the botanist advised 'my friend, look out for a rich English girl, who can provide for you and your Family.'

After Reinhold had fallen out with the Admiralty over the account of the *Resolution* voyage, he had failed to procure the well-paid position he had expected to be given at an academic institution. When the librarian at the British Museum died, for example, a friend had made enquiries on Reinhold's behalf, but was rebuffed with the argument that 'the man was *quarrelsome*'. No one wanted to employ a man who had the reputation of picking fights with his superiors. So, by the end of 1777, when George had returned from Paris, debtors and bailiffs were knocking at the door of Percy Street, and Reinhold found himself begging Joseph Banks for a loan, writing that the 'horrors of a Jail stare into my face'. In January 1778, George also reached out to Banks, explaining that 'our situation here is the most disagreeable & most precarious'. But his appeal went unanswered. A few weeks later, he set off to Banks' elegant new house at Soho Square – just a short seven-minute walk from Percy Street – to plead their case in person. Upon arrival, he first had to step onto some scales. Banks, ever the inquisitive scientist, had recently begun weighing all his guests, a practice he would continue for decades. Every name, date and weight was meticulously noted in a leather-bound ledger. George registered at 10 stone 3 pounds – only then could he speak on his father's behalf, but Banks, who had already lent Reinhold £250 on a previous occasion, was not willing to contribute any more.

Reinhold didn't make it easy for himself. Georg Christoph Lichtenberg had already noted, shortly after the return of the *Resolution*, that Reinhold was 'unforgiving when he was insulted'. Always mistrusting, his father believed that people wanted to harm him, George told a friend, and had a 'tendency toward self-love, pride, and a certain scholarly vanity'. Over the years, George described his father variously as impatient, fiery, short-tempered, obstinate and haughty. Those who lived with him had to endure hardship and embarrassment. And it wasn't just family and friends who suffered – Reinhold even shouted at people who talked too noisily during a play.

Then, in early 1778, William Wales, the astronomer on the *Resolution*, published a forty-page attack on *A Voyage round the World*, aimed at Reinhold rather than George. In fact, Wales believed that Reinhold Forster must have been the author for it was 'written with so much arrogance, self-consequence, and asperity' that it could not have come from young George's pen. Page by page, paragraph by paragraph, and sentence by sentence, it was a petty and vicious rebuttal of what George – or in Wales' interpretation, Reinhold – had written.

According to Wales, the book was riddled with factual errors: 'Dr Forster says, Turtle Island was about seven miles long. I believe it might be about two miles and a half long', or a reef was to the north-west of an island, not to the south where *A Voyage round the World* located it. Instead of saying '*We* hoisted a boat out', Reinhold should have written 'a boat *was* hoisted out'. How could the waterspouts at the New Zealand coast have been illuminated when the sun hadn't been out? And why did Reinhold criticize the sailors?

The whole book was full of cruel misrepresentations, Wales claimed. He also disliked its critical depictions of white Western men – 'the Doctor is always so eager to blame the Europeans.' Wales disputed that muskets had been used frequently and claimed that they were fired *over* not *at* the indigenous people. The bloody account of catching one of the islanders with a boathook in Tonga was untrue, he wrote, because a boathook, 'which every one knows is as blunt as one's fingers, slightly scratched his side'. And the telling of the murder at the beach in Tanna was absurd, Wales wrote – the marine would have been a fool had he not shot at the islander who had crossed the line in the sand and aimed an arrow at him. Wales' allegations went on and on. The astronomer wanted to 'cut, slash, and hack my work to pieces', George said.

Not only did Wales tear apart *A Voyage round the World*, he didn't even think George capable of writing it. He was still just his father's son and assistant. So it was George who put his name to the counter-attack in February 1778. His response was light-hearted, but infused with barbed humour.

'It is time,' George wrote, 'to turn to the *faulty passages of my work.* I can only lament, that after so much assiduous toil on the part of Mr. Wales, their number is not quite so copious, as he may wish' – and then he happily conceded that some of the geographical positions were not exact because Wales had refused to share his calculations. But George wouldn't accept being slandered for his own opinions, judgements or conjectures. He did believe, for example, that the indigenous people had souls, even if Wales disputed whether they had been able to communicate such a concept to him. George did not support the claim that Europeans were inherently better, even if the Spanish had defended 'their butcheries in America' by denying that the Aztecs and Incas had souls. He might just be a 'poor shortsighted youth', but Wales was no great philosopher himself – after all, an astronomer's mind had to be equipped for tedious and laborious calculations, not for visionary thinking.

This was George's first public dispute. The next came a few months later, when his father made him publish an angry letter to the Earl of Sandwich, the First Lord of the Admiralty – twenty-five pages of grievances and complaints about how the Forsters had been treated since the *Resolution*'s return. Already a few months previously Reinhold had warned Banks that he would 'informe all England of this dark iniquitous transaction'. George tried to convince Reinhold not to publish the letter but failed – the 'unequal contest was evident to all but my father'. And so, he put pen to paper to appease him and to expose how the English government had wronged them when Sandwich had not permitted Reinhold to compose his own account of the voyage. *A Letter to the Right Honourable The Earl of Sandwich* makes for painful reading – partly because it illustrates how unfairly the Forsters had been treated, but also because this public argument vanquished all chances of reconciliation. Not only did they attack Sandwich, the Admiralty and other wealthy patrons, but they also accused the king of ignoring their pleas after 'your Lordship ventured to abuse the ear of his Majesty with false and injurious aspersions'. Nor did it help that Reinhold demanded another £4,000 as compensation. 'I know a man,' George later said, 'who never blames himself, but who has a gift of blaming others for all his failed projects.'

Life in London became difficult. It was time to escape his overbearing father, and with no prospects in England, George decided to try his luck in the German states. During the previous few months his publisher Karl Spener had suggested that George should come to Berlin to translate some volumes of Buffon's *Histoire naturelle* from French to German. He didn't know how to tell his father and was reluctant to leave his long-suffering mother and siblings, and further expose them to Reinhold's terrible temper. After some back and forth, George decided he must go. Perhaps he could earn enough to assist his mother financially, but Spener would have to send a letter explaining the situation to his father – a letter 'that presents everything sweet and poignant, and beneficial for the *whole* family'. Other correspondence should not be sent to Percy Street, but to a local bookseller where George could pick them up unbeknown to his father, who otherwise opened and read all letters addressed to his son.

Spener, who knew Reinhold well by now and was only too aware how much George suffered, obliged, and the subterfuge worked. Two months later, just before midnight on 21 October 1778, George left London for Harwich on the east coast of England. It was dark and his luggage was cumbersome – 34kg of plant specimens, a trunk filled with manuscripts, and a collection of South Pacific objects which weighed almost 150kg. As the carriage rolled out of London, George felt guilty at leaving his family in such an uncertain financial situation, with his father facing debtor's prison and his mother at a loss for how to put the next meal on the table. Weighed down by worries, George sailed to the Netherlands, from where he would travel on to Germany. 'Are you healthy, dear Mother? Are you calm? Is God sending you comfort and courage?' he wrote to London, 'has no new adversity befallen our troubled home?'

Staying in cheap taverns, he found himself shaking off fleas at night, yet was courted during the day by princes, aristocrats, politicians, writers and scholars. In Rotterdam, The Hague and Amsterdam twenty-three-year-old George shuttled from dinners to laboratories, and from libraries to the Prince of Orange's natural-history cabinet. 'People are clamouring for me,' he wrote to Spener in mid-November. Still so young, George was thrilled by the attention. Deliberately stepping outside his father's shadow, he began to feel alive. He was George Forster, famous explorer, fearless adventurer, and acclaimed author of *A Voyage Round the World* – so much more than just his father's son.

From the Netherlands he went on to Germany, where the prominent playwright Gotthold Ephraim Lessing invited him to dinner and Christoph Martin Wieland, the writer who had reviewed *A Voyage Round the World* so favourably, hoped to meet the 'young argonaut'. There had been English, Spanish and Dutch circumnavigations of the globe, but the

Philosopher Friedrich Heinrich Jacobi

Forsters were the first Germans who had sailed on such a voyage – and no one wanted to miss the chance to speak to him. In one town he chanced to overhear an artist talk about 'Forster who travelled around the world', and told him 'that is me'. Strangers bought him drinks and invited him to meals. 'A truly noble person', one new acquaintance said, 'always true to himself, always open and free'. There was an honesty and openness about him that belied his fame. 'Never was I enough of a statesman,' George admitted to Spener, 'to shroud my heart in the darkness of pretence so that I could not be deciphered at first glance.' When he arrived late in the evenings in small towns or large cities, people woke each other so as not to miss him. 'How can you sleep, if George Forster is here?' one asked.

In Düsseldorf he was introduced to Friedrich Heinrich Jacobi, a well-known philosopher who seemed acquainted with every illustrious German poet and thinker. 'He is a magnificent young man,' Jacobi told a friend, 'I have not seen anyone in a long time who has won my heart as much as this Forster.' Come quickly, Jacobi wrote to George, demanding that they share every meal – and stressing 'do not speak a word to anyone that I do not hear'. They would become close friends.

It was a relief not to be in London. Away from his father and the demands of bailiffs and work, George felt almost content, although he wrote to Reinhold that 'it would be dangerous to allow oneself to be intoxicated by these deliciously flattering moments'. When he sat next to Jacobi's sisters, who always fussed over him, he was reminded of his sisters Virginia, Wilhelmina and thirteen-year-old Justina.* 'What will become of them? Who do they have to pour out their hearts to, as they used to do to their brother?' he wrote to his father.

People liked him – 'a youth with the knowledge and maturity of a man', said one German writer. There was a charm to the way that his slight physique and gentle manners gave him an air of vulnerability at odds with his intrepid travels. George was naturally modest but still at ease in the company of intellectuals and aristocrats. Philosophers, poets, artists, politicians, elderly ladies and beautiful young women vied for his attention. One professor, surrounded by three yapping little dogs and a dense cloud of tobacco smoke issuing from a pipe that never seemed to go out, questioned him for a whole afternoon about Tahitian dogs. Even children were drawn into the whirlwind. 'We had a great man here,' wrote Jacobi's sister Lotte to her ten-year-old nephew, George was an explorer who 'had seen ice islands and wild people and countries where bread grows on trees, and people only need to pick and roast it, like you roast chestnuts or potatoes'.

Passed from one admiring person to the next, George moved from city to city across the German states, drinking exquisite champagne and eating fine food. He was celebrated in every imaginable way, he wrote to London three days before his twenty-fourth birthday. In Wörlitz he spent three days 'en famille' with the Prince of Anhalt-Dessau, the young ruler who had visited the Forsters in London. The Prince was so inspired by George's stories and the South Pacific objects the Forsters had given him that he commissioned a garden pavilion to exhibit them. In Göttingen, a city known for its thriving university, George stayed with Georg Christoph Lichtenberg, the professor who he had met in London. In his guest's honour Lichtenberg organized a large dinner to introduce – and to show off – the young explorer to his colleagues.

Sometimes all the attention became too much. In Berlin, where George stayed with Spener, he attended over fifty lunches and dinners

* George's twenty-year-old sister Antonia had also left London and now worked as a governess for a wealthy banker in Vienna. She would later travel to Suriname in South America as a companion to the governor's wife and governess for their children, as well as working in Copenhagen.

Professor Georg Christoph Lichtenberg

in five weeks. By the end of his stay, he was exhausted by telling the same stories over and over again, only to be confronted by another round of questions. 'The empty, insipid heads, these wig stands,' he said, 'almost tortured me to death.'

No matter how many parties he attended, George couldn't quite forget that his father had been left growling in London. 'I know my father,' he admitted to Spener, 'he will of course accuse me of abandoning him to his misfortunes, and to only care for myself, without regard for the suffering of others.' Yet as the loyal Woide pointed out, Reinhold's 'affairs are so entangled that I cannot presume a happy outcome for him here in England'. George would have to search for a job for his father so that everybody could find some peace. Meanwhile Reinhold, now drowning in debt, bombarded the Earl of Sandwich, begging for money and support. An avalanche of letters arrived at the Admiralty, but Sandwich couldn't forgive the querulous naturalist for his public attack and finally replied that 'there is no business depending at this time between you and me'.

When the Minister of State of Hesse-Kassel, who had also visited the Forsters in London, invited George to Kassel, people were so enthusiastic that his arrival was announced in the local newspaper. He had hoped to find employment for his father here, but instead the ruler, Landgrave

Friedrich II, offered George himself a position as professor of natural history at the Collegium Carolinum in Kassel. When George accepted, Reinhold was furious. The family couldn't survive without his eldest son, who had always provided the only steady source of income. It was unbelievable, George wrote to Spener, 'no one has ever been treated like this by their father'.

What Reinhold didn't realize was that George had only agreed to work in Kassel so that he could support the family. 'Without any ties, without concern for anything beyond myself,' he told Spener, 'I would not have allowed myself to be bound.' Despite Reinhold's complaints, George continued to lobby on his father's behalf. As he moved from one city to another, he tried the King of Prussia, the king's sister, ministers, the Duke and Duchess of Braunschweig, Prince Charles of Hesse-Kassel and many others. No one wanted to employ the notoriously difficult Reinhold Forster.

13

'I am far too restricted for my way of thinking'

Kassel: 1780–1784

By the late summer of 1780, the sun had baked Kassel's gardens for weeks. When the dead elephant was wheeled through the streets it was yet another hot day. A pulley system had been set up to move the huge corpse from the menagerie across the river to the anatomy theatre – normally a brisk fifteen-minute walk but a complicated and slow enterprise with an elephant weighing four tons.

Whenever an animal died in the landgrave's menagerie, it was donated to the professor of anatomy to be dissected. Over the past year there had been a camel, a baboon, a leopard, a seal, a monkey, a porcupine and now the elephant. It had been the landgrave's particular favourite. Friedrich II had even tried – but failed – to have it perform at the opera. Previously, only the camel had been willing to do so. George Forster was excited to join the dissection, but when his friend the professor of anatomy Samuel Thomas Soemmerring opened up the elephant's head, they found the brain smoking and liquidized from the heat. When they cut into its bloated belly, the dead animal exploded with a bang and there was blood, faeces and decomposing flesh everywhere. The smell must have been unbearable.

Over the following months, the skeleton was prepared for display. When Goethe, Germany's towering poet, heard about it, he was so keen to investigate the elephant's skull that he asked Soemmerring to send it to him. In 1774, Goethe had shot to international fame with *The Sorrows of Young Werther* – the novel that had so moved George in

London after the return of the *Resolution* – but he was also fascinated by the sciences. He was interested in geology and the origins of Earth, and had spent weeks in the anatomy theatre of the university of Jena, dissecting everything from mice to humans. Soemmerring obliged – when Goethe asked for a favour, it was usually granted. 'I'm keeping it hidden in my most private room,' Goethe wrote after receiving the elephant's skull, 'so that no one thinks I'm mad. My landlady believes there is porcelain in the enormous trunk.'*

Goethe had first met George in Kassel in September 1779, six months after the young explorer had taken up his new job. It had been a short visit but they had talked all night and the next day. 'Much asked and chatted,' Goethe wrote in his diary, telling a friend that he had grilled 'young Forster' about the South Pacific islands. 'You know him,' George wrote to Jacobi, 'and know what feeling it can be to see him only for a few hours, to speak with him alone just a few minutes, and then to lose him again like a meteor.' The two men remained correspondents for many years.

Nestled into a wide valley along the winding Fulda river and surrounded by meadows, orchards, vegetable gardens and gently undulating forested hills, Kassel was the capital of the small Landgraviate Hesse-Kassel around ninety miles south of Hanover. With 20,000 inhabitants, the city wasn't exactly a metropolis, and George missed the thrill of new lands and people. After his three years in London, following the *Resolution* voyage, all German cities would feel parochial. 'No one reads in Cassel,' he told Jacobi, and though there was a library which was open to everybody, it had few scientific titles and was small compared to a university library such as the one in Göttingen. The tail end of winter was long and dark – 'the most miserable weather in the world, a fog like at the South Pole'.

Even more depressing was the news that George's remaining luggage, which he had arranged to have shipped from England, had been shipwrecked off the coast of Denmark. His trunks had been rescued but when

* The skeleton of the elephant is still on display at the Natural History Museum in Kassel, the same building where George Forster taught at the Collegium Carolinum. Today the animal is often referred to as 'Goethe's elephant.'

he received them after several months, he found his plant collection destroyed, instruments broken, and all his books mouldy. 'A complete herbarium from the South Sea such as has never been seen before, and perhaps will not be collected again in this century,' he wrote to Spener in Berlin, 'all entirely rotten'. Books could be bought again (and he went into huge debt to do so), but his herbarium – the plants he had gathered during the *Resolution* voyage – was irreplaceable. Miraculously, the mahogany desk, which had travelled with him around the world, had survived. This small and unassuming desk had become a trusted companion, a quiet fixture in the turbulent years during and after the *Resolution*. It gave him reassurance to work on its narrow drop leaf.

And he was also glad to have Soemmerring in Kassel. It had been George who had urged him to pursue the vacant position of anatomy professor at the Collegium Carolinum. As the son of a doctor, Soemmerring had studied medicine in Göttingen – but unlike his father, he chose an academic career in anatomy rather than to work as a practising physician. He was a keen student who caught his professors' attention with his gift for observation and his skill for drawing – qualities which would make him a brilliant anatomist. His dissertation on cranial nerves proposed a classification still in use today. After completing his degree in Göttingen, Soemmerring continued to focus on his research

Anatomist Samuel Thomas Soemmerring

and embarked on a study trip to Holland, England and Scotland. In the summer of 1778, a few months before George had left for Germany, he had arrived in London. Nearly the same age – Soemmerring was only two months younger – the two men had liked each other immediately. A quiet and sensitive man with a love for science, Soemmerring had found a kindred spirit in George, and together they had spent many days botanizing in the countryside on the outskirts of London. Soemmerring had then travelled north to Edinburgh to further his medical and anatomical studies, before returning to Göttingen. Without a job and income, he had been easily persuaded to apply in Kassel and was appointed a few weeks later.

Overshadowed and controlled by his father, George had never formed close friendships, but when Soemmerring moved to Kassel they became inseparable. 'Forster is my most intimate friend,' Soemmerring told his father. They shared their passion for science, knowledge and nature but also confided their thoughts, fears and emotions. It was an age when it was not uncommon for men to declare passionate feelings of love in their platonic friendships, but there were also rumours of homosexuality – people were talking about it, as one visitor noted in his diary. Whatever the connection, theirs was a relationship built on love, tenderness, trust and respect. Soemmerring lived in rooms in the new anatomy theatre south of the Fulda river and George moved from his lodgings near the Collegium Carolinum, where he worked, to an apartment close by. Even if it was in an unfashionable part of the city and further away from his workplace, George preferred the proximity to his friend just at the end of his street.

As he walked several times a week to the Collegium Carolinum, George could see how the rulers of Hesse-Kassel had spent extravagantly on buildings, gardens, public spaces and avenues. Next to the Collegium Carolinum was the Fridericianum, the first building in the Holy Roman Empire to be constructed as a public museum. It opened the year George arrived in Kassel and stretched almost 80 metres – its neo-classical façade was all columns and windows with a commanding portico as its entrance. Making his way home after work, George would also have been able to catch a glimpse of the Orangerie, a palatial baroque building that not only housed tender plants in the winter but was also used for lavish balls

View of the Orangerie

and masquerades. It was situated in a huge formal garden with canals, fountains, statues and immaculately clipped trees and hedges next to the river where George sometimes enjoyed the fresh air during an early morning walk. Long allées radiated out from the Orangerie, proclaiming the power of Landgrave Friedrich II like a mini-Versailles.

Even in Kassel, George could not escape from his father's dark presence. Reinhold remained exceedingly difficult. He was now so much in debt that the family was in danger of starving and he had to sell his beloved library. 'I need not tell You his story; You are well acquainted with his heat & impetuosity,' George appealed once again to Joseph Banks in London, but he was begging him 'to save a perishing family'. Soon afterwards, Reinhold was sued by one of his creditors at the King's Bench Court and ordered to pay what he owed him – £160 – plus damages. He was only one of many claimants: altogether, Reinhold owed between £700 and £800, including the money that Banks had previously lent him. 'I have written several hundred letters on the matter this year,' George told Spener. Finally, at the end of 1779, the Duke of Braunschweig agreed to pay some of Reinhold's debts and employ him at the university in

Halle, some 120 miles east of Kassel. 'Whether he will be happy in Halle,' George said, 'is another question.'

George's life had become predictable and constrained by the monotonous academic routine. He taught natural history to students at the Collegium Carolinum, as well as instructing the younger boys, who attended the military academy, in geography and German for several hours a week. Lectures had to be prepared, written and presented, and essays and translations had to be completed. He translated one of the volumes of Buffon's *Histoire naturelle* but he didn't like teaching. 'I'm Buffon's translator,' he wrote to Spener in Berlin, 'I correspond with princes and I'm writing a handbook of natural history, I've sailed around the world and end up in Kassel to instruct unruly twelve-year-old boys how to spell in their mother tongue.' To earn more money, he also agreed to oversee the landgrave's natural-history collection, a decision he soon came to regret as the ruler expected to be entertained daily by his in-house explorer. George did not enjoy the visits as the landgrave expected obsequious behaviour. 'You can never stuff His Highness with too many compliments,' he told Soemmerring.

In addition to his regular work commitments, he compiled a catalogue of the natural-history collection – which 'my drunken predecessor left in the utmost disorder' – and gave talks in French at the Société des Antiquités in Kassel on subjects ranging from the Greek Phoenix mythology to the happiness and fulfilment of humanity (though George admitted that the latter had nothing to do with antiquity). He translated from English into German his father's book of natural-history observations made during the *Resolution* voyage, but struggled because it was pedestrian, dull, and full of contradictions. 'To write learnedly and to write beautifully are two different things,' George told Spener in Berlin. His father had given birth to a hydrocephalus and if anything would put him off writing, it was this book.

His father continued to demand that his son be at his service. When Reinhold asked Lichtenberg in Göttingen to publish an English article that he had written about Russia, he added: 'my son in Cassel can scale down the map and translate the English for the magazine.' As if he didn't have enough to do, George also edited a new journal together with Lichtenberg – the *Göttingisches Magazin der Wissenschaften und Litteratur* (*Göttingen Magazine for Science and Literature*) – as well as contributing several articles. Often the days were far too short. 'My dearest, I am writing half-asleep, now at 1 o'clock in the morning,' George wrote to Jacobi, 'but I have no other time for my most necessary correspondence.' When Spener complained about delays, George asked for patience. He would need ten hands and three heads, he replied, to finish everything on time.

George was becoming a public intellectual, sure of his ideas and analysis, and buoyed by scholarly recognition. Two of the most important scientific societies in Germany, the Göttingen Academy of Science and the Leopoldina in Halle, elected him as a corresponding member. Professor Christian Gottlob Heyne, a classical scholar and director of Göttingen's university library – whose influence in the learned world was so great that George described him as the man 'who brings rain and sunshine' – asked him to review travel books for the *Göttingischen Anzeigen von gelehrten Sachen,* which he published. Who better than the legendary explorer and travel writer, Heyne thought. The learned audience in Germany wanted to hear what George Forster had to say.

He wrote essays, including one about Tahiti which was supposed to be based on a short manuscript by Domingo de Boenechea, the captain of the Spanish *Áquila*, who had first travelled to the island in November 1772 and then died there during a second voyage in January 1775. Instead of translating the account, George used the opportunity to substantially extend, comment and correct, making it his own work. Where other Enlightenment thinkers firmly excluded emotions, George once again stressed that a subjective viewpoint – like coloured lenses shaped by culture, education and individual experience – wasn't to be avoided but was part of being human and therefore important for observations. In his essay about Tahiti, he wrote that 'everyone has had opportunities to see in ways that were unique to them and that were not available to anyone else. But everyone also has their own way of seeing.'

George's translation of volume 6 of Buffon's *Histoire naturelle* also illustrates his confidence, for he didn't hesitate to criticize the revered naturalist, adding a large number of corrective footnotes, which often ran several paragraphs long. Much of Buffon's work was based on comparisons between flora and fauna from different continents – with the European specimens always coming out bigger, stronger and better – which contributed to the well-accepted theory that certain climates produced a 'degeneracy' in animals, plants and inhabitants. Building on the experience of his own travels and the many travel accounts he had translated and reviewed, George found it easy to provide countless examples that refuted Buffon. When the French naturalist claimed that dogs became smaller in colder climates, for instance, George wrote a long note about the size and strength of Newfoundland dogs. Or when Buffon declared that Native Americans were weak and cowardly – characteristics apparently embodied in a hairless feeble physique – George launched into a long correction. The indigenous people of North America were not only strong and brave, but they plucked and shaved their hair for cleanliness. If one compared them with the supposedly civilized Europeans, he wrote, 'one cannot possibly be so blind as to consider the latter, who are half emasculated by luxury and effete slack customs, as the strongest and healthiest'.

Still only in his mid-twenties, George had seen more of the world than anyone else in Germany. He had boarded the *Resolution* as a botanist and draughtsman, focusing then on plant and animal specimens, classifying and depicting. But as he had travelled, observed and written about the voyage, he changed the way he understood and investigated the world around him. In 1781, two years after moving to Kassel, he delivered a lecture – later published as *A View into the Whole of Nature* – about nature and the sciences which illustrated how radically his ideas were evolving. In an age when most scientists looked at nature through the narrow lens of classification, George wrote:

> The sciences have become fragmented, and people believe that every difficulty has now been overcome. Disciplines have emerged, and within them almost innumerable subdivisions and subjects. Each individual branch of human knowledge has been assigned its own observers, who ignore the whole and devote themselves solely to their part. Thus, the beautiful soul has escaped from the beautiful body.

Natural history, he told his students, 'has been turned into a meaningless drivel of nomenclature, artificial terms and systems'. Scientists had become 'minute enquirers, whose life is wholly spent in the anatomical dissection of flies, from whence they never draw a single conclusion for the use of humankind'. It was important to look at nature as a whole, not just at the individual parts. He was not the only one who perceived nature as a dynamic unity – Buffon also did so – but most botanists and zoologists favoured the neat categories of classification over an unruly web of entanglements. At a time when others were forcing nature into a rigid system of taxonomic units, George wrote of context, relationships and reciprocity. It had been the *Resolution* voyage, he later wrote, that encouraged this endeavour 'to bring my concepts back to a certain universality, to bind them together into a unity'. What he had seen as he had circumnavigated the globe changed the way he grasped the world.

Everything was dynamic, changeable and interdependent – 'the great connections have brought forth all the smaller, subordinate relationships'. The rotation and axis of the Earth, day and night, summer and winter, atmosphere, water and soil, shaped plants and animals. Nothing could be seen in isolation. He mocked thinkers who were only interested in the names and classification of snails, butterflies and plants because they didn't look at the interconnected whole. Nature was neither a dead aggregate nor an accumulation of separate elements but an 'active living power', created by the almighty hand of God. Nature, he wrote three years later, was a 'magic net of countless threads joined by countless knots, where each thing is connected to all and all to each, a system of divine concordance'.*

George worked hard, but he had also inherited his father's inability to control his expenses. Though his yearly salary in Kassel was 450 taler (increasing to 800 after 1781), in addition to the income from teaching the cadets, looking after the natural-history cabinet and his writing, his debt rose to 2,000 taler – an enormous sum at a time when a cook only earned 12 taler a year and a manservant between 50 and 60. His

* Alexander von Humboldt would later consolidate many of these ideas into his visionary concept of nature that still shapes our thinking today. He described nature as a living organism, a web of life where everything was connected. Unlike George Forster, who saw nature as the product of God, the divine architect, Alexander von Humboldt believed in nature as the life force itself.

publisher Spener helped where he could, giving him loans and generous advances but it was never enough.

'I am far too restricted for my way of thinking', George complained. He disliked the fact that days away from Kassel had to be agreed by the landgrave. The years in London after the voyage had been difficult but at least England was relatively free. The English Parliament was strong, the king was accountable, individual liberties were protected, journalists were free to write (almost) anything they wanted, and dissent was (mostly) tolerated. By contrast, Hesse-Kassel was controlled by an absolute ruler who even sold thousands of his subjects as mercenaries. The landgrave was a 'monster', George wrote to a friend, 'who now engages in the abhorrent trade of soldiers, selling to England the sweat, blood and freedom of his subjects to satisfy his infamous desires'. The landgrave's insatiable appetite for women, art, castles and lavish gardens proclaimed his ambitions and power, but the price was paid in the limbs and lives of his subjects. Some 17,000 men had been sent from Hesse-Kassel all the way to North America to fight side by side with British soldiers – almost as many as the inhabitants of the city of Kassel (the entire population of the small state was only 300,000). So many Hessians died on faraway battlefields that children begged in the streets of Kassel, crying 'I am a poor orphan, my father perished in America.'

In the German states, as in other European countries, ordinary people had few rights. Deeply personal decisions such as choice of profession, marriage, financial matters, and where to live were often dependent upon the approval of one's ruler. Destiny was determined by birth and the arbitrary will of the head of state. Serfdom still existed in some German territories and taxes were raised according to a sovereign's needs, rather than being measured by the income of his subjects. Rulers were all at once law, police and judge, and could imprison, censor and refuse marriage permissions. Playwrights were incarcerated for their plays, professors could lose their positions for speaking up, philosophers were silenced for their ideas, and books were pulped. After the South Pacific, life in Germany couldn't have been more different.

As often as possible, George rode the thirty miles to Göttingen, sometimes with Soemmerring. When he needed company, he would

Library of the University of Göttingen

visit for a few days, often falling asleep on his horse as it trotted for hours through the night. With just 6,000 inhabitants Göttingen was small – it only took half an hour to walk around the town on the earth ramparts which had been turned into a promenade – but it was the seat of one of Germany's finest universities. There were around 900 students, professors were well-paid, and the library was one of the best in the German states. Here George was able to borrow books and discuss the latest ideas with his many new friends.* In Göttingen, he was always busy, rushing through narrow streets that teemed with the dogs owned by the students, from one meeting to another, and from dinner to party.

Whenever he went, George stayed in Lichtenberg's apartment near the university. Lichtenberg was endlessly curious, known for his wit and fiery temperament. Short, gangly, with thin legs and an enormous head, Lichtenberg was certainly not handsome, but he surprised his

* George would have liked to work in Göttingen (situated in the Electorate of Hanover), but the town had been closely linked to England since the Prince-Elector of Hanover had become King George I of Great Britain in 1714. The administration in Hanover – and in particular its financial decisions – was overseen by the English king. George III remained the Elector of Hanover, and after Reinhold Forster fell out with the Admiralty, his son never had a chance of employment there.

contemporaries by having affairs with several young women. He was also hugely popular with the students, who were entertained by the many theatrical experiments he conducted during his lectures.

George was dazzled by the older man. The admiration was mutual and Lichtenberg described George later as a 'wizard of prose'. During one two-week visit, when Soemmerring joined them, the three men experimented and talked without a break. It was glorious, Lichtenberg told a friend, even mealtimes became scientific investigations – a pike steamed in a cooking pot waiting to be eaten, while they dissected its raw head to investigate the brain nerves. In the fireplace a cauldron bubbled with varnish for the taffeta they were using to make a hot-air balloon. Inspired by the French Montgolfier brothers, who had attracted huge crowds when they flew the first balloons over Paris, George, Soemmerring and Lichtenberg attempted to trap hydrogen in their taffeta balloon but the gas kept escaping. Finally, they succeeded in flying pig bladders so high that they disappeared out of sight. 'I have never lived happier days in Göttingen,' George wrote to Lichtenberg afterwards, 'I have enriched my mind with many new ideas'.

Göttingen's additional attraction was the presence of the 'university-mademoiselles', a group of highly educated professors' daughters who George had already met during his first visit in December 1778. Among them was Therese Heyne, daughter of Professor Heyne; Caroline Michaelis, daughter of a respected orientalist and theologist; and the poet Philippine Gatterer, daughter of the professor of history.

Having observed women in different cultures, George had concluded that the worse a nation treated its women, the less civilized were its people. 'It is the practice of all uncivilized nations to deny their women the common privileges of human beings,' he had written in *A Voyage Round the World*, 'and to treat them as creatures inferior to themselves.' The Māori, as well as the men in Tanna and New Caledonia, all behaved towards their women with unkindness and used them as 'beasts of burden'. In George's eyes, this attitude made them less civilized than the people of Tahiti and Tonga, where women seemed to be more respected and enjoyed greater freedom. There was a 'higher degree of culture', he explained, 'where the understanding is sufficiently enlightened to remove the unjust contempt shewn to the fair sex'.

1. HMS *Resolution*, Captain Cook's ship on which George Forster travelled around the world from 1772 to 1775.

2. Reinhold Forster (*left*) and George Forster (*right*) in New Zealand. Jean-François Rigaud portrayed Reinhold with *Forstera sedifolia*, a small New Zealand perennial named after them, in his hatband, and the bellbird (*Anthornis melanura*) in his hand. George, who was the expedition's draughtsman, is ready to sketch the bird.

3. George Forster's drawing of the *Resolution* and *Adventure* among the icebergs in the Southern Ocean. The Southern Lights are visible in the sky.

.. An atmospheric watercolour of Dusky Sound on New Zealand's South Island sketched by he expedition artist William Hodges in 1773. It shows the wild scenery with mountains and ocky islands, as sunbeams break through the clouds.

;. Pickersgill Harbour in Jusky Sound – named after he third lieutenant Richard Pickersgill – where the *Resolution* anchored from he end of March to mid-May 1773. In the distance, between two trees, the observatory tent is visible. Note the laundry drying on ines and the tree used as a gangway to the ship. The tree still exists today.

6. George Forster's drawing of a blue petrel (*Halobaena caerulea*) in the Southern Ocean.

7. George Forster's drawing of a tūī (*Prosthemadera novaeseelandiae*) in New Zealand.

8. George Forster's sketch of a Cook's scorpionfish (*Scorpaena cardenalis*) – one of the many fish the Forsters collected in Dusky Sound.

). A scene with the Māori at Ship Cove in Queen Charlotte Sound at the northern part of New Zealand's South Island. The *Resolution* stopped here three times during its voyage.

10. George Forster's beautiful drawing of a fantail (*Rhipidura fuliginosa*) in New Zealand.

11. Matavai Bay in Tahiti, painted by William Hodges. Note the warrior with the towering helmet standing on the raised platform on one of the canoes. These helmets were made of wicker, covered in bluish green feathers and crested with long bright tail feathers, which created the effect of a radiant halo.

12. The breadfruit tree (*Artocarpu communis* J. R. & G. Forst.), which George first encountered in Tahiti and which eventually led him to develop a theory of Polynesian migration 200 years before DNA and archaeological studies confirmed it.

13. Parrots from Tonga (*Prosopeia tabuensis*) – this one drawn by George Forster – provided the red feathers that were hugely popular in Tahiti, where they were regarded as signs of divinity. Hitihiti, the young man from Bora Bora who travelled with the *Resolution*, advised the crew to collect the feathers in Tonga to trade for valuable objects in Tahiti

14 and 15. The details on the feathers of the New Zealand green kākā (*Nestor meridionalis*) show how George's skills as a draughtsman improved over the course of the voyage.

16. When the ships were anchored, George usually only had time for quick pencil sketches, leaving the colouring in for the long weeks at sea. This drawing of an Atlantic yellow-nosed albatross still has George's detailed notes including 'Irides Brown. Under Eyelid White. Head dark pearly grey, gradually & very softly vanishing in to a fine clear white at the neck,' and 'This leg is something too large.'

17 and 18. These two drawings again show how George Forster's artistic skills developed during the voyage. A penguin drawn in 1773 stands rigidly on the ice, but the spotted eagle ray from the second visit to Tahiti, in May 1774, exhibits fierce energy.

19. A stunning blue morning glory (*Ipomoea indica*) collected on 9 August 1774 in Tanna and painted by George Forster.

20. A new passionflower (*Passiflora aurantia*) that George Forster found in New Caledonia on 8 September 1774.

21. The Forsters found this magnificent tree in Tahiti – drawn by George – and named it *Barringtonia asiatica* after one of their patrons. As the vice president of the Royal Society, Daines Barrington had helped with Reinhold's appointment as the naturalist on the *Resolution*.

22. This portrait of George Forster, attributed to Johann Heinrich Tischbein the Elder, was painted in 1784, shortly before he left Kassel for Vilnius at the age of twenty-nine.

23. A view of the Strand in London, famed for its many shops and near Somerset House Stable Yard, where the Forsters lived before the *Resolution* voyage.

24. The garden walk at the Palais Royal, where George Forster liked to shop when he visited Paris in 1777.

25. At the centre of this coloured engraving is the imposing Fridericianum in Kassel, the first building to be constructed as a public museum in the Holy Roman Empire. Immediately to its right – the building with the rounded gable – is the Collegium Carolinum, where George Forster taught his students.

26. A view of Mainz across the Rhine, where George lived from 1788 to 1793, and where he became a co-founder of the Mainz Republic.

27 and 28. In 1789, while living in Mainz, George and Therese Forster commissioned two portraits – companion pieces that projected a wealth that they did not possess and marital harmony that no longer existed.

This may be why he was so often drawn to strong-minded women. In Kassel, he had met Princess Amalie von Gallitzin, a woman in her early thirties who defied convention. She was separated from her husband, wore her hair short, liked to swim in rivers, and draped herself in loose-fitting garments like a Greek statue. An accomplished scholar, she was generally accompanied by a servant who carried a big pile of books. 'An extraordinary woman,' George wrote, 'a true marvel of *profound* scholarship . . . I know few professors who can equal her.' Never afraid of women who were intellectually his equal, he had initially been attracted to Philippine Gatterer, whose poetry he had read, but she had married someone else. Caroline Michaelis had also caught his attention and he had given her a piece of white Tahitian cloth which she sewed into a shepherdess dress for a ball. But on his first visit at the end of 1778, he had somehow failed to notice Therese Heyne's infatuation with him.

Perhaps it had been her age but since then the fourteen-year-old girl had become a quick-witted and confident young woman. Her father had neglected her formal education, but he allowed her to participate in discussions with his fellow professors, with subjects ranging from archaeology, natural sciences and anatomy to politics and history. She listened and argued, she later explained, and 'I read, read, read'. When she was only seven, Heyne had attempted to curb her obsessive reading by locking all

Therese Heyne as a young woman in Göttingen

the family's novels in a cupboard. Therese could not be stopped, however, pushing in the canvas panel of one of the doors to open the latch from the inside, and read what she wanted. She learned from the students who rented rooms in her father's house and as the daughter of the university's librarian, she had the library's 100,000 books at her disposal. 'The loss of the library would make me a most wretched creature,' Therese said, 'for reading is as indispensable to me as food.' She was not an obvious beauty but her eyes sparkled with curiosity and her lips were often drawn into a knowing smile. Wild, unpredictable and curious, she was 'a girl full of fire', remarked a female visitor in Göttingen. One of her best friends explained that she was 'a strange mixture of nobility, greatness of the soul, and a thousand follies, to which vanity and sentimental infatuation lead her'.

The young women adored the slender adventurer. It was his voyage and a certain 'strange, foreign quality', Therese later said, that aroused her interest. George seemed to carry the physical scars of his journey lightly. Smallpox had blemished his skin since childhood and scurvy had not only decayed his teeth but also yellowed the whites of his eyes. Yet Therese described how his face became handsome and alive the moment he talked. 'As soon as he was animated by conversation, his features became vividly expressive,' she said, 'and I have rarely seen a face that could be so greatly transformed by intellect and emotions.' He was gentle and sensitive, different from other men and unlike the boisterous students. But when rumours reached friends that George might be looking for a wife in Göttingen, he laughed and dismissed them all, insisting that 'my bride is certainly and truly none other than the Göttingen library'.

Instead of women, George became caught up in a flirtation with the Rosicrucians, an enigmatic brotherhood of alchemists, loosely associated with the freemasons. Since the return of the *Resolution*, he had already entered freemason lodges in Paris, London, Braunschweig and Kassel – a world of secret names, codes, oaths and ceremonies – but the Rosicrucians guarded their rituals and activities even more closely. One of their pursuits was to find the philosopher's stone which could turn base metals into gold – and with George's debts mounting steadily that was certainly an appealing prospect. Another objective was to find God through the study of nature. Since God had created the natural world, they believed, it was through the knowledge of nature that one could

A vignette from a 1779 Rosicrucian book, illustrating their emphasis on scientific observation of nature

find and come close to the divine. The foundation of everything, George wrote to a fellow Rosicrucian, was that 'the omnipresent God is inseparable from nature' – God was the unity of the whole. This theme had also informed his *A View into the Whole of Nature*, in which he declared that nature 'remains always the first direct revelation of God'.

George was attracted to the brotherhood's attitude to religion. Unlike his father's dry Protestantism, their approach was built on emotion. 'True religion,' George wrote to his youngest sister Justina at the time, 'was boundless love that transcends all other love', and happiness could only be achieved by being close to God. He had been so lonely as a child and adolescent, he later explained, that he was prone to 'religious fervour'. He wanted to discover the truth about the world and to feel God, for 'nothing is more intoxicating . . . than the joy of beholding the great plan of creation'.

Soemmerring had introduced him to the order probably already at the end of 1779, but from 1781 the two friends spent most of their spare time in the Rosicrucians' laboratory. Surrounded by several special ovens, an array of vessels, vials and cauldrons – as well as pestles and mortars, filters, metal tongues, sheep intestines and bladders – they melted metals, concocted new chemical combinations, and heated mercury and acids. They dissolved, boiled, distilled, crystalized different components, and sometimes didn't leave the room for the entire day, their notebooks filled up with the symbols for saltpetre, sulphur, ethanol, antimony, and other chemical elements. On clear nights, George trudged through wetlands and forests, trying to find so-called star jelly – a mysterious substance that was believed to originate from a mythical confluence of rays of sun and moon, and celestial vapours – needed for the creation of the philosopher's stone.

Their feverish intoxication lasted a couple of years but by September 1783, George and Soemmerring had left the brotherhood. Soon George was warning others. It had all been false enthusiasm. Perhaps they had been too young, too inexperienced, too curious, and too gullible, he told Soemmerring, but they had to escape the Rosicrucians' maw for they already had wasted too much time and money. 'What is left,' he asked, 'but to investigate for oneself and accept nothing in good faith?' Alchemy had failed to quench his 'burning thirst for certainty'.

He might have been disillusioned, but George didn't despair. 'Children learn to walk through much falling and getting up again,' he wrote to a friend shortly after leaving the Rosicrucians, 'that is my consolation! One must never stop, never grow tired of getting up again when one has fallen.' He remained curious, interested in everything – exploration, natural history, ethnography, and many other subjects. He and Soemmerring experimented with fireflies, placing some into jars with normal air and others with pure oxygen to investigate the strength of their illumination. Those breathing oxygen shone brighter and one firefly created enough light to read the *Göttingischen Anzeigen von gelehrten Sachen* at night. But while Soemmerring doggedly collected data about one subject, George was already rushing off to the next. He didn't limit himself to just a slice of the world, he wanted to understand its entirety. 'Let us seek the truth,' he wrote to Jacobi, 'to embrace and kiss it.'

'I would be far more useful to the world if I were to embark on another great voyage,' he told a friend in November 1783, a few months after leaving the Rosicrucians. Weren't there enough people who could sort, classify and regurgitate what had already been discovered? But if he couldn't travel to distant continents and islands, he could explore them with his mind and imagination – and in Kassel in early 1784 he published his groundbreaking *About the Breadfruit*. In what was ostensibly a botanical treatise, he illustrated how the tendrils of botany reached into culture, ethnography, history, linguistics and human migration. A brilliant and original piece of scholarship, *About the Breadfruit* reveals George's visionary thinking, the work of a man way ahead of his time.

George had first encountered the breadfruit during the *Resolution* voyage.* It was a tropical fruit which grew on large trees on many of the South Pacific islands they had visited. He had enjoyed the dishes made with the abundant breadfruit – cooked on hot stones or fermented into a dough which was baked like bread – but he had also noticed that they had been seedless. With no seeds, the breadfruit trees on Tahiti, Tonga, Tanna and Malakula, George explained in his essay, could only be propagated by cuttings from suckers that grow off the tree's roots. During the many months they had spent in the region, George had not seen a single wild breadfruit tree – all of them had been planted by humans.

That made him wonder where breadfruit trees originated and how they had arrived on the islands. Searching Göttingen's vast library, George had then discovered several botanical volumes which contained descriptions of wild specimens with seeds and small fruits with little flesh from Indonesia and the Philippines. If Tahiti, Tonga, Tanna and Malakula had no indigenous breadfruit trees with seeds, the only explanation was that they must have been exported from Southeast Asia, travelling thousands of miles across the ocean to the South Pacific islands. For George this proved two things. Firstly, the sophistication of the islanders' agricultural methods – as there was apparently no seedless variety in Southeast Asia, they must have bred and transformed the originally small fruit into the large nourishing crop he had tasted. Just as cereals and fruits had been domesticated through selective breeding in Europe, so the South Pacific islanders had used cuttings from trees with larger fruits to facilitate the slow changes over the centuries – 'bit by bit'.

His second conclusion was even more striking, for the history and movement of the breadfruit enabled George to develop a stunning

* As the first to publish the botanical description of the breadfruit from the South Pacific islands shortly after their return in 1775, George and Reinhold had their name attached to it for posterity – *Artocarpus communis* J.R. & G. Forst.

understanding of Polynesian migration. The breadfruit's journey, and its cultivation from a small fruit with spiky skin, seeds and little flesh, to the larger seedless variety found in Tahiti, Tanna and the other islands, was proof that the Polynesians had migrated east from Southeast Asia across the Pacific – a theory confirmed more than 200 years later by DNA and archaeological studies. As people had boarded their canoes to travel to distant islands, they had packed their most valuable crops and animals. 'The breadfruit tree,' George wrote, 'could only have been brought eastwards by humans.'

About the Breadfruit also illustrates how differently George thought from other scientists and explorers of his day. During the *Endeavour* voyage Joseph Banks had also taken note of breadfruit trees but his interest was economic. Struck by the ease of cultivation and rich harvests – 'Bread fruit is procurd with no more trouble than that of climbing a tree,' he had written in his journal during the *Endeavour*'s stay in Tahiti – Banks lobbied both George III and Parliament to send an expedition to the South Pacific to transfer breadfruit tree seedlings from Tahiti to the West Indies in order to feed the slaves on British sugar plantations.* Where Banks saw a nutritious high-yielding food plant that could fuel the engine of the British Empire, George Forster saw evidence of Polynesian migration.

The kernel of George's theory of Polynesian migration was already in *A Voyage Round the World*, where he had looked at the different languages spoken in the South Pacific. First, he had noticed that almost all the languages which the *Resolution* crew had encountered were variations or dialects of one language – with the noticeable exception of those spoken in Vanuatu and New Caledonia. Often only a letter or a sound was different. The Tahitian word for 'to sit' is *noho* and in Tonga

* Banks would finally convince them and sent Captain William Bligh on the *Bounty* to Tahiti in 1787. The venture didn't go according to plan when the mutineering crew put Bligh and eighteen other men in the *Bounty*'s launch in the middle of the South Pacific in April 1789. The last thing Bligh saw of his breadfruit trees were 1,015 saplings neatly planted in his Great Cabin. They then sailed almost 4,000 miles in the 23-foot open boat to Timor in the Dutch East Indies from where Bligh chartered a boat and then made his way back to Britain, where he arrived in March 1790. Seventeen months later, in August 1791, Bligh set out on his second breadfruit expedition, delivering more than 600 thriving saplings to Jamaica and St Vincent.

it is *nofo*, while 'woman' is *vahine* in Tahiti, *wahine* in Māori and *fefine* in Tonga. Or the sound for 'k' in Māori and Tongan words doesn't exist in the corresponding Tahitian terms where it's replaced with a glottal stop – for example, 'canoe' is *vaka* in Tonga, *waka* in Māori and *va'a* in Tahiti. Similarly, at the Marquesas Islands, George noted, 'their language [was] much nearer the Tahitian, than any other dialect in the South Sea, with this difference, that they could not pronounce the *r*.' This affinity, he was certain, demonstrated that the different islanders 'must have had one common origin, perhaps in the mother country, from whence both these colonies issued'.

He had not been the first to notice language similarities. During the *Endeavour* voyage, when Tupaia had communicated with the Māori, Cook and Banks had also realized that languages across vast distances were related. 'This is a sufficient proff that both they [the Tahitians] and the New Zelanders have had one Origin or Source,' Cook had written in his logbook in March 1770, 'but where this is, even time perhaps may never discover.' He had left it at that, and neither Cook nor Banks had pursued these speculations any further. During the years on the *Resolution* George had most certainly discussed these ideas with Cook, but his systematic investigation into the spread of languages and the breadfruit tree turned these initial insights into an original and bold analysis of Polynesian migration.

In 1778, Reinhold had published 'A Comparative Table of the Various Languages in the Isles of the South-Sea' in his *Observations Made During a Voyage Round the World*, which George had translated into German. As its title reveals it was a list of words which the Forsters had collected during the *Resolution* voyage. Not only did it include vocabulary from the South Pacific islands they had visited but also Malay words – a language spoken in Indonesia. When the Forsters had noticed the presence of Malay words in the Polynesian languages, they had worked out that the further east an island was located, the fewer Malay words its language contained. This meant that islands such as Tahiti or Easter Island, which were far further east from Indonesia, must have been colonized later than western islands such as Tonga, where they had identified more Malay terms. Why? They deduced that Polynesian and Malay must have originally developed from one language, meaning that when the Polynesians had arrived at the western Polynesian islands their language had begun to separate and change. As the Polynesian settlers then moved further east over the next centuries, more of the original Malay words disappeared, or changed so radically that they were no longer recognizable.

Even their deities revealed this migration. Māori gods, for example, George wrote, are 'so correspondent to those of the Tahitians, that their system of polytheism must be of very ancient date, and seems to derive its origin from their common ancestors'. Wherever they had stopped on the voyage, George had looked for similarities or differences. There were two distinctive groups of people in the South Pacific, he realized, different in appearance, language and culture. The people in Vanuatu and New Caledonia had darker skin and spoke languages which were quite unlike those in the Society Islands, Tonga, the Marquesas, Easter Island and New Zealand. 'They appear to be of a race totally distinct of these,' he wrote about the islanders from Vanuatu, but 'the natives on some parts of New Guinea and Papua seem to correspond in many particulars with what we have observed.' It was possible that the islanders from Vanuatu and New Caledonia might be related to those of Papua New Guinea.

Today it's thought that around 45,000 to 50,000 years ago, when Australia, Tasmania and Papua New Guinea formed a single landmass known as Sahul,* the first humans – descendants of people who had migrated from Africa through Southeast Asia – reached and settled in what is now Papua New Guinea and later in the Bismarck Archipelago. These early inhabitants and their descendants lived there for tens of thousands of years before the next great movement of people. Roughly 3,500 years ago (1500 BCE), there was a second, different wave of migration, this time from Southeast Asia, pushing eastwards across the Pacific. Long before the earliest European expeditions, the ancestors of today's Polynesians set out from regions which include present-day Taiwan, the Philippines and Indonesia. They sailed vast distances in outrigger or double-hulled canoes loaded with hogs, chickens, root vegetables, coconuts, bananas and breadfruit seedlings. Masterful navigators,

* Around 8,000 years ago, when sea levels rose after the last Ice Age, New Guinea was separated from Australia.

they used stars, birds, disruption in ocean swells, cloud formations and wind patterns as their guides as they crossed the Pacific. Today their progress across these vast distances can be tracked through DNA but also through crops and agricultural methods such as the domestication of dogs, chickens and pigs – as well as through archaeological records, including the spread of uniquely ornamented Lapita pottery.

Exact dates are disputed, but it's believed that they first settled between 3,400 and 3,200 years ago (1400 and 1200 BCE) in parts of coastal Papua New Guinea, the Bismarck Archipelago and then the Solomon Islands. Soon after, around 3,000 years ago (1000 BCE), they moved south-east to Vanuatu and New Caledonia – islands that had not previously been inhabited – where they later came into contact with and were joined by descendants from the first migration wave who were living in the Bismarck and Solomon Islands. Over generations, these communities blended and differed both in appearance and culture from those who had continued to sail further east.

The eastward expansion brought the Polynesian ancestors to Fiji between 3,100 and 3,000 years ago (1100 and 1000 BCE), and then on to Samoa and Tonga where they arrived around two hundred years later (900 and 800 BCE). Migration then paused for almost two millennia, before navigators set out again, reaching the Tahitian, Cook and Marquesas Islands around 1,000 years ago (1000 CE). Then in a final push, they sailed to Hawai'i, Easter Island and New Zealand. Several centuries before Columbus and Magellan embarked on their voyages in the fifteenth and sixteenth centuries, Polynesian ancestors sailed some 2,500 miles through storms and unknown waters and arrived in New Zealand around 700 to 800 years ago (1200 to 1300 CE).

The differences George observed in the people of Vanuatu and New Caledonia, compared to those on more easterly islands, was the result of intermingling between the descendants of the first migration wave and later Polynesian settlers. George could have not known the complex details of these migration patterns, but more than two centuries ago he worked out the broad outlines by studying the diaspora of Polynesian languages and the history of the breadfruit tree. He could only guess their reasons – 'oppression by their own people, or foreign conquerors, or superstitious legends, or some other cause' – but he was convinced that these great ancient navigators and their families had set out on purpose to find new islands to colonize and had not drifted there by accident. 'I cast a glance at a map of that part of the world,' he wrote in *About the Breadfruit*, 'I survey the vast Pacific Ocean, and find that the most distant, solitary, and scattered islands are not only inhabited by people, but occupied by the very same people . . . I confess, I cannot convince myself that a storm, or a series of similar coincidences, is sufficient to satisfactorily explain this widespread dispersion of one and the same people across such a vast ocean from New Zealand to Easter Island.'

The people of the South Pacific, George realized, were connected rather than separated by the ocean.* Where others saw tiny islands spread across the vastness of the Pacific, he brought them together with the threads of migrations. Building on what he had seen as a young man, George had matured into a bold and original thinker. It would take more than two hundred years for the world to catch up with him.

* This connectedness was beautifully evoked by the Tongan historian Epeli Hau'ofa in the late twentieth century when he talked of 'Oceania' instead of remote South Pacific islands. It was a 'sea of islands,' not islands in a far sea but a large interconnected world where people sailed, mingled and belonged, not constrained by the boundaries of land surfaces.

14

'The decision, then, is made, and all that is wanting is the subject'

In Search of a Wife: 1784

At almost thirty, George Forster decided that he needed a wife. She should be young, innocent, healthy and ideally wealthy, he thought, and while she didn't need to be beautiful, she should also not be too ugly. 'I expect nothing perfect in marriage,' he told his publisher Karl Spener, but something 'to soothe my imagination and my desires'. In recent years, Spener had become a close friend, a steadfast supporter as George had emerged from his father's grip. George asked Spener for advice and guidance, but also shared his feelings, insecurities and frustrations about his work and father. Only five years older, Spener was like an older brother who listened and cared. He commissioned George's work (though he could also be a critical editor), lent money, and supplied books – and even named his son after him.

'You're a husband, – and I could become one; I believe I am suited to it; my heart is soft and tolerant,' George wrote to Spener, adding that his wife should love him for himself, not his fame. Over the next few months many letters shuttled back and forth between Kassel and Berlin with questions, instructions, possible candidates and more questions. 'I've gone over everything again and again,' George finally told Spener in September 1783, 'the decision, then, is made, and all that is wanting is the subject. But where do I find one? Where do I look? How do I begin the search?' In early March 1784 he even ordered a library for his unknown future bride – books 'which my wife (I must have a wife soon, soon) can read and use', he wrote.

Since his move to Kassel in March 1779, George had often made the thirty-mile trip to Göttingen, becoming a regular visitor at the Heyne family home. Christian Gottlob Heyne had become a fatherly friend. Twenty-five years older than George, and of a much gentler disposition than Reinhold, Heyne listened and advised. 'I revere Heyne as one of the most respectable men,' George told Jacobi, 'a man who is not merely the soul and mind, but also the very heart of Göttingen.'

George also enjoyed the company of Heyne's oldest daughter. Now nineteen, Therese was slender with curly brown hair, her fiery eyes betraying her passionate nature. She talked quickly, so fast, one of her father's students noted, that she ran out of breath as her words could barely keep up with her ideas. Many remarked on her liveliness and her curious mind. She was a born storyteller too – 'I have never heard a woman speak more beautifully,' one visitor remarked – and Therese's friend Caroline Michaelis thought that she talked incessantly but always wittily. Even as a teenager, Therese's letters were evocative, funny and clever – she wrote, a friend said, as if 'her paintbrush was dipped in a hundred different colours'.

She was a wild, free-spirited young woman, and had no interest in idle

Professor Christian Gottlob Heyne

chitchat. How could people spend so much time on silly and unimportant trifles, Therese despaired, bored when they talked 'only of what they had eaten, drunk, and what others had worn'. Her father had encouraged her to think and learn, even giving her his students' essays to correct and comment on. She delighted, she laughed, 'in being the secret critic of these young men' but grew frustrated when her older brother, who studied in Kassel, was lazy. He had only a tenth of her ambition – an ambition, she said, 'which is of no use to me as a girl'. She was self-assured enough to have heated discussions about religion with one of the professors. There was no doubt, she later admitted, that 'a spirit of independence was awakening in me, which had great influence on my destiny'.

Yet Therese also sometimes felt insecure. She worshipped her father but the relationship with her unconventional mother had been complicated. Her mother had neglected house, husband and her three children, Therese later said, and taken a young lover. It had been an unhappy childhood from which Therese had escaped into books, learning to read and write at the age of four. When she was twelve, her mother died and Heyne married a woman only eleven years older than his daughter. Therese liked her new stepmother but worried that the steadily increasing number of stepbrothers and sisters – already four in five years – might reduce her father's love for her. As a little girl, she had often played with her doll in the reading room of the university library where Heyne worked, asking, learning and listening. Her father loved her but also knew that she was irrepressible and thought that he had somehow to constrain her intensity. In his presence, she admitted, she tried to control her emotions, feeling like an untamed horse harnessed by tight reins.

Therese might have been loud, bold and unruly but she felt lonely. 'Since I see no soul around me that understands me,' she confided to her older friend Luise Mejer, 'I must withdraw, and retreat into myself.' Over the past couple of years Therese had fallen in and out of love. At fourteen she had been smitten with George, but when he hadn't noticed, she had turned her attentions to the students in Göttingen. There had been one in particular who had courted her but then he became interested in another young woman. 'I weep for a man who has forgotten me,' she confided to Luise. But soon he was replaced because she loved to be admired and courted.

'She built castles in the sky,' Luise warned, and was prone to 'a thousand follies'. Therese herself was confused how she could love one suitor but at the same time feel 'so easily interested in so many other men'. It was as if she had two souls, she confessed, one that loved deeply and another that flitted around like a butterfly. Maybe she had talked to George about this, or he to her. At exactly the same time, George told Jacobi he had two souls – one that did what he didn't want, and another that wanted what he didn't do.

By the summer of 1783 Heyne had had enough and sent his daughter with relatives to Switzerland – to get her out of Göttingen, where she was tangled up with too many students, and to calm her feelings. In a long letter of advice he warned her about the risks of being too frivolous and enthusiastic. Be gentle, don't fall for people immediately, and don't show off, he counselled. Instead of finding peace, Therese stumbled into the next emotional turmoil. She felt awful for failing everybody, she wrote from Switzerland to Luise, 'I'm a terrible creature!' Her father was going to be disappointed because she was neither calm nor virtuous – 'why am I condemned to extraordinary follies?' she berated herself. 'Luiße, don't ask,' she wrote, 'but mourn my heart, which did nothing wrong, yet still lost its innocence!' Another man, another love. Luise hardly knew how to reply and felt sorry for Therese and those around her.

People in Göttingen began to talk and Lichtenberg believed that Therese was pregnant. 'People are saying,' he told a colleague, that she 'only went to Switzerland to rid herself of a certain burden.' There had been talk of marrying her off to an elderly widower in Switzerland or to the brother of her stepmother. Heyne was certain that only a husband could tame his capricious daughter. Therese had her own ideas and decided that if she was going to be chained to a man, he would have to be an interesting one: George Forster. Since their first meeting, five years previously, she had been fascinated by him and the tales from his voyage – 'he was Therese's first love,' Luise said. Here was a man who had seen the world – adventurous and curious about everything.

Driven by her 'desire for something extraordinary', it might have even been Therese who proposed to George – which would have been a highly unusual step at the time. Neither Therese nor George wrote about the details of their engagement, but a friend noted in his diary a few weeks later: 'about Forster, and Therese Heyne, who was the first to confess her love to him, and he accepted. The good man!' They became engaged on 18 April 1784. Heyne had no objections. Though George was not rich, he had a brilliant mind and a bright future – the 'nation's favourite writer', Heyne would say. George didn't tell his father. Why do so, he explained to Soemmerring, when Reinhold Forster would only take advantage and come up with 'an extravagant demand on his part to ruin all my happiness and rob me of the dear girl'.

George was enchanted by Therese – she was well-read, witty and thrillingly mercurial – but immediately after their engagement he had to leave for Vilnius (then part of the Polish-Lithuanian Commonwealth, today the capital of Lithuania). A few months earlier, the newly established university of Vilnius had offered him a position as professor of natural history. In fact, the university had first approached Reinhold, whose demands had been so outrageous that they turned to George instead. He too had a long list of conditions. Vilnius wasn't exactly the centre of scientific thinking or intellectual exchange, but knowing that an illustrious explorer and popular writer would gild their young institution, the university had accepted George's requirements: the salary was almost twice that of Kassel, there was an annual allowance for the maintenance of a botanical garden and natural-history library, free lodging, and a budget for the move and travel expenses. Best of all, the Vilnius authorities had agreed to pay off his huge debts. In return, George was contracted to stay eight years.

After consulting his future father-in-law, George accepted. He didn't feel he had much choice because he was broke and struggled to make a living in Kassel. 'That cursed money!' he told Soemmerring, 'or rather, the misfortune that I cannot manage it properly!' And as if to compensate for the prospect of moving to Poland, he ordered lots of books and even bought himself a carriage.

The day after their engagement, George left his fiancée in Göttingen, promising to send for her once he was settled in Vilnius and they could marry. 'I am shattered beyond measure,' George wrote to Spener, 'saying goodbye from Göttingen has torn my heart asunder.' He returned to Kassel to pack and bid an emotional farewell to Soemmerring. The two young men had become so close that the thought of separation terrified them. During their time in Kassel, they had always discussed their ideas, experimented together and challenged each other. Instead of spending almost every day together, they would now have to wait for several months for their letters to arrive.

On 23 April, George left Kassel and stopped in Göttingen for one final night. He wasn't allowed to see Therese – probably because her father had decided it would draw too much attention. Heyne wanted to be sure that his future son-in-law succeeded in Vilnius before making the engagement public. It was ten at night when George's carriage rattled along the cobblestones. Across from the library, he could make out the shape of the large Heyne residence beside the little river that ran through town. Tall trees and a small hexagonal pavilion stood in the garden behind the large three-storey timber-framed house. Candles still flickered in Heyne's study – 'I saw his light, and could imagine him sitting there working! The good man! Five steps away from me, and

The half-timbered Heyne house is just visible to the left of the large trees, with the garden pavilion in front

yet so far away and so separated; and then dear Therese! The pain was almost unbearable.'

As always he stayed in Göttingen with Lichtenberg, less than 200 yards from the Heyne residence. The two men talked all night, as if George was trying to fill up his well of friendship. The next morning, they stood in silence. George departed with a heavy heart, saddened to leave friends and fiancée behind. 'I am still dazed by the shock of our separation,' he wrote the next day to Soemmerring. 'Unfortunately, my dear Forster is already gone,' Soemmerring himself wrote to a mutual friend, 'his loss can be replaced by nothing but himself.' Nor was he alone in mourning George's departure. How could he move to a place so far away, some asked, 'God save poor Forster.' Germany had 'lost one of the most celebrated scholars and writers', reported one of the regional magazines, and a London friend wrote that 'England lost this remarkable man, and now Germany has lost him too.'

It was 850 miles from Göttingen to Vilnius – a journey that he could have made in as little as three or four weeks – but it took him seven months. As though avoiding his destination, George now embarked on a circuitous journey around the German states. As he travelled, he began to reflect once again on his time with the Rosicrucians, as if every mile that he moved from Kassel provided a new clarity. He was glad to have escaped them, he wrote to Soemmerring in mid-May from Leipzig, for 'we weakened and paralyzed our powers of thought, impoverished our understanding, filled our mind with useless trifles, and undermined and corrupted our principles.' So much time had been wasted on useless alchemical experiments and secret meetings with the Rosicrucians.

As he crossed the German states, George reconnected with old friends and made new ones. But when his father came from Halle to see him in Leipzig (where George attended the Leipzig Book Fair with Spener), their meeting ended in a heated altercation outside a beer garden in front of other guests. 'Scene with my father after lunch with a headache and burning sun in the meadow,' George noted in his diary, 'ends with me lending him 100 Reichstaler which I urgently need myself.' It had been one of their worst fights. His father believed that one of the Leipzig publishers owed him some money, but as so often had miscalculated his earnings. Furious, he had then forced George to ask Spener for a loan. When Spener refused, Reinhold exploded, shouting at him and his son. As so often, it was never Reinhold's fault. Nor did things improve much during George's subsequent visit to Halle to see the rest of the family.

His father had the unfailing talent of making the world his enemy, George wrote to Soemmerring. Convinced as he was of his own abilities – 'always completely satisfied with himself' – Reinhold Forster regarded everybody else as less important and capable. Nothing had changed. Once again George felt terrible about leaving his mother and siblings exposed to Reinhold's temper, but he could only endure his father for a few days.

During his journey he sent long letters to Therese in which he tried to describe his own personality. He wanted to be honest with her. A few days after the encounter with his father he wrote Therese a long letter:

> I believe suffering has significantly shaped the way I think. You know that I have endured much from a young age, that I carried the worries of a large and unhappy family. That at an age when one typically follows the cheerful, inviting allure of nature – when one tends to be led by feelings, with no responsibility other than enjoying life and preparing for that enjoyment, I worked continuously. As a result, I led a rather gloomy and burdensome life as a boy and young man, one that drained both my physical and mental energies. This drove me towards the only thing left to me: religious fervour, and I gradually became accustomed to viewing suffering as good and beneficial, and pleasure as dangerous, if not outright harmful. My naturally lively and impulsive temperament was curbed and brought under control by the chastisement and pressure of a more volatile temperament, and by being a constant witness of the misfortune which this temperament brought upon himself when left unchecked. This force of opposing powers and principles ultimately restrained and subdued my nature, so that it now appears calm, peaceful, indifferent, or at least imperturbable ... For the past six months, I have begun to live and think as I wish I had lived and thought over the

> past five to six years. But I now feel and realize that this was simply part of the path I had to travel before I could emerge from darkness into light. I am proof enough to myself, as you are to yourself, that the path which Providence took me on was the best one, the only way a person like me, and in my situation, could remain uncorrupted and ultimately gather the experience that guided me in the right direction.

Where Therese expected passion, George delivered life lessons. Sometimes he doubted whether he was good enough for her. 'I wonder,' he asked Soemmerring, 'what right I have to want to entwine the fate of that dear angel with my own unhappy one?' When his thoughts turned too dark, he found distractions. Wherever he arrived, scholars, writers, poets and scientists sought his company. George enjoyed their conversation and showed off the large portfolio of engravings from Cook's third voyage, which he had received from Joseph Banks shortly before his departure from Kassel. Banks had sent them because Spener had commissioned George to translate the account of Cook's third voyage and would need the illustrations so they could be reproduced in the German edition.

In July 1776, exactly a year after the *Resolution*'s return, Cook had left on his third expedition, supposedly to return Mai to the Society Islands but also in an attempt to find the fabled Northwest Passage – a (then) hypothetically navigable path connecting the Atlantic and Pacific Oceans through the Arctic Ocean in the far north. Discovering such a passage would make the long and dangerous route around Cape Horn at the southern tip of South America unnecessary. Mai was successfully taken home, but Cook was once again blocked by ice after sailing north through the Bering Strait between Alaska and Russia. On their return south, they had stayed in Hawai'i in January and February 1779. After an initially friendly welcome, tensions rose and when a small boat was stolen from one of the expedition's ships, Cook had tried to take the local chief hostage for ransom. In the ensuing skirmish Cook was stabbed and killed by the Hawaiians, his body dismembered, disembowelled, and partly burned according to traditional rituals. 'His most unfortunate & much-to-be-lamented End,' George had written to Banks on hearing the shocking news, but he also believed that Cook had been careless and had provoked the islanders – 'to fire at them, surrounded by a crowd of people with only ten men! Surely, that was reckless.'

George mistakenly thought that the engravings were a present and was later firmly reminded by Banks that they were not his to keep. But for now they were in his possession – fifty engravings depicting landscapes, indigenous people and artefacts from the South Pacific. 'Something so marvellous cannot be imagined, much less described,' George had told Lichtenberg. Finally he was able to *show* his friends and acquaintances what he had seen rather than just rely on words.

'I am very well here,' George wrote from Dresden, 'and I am carried as if upon hands.' Dresden – or the 'German Florence' as it was called – was the capital of Saxony. Its skyline was dominated by richly ornamented baroque buildings and the huge dome of the Lutheran Frauenkirche, one of Europe's largest churches. Parts of the city had been built in the early eighteenth century during the reign of August the Strong, who had also assembled sumptuous art collections after his grand tour of France and Italy. It was one of the most dazzling cities in Europe.

As soon as he arrived, George went sightseeing. The broad sandstone

One of the engravings from George's portfolio of Cook's third voyage, showing a dance in Tahiti

bridge that spanned the river reminded him of Westminster Bridge in London and he enjoyed the views from the elegant promenade built atop the old fortifications. On still days, when the river was calm, its surface perfectly mirrored the city's spectacular silhouette. He wandered among ancient marble sculptures, inspected the natural-history collections in August the Strong's opulent Zwinger palace, listened to renowned musicians in packed concert halls, and visited the library. When George entered the majestic Grüne Gewölbe – the Green Vault – he couldn't believe his eyes. This theatrical *Wunderkammer* was filled with treasures: royal jewellery, glittering baroque objets d'art, and elaborate tableaux in gold and silver, encrusted with thousands of precious stones and pearls. Its displays included gold-plated automatons, sparkling diamonds (among them a rare 41-carat green diamond, the largest of its kind in the world), as well as rubies, emeralds, sapphires, black onyx, garnet and many more – it 'surpasses all the profusion of gemstones I have ever seen in Europe,' he told Soemmerring, 'and which, unless one has seen it, cannot truly be imagined'.

In the Gemäldegalerie, Dresden's popular picture gallery, George was astonished by the sheer number of masterpieces, listing them in his diary with increasing excitement: Holbein, Rubens, Rembrandt, Carracci, 'Italian Venus by Titian!!', 'Raphael!!!', and then 'a *glorious* collection'. He was invited to dinners where he was asked to read from his *Voyage* and he inspected the mining academy in nearby Freiberg. For a few days he also travelled with new acquaintances to a spa town where he lived on a diet of milk and strawberries in the hope of soothing his scurvy-damaged stomach and curing the rheumatism in his leg.

In Dresden, George was painted by Anton Graff, one of Germany's leading artists, because Spener had asked his bestselling author to sit for a portrait. It was not the first that year. George had already had one done in Kassel by the celebrated Johann Heinrich Tischbein (the Elder), but he wasn't satisfied with the result because the painter's eyesight was by then so bad that even the colours on the palette had to be pointed out to him. But he liked his Dresden portrait. 'Graff captured me perfectly,' George reported to Soemmerring, 'down to the smallest features and nuances.' It shows an earnest man with a high forehead and fine eyebrows. He wears a carefully coiffed wig and fashionable white necktie.

Engraving after Anton Graff's Dresden portrait of George Forster in 1784

George looks older than his twenty-nine years, more a handsome scholar than an intrepid adventurer.

Despite the whirlwind of meetings, dinners and other social engagements, George often felt lonely and went for long walks. Nature had always consoled him. In mid-July he wrote in his diary: 'the beautiful secluded shadowy path, between the moss-covered rocks, through the tall beeches, and poplars and firs, down along the murmuring, rushing and gurgling forest brook, ha! it embraced me, drawing me away from the tangled vastness of the world before me, pressing me closely to the bosom of Mother Nature ... thus nature knew how to pour balm and cure for every sorrow into the eternal diversity of her creations.' For a brief moment, he forgot the new reality that lay ahead of him.

Sometimes his escape took him somewhere else – 'took a bath at 4 o'clock, splashed about lustfully, and despite all my earlier good resolutions, it once again led to *purgatio*' and 'succumbed to *masturbation*'. Even when reading French natural-history books, he couldn't stop himself and noted 'Read Büffon, and during it (*purgatio*)! – finished reading Büffon.' Missing Therese, he carved the letter T into the bark of a tree and began to talk to her silhouette which she had given him. 'O God, O God! When shall we meet again?' he exclaimed to her profile cut in black against the white paper, 'when shall I press you dear, dear girl to my burning chest?'

15

'Good heavens, the way I'm celebrated here shouldn't be allowed'

Detours to Vilnius: 1784–1785

After the weeks in Dresden, George Forster went to Prague for a few days and then on to Vienna, the de facto capital of the Holy Roman Empire. On 28 July 1784 the large number of carts and carriages moving along the road on which he was travelling announced the city long before George saw Vienna's church towers the next morning. He lodged at the White Swan, an elegant hotel at the centre of town, and bought a map. With 200,000 inhabitants and being the Habsburg emperor's home, Vienna was a vibrant centre for the arts, science and music. George wanted to explore. On his first day he went to the Prater, a large public park beside the Danube, to meet some acquaintances from Dresden. It was a hot summer evening and together they watched the launch of a hot-air balloon, and when darkness fell spectacular fireworks illuminated the city's many church spires. It was the beginning of seven invigorating weeks in Vienna.

Fame eased his entrance into society, but he had also brought letters of recommendation and knew plenty of people from his time in London and his travels through Germany. He described his days across page after page in his diary: up early, powdered and dressed; a quick breakfast of strawberries and milk; then dashing to a coffee house to read the papers and chat to a new acquaintance; a quick morning visit to a *comtesse* or one of his many female admirers – 'to give compliments with a bon coeur'; followed by a meal with several famous scientists, sharing discoveries and ideas; then a quick carriage ride to the imperial

The Prater in Vienna

botanical garden to inspect the glasshouses and talk to the emperor's gardener; or to a tastefully furnished parlour where a fashionable hostess introduced George to her friends, reminding him to bring the engravings from Cook's third voyage, 'all interrogating me mercilessly until Gemmingen [a friend] rescued me'; back to his lodgings to change and freshen up for the theatre or opera; and afterwards another meal with his ever-growing group of acquaintances. Among them were Austrian politicians, a Russian minister, the Portuguese ambassador, a French diplomat, a professor of anatomy, an alchemist who wore his wig only an inch above his eyebrows, a young count, the director of the Vienna observatory, a German prince, generals, musicians, artists, poets, writers, chemists, minerologists, botanists, dukes, princes and many others – including numerous women.

'Beautiful women and lovely girls abound here,' he wrote undiplomatically to Therese. He always had time for the *Gräfinnen*, countesses and young women who called him 'our seafarer'. There was the witty Mimi, who adored him; and Laura, whom he adored for her musical voice, knowledge and collection of rare minerals; and Laura's sister, Jeannette, who 'has lovely eyes in which I gladly lose myself'. One sister sang beautifully, he told Soemmerring, the other was beautiful. He saw Countess Maria Wilhelmine von Thun almost daily – a gifted musician, ten years older than George, who hosted an exclusive Viennese salon – 'the greatest woman in the world and her three graces of daughters, each one an angel of her own kind' (again to Therese). He played badminton and *boules* with yet more countesses – Caroline, Christiane, Josephe and Antoinette – and recited English poems for them. For the first time in his life, George allowed himself to be frivolous, boisterous and relaxed. He was always going to be an honest man who loved his fellow human beings, he wrote to Soemmerring, and would always try to help others, but he no longer believed that one had to renounce joy in order to be a good person, adding that 'in my opinion, true happiness is now to enjoy everything that is allowed'.

One night, after seeing the celebrated actress Katharina 'Kitty' Jacquet perform in the national theatre, he was introduced to and fell for 'beautiful dear Kitty'. She was so alluring, she could have stepped out of a novel, George thought, and once again he unpacked his Cook engravings to show off as the adventurous hero. The flirtatious women excited him so much that he doggedly recorded his sexual arousal in his diary: 'I was overcome today between 2 and 3 p.m. after lunch' or '*masturbation* despite my best intentions!' He couldn't help himself. 'Coquettish with Mimi,' he confided to the pages on 1 September, a month after his arrival, and on the same day: 'Têtc à tête with poor Jeannette who is all tender and cries.' 'Dearest Vienna,' he wrote in his diary, 'what kind of chains of roses are you winding around poor Forster?' He couldn't get enough. 'I believe that Kitty was particularly affectionate to me today,' he wrote on 5 September, after seeing her in the theatre, but on the same day Laura allowed him to hug and kiss her – 'she let me do *everything*, kisses on the bosom, embraces etc.' He had to be less reckless, he reprimanded himself, adding a note in his diary after a particularly flirtatious day – 'be careful'.

Vienna was one great whirlwind of invitations, visits, parties and balls, so many dinners, picnics and convivial meals that 'all buttons are popping off my shirts and all my coats and waistcoats are too tight'. He could live in this marvellous city, he admitted, and tried to forget that he was expected in Vilnius. 'Vienna is a paradise,' he wrote to Soemmerring. He couldn't stop himself from telling Therese how happy he was.

'Imagine your clumsy Forster,' he wrote to her after dancing all night at a ball, 'who was suddenly and despite all protestations grabbed by the arm and pushed from one dancer to the next.'

With every letter, Therese became more worried. 'He's in love with Vienna,' she confided to Soemmerring, and 'I think also with Countess Thun'. Her fiancé didn't seem to miss her, nor have any hesitation at flirting with dozens of women. So in her letters to George, Therese hinted that she had admirers of her own, turning her attention back to the students and young men in Göttingen. When she kissed Caroline Michaelis' brother – 'all without consequences' – she even mentioned it in a letter to Soemmerring. 'I don't fear Michaelis when it comes to my Therese,' George replied to Soemmerring, confident that she would wait for him.

But by now Therese was having second thoughts. If George were to write to her again about other women, she quipped, she would 'flirt with all the counts, barons and princes'. Already bored by Caroline's brother, she had quickly found another student. He was young and passionately in love with her, but, Therese later admitted, 'his vehemence exalted my head'. Her behaviour became worrying enough for Heyne to send her to Gotha, some seventy miles south of Göttingen, to stay with Auguste Schneider, one of her female friends. 'Protect her from all infatuation,' Therese's stepmother wrote to Auguste, and 'do not let her read or write too much'. It was a strange choice since Auguste was the mistress of the Duke of Saxe-Gotha.

Soon Auguste's physician began to court Therese. Older than the students she had flirted with in Göttingen, Therese's new suitor showed her respect rather than ardent declarations of love. He gave her more self-confidence, Therese said, than the younger men. Completely unaware of what was going on in Göttingen and Gotha, George wrote to Soemmerring, 'Therese will make me very happy, of that I am certain'.

One of the men who had invited George to Vienna was Ignaz von Born, an esteemed geologist and mineralogist with a keen interest in exploration.* Despite a mining accident which had left him unable to

* The copper ore mineral Bornite is named after Ignaz von Born.

walk without help, Born was active, well-connected and according to George, always in a good mood – he was also the father of the flirtatious Mimi. Born had met George during a visit to London and liked him so much that he tried to find ways for him to stay in Vienna. The professor of natural history at the university was already seventy or older, Born told George, and he suggested waiting for him to retire or die. He also made sure that his guest met all the important and potentially useful people. 'From the Emperor to the savants,' George proudly told his future father-in-law, 'everybody hopes to see me move here.' The interest was unsurprising, for few people had any first-hand knowledge of foreign countries, let alone remote islands in the South Pacific. Botanists wanted to know about the plants he had collected, zoologists about the animals, geologists requested information about volcanoes, and others just wanted to listen to daring adventures. George soaked up the attention.

As the leading freemason in Vienna, Born also introduced George to his lodge 'Zur wahren Eintracht' ('True Concord'). 'The best minds of Vienna – both among scholars and poets – are members,' George wrote to Soemmerring, 'and have transformed the whole thing into a society of scientific, Enlightenment-loving men, free from all prejudice.'* Many brothers were scientists, writers, poets and politicians who wanted to establish a kind of academy of science and art. Despite his experience with the Rosicrucians, George became a member and justified his decision to Soemmerring by explaining that it was a strategic move. He accepted Born's invitation 'for political reasons, because in this way I secure myself a following. All the brothers are fond of me to the point of adoration, and would do anything to have me brought here for good.' But no matter how much everybody tried, there was no available position for George in Vienna at the time.

It was at Born's house that George met Angelo Soliman. As a child, Soliman – or Mmadi Make as he was originally called – had been captured in West Africa and then sold and resold until he eventually became a valet of the governor of Sicily and then of an Austrian prince.

* A few months later, composer Joseph Haydn would also be initiated and Mozart, visiting from his main lodge lodge 'Zur Wohltätigkeit' (Beneficence), received the second degree of Fellow Craft on 7 January 1785.

Unlike other slaves, he had then ended up a free man at the Viennese court, where he tutored princes and received a substantial salary. Now in his early sixties, Soliman wore expensive and elegant clothes, spoke six languages fluently, and read Cicero. He knew Mozart, was highly educated, married an Austrian baroness, was a member of the 'Zur wahren Eintracht' lodge and very much part of Vienna's high society – he seemed the epitome of the equality of races.

One contact led to the next. George spent a great deal of time with Jan Ingenhousz, an internationally respected Dutch doctor and chemist. Ingenhousz had recently discovered photosynthesis, was a member of the Royal Society in London, and had inoculated George III. Now working as the court physician in Vienna, he introduced George to Nikolaus Joseph Jacquin, the botanist-explorer and director of the botanical garden who subsidized his income by selling greenhouse-grown asparagus and pineapples in winter. And also to Alessandro Volta, a physicist and chemist who had identified methane and would later invent the first electric battery.* A tall, athletic man, Volta spoke so bluntly and directly that George hoped never to have a disagreement with him.

This was a particularly thrilling moment to be in Vienna, which had become a hub of the Enlightenment, energized by Emperor Joseph II's sweeping reforms and a period of relative political stability. It was a time of unprecedented religious freedom and intellectual enquiry – only three years earlier, in 1781, Joseph had issued an Edict of Toleration and relaxed strict censorship rules. Since then, more radical ideas about liberty, religion and government had begun to circulate widely. Vienna emerged as a centre for publishing, with literary salons, coffee houses and reading societies where these new ideas were debated. It was also a city of open spaces where people from all social backgrounds mingled during the summer months. The emperor had opened several parks to the public and the Viennese delighted in firework displays in the Prater and enjoyed sitting outside the many coffee houses. This lively atmosphere fostered a sense of optimism and curiosity that excited George's very being.

* The unit by which electrical potential difference is measured – volt – is named after Alessandro Volta.

Some days he had a dozen appointments, parties and other engagements. Even Soemmerring had to wait for letters. Rushing through Vienna's streets and parlours (always carrying the Cook engravings), George was in constant demand. 'Oh, if only we had Forster with us forever!' they said, 'yes, he must, he must stay with us!' He was a popular guest, charming and entertaining. 'How are you my dearest?' one of the princes at court asked, 'is the air in Vienna treating you well? . . . How long do you intend to remain with us? . . . And do you proceed straight to Poland thereafter? . . . Well, should you not like it there, do come back to us!!!'

Even Emperor Joseph II asked to see him. Early one morning George rushed to the Hofburg, the emperor's palace in the centre of Vienna. As he was ushered through endless corridors, watchful eyes of generations of Habsburgs followed him from gilded frames. After a two-hour wait in an antechamber, the doors opened and George finally met the emperor, who bombarded him with questions:

'You went on the great voyage?'

'Yes, Your Majesty.'

'Did you suffer much?'

'I returned with a weak stomach.'

'Did seasickness cause you much discomfort?'

'No, Your Majesty, I was ill for eight days, and then I was fine.'

'Was Cook very particular about cleanliness? Did the Sauerkraut serve you well?'

'Yes, Your Majesty.'

'What kind of man was Cook?'

'A magnificent navigator.'

Unlike his father (who had told the chamberlain of the Prussian king, Friedrich the Great, 'I have seen five wild kings and two completely tame ones in Europe'), George tried not to offend.

The emperor was confounded by George's plans for Vilnius.

'You're going to Poland?'

'Yes, Your Majesty.'

'Is there a university?'

'Yes, Your Majesty.'

'Do you know anyone in Poland?'

'No, Your Majesty.'

'Can you speak the language yet? Have you been to Poland before?'

'No, Your Majesty.'

'What do you intend to do there?'

'Teach natural history.'

'I should think, instead of sciences, you'd need to teach them the ABCs first.'

Surprised that the celebrated George Forster would move to Poland, the emperor predicted, 'If you want to work, you will not endure it there. I think I shall see you again soon.'

And so the carousel turned: George took sisters Laura and Jeannette to the opera, only to flirt with another woman as he scanned the balconies; he enjoyed several dinners with the libertine Giacomo Casanova; Kitty Jacquet gave a performance at the theatre in his honour; he ate copious amounts of ice cream in the Graben, Vienna's most fashionable street; he danced under hundreds of candles at a masked ball and delivered forget-me-nots to his female admirers. Carriages filled with men and women dressed in their best clothes and wearing their finest jewellery rolled through the streets of Vienna to

The Graben in Vienna

attend parties given in George's honour. 'Good heavens, the way I'm celebrated here, shouldn't be allowed,' he noted in his diary, hoping it never stopped. It wasn't just the parties: he meandered through the emperor's opulent gardens at the Schönbrunn Palace, attended large picnics in the formal parterres of the Augarten, one of Vienna's public parks, and was invited to large country houses set in huge gardens overlooking the Danube. He studied art, examined botanical specimens, and inspected the imperial natural-history collection (which consisted mainly of rocks as the emperor couldn't bear the sight of stuffed animals, he told Soemmerring).

And there were more concerts, plays, dinners and country excursions. Wide petticoats brushed against his legs, ringed fingers fluttered over his arm, and sweet perfumes enveloped him as hushed voices whispered in his ear. The men were more serious, the women encouraging. Here was an arm that led him into the gardens, across wooden bridges, over little gurgling streams, into shaded groves and hidden grottos. There, they sat down on stone benches cushioned by moss. Servants laid out delicious picnics under tall trees. He went to bed late, often after midnight, and woke up with champagne headaches. But he was happy.

Then it was almost over. Vilnius could no longer be delayed. There was just enough time for a few more parties and a picnic outside Vienna for which he and his new friends all squeezed into several carriages. They walked, ran, ate, drank and sang – the women chasing George across meadows. By the end he was exhausted but went back home, had his hair brushed and powdered, and went out again. It took several days to say goodbye and on his last day George delivered his silhouettes and wax portraits – all commissioned in Vienna – so that his new friends would not forget him. There was one last breakfast with Kitty and more than twenty other visits, until the day ended in Laura and Jeanette's parlour, where all three cried when he bid his farewell. The next morning, 16 September 1784, after seven weeks, George left Vienna. 'At 9.30 a.m. bleary, shattered and desolate off in my carriage,' he wrote in his diary.

He still didn't rush. It took George another two months to travel the 750 miles to Vilnius along muddy and sandy roads, interrupted by a three-week stop in Warsaw and a visit to Grodno (today in Belarus but then an important city in the Polish-Lithuanian Commonwealth), where Parliament was meeting. Grodno was a royal residence and Stanisław II August, the Polish king, had requested George's attendance. Dining there several times with the king, George inevitably found himself questioned again about the *Resolution* voyage. By the end so many people had leafed through his engravings, he told Spener when he finally and reluctantly forwarded the portfolio to Berlin, that 'the girl from the Sandwich Islands has been practically ravished, so thin and soft has the paper become'.

It was always the same, he told Therese, and terribly boring to tell the same stories again and again. To his great surprise he also met a fellow explorer in Grodno, the flamboyant Prince Nassau-Siegen who had travelled with Bougainville to the South Pacific and was now married to a Polish countess. 'A handsome man, bald head, a stork's nest hairstyle,' George wrote that evening in his diary, referring to the prince's wig. Of course, they talked about their voyages and shared tales from Tahiti and the South Pacific. But George disliked the endless formalities at court – 'my back, being unaccustomed to the exercise, aches especially from all the bowing,' he joked in a letter to Countess von Thun. 'Nobility is a mere illusion invented by people,' he wrote to his father, 'title and rank, considered in themselves, are certainly the most miserable things in the world.'

The portrait of the woman from Hawai'i (then called Sandwich Islands by the Europeans) which George mentioned in his letter to Spener

After two weeks in Grodno he set off and three days later, on 18 November 1784, George caught his first glimpse of his new home. Built into a valley surrounded by forested hills, Vilnius was bigger than he had expected. Large buildings and church spires gave the skyline a grand feel, but when his carriage entered the city George quickly realized his mistake. The narrow streets were covered in dirt, mud and dung, while fires had left many houses in ruins. In the eighteenth century alone there had been ten major fires – the last one only four years previously – which had destroyed three-quarters of all the city's buildings. The ancient walls were crumbling and the once populous city was dwindling – only a quarter of the former 80,000 inhabitants remained. After Vienna, Vilnius seemed drained of colour. The Polish-Lithuanian Commonwealth had seen better times. In the sixteenth and seventeenth centuries it had been one of the largest states in Europe, but much of its territory had been divided between Russia, Prussia and Austria in the first Polish partition in 1772. Since then, the country and Vilnius had suffered a steady economic and political decline. In 1773 the thriving Jesuit academy, which had been the intellectual centre of the city, had been closed when the pope had suppressed the Jesuit order.

View of Vilnius from the distance

But Stanisław II August prided himself on being a great patron of the arts and sciences and he had founded the Commission for National Education – the first Ministry of Education in the whole of Europe. The king's ambition was to educate his country with a reformed school system and new universities. Vilnius was to become a centre of scholarly learning and in 1781 the Commission had reopened the former Jesuit academy as the University of Vilnius. One problem, however, was the lack of professors, as most of the faculty were ex-Jesuits – the reason why the king and the Commission had invited George.

Like the city, the university looked imposing enough from the distance – the main complex was a large three-storey building with arched arcades around an open courtyard, dating from the seventeenth century, and a more recent central tower of almost 70 metres, the highest structure in town. On closer inspection, however, the university was disappointing. The professors lived in former student lodgings, George told Soemmerring, which 'consists of various buildings, haphazardly stuck together as needed, without order or symmetry'. When he walked through his new apartment, George found a maze of little rooms, split-level landings and narrow corridors in a state of disrepair. None of the stoves were working properly, the hearth in the kitchen needed new stones, the windows had

The Grand Courtyard of the University of Vilnius at the time when George taught there

to be repaired, walls had to be papered, and one of the staircases had to be replaced because it was so worn that it was a danger to use. On the ground floor was a kitchen, storage rooms, some smaller chambers and a laboratory. On the first floor, situated above the laboratory and overlooking the garden, were the two best rooms with high ceilings and large windows, but they housed the university's natural-history collection – a collection so small that one couldn't call it such. Further up were more bare rooms with some broken windows and an attic with just a hole for access. The ceilings in some of the rooms were so low that George could touch the beams. There was no furniture, wallpaper or curtains.

The rest of the university was no better. The seminar rooms needed renovation and the so-called botanical garden behind his lodgings consisted of a few empty flowerbeds: 'barely big enough to plant a few cabbages', George informed his father. Nor was he impressed by the professors and their wives. The only interesting and educated woman was the widowed Countess Przezdziecka, he told Therese, and 'once you can pronounce it, half the Polish language has been conquered'. The servants were drunk, dirty and lazy, he complained, the craftsmen were slow, and the local aristocrats had no manners – countesses picked lice from their heads in public and knights blew their noses into their fingers rather than handkerchiefs. Not even the women pleased him. They were flirtatious, he told Soemmerring, and demanded to be caressed and touched – 'one may kiss a woman upon the bosom without scandal!' – but they weren't entertaining or attractive.

Vilnius felt provincial and backward. Though Stanisław II August had attempted reforms, the feudal system still shackled peasants to their land and lords. They were treated like cattle and lived in abject poverty. 'Oh, this wicked serfdom is an ugly thing,' George wrote to Therese, 'it kills and dulls humanity down to the root.' Dismayed by the 'half-wildness and half-culture of the people', he even found the language barbaric. Tahitian, he said, was more beautiful than Polish, a language riddled with superfluous consonants.

Vienna 'seems just a sweet dream', he wrote to Countess von Thun. He bitterly missed Soemmerring – 'my only, my most dearly loved, my often longed-for and sighed-after friend.' Nothing pleased him and every day was the same. Rising at 4.30 a.m., George worked until lunch, returned to his desk until 7 p.m., had dinner, read some more, and went to bed. Thankfully, the university was still small, and with only thirty students George's obligations weren't onerous. But he had to teach in Latin, which made him so nervous that he wrote and read aloud every single word in advance. 'It's an insurmountable weakness, a kind of shyness that drives me mad,' he admitted to Therese's father. The long and dark winter weighed on him and he dreamed of a warm climate. Since the *Resolution* voyage, he couldn't bear the cold any more. Even the postal service was unreliable, and he often had to wait months to receive letters, or the books and newspapers he had ordered. How could he think or write 'if there was a wall in front of my mind,' he told Therese in February 1785, three months after his arrival.

Without a wife, he would not survive. He needed someone to talk to. 'My head remains too empty,' he explained to Soemmerring, 'and since I can't have you, Therese is the second on the list. I can't work, I can't sit at home, I am gloomy, restless, dull, have no ideas, and suffer unspeakably; in short, I lack all motivation.' He also yearned for a beautiful body in his arms – 'a full firm bosom, a fair eye, and a mouth that promises heaven'. It was time to go and get his bride. But before he left, he ordered furniture and other household items from Berlin, asking Spener to organize the shipping and the financial arrangements – a dressing table for Therese, two nightstands with chamber pots, new bedding, an elegant tea urn, silver cutlery, pots and pans, lamps and candlesticks. He also ordered a yellow tea and dinner service from England – if they had to live in Vilnius, at least they would be surrounded by beautiful things.

By now Therese had returned from Gotha and was flirting with the assistant librarian at the university in Göttingen. Twenty-seven-year-old Friedrich Ludwig Wilhelm Meyer – she called him Willie – was charming and confident. His unpowdered blond hair was tied into a pigtail and his handsome face was dominated by a prominent nose. Meyer was always smiling and impeccably dressed in a striped coat – his 'Zebra Coat, in which he was so famously beautiful', Therese's friend Caroline Michaelis later said. He was an amateur poet who used his quill to seduce women, and his letters to Therese during the summer 1785 were full of melodramatic flourish – he was pining for her, his face was covered in tears, he

Silhouette of Wilhelm Meyer

preferred to die than not be loved by her and despaired that she couldn't be his. 'You break my heart, you tear it apart, you pierce it,' he wrote, and when Therese told him that she was engaged he was undeterred. They met secretly. When the church bell rang, Therese would pretend to go for a walk and then serendipitously bump into Meyer. Oh good day Herr Meyer, she said. Madame Therese, he nodded, before strolling on together, their hands ever so slightly brushing, just a feather of a touch but electrifying nevertheless. Therese, he said, was the 'purest, simplest creature, which no poet's imagination could ever have conjured up'. At night he stared longingly at the light in her window – 'Oh, that I were among the dreams that now flutter around you, that I might float in the air you breathe.'

In stolen moments at her house, Therese let him hold her. Her head on his chest, she could hear his heart. Kiss me, he said, and when she refused, she instead pressed her lips on his forehead. Let me kiss your feet, he demanded, and carefully removed her shoe before moving his head towards her stockinged foot. That was all she let him kiss, Therese later stressed, nothing more, but her family and friends were worried. 'Therese can't remain faithful to Forster in Göttingen,' said her friend Luise, 'because her heart or her mind is like a butterfly.'

'For the first time,' Therese recalled later, 'I loved all-encompassing, beyond words and blissfully.' Meyer's commitment, though, remained elusive for he was as changeable in his passions as in his profession. After his studies in Göttingen in the late 1770s, he had tried his luck as a private secretary in St Petersburg, then in Berlin, Vienna and Stade, before returning to Göttingen in early 1785. Why should he be 'unfaithful to the entire sex just for one woman,' he told a friend, there was nothing wrong with courting several women at the same time.

And what of George? Did Therese think about him? Their different temperaments leapt off the pages of their letters. Therese couldn't understand his quietness and modesty, his willingness to accept sadness, his refusal to become upset, and the way he was always so understanding. When she worried that his mood was too dark, he replied, 'I regard gloom, sorrow, trouble and suffering as the spices which improve the true joy of life.' And no, he was neither cold nor unmoved, nor indifferent to pain, nor indeed to joy. 'Forgive me for the cold philosophy as you always call it,' he wrote, for 'it is the philosophy of a warm heart.' In one of the last letters that he sent before leaving Vilnius to meet Therese in Göttingen, he mused about his ideas of friendship, marriage and trust – 'blind love, foolish, born out of whim, arrogance, recklessness, of an excitable sensual feeling, grown into a dangerous passion, has no place here'. Drawn into Meyer's hypnotizing fire, this was not what Therese wanted to hear.

After less than four weeks of travelling (with an eight-day stop in Warsaw and a few days in Dresden), George arrived in Göttingen on 21 August 1785. He couldn't wait to hold Therese in his arms. Did he first stop at his lodgings to brush off the travel dust or did he rush to the Heyne house, up the stairs and into the parlour? Either way, when he entered the room, he must have realized that something was wrong. Therese was bent over her needlework and didn't even look up. Her eyes were red and swollen, her sorrows written across her face. Heyne took her hand and led her to George. She tried to suppress the tears but when he touched her, she couldn't stop crying.

As a young woman in the eighteenth century, Therese had little say in her future. At a time when fathers decided the fate of their daughters, she knew that regardless of her sense of independence, her wishes were ultimately not important. Besides, Meyer had made it clear that he was not interested in an ordinary life and she had accepted her fate to marry George. 'It never occurred to me to be Meyer's wife rather than Forster's,' she told friends years later, 'it seemed unnecessary for love.'

Eventually, she confessed her feelings for Meyer to George. So, he now knew that his bride didn't return his affections but he was still mesmerized by her, by her energy and mind. He would do anything to make her smile again – 'my overly tender, soft love, which only sought to ensure Therese's happiness, and in that alone I believed I could be happy'. And the only person who seemed to bring her joy was Meyer – the moment he entered the room, her face lit up. For much of his life and in the shadow of his father, George had become accustomed to ignoring his own wishes. For years he had learned to adapt to the demands of his father, so why not to those of the woman he loved. Self-denial almost felt natural, he said. Maybe Therese persuaded him, maybe it was his own suggestion, but over the next days George came to accept that he had to share her with Meyer. Therese was allowed to adore Meyer and George hoped that eventually she would extend her feelings to him. The fact that he would be taking Therese to Vilnius helped – far away from Meyer where their love could only be played out in letters.

In a society where husbands controlled all aspects of their wives' lives, George was notably tolerant. A woman's role and domain were the children, the household and her husband's well-being. The man was the head of the family, while the wife had to follow his decisions, be gentle, malleable, and create a peaceful home life. But George believed in equal rights and that 'equality is the inescapable condition of love'. Earlier that year he had written to Therese from Vilnius that 'I hate everything that gets in the way of freedom', a statement that applied to men and women.

In Göttingen, George, Therese and Meyer spent long afternoons in the garden at the back of the Heyne house or went for long walks, talking about the future and their desires. It was all strange, new, and somehow thrilling – this world of fevered emotions, 'those days of intoxication', as George called them. 'I masked my bleeding heart with romantic rapture, Meyer remained steadfast,' Therese later wrote,

'Forster was more carried away than the two of us, had us swear eternal love to each other, as equals, and never asked for a kiss I hadn't also offered to Meyer.' It was, Therese thought, like stepping into the passionate whirlwind of a romantic novel. And indeed, two decades on, she would turn this peculiar love triangle into a book – her novel *Mehr Glück als Verstand* (*More Luck Than Sense*) – which was so autobiographical, she admitted, that the protagonists were 'drawn from nature, even in the smallest of details'.

Promising each other everlasting devotion, George, Therese and Meyer now called themselves an 'alliance of the trinity'. Therese 'is the link in the chain that binds us forever,' George told Meyer, 'let us love each other above all else, and one in the other, let us love each other as brothers and friends of our Therese, let us love Therese as the only and best woman who ever graced this earth!' Looking back, George came to believe that he had been too young and inexperienced to truly understand the repercussions of letting Meyer into their relationship. Therese was so different from other women and somehow he believed that she would be able to give him what he yearned for in this entanglement of three hearts. 'I imagined an equal sharing,' he explained, 'with no lessening of my own rights.'

On 4 September 1785, two weeks after George's arrival in Göttingen, they married – with Meyer as their witness.

16

'A tremendous number of frozen heads'

Exiled in Vilnius: 1785–1786

George and Therese Forster left Göttingen the day after their wedding. As always, George took his time. He seemed to take pleasure in the actual activity of travelling, rather than seeing it as simply getting from one place to another. As landscapes, villages and towns rolled by, he observed everything. He enjoyed meeting people – strangers and old friends alike. On their way to Vilnius, the newlyweds stopped for two days at Weimar to visit Goethe. The poet invited them for dinner where they also met Christoph Martin Wieland (who had reviewed *A Voyage Round the World* so favourably) and the eminent philosopher Johann Gottfried Herder. 'Goethe was lively and kind, and Wieland witty and endearing,' George wrote to Meyer from Weimar, but he was particularly excited to meet Herder, whose recently published *Ideas for the Philosophy of the History of Mankind* he and Therese had read. 'The book has a great value for me,' he had written to her in the previous year, 'and Herder has become even dearer to me as a result than he was before.' He was no doubt pleased that the philosopher had cited him in his chapter about Africa – 'what a boon for natural history and anthropology would be a company of men possessing Forster's acuity, Sparrman's patience, and the learning of both, to explore this undiscovered country!'

At forty-one, Herder was the head of the clergy in the Duchy of Saxe-Weimar but also a strikingly original mind whose works were read by almost every German intellectual of the day. Like George, he was interested in language, cultures and humankind. In 1772, the same year George had set sail on the *Resolution*, Herder had published *Treatise on the Origins of Language*, arguing that language set humans apart from animals, and that it was a 'natural organ of the understanding, a sense of the human soul'. George would later use similar arguments in a number of his own essays. For both men, language was inseparable from human and cultural identity.

In *Ideas for the Philosophy of the History of Mankind*, Herder widened his scope and examined the interplay between climate, plants, animals and people. He sought to understand what made humans human – including our ability to reason and speak – and believed that each nation and culture had to be seen within its own particular setting and history. Humanity's progress was neither hierarchical, nor did it move along a single trajectory, but was built on cultural diversity and the unique spirit of each people (*Volksgeist*), shaped by geography, language and experience – exactly what George had realized during the *Resolution* voyage.

Herder spent most of the two days in Weimar with George and Therese – 'I found in him a man who far exceeded my expectations, so open was he, and so sympathetic, and so free from all kinds of prejudices,' George wrote afterwards to Heyne. The proud husband watched his bride shine. Everyone seemed to adore her, George told his father-in-law, 'for who can see and hear our wonderful Therese without loving and appreciating her'? They went on to Halle for a brief visit to George's parents who had not met Therese before – one can imagine his trepidation, but for once it didn't end in a fight with Reinhold – then to Berlin for eight days, staying with the trusted Spener before travelling on to Warsaw, where they remained for two weeks.

Therese was the soul of the gatherings, George thought, she had 'a mind and heart as I had never hoped to find'. He also dispatched her silhouette to Meyer with the instruction that he 'kiss this image of our worshipped Therese'. George believed that everybody admired his bride, but his Göttingen friend Lichtenberg disagreed. Lichtenberg – a man who had had numerous affairs of his own – compared Therese and her tattered reputation to a ship on fire. 'I also believe this fiery little ship will become a rather good fishing boat,' Lichtenberg told Soemmerring, 'as long as Forster frequently boards it, carefully plugs the main leak, and throws the combustible materials overboard.'

*

For all the display of happiness, it wasn't an easy beginning. Therese liked George as a friend – admiring his mind, respecting his integrity and kindness – but she was in love with Meyer. She knew what was expected from her as a wife but would always despise the physical aspect of her marriage. Whenever George turned to her at night, she flinched. 'I only became a wife four weeks after my wedding,' she explained many years later, 'because nature had not destined us to be husband and wife.' When she finally had sex with George, she hated it. 'I wept in his arms and cursed nature which had created this torment for lust,' she told her friend Caroline.

But in Vilnius, far from Göttingen and the intellectual discourse to which they both were accustomed, the couple grew to rely on each other and became close. They went on long rambling walks in the nearby forests, talked for hours, and George taught Therese botany. 'Had I not a wife who replaces everything that I have left behind and that I now lack, I would not be able to bear it here,' he admitted to Lichtenberg.

Therese took to calling him 'Försterchen', an affectionate diminutive of 'Forster' and wrote cheerful letters to her parents, describing her first home in great detail. George had instructed the university to make some improvements in preparation for the arrival of his new wife. Functioning stoves had been installed and finally a new staircase, the natural-history collection had been moved into one of the smaller chambers so that the two spacious rooms with the large windows, overlooking the garden and above the laboratory, could be turned into a parlour and bedroom. 'Green wallpaper, very pretty green chairs, a good brand-new sofa, a lovely mahogany bureau that travelled around the world with Forster,' Therese described their parlour – George had given her his beloved desk to sit at when she was writing her correspondence. On the next level up, along a narrow corridor, were the servants' quarters (one for George's valet and his wife, the cook, and another for Marie, Therese's maid who had come from Göttingen). Next was George's herbarium and then a few more steps up his study – two rooms with cabinets and several tables to work on, as well as a small sofa – with the library next door. It was a confusing warren of corridors, stairs and split-level landings, Therese wrote to her stepmother shortly after their arrival, and 'I'm still so unfamiliar with my own house that I've already got lost among the different levels'.

The couple shared every meal and spent their evenings in the green parlour, reading books to each other. During the day, George taught, prepared lectures, wrote and translated, while Therese made curtains and organized the household. She sewed shirts for her husband and dresses for herself, knitted socks, and planted herbs and sweet-smelling flowers in pots to bring nature inside. But she also read scientific books so that she would become a worthy partner for her husband. Nonetheless, both felt cut off from the world, asking friends and family in every letter for books, magazines and further letters. He couldn't work when starved of literary sustenance, George told Spener, while Therese begged her stepmother for book recommendations and news.

Letters to friends painted a portrait of a marriage built on trust, kindness and shared interests. 'Forster is an angel disguised as a human,' Therese wrote to her stepmother. Unlike most husbands at the time, George couldn't understand men who refused to take women seriously – 'so, I'm asking for your opinion which I will gladly make into law,' he had told Therese after their engagement, promising always to consult her. And Therese respected him for accepting Meyer in her life. 'I love you more every day,' she told her husband, 'and the more I love you, the larger my heart grows, for you do not pull me away from those I loved before.' In Vilnius, they only had each other. 'Forster and I are one world,' Therese wrote to Göttingen, and they would simply have to survive their exile.

To compensate, they renovated their apartment – the new wallpaper fell off during the damp winter months – and they bought fine furniture, books, horses and a carriage, spending money they didn't have. With a spendthrift father, George had never learned how to budget and their debts mounted. They built a wall in one of the corridors to partition off a little antechamber where visitors' servants could wait – otherwise, Therese told her stepmother, they would linger in the kitchen and steal food. 'In just fifteen minutes, his pockets were bulging – bread rolls, cakes, bones from the roast – everything went in,' she complained about a particularly brazen servant. When spring finally thawed the snow and the soil warmed, Therese planted a garden – 'which makes me as happy as a child', she reported home.

Therese worried about her husband. During those first months of marriage, she had realized just how much he had suffered under his father's yoke. 'How often must his heart have been wounded,' she wondered, 'without a kind hand to heal it.' She was also concerned that George focused all his energy on her – how would he survive, if something happened to her, she wrote to Soemmerring, 'it is not entirely wise to tie one's happiness to one person and enjoy the rest of the world through her'. But her husband didn't care. 'I am fully persuaded that marriage is the happiest state upon earth,' he now said. He loved sharing his life with her and he admired her curious mind – 'her entire mode of thinking' – even encouraging her to write books or essays. But she couldn't, she said, because she wasn't able to write as quickly as her thoughts. The 'sparkle of my ideas is stifled by the slowness of my quill', she explained, 'I have whole volumes in my head, yet not a single line upon the paper.' Instead Therese composed long and entertaining letters to friends and family at home.

Meyer continued to write too, as did the young couple to him, but over the next few months George's letters became fewer and less passionate – perhaps because Therese was pregnant. The child 'was conceived during our journey', he proudly declared, 'and probably owes its existence to a most wretched night's lodging'. Therese, George now wrote to Meyer, was 'your tenderly loving sister', affirming his own position as the husband.

On 10 August 1786, less than a year after their wedding, Therese gave birth to a daughter – named Therese after her mother but nicknamed Röschen, Little Rose. Instead of employing a wet nurse, Therese breastfed the baby herself, ignoring the reproachful expressions of their Polish neighbours. George was devoted to his daughter. Baby Röschen was perfect, he told Lichtenberg, for 'the little devil has a full round face and her mother's vivacity'. He watched her become aware of her surroundings and develop her personality, wondering what came from nature and what from nurture. He didn't believe that babies were born with pre-existing ideas in their mind, he wrote to Herder in Weimar, but speculated if there was perhaps a certain inherited sensitivity or receptiveness. In any case, he believed that his daughter should be educated. 'I don't see,' he said, 'why a girl should not read, write, talk, think what and how she wants', and he couldn't understand why most men preferred sons. To him, his little family, wife and baby daughter, was his greatest joy.

Intellectually and professionally, George still felt isolated. Surrounded by a 'tremendous number of frozen heads', as he described his fellow professors to Lichtenberg, he feared that he 'couldn't keep up with his distant colleagues'. He read as much as he could, but books and letters couldn't replace real discussion. His mood only lifted when, in the summer of 1786, he read Immanuel Kant's latest treatise 'Determination of the Concept of a Human Race'. Here, finally, was an intellectual gauntlet that George could pick up from Vilnius.

Then in his early sixties, Kant lived in Königsberg (today's Kaliningrad in Russia, but then part of Prussia and some 100 miles east of Gdansk) and was one of the most revered philosophers in Europe. His widely discussed *Critique of Pure Reason* (1781) was an analysis of what we can know – the possibilities and impossibilities of metaphysics – and is today recognized as one of the most important works in the history of philosophy. Famed for his ideas on reason, freedom, and how we understand the world, Kant was also notorious for never once having left his birthplace.

Now, in 'Determination of the Concept of a Human Race', Kant declared that humankind had adapted and developed over countless generations into four different races – 'the *whites*, the *yellow* Indians, the *Negroes*, and the *copper-coloured red* Americans' – according to different local environments and climates. Kant also believed in a hierarchy based on skin colour: white people were the pinnacle of creation, while the indigenous people of the Americas were 'incapable of any culture' and 'far below the Negro, who undoubtedly holds the lowest of all remaining levels that we have designated as racial differences'.

As a traveller, George Forster had met and seen a great many people who didn't fit into Kant's categories. Skin colours were not sharply delineated but gradual shades, he said, 'everything in creation is interconnected by nuances'. This was an idea that Herder had recently discussed in the second volume of his *Ideas for the Philosophy of the History of Mankind*, published in April 1785. Skin colours blended into each other, Herder had written – 'on the whole all ultimately become shades of one and the same picture, spread over every age and every place on earth'.

'Race' was itself a relatively new concept, initially employed as a scientific ordering or classifying principle. Scientists had used geographic location, skin colour, size and hair as taxonomic data, but these traits were quickly becoming associated with moral judgements and claims of racial superiority or inferiority. Black people in Germany and Europe lived in a world so deeply steeped in racism that even the Scottish philosopher David Hume, a so-called 'enlightened' thinker, didn't hesitate to write in his essay 'Of National Characters': 'I am apt to suspect the negroes, and in general all the other species of men ... to be naturally inferior to the whites. There was never a civilized nation of any other complexion than white, nor even any individual eminent either in action or speculation ... There are NEGROE slaves dispersed all over EUROPE, of which none ever discovered any symptoms of ingenuity.' Similarly, the esteemed art historian and archaeologist Johann Joachim Winkelmann wrote without scruple about the 'turgid puffed-up mouth which the moors have in common with the apes in their country'. Having never liked the term 'race', George used it only because Kant had. Kant classified all South Pacific islanders into one category and George picked up his pen to prove him wrong. A fight would also be excellent publicity, he wrote to Soemmerring, 'if the public has to recognize that I am right, that I am right against *Kant*, then that can also be considered victory'.

His reply to Kant, 'Something More about the Human Races', was a polemical essay published in November 1786 in *Teutsche Merkur*, an important German literary magazine based in Weimar and published by Wieland. In his essay George argued that philosophers should work from observation rather than develop abstruse theories with no foundation in reality. He was incredulous that Kant could make such statements without ever having travelled. George's essay was as much an attack against Kant's racial ideas as his philosophical method – this 'armchair philosophy', as he called it. Abstraction led one down the wrong path and like so many other philosophers, Kant had tried to mould the world to his pre-conceived ideas. Already in *A Voyage Round the World*, George had ridiculed thinkers who presented 'a few circumstances as facts; and wresting even those to suit their own systems' – in doing so they 'have built a superstructure which pleases at a distance, but upon nearer examination partakes of the illusive nature of a dream'. Where Kant argued that one had to have an idea or theory to know what to search for, George said that pre-existing concepts manipulated our understanding of reality to such a degree that it shaped the world according to what we expect it to be. But 'nature's order doesn't follow our divisions'.

Kant maintained that the four races had developed from one original line, but George argued that the possibility of separate origins of humankind should not be dismissed. He was quick to explain to Herder that he was 'still far from believing that humankind really had multiple progenitors' – such a theory went against all his ideas about the unity of humans – but he stressed that every option had to be examined. It could be useful, he wrote to Herder, 'to look at the issue from another perspective'. The entire discussion of the origin of humankind was based on guesswork. 'That all humans are of one species is well established,' George said, but that they apparently all originated from one ancestor was simply a '*matter of faith*'.

Not only did George challenge Kant, but he also contested the authority of the Bible and its creation myth of Adam and Eve – 'an old book against which no one may write'. How would anyone be able to prove humankind's beginnings? One original set of parents in one place was as likely or unlikely as hundreds in different locations across the globe, and in any case, where would this one paradisical spot be 'which contained within itself the whole storehouse of nature, providing for every climate and every element?'

But even if there *had* been different local creations, George wrote, no one race had the right to oppress another. Nor had the belief in *monogenesis* – the idea that all humans had derived from one original Adam and Eve – ever stopped white people from subjugating others. 'Let me rather ask,' he wrote, 'whether the thought that Black people are our brothers has ever once caused the lifted whip of the slave driver to sink? Did he not, in full conviction that they were of his blood, torment the poor patient creatures with executioner's fury and devilish joy?' And being of the same skin colour had never stopped

Europe's many despots from ruling with brutality over their fellow humans.

When his essay was published in October 1786, George dispatched a flurry of letters from Vilnius across the German states, asking friends and acquaintances for their opinions. 'I desire your judgement ... without reserve,' he demanded in one note, and from another friend 'your candid opinion on the matter'. He wrote to Spener, 'I beg you to be attentive to the impression the article makes upon those whose judgement carries weight in the learned world.' Delighted by the overwhelmingly positive response and with people waiting for another instalment, George felt good for the first time in months. That he was accused of heresy for challenging the biblical origin story of Adam and Eve didn't seem to bother him. Since he had left the Rosicrucians three years previously, George had turned his back on religion. 'Adam,' he would later say, was the 'creature of some oriental fantasy.' He would never bow before orthodoxy or doctrine, he told Soemmerring, 'because I consider it my good fortune to be able to express freely those thoughts I hold to be true'.

Kant was not pleased and replied with an article bristling with so many abstract philosophical concepts and terms that George thought its language as prickly and abrasive as a frightened, curled-up hedgehog. Kant now accused the young explorer of 'purely empirical groping about without a guiding principle that might direct one's search', and relying on observations alone. Travel writers like George Forster, Kant wrote, couldn't comprehend what they were seeing because they didn't know what they were looking for. George disagreed. Only experience could be the foundation of theories.

But George soon became uncomfortable with parts of his argument because the idea of multiple origins could be used to promote the idea of superior and inferior races. Soemmerring had recently published a treatise on the anatomical differences between Europeans and Africans, concluding that the 'Moor seems closer to the monkey than the European' – though he had quickly printed a second edition in which he asserted that Africans were still 'true humans, just like us'. As absurd as the discussion seems today, at the time some scientists believed that Africans were the offspring of humans and monkeys. George had reminded Soemmerring that the ability to speak and think was the defining factor of humans. 'I am far from thinking,' he wrote, 'that any ape could have played a role in the formation of the Negro'. The differences between Europeans and Africans were too minor to make them two species – they 'stand very close to one another'.

George was concerned that his views could be misconstrued as an argument for a hierarchy of races and didn't include 'Something More about the Human Races' in an essay collection he published three years later. His ideas would develop further and he was already working on an essay about Captain Cook in which he underlined the unity in human diversity. Human appearance might differ depending on where a person was from, he explained, but in terms of their instincts, biological developments and morals, all people were the same.

As always, George was busy with various projects at the same time. In his study in Vilnius he had several small tables piled high with different books, papers and inkwells for each undertaking. He stepped from one table to the next without having to move any of his material – 'entirely in factory style', he told Spener, 'but the work itself need not be factory-like'. In 1786 he worked on his article against Kant, two botanical treatises in Latin, lectures on zoology and mineralogy for his students (also in Latin), an essay about Botany Bay in New Holland (today's Australia), and a German translation of Captain Cook's account of his third and last voyage which had been published posthumously in four volumes in England.

Getting up at 6 a.m. every morning, he worked on the Cook project until lunch, and after a quick meal returned to his study (and to a different table) to work on other essays, books or lectures, before he went back to the Cook manuscript. As so often he edited the original when he felt he could improve it. He added annotations, shortened the footnotes – 'many castrated' – and deleted the English editor's preface. Every evening, he emerged from his study and gave Therese the pages he had translated. She then read them, added comments, and made suggestions. He was exhausted and struggled for months with a stubborn cough, but he persisted because in Vilnius writing and publishing became more important than ever to him. 'I regard these smaller works as necessary,' he wrote to Lichtenberg in Göttingen, 'in order not to be completely forgotten in the learned world.'

Lichtenberg admired George's mastery of words, even his correspondence was formidable. 'It is true, this man writes letters as though they were printed,' Lichtenberg wrote to Soemmerring, 'truly, in all seriousness, most excellent.' When the first Cook volume rolled off the printing press many important German journals reviewed it – twelve reviews in nine different papers – praising the translation as 'vivid and beautiful', 'excellent' and 'unrivalled'. The copious annotations, one reviewer thought, made the translation better than the original, and another wrote that there was no German writer better suited to translate Cook than the famous George Forster.

George also wrote his own introduction for the German edition, a brilliant essay entitled 'Cook, the Discoverer', which one reviewer described as a masterpiece. The text was not only a monument to Cook's scientific and geographical achievements, but also to his steadfast character. Across almost 200 pages, George recounted the successes and accomplishments of the man with whom he had sailed – ranging from Cook's navigational feats to his defeat of scurvy. He praised Cook's dispassionate judgement, courage, and 'his respect for human rights', but also his triumphant rise from a modest background. 'His active mind, firm in decisions, bold and quick in execution,' George wrote with admiration, 'broke the chains that had been placed upon him.'

There was also criticism. He couldn't understand why Cook had introduced horses to Tahiti during his last voyage, for example. There was no agricultural use for them in the local plantations and they would become a luxury which would only foster inequalities. Horses increased the wealth of a few without advantages for the general population – 'the nobles, whose feet no longer touch the ground, will eventually come to consider themselves entirely different creatures from the pedestrians.'

The essay illustrated George's deepening philosophy (and his reading of Herder). What does it mean to be human? What distinguishes humans from animals? And what do humans have in common? 'There is indisputably no subject closer to a human being than human beings themselves,' he wrote, 'in all their diversity in appearance, in development, in disposition, and in time and place.' Here again was the theme that had driven his thinking since he had boarded the *Resolution* at the age of seventeen.

What made humans human, George explained, was reason, morality, and the 'awareness of an abstract *self*'. There was no nation or tribe without language, he wrote, and because there was no language without reason, no human could be an animal or even close to animals. In this 'ocean of humankind' there might be 'countless shades', but no matter where they lived, how they looked or what they believed, all humans were the same species. It was irrefutable, he wrote in 'Cook, the Discoverer', that the 'nature of man may differ depending on the climate . . . but in essence all are specifically the same' (he chose the term 'specifically' deliberately to imply the concept of 'species'). Whatever others said, George doubted the utility of ascribing certain traits or qualities to particular nations or groups. Doing so would be unfair, he wrote elsewhere, because the 'characters of every nation are so manifold'.

The essay also attacked slavery. The transatlantic slave trade which kidnapped and transported African people to the Americas had fuelled European economies since the sixteenth century. Today, George wrote, economists were able to calculate with 'arithmetical precision how many drops of negro sweat are needed for a spoonful of sugar'. The greed for gold, silver, tobacco or spices had brought devastation, death and exploitation to distant countries. 'We're engaged in slavery,' he accused in another essay around the same time, 'so that we can enjoy a few delicacies such as sugar and coffee.'

The German states might not have been directly involved but for centuries trade routes crossed the Mediterranean Sea from Africa to Europe. There were hundreds of slaves – but also free Africans – in the German territories. In Kassel, George would have encountered some of them because there were several slaves at the court, dressed in colourful red and blue liveries with silk stockings and yellow boots. In addition, more than one hundred African Americans had enlisted with the Hessian regiments in America during the War of Independence and later arrived as free men in Kassel at the end of the war in 1782 and 1783. Some were joined by their wives and children, while others were brought by the Hessian soldiers as wives, mistresses and servants. Some

A black drummer in a Hessian regiment in the 1780s

married white women and several became musicians in the landgrave's personal regiment. Their presence in Kassel had enabled Soemmerring to prepare his treatise on the anatomical differences between Europeans and Africans. Whenever an African died, he or she was brought to Soemmerring's anatomy theatre for dissection.

German rulers bought slaves directly from sea captains or trading companies in Europe – young boys, mostly, but also girls, who were kept at various courts as musicians, grooms, footmen, servants and dancers. Sometimes depicted wearing elaborate 'oriental' costumes, turbans and jewels in paintings, these so-called 'Kammermohren' ('chamber-moors') became status symbols, proclaiming their owners' wealth and power. Some eventually became court favourites, learning to read and write, yet most remained property – and could be sold or given away.

A few became famous and were freed. Anton Wilhelm Amo, for instance, Europe's first African professor, taught at universities in Wittenberg and Jena in the 1730s and 1740s. Abducted as a young boy in

Angelo Soliman

today's Ghana, Amo was given as a present to the Duke of Braunschweig, who conducted an 'experiment' to see how much a Black person could learn when given the best education. Having studied at the best German universities, Amo became fluent in several languages and wrote a thesis in Latin entitled *The Rights of Moors in Europe* and later treatises on the dualism of mind and body. Yet despite his obvious achievements, he struggled to earn enough money after the Duke of Braunschweig died, and he experienced racist prejudice. In his mid-forties, he returned to West Africa where he lived until his death.

There was also Angelo Soliman, the African freemason whom George had met in Vienna. Married to an Austrian baroness and widely respected, Soliman was part of Vienna's high society. But even Soliman suspected that he had been purchased 'in order to find out whether Culture educates a negro in the same way as it educates a white European'. Free, wealthy, assimilated, and always elegantly dressed, Soliman nonetheless became the most gruesome embodiment of the age's underlying racism. After his death the emperor had his body skinned, stuffed and exhibited as a 'noble savage' in the Imperial Natural Collection in Vienna, wearing a feather skirt and a necklace made of porcelain snails next to a stuffed capybara, tapir and birds. When Soliman's daughter begged for her father's remains in order to give him a proper burial she was refused.

As slavery didn't officially exist in the German states, the legal status of Black residents was particularly nebulous. George Forster believed that slaves should automatically be freed when they stepped onto German soil, but his contemporaries had other ideas. A few years earlier, in 1783, one of Germany's most prominent legal scholars, Ludwig Höpfner, had published a book that systematically undermined any rights that slaves might have. Höpfner, a friend of Goethe's, had taught at Kassel in the years before George arrived there, and had since become legal advisor to the ruler of Hesse-Darmstadt. His book became the most influential legal textbook in Germany in the second half of the eighteenth century. 'The King of Prussia has confirmed,' Höpfner wrote, 'that a Moor purchased in Copenhagen and brought to the Prussian lands cannot demand freedom simply because he is now living in Prussia.'* To underline his argument, he claimed that Black people were 'not regarded as persons but as things'.

George disagreed profoundly with anyone who 'degrades man to a beast'. He was always going to say and write what he believed, he told Soemmerring, who had warned him to be careful. As long as he could hold a quill and write, he would do what he could 'to contribute to the true happiness of humanity'. Silence was not an option, 'for what do we fear?'

* Just before the *Resolution* had left in July 1772, a dramatic case gripped London in which Chief Justice Lord Mansfield ruled the opposite. A customs officer named Charles Stewart had brought the enslaved James Somerset from Boston to England. When Somerset escaped, he was recaptured and forcibly detained on a ship bound for Jamaica, where Stewart intended to sell him. Abolitionists intervened and brought the case to court, arguing that English law didn't recognize the existence of slavery in England and therefore Somerset had to be freed. They won the case and *Somerset vs Stewart* became a landmark judgement, widely discussed in London when George had still been in the city.

PART IV

Revolutions

17

'So, I wait for better times'

Upheavals: 1787–1788

On 3 June 1787 a Russian officer knocked on George Forster's door in Vilnius. In his late twenties, Captain Grigory Ivanovich Mulovsky was the illegitimate son of the vice president of the Russian Admiralty and he brought momentous news: Catherine the Great, Empress of Russia, had commissioned Mulovsky to lead a five-ship expedition to the South Pacific, Japan, China and America, and had requested the renowned George Forster to take charge of the scientific aspects. The voyage would take around four years, Mulovsky told George, and was scheduled to depart the following March from England. George couldn't believe his luck but didn't quite dare to let himself be swept up by the 'sweet thrill of the idea'.

Over the next week, he and Mulovsky negotiated the terms. George wanted an annual salary of 3,000 roubles and on his return a yearly pension of 1,500 roubles. If he died, Therese should receive the money, and if she died, it should be transferred to their daughter, Röschen. He also insisted on money to purchase the necessary equipment and that the Russians would buy him out of his contract with the university in Vilnius – all of which would amount to 5,400 roubles.* And he wanted to choose a team of scientists and artists to accompany the expedition. When the Russian Admiralty received his terms, they didn't hesitate – Catherine simply signed the request: 'So be it.'

Five weeks after Mulovsky's visit, the contract and official commission

* 4,000 roubles for the equipment and 1,400 roubles to pay off the university, in addition to his salary.

arrived from St Petersburg. All his conditions had been accepted, George told his father-in-law on 19 July 1787. It was a princely offer – the chancellor of the Russian Empire, for example, the highest paid civil servant in the country, earned 7,000 roubles a year and could afford a castle with one hundred servants. George would be able to pay off their substantial debts and Therese would be well cared for while he was away. George was finally free to leave Vilnius.

It hadn't been easy over the past year. Even though Therese had done her best to provide intellectual stimulation, George continued to feel isolated from the scholarly life of Europe. His letters were filled with dark thoughts. With deadlines looming and their debts increasing, he was so overworked that he had to get up at 5 a.m. to write until 8 p.m., and then collapse into bed. 'This wretched land will be the death of me,' he had told Spener in February. The previous winter had been particularly hard. He had been ill for three months, unable to get rid of a persistent cold. The local physician was concerned and Therese worried. 'I saw Forster pacing the room for weeks with a gloomy countenance,' she wrote to Spener, 'sullen, gaunt, without appetite.' George had never been good at hiding his feelings. Therese once compared him to a 'mirror in which everything is reflected . . . or like a water surface that reflects back but that is also ruffled by every wind'. His emotions were open, raw and vulnerable, his unhappiness obvious.

Mulovsky's offer now lifted the veil of darkness. Over the following weeks, George wrote enthusiastic letters to friends and acquaintances, asking for recommendations of people who might be interested in joining the expedition – surgeons, astronomers, botanists, artists, scientific assistants and hunters – including Soemmerring. It would be thrilling if they could both travel together. 'Now, my brother, answer in haste,' George wrote to Soemmerring the day after Mulovsky had arrived, 'let the reply fly.' They would be united, working together, seeing the world, and the salary would be good. 'Without any question, I shall come with you,' Soemmerring replied, 'even if I receive no salary, but only room and board' – though by the last page of the letter the amount had risen to 1,500 roubles, then to 2,000 and finally to 3,000 roubles.

There was a breathless excitement in the flurry of letters that raced between Vilnius and Mainz, where Soemmerring had moved from

Kassel to become professor of anatomy at the university. 'I am still intoxicated with joy,' Soemmerring wrote. Was George going to take a servant? he asked. What kind of equipment? A sword? Bedding? How much paper? How were they going to receive their money? Which books should he take? Were the meals free on board? Should he pack his fancy black silk coat? And how many shirts? Don't spend any money on a wardrobe, George replied, for 'what do we need clothes for on the ship?' But he urged Soemmerring to pack enough shirts and socks. Soemmerring seemed to have been so concerned that Therese became involved, listing what her husband was taking: '18 nightshirts, 18 with cuffs, 18 without, and another half dozen of the second sort of day shirts which are older. 3 dozen handkerchiefs, 2 dozen linen and 1 dozen woollen stockings', as well as three sets of bed linen, napkins, towels and washcloths. George dispatched a long list of books that he was packing to avoid taking duplicates and advised Soemmerring to sell his furniture and scientific collection. They could buy equipment and books in London from where the expedition ships would depart.

Therese's father, Christian Gottlob Heyne, was glad for George but feared that Forster senior might interfere. 'I hope your good father is not getting involved,' Heyne wrote at the end of June, 'don't let anything get to him too soon.' George waited until the beginning of August to inform his father in Halle, who reacted predictably with an angry letter. He hadn't heard from his father for more than a year, George told Soemmerring, and had already wondered if the reason was that 'he knows that I cannot part with any cash at this moment'.

Instead of congratulating his son, Reinhold strongly advised against working with the Russians. They were terrible navigators, he claimed, temperamental, inexperienced, offered wretched accommodation, and sailed with insufficient provisions. Reinhold included a long and patronizing packing list, advising George to take a brass washbasin, lemon juice, thread and needle, coffee, spare buckles, razors, scissors, candles, guns and shoe polish, as well as instructing him to demand a large cabin with a lock – as if his son had never been on an expedition himself.

Reinhold also suggested that George recruit his younger brother William as a surgeon for the expedition. When George objected that William didn't have enough experience, his father replied angrily, 'as to surgical Operations, though William has not yet had opportunities to practise Surgery, he is however well acquainted with all the operations, in cadavers.' Reinhold's talent for interfering in his son's life never ceased. The previous year, George had enquired about a position in Berlin and one in Marburg, only to be informed by Soemmerring that his father had also applied. 'The man ruins everything for his son,' Heyne wrote to Soemmerring, and George was frustrated 'that I always and everywhere clash with my old father!'

In Vilnius, George and Therese had to sell their furniture, pack up the house, and finalize their financial matters. 'I'm dizzy from all the ideas that race through my head,' George told Heyne, who was more of a father to him than Reinhold had ever been. They also decided that during George's absence Therese and Röschen should live in Göttingen, near her parents. So at the end of August 1787, three months after Mulovsky's visit and less than three years after George had first arrived in Vilnius, the Forsters and their three servants climbed into their carriage in Vilnius. In their euphoria, they barely noticed that Turkey had declared war on Russia on 24 August.

They stopped in Warsaw for a few days, from where George sent a note to Herder, proposing that they meet in Weimar to discuss 'my forthcoming journey, which will be of interest to you in light of your studies on the human race'. And so they did. Herder felt invigorated after their visit, buoyed by their conversations and by George's offer to send observations about any nations or indigenous peoples he might encounter during the expedition. 'I am turning over all sorts of things in my head,' Herder wrote to Therese afterwards, 'and mean to furnish him with a large cargo of questions.' Goethe, who was in Italy at the time, was informed of the plan by Herder and began considering what he too might ask George.

They reached Göttingen on 16 September 1787, in time for the fiftieth anniversary celebrations of the university.* Everybody was

* On that day, seventeen-year-old Dorothea Schlözer, daughter of one of the professors at the university of Göttingen, was the first woman to receive a doctorate in Germany. Unlike most of his contemporaries, her father believed that women were as intelligent as men and conducted an experiment by providing his daughter with a rigorous education. At the age of four Dorothea could read and at five she

delighted to see George. The Göttingen Academy of Sciences elected him as a full member, and three sons of the British king, George III, who were studying in Göttingen, invited him several times for dinner. George was surprised not to find any letters from Mulovsky, but having read in the newspapers about the conflict with Turkey, he assumed that the Russian Admiralty was distracted by war efforts.

In Mainz, Soemmerring was becoming nervous. 'All trunks and chests are repaired and ready,' he reported on 18 September, 'shirts and stockings are taken care of.' Four days later he wrote again, and again a week later. What should he do? Should he hand in his notice? Buy wood for the winter in Mainz? 'I am eagerly awaiting your advice.' George remained unruffled. Trying to calm his friend, he reassured him that the Russian war with Turkey was not going to affect their plans. Nothing would spoil his happiness. 'I am free!' he told Spener, and he felt healthier than he had been for a long time.

George focused on the arrangements for the expedition – books had to be ordered, to-do lists compiled, and an artist and another naturalist remained to be found to join the expedition. 'Since all is uncertain,' he told Spener, 'I proceed as if everything is going according to plan.' But in mid-October there were newspaper reports of riots in Holland, and George read that Britain had declared war on France, which, although untrue, only added to his confusion and sense of uncertainty because the Russian expedition was meant to start in England.

There was still no news from Mulovsky at the beginning of November. As doubts crept in, George walked several miles every day to strengthen his body for the exertions of the expedition. They had rented rooms for Therese and Röschen, but there was hardly space for all of them as George was supposed to have gone by now. He didn't work much – too many distractions, too many letters to write, and too many visitors. He doggedly continued his preparations. At the beginning of December, still nothing.

His father, though, was dispatching long letters from Halle to Göttingen in which he suddenly detailed *his* conditions for joining the

was taught by the university's professor of mathematics. She spoke ten languages fluently and was proficient in zoology, mineralogy and botany.

expedition – ignoring the fact that his son had never invited him and that he had advised George not to go either. George didn't know what to do. His father's demands were so unreasonable that the Russians were unlikely to employ him – in which case he would be furious with his son, but if Reinhold came along, George wrote to Herder, 'I foresee endless vexation throughout the entire journey!'

On 23 December, with still no news, George received a letter from a Spanish acquaintance he had met three and a half years previously in Dresden, enquiring if he might be interested in an expedition to the Philippines. He was still committed to the Russians, George replied, but he knew just the man for the Spanish expedition: his father. If the Spanish would engage Reinhold for their Philippines expedition, George quietly plotted, he would not have to deal with him any more. He also used the opportunity to find out if there might be a position in Madrid for him in case the Russian expedition was cancelled. The long letter read like a resume in which he described his interests, qualifications and personality, but it also openly reveals George's sense of himself:

> I am 33 years old and healthy. My face, while unremarkable, is at least not displeasing. I accompanied Cook on his second voyage around the world and later wrote about it. The field of science I have most particularly applied myself is the study of nature in its broadest scope, including some aspects of physics and chemistry. I can draw animals and plants tolerably well. I have a taste for philosophy, the fine arts, and the humanities. Geography, history, politics, statistics, and public affairs are among my favourite subjects that have always filled my spare time. I know as much Latin as is expected nowadays of a scholar whose primary field is not philology. I speak and write German, French, and English fluently. I read and understand Dutch, Italian, Spanish, Portuguese, and Swedish. I have some knowledge of Polish and a basic understanding of Russian. I believe myself competent to write correspondence and business documents as well as to manage business assignments entrusted to me. I enjoy talking, but rarely do so; I communicate openly yet maintain self-control. I am gentle and cheerful, yet serious. I am bound by neither prejudice nor

> a dogmatic notion of duty, but rather by an inner sense of self-respect and a deep urge to be happy by making others happy.

On 24 December, George travelled seventy miles to Hanover to ask a friend of his father-in-law, the royal physician Johann Georg von Zimmermann, for help in contacting the Russians. Zimmermann had treated the two 'Greats' – Friedrich and Catherine – and after listening to George's concerns, promised to forward his letters to St Petersburg and the Empress. But when George returned to Göttingen in early January, a letter from Mulovsky was already waiting for him. It was brief and devastating – because of the war with Turkey, the captain wrote, the expedition had been cancelled.

There was another blow. Since their arrival in Göttingen, Therese had once again found comfort in the arms of Wilhelm Meyer. She was still in love with him and George quietly accepted Meyer's presence in her life – knowing that he was about to embark on a dangerous expedition from which he might never return.

Shortly after George came back from Hanover, their marriage finally cracked. Perhaps it was disappointment that her husband was staying, or perhaps Therese and Meyer had overestimated George's seemingly never-ending patience and forbearance. In Vilnius, George had succeeded in suppressing any feelings of jealousy, but in Göttingen, where Meyer and Therese had taken few precautions to hide their feelings, it was different. 'You lived in the rapture of passion,' George wrote to Meyer later, 'and when you were together, the world vanished for you.'

To prove to himself that his wife was still his, George decided, as he described it, to 'exorcise passion through passion'. The result was unsurprisingly the opposite of what he had hoped. Therese turned away, emotionally and physically. But when she refused to sleep with him, something exploded in George and all the pent-up unhappiness came tumbling out. For two long days, through the weekend of 19 and 20 January 1788, the couple fought. Therese accused George of forcing her to have sex with him, and he demanded she end her relationship with Meyer. They shouted, cried and shouted more. George was distraught and Therese became ill.

She was adamant that he leave Göttingen. There was no future for them, she said. After just over two years, their marriage seemed to be over. The next day he departed for Berlin, some 200 miles to the north-east of Göttingen, shattered at the prospect of life without her. As always, he stayed with his old friend and publisher Spener and tried to distract himself by going to the opera and meeting friends, but after a few days he simply collapsed. He suffered from fevers, diarrhoea, cramps and general exhaustion. His health had never quite recovered after the *Resolution* voyage. Violent headaches and rheumatism often left him unable to walk or even to hold a pen, and stress or emotional upheaval triggered more serious illnesses – this time, he told a friend, it was 'the result of the vexation that brought me here'. Spener and his wife looked after George, nursing him and calmly listening to his woes.

When Reinhold heard that his son was in Berlin, he was furious that George had not stopped in Halle en route, and he dashed off two letters in three days. 'Your mother finds it very hard, that You shun *and* avoid us so much,' he fumed. In any case, what was he doing in Berlin? If he was trying to find a position or obtain funds for Reinhold, it was a waste of money and time because the people in Berlin were 'cringing Toadeaters' – 'for God's sake, be a Man, don't cringe for these base wretches'. The letters were a long list of grievances about *himself* – *his* life was terrible, *he* needed money, *his* professional obligations were too great. 'I hope God will deliver me from the house of bondage *and* ignominy, to which those would-be learned men have doomed all the Professors of this University.'

The news from Göttingen was no better. A few days after George had left, Therese wrote a short and unambiguous note to her husband:

> My heart bleeds for the step I forced you to take because you did not yet feel its necessity. Humanity and magnanimity will soon convince you of this, and courage shall support you. My health is now without pain, but my chest has received a shock I cannot explain, weak voice and fatigue have not yet left me. My heart is broken, pity once again battles with reason, but I count on the future because at present I can't think of happiness. Preserve your health for the sake of your child and your friend, seek distraction, and know that the news which declares you content is the most welcome to me.

The letter ended with a cold 'your Therese Forster'.

Meyer wrote a long letter to Therese's father, justifying his behaviour: he had never flirted with his daughter, they had never acted in secret, and George was never going to find true happiness with her. 'I have used none of the arts that beguile women and debase men,' he added.

Heyne tried to mediate but couldn't comprehend what was going on. Everybody involved told a different story. He loved George like a son, and had always been troubled by his daughter's high-spirited and hot-tempered character. 'It would be good for her,' he wrote, 'to stop a few degrees below boiling point.' Heyne confronted her, but Therese fought back. She accused George of lying and begged her father to listen to her side of the story. She had never loved George but had married him out of duty to relieve Heyne of the burden of supporting her, she now said. She had never slept with Meyer – 'I have been wrong and erred but never been unfaithful.' Heyne urged that she should not leave George, and she eventually agreed to write to Berlin to ask him to return. Years later, Therese had a different perspective, telling her father that Meyer had blinded her and that he 'was a wicked man who sought to ruin me'. He was like a comet, Therese wrote in her autobiographical novel, a brilliant but chaotic force that moves on its erratic path, threatening the destruction of a world and the eternal harmony of the universe.

From Berlin, George wrote a long eleven-page letter to Meyer, laying out his demands while at the same time showing an almost inhuman forgiveness and kindness. 'I love you with the heart with which I love my dearest friends,' he told Meyer, but for the first time in his marriage he also asserted himself. Yes, he would help Meyer find a job in Berlin, and, yes, he could remain in Therese's life, but only as a friend and certainly not in Göttingen. 'My contentment as a fiancé and husband, the long habit of self-denial', he wrote, had made them all (including himself) believe that 'a man of my disposition and sensibility requires but little, does not feel the lack of what he has to forgo, and is therefore amply rewarded with whatever is offered to him.' It had been a mistake to accept this strange triangle of feelings. 'What should have remained friendship became love,' he now said, 'and oh, the folly of believing that two loves can coexist in one heart!' He was glad that his wife had asked him to come home but it was time for some rules. He was Therese's husband, not Meyer. 'Your love must turn into friendship, her friendship for me into faithful conjugal love.' He wanted Therese's passion, not her pity.

Meyer agreed to leave and at the end of February 1788, George travelled from Berlin for Göttingen, stopping for two days in Halle to appease his father. Thirty-five miles west of Halle, he almost died when his carriage crashed down a steep embankment, overturning several times. When the carriage finally came to a stop, it was upside down with its doors blocked. George was stuck inside and had to wait until some locals turned the vehicle over so he could crawl out on all fours. The next day, at 11 p.m., he finally arrived in Göttingen, exhausted and bruised but with no broken bones.

Relieved to be home after a separation of six weeks, George forgave Therese and she promised 'to be happy with me from now on', he wrote to Spener, also thanking him and his wife 'for the patience and forbearance you have had with my melancholy or hypochondria*, or whatever you wish to call it'. It would take time to heal but George was determined to win back Therese's feelings. The fight and separation had shaken him. During those cold grey weeks in Berlin he had been ill and depressed, but as winter gave way to spring he turned to nature for hope. 'Spring infuses all living creatures with new fire and new vitality and with them new desires,' he told Soemmerring in May, and perhaps it was the same with his marriage. His love for Therese ran deep, and he would gladly sacrifice his life for a few happy years with her. Joy had to be balanced with sadness. 'Maybe life should be like a cheerful dance, where at times some rest, until the rules of the dance call them back into motion and they rejoin the others,' George said, 'meanwhile the others continue to dance confidently, knowing that by the time they have completed their turn, they may again offer their hands to those at rest.'

Therese was devastated when Meyer left Göttingen in June 1788, unable to forgive him for abandoning her and despising George for loving her. Whenever her husband tried to touch her, she retreated. He

* In the eighteenth century, hypochondria was not an imagined illness in the way it is thought of today, but referred to what was believed to be a real abdominal condition triggered or worsened by melancholy or anxiety.

was still her friend but she couldn't endure physical contact. At night, when he turned to her, 'I had to grit my teeth,' she confessed to Caroline, 'to me, it felt like a humiliation of humankind.' Over time this feeling turned into bitterness and resentment. The more he showed his feelings, the more she pulled away. 'All love in her bosom is extinguished,' George wrote in his last letter to Meyer, 'and towards me, she remains cold and indifferent, almost to the point of repulsion.'

He was heartbroken and withdrew too – 'so, I wait for better times'.

18

'Freedom, freedom, boundless freedom in everything'

Mainz: 1788–1790

George Forster needed a job. He had paid off his debts with the 4,000 roubles the Russians had allowed him to keep but a regular income was essential. Having cancelled the expedition, Catherine the Great was still keen to employ George and offered him a position at the aristocratic military academy in St Petersburg. He politely declined – the harsh climate, strict hierarchy and etiquette of Russian society, as well as the expenses, lack of scholarly exchange and court intrigues were not appealing. Life in Russia, George said, was unsuitable for 'a quiet, freedom-loving man'. Heyne agreed. Not only would his son-in-law's talents be wasted in Russia, but he was concerned about Therese: 'my daughter in Petersburg, the seat of opulence and depravity of morals!'

When Heyne heard that the university of Mainz was looking for a new head of the library, he suggested George to the outgoing librarian. A few days later the librarian wrote to the ruler of Mainz that 'it is quite beyond doubt that the mere name of a man as illustrious throughout Europe as he is would at once bring new and great prestige to Your Electoral Highness's university.' George Forster, the librarian added, would enrich the international reputation of Mainz more than twenty other scholars taken together. And so, in April 1788, a few weeks after his return from Berlin, George travelled from Göttingen 150 miles south-west to Mainz to present himself. Maybe this could be a new beginning, a fresh start far away from all the dark memories. It wasn't the most thrilling role, but at least he would be in the same city as Soemmerring.

The decision was quickly made and George accepted the position three days later. At the end of August 1788, after an intensive three-month course in the management and organization of libraries with his father-in-law in Göttingen, George sent their furniture, his books and other belongings to Mainz. Four weeks later he travelled with Therese and two-year-old Röschen to their new home, where they arrived on 2 October 1788.

Mainz, situated in the western part of the Holy Roman Empire, was only around seventy miles from the French border and twenty miles west of Frankfurt. It had been the home of Johannes Gutenberg, the pioneer of the printing press, and with 28,000 inhabitants it was not a small city by the standards of the time – Frankfurt, a thriving commercial centre and trade hub with 30,000 people, was not much larger. It was the capital of the wealthiest of the German Electorates – an ecclesiastical state with a population of 400,000, ruled by the Prince-Elector Friedrich Karl Joseph von Erthal, one of the eight individuals entitled to elect the emperor of the Holy Roman Empire. Being an elector was a position of immense prestige and influence within the imperial structure – so important, in fact, that major powers such as Russia, France, Prussia and Austria posted diplomats to Mainz.

George didn't care for the political intricacies and courtly organization of the Electorate, but he liked the views from Mainz over the expansive vineyards and surrounding orchards, and towards the low Taunus mountains to the north. The city's skyline was defined by an imposing red sandstone cathedral and many church spires. As the capital, Mainz was also the seat of the elector's court with a large city castle and a resplendent baroque summer palace with elaborate formal gardens just outside the old city walls. The mighty Rhine, one of the longest and most important rivers on the continent, was a vital trade and transport artery that connected Mainz to other German states and to Europe. Wide promenades and elegant buildings lined the river but inside the old city centre a warren of narrow cobbled streets were reminders of Mainz's medieval past.

George had heard that the Elector of Mainz was an enlightened ruler who prided himself on having abolished serfdom and founding the new university, just four years previously in 1784. Although head of

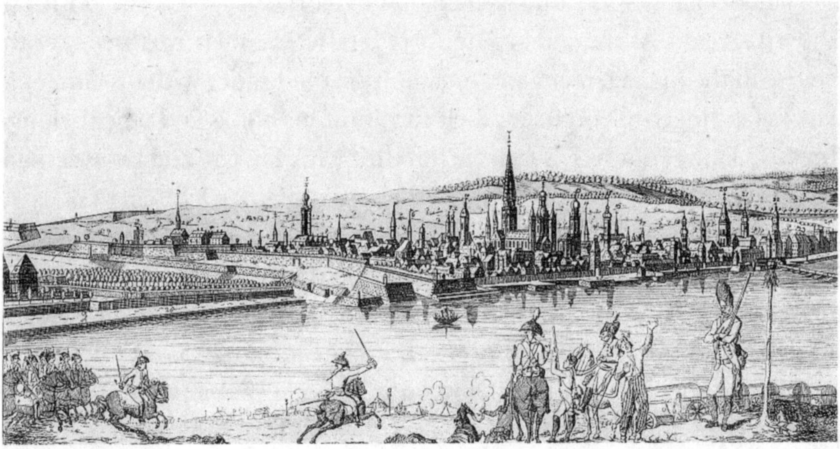

View of Mainz across the Rhine

the Electorate's Catholic Church, the elector was known for an unusual openness to other religions. Unlike other universities in Catholic states, some professors in Mainz were Protestant, and even more unusually Jewish students were admitted. But unlike Göttingen, where class boundaries were relatively fluid, Mainz remained rigid. With a large court and many courtiers, society's divisions were more distinct there – the aristocracy didn't mingle with professors, merchants, or other members of the middle classes.

When George came to inspect the library, he was disappointed. Books from a monastery and a dissolved Jesuit college, which were meant to be consolidated for the new university, were spread across three different locations in the city and stored in large piles on floors covered in dust and papers. There were no desks to work at and no storage cupboards. The windows hadn't been opened for years and some of the rarest books had been half eaten by beetle larvae. The catalogues were fragmentary and there were so many double and triple copies that it was impossible to find out how many books the library actually owned. Scanning the titles, George also realized that they were mainly books of theology. The library's benefit for professors and students, he wrote to his father-in-law, was non-existent, and the budget for new books was small. No one in the administration seemed particularly interested in its advancement. He was obliged to sort the books and compile a catalogue, but George hoped that his other duties would not be too onerous. He wanted time to think and write.

During his first visit to Mainz, he had found a spacious newly built three-storey terraced house in Neue Universitätsstrasse, not far from the university and only a fifteen-minute walk to the Rhine. Most importantly, it was next to Soemmerring's lodgings. They put up new wallpaper, Therese sewed curtains, and George had shelves made for his many books, and eight framed engravings of views of Tahiti adorned the walls. After the emotional turmoil of Göttingen, George felt much calmer and little Röschen was the joy of his life. She often sat with him at his desk and he was proud when she began to draw and scribble, watching her little hand hold the pen tightly.

Friends and acquaintances visited. The first was Wilhelm von Humboldt, a twenty-one-year-old Prussian aristocrat who was a gifted linguist and the older brother of Alexander von Humboldt.* Wilhelm had studied in Göttingen and arrived in Mainz only a few days after the Forsters. George spoke about his time in Vilnius and read from his unpublished works. He also showed Wilhelm the proposal for a book he was planning to write about explorations. Like a manual for future travellers, the book would provide suggestions as to which countries to study and which topics to focus on. It would include information about ethnographical observations, botany and geography, as well as practical tips about scientific instruments, books and useful clothing – 'it was very beautifully written,' Wilhelm said. Having read George's essay 'Something More about the Human Races', Wilhelm believed that he 'was certainly the only one who could achieve anything here. For very few have seen what he has seen, and those few, such as his father, do not have the brilliant genius, the philosophical mind'. George's intellect was expansive, his heart open, and his writing masterful. Fascinated by languages himself, Wilhelm was also impressed by George's exceptional aptitude – 'he must indeed have a special talent for languages, as he writes equally well in French, English, and German.'

Wilhelm von Humboldt also enjoyed Therese's company. A quiet and kind man, he listened when she opened her heart. When she described a man who had consoled her but had made clear that nothing could be

* To avoid confusion between the brothers, I refer to Wilhelm and Alexander von Humboldt by their first names rather than by their surname alone.

changed about her situation, he was certain it was Meyer whom he knew from Göttingen – 'that seems, I think, to be in Meyer's character,' he noted in his diary. Wilhelm admired Therese's lively spirit, erudition and strength. There was something unusual about her conviction that she was a 'completely self-sufficient being' – he found her a remarkable woman but disapproved of her wearing too much make-up. Therese flirted with him as they talked about love, friendship and marriage, warning him not to fall in love with her. That he was called Wilhelm, like Meyer, made her like him even more, she admitted. He spent four days with the Forsters in Mainz. They went for long walks along the Rhine, enjoyed congenial meals, and on a cold and clear night they went out to look at the stars.

But unlike others, Wilhelm von Humboldt noticed the pretence of it all. Therese was trying to make everybody believe that she was happy. She entertained, laughed, steered spirited discussions, but just as her make-up couldn't hide her pale skin, so her laughter couldn't hide her pain. Where she was restless and animated, George was quiet and calm. He was 'kind, gentle, clever, learned, and deeply in love with her', Wilhelm wrote to a friend in Berlin, but Therese thought her husband weak and disliked him for it – 'so she doesn't love him'.

In Mainz, George and Therese had their portraits painted, companion pieces proclaiming a unity that didn't exist. Husband and wife were both dressed in elegant and fashionable clothes. Whereas George had worn a plain grey suit in his Tischbein portrait, he now chose an elaborately embroidered colourful waistcoat with flowers and gold stitching as well as a shirt with flamboyant lace cuffs. He looked serious, a man of gravitas, affluence and social standing. Therese wore a sumptuous blue silk dress richly embroidered with flowers – a wide petticoat, her waist cinched, and the tight sleeves opening at the elbow into a wide layered lace trim. Like George's clothes, her outfit with large earrings and a matching ring exuded wealth that the Forsters didn't have. With her cleavage primly hidden by lace, and her hair carefully coiffed and tamed, her portrait conveyed the image of a conventional wife, which she certainly wasn't.

No matter how much she professed to have come to terms with her marriage, Therese was miserable. It was, as she later admitted, the 'most dreadful period of my life'. George felt rejected. 'My heart has suffered so much this year,' he admitted to his father-in-law, and Therese rebuffed him so vehemently that he gave up any hope of reconciliation. Heyne was concerned that his daughter had still not accepted her role as wife and stoically advised fresh air, walking, and no books that might stimulate imagination and emotions. Despite all this, George and Therese remained friendly and civil with each other. They lived quietly, preferring the company of a few friends to large gatherings. In the evening they talked and read together, and when they had guests Therese read aloud.

George had his best friend next door, but he also renewed his friendship with the philosopher Friedrich Heinrich Jacobi, whom he had met during his hectic tour of the German states at the end of 1778. Though Jacobi lived 130 miles away in Düsseldorf, George visited him regularly. He had never minded travelling in carriages – 'to let myself be jolted around for a day every now and then,' he joked, 'always does wonders for the bowels'. In Mainz, like in so many cities before, almost everyone liked George immediately. A Danish poet who spent a few days in town raved about him. 'With gravity on his brow, wit in his eyes and love around his lips, he captivated me completely,' he wrote, describing George as an intellectual giant and as '*cosmopolitanism* personified'.

A new acquaintance was twenty-four-year-old Ferdinand Huber, a low-ranking diplomat from Saxony at the Mainz court and a close friend of the acclaimed playwright Friedrich Schiller. An unpublished writer

Ferdinand Huber

with ambitions much larger than his talents, Huber was unhappy in Mainz. His daily work was mind-numbingly repetitive, he complained, consisting mainly of copying bureaucratic records and letters. Instead of composing plays in his spare time as he told friends, he mostly procrastinated: sorting his papers, jotting down ideas he already had noted, counting his linen, eating and gambling.

Huber made an awkward first impression. He couldn't ride or dance and became dizzy so easily that he wasn't even able to climb on a stool to reach a book on a shelf or walk down a steep hill. Perpetually unsure of himself, he compensated by peppering his conversation with endless quotations from poems while constantly referring to his friendship with Schiller. Craving intellectual stimulation and the reflected glory of famous people, Huber had keenly awaited George Forster's arrival. Nervous when they finally met, Huber was shy and clumsy but didn't give up. 'I have set a slow plan of conquest upon him,' he said, determined to be his friend because 'Forster seems to be a truly good man, full of fire and pure emotion'. The strategy worked and Huber (who was ten years younger) soon spent most of his free time in the Forster house in Neue Universitätsstrasse. George took him under his wing, encouraging him to return to his literary ambitions.

George Forster had brought him back to life, Huber told Schiller at the end of December 1788, like rain falling on a withering plant. His presence in Mainz changed everything. 'Forster is one of the best people I know,' Huber continued, he was uncorrupted, unprejudiced, and combined a good heart with strong intellect. Like Wilhelm von Humboldt, Huber also admired Therese – 'she has an excellent mind, and her great fondness for caprices makes her captivating'. There was never a boring moment with her.

George worked hard. He tried to bring order to the university library but also wrote many book reviews, translated travel accounts, and compiled a collection of his previous work which included 'Cook, the Discoverer' and *About the Breadfruit*. Lacking time to write his own books, he often used his reviews, and the prefaces and annotations of translations – as previously with 'Cook, the Discoverer' – to present his own ideas. He had been commissioned, for instance, to translate an account of a shipwrecked English merchant ship at one of the Palau islands in the western Pacific Ocean, and in its introduction he returned to the widely held prejudice that Europeans were superior to others. The idea had no foundation in reality, he argued, because the indigenous people of Palau had treated the marooned English crew with kindness and hospitality, helping them build a new ship. They had dignity and humanity, but they were not examples of Rousseau's happy, peaceful savage because they had also been at war with their neighbours. One couldn't judge a nation's virtue by the physical appearance or the level of education, George insisted, 'man is neither good nor evil by nature; but the circumstances into which fate places him, from his very earliest beginnings, can make anything of him.' This was one of the convictions that had defined his thinking and interests from earliest adulthood.

His work was so much respected that even these introductions were read with interest by scholars and the general public alike. 'The audience is used to eagerly devouring everything that comes from the pen of the famous world traveller,' an enthusiastic reviewer declared in a leading literary journal. George Forster was a 'great storyteller,' wrote another, while a third hailed him as a 'glorious writer'. Goethe thought it was always a 'special pleasure' to read what George had written, and Lichtenberg wrote from Göttingen 'what I so greatly admire in your letters and essays, the straight, consistently strong line – I recognize it, and it delights me as much as the gait of a beautiful girl'. Schiller didn't always agree with George, but he approved of his writings and published some of his pieces in the literary magazine he edited. 'Even his most untenable opinions are presented with such elegance and liveliness,' Schiller told Huber, 'which makes reading them an exceptional joy.'

Money remained tight and George had to publish as much as he could. Just as in Vilnius he often rose before sunrise and began to write at 5 a.m. Never able to sit still, he paced up and down his study, sitting down, getting up to think, pulling out a book, sitting down to write, pacing again. He felt 'shackled to the quill as in a galley', frustrated that he had so little time to compose his own essays and books. The long hours at his desk took their toll and George hated the cold German

A caricature of George Forster as an overworked translator. There are many indications that it was him: the title of the open book 'a new Voyage 1775', Bailey's English–German dictionary, the South Pacific objects on the wall and the first sentence of the manuscript he's writing is 'from the English'

winters, heating his study to the point that it was as warm as a hothouse for tropical plants. He was almost imprisoned there, he told Jacobi, and 'my head is empty, I have nothing more of my own to say of the world.' If only he could travel again and see the world with his own eyes, because 'the paltry twenty-four *letters* are not enough'.

He was thirty-four, yet despite the public acclaim George still doubted his abilities and worried that the best part of his life was over. Others seemed to find it easy to constantly come up with something new, but he worried that he might just be mediocre and questioned what he had really achieved. 'There are people,' he wrote to Jacobi, 'who have ideas with a life on their own – ideas that move of their own accord in the mind, uninvited, crossing paths, colliding, bumping, running into each other, uniting and hatching new ideas.' How he wished he could think like that. 'My ideas lack this agility; when I need them, I must summon them, laboriously, with tremendous effort, tease them out of their hiding places, and when at last I want to string them together, they show no affection for each other because they have a natural resistance that seems insurmountable – they refuse to unite and remain barren and unproductive.'

'What do you think of the revolution in France?' George wrote on 30 July 1789 to his father-in-law. With Mainz close to the French border, the *Privilegierte Mainzer Zeitung* had been the first German newspaper to report what was happening in Paris. On 12 July the Paris correspondent wrote that thousands of people had taken to the streets, supported by defected and armed soldiers. For two days and nights drums and musket shots had echoed through the city. As their numbers increased, so did the rioting. A large grain depot was plundered, as well as the Hôtel des Invalides – the military hospital which not only housed injured soldiers and veterans but also some 30,000 muskets and several cannons. '36,000 citizens banded together,' George could read in the *Privilegierte Mainzer Zeitung*, 'and attacked the patrols, murdering anyone who resisted.' On 14 July they had stormed the Bastille, the Parisian prison that symbolized the authority of the French king. The numbers were exaggerated, but the result wasn't – Paris was in the hands of the French people, not Louis XVI.

Troubles had been simmering in France long before the first stones were thrown or barricades built. Over the past four decades, ordinary men and women had become disillusioned with the monarchy and aristocracy. In bustling cafés and on the grounds of the Palais-Royal – where George had gone shopping during his visit in 1777 – people dissected the queen's supposed affairs and seemingly insatiable appetite for luxuries with as much fervour as the rising food prices and embezzlement by ministers. They shouted, interrupted, agreed, applauded, took sides, and expressed outrage – 'every person down to domestic servants and water carriers is involved in debating,' one observer noted. Year after year, each scandal, political failure, or display of arbitrary power had left its mark, slowly shaping public opinion and steadily undermining royal

Storming of the Bastille

authority. It was, as the same commentator described, like a 'murmur' echoing through Paris.

During these decades Enlightenment ideas such as natural rights, liberty and equality took hold. These were not just the dreams of philosophers in their studies, but topics discussed by many in salons and cafés. Parisians were easily incited and spilled into the streets to protest – the city was no stranger to riots, known as *émotions populaires*, collective outpourings of feeling that often erupted into violence. The events of 14 July didn't arise overnight but had gradually been building up over the years.

Amid this growing tension, France was grappling with an ongoing economic crisis that had pushed the country to the verge of financial collapse. The monarchy's coffers were drained by years of war and royal extravagance, yet the burden of taxation fell not on the nobility or clergy – who were largely exempt – but on the backs of the common people. A series of catastrophic harvests and soaring bread prices plunged families into hunger. Then came the winter of 1788–9, the coldest in living memory when the thermometer plummeted to –23° Celsius. Fires went out, food grew scarce, and people became destitute.

In 1788, when the *parlement** of Paris – a powerful judicial body made up almost entirely of nobles – had refused to authorize new taxes without the consent of the Estates General, which had not met since 1614, it set off a chain of events the king could no longer control. The structure of the Estates General – three chambers for Nobles, Clergy and the Third Estate – was, however, a relic of a past that didn't reflect France's social reality. 98 per cent of the population – including peasants, workers, craftsmen, tradespeople and the rising bourgeoisie – were nominally represented by the Third Estate, but as each chamber had an equal vote, the voices of the vast majority were easily drowned out by those of the privileged.†

And so, when the Estates General had convened in Versailles in May 1789, the old choreography unravelled. The Third Estate demanded more delegates, and crucially that votes be counted by head, not by estate to ensure fairer representation. When they were rebuffed, they did something that would have been unthinkable in 1614. On 17 June 1789 they took matters into their own hands, declaring themselves the National Assembly, a body that, they stressed, held the true sovereignty of the nation rather than the king. 'Voilà, the word Estates General abolished,' one observer commented, 'that is much more important than you might think. In changing words, one changes ideas; and in changing ideas, one changes things.' Three days later, after being locked out of their meeting hall by the king's command, the delegates gathered in a nearby indoor tennis court and swore an oath 'never to be separated until we have formed a solid and equitable Constitution'. The Tennis Court Oath, as it would come to be known, reverberated across France. Only thirteen years earlier, on the other side of the Atlantic, the American colonists had proven that it was possible to challenge a king and to free a nation of its despotic shackles. And so could the French.

News raced from Versailles to Paris as spectators hurried home to report on the proceedings. There were also rumours of a looming military coup, of the king paying saboteurs to ruin the next harvest,

* The *parlement* – not to be confused with the modern term 'parliament' – was a court of appeal which had to give assent to laws and edicts issued by the king.

† Even within the Third Estate, representation was skewed, with a large proportion of the delegates being lawyers, notaries and magistrates.

of plans for an engineered famine. By late June, thousands of Parisians gathered daily in the gardens of the Palais-Royal to listen to fresh dispatches from Versailles and discuss feverish speculations, including claims that the First Estate was plotting to assassinate delegates from the Third Estate. The atmosphere became increasingly charged until it ignited on 12 July when word spread that the king had dismissed Jacques Necker, the Finance Minister seen as being sympathetic to the Third Estate. Parisians took to the streets. Two days later, the Bastille was stormed. Almost one hundred people died and its governor was beaten to death, his head paraded through Paris on a pike.

The reports that arrived in Mainz about what was happening in France were perplexing and often contradictory: one article in the *Privilegierte Mainzer Zeitung* stated that Paris had been burned to ashes and there were varying reports about the king's reduced role and powers. One dispatch claimed that order had been apparently restored but was followed by the news of more murders and 200,000 armed citizens. Even the Paris correspondent of the *Privilegierte Mainzer Zeitung* seemed confused. On 22 July he feared the beginnings of a civil war, but a week later he proudly announced that 'the English have worked for centuries on their liberty, while we haven't even worked for eight days', only to report two days later the brutal lynching of one of the king's ministers by the Paris mob. George and his circle could think of nothing else. It was like watching the unfolding of a gripping drama on stage, Huber explained to a friend nine days after the storming of the Bastille.

When the French abolished the feudal system and the privileges of clergy and aristocracy on the night of 4/5 August, an enthusiastic George wrote to Heyne 'what a session it was of the French National Assembly!' Then, on 26 August, the new French Parliament adopted the *Declaration of the Man and of the Citizen*.* Already two weeks earlier George had been able to read the draft text printed in the *Privilegierte Mainzer Zeitung*. The *Declaration*'s first article proclaimed 'Men are born and remain free and

* The first draft of the *Declaration of the Rights of Man and of the Citizen* was written by the Marquis de Lafayette with the help of Thomas Jefferson and was presented to the National Assembly on 11 July 1789. After that, a committee of deputies that included Abbé Sieyès, Mirabeau and Talleyrand revised it extensively before it was adopted.

equal in rights. Social distinctions may be based only on considerations of the common good.' After centuries of rule by despotic monarchs, the French had asserted the individual's right to liberty, property and freedom of speech, and laws to protect them, enshrining the ideals of the Enlightenment. Sovereignty, the *Declaration* decreed, resided in the Nation, for 'no body, no individual may exercise any authority which does not proceed directly from the nation'. Although France was still a monarchy, the absolute rule of King Louis XVI was over and the French nobility had lost its power. The *Ancien Régime* had collapsed. In an essay that autumn George wrote that 'France is shaking off its death slumber and will be free'.

Everyone looked to France. Direct reports came early in September 1789, seven weeks after the storming of the Bastille, when Wilhelm von Humboldt arrived in Mainz with his former tutor, Joachim Heinrich Campe. The two men had just spent more than three weeks in Paris where they had met revolutionaries, visited the sites of the revolution, and witnessed the sessions of the National Assembly. 'The Bastille lies in ruins,' Wilhelm wrote in his diary on 9 August, after watching how hundreds of people removed brick by brick from what he called this 'bulwark of despotism'. They saw girls hanging flower bouquets on soldiers' bayonets and heard young boys speak of freedom and civic rights – 'even as a mere spectator, you feel here, in all your senses, in all your powers and abilities – I don't know how – at once elevated and ennobled'. It was like disappearing into an ocean of humanity, Wilhelm said, 'one gets swept away in the current so much that one feels like a drop in that ocean. I like that.'

Campe left Mainz that same day, but Wilhelm stayed for more than two weeks with the Forsters. Heavily pregnant with her second child, Therese was glad to see him and hear his news. 'When will other nations begin to follow such an example,' Wilhelm had already written to George from Paris. What had happened in France was nothing less than a revolution of ideas and proof of the power of philosophy. 'It's wonderful to see,' George wrote to his father-in-law, 'what philosophy has put into people's minds and then brought to fruition in the state.' Wilhelm and George couldn't stop talking. Those days together in Mainz 'were perhaps the happiest of my entire life,' Wilhelm von Humboldt later said, 'there are few other people with whom I feel such deep understanding as I do with you . . . you cannot know how much I admire the fruitful abundance of ideas that come to you with every subject, the vivid clarity with which you present them.'

No one in Europe was unaffected by the French Revolution, its echo reverberated across borders and classes. The French had given themselves a voice, and people from across Europe travelled to Paris to see how this new reality was built. The rallying cries of the revolution – liberty, equality and fraternity – promised a different future. Students in German cities shouted 'Vive la liberté!', poets wrote poems in celebration of the revolution, and philosophers saw the principles of the Enlightenment codified into a new state. After reading the *Declaration of the Rights of Man*, Kant declared, 'I have seen the glory of the world'. Nineteen-year-old Wilhelm Hegel, long before he shaped modern philosophy, sang the *Marseillaise* and secretly read French newspapers, hailing the French Revolution as the 'dawn of freedom'.

But many others feared the contagious power of the French ideas. Rulers of the German states that constituted the Holy Roman Empire were deeply worried, as were those who dreaded the collapse of the political order, foreseeing chaos and anarchy. French pamphlets were soon forbidden and private letters were opened. In England, the conservative statesman and philosopher Edmund Burke warned against 'pulling down an edifice, which has answered in any tolerable degree for ages the common purposes of society', while reactionary voices in the German states feared that the French were demolishing the very pillars of society.

George's own political beliefs were rooted in his experiences as a ten-year-old boy in Russia, when he had been moved to hear from the impoverished German settlers along the Volga how the governor in Saratov had tyrannized them to line his pockets. A decade later, in Tahiti, he had spoken of revolutions as a 'natural circle of human affairs', comparing the overweight man he had seen being hand-fed by a woman to a European aristocrat who exploited others. He regarded Tahitian society as relatively egalitarian but warned that some of the islanders would eventually revolt against grievances – a 'proper sense of the general rights of mankind awakening in them, will bring on a revolution'. After his return from the voyage of the *Resolution*, George had supported the American revolutionaries during the War of Independence, and he esteemed Benjamin Franklin so much that he kept his portrait in his room.

When he had lived in Kassel, George criticized the Landgrave for selling his soldiers as mercenaries to the English in their fight against the United States. And later, in Vilnius, he had seen the detrimental effects of despotism and the feudal system, noting that the Polish clergy and aristocracy treated peasants like slaves or cattle. So, while many German thinkers welcomed the French Revolution, George's global perspective was unique. Freedom and equality had always been important concepts for him, but they now became reality, only seventy miles from the Rhine at the French border.

George didn't yet believe that the German states needed a revolution – reforms certainly, but not a radical upheaval – though his writings became more overtly political. In September 1789, while Wilhelm von Humboldt stayed with them, George worked 'On Proselytism', an essay in which he equated religious and political freedom. If rulers or states shackled their citizens' beliefs, he warned, 'then all free discussion will come to an end'. Truth and the ability to make moral choices would disappear. 'To be free, means to be human,' he declared. 'Let everyone *believe* as little or as much as they can,' he wrote to Jacobi, 'and let everyone speak freely and without fear what they believe.'

The French Revolution also made George think about a writer's impact. If a popular book influenced readers' thinking, didn't that affect society at large? He had always emphasized the supreme importance of freedom – 'therefore let us not stop shouting: freedom, freedom, boundless freedom in everything,' he had written earlier that year to Jacobi – and perhaps he could make a difference. He was no Hercules, but he could fight with his pen. 'A hundred thousand people, who could and should be happy, are miserable,' he had told Therese during their courtship, 'but if I can make fifty, twenty, ten, or even *one* happier than they would have been without me; should I refrain from doing so because I can't relieve the wretchedness of the hundred thousand?'

In his correspondence with Jacobi, George's tone now became impatient. What was the point of metaphysics at times like these: 'apart from its usefulness in sharpening the faculties of the mind, it seems to be quite dispensable in life!' Philosophers who were too certain about their own insights were mistaken – 'I've never liked despotism, not even one that was based on *generally valid principles*.' George had always bought and borrowed books, but in the months after the revolution he ordered and read even more. Parcels flooded in from friends and publishers across the German states and from abroad. Adam Smith's arguments in *Theory of Moral Sentiments* that humans are social creatures guided by empathy resonated with his own ideas. Our self-interest, Smith wrote, was restrained by our feelings for others, for our morality is based not on reason but on our nature as social beings. On the other hand, George considered Edmund Burke's recently published *Reflections on the Revolution in France* – which condemned the tumultuous events in France – a terrible book full of 'insipid, pedantic and unsatisfying drivel'.

George was also once again embroiled in a public debate about race. This time his opponent was Christoph Meiners, a respected Göttingen historian who believed that there were two separate races: white people, who were beautiful and virtuous; and dark-skinned people ('half-humans') who were repulsive and debased. Meiners published widely and regularly, using his racist ideas of what he believed to be the 'natural inequality' of humankind to justify slavery. 'For a long time, nothing has outraged me like this,' George told Heyne in September 1789.

Already three years earlier, George had contested Kant's racial theory with his 'Something More about the Human Races' but had long since abandoned the notion of *polygenesis* – the theory of multiple, independent origins of humankind. He had quickly grown troubled with the concept of separate species and Meiners' publications proved how easily it could serve as justification for a hierarchy of humankind and for racist denigrations. This hypothesis of two types of humans – those who were apparently 'morally and physically perfect, and those who were ugly by nature and evil by inclination' – was absurd, George now wrote to Jacobi, adding he could just as easily paint a hideous portrait of Europeans. 'If one were to collect characteristic traits of European peoples from travel writers and historians,' he wrote in a long review of Meiners' work, 'would it not be possible to compose an abhorrent picture of superstition and stupidity, of greed and selfishness, of clumsiness and obstinacy, of lust, excess, extravagance, insensitivity and malice?' Why even try to divide humankind into 'white, black, yellow, copper-red – who thinks nowadays in such outdated concepts?'

'Instead of merely noting similarities and differences, like Mr. M. does, and examining all peoples a hundred or more times to tell us where this or that vice (by European standards) is particularly noticeable,' he wrote in his review, 'it would have been fairer to consider each nation on its own, to describe it in all its aspects, and carefully study how it fits into the place it occupies on Earth.' Point by point, George dismantled Meiners' arguments, filling two entire issues of the *Allgemeine Literatur Zeitung*, Germany's most important literary journal. It was wrong to apply ranking or hierarchy. To be a good or great person, he concluded, 'is not bound to any particular place on Earth or to a privileged tribe'. That the editors of the *Allgemeine Literatur Zeitung* decided to give George Forster such an unusual amount of space showed how highly he was regarded.

He also began to select books on slavery to review, so that he could either eviscerate or support their arguments. He reviewed *Africa and the African People* by a French pro-slavery commercial agent in Senegal. Counter to the book's portrayal of Africans as unable even to grasp the value of freedom, George argued that there were plenty of examples of their abilities and intellect. On the other hand, in a review of a book about the United States by the French revolutionary and abolitionist Jacques Pierre Brissot, George agreed with the author and denounced slavery as inhuman, unnatural and truly abominable – 'there is no difference ... in a black and a white head'.

For George, the discussion of race was deeply political. As he followed the fast-moving events in France, he also applied his ideas about humankind's equality to European societies. 'We have, after all, examples of slavery in abundance which teach us how deeply humanity can be degraded, even in our own society, and how greatly the power of thought can be stifled.' That European princes insisted on 'hereditary differences' between themselves and the so-called lower classes, he said, was just as bizarre as Meiners' belief in the inferiority of some races. In *A Voyage Round the World*, George had written that 'the same instincts are active in the slave and the prince' – he didn't mean that everybody was the same but that everybody should have the same rights.

On 21 November 1789, Therese gave birth to another daughter, Clara. It had been a difficult pregnancy in which Therese had talked openly about her reluctance to have another child. Röschen had grown into a serious three-year-old with blond hair and brown eyes, while Clara was an excitable creature with brown hair – 'a little blue-eyed mercurial imp', as Therese said six months after her birth, driven by an 'all-encompassing recklessness'. Unlike other middle-class parents, who tucked children away in a nursery with a maid or governess, Therese and George made their girls part of their daily life. Röschen ran around the house and visitors found themselves playing with her. Wilhelm von Humboldt let her ride on his legs until he was exhausted. 'Röschen, the foot is tired,' he said, but she laughed and kissed his foot – 'now it's no longer tired' – and continued riding.

It gave him pleasure to see his loved ones happy and near him, George told his father-in-law in January 1790, but he was still overworked. Deadlines loomed and he disliked spending his days in the library, where he had to share a table with colleagues who drank so much in the evenings that they stank the next morning. He missed travelling. In need of a break and fresh inspiration, he decided to visit England – 'this homeland of his mind and heart' as Therese described it – to renew old friendships in London. Taking it slowly, he would travel through the Netherlands to see towns, meet people, visit galleries, and inspect natural-history collections on his way. Most importantly, it was time to see what was happening in revolutionary France.

19

'As if I carry the world within me'

Travels: 1790

Wilhelm von Humboldt's younger brother Alexander had time and money, and when George suggested to travel to England, the Netherlands and France, he immediately agreed. It would be a trip that changed Alexander von Humboldt's life. Like George, he had also found solace in nature as a boy, sketching and collecting plants and animals. Unlike his calmer older brother, he was impatient and unpredictable. While Wilhelm had focused on his studies, Alexander dreamed of adventures and expeditions. Already as a boy he had read about Cook's voyages and had been excited to meet the great explorer George Forster, even dedicating his first book to him. Following in the footsteps of his brother, the twenty-year-old

Alexander von Humboldt

had also studied in Göttingen and had stayed with the Forsters in Mainz for a few days the previous autumn. George was fond of the younger man, who was driven by a deep-seated curiosity and a fascination for the natural sciences. Fifteen years older, George became a mentor to Alexander von Humboldt, who would later say that it was their time together that had ignited his longing for his own expedition to South America in 1799.

Equipped with letters of recommendation and the elector's permission to depart, George left Mainz on 25 March 1790, leaving behind Therese with three-year-old Röschen and four-month-old Clara.

Sailing north-west along the Rhine, Alexander and George sat on deck, watching the villages, vineyards and fields pass by. Alexander begged for stories from the South Pacific and they discussed islands and islanders, expeditions, botany, geology and much more. In the evenings George filled his diary and composed long letters to Therese, describing everything they had seen but also declaring his deep and continuing love for her. 'Dearest, most loving and adored soul!' he wrote, 'I think of you a thousand times a day.'

Stopping at the cities along the river, they examined the natural-history collections in Bonn, the unfinished cathedral in Cologne, and the art gallery in Düsseldorf which was filled with Flemish, Dutch and Italian art. In Düsseldorf they also visited Jacobi, who welcomed them with open arms. George was overjoyed to spend time with his old friend. 'When I carry a great and good person in my heart and mind,' he told Jacobi afterwards, 'it feels as if I carry the world within me.'

From Düsseldorf they continued their travels in a stagecoach and George entertained himself by chatting with their fellow passengers: a miserly French aristocrat and his maid; an amusing engraver from Flanders who within half an hour had revealed his entire family history, financial circumstances and health problems while cradling a pot with a special tincture he needed for his engravings; and a young Irish Franciscan monk who couldn't believe that he was travelling with the celebrated George Forster 'about whom he had heard and read so much in Ireland'.

George enjoyed Alexander's company, even if the young man sometimes slept too much. 'Once Humboldt is in bed, I can't get him back out again,' George wrote to Therese, and he had never met anyone who could so easily fall asleep in a rattling carriage – but when Alexander was awake, he noticed more than someone who never slept. With his travel companion nodding off, George's thoughts flew to his wife and 'I dream myself back into the life I once lived with you.'

As they rolled through the German territories and then west into the Austrian Netherlands,* George was surprised how openly the people here talked about revolutions and politics. 'The multitude of ideas now circulating,' he noted, 'would have caused quite a stir just ten years ago.' Here, demonstrations against the rule of the emperor had grown into a full-blown revolution and resulted in the declaration of an independent Belgium in 1789. But unlike France, the short-lived 'United States of Belgium' were ruled by conservative Catholics. Just when George and Alexander arrived in Brussels, the ruling party had rejected the creation of a truly representative national assembly with the words 'we don't want to be free'. George was disappointed but not surprised, for it was religion – not political convictions – that had been the driving force of this revolution and ultimately caused its failure.

From Brussels, they crossed briefly into France on 12 April, chasing rumours of a counter-revolution in Lille. France was in flames, people said, warning George not to go. 'We assured them that our aim was simply to watch the spectacle of great events,' George drily noted. But when they arrived in Lille all seemed normal – the shops were open and people went about their business, only the theatre was closed. As so often the newspapers had exaggerated. 'Good heavens!' he wrote to Therese, 'we couldn't even catch so much as a little skirmish in Lille.'

Paris, some 140 miles south of Lille, would have to wait, as they had decided to visit the French capital on their return journey – saving the most exciting bit for last. First they would continue through the Netherlands and then on to England. From Lille they went north to the coast on their way to Antwerp, Rotterdam and Amsterdam. Seeing the beach and the pounding waves, George felt transported back to the

* The southern region of the Netherlands (which later became Belgium and Luxembourg) was controlled by Austria. The northern part was the Dutch Republic – a confederation of several provinces which gained their independence from Spain in the late sixteenth century after a long-drawn-out war.

Resolution – 'those three years I spent on the ocean, and which shaped my entire life'. But the stormy sea was also a political metaphor. Each person was like an individual wave, appearing and disappearing, 'while the whole continues its course in immutable unity'.

They now travelled on barges along canals which were lined with tall poplars, elm trees and willows. Windmills turned gracefully on green fields and the horse-drawn barges were much more comfortable than bumping along in carriages. It was so smooth that George had time to write letters and fill the pages of his diary. He observed nature, culture and people. When they saw a young woman dressed in traditional costume which included a pointed white bonnet with turned-up flaps over the ears, he quipped that had an explorer seen her on a tropical island, 'he would have described her barbaric headdress and made a drawing of it; only we don't realize how similar we Europeans are to the savages.'

From Brussels they had already sent their luggage to Antwerp so that they could travel lightly with just a small bag to avoid the constant and protracted custom inspections at every town. By the time they were reunited with their trunks, they were in urgent need of a change of clothes, George wrote to Therese, because 'we both looked rather slovenly'. Doors

Canal and windmills near The Hague

seemed magically to open when George Forster arrived and they met so many people that it was almost too much. 'Forster's name, which sparks widespread interest,' Alexander wrote to a friend, 'secured us access to all the important people.'

There was so much to see and do: paintings in Antwerp – Rembrandt, Rubens, Correggio, Van Dyck – a night on the luxurious yacht belonging to the mayor of The Hague and dinner with the English ambassador. It was obvious, George said, 'that I'm much paraded about, largely out of curiosity'. They received free tickets for the theatre and George made fun about the overacting actors – if the Dutch were honest 'they would admit that they have learned to gesticulate from windmills'. They saw the skeleton of an orangutan, visited the botanical garden in Leiden and admired the flamboyant display of tulips in Haarlem.

But all this fame felt hollow. 'I would trade the veneration from the entire world for one more spark of love,' he told Therese at the end of April. Surrounded by all the hustle and bustle, there were moments when this carousel of activities and sights seemed to suddenly turn silent and George felt as if he had stepped off. As the world raced by, he became quiet and thought of his girls, Therese and his marriage – 'the past, present, and future of my circumstances' – but then he pulled himself together, smiled and met yet more people.

In The Hague, George ran into a colleague from Mainz who told him that Therese had inoculated Röschen against smallpox. George was anxious and taken aback that his wife had made such a decision without consulting him. Since the early eighteenth century, European physicians (following the lead from China and the Middle East) had removed pus or scabs from a pustule of an infected person and rubbed it into a small skin incision of the person to be inoculated. Instead of being infected by air with the virus moving through the respiratory tract before spreading through the rest of the body, the hope was that an infection through the skin was milder and more localized – while at the same time giving immunization against the smallpox virus. Though not an unusual procedure any more, it was dangerous and many children died.

There was more that Therese was concealing. She had also embarked on an affair with George's friend the Saxon diplomat Ferdinand Huber.

That was not what George had in mind when he had ended one of the letters to his wife with: 'and may you bring joy to everyone around you'. Ten years younger than George, Huber was in his mid-twenties and the same age as Therese. Since the Forsters had moved to Mainz, one and a half years previously, Huber had spent every free minute in their house. Every morning during the warmer months, he and George would swim in the Rhine, before having breakfast and working together. But with George away, Huber had sought other diversions.

Unaware of what was going on at home, George continued to dispatch long letters to Therese. 'We shall be happy, my dear wife,' George wrote with impeccably bad timing, 'my soul can sense and foretell it.' Just as he was starting to believe again in their future, Therese was beginning a new life with Huber. As George opened his heart, Therese shuttered hers. In light of their marital problems and Therese's propensity for flirtation and entanglement, it had probably been naïve of him to be away for so long.

On 5 May 1790, six weeks after they had left Mainz, George Forster and Alexander von Humboldt boarded a ship on the Dutch coast and sailed to England. In London, he stayed with his sister Virginia who had remained there when her parents and younger siblings had left for Halle ten years previously. Now in her early thirties, Virginia was married to a German pastor who preached at the Royal German Chapel at St James's Palace and had tutored King George III's daughters. George was glad to see his sister and her children but was tortured by her husband's constant Bible references and court gossip. 'I wasted the first fourteen days, and my good mood along with them,' he wrote to Jacobi, 'at my brother-in-law's, who is a clergyman of the most common sort.' But the whole Forster family had been excited when they heard about George's trip to England. His mother wanted to know everything about her daughter and grandchildren, and Reinhold had of course dashed off a long to-do list for his son.

In London, George and Alexander saw William Hodges, the artist on board the *Resolution*, and met Captain William Bligh, who had finally arrived in Britain in March 1790, following the mutiny on the *Bounty*. They also visited the astronomer William Herschel just outside London to see his giant forty-foot telescope and rushed from one dinner to the next. Their days were packed. Reinhold had asked his son to buy books, rocks and minerals as well as obtain some money for him from the English government – 'naturally You will do me the favour to urge *and* negociate'. He also wanted him to speak to England's leading ornithologist, John Latham, who had consulted George's bird drawings that Joseph Banks had bought.* Astonishingly, Reinhold still referred to them as 'our drawings'. Latham had promised a copy of his book but had failed to dispatch it. 'Be so kind,' Reinhold wrote to his son, as 'to clear this affair up'.

They saw Banks, who had by now become the most influential scientist in England – confidant of King George III, nominal director of the royal botanic garden at Kew and President of the Royal Society. Polite, yet cold and distant, Banks was still waiting for Reinhold to pay back the money he had lent him more than ten years previously and had no intention of assisting his son.

If George could only convince an English bookseller to commission a book about South Pacific plants, he might make some money and re-establish himself in the English-speaking publishing market. But no one was interested. 'Fear of a man like Sir Joseph Banks, who believes he has the monopoly on South Sea plants,' he told Jacobi, 'held them back.' It was common knowledge, George said, that Banks hated everybody who knew anything about the South Pacific. It didn't help that people remembered the quarrelsome Reinhold Forster – 'for some of the odium spreads from the father to the son,' George told his father-in-law.

Unaware that Huber was amusing himself with his wife in Mainz, George wrote warmly to him from London: 'May the good spirit of my Therese, whose benevolent influence you now enjoy, be your protection, my dear friend!' At least Soemmerring missed him. 'Your absence,' Soemmerring wrote from Mainz, 'makes me sleepy and drowsy and completely

* In the 1780s, Latham had published *A General Synopsis of Birds*, the first systematic attempt in England to describe and illustrate birds from around the world, including many collected during the Cook voyages. The book Reinhold was referring to was Latham's *Index Ornithologicus* in which he provided scientific binominal names for all the birds he had previously described. Latham didn't travel himself but relied on specimens and drawings from others, including those from the Forsters.

uninterested in anything' – he was looking forward to George's return in order to feel energized again. George was also relieved when Soemmerring sent news about Röschen. She was doing well after the inoculation, the infection had been very mild, and no scars would be left.

After a busy month in London, George Forster and Alexander von Humboldt set off for Bath, Bristol and Birmingham. Wherever George went, he carried his journal and pencil, scribbling notes in narrow lines, filling the pages. As the post-chaises rolled through the English countryside, passengers from all walks of life boarded. There was an elegant lady who, upon taking off her hat, shook out her blond curls for so long that the entire carriage filled with her strong and sweet perfume, and a farmer's wife who shouted out the names of all the local farmers she knew whenever the carriage passed a field. Some passengers were quiet, others talked incessantly. 'Bath is the most boring town in the world,' one began, before launching into a long disquisition about England's most fashionable spa town, while another couldn't stop praising Gloucestershire cheese. Some tried to sleep, while others annoyed everyone by constantly opening and closing the window. Rattling along bumpy roads for many hours a day, thrown against his fellow passengers, George made the most of these long journeys and talked to everybody. Just as he had observed the indigenous people during the *Resolution* voyage, he interrogated his fellow passengers about customs and manners.

In Birmingham, they inspected the innovative Soho Manufactory and Mint where a thousand workers mass-produced buttons, coins and other metal objects. This was at the heart of the Industrial Revolution, but George wasn't interested in steam engines and increased productivity. He saw the people and observed 'how much the labour of certain mechanical arts dulls the soul'. He found it strange that a city such as Birmingham, with 60,000 inhabitants, wasn't allowed a representative in Parliament in Westminster.* They didn't just visit English cities but

* The electoral system in Britain was outdated and had no proportional representation – small villages with few eligible voters could send an MP to Parliament but large and fast-growing cities such as Birmingham or Manchester couldn't. Changing that wouldn't begin for more than 40 years with the Reform Act of 1832.

Peak District in Derbyshire

also popular gardens – the design of one was so formal that George compared it to a lady squeezed into an opulent ballgown and corset, while another was planted so naturally that it reminded him of a woman in a negligee who needed no make-up to be beautiful.

At one stop somewhere between Birmingham and Derbyshire, so many people boarded that George offered to sit outside the carriage at the back on a narrow seat. The view was better there, although he had to hold tight to a small metal rod that was fixed to the side like a low railing. He tried to wedge his feet between the carriage and the seat for some stability, but the bench was set high and had no cushions. With his slight body bouncing up and down, he felt every pothole. When they finally arrived at the next stop, he was relieved to step off the carriage and eager to explore Derbyshire. As they walked through forests and the high moors of the Peak District, the joy of nature filled George's diary pages. There was magic in nature, he wrote, and everybody could feel it, even if they didn't understand the workings of the natural world. 'I've had the happiest journey of my life,' Alexander von Humboldt wrote to a friend as the English part of their trip came to an end, 'Forster's personal qualities and his name have been infinitely advantageous to me'.

After almost two months in England, the travel companions left for France on 29 June 1790, and crossed the Channel from Dover to Calais. As the stagecoach clattered along French country lanes and through villages, their fellow passengers opened the windows and shouted 'Vive la Nation!' George was astonished to hear ordinary people openly talking about their rights and liberties.

None of the letters that George wrote to Therese from France or any of his diary entries from those days have survived, so we don't know if he visited some of his old acquaintances, but they arrived in Paris on 1 July, just before the celebrations of the first anniversary of the storming of the Bastille. The revolutionaries had decided to stage the festivities on the Champ de Mars, where Louis XVI's soldiers had once paraded. They wanted to build the largest amphitheatre in the world, and this

Volunteers building the amphitheatre at the Champ de Mars in Paris in preparation for the first anniversary of the storming of the Bastille in July 1790

vast open space – south of the Seine on the western outskirts of Paris – was the perfect location. But with time running out, an urgent call went out for volunteers to help. More than 200,000 people carted sand, gravel and soil to build the massive tiered earthen stands to seat the audience.

George and Alexander joined in for a day. It was electrifying to see how people from all classes and backgrounds – young and old, men and women, farmers with floppy hats and aristocrats in embroidered waistcoats, nuns and monks, maids in aprons, and scholars who had left their books on desks at home – had come to help. They were working side by side in a 'frenzy of freedom', George later wrote. As he shovelled sand, he watched shopkeepers, actors, chimney sweepers, dukes, artists, carpenters, labourers and students arriving arm in arm, often singing, with spades on their shoulders. As if this wasn't already a singular sight, suddenly Louis XVI appeared in the crowd without his guards, taking a shovel and filling a wheelbarrow with sand. Everybody was clapping – the king was one of them. 'To be human was the glorious pride of twenty-five million people,' George said, 'the first and last goal of their liberation.' France was becoming a 'Menschenrepublik', a republic based on the idea of humanity. Until this visit to Paris, the French Revolution had been a dramatic yet still abstract event for George, but to see the enthusiasm of the people, he now wrote to his father-in-law, was deeply moving.

They left the French capital on 6 July because George had already overstayed his leave by a couple of weeks, and arrived five days later in Mainz, after almost four months of travelling.

It was not the homecoming George had expected. Since parting from Meyer, Therese had been dejected, but after Clara's birth in November 1789, George had begun to hope again. They were a family, and their baby daughter was proof. During his travels, it had been easier to imagine a harmonious marriage – he had painted himself into her heart again – but shortly after his return from France, George discovered Therese's affair with Huber. This wasn't just a passionate interlude. Therese was in love with Huber, and Huber with her. How long had she lied to him? Why had she fallen for Huber at all? He was soft-spoken and slightly awkward, exactly the opposite of Meyer, who had wooed her with his swagger and dramatic declarations of love. Cerebral and shy,

Huber didn't stand out, but perhaps that was his attraction. Therese could shine and sparkle against his bashfulness. He was, Therese later wrote, 'a person who understood me completely, who accepted me completely'.

By mid-September, two months after his return, George told Jacobi that a 'grievous domestic matter is now resolved'. How exactly is not clear. There were fights and tears, but Therese didn't break up with Huber – he remained in their life, not only as her lover, but also assisted George with his translations. By early November, Huber had even moved into their house, supposedly as a lodger. Once again, George accepted that there were three people in his marriage.

Concentrating on work, George did what he always did and pushed his pain away – 'to accept things as they are,' he had told Therese a few months earlier, 'that's the only philosophy'. When he couldn't sleep, he took camphor and salammoniac pills, but the tension in the house became too much for Therese and by the end of the year she was ill. It had started with a toothache and a cold, and then turned into a more serious pneumonia. The doctor prescribed a regime of blood-letting, poultices and daily hot baths. George was worried, as was Heyne, who feared that his daughter 'consumes herself through her constant agitation'.

Yet somehow, in the midst of all this turmoil, George finished the first volume of *Views of the Lower Rhine, from Brabant, Holland, England and France* – the account of his travels through Europe and England. It was a bittersweet experience. On the one hand he enjoyed working on a proper book again, rather than just a review or a translation, but it also marked the end of his long friendship with his publisher Karl Spener. When George proposed the project for a much higher fee than per their usual agreement, shortly after his return from France, Spener had been hesitant. George then looked elsewhere, telling Spener in early September that six other publishers were keen. Spener didn't reply. Following up with several more notes, George finally gave up two months later and signed a lucrative contract with Christian Friedrich Voß, another publisher in Berlin. 'I honour, esteem and love you as always, and wish you all the best,' George wrote to Spener, but he was disappointed 'that you value my works far less highly than other publishers'. It was his last letter to a man who had launched his work in Germany more than a decade earlier.

The first volume of *Views of the Lower Rhine, from Brabant, Holland, England and France* was published in February 1791 (the second followed in April 1792). The word 'Views' in the title – *Ansichten* in German – had two meanings: how something looks, but also a personal opinion or viewpoint. It was deliberately ambiguous. Rather than a straightforward travel account, George had composed the book as a series of letters which he addressed to his readers, writing them into an unfamiliar world of revolution and republican movements. As they turned the pages, they encountered people discussing their rights over a bottle of beer and reading political newspapers in taverns. This was a book about a new reality.

Even art had to develop, George explained, revising his long admiration for ancient Greek art. He had always been open to reassess his opinions and adjust his beliefs when circumstances changed, for 'any truth that shuns the light is either a phantom or a piece of trickery,' and he valued his ability 'to be inconsequent and unpredictable'. Now that the world had changed, the Greek gods carved from white marble which he had previously revered were no longer an appropriate expression of humanity – as alien as Greek words in modern poetry. 'The idealized gods and goddesses are no more,' George wrote, 'they have been replaced by people with unique, individual character; by people marked by prevailing passions and temperaments.' Art should be about humanity. Where Greek art had been the embodiment of the beautiful – the perfected, harmonious and exquisite – the soaring columns of the half-finished cathedral in Cologne, for example, he wrote, 'stand like apparitions from another world, like fairy palaces, to bear witness to the creative power of humans'.

Views of the Lower Rhine, from Brabant, Holland, England and France, Lichtenberg told Soemmerring, was 'a book about humans'. Instead of describing tourist sights, George commented on politics, society and the living conditions of ordinary people. When he visited the towering Ehrenbreitstein fortress on the Rhine near Koblenz, for example, he didn't write about the imposing building or the expansive views but about the emaciated prisoners held there, rattling their chains and

Ehrenbreitstein fortress near Koblenz

holding out spoons to beg for food. There was no need to mention if they were murderers or petty thieves. In George's eyes, they were all humans, all with a right to happiness and liberty. 'The freedom of an individual,' he urged, 'is indisputably a right tied to the human condition, and therefore inalienable.' In the process, he shifted the reader's attention from tourist attraction to the grim reality of life in the German states. This contrast, between the fortress as an emblem of state power and George's empathy for the prisoners, was characteristic of his approach in the book.

Much as he wanted to educate his readers about the new political climate in Europe, he had to be careful not to upset the authorities. German rulers in the various territories of the Holy Roman Empire remained concerned about the fires that French ideas might ignite in their home states. Just when George had returned from his travels in the summer of 1790, thousands of peasants had revolted in Saxony and students in Göttingen had taken to the streets. 'The ferment is everywhere,' Reinhold told his son. In late August students had roamed through Mainz, breaking windows and injuring a professor. The authorities in the city feared that the situation could escalate and deployed 800 soldiers to control the students. 'So, you also had the freedom influenza in your city?' Lichtenberg wrote to George when he heard the news. He had to tread lightly, George told Jacobi when he sent *Views*, 'and sow the good seeds so subtly that no one around notices the sowing'. His father-in-law was troubled about George's increasingly political publications – 'you're walking on hot coals,' Heyne wrote.

His concern was not unreasonable. George's chapter on the rebellion in Liège, for example, was the opposite of cautious. In August 1789, a month after the storming of the Bastille, and inspired by the news from Paris, the inhabitants of the Prince-Bishopric of Liège, an ecclesiastical principality in the Holy Roman Empire (now part of modern-day Belgium), had rebelled against the ruling prince-bishop and established a republic. The revolutionaries in Liège had placed sovereignty in the hands of the people, George explained, and this momentous transformation had not been achieved by peaceful negotiations – 'violence, then, not the gentle persuasion of reason, but the superiority of physical power … brought about all the changes in this small state'. He also accused commentators of exaggerating the violence carried out by revolutionaries, while ignoring 'the systematic murder of thousands through the ambition of warring despots'. It was a sad world in which one had to choose between the two evils, but the 'consequences of anarchy,' George wrote, 'are mere child's play compared to the atrocities committed by insulted slave-drivers'. He was walking a dangerous tightrope.

Alexander von Humboldt was certain that the book 'will cause a stir in the world'. Almost two decades later, after his own five-year expedition to South America and influenced by his mentor's narrative-driven and expressive writing style, he even adapted George's title for his best-selling *Views of Nature.* Goethe, who didn't agree with George's political views, enjoyed *Views of the Lower Rhine, from Brabant, Holland, England and France* so much that he reread the book the minute he finished it. One 'wishes to travel with such a good and well-informed observer,' Goethe said, while Lichtenberg declared it 'one of the foremost works' in Germany.

The book might have been political and sometimes even radical, but it was no call for a revolution. George suggested that it might be better to improve, rather than replace, the flawed old constitutions of the German states. 'We're not at a point where a violent revolution could help or benefit us in the slightest,' he wrote to a friend in April 1791.

20

'As empty as a hollowed-out pumpkin'

Troubles: 1791–1792

Nonetheless, George and Therese's parlour in Mainz became a centre of revolutionary ideas. In the privacy of their home, everybody felt free to speak their mind and even to criticize the Mainz government. Visitors appreciated George's intellect and Therese's wit. At twenty-seven, she was still young and hadn't lost her desire to be extraordinary. She enjoyed her role as the hostess of these small gatherings and there were still aspects of her marriage that she valued. In theory, she liked being George's wife – he was famous and, as her friend Caroline said, Therese carried his name with pride. Huber continued living with them, feeling comfortable in his role as lover of the wife and friend of the husband. He had put on weight and worked as little as possible. At least Therese and Huber were discreet – so discreet in fact that visitors didn't realize what was going on.

Every day at around 7 p.m. friends arrived at Neue Universitätsstrasse. There was the inner circle who came every day, and then those who stopped in Mainz on their travels. 'You will believe me,' one young man wrote home, 'that it is rare to find oneself in such interesting company.' Reading the latest French newspapers, they debated the events in France, the concept of freedom, and the current climate in the German states. Politics in Mainz consisted of 'deceiving everyone, negotiating with everyone, and keeping no promises', George wrote to Jacobi.

'In Germany, the princes fear the fever of freedom,' George told a friend. The elector, once so proud of his reforms, now prohibited his subjects from speaking out against religion, government and his decrees. Post was intercepted and a new censorship bureau established. 'Letters are opened; Masses are held for the downfall of the French constitution; all foreigners are closely watched; all public speeches on religion and state are strictly forbidden! All movements are monitored by cunning spies,' one young man wrote to his father after an inspiring evening of resistance at George and Therese's house.

In Göttingen, Therese's father was getting nervous about the radical leanings of his daughter and son-in-law. George's letters and reviews were becoming increasingly alarming. 'I'm familiar with your fine, noble enthusiasm, which is sometimes stirred up more than is good in your house,' Heyne wrote, and advised George against the translation of a book by Jacques Pierre Brissot, one of France's most outspoken revolutionaries. George had already reviewed it so positively that people were talking, Heyne warned, asking him to rein in 'your own zeal for liberty'. The authorities in Göttingen, where Heyne published the *Göttingischen Anzeigen von gelehrten Sachen*, were not pleased. If that was the case, George replied, he would no longer be able to review for him any more – 'I can remain silent, but I cannot write against my conviction and insight.'

He continued to follow the events in France closely. In late June 1791, the *Privilegierte Mainzer Zeitung* reported that Louis XVI had tried to flee from France during the night of 20 June. The king, his wife Marie Antoinette and their children hadn't travelled far before they were recognized in Varennes, a small town some 150 miles east of Paris. Pursued by large crowds shouting insults and threats, the royal family had then been returned to Paris and placed under guard at the Tuileries Palace. This was a turning point. Even after the revolution France had remained a monarchy – the king was still king, albeit with far less power than before – but the mood was changing. By attempting to flee, Louis XVI had lost any remaining trust. Tensions were also rising between the more radical French revolutionaries, the Jacobins,* who demanded the

* The Jacobins were named after their meeting place at the former Dominican monastery, Couvent des Jacobins de la rue Saint-Honoré in Paris.

abolition of the monarchy, and the moderates who argued that the king should have a role.

'The flight of the king has very much strengthened the power of the National Constituent Assembly,' George wrote to Heyne on 9 July. In Germany even those who had supported the French Revolution were becoming increasingly worried. A constitutional monarchy with a Parliament that ensured the rights of its citizens was one thing, but a full-blown democratic republic in the hands of radicals was too much for most Germans, no matter how liberal. George, though, maintained his support. He was impressed that the French, who had been ruled for so long by despots, could still remain measured and calm. 'This moment in which we live now is extremely important and interesting,' he told Heyne at the end of July, for 'all cogs and wheels of the old order are stalling. The ignorant nobility must give way to the better, nobler middle class.'

German rulers feared the worst. At the end of August 1791, the Prussian king, Friedrich Wilhelm II, and Leopold II, the emperor of the Holy Roman Empire and brother of the French Queen Marie Antoinette, issued a joint declaration, proclaiming 'the situation in which His Majesty the King of France currently finds himself is a matter of common interest to all the sovereigns of Europe'. If the French king's powers were curtailed, they would take action. Not quite a declaration of war, but certainly a warning.

There were also troubles at home. Two weeks before Louis XVI's attempted escape, Therese had given birth to a third daughter, Louise. She was not George's child. A few months later, the baby and two-year-old Clara were inoculated against smallpox, just as Röschen had been in the previous year. But this time both girls became gravely ill. As Clara's fever rose, George feared for his strong and wild daughter. She pulled through, but the baby died. George was deeply saddened. 'You do not know how painful it is until you have experienced it,' he wrote to Heyne, but he might have already suspected that Louise was Huber's child because 'losing the elder one would have been ten times harder for me'. Had Clara died, he admitted, 'I'm not sure how I would have endured the loss'.

By the time Louise died in November 1791, Therese was pregnant again, and again not with George's child. George spiralled into melancholy and illness. He suffered from fevers, vomited and coughed, and his gums became so infected that he almost lost his teeth. Maybe, he told his new publisher, his sickness had been triggered by 'a certain quiet sorrow'. He was tired and despondent and admitted to Jacobi, 'I have perhaps never found myself in a more difficult situation than now.' The family's increasingly precarious financial situation added to the misery – they were spending more money than George earned from his university salary and his writing. Every day he forced himself to his desk, working for the library but also translating and writing, desperately trying to earn money and to forget that his marriage had failed. 'My strength is depleted,' he told Jacobi, 'my body no longer able to bear any exertions, my mind is paralyzed.' Winter always made him feel depressed, but that year George couldn't seem to shake off his dark mood even when spring arrived. As Therese's belly grew, so did his sense of being rejected. His exhaustion combined with 'several painful experiences I have endured over the past few months', as he wrote to Heyne with considerable understatement, was just too much.

Only his daughters made him feel at peace. Five-year-old Röschen, the eldest, was gentle and sensible, but also inquisitive, always asking and keen to learn – like George in many ways. Little Clara was his favourite, 'a wild untamed rascal', he wrote to his father-in-law, 'just as I imagine the dear mother might have been at that age'. Everything about Clara reminded him of Therese: 'she's brunette like the mother, fiery and lively like the mother, and intuitive like the mother'.

By spring 1792, everybody was ill – coughing, wheezing, battling fevers – George, Therese but also the girls, Huber and the servants. 'Today, I am as feeble as a fly,' George wrote to his publisher on 27 March 1792, but his greatest worry was Röschen, who had pneumonia. For weeks he feared for her life, but she survived. In the midst of all this came the news that France had declared war on Austria on 20 April, when the Holy Roman Emperor refused to withdraw his troops from the French border. It was only a matter of time before Prussia and other German states would be drawn into the conflict. The day after France's declaration of war, Therese gave birth to a son. They named him Georg, probably to keep up the pretence that the first-born son was named after the father.

A week later, France invaded the Austrian Netherlands. George seemed unperturbed. 'Things that cannot be changed must be endured,' he said, 'like thunderstorms, frost and snow, rain and stormy weather.' Others were more anxious. War not only meant guns and cannon fire on the battlefields, but also hungry armies who emptied grain stores, wine cellars and vegetable plots. Officers were billeted in private homes, soldiers had to be fed, horses were confiscated, jewellery was stolen and women were raped. Jacobi prayed that the 'French lava would not reach the banks of our Rhine', and in Mainz the old fortifications were repaired, the moat filled with water, and the food stores checked.

Worse, at least for George, his wife held the baby of another man in her arms. George tumbled into darkness. 'Sometimes I think . . . that I'm nothing to my dearest friends to whom I would like to be so much,' he wrote to Heyne at the beginning of May, adding 'that my mind and heart do not interest them, and I'm in their way'. He felt as if he had aged by twenty years from one day to the next, he wrote to Lichtenberg in Göttingen in mid-May, like a plant killed by a sudden frost. His head was 'as empty as a hollowed-out pumpkin'. Heyne, concerned as always

Caroline Michaelis-Böhmer (later Schlegel-Schelling)

about his unpredictable daughter, tried to advise George: 'Stand your ground, and let others just stand there like penguins.'

Amid all this darkness, some relief came from two women who had joined their circle in Mainz: Meta Wedekind-Forkel and Caroline Michaelis-Böhmer, Therese's old childhood friend. Therese, Meta and Caroline were daughters of prominent scholars in Göttingen and now in their mid and late twenties. All three were highly educated, fiercely independent and unconventional women. Since the summer of the French Revolution in 1789, Meta had come for long visits to Mainz, where her brother lived, and Caroline had moved there in February 1792.

Trapped in a loveless marriage, Caroline had been widowed at the age of twenty-four. She was small and slender, with brown hair that tumbled in thick curls around her face. She was confident and beautiful, and arrived in Mainz with her young daughter to be near her friend Therese. Caroline relished her new freedom and had no interest in marrying again. 'I am definitely happier the freer I am,' she had said to a friend who wanted to introduce her to a prospective husband. George enjoyed her company – 'she's a clever woman who enriches our domestic circle,' he told Lichtenberg. She liked him, too. George Forster was the 'most wonderful man', Caroline thought, intelligent, humble and altruistic – but also weak because he depended too much on Therese's approval and love. It pained Caroline to see how much George suffered in his marriage. He 'pines for love', she wrote to Wilhelm Meyer, Therese's former lover, and 'her ungracious selfishness condemns him to eternal torment'.

Meta had been married at the age of sixteen to a man twice her age who reputedly had been the lover of Therese's mother – at least according to Therese. She had then caused a scandal when she embarked on a public affair with Gottfried August Bürger, a prominent German poet, while also taking a second lover. Upon discovering that Meta's husband was not his only rival, Bürger had retaliated by publishing a series of spiteful poems about her. Instead of staying with her husband in Göttingen, Meta moved to Berlin with her second lover and then returned to Göttingen in autumn 1791, where she fell in love with a young student. When she became pregnant by him, she secretly had the baby in a village

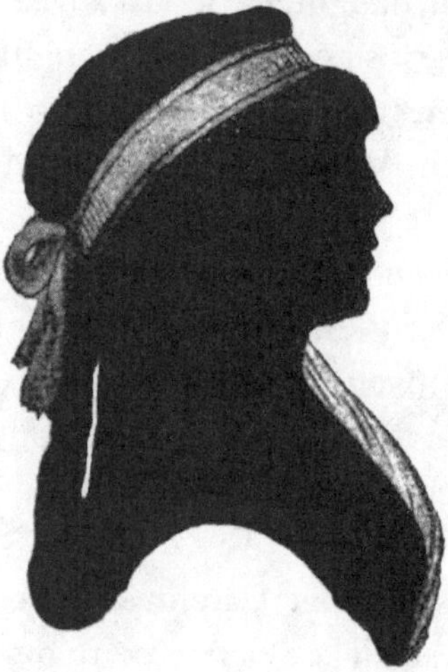

Meta Wedekind-Forkel (later Liebeskind)

150 miles south of Göttingen. A few days after giving birth, she moved alone with her newborn to Mainz and shared lodgings with Caroline. Her reputation may have been ruined but George didn't care. 'She is certainly much more to be pitied than blamed,' he told Heyne. Whenever Meta left Mainz for Göttingen, George missed her, 'you are a more forgiving friend to me than all others around me,' he told her.

Meta, who had published a novel a few years previously, also became an important literary collaborator, translating numerous books for and with George. Their partnership relieved his workload and gave Meta financial independence. Among the translations, on his urging, was Thomas Paine's *Rights of Man*, which had been published in Britain in March 1791. The bestselling English-born writer and revolutionary, who had played a key role in convincing American colonists to declare independence with his 1776 pamphlet *Common Sense*, had written another radical book.

In *Rights of Man*, Paine defended the French Revolution and declared all men equal, born with natural rights such as liberty and resistance to oppression. The important word was 'natural' as these rights could not be granted by a government but were inherent and universal for everyone, Paine explained. The pamphlet manifested what George had been thinking for a long time. Paine's insistence on the unity of humankind appealed to him, yet George did not dare publish a translation of his own. Instead, he wrote a preface to the German edition, albeit anonymously, knowing that the Elector of Mainz would not have been pleased if his university's librarian endorsed the work of a revolutionary. But it was no coincidence that George once again mentioned the term 'human rights' that same year. 'What distinguishes human beings from animals is the divine spark of self-conscious reason, reflected back through language,' George wrote in 1791 in an essay about North America, 'all rational beings are human, and human rights require us to recognize them as such on the basis of this capacity, and not through some unverifiable ancestry.'

Caroline and Meta spent every evening in the Forster house, joining in the discussions on the French Revolution, politics and literature. In late spring 1792 everybody was trying to puzzle out what was happening with the French war effort. On 15 May, George wrote to Heyne, speculating that England would probably stay out of the war but he was less sure about Prussia. Eleven days later, on 26 May, he was certain that Prussia would fight against France. But no one seemed to know what was really going on. Heyne reported rumours of a ceasefire between France and Austria, but less than three weeks later the Prussian army was marching through Göttingen. Soon Prussia would officially join Austria in the fight against France. The war, George predicted, was going to turn the revolution into a bloodbath and he had little hope for the lives of the French king and his family.

In Paris, the revolutionaries split into ever hardening factions. On one side were the radical Jacobins who wanted a republic and championed the cause of the common people with fervour. On the other were the Girondins,* more moderate in their views, who favoured a constitutional monarchy, defended private property, and sought to achieve revolutionary change through legal reforms rather than turmoil and upheaval. 'All government, to be good, must embrace the principle of stability,' one of their delegates in the National Assembly declared. Meanwhile thousands of Parisians rioted in protest against both king and monarchy. 'Democratical licentiousness is a devilish thing,' Reinhold Forster wrote to his son, the French 'are now governed by the worst *and* most wretched rabble'. Yet when Heyne dismissed the Jacobins as the 'most despicable people

* The Girondins were a loosely organized group, named for several of their prominent members who came from the Gironde, a *département* in south-western France.

on God's Earth', George disagreed. If he had to take sides, he replied in a long letter on 5 June 1792, 'I gladly confess that I'm always rather *for* than *against* the Jacobins.' Without them, he pressed, the revolution would have been crushed.

While the French revolutionaries were debating whether to dismantle the monarchy, the Holy Roman Empire was cementing its own. In March 1792, a few weeks before the French had declared war on Austria, Emperor Leopold II had suddenly died. Even though the title had been held for centuries by the Austrian Habsburgs, and was de facto hereditary, eight Prince-Electors from the German Electorates* had formally to vote on the next emperor. On 14 July 1792 – the third anniversary of the storming of the Bastille – Leopold's son was duly crowned Francis II in Frankfurt. Five days later, Germany's entire aristocracy seemed to descend on Mainz when the new emperor arrived after his coronation.

The Favorite, one of the elector's palaces where the festivities were held

* These were the Electorates of Mainz, Trier, Cologne, Hanover, Saxony, Brandenburg and Bavaria, as well as the Kingdom of Bohemia. The Elector of Brandenburg was the Prussian king, Friedrich Wilhelm II, and the Elector of Hanover was the British king, George III. The 1792 imperial election was the final one as the Holy Roman Empire was dissolved by Francis II in 1806.

Friedrich Karl Joseph von Erthal, the Elector of Mainz, put on a show that would become the last dance of the old order – opulent, lavish and extravagant. The Forsters and their friends watched as hundreds of gilded carriages rolled into the city. Some ten thousand people arrived, George said, and the streets were so crowded that Mainz felt like a busy capital of a large country. Horseshoes clanked noisily on the cobbled stones, exuberant children ran shouting after the carriages, and the new emperor and his wife appeared on the castle's balcony. But when the Prussian king entered Mainz with his entourage, it suddenly began to rain 'as if all the democrats of France were emptying their chamber pots', one observer joked.

Cannons were fired, drums were played, and church bells rang all day long. So many princes and dukes arrived that there were not enough rooms in the elector's palaces. Instead of sleeping in elegantly carved beds with sumptuous silk curtains, they were lodged in the city's taverns. There were balls, concerts and banquets, and for several days Mainz became the centre of the Holy Roman Empire. Fireworks, torches and lamps illuminated the palace gardens and bridges. On the third night, music drifted over the water as nine large yachts, lit by thousands of candles in drinking glasses, sailed along the Rhine. In between, dozens of smaller vessels – also bathed in light – ferried back and forth, bringing the river to life. Night was turned into day in a decadent display. This was everything the French revolutionaries had fought against. George thought that the festivities were a 'barbaric finery . . . of feudal arrogance'.

A few days later, on 24 July, Therese fed baby Georg in the late morning and put him to bed. She went downstairs to entertain her many guests who were still in Mainz for the festivities. A couple of hours later Huber brought news that the boy was ill. By the time Therese had rushed to the nursery, he was barely breathing. She and Huber sat with him as he continued to decline. They couldn't do anything but watch him struggle. Five hours later the baby was dead. He had been only three months old. When the small body was taken to be buried, Therese couldn't stop crying. George couldn't bear her tears and said 'until I am carried there too, nothing will improve'. Therese couldn't even look at him any more. It was all too much for her. First baby Louise had died after the smallpox inoculation and now, only eight months later, her little boy.

A day later, on 25 July, the commander of the allied army declared that if anything happened to the French king and his family, they would destroy Paris and civilians would suffer. Then Austria and Prussia invaded France. To support the allied cause, the Elector of Mainz also dispatched 2,000 soldiers, nearly two-thirds of his entire military force. Meanwhile Paris descended into chaos. On 10 August 1792 a mob of around 20,000 stormed the royal Tuileries Palace, killing more than half of the 900 Swiss Guards stationed there. Many were hacked to death with knives, pikes and hatchets, their uniforms torn to shreds and kept as souvenirs. The king fled to safety, but it was another decisive moment in the revolution. Three days later Louis XVI and his family were imprisoned in the tower of the medieval Temple fortress in Paris. It was the beginning of their end.

At the end of August, Goethe stopped in Mainz on his way to join the troops of Duke of Saxe-Weimar at the front. He would have much preferred to stay at home in peaceful Weimar, but he was the duke's privy councillor and his ruler had demanded his presence, no matter if he was Germany's most notable poet or not. 'Goethe with the army!' wrote Heyne, 'what a profanation!' Goethe spent two evenings with the Forsters and their friends, but everybody avoided the topic of politics as their guest was on his way to the front. Goethe abhorred war and the French Revolution. Even if he believed that reform was necessary, he didn't support a volatile and violent revolution. Like many other Germans, he thought change had to happen within the existing structures. Instead of reading the latest French newspaper and discussing the revolution, the friends talked about literature, art, science and travels with him. 'I finally got to meet Goethe,' Huber wrote to a friend a few days later, 'on the first evening, we were all in good spirits thanks to the fine wine, he mixed witty ideas with reasoned reflections and was truly animated . . . on the second evening, we drank beer, whereby much was lost for the general conversation, but he told some very charming and humorous stories about Italy and was altogether easy and good-natured.'

In early September, not long after Goethe had left, news trickled in that Paris was running with blood. Around 1,200 prisoners had been

September Massacres in Paris in 1792

butchered – priests, aristocrats, politicians, former judges, and those refusing to follow the revolutionaries, but also many who had been imprisoned for non-political crimes. 'Let the blood of the traitors flow,' Jean-Paul Marat, a leading Jacobin, declared. For five days, revolutionaries broke into prisons and left behind a grisly trail of hacked-off limbs, genitalia and slashed faces. Naked corpses were dragged through the streets and thrown on piles, and some revolutionaries even pinned their victims' ears to their clothes as a gruesome badge of honour. It was carnage. The Paris correspondent for the *Privilegierte Mainzer Zeitung* was horrified – 'the strangling and murdering,' he wrote on 6 September, 'has not yet come to an end.'

The Legislative Assembly was dissolved and a new Parliament – now called the 'National Convention' – was elected by universal male suffrage.* On 21 September 1792, the National Convention declared the end of the monarchy, established the French Republic, and decided to put the king

* The National Convention was the third revolutionary legislature, following the National Assembly (June 1789–September 1791), which had drafted the constitution, and the Legislative Assembly (October 1791–September 1792), which had governed under the constitutional monarchy. Every independent male French citizen over the age of twenty-one was allowed to vote for the National Convention – except servants and the unemployed.

on trial. Even those who had welcomed the uprising of 1789 were mortified. For many, the ideals of the French Revolution had become tainted with blood. Across the border, staunch supporters such as the Weimar writer Wieland turned away, repelled by the brutality, now asserting that the French people were 'not yet ready for freedom'. George disapproved of the violence but he never hesitated. 'The lava of revolution flows majestically,' he would later write, 'a state shaken by revolutions resembles a fever-stricken patient; a vigorous life force struggles in a fierce battle against the alien substance which it must either expel or to which it must succumb to: salutary crises and raging paroxysms constantly alternate with one another.' To exorcise despotism, the French had first to suffer.

21

'The final hour of tyranny has come'

Mainz Republic: 1792–1793

Maids wrapped silverware and porcelain, servants carried trunks filled with clothing and bedding, furniture was lifted, paintings were taken off the walls, wine bottles were packed into carriages, money was counted and jewellery hastily grabbed. Traffic on the roads leading out of Mainz came to a standstill as hundreds of carriages, carts, drays, chaises, hay wagons, barrows and horses loaded high with possessions tried to leave the city. Every available horse and vehicle was used. The Rhine itself was clogged with boats of all sizes – captains were bribed and transportation costs rose tenfold in one day. With the French army marching towards the city, all the aristocrats, *émigrés*, clergy and civil servants were fleeing, taking their valuables and belongings. In the middle of the night, the elector himself joined the exodus after having the coat of arms scratched off his carriage, taking with him furniture, paintings and the cathedral's treasury gold, as well as his jewellery-encrusted liturgical vestments and cash boxes filled with funds intended for Mainz's widows and orphans.

Four days earlier, on 30 September 1792, the French had taken Speyer, a German town only sixty miles south of Mainz, soon followed by news that the troops were occupying Worms, halfway between Speyer and Mainz, and then apparently Oppenheim, just fifteen miles away. Reports were confusing with newspapers writing one day of battles and the next of a ceasefire, only to report more battles. No one really knew where exactly the French were moving but they were certainly coming closer. A thousand farmers were forced to repair and strengthen the crumbling Mainz ramparts, but with two-thirds of the Electorate's army away fighting with the Prussians against the French, the city was not in a position to defend itself. Almost a third of the city's 28,000 inhabitants left in three days.

'We're prepared for anything,' George Forster wrote to Heyne, 'who can escape their fate?' The French, he was certain, wouldn't harm ordinary citizens – only tyrants and aristocrats. This was the 'last gasp of a dying despotism', he said.

Prussia and Austria were at war with France but nothing had gone according to plan. The allied armies had marched towards Paris confident in their success, but on 20 September 1792 the French had defeated the Prussians at the Battle of Valmy. It had rained incessantly for weeks and as the Prussians retreated, they had to walk across flooded meadows and roads that turned into an ankle-deep quagmire of mud and manure. There was no food, and soldiers were dying of dysentery, typhus and exhaustion. The sick and wounded were left behind, piled up by the road. Uniforms were caked in mud, swords and muskets rusted, and morale was low. 'No pen and no tongue can describe the misery of the allied army', Goethe wrote to his mother from the front. The allied armies were humiliated by the French, who now moved into German territory.

By 9 October, five days after the panic in Mainz had started, only one other house remained occupied in George Forster's street. Even Soemmerring was away. Recently married, he was on his honeymoon, but his in-laws sent a note to George asking him to pack up any valuables, manuscripts and clothes, and to dispatch everything to Frankfurt where they lived. 'I will not move anything in my house,' George wrote to Soemmerring, doubting that the French would plunder the city. As he updated friends and family in daily and sometimes even twice-daily letters, George's reports were infused with a sense of excitement which had been missing for a long time.

Those who had stayed in Mainz readied themselves for the invading army. On 19 October the French arrived and set up camp outside the city walls. The next morning, George climbed a church tower to see what was going on. There, just beyond gunshot range, thousands of tents formed a huge half circle around the city. Some 12,000 French soldiers had already assembled when news reached Mainz that another 20,000 more were expected that day, bringing heavy artillery. Mainz had only 3,000 men to defend it, most of them inexperienced. 'We're quite calm here . . . and have nothing to fear,' George wrote later that morning to his father-in-law. Mainz would have to surrender and embrace the French and their revolutionary ideas. The days of autocratic rulers seemed finally to be over. As a precaution, however, the household now carried buckets of water up to the attic in case of fire. When he went outside the city gate, George saw French soldiers playing boules with cannon balls and he greeted them with an enthusiastic 'Vive la république!' That afternoon, he sat down at his desk and tried to work.

Two days later, on 21 October 1792, the city surrendered without a fight, and General Custine, the leader of the French troops, moved into the elector's castle. Fondly known as 'Général Moustache' by his soldiers, Custine promised freedom to those who joined the revolution. He gave a speech in which he asked the people of Mainz to choose between despotism or becoming a free republic with French support. Watching their interaction, George remarked how officers and ordinary soldiers were 'like brothers, one heart and one soul' – even eating at the same table. This really seemed to be a new world. Those who remained in Mainz pinned red, blue and white cockades to their hats as a symbol of the revolution, and shouted 'Vivre libre ou mourir' – 'Live free or die' – as they marched through the streets. On 23 October, two days after the capitulation, the Mainz revolutionaries assembled in the most regal room of the elector's castle and founded the 'Society of the Friends of Liberty and Equality' – commonly known as the Jacobin Club after their French namesake – with the goal of establishing a German republic.

Over the following days, the French army captured numerous other German cities within a fifty-mile radius of Mainz, including Frankfurt, Mannheim and Koblenz. In Mainz the *Privilegierte Mainzer Zeitung* was taken over by the revolutionaries and became the pro-French *Mainzer National-Zeitung*. In the past George had often procrastinated. 'What I think, I do not always do,' he had said earlier that year, 'in my opinion, that requires a more passionate temperament than mine.' Once again, he took his time to decide whether to join the German revolutionaries.

Ever since the *Resolution* voyage, George had believed in the unity of humankind. Equality was a reality for him. The voyage, the young literary critic Friedrich Schlegel observed a few years later, had been the '*Urkeim*' – the first seed – from which George Forster's deep belief in freedom developed. In Tahiti, for example, he had seen how a chief had worked alongside others and rowed his own canoe. Almost twenty years later, in Paris, George had witnessed something similar when Louis XVI had carted and shovelled sand, just like the other 200,000 volunteers, to build the earthen amphitheatre at the Champs de Mars for the first anniversary of the storming of the Bastille. George had been elated to see the French king working among his fellow citizens, much like the Tahitian chief.

The situation in Mainz, he now decided, was an opportunity to change Germany's future. 'Since the beginning of Christianity there has been nothing like it,' he wrote to his publisher Christian Friedrich Voß, 'nothing can resist the enthusiasm of the advocates of freedom.' It was the moment to choose sides. For the first time in a long while, he felt alive. Germans should finally 'feel human and liberated'. In Göttingen, his father-in-law was shocked by George's news. 'For heaven's sake,' Heyne wrote on 31 October 1792, 'exercise moderation, caution and prudence', there was no guarantee that the allied armies wouldn't retake Mainz. By siding with the French, George was committing treason, and it was short-sighted to assume that the elector wouldn't return.

It was too late. On 5 November 1792, a little more than two weeks after Mainz had surrendered, George Forster became a member of the Society of the Friends of Liberty and Equality. It was impossible to remain neutral in such a situation, he told his father-in-law. Five days after that, on 10 November, he told his publisher that he was ready to become a French citizen. Custine was delighted by the coup, as he called it in a letter to Paris, of 'attaching Mr. Forster, one of Cook's companions, to the interest of the nation'. With every letter Heyne urged moderation, but George was already on the front bench of the revolution. 'We live in strange times,' George said, 'when the measure by which we used to judge each other . . . has to be broken, and only one measure, humanity alone, remains.'

A routine soon developed in which the members of the Society of the Friends of Liberty and Equality lectured and educated the citizens of Mainz on the principles of democracy and their rights over several nights a week. On 15 November, George himself delivered a speech which was published and distributed across the German states. Standing at a lectern under chandeliers in the beautifully panelled castle room where the society met, he advised the people of Mainz to accept the freedom the French offered and to become part of the French Republic. Though they spoke different languages, he said, terms such as *liberté* and *egalité* had the same importance in Germany – 'what is true, remains true in Mainz or in Paris'. The decision was easy, one between 'ruin and poverty and slavery – or happiness, prosperity, and freedom'. Despots and monarchs – 'the scum of the human race, these degenerate, imbecile privileged people' – claimed that only a few were born to rule and to own property, while the majority were destined to obey. But all that was in the past. The people of Mainz had transformed themselves 'from oppressed, abused, and silently obedient subjects into proud, outspoken and free citizens, daring champions of freedom and equality'. They were the first of all the German states to break the yoke of despotism. 'Be free, fellow citizens, give yourselves a free constitution, and the French promise you their protection; from that moment on, they are no longer

George Forster giving a speech at the Society of the Friends of Liberty and Equality

conquerors, but brothers,' he proclaimed, 'we kindle the sacred flame, we press on toward the great goal, we shall not rest until freedom and equality have been recognized as the inviolable principles of human happiness.'

With that, one of Germany's best-known public intellectuals became the spokesperson and public figurehead of the revolution, carrying the message far beyond the Electorate of Mainz, thereby risking his life and livelihood. George was one of several leading revolutionaries in Mainz – a group that also included Caroline Michaelis-Böhmer's brother-in-law, Georg Wilhelm Böhmer, and Meta Wedekind-Forkel's brother, Georg Wedekind. George was the most prominent, amplifying their voices. If we are one species, united by our shared humanity, he believed, everybody should have the same rights. This was why he embraced the revolution wholeheartedly.

On 20 November, General Custine made George Forster vice president of the provisional government. Fluent in French, George became responsible for food provision, street lights, billeting and fuel, as well as coordinating the new administration and promoting a sense of community. For years he had struggled with self-doubt. Just the previous winter, he had confided to Jacobi that 'nothing prospers for me, the more I labour . . . the more everything slips through my fingers, and now I stand empty-handed'. After the thrill of the *Resolution* voyage, his adulthood had been measured out in difficult, anxious years. 'There is too much writing and too little action in the world,' he had complained when he had felt chained to his desk three years earlier. But now the revolution in Mainz gave him meaning and energized him. 'It is downright impossible for the rotten dams to withstand the waves of freedom,' he declared.

George Forster was back in turbulent waters.

In 'Cook, the Discoverer', the long essay he had published in 1787, George had described a state or a nation as a 'living organic whole'. Parts could rot and die off but new ones would grow. In much the same way, a revolution is 'a natural phenomenon', he explained, 'which cannot be confined or determined by rules of reason, but must take its natural course'. And because a revolution was a natural force, he was not shocked by its raw power. 'All creation is chaotic,' and what happened in France would clear the air like a storm. Revolutions were part of the natural cycle of nations and he would play his role.

When the news spread that George had joined the French administration in Mainz, friends and family were troubled. Was it really necessary to publish the speeches of the Society of the Friends of Liberty and Equality so that all of Germany could read them, Heyne asked. Reinhold also disapproved. George didn't care. 'My opinions are my property,' he wrote to his father in Halle, and he was now a citizen of the French Republic. If Reinhold was anxious about repercussions for himself, he could simply declare that he wasn't responsible for his son's actions. Similarly, his Berlin publisher Voß was concerned that his newly signed bestselling author was now an outlaw. 'Do not fear that I have the desire, strength or urge to play a violent role,' George wrote, but Voß wasn't reassured, reminding him that he was Prussian. He never felt like a Prussian, George replied, and in any event, he had left his birthplace of Hochzeit-Nassenhuben before the Prussians annexed it, so 'in this respect, therefore, I'm not a Prussian subject.' Since then, he had lived in Russia and England, circumnavigated the world, and worked in Kassel, Vilnius and Mainz, none of which were part of Prussia. He felt no allegiance to a country which had never assisted him or his father. His loyalties were determined by his beliefs, not by place. He would '*live and die as a republican*', he told Voß, highlighting the sentence for emphasis.

Many disagreed. Soemmerring, for one, was unsettled by the chaos in Mainz when he returned from his honeymoon. This was anarchy not democracy, he wrote to an acquaintance. French soldiers were everywhere, and several officers had even been billeted in his house. The streets were filthy, grain stores were emptying rapidly, and distressingly, George resented him for not taking part in the revolution. 'My friends are all gone,' Soemmerring lamented, 'except one! who is hostile because I'm not enthusiastic.' George couldn't understand why Soemmerring was trying to remain neutral, refusing to fight for equality, liberty, and the future of humanity. For years they had been best friends, but politics now drove a wedge between them.

Accustomed to glowing reviews, George also had to adapt to criticism of his books. When his *Memories from the Year 1790* – an illustrated calendar of the events of 1790, which included his first-hand testimony of the preparation of the anniversary of the storming of the Bastille in Paris – was published just as the French took Mainz, reviewers were appalled by his positive depictions of the revolution. One critic complained about the 'fashionable democratic drivel', while another was confounded by George's sudden metamorphosis from 'calm observer to wild enthusiast'. Those who knew George Forster's other work, the reviewer wrote, 'would find it hard to believe that these *Memories* came from his pen'. But there were more important things than the approval of critics. 'Freedom has always been, and always will be, the greatest and most precious of all goods,' George said in mid-November 1792, 'without it, in my opinion, there can be no true happiness, no public welfare'.

But supporting the French Revolution remained extremely risky. Exactly how risky became clear in early December when the Prussians recaptured Frankfurt, only twenty miles to the east of Mainz. The front had advanced alarmingly close and people in Mainz suddenly became reluctant openly to endorse the revolution. Huber – who as a diplomat from Saxony had been forced to leave Mainz to keep his government's papers safe – urged George to send Therese and the children away. At first hesitant, George agreed when Therese convinced him that it was too dangerous for the family in Mainz, 'I feel that I cannot demand the sacrifice from Therese to live and die with me,' George wrote to Huber on 4 December.

This was the opportunity she had been waiting for and so, on 7 December 1792, Therese travelled with their two young daughters to Strasbourg in France, some 120 miles south of Mainz. As the wife of a revolutionary and traitor she was not safe in Germany any more. George hoped she would be out of danger in France, and friends promised to look after them. As their carriage rolled south, three-year-old Clara leaned out of the window and shouted 'bon jour, citoyens!' whenever they saw French soldiers. A month later, Therese moved on to Neuchâtel in today's Switzerland, where old friends of the Heyne family offered refuge – a move with grave consequences for George because it was under Prussian control. Regarded as an enemy of the state by the Prussians for his support of the French in Mainz, George would not be able to see his wife or children in Neuchâtel. What he didn't know was that Huber was planning to join Therese as soon as he could remove himself from the Saxon administration.

Caroline Michaelis-Böhmer, who had remained in Mainz, didn't understand how Therese could even consider fleeing or how she could leave George. It was cowardly, disloyal behaviour. 'Many suspect separation plans,' Caroline wrote, and if that was the case Therese should be honest with George. Eventually, Caroline convinced Huber and Therese to tell the truth. When the letter was sent, Therese felt relieved. For the first time since her marriage, she told her father, she could give George 'what I always gladly gave, and he never happily accepted – my respectful friendship'. If only he had been her brother and not her husband. George was devastated but agreed to the separation – unlike most of his contemporaries he didn't believe that he could force his wife to remain tied to him. He continued to correspond with her, sharing his feelings, thoughts and political news. He even remained Huber's friend.

Divorce was a scandalous solution that would bring gossip and a tarnished reputation, and Therese tried to control the narrative. Since George needed love and she couldn't provide it, she now insisted that their separation would make him happy. Huber also tried to rewrite what had happened when he told Heyne that he had rescued Therese from the dangerous consequences of being the wife of a revolutionary. Her escape from Mainz had not only benefited her and the children but apparently also George. 'I may say,' he wrote, 'that I deserve the thanks of all those who are interested in these four people.'

Heyne was bewildered. When his daughter explained that she had always loved George as a friend, but never as a husband, he refused to understand. 'A thousand virtuous wives have found themselves in unhappy marriages,' Heyne wrote, 'as well as a thousand husbands – each one uses common sense to make their situation bearable.' Wives, he later said, should be quiet and focus on domestic matters. Determined to justify her behaviour, Therese even told her father that 'nature did not intend for us to be spouses in a sensual way'. Whenever George demanded 'what was his right', she said, 'I was unbearably repulsed'. Her father ignored her explanations. He could not comprehend that she had invited Huber to live with them in Mainz and destroy her husband's happiness, nor why George had not thrown her lover out of his house.

Her unruly enthusiasm, Heyne now accused Therese, had made many people miserable. The only solution out of this labyrinth of immorality was to return to George. 'God, how I have always loved you,' Heyne said to his daughter, but she had sorely disappointed him.

At least Caroline and Meta were still in Mainz, although both embroiled in their own scandals. Meta already had a child by her lover and Caroline would also soon find herself pregnant after a one-night-stand with a young French soldier. They were all drunk on the idea of equality and a new social order. If men were free, surely women should be too. One particularly wild occasion was on 13 January 1793, when the Mainz revolutionaries erected a twenty-one-metre high 'Tree of Liberty', a column painted in the revolutionary colours on the market square. Several thousand people, George, Caroline and Meta among them, joined the dancing and singing that went on all day and night. Cannons were fired, the *Marseillaise* was played, and they all shouted 'Long live freedom! Long live the nation! Long live the republic!' They also learned to sing *Ça ira* – 'It'll be fine', the revolution's unofficial anthem – and dance the

Ball of Freedom and Equality in Mainz on 13 January 1792

wild *Carmagnole*, a popular song with the French revolutionaries. The women wore red, blue and white ribbons in their hair, and Caroline claimed that she couldn't wait to tell her future grandchildren that she was witnessing the greatest upheaval of all time – 'for my very life I would not leave here'. The atmosphere was exhilarating.

In his speeches George was vocal and bold. He was a transformed man. With renewed confidence, he stood up and swept up the audience with his enthusiasm. When he spoke of breaking the iron chains that had shackled them for centuries, he was not talking only about the revolution in Mainz. There was something deeper, more visceral in his words, something fundamentally related to himself. For the first twenty-two years of his life, his father had controlled George's every step. Reinhold's volatile personality and his constant lack of money had shaped his son's future. George had learned to ignore his own wishes and focused on trying to bring joy to others – that 'burning desire to see happy people around me'. In his marriage some of these patterns had been repeated but now he seemed finally to have unfettered himself. Tyrants had suffocated their subjects, robbing them of their freedom and self-determination, he told the Society of the Friends of Liberty and Equality. Despots had reduced people 'into a blind, lifeless instrument of their whims and desires'. Enough. 'Vengeance! Vengeance,' he shouted from his lectern, 'vengeance upon the murderers of our souls'.

Nothing curbed his fervour, not even the news that the French had executed their king on 21 January 1793. A week later, George read in the *Mainzer National-Zeitung* that 'today people have finally realized that a king is only a man and that no one is above the law'. The explosive trial of Louis XVI – Citizen Louis Capet as he had been called since the proclamation of the French Republic in September 1792 – had begun on 11 December 1792 and lasted a little more than a month. The National Convention unanimously voted the king guilty – unsurprisingly given that the Jacobins were now in the majority. Thousands had watched when the guillotine's twelve-inch blade severed the king's head. 'Peoples of Europe! Peoples of the Earth,' the *Mainzer National-Zeitung* declared, 'behold the thrones, see that they are nothing but dust.' Europe's monarchs were stunned. 'We hurl at their feet, as a gauge of battle, the French king's head,' the revolutionaries shouted and declared war on

Execution of Louis XVI on 21 January 1793

Britain, the Dutch Republic and Spain. Almost all of Europe was now fighting against France.

This wasn't a moment for moderation, George wrote to Therese, quite the opposite, 'it even becomes a duty to resort to extremes at times.' The death of the king was necessary for the security of France and not based on the 'code of law but on natural law'. As a tyrant, he had had to die.

It was one thing to proclaim his opinions in private correspondence, but he now openly turned against German rulers. Gone were the days when he had tiptoed between his beliefs and his public persona. Less than two years previously, he had not dared to translate Thomas Paine's *Rights of Man*. Now he discarded all caution. He called the emperor of the Holy Roman Empire 'Weakling Franz' and pronounced the Elector of Mainz – or Friedrich Karl Joseph as George now referred to him, purposefully dropping his title – a 'torchbearer of discord and despot's fury'.

Schiller told a friend, 'I'm predicting that he [Forster] will only derive shame and regret from this matter.' Even Wilhelm von Humboldt, initially so enthusiastic about the French Revolution, wrote that George's open political engagement was 'incomprehensible to me'. There was a profound difference between supporting what was happening in France and initiating a German revolution, Wilhelm told Schiller. Reinhold couldn't make sense of his son's behaviour and told anyone who listened that he would happily see him on the gallows, while Jacobi was advised by a friend to break off all contact.

Soemmerring believed George had lost his mind. 'He can't be saved for Germany,' Soemmerring wrote to Heyne. This was treason. The two friends had finally fallen out when Soemmerring had moved to Frankfurt to live with his wife's parents after the Prussians had recaptured the town from the French. When Soemmerring asked his old friend to safeguard his house in Mainz, George had replied with an angry letter. Why should he be his protector, George wrote, 'I would have to station myself at the cellar door as a guard.' All would have been fine 'if only you had been determined to share all good and ill with us here'. It pained him that they had such different opinions about French revolutionary politics but he couldn't do more than put a lock on Soemmerring's house. The letter marked the end of their long friendship.

They all judged him wrongly, George told his publisher. His beliefs in freedom, equality and humanity had always been apparent, and 'what I have done since then can only prove that I was capable of *acting* according to what I *think*.' He was willing to sacrifice his happiness, career, health and life for freedom in Germany, he explained, and if others were to condemn him, so be it. Only his own conscience could be a judge of his behaviour. When he went to Paris with Alexander von Humboldt, he had seen with his own eyes how the lives of ordinary people had changed. It had been uplifting to witness their enthusiasm and belief in a better world. There were setbacks and struggles, of course – a war, high food prices, political infighting, an economic crisis – but the revolution had changed everything. Peasants in France were no longer shackled to a feudal lord, urban workers were allowed to vote, and the middle classes began to assert their political rights. He had been moved by what many French citizens had told him: they endured much, faced hardship, and had less money in their pockets, but they believed it was all worth it, because 'our children will thank us, for they will benefit from it'. The past was over and the future was theirs.

George cut off his ponytail to show his republican sympathies, because those who wore their hair short didn't need a servant to style and powder it. 'Here is some hair to prove it,' he wrote to Therese, enclosing the locks.

As the newly elected president of the Society of the Friends of Liberty and Equality and the vice president of the provisional administration, George was at his desk by 5 a.m. and in bed after midnight. As he tried to coordinate provisions and other logistics, he sometimes felt like a 'businessman en miniature'. There was so much to do, write and organize. He convinced the French not to take the elector's library to Paris because it now belonged to the citizens of Mainz, and he persuaded Custine not to destroy any of the ecclesiastical monuments as they had done in France because they were important cultural artefacts.

As if he were not busy enough, George also founded a newspaper – *Neue Mainzer Zeitung oder der Volksfreund* (*The New Mainz Newspaper or Friend of the People*) – proudly announcing in its launch issue that 'finally freedom of the press reigns within these walls, where the printing press was invented'. He was not only the editor but wrote most of the articles, predominantly focusing on political news and reports about revolutionary developments in Germany and the rest of Europe. His editorial principles, he explained, were truth, republicanism, and the advancement of happiness, liberty and equality, and the 'most noble struggle ever fought for with pen or sword, the cause of humanity'.

Then in February 1793 the provisional government finally announced the first elections in Mainz which George had long requested. His name was also on the ballot papers – he wanted to build this new world, a politician who would shape the future. It had been almost two decades since he had returned from his voyage on the *Resolution*. Since then he had written widely about the human condition, but standing for election was altogether different. If elected, he would be a part of the structure of power and able to transform the way people lived.

All men aged twenty-one and older – except servants and farm hands – were allowed to cast their vote, while women were excluded. But when the French authorities required constituents to swear an oath to freedom and equality, people refused, disqualifying themselves from the vote. George grew frustrated. It was infuriating that his fellow citizens couldn't see the advantage of free elections. He travelled from village to village to convince people to vote but in a letter to Therese he complained that 'in the end, we will have to graciously command them that they shall and must be free.'

The election fell on a Sunday, 24 February 1793, and in the early morning bells rang out in the city's six churches, calling all eligible men to exercise their right – the first ever such vote in a German state and the 'most solemn act', as George wrote in the *Neue Mainzer Zeitung* two days later. But only 8 per cent of those who were allowed to participate went to the polls, with the powerful guilds in which many trades were organized, clerics and civil servants boycotting the election, and many others refusing to take the required oath. 'Such stupid, heartless and mindless people!' George complained to Therese in a long letter. Some of those who had refused the oath were expelled from the city – a step which George compared to an amputation of an infected limb. Just as gangrenous tissue had to be excised from the body, so these men had to be removed.

Less than a month later, on 17 March 1793, the newly elected Parliament met for the first time, and the next day founded the Mainz Republic – Germany's first independent republic. At a time when the other heads of state in the Holy Roman Empire ruled for life, usually by hereditary right, the people of Mainz had voted for their government. This was the moment George had been waiting for. 'The final hour of tyranny has struck,' he declared in a speech, and 'the dying monster writhes at our feet.' Elected as vice president, he promised to use his power wisely.* He was the heart of the Mainz revolution, Meta wrote, 'a mighty leader for politics and democracy'. His colleagues called him the soul of the new Parliament.

On 21 March, George addressed his fellow members of Parliament, warning that the elector would take back his power if the young republic didn't unite with the French. 'Oh rescue, rescue quickly by a wise decision, life, happiness, freedom,' he said, 'secure for ever a good

* Philosophy professor Andreas Joseph Hofmann was the president. Hofmann was a great orator, known for his passionate speeches and thundering accusations. He was opinionated, argumentative, and unwilling to compromise.

people that cannot protect itself against all deceit and murderous desire of the enemies. Keep your liberators, your protectors in the country; hold tightly to them, do not release them from your embrace, swear to them eternal brotherhood, and receive the same from them; speak the great decisive word: *the free Germans and the free French are now one inseparable people*!'

Four days later, he left for France with two other delegates, entrusted with the task of travelling to Paris to ask the French government for the Mainz Republic to become part of France. 'I'll probably be back in three weeks,' he wrote to Therese.

22

'What happens, *must* happen'

Paris: 1793–1794

It took them only four days to cover the almost 350 miles from Mainz to Paris. Travelling day and night, the Mainz delegation arrived on 29 March 1793 and the next day George Forster went to the Manège, the former riding hall at the Tuileries Palace where the French National Convention met. The different political factions had divided the ascending rows of benches along the building's sides. The radical Jacobins sat in the upper rows – hence becoming known as the 'Montagnards' (the Mountain party) – whereas the more moderate Girondins occupied the

The Manège, where the French National Convention convened in Paris

lower seats. Acoustics were terrible in the long vaulted room and George had to shout to be heard when called to give his speech. He kept it short. The free Mainz Republic wanted to unite with their French brothers and were seeking accession to France. Amid war and chaos, George declaimed, they had voted to be free and would never forget that it had been France which had broken their chains. With strong applause, the National Convention granted the request.

But by the time George had arrived in Paris, the Prussians and their allies had already laid siege to Mainz and driven a wedge into the French troops. While Mainz remained under General Custine's control until the summer, the territory between the city and France was in the hands of the anti-revolutionary allies. George was also dismayed when news reached him that Caroline Michaelis-Böhmer and Meta Wedekind-Forkel had been arrested by the Prussians as revolutionary sympathizers, and incarcerated with their children in a fortress not far from the city. There was nothing he could do for them. As a founder of the Mainz Republic, George was considered a traitor and it was impossible to travel home.

In Paris, George lived together with one of the other Mainz delegates, Adam Lux, in a small garret in the Rue des Moulins near the Tuileries Palace. He had only the six shirts he had brought with him, and the breeches and coat he wore. His books, manuscripts and papers were all out of reach. 'I'm starting all over again, without knowing how and with what,' he wrote to Therese in Neuchâtel, 'since I'm cut off from all of Europe, burdened with debts, without any means, without support, and almost without hope.'

Proximity also bred disappointment: the revolution was not what he had believed. 'From a distance, all seems different than on closer inspection,' he wrote to Therese shortly after reaching Paris, 'everything is blind passionate rage, frenzied partisanship and quick temper.' Under the leadership of Maximilien de Robespierre and Jean-Paul Marat the Jacobins were becoming more radical and violent, and the chasm with the moderate Girondins was widening. On 10 March 1793, less than a month before George arrived in the French capital, the Revolutionary Tribunal – a court with a jury of twelve, five judges and a prosecutor – had been established by the National Convention in response to what it perceived as internal threats and counter-revolutionary activity. Founded to provide a legal process when dealing with the revolution's enemies in place of mob justice and violent outbreaks, the Revolutionary Tribunal would soon become a symbol of terror, its name whispered with dread. Thousands, including many from within their own revolutionary ranks, would be convicted and sent to the scaffold. One of the Girondins warned the National Convention with almost prophetic foresight: 'Citizens, we have reason to fear that the revolution, like Saturn, will devour successively all its children.'

Paris felt very different to George compared with his last visit in the company of Alexander von Humboldt, almost three years previously. 'We live in uncertain and dangerous times,' he now said. Everybody had to be careful as loyalties and alliances seemed to shift at any moment. At the end of April he wrote to Therese, 'whoever rises to the top, steers the helm until someone else, who is stronger at that moment, pushes him aside. If one can't persecute, denounce, and have others guillotined, one is nothing.'

Gone were the optimistic days of the revolution's beginning. In February 1793, France had declared war on the Dutch Republic and Britain, thereby further expanding the conflict as part of the British navy arrived from the Mediterranean. The French army's initial victories had been reversed, as the allied armies – now composed of the Holy Roman Empire, Britain, Spain, the Dutch Republic, and others – launched offensives from several directions. They advanced from the north-east into France, while General Custine was retreating from Prussian forces in the east (Mainz, however, was still in French hands but under siege). From the south, the Spanish prepared to push across the Pyrenees. In early April, General Dumouriez, a French general aligned with the Girondins and one of the victors at the Battle of Valmy, was defeated by the allied army in the Austrian Netherlands. When he abandoned his troops and fled – riding through a hail of French bullets to reach safety behind the enemy and defect to the Austrians – it only fuelled the Jacobins' conspiracy theories. For the Jacobins, Dumouriez's behaviour confirmed that the most dangerous enemies were within France. Other evidence of internal threat – this one in plain sight – was the revolt of royalist insurgents in the Vendée, in the west of the country, which quickly descended into a brutal civil war. 'We will give death to our enemies,' Marat warned, 'we will erase them.'

'I cannot do it,' George replied, when Therese asked him to write a history of the revolution, 'ever since I realized that there is no virtue in the revolution, it disgusts me.' It felt wrong to be a chronicler of these events. On the long walks he took in Paris, George sought refuge in nature as so often. Soon after his arrival, in early April, he watched the first unfurling leaves of spring, the green so bright that their sight made him feel alive again. At dawn, he listened to the nightingales, their song reminding him 'how beautiful nature is'. In mid-May he went to Versailles, the late king's great palace and estate which had become a public park. That ordinary Parisians now walked where the royal family and their courtiers had enjoyed their privileged lives was a reminder of just how much had changed. It was a gloriously sunny day. All the fountains were flowing, and as George meandered along the gravel paths he watched the water spouting from the mouths of sculpted lions and dragons, and sparkle in a golden light.

He didn't have a lot of money but he sent what he could to Therese and the girls. The French government paid him a small stipend, and at the end of June 1793 he translated the new French constitution into German and English. It was a bold document that promised radical redistribution of wealth by taxing the rich, state education for all, and universal male suffrage. As the delegate of the Mainz government, George accepted the constitution on behalf of the beleaguered Mainz Republic and urged the French to send military support to the city. The new constitution, though, never came into effect because the National Convention decided to wait until peace had been re-established.

Notwithstanding the political turmoil and unrest, Parisians went about their daily lives, and although George complained about loneliness he did go out regularly. He avoided members of the French government – 'because until now I could not and would not belong to any party' – and sought out fellow foreigners instead, meeting old and new friends who invited him to dinners, small parties and the theatre. Since the summer of 1789, the French Revolution had attracted a motley group of people to Paris, but many had left by now, fearful for their lives. George enjoyed in particular the company of some of the few remaining British people and their 'calm sense of liberty' – though liberty also seemed to mean the freedom to choose lovers at will.

There was the young Scottish radical writer Thomas Christie, in Paris not only with his new bride but also followed by his married mistress and their illegitimate child. As if this was not entanglement enough, he tried to set George up with his sister, despite her already being engaged. George attended the salon of the poet Helen Maria Williams, where moderate revolutionaries gathered on Sunday evenings – she herself was involved with a married man. He also met Mary Wollstonecraft, a close friend of Christie, who was in Paris with her American lover, Gilbert Imlay. Aged thirty-four, Mary Wollstonecraft was an outspoken supporter of the French Revolution and as known for her unconventional life as for her writings. She had just published *A Vindication of the Rights of Woman*, an explosive book that advocated female suffrage. 'I shall first consider women in the grand light of human creatures, who, in common with men, are placed on this earth to unfold their faculties,' Wollstonecraft wrote. George had bought the book shortly after publication and liked her immediately.

Another formidable woman who impressed him was Théroigne de Méricourt, a Belgian revolutionary and former courtesan. It was later said that she had joined the outraged women who had besieged Versailles in October 1789, dressed in a blood-red riding-coat, sabre in hand, and astride a black horse. The theatrical image was exaggerated but Théroigne de Méricourt was a fierce advocate of the revolution and of women's rights. Imprisoned for a time by the Austrians, she returned to Paris in January 1792 after her release where she aligned herself with the Girondins – only to be brutally attacked by a group of women associated with the Jacobins. She was a 'martyr of freedom', George thought, and despite suffering from constant headaches since the attack she was still driven by a passionate fervour. 'Imagine a 25- or 28-year-old brown-haired girl with the most open face,' he wrote to Therese, 'with features that were once beautiful, are still partly so, and reveal a simple, noble, resolute character full of spirit and enthusiasm; a particularly gentle expression in her eyes and mouth. Her entire being is imbued with her love of liberty; she speaks constantly about the revolution, and it's worth noting that all her judgements expressed yesterday were accurate, without exception clear, decisive and to the point.'

In Paris he was also introduced to Thomas Paine, the English revolutionary who by now had been elected as a member of the French National Convention. George admired his work – 'God Paine', he and Meta had called him after reading *Rights of Man* – yet thought him disappointing in person. 'I found not much remarkable in Thomas Payne,' he wrote to Therese in mid-May, 'he is better appreciated in his writings.' Paine's face, George noted, was bright red and covered with purple spots, but his eyes burned with a fiery intensity that revealed the force of his ideas.

George missed his wife and daughters, but Therese had made it clear that she would not leave Neuchâtel. 'I don't want to return to you. I respect you, I honour you, you will always be my friend and confidant,' she wrote in June 1793, 'but I can no longer be your wife.' In July, and after much delay, Huber finally arrived in Neuchâtel (though he moved into separate lodgings from Therese to keep up appearances), and it was as if George only now realized that his marriage was truly over. 'What has happened, my friend, cannot be changed,' George wrote to Huber, but he had done him the greatest injustice – 'your action ... brought a man, who only knew one kind of happiness, to lose all hope for the future'. Even so, George was grateful for Huber's assurance that he would care for his daughters, ending his sad letter, 'so you also inherit my last and only fortune'.

He still longed to embark on another expedition. Yearning for distant countries, he ended a long letter to Therese on 13 July 1793 with the sentence: 'Today, 21 years ago, I embarked with Cook.' He wrote only to her, and to none of his friends, with the occasional exception of Huber. Counting the days until the post arrived, he thanked her for news of his *Herzenskinder*, his darling children. 'Since I can't be near them,' he said, 'there is no better substitute than the most detailed news about their coming and goings and their well-being.' From Paris he sent what little presents he could afford for the girls and letters in which he told them how desperately he missed them. 'I would so love to be with you and your sister and your mother,' he wrote to his eldest daughter, Röschen (or Therese as they now called her), shortly before her seventh birthday, 'mother will kiss and love you in my name and if you want to embrace your father, just run to her and send me your kisses.'

On 13 July 1793 the already tense Paris atmosphere turned volatile when twenty-four-year-old Charlotte Corday, a fervent Girondin, stabbed and killed Jean-Paul Marat, the prominent Jacobin, at home in his bath. Four days later, on 17 July, George witnessed her execution at the Place de la Révolution beside the Seine, not far from his lodgings. As the summer sky darkened and heavy rain soaked Charlotte Corday's purple prisoner's shirt, George was stirred by her dignity and calm. Tall, with her dark brown hair cut short, she walked up the steps to the guillotine with her head held high. 'She was radiant, ravishingly beautiful,' George wrote to Therese.

Adam Lux, the Mainz delegate who lived with George in his garret, was so entranced by Corday's beauty that he declared her a martyr and immediately printed a leaflet defending her crime and accusing the French government of betraying the revolution's ideals. Eleven years younger than George, twenty-seven-year-old Lux had written his doctoral thesis on the subject of 'Enthusiasm', so his fervour may not have surprised those who knew him. They had lived together for four months, but George still didn't understand Lux. 'His intention is noble, his courage heroic, his feelings right and beautiful,' George wrote to Therese, but publishing the pamphlet was too dangerous 'given the prevailing general *mistrust*'. Worries crept in that he might be implicated because they shared lodgings and were colleagues from Mainz. 'Are my letters to you being intercepted?' George asked Therese, 'yours to me have been opened for some time now.' It probably meant nothing, trying to reassure himself, 'I don't deserve any suspicion, and my whole life is proof that no one holds a truer and warmer concern for humanity at heart.'

Within a week Lux was detained. In the early morning hours of 24 July the agents of the Committee of Public Safety stormed up the stairs to the garret in the Rue de Moulin. Lux was prepared to sacrifice himself – 'the good man has completely lost his head over the girl and knows nothing more blissful than to die for her,' George wrote to Therese. George hoped that imprisonment would be Lux's punishment, but the Revolutionary Tribunal sentenced him to death. A little more than three months after his arrest, Lux would be guillotined along with others who criticized the Jacobins. 'This court of blood is a disgrace of the revolution,' George told Therese, but Lux had acted unwisely – 'he *jumped* onto the execution scaffold.'

But despite the bloodshed and his initial shock when he had arrived in Paris, George believed in the '*importance* of the revolution'. As the weeks and months went by, the disgust and disappointment he had felt subsided into something different. Yes, the brutality was terrible but the alternative – a return to despotism – was worse. Maybe the enthusiasm and idealism of the early months of the revolution had given way to something darker, but even the measured Thomas Jefferson, known for his principled restraint and thoughtful deliberation during the American Revolution, had said that the 'tree of liberty must be refreshed from time to time with the blood of patriots and tyrants. It is its natural manure.' France had thrown off the shackles of tyranny and what mattered was the emancipation and liberation of the people. There was no guarantee that the revolutionaries would be able to hold on to power. Counter-revolutions, war, economic problems and social unrest could destabilize or break the fragile new order – to survive France had to 'swim in blood and tears'.

The news from Germany was also discouraging. On 23 July, after a long siege and then relentless bombardment, the Prussians finally wrenched Mainz from the French. Houses burned, church towers collapsed, and the cathedral lay in ruins, as did its library of valuable manuscripts. The fire that had ravaged the city during the battle had been so ferocious that Soemmerring saw the light of the flames against the dark sky from Frankfurt, some twenty miles away. The Mainz Republic had lasted only a few short months and the elector returned to rule. The dream of freedom and equality vanished together with George's chance of going back. He also received word that the Prussians had broken into his house and confiscated all his books, manuscripts and papers. His work was now in the hands of the enemy. France became his only home.

At the end of July 1793, the French government sent George to the northern front, thirty miles south-east of Lille, to facilitate a prisoner-of-war exchange with the English. He stayed in a town some twenty miles behind the front line. His mattress was infested with bedbugs and provisions were scarce with only dry bread for breakfast. It soon became apparent that there was nothing to do as the English refused to engage in any negotiations. Certain that his political career was over, George picked up his pen again. Therese had finally convinced him to compose an account of the revolution in Mainz. He struggled with the work, however, because the Mainz Republic didn't exist any more – 'I write what I no longer believe' – but his faith in the ideals of the revolution remained intact. There would come a time, he declared, when it was no longer true 'that coincidence, which forced a free man to become another's slave, should be binding for all future generations, or that the rational son should not be allowed to assert his independence because his weak father let himself be robbed of his own' – the last part certainly a stab at his own father.

In another essay that he wrote at the time, he railed against the corrupting influence of tyranny and the importance of dignity. Despotism, he argued, reduced people to automatons, stripping away their humanity. 'Instead of promising us happiness, let it be your sole concern to remove the obstacles that obstruct the free development of our powers; open the path for us, and we will walk it,' he demanded – autocratic rule eroded human dignity, the very foundation of being a free individual. Without dignity, there could be no true happiness, freedom and self-realization.

With little else to do, he had time to think and write. On his walks along a canal shaded by tall silver poplars, he thought of Therese and his daughters. Imagining them, the feeling was so strong, he told her, that he could see the girls jumping up and down in the grass. He hoped that his daughters were in good spirits. 'Happy children make happy adults!' he wrote at the end of August, 'all disaffection has its most likely root in early impressions!' Maybe he was also thinking about his own childhood. When Therese wrote about the similarities in temperament between her, George and the girls, he disagreed. 'Children cannot and should not become what their parents were,' George replied, 'every person has their own individuality' – and those differences had to be fostered and supported. The separation from his daughters was the most painful aspect of his exile. More than anything, he longed to laugh with them and be their teacher. 'No opportunity that invites them to think for themselves must be neglected,' he reminded Therese, and sent pressed forget-me-nots so they would remember him.

At the end of September, two months after his arrival, he still hadn't heard anything from the English. He dispatched political news to Therese – reports about the French war efforts as well as domestic and regional government policies. The situation became increasingly chaotic as the French troops struggled against the advancing allied armies and anti-Jacobin uprisings broke out in Lyon, Marseilles and Bordeaux. The revolt in the Vendée continued, and further south, French royalists welcomed the British fleet, willingly surrendering the important Mediterranean port of Toulon. As long as Europe's rulers were trying to destroy France there was no hope for peace, George believed, the fate of the whole continent was unpredictable because it was in the hands of 'mad unruly caprice and raging passion' – and he was not referring to the revolutionaries in France but to Europe's rulers and military commanders.

Back in Paris that October, though, George realized just how unpredictable life had become. Letters were opened, houses searched, and people were watched as Robespierre's Revolutionary Tribunal imprisoned and killed anyone they thought suspicious. This was different to what had happened to his colleague Adam Lux, who had known what he did when he provoked the government. In the previous month the National Convention had passed the so-called 'Law of Suspects' under which anyone deemed an enemy of liberty, 'either by their conduct, their contacts, their words or their writings', could be imprisoned and face execution. The law was so broadly framed that it could be applied to almost every citizen and foreigner in France. It was the beginning of the so-called Reign of Terror, which would last until July 1794, and during which many thousands lost their lives to the guillotine.

As the prisons became even more overcrowded, everyone George met knew someone who had been executed. Foreigners, politicians, priests, revolutionaries – no one was safe any more, and a pervasive atmosphere of paranoia settled over France. At any hour, government agents or local surveillance committees could knock on the door to take an unsuspecting resident into custody. Their authority was sweeping, requiring no formal warrant. Arrest, trial and punishment often followed at

The execution of the twenty-one Girondins in October 1793

an alarming speed – and denunciations became a defining feature of daily life. Even men with impeccable revolutionary credentials, such as Thomas Paine, were detained, along with George's friend Thomas Christie and Helen Maria Williams – whose salon he had attended – and other English acquaintances. In early October, in one night alone, 250 British citizens were apprehended as spies and counter-revolutionaries. Even General Custine had been recalled from command and was sentenced to death for losing Mainz to the Prussians. On 16 October 1793, Marie Antoinette, the former queen, was beheaded. Two weeks later, on 31 October, twenty-one leading Girondins were guillotined – it took the efficient executioner only forty-three minutes to chop off their heads. During the Reign of Terror more than 2,600 people were guillotined in Paris – most by the hand of seasoned executioner Charles-Henri Sanson – and another 13,000 or 14,000 in the provinces. The rise and fall of the guillotine's blade had become France's metalled heartbeat.

In late October 1793, George travelled more than 250 miles from Paris to Pontarlier, a small French town near the Swiss border where he had arranged to meet Therese, Huber and his daughters – their home in

Neuchâtel was only thirty miles to the east. The plan was to finalize their divorce in France, as the Swiss still didn't allow it. But when he arrived in Pontarlier, George realized that as German subjects his family couldn't cross into what was now enemy territory. With Therese unable to enter France, they would have to stay married.

In possession of a French passport, at least George could enter Switzerland –it was risky, as his papers only permitted him to travel to negotiate the exchange of prisoners of war. They would have to be careful and keep a low profile. Therese's Neuchâtel friends found a remote country inn in Travers, a Swiss village just across the French border, where they spent four days. It had been almost a year since George had seen his family. The weather was cold and the mountains covered in snow. Nothing could dim his joy at seeing his daughters. Therese, his eldest, was now seven years old, and Clara would turn four a few days later. As they played, sang and read together, George was delighted at how well the girls had learned to speak French in Neuchâtel. At night, once the girls had gone to bed, the adults sat together, talking and planning. Once again George suggested that they all live together – perhaps in Paris when the situation in France had calmed down.

When they left, he couldn't stop crying – 'Oh my children! How my heart bleeds at this farewell!' He tried to be strong but the visit was just too short. He lingered in Pontarlier for another two weeks and, reluctant to leave, began to write *Parisian Sketches*, a political text composed as letters which explained the situation in France to a fictional German opponent of the revolution. In it, George defended France and stood by the revolutionaries who had sacrificed themselves for the rest of Europe – 'our true martyrdom, for the benefit of other nations of Europe'. What was happening in France was the greatest and most important revolution of all times, he wrote, 'all idols lie in the dust; all prejudices have been shattered; wealth has lost its allure, and corruption its power.' Those who denounced the revolutionaries as immoral and bloodthirsty were wrong, because violence and depravity were the cause, not the fruit, of the revolution. For centuries, the French had been tied to the brutal yoke of despotism, and only force could break those chains. He had never condoned violence, but with royalist uprisings and defeats against the allied armies there was a real danger that the revolution could fail. 'Welcome, Revolution, with all your ills and abominations!' George wrote to Therese from Pontarlier. It was the price for freedom.

One can't deny millions of people reason and virtue and declare everything that happened to be the work of evil and darkness, he underlined. 'Without the rivers of blood, the benefits of the revolution which the world so desperately needs, would never have been realized' – this was the 'raw power of the crowds' and not the work of an individual. Just as a single firefly wasn't enough to bring light to darkness, so the revolution wasn't driven by a Robespierre or any other political leader but by 24 million French people – 'thus the individual little creatures vanish before the eye of the beholder; their light only matters together, where it is multiplied by 24 million.' There was a renewed vigour in George's words as if seeing his daughters and Therese had restored his strength.

When he returned to Paris at the end of November 1793, George was sanguine about the future. Meeting friends and informed acquaintances, he was convinced that despite military setbacks France would survive. 'The ground still trembles beneath our feet, the earth is still burning,' he wrote to Therese and Huber on 2 December, 'but that the Republic will endure is beyond doubt.' In Germany, old friends remained concerned – 'do you hear anything about Forster?' Goethe asked Soemmerring in early December, while Heyne still tried to fathom why his son-in-law had sided with the French revolutionaries. Even when he became bedridden with a debilitating chest infection, George remained positive. Wrapped in blankets and a fur coat, he sat alone in front of the smoky fire in his garret, continuing to write *Parisian Sketches* and long letters to Therese, resting the sheets of paper on his knees. 'In any case, let us wait and see what time shall bring,' he wrote on 11 December, but by then he could barely walk, and dressing and shaving exhausted him so much that 'I lie here like a fly in an armchair.'

On 19 December he felt well enough to visit a friend in another neighbourhood, but on his way home failed to find a carriage and had to walk back across Paris on a cold and foggy winter evening. His health began a precipitous decline: stomach cramps, fevers, vomiting, and pains in limbs and joints. 'I'm completely exhausted and emaciated,' he wrote to Therese on 27 December, and as his body surrendered, his mood darkened. Surviving felt pointless if no one cared. His hopes had too often been disappointed, he told Therese, there was no reason for him to get better. 'For what? For miserable self-preservation from one day to the next in an existence devoid of pleasure and joy.' Therese's letters from this time are lost, but his replies implied that she was annoyed by his constant questions about her and Huber's plans, and that she had pushed back against his ideas about moving to France. When his doctor diagnosed a 'sickness of the mind', George was certain that his illness was related to the constant disappointment and Therese's refusal to engage in a shared future.

With the pain unbearable and sleep elusive, he took opium to disappear from reality as the year began to turn. Outside, the guillotine blades continued their grim, daily work – thirty-two heads in twenty-five minutes on the last day of 1793 alone, according to the executioner's tally. 'The Revolution is a hurricane, who can stop it?' George wrote to Therese and Huber on 28 December, but 'what happens, *must* happen.' Although he could barely hold his quill, he forced himself. 'I have no strength left to write. Farewell!' he wrote on 4 January, 'kiss my *Herzblättchen*'. The letter was his last.

Six days later, on 10 January 1794 at 5 p.m., he died. George Forster was thirty-nine years old.

The obituary in the French *Moniteur* newspaper stated the long-term effects of scurvy and 'domestic sorrows' as the causes of George's death, briefly summarizing his life and underlining that he had been a staunch supporter of the revolution. The English also wrote of 'some domestic uneasiness of the conjugal kind', but in Germany few publicly mourned George. Even close friends refused to write tributes about a revolutionary and declared traitor.

Lichtenberg, a man known for his biting aphorisms, feared possible repercussions – 'I'd rather keep silent,' he said. 'Oh, how gladly, how most gladly would I have dedicated a few pages to him,' he told Soemmerring, 'were I still that childless being, unconcerned with the future, free in thought and free in writing, as once I was.' Even Wilhelm von

Humboldt, such a trusted friend and regular house guest, found himself unable to forgive George's treason – he too remained quiet. Friedrich Schiller called George a 'raging fool' and published several satirical couplets with Goethe. One of them, titled 'Unhappy Hastiness', mocked what they saw as a rash decision to join the Mainz Republic – for them a metaphorical plunge into madness:

> Ah, when they shouted of *freedom*, of *equality* – I hastened to join;
> Yet finding the stair too long, I leapt from the rooftop instead.

In February 1794, Goethe wrote to Soemmerring, 'so, poor Forster had to pay for his mistakes with his life! Even if he escaped a violent death! I'm sincerely sorry for him.' But when Jena's *Allgemeine Literatur Zeitung* praised George Forster as one of the greatest writers in Europe and reprinted the *Moniteur*'s obituary, the ruler of the small Duchy of Saxe-Weimar, where the journal was based, was furious. The journal's editors were forced to print a counter-statement in the following issue – written by Goethe – distancing themselves from the celebratory tone of the original obituary.

When Therese heard about George's death, she immediately dispatched a letter to her father, claiming that her husband's happiness had always been her greatest wish. 'Oh, he was so very much loved, and greatly revered,' she wrote. A few lines later, though, she announced her plan to marry Ferdinand Huber as soon as possible. Heyne was appalled by his daughter's behaviour and desolate about George. His many letters were filled with grief:

> Since the news I received yesterday, which completely stunned me, I have not yet been able to collect my thoughts again; I am inconsolable over the loss of my Forster. Truly, he was my Forster; I loved him beyond all expression! So many feelings came together! His worth – ah, never shall the world find his like again! Such vast and varied knowledge united in one man will scarce again be seen. The noblest character, the best heart, and always the object of my sorrows, of my pity; – I always thought of him with deep emotions, he deserved to be happy more than a thousand others, yet he never was, he was so deeply unhappy! It is beyond my comprehension that I shall never see him again.

George would always remain 'the dear unforgettable Forster', Heyne told his daughter, for 'with all his faults, he was the most noble man and a scholar of a kind of which I know no other.' He was 'one of our best and finest writers', Heyne wrote in his private correspondence – but never dared to say the same in public.

In the weeks and months after George's death, letters zigzagged across the German states. Sophie von La Roche, Germany's most successful female novelist, wrote to Soemmerring – 'is it true that our dear, long-beloved Forster has perished in Paris?' He had been far too young, she said, 'and I shed a heartfelt tear for him'.

On 6 February 1794, Alexander von Humboldt also wrote to Soemmerring, 'Oh, but our Forster, is he truly no more? Those times of our lives we spent with him were beautiful!'

Epilogue

After George's death, Therese began to rewrite history. At the end of February 1794 she sent a long rambling letter to her old friend Caroline Michaelis-Böhmer, explaining their relationship – 'he never possessed my love, never my desire, but from the moment of our union, he had my wistful tenderness, my anxious care. His happiness was necessary for my peace.' She and Huber had planned to move to France to be near George, she suddenly claimed, 'he was to us what God is to Christians – we had to be devout and joyous for his sake.' Had George demanded she leave Huber, she would have done so, 'I would have never resisted'.

Friends and family tried to rescue George's manuscripts, which had been confiscated by the Prussian authorities since their recapture of Mainz. Heyne, Therese, Reinhold Forster and Soemmerring were all involved. On 25 January 1794, only days after receiving the news of his son's death, Reinhold wrote to Voß, George's publisher in Berlin, urging him to help – not so much to honour his son's legacy but to repay George's debts. They had to act fast, Reinhold urged, as Heyne was already conspiring to claim George's effects for Therese. He also wrote to the Elector of Mainz, blaming Therese – 'the wicked snake' – for George's revolutionary leanings, treason and his financial woes. It was Soemmerring who saved them, eventually convincing the Prussians to release a traitor's correspondence and manuscripts. The two friends had never spoken again after George became the leading voice of the Mainz Republic, but Soemmerring still loved the man who knew him best.

Over the next years Therese invented, embellished and lied to present herself as the mistreated partner in her marriage. When her oldest daughter was sixteen, she told her that Caroline had seduced George. 'I fear we have reason to reproach him for behaviour that was far from delicate in every respect,' she said, though it was Therese who had betrayed her husband, and Caroline had only ever been George's friend.

The two women, friends since childhood, became estranged. 'Therese has done me such infinite harm, of which I discover new traces almost daily,' Caroline wrote, 'that it would be disingenuous for me to love her.'

Therese married Huber on 10 April 1794, exactly three months after George's death. She had six more children, only two of whom reached adulthood. Huber himself died at the age of forty, in 1804. After his death, Therese published Huber's correspondence together with a description of his life. Before doing so, she edited and altered the letters, presenting her second marriage as a selfless act in which Huber had taken care of a widow and her children. Caroline was appalled and wrote a furious note to their mutual friend Meta – 'what does Therese want with all these undertakings? other than to justify herself.' It was a 'bizarre work of art in its omission and concealment,' Caroline said, 'which has left me feeling sick and disgusted'.

In Weimar, Goethe read Huber's letters and the biographical essay with great interest. 'I believe,' he wrote to a friend, 'that one could write a fascinating novel from these characters, relationships, and events, because then one could focus on what had to be hushed up here.' A few months later, he began to jot down the first ideas for his novel *Elective Affinities* in which the relationship of a couple breaks apart with the arrival of another man and woman. When Goethe had spent two days in Mainz in August 1792, he had seen George, Therese and Huber as well as Caroline – they had been quite possibly an inspiration for his turbulent novel in which the four protagonists are torn between passion and convention.

Therese had a talent for upsetting people. When her daughters Therese and Clara were in their thirties, they dared to stand up to their mother, reproaching her for being controlling and manipulative. 'Do you see in everything I have ever written hatred towards humanity and the world,' Therese replied to their accusations – 'you treat me like a tyrant you must tiptoe around.' Like Reinhold, Therese never found fault in her own behaviour, saying 'I always only wanted to do good'.

Therese needed to make a living and so she began to write novels, at first under Huber's name and anonymously, and then, after her father's death, under her own name. She also wrote articles for a literary and cultural daily, the *Morgenblatt für gebildete Stände* (*Morning Paper for the Educated Classes*). In 1817, aged fifty-two, she became the editor of the *Morgenblatt* – the first woman to run a newspaper in Germany – and made the journal hugely successful. In 1824 she told a friend that she had burned almost all her letters to George – 'a large laundry basket full' – but five years later, shortly before her death, she published his correspondence with others and a long biographical sketch. This again was a sanitized portrait, for Therese had not only eliminated but also heavily edited many of his letters to conceal her affairs and plans for a divorce – 'I prune everything that is just sentimental effusions,' she admitted. 'It was Forster's greatest misfortune to be survived by Therese Huber,' one early biographer said, and her manipulations certainly cast George in the light she preferred. We rarely see him confronting or reproaching her for infidelity – but any such accusation in a letter she would most likely have consigned to the fire, along with any version of their story that didn't suit her designs. When she died on 15 June 1829, aged sixty-five, she took the truth with her to the grave.*

Reinhold Forster was one of the few who dared to write about George in public. Even if he had disagreed with his son's political decisions and at one point had said he wanted to see him hanged, Reinhold was shocked by his son's death. He published an account of George's life, but one focused on the early years. The father who George had once described as someone with 'a propensity for self-love, pride and a certain scholarly vanity' managed to write more about himself than his son – focusing on his own achievements in Russia and on the *Resolution* rather than George's experiences. According to Reinhold, he was the mastermind behind his son's literary success and fame – he had 'trained him to become the great light of Germany', he told Wieland a few years later.

Another who refused to stay quiet, but who expressed himself in a very different tone, was the philosopher Herder. Fearing that Germany was manoeuvring itself into intellectual isolation, Herder mourned his friend's death and open mind. 'How much have we lost in this respect

* In 1843, George Forster's beloved eldest daughter Therese published several edited volumes of his collected works. They included his account of the *Resolution* voyage, his *Views of the Lower Rhine, from Brabant, Holland, England and France*, and three thick volumes of essays and treatises (including *About the Breadfruit* and 'Cook, the Discoverer'), as well as revolutionary and political writings such as *Parisian Sketches* and for the first time *Account of the Mainz Revolution* (which had not been published during his lifetime).

when Georg Forster died!' he wrote, 'an evil genius seems to be at play, trying (and against what?) to tear the thread that connects us with the ideas of other nations.'

Even after his death George continued to inspire, his work reaching a younger generation. In September 1798, less than five years after his death, the twenty-five-year-old English poet Samuel Taylor Coleridge published *The Rime of the Ancient Mariner*, a long narrative poem about a sailor who, after killing an albatross, brings misfortune upon his ship and is then condemned to wander the world telling his harrowing tale. The poem broadly follows the route and description of *A Voyage Round the World* – and to some extent, mirrors the sequence of events, moving from the violent storms that drove the *Resolution* south into the labyrinth of icebergs near the South Pole to the dead calm seas of the tropics.* George's spectacular descriptions of the groaning blue and green icebergs seemed to have fed straight into Coleridge's verses.

> And now there came both mist and snow,
> And it grew wondrous cold:
> And ice, mast-high, came floating by,
> As green as emerald
> . . .
> The ice was here, the ice was there,
> The ice was all around:
> It cracked and growled, and roared and howled,
> Like noises in a swound!

Where George had written of how phosphorescence lit up the ocean and illuminated the shapes of fish swimming next to the *Resolution*, Coleridge composed:

> Beyond the shadow of the ship,
> I watched the water-snakes:
> They moved in tracks of shining white,
> And when they reared, the elfish light
> Fell off in hoary flakes.
> Within the shadow of the ship

* Coleridge's maths teacher had been William Wales, the *Resolution*'s astronomer.

I watched their rich attire:
Blue, glossy green, and velvet black,
They coiled and swam; and every track
Was a flash of golden fire.

When he wrote *The Rime of the Ancient Mariner*, Coleridge had never crossed the Channel, let alone an ocean, yet his evocations of storms and icebergs are as haunting as if he had been on the *Resolution*.

There was more in George's work that appealed to Coleridge. In *A Voyage Round the World*, George had ridiculed scientists who simply collected data – 'they received a confused heap of disjointed limbs, which no art could reunite into a whole; and the rage of hunting after facts soon rendered them incapable of forming and resolving a single proposition.' Coleridge too despised these 'Little-ists', as he called them, decrying the fragmentation of science. 'This devotion to the fractional materials of knowledge,' he said, 'did weaken the connective powers of the understanding.'

Alexander von Humboldt agreed. When he embarked on his epic five-year voyage to South America in 1799, he often cited his old mentor as his inspiration. Unlike his brother, Alexander von Humboldt never stopped talking about the 'ingenious Georg Forster'. For the rest of his long life – in his letters, conversations and books – he credited George for guiding his thinking about the natural world and politics. 'What I owe to your son,' he wrote to Reinhold three years after George's death, 'for that, alas! I can now only thank his excellent father.' Whenever someone mentioned George, Alexander reminisced about their friendship. 'A world of memories and deepest gratitude is attached to this name for me,' he wrote in 1856, at the age of eighty-seven.

In his hugely popular travel account *Personal Narrative*, Alexander von Humboldt wrote that his view of nature had been shaped by George Forster. And in 1845 he told Wilhelm Grimm (one of the famous folklorist Brothers Grimm) that *A Voyage Round the World* had been an inspiration for his own international bestseller *Cosmos*. He gave George a rousing memorial in his second volume:

> Through him has been commenced a new era of scientific travelling, having for its object the comparative knowledge of nations and of

> nature in different parts of the earth's surface. Gifted with refined aesthetic feeling, and retaining the fresh and living pictures with which Tahiti and the other fortunate islands of the Pacific had filled his imagination (as in later years that of Charles Darwin), George Forster was the first gracefully and pleasingly to depict the different gradations of vegetation, the relations of climate, and the various articles of food, in their bearing on the habits and manners of different tribes according to their differences of race and of previous habitation. All that can give truth, individuality, and graphic distinctness to the representation of an exotic nature, is united in his writings: not only his excellent account of the second voyage of Captain Cook, but still more his smaller works, contain the germ of much which, at a later period, has been brought to maturity.

Friedrich Schlegel, one of the Young Romantics who came together in the small university town of Jena in the mid-1790s, also chose to acknowledge George's achievements publicly. It helped that Schlegel had never cared what others thought. 'Shackles, walls and dams could not stop this *free* spirit,' he wrote in 1797 in a long essay about George, insisting that one couldn't read his works 'without feeling not only invigorated to think for oneself and enriched, but also feeling *expanded*'. He was one of the greatest German writers, Schlegel said, 'undoubtably Forster was an *artist* in the fullest sense of the word'.

Therese's old friend Caroline Michaelis-Böhmer was at the centre of this group of rebellious young thinkers and poets in Jena – so, maybe it wasn't surprising that they read and appreciated George's work. His fight for freedom and equality, and his emphasis on the importance of emotion, resonated with their sensibilities and ideals. Already in *A Voyage Round the World*, George had stressed the value of feelings and subjectivity. 'For me to feel is more than to know,' he wrote, underlining that each person sees the world through their own mind and heart, rather than submitting to some kind of objective truth. At a time when Enlightenment thinkers celebrated the power of reason, he had warned that submitting to its supremacy demanded unconditional obedience – the reliance on reason alone would turn people into empty 'human shells'.

His ideas laid down some of the first stepping stones between the Enlightenment and Romanticism. 'Don't forget that the path to reflection leads through imagination,' he had written in 1792, and this new focus became important for the Young Romantics, who believed that the world had been stripped of poetry and reduced to a monotonous machine – a vast millwheel grinding itself to dust. Nature, they felt, had been diminished to something that could be measured, classified, rationalized, dismantled and exploited, robbed of its awe and wonder. 'The sciences must all be poeticized,' the young poet Novalis declared in 1798. For centuries, imagination had been assigned a subordinate place in the discipline of philosophy. Descartes, Spinoza and Leibniz had regarded it with suspicion, believing it to be unreliable and obscuring the truth. Samuel Johnson had called it 'a licentious and vagrant faculty', but George Forster believed that imagination was essential for true knowledge.

'Reason, feeling and imagination, united in the most beautiful dance, are the three Graces of life,' he had written in an essay in 1791, his words encapsulating this new understanding of the world.

Yet for most Germans, George Forster remained a traitor. As Germany turned inward after Napoleon's victories in the first decade of the nineteenth century, he was written out of history. But those who believed in freedom and equality didn't forget. The poet Heinrich Heine – himself forced to leave Germany for Paris in 1831 because of his radical political opinions – even made a pilgrimage to the garret room where George had died. In November 1845, three years before he wrote the *Communist Manifesto* with Karl Marx, the German revolutionary Friedrich Engels published an article in the newspaper *The Northern Star* in which he asked the English to remember George's legacy – 'why not glorify George Forster, the German Thomas Paine, who supported the French Revolution in Paris up to the last, in opposition to all his countrymen?' One hundred years later, another communist, Egon Erwin Kisch, praised George as the most important German writer, albeit one who had been eradicated from the canon as 'the imperial ban against revolutionaries applies in all realms and does not expire even after a century and a half'.

The few who presented him in a positive light often focused on the private man or the explorer, sacrificing the political thinker and writer. An early biographer remarked in 1915 that 'we should leave the politician Forster to the French.' Decades after his death, his support for the revolution and belief in freedom and equality still evoked disdain. 'He forgot his fatherland for the sake of freedom and joined the fools and villains,' one critic wrote, 'but he soon realized his error and died.' Another published an article in a popular magazine with the title 'Georg Forster, Naturalist and – Traitor to the Fatherland'. In the 1930s, the German philosopher Walter Benjamin included him in his anthology of letters, *Deutsche Menschen* (*German People*), but it was mostly George Forster's absence that was notable in Germany.

It was only in the late 1950s, two centuries after his birth, that historians in East Germany became interested in George's role in the Mainz Republic. That led to an ambitious research project at the Academy of Sciences of the German Democratic Republic in East Berlin, culminating in the publication of a comprehensive eighteen-volume edition of his works and letters.* This edition fostered more research and West German historians also began to rediscover his work, but the English had almost entirely forgotten him – a German who had criticized Britain's imperial ambitions was never going to be popular. There is a bitter irony in the fact that a man who described himself 'as a human, a citizen of the world' should have remained unknown in the rest of the world.

For me, George Forster's most important legacy was his unshakeable belief in humankind – this messy, uncontrollable and incomprehensible thing that is us. More than eight billion of us – so utterly different, yet so alike. At times like ours, when the world seems to retreat behind national boundaries, when discord is fostered and division emphasized, I see George Forster as a light in the darkness. Not a flawless shining hero, but a human being full of contradictions and faults who nonetheless tried to make the world a better place, with one word and one sentence after the next. He was far from perfect – he made mistakes and misjudged situations. He was a product of his age, yet he shook off its

* In 1987, the GDR also named the first German Antarctic station after George Forster.

chains of prejudice. He saw unity behind our diversity – not a sameness that made us all alike but a bond that should hold us together. A perpetual outsider, always travelling, George Forster never felt that he truly belonged, but that was also why he embraced the otherness of others. He was a traveller who opened his heart, eyes and his mind.

He defied the limitations of his short life. He was an original thinker and a man of enormous compassion. 'Oh, if only one could see into my heart!' he wrote in 1784, 'it is a heart that loves humankind!' Humans are like harp strings, he had once explained, from which a great variety of melodies and harmonies can be produced because of their different lengths. Were the strings all one length, the richness of the music would be lessened. Our differences produce the symphony that is humankind. For George Forster, these differences should never be a cause of hatred, racism or oppression, because our diversity is fundamental to our human species – it makes us who we are. 'Freedom and equality? My entire life is proof to myself . . . that these principles are and always have been intimately interwoven with my way of thinking,' he had said in 1793. 'I can and will never deny them.'

Abbreviations

Unless otherwise referenced, letters to and from George Forster and Therese Heyne-Forster-Huber are published in *Georg Forsters Werke. Sämtliche Schriften, Tagebücher, Briefe* (AA vols. 13–18) and *Therese Huber. Briefe*, ed. Magdalene Heuser, Berlin: De Gruyter, 1999–2013.

All translations of German letters and George Forster's German publications are mine.

PEOPLE

AH: Alexander von Humboldt
CS: Caroline Michaelis-Böhmer-Schlegel-Schelling
GF: George Forster
JRF: Johann Reinhold Forster
TF: Therese Heyne-Forster-Huber
WH: Wilhelm von Humboldt

SOURCES AND ARCHIVES

ALZ: Allgemeine Literatur Zeitung
BBAW VA32182: Documents related to Mulovsky's expedition from the Central State Archive of the Navy, St Petersburg, at Brandenburgische Akademie der Wissenschaften
BBAW: Brandenburgische Akademie der Wissenschaften
BF online: Papers of Benjamin Franklin, https://franklinpapers.org
BL: British Library
GNM: Germanisches Nationalmuseum Nürnberg
Gotha: Forschungsbibliothek Gotha der Universität Erfurt
HMC: Harris Manchester College, University of Oxford
KSW: Klassik Stiftung Weimar
NHM: Natural History Museum, London
NMM: National Maritime Museum, Greenwich
RS: Royal Society, London
RS CMRS: Council Meetings, Royal Society, London
RS JBRS: Journal Books, Royal Society, London

SAL: Society of Antiquaries of London
Stabi Berlin: Staatsbibliothek Berlin
SUB Göttingen: Staats- und Universitätsbibliothek, Göttingen

WORKS

AA: (Akademie-Ausgabe) Forster, Georg, *Georg Forsters Werke. Sämtliche Schriften, Tagebücher, Briefe*, published and edited by Akademie der Wissenschaften der DDR, Berlin: Akademie-Verlag, 1958–

GF Ansichten 1791–92: Forster, Georg, *Ansichten vom Niederrhein, von Brabant, Flandern, Holland, England und Frankreich im April, Mai und Junius 1790* (1791–92), AA 9

GF, 'Geschichte der Reisen' (1791): Forster, Georg, 'Geschichte der Reisen die seit Cook an der Nordwest- und Nordost-Küste von America und im nördlichen Amerika selbst von Meares, Dixon, Portlock, Coxe, Long u.a.m unternommen worden sind' (1791), AA 5

GF Letters 1829: Forster, Georg, *Johann Georg Forster's Briefwechsel, nebst einigen Nachrichten von seinem Leben*, ed. Therese Huber, Leipzig: F.A. Brockhaus, 1829

GF Speech 15 November 1792: Forster, Georg, 'Über das Verhältniß der Mainzer gegen die Franken,' 15 November 1792, AA 10. 1

GF Speech 1 January 1793: Forster, Georg, 'Anrede an die Gesellschaft der Freunde der Freiheit und Gleichheit am Neujahrstage,' 1 January 1793, AA 10. 1

GF Speech 21 March 1793: Forster, Georg, 'Rede über die Vereinigung des rheinisch-deutschen Freistaat mit der Frankenrepublik,' 21 March 1793, AA 10. 1

GF Voyage 2000: Forster, George, *A Voyage Round the World: George Forster*, ed. Nicholas Thomas and Oliver Berghof, Honolulu: University of Hawai'i Press, 2000

JRF Journal 1982: Forster, Johann Reinhold, *The Resolution Journal of Johann Reinhold Forster, 1772–1775*, ed. Michael E. Hoare, London: Hakluyt Society, 1982

JRF Map Volga, 1768: Forster, Johann Reinhold. 'A Letter from Mr. J. R. Forster, F.A.S. to M. Maty, M.D. Sec.R.S. containing some Account of a new Map of the River Volga,' *Phil. Trans.* RS, 1768, vol. 58

JRF Natural History Volga, 1767: Forster, Johann Reinhold, 'A treatise on the natural history of the river Volga,' 1767, RS, Letters & Papers, 4/394

JRF *Philosophischer Anzeiger*, 1795: Forster, Johann Reinhold, 'Ueber Georg Forster,' *Philosophischer Anzeiger*, 1795

JRF Specimen Volgensis, 1767: Forster, Johann Reinhold, 'Specimen Historiae Naturalis Volgensis,' *Phil. Trans.* RS, 1767, vol. 57

Phil. Trans. RS: Philosophical Transactions of the Royal Society

Notes

AUTHOR'S NOTE

xxi. spelling of George vs Georg: Some examples are, JRF, 13 September 1773, JRF Journal 1982, p. 363, JRF to T. Pennant, 17 October 1768, Uhlig 2000, p. 55; JRF to Spener, 14 February 1777, AA 13, p. 921; Spener to Banks, 14 August 1784, Banks 2008, vol. 2, p. 68; GF to Spener, 22 September 1775 and 2 April 1776; TF to GF, 8 November 1785; TF to Spener, 21 January 1787; GF to TF, 2 April 1790; TF to F.J. Bertuch, 11 May 1790; JRF to GF, 29 April 1792; AH to JRF, 24 September 1790, Humboldt 1973, p. 108; CS to Meyer, 15 June 1793, Schlegel-Schelling 1913, p. 295; TF to G. Reinhold, 6 July 1810.

PROLOGUE

1. 'he is killed': GF, 19 August 1774, GF Voyage 2000, p. 550; GF records *marokee* as '*markom*'; see also footnote 66, p. 822. **1. GF with the islanders:** GF in Tanna, GF, 5–20 August, GF Voyage 2000, pp. 508–56. **1. 'members of one great'**: GF, 19 August 1774, GF Voyage 2000, p. 549. **2. account of islander's murder**: Ibid, pp. 549–50; Cook, 19 August 1774, Beaglehole 1961, pp. 498–500; Sparrman, August 1774; Sparrman 1953, pp. 150–51; Elliott Journal, August 1774, Holmes 1984, p. 34. **3. 'Instead of making amends'**: GF, 19 August 1774, GF Voyage 2000, p. 551. **3. 'the intercourse which has'**: GF, 21 August 1773, GF Voyage 2000, p. 168. **3. 'have by nature no'**: Kant, 'Observations on the Feeling of the Beautiful and Sublime' (1764), Kant 2011, p. 58. **4. 'what is tolerance'**: GF to Soemmerring, 5 April 1787 **4. 'I have spent half'**: AH to Heinrich König, 28 July 1858, Bruhns 1872, vol. 1, p. 104. **4. 'So many men seem'**: GF to TF, 25 July 1784 **4. 'I thank God that'**: GF to A.F. von Veltheim, 19 January 1780. **4. 'nothing is so irresistible'**: GF to T.F., 3 September 1784; see also GF to Jacobi, 16 November 1783, and GF to Soemmerring, 19 February 1787. **5. 'aching feelings of'**: GF to JRF, 2 March 1783. **5. 'I also feel voids**': GF to S.H. Jacobi, 9 March 1784. **6. 'to throw more light'**: GF Voyage 2000, p. 9. **6. 'beautiful manifestation of'**: GF, 'Über lokale und allgemeine Bildung' (1791), AA 7, p. 49. **6. 'One is either for'**: GF to TF, 4 February 1793. **6. 'of the rights which'**: GF Voyage 2000, p. 9. **6. we're all the same**: GF, 'Cook, der Entdecker' (1787), AA 5, p. 280. **6. 'brings all individual chords'**: GF, 'Über die Beziehung der Staatskunst auf das Glück der Menschheit' (1793), AA 10. 1, p. 580. **6. 'the real guide to how'**: Ibid, p. 591.

CHAPTER I

9. a magnifying glass: JRF, Specimen Volgensis, 1767, vol. 57, p. 341, 324. **9. 700 specimens**: JRF, Natural History Volga, 1767, 4/394, pp. 11–12. **9. GF in Russia**: JRF, *Philosophischer Anzeiger*, 1795, col. 14–15; JRF, Natural History Volga, 1767, 4/394; JRF Specimen Volgensis, 1767, vol. 57; JRF Map Volga 1768, vol. 58, p. 215; Steiner 1968, vol. 2, pp. 254–6; GF Letters 1829, pp. 6–11; J.H. Merck to Duke Carl August of Saxe-Weimar, 9 May 1781, Merck 1911, p. 97; Hoare 1976, pp. 27–32. **9. wildfire in Russia**: GF, 'Neuholland und die britische Colonie in Botany-Bay' (1786), AA 5, p. 168. **9. animals GF saw in Russia**: JRF Specimen Volgensis, 1767, vol. 57, pp. 342–3, 348. **9. dugouts in the ground**: Beratz 1923, pp. 68–71; Züge 1802, vol. 1, pp. 153–54. **10. Lake Elton**: JRF Natural History Volga, 1767, 4/394, pp. 8–9. **10. Ryn Desert**: JRF Map Volga, 1768, vol. 58, p. 215. **10. 'of a nauseous or'**: JRF Natural History Volga, 1767, 4/394, p. 23; for wild asparagus (*Asparagus officinalis*) and bog cranberries (*Vaccinium oxycoccos*), JRF Specimen Volgensis, 1767, vol. 57, pp. 329–30. **11. GF's childhood**: JRF *Philosophischer Anzeiger*, 1795, col. 12; see also JRF to GF, 29 April 1792; GF Letter 1829, p. 6ff; GF to J.G. v. Zimmermann, 30 December 1787. He was baptized Johann George Adam Forster. **11. GF's family home**: George Forster's home in Hochzeit-Nassenhuben after a photograph by Damm at bpk-Fotoarchiv, Nr. 10028381; JRF to K.F. v. Irwing, 19 February 1763. **11. GF's education**: JRF *Philosophischer Anzeiger*, 1795, col. 12–13; see also GF Letter 1829, p. 6ff. **12. classroom outside:** Turner 1799, p. 420. **12. another with the whip**: GF Letter 1829, p. 7; TF to F. and J.G. Reinhold, 6 and 8 May 1806. **12. 'I had no say'**: GF to Jacobi, 29 August 1783. **13. GF making others happy**: GF to F. d'Elhuyar y de Suvisa, December 1787 (draft) and 23 December 1787; for JRF's temper, e.g. Lichtenberg to J.A. Schernhagen, 16 October 1775 and 23 December 1782; Lichtenberg 1983–2004, vol. 1, pp. 566–7, and vol. 2, p. 489; GF Letter 1829, p. 7; Elliott Journal, March 1775, Holmes 1984, p. 44. **13. JRF's upbringing**: Hoare 1976, p. 9, for JRF's marriage, p. 15. **13. JRF and scholars in Europe**: Ibid, p. 24ff. **13. JRF falling asleep**: Turner 1799, pp. 418–19. **13. 2,500 fine volumes**: Hoare 1976, p. 16; for JRF ignoring practicalities of daily life, J.H. Merck to Duke Carl August of Saxe-Weimar, 15 June 1781, Merck 1911, p. 100. **13. GF's siblings**: Anonymous 1804, p. 805. **14. 'made use of our own Thoughts'**: John Locke, *An Essay Concerning Human Understanding* (1689), Locke 1894, p. 115. **14. 'Reason determines the philosopher'**: Diderot and D'Alembert, *Encyclopédie*, 1765, vol. 12, p. 509. **15. '*Sapere aude*'**: Immanuel Kant, 'An Answer to the Question: What is Enlightenment?', 1784. **16. 'Come, ye philosophers'**: Voltaire, *Poème sur le désastre de Lisbonne*, Molesky 2016, p. 328. **16. Russian troops near Gdansk**: Turner 1799, p. 422. **17. JRF applied immediately**: JRF heard about the commission from H.W. Rehbinder, the representative of the Russian government in Gdansk; JRF *Philosophischer Anzeiger*, 1795, col. 14; JRF to J.D. Michaelis, 26 January 1765, SUB Göttingen. **17. JRF's character**: GF Letters 1829, p. 5. **17. 'my little travelling companion'**: JRF to J.D. Michaelis, 26 January 1765, SUB Göttingen. **17. GF**

and JRF's travels in Russia: JRF *Philosophischer Anzeiger*, 1795, cols 14–16; JRF Natural History Volga, 1767, 4/394; JRF Specimen Volgensis, 1767, vol. 57; JRF Map Volga, 1768, vol. 58, p. 215; Steiner 1968, vol. 2, pp. 254–6, GF Letters 1829, pp. 6–11; J.H. Merck to Duke Carl August of Saxe-Weimar, 9 May 1781, Merck 1911, p. 97; Hoare 1976, pp. 27–32. **17. Catherine's invitation for German settlers**: Beratz 1923, pp. 22–8; Steiner 1968, vol. 2, p. 249. **18. not as golden as her pledges**: Count Orlov to Catherine the Great, May 1765, Steiner 1968, vol. 2, pp. 251–2; Hoare 1976, p. 27. **18. visiting colonies en route**: Nišnaja Dobrynka (founded 29 June 1764), Talovka (10 August 1764), Ust'-Kulalinka (12 August 1764), Sosnovka (14 August 1764), Svastjanovka (7 September 1764), Verchnaja Kulalinka (26 May 1765), Steiner 1968, p. 431. **18. brown bears and wolves**: JRF Specimen Volgensis 1767, vol. 57, p. 342. **18. conditions were abysmal**: Beratz 1923, pp. 68–71, 76–7; Züge 1802, vol. 1 pp. 141–56. **18. corrupt governor**: The governor was Nikita Stroev; Bartlett 1975, p. 491; JRF *Philosophischer Anzeiger*, 1795, col. 16; Züge 1802, vol. 2, pp. 51–2. **18. 'these graves of the living'**: Züge 1802, vol. 1, p. 154. **19. 'So this is the paradise'**: Ibid, p. 144. **19. 'my inclination to observe'**: GF to TF, 25 July 1784. **19. 'a wicked, despotic'**: GF Letters 1829, p. 9. **19. 'everything that happens'**: GF to Heyne, 5 June 1792. **19. 'very fat in autumn'**: JRF Natural History Volga, 1767, 4/394, p. 25. **19. otters, Tatar coins and caviar**: JRF Specimen Volgensis, 1767, vol. 57, pp. 342, 354; JRF's paper about 'Tartarian Antiquities' at the Society of Antiquaries, 26 February 1767, Minute Book, SAL, vol. 10, pp. 267–78. **20. natural history collections at Volga**: JRF Natural History Volga, 1767, 4/394, pp. 11–12. **20. turned against . . . Cossack escorts**: Report of Chancellery for the Guardianship of Foreigners, enclosed in a letter from Lord Cathcart to the Earl of Halifax, 17/28 June 1771, Bartlett 1975, p. 495. **20. JRF's troubles in St Petersburg**: JRF *Philosophischer Anzeiger*, 1795, col. 16; J.H. Merck to Duke Carl August of Saxe-Weimar, 9 May 1781, Merck 1911, pp. 97–8; JRF to J.D. Michaelis, 24 August 1775, Michaelis 1796, vol. 3, p. 376; for the Chancellery, Beratz 1923, p. 95ff. **20. GF at school**: JRF *Philosophischer Anzeiger*, 1795, col. 121; Steiner 1968, p. 261. **21. threatening to publish a letter**: Marquis de Bausset to Duc de Choiseul, 29 August/10 September 1766, *Sbornik Imperatorskago Russkago istoričeskago obščestva* (SIRIO), 1913, vol. 141, p. 145. **21. 'We are almost Englishmen'**: JRF to J.D. Michaelis, 24 August 1775, Michaelis 1796, vol. 3, p. 375; for Forster family ancestry *Philosophischer Anzeiger* 1795, col. 10; Hoare 1976, p. 1. **21. 'George', rather than 'Georg'**: Hoare 1976, p. 16. **21. 'So I went to'**: JRF to J.D. Michaelis, 24 August 1775, Michaelis 1796, vol. 3, p. 376. **21. 'himself transported to'**: Archenholz 1790, p. 2. **21. selling books to buy food**: JRF to C.A. Böttiger, 9 January 1798, GNM.

CHAPTER 2

22. 3 ½ guineas: Hoare 1976, p. 36; for costs of lodging: the German tourist C.P. Moritz paid 12 and 16 shillings for his lodgings in London, C.P. Moritz in 1782,

Moritz 1983, pp. 27, 188. **22. shops in London**: Lichtenberg to E.G. Baldinger, 10 January 1775, Lichtenberg 1938, pp. 63–4; C.P. Moritz in 1782, Moritz 1983, p. 33. **22. 'an atrocious mess'**: C.P. Moritz in 1782, Moritz 1983, p. 35; for liquor p. 33 and Archenholz 1790, p. 204. **22. Woide generously organized**: C.G. Woide Diary, 4 and 6 October 1766, 14 January 1767, Woide Papers, BM Add 48,700 f. 100, BL; for lodging in Denmark Street, Gordon 1975, p. 11. **23. boisterous, frenzied and dirty**: Lichtenberg to E.G. Baldinger, 10 January 1775, Lichtenberg 1938, pp. 63–4. **23. 'By your leave'**: Ibid, p. 64. **23. 'Indeed one can have'**: Lichtenberg to J.C. Dieterich, 19 April 1770, Lichtenberg 1938, p. 49. **24. lanterns outside the houses**: Titius (1777) 1783, vol. 10, p. 181. **24. St James's Park**: C.P. Moritz in 1782, Moritz 1983, p. 30. **24. 'keen-eyed assistant'**: JRF to J.D. Michaelis, 26 January 1765, SUB Göttingen. **24. GF had picked up English**: JRF *Philosophischer Anzeiger*, 1795, col. 123. **24. Society of Antiquaries**: 21 May 1767, SAL/02/010/062, Minute Book, SAL, vol. 10, pp. 346-7; Gordon claimed that the Forsters also went to the RS that afternoon but the RS Minutes of the Meeting list 'Revd Mr Forster' not 'Mr Forster' (which is how JRF was always listed). JBRS, vol. 26, 21 May 1767, p. 611; Gordon 1975, p. 30. **25. Warrington Academy**: C.G. Woide Diary, 22 May 1767, Woide Papers, BM Add Ms 48,700 f. 142, BL; see also JRF *Philosophischer Anzeiger*, 1795, col. 123; for £60 salary, Minute Book, 25 June 1767, Minutes of the Proceedings of the Trustees of the Warrington Academy, vol. 1, HMC MS. Warrington, 2, p. 133; JRF was also allowed to charge each student 2 guineas. **25. 'agreeable and easy'**: A Report of the State of the Warrington Academy, Annual Meeting, 25 June 1767, HMC Warrington Academy Reports Book, p. 3. **25. apprentice to a merchant**: JRF *Philosophischer Anzeiger*, 1795, col. 124; J.H. Merck to Duke Carl August of Saxe-Weimar, 15 June 1781, Merck 1911, p. 98; Gordon 1975, pp. 42–5; JRF left London on 22 June 1767, C.G. Woide Diary, 22 June 1767, Woide Papers, BM Add Ms 48,700 f. 147, BL. **26. Justina Elisabeth Forster's character**: 'Obituary Justina Elisabeth Forster,' *Hallisches Patriotisches Wochenblatt*, 15 December 1804, p. 806. **26. Justina Elisabeth's arrival**: C.G. Woide Diary, 4 September 1767, Woide Papers, BM Add Ms 48.700 f. 165, BL. **26. journey north in the stagecoach**: Woide took them to Newgate Street on 6 September 1767, C.G. Woide Diary, 6 September 1767, Woide Papers, BM Add Ms 48.700 f. 166, BL; JRF *Philosophischer Anzeiger*, 1795, col. 125; J.H. Merck to Duke Carl August of Saxe-Weimar, 15 June 1781, Merck 1911, p. 98. **26. JRF decided to let him stay**: JRF *Philosophischer Anzeiger*, 1795, col. 125. **26. six young students**: Gordon 1975, p. 50. **26. GF attended lessons**: JRF *Philosophischer Anzeiger*, 1795, col. 125. **26. 'I intend to come'**: JRF to T. Pennant, 17 October 1768, Uhlig 2000, p. 55; GF as tutor, GF Letters 1829, p. 13; JRF *Philosophischer Anzeiger*, 1795, cols 125–6; J.H. Merck to Duke Carl August of Saxe-Weimar, 15 June 1781, Merck 1911, p. 99. **27. 'this worthless set'**: JRF to T. Pennant, 21 April 1769, Gordon 1975 p. 108. **27. 'confined to a wretched school'**: JRF to T. Pennant, 12 December 1768, Uhlig 2004, p. 30; see also Gordon 1975, p. 87; for disobedience of students, Minute

Book, 26 January 1769, Minutes of the Proceedings of the Trustees of the Warrington Academy, vol. 1, HMC MS. Warrington. 2, p. 139. **27. 'agreeable and easy'**: A Report of the State of the Warrington Academy, Annual Meeting, 25 June 1767, HMC Warrington Academy Reports Book, p. 3. **27. 'no foreigner has ever'**: Archenholz 1785, vol. 1, pt. 2, p. 592; see also Aikin 1803, vol. 4, p. 171. **27. 'I was yoked too early'**: GF to J.G. Herder, 21 July 1786, AA 14, p. 513. **27. Pehr Osbeck**: The translation of Osbeck's *A Voyage to China and the East Indies* was published in early 1771. **28. Kalm's three volumes**: The translation of Kalm's *Travels into North America* was published in late 1770. **28. Bougainville's rapturous portrait**: The translation of Bougainville's *Voyage Round the World* was published on 18 January 1772. **28. 'to travel with them'**: GF, 'Des Abbés Rochon Reise nach Madagaskar und Ostindien' (1792), AA 5, p. 625. **28. 'carelessly dropt a cloth'**: Bougainville 1772, p. 219. **28. Forsters moved back to London**: C.G. Woide Diary, 10 December 1770, Woide Papers BM Add 48.700 f. 200, BL; Gordon 1975, p. 109. **28. JRF and GF at Royal Society**: JBRS, vol. 27, 13 December 1770, p. 404ff. **28. JRF presented GF's translations**: JBRS, vol. 27, 13 December 1770, p. 405. **28. meeting room at RS**: Mylius 1787, pp. 73–4. **29. portraits of previous fellows**: *Gentleman's Magazine*, 1768, vol. 38, p. 63. **29. At these meetings**: JRF and GF were at the RS on 13, 20 December 1770, 10, 17, 24, 31 January, 7, 14, 21, 28 February and 7 March 1771, and more dates, JBRS, vol. 27, pp. 404, 413, 415, 418, 420–423, 428, 432, 438, 443, 451, 453; for collections at RS, Mylius 1787, p. 75. **29. Reinhold was elected a fellow**: JRF, Election Certificate, 27 February 1772, RS, EC/1772/09. **29. translating eight volumes**: Pehr Kalm's *Travels into North America*, 1771 (2 vols); Pehr Osbeck's *Voyage to China and East Indies*, 1771 (2 vols); Jean Bernard Bossu's *Travels through that part of America formerly called Luisiana*, 1771 (2 vols); Louis Antoine de Bougainville's *Voyage Round the World*, 1772; Johann Hermann von Riedesel's *Travels through Sicily and that part of Italy called Magna Graecia and A Tour through Egypt*, 1773; JRF dedicated books to influential scientists and people: *Novae Species Insectorum Centuria*, London: T. Davies & B. White, 1771 was dedicated to Banks; *Flora Americae Septentrionalis*, London: T. Davies & B. White, 1771 to Solander; and the translation of Bougainville's *A Voyage Round the World* was dedicated to James West, president of the Royal Society. **30. 'If I didn't have a son'**: JRF to J.D. Michaelis, 30 October 1771, Michaelis 1796, vol. 3, p. 344. **30. 'translation-machine'**: GF to Spener, 28 July 1779. **30. 'He writes our language'**: *Critical Review*, 1771, vol. 31, p. 127. **30. 'superior to the original'**: Ibid, 1772, vol. 33, p. 71. **30. 'in a very mysterious manner'**: JRF, 26 May 1772, JRF Journal 1982, p. 123. **30. Banks had paid £10,000**: J. Ellis to Linnaeus, 19 August 1768, Smith 1821, vol. 1, p. 231; for Banks' *Endeavour* cabin: Plan of His Majesty's Bark *Endeavour* as fitted at Deptford in July 1768, ZAZ6590, NMM. **30. Banks and the *Resolution***: Beaglehole 1961, pp. xxviii–xxxi; see also Lord Sandwich to Banks, 20 June 1772, Banks 2008, vol. 1, pp. 135–6. **30. too dangerous to sail**: Cook to P. Stephens, 14 May 1772, Beaglehole 1961, p. 930. **30. 'He swore & stamp'd'**: John Elliott,

'Memoirs of the Early Life of John Elliott, of Elliott House, Esq. And Lieut of the Royal Navy,' 1772, BL Add 42714, f. 10v. **30. withdrew from the expedition**: Navy Board to Admiralty, 22 May 1772 and Admiralty to Navy Board, 28 May 1772, Beaglehole 1961, pp. 934–5. **31. JRF immediately agreed**: JRF, 26 May 1772, JRF Journal 1982, p. 123. **31. RS lobbied the Admiralty**: JRF, 6 June 1772, JRF Journal 1982, pp. 124–5. **31. Forsters were officially appointed**: JRF, 11 June 1772, JRF Journal 1982, p. 125; Admiralty Secretary to Navy Board, 12 June 1772, Beaglehole 1961, p. 940. **31. JRF received £4**, 000: GF Voyage 2000, p. xxxviii. **31. 'unacquainted with the peculiar'**: JRF, 13 June 1772, JRF Journal 1982, p. 126. **31. father and son bade farewell**: JRF, 26 June 1772, JRF Journal 1982, p. 127; C.G. Woide Diary, 26 June 1772, Woide Papers BM Add Ms 48.701, f. 56, BL; for Woide as guardian, JRF, 20 June 1772, Woide Papers BM Add Ms 48.706 f. 115, BL. **31. Woide took his**: C.G. Woide Diary, 29 June, 31 August and 1 September 1772, Woide Papers BM Add 48.702 f. 56, 65, BL. **32. 'provided they shall'**: JRF, 20 June 1772, Woide Papers BM Add Ms 48.706 f. 115, BL.

CHAPTER 3

35. Departure *Resolution* and *Adventure*: GF, 13 July 1772, GF Voyage 2000, p. 18. **35. under the age of sixteen**: e.g. midshipman John Elliott (b. 11 January 1759), cartographer Henry Roberts (1757), midshipman and future explorer George Vancouver (22 June 1757), Cook's mate Edward Barrett (1756), Alexander Hood (baptized 23 April 1758) and several others born in 1755 and 1754. Beaglehole, p. 874ff; and the Muster for H.M.S *Resolution* 1772–1775, PRO Adm. 36/7672 compiled by the Captain Cook Society (https://www.captaincooksociety.com/Portals/ccs/Files/Documents/Musters/3resolution2muster1.pdf). **36. *Resolution* was larger than the *Adventure***: The *Resolution* was 462 tons and the *Adventure* was 340 tons. Many books list 112 men on the *Resolution* and 81 on the *Adventure*, but those are only the crew members without the supernumeraries. The supernumeraries were: astronomer Wales and his servant, artist Hodges, the Forsters and their servant on the *Resolution*, and astronomer Bayly and his servant on the *Adventure*. Cook, 13 July 1772, Beaglehole 1961, p. 12. **36. provisions *Resolution***: Cook, 13 July 1772, Beaglehole 1961, pp. 13–17; Admiralty Secretary to Cook, 11 April 1772, p. 923. **36. for preserving animal specimens**: Admiralty Secretary to Victualling Board, 18 June 1772, Beaglehole 1961, p. 941. **36. The deck itself was crowded**: GF, 'Cook, der Entdecker' (1787), AA 5, p. 238. **36. layout *Resolution* and cabins**: Ibid, pp. 240–1. **36. *Resolution* crew**: Beaglehole 1961, pp. 874–87; for men on *Endeavour*, p. xxxiii. **37. canvas bags**: Cook to Navy Board, 9 April 1772, Beaglehole 1961, p. 922. Cook thought that the usual trunks would take up too much space – instead he had ordered canvas bags which were one yard long. **37. GF's cabin**: GF, 'Cook, der Entdecker' (1787), AA 5, p. 240; for location of the cabin: GF, *A Letter to the Right Honourable The Earl of Sandwich*, London, 1778, GF, AA 4, pp. 70–1; JRF, 10

April 1773, JRF Journal 1982, p. 251; Cook to Navy Board, 15 June 1772, Beaglehole 1961, p. 940. **37. library into storage**: Hoare 1976, p. 82. **38. 'Floods of saltwater'**: JRF, 27 November 1772, JRF Journal 1982, p. 184. **38. JRF tried to swap cabins:** Wales (1778) 2000, p. 701. **39. Cook had studied charts**: Beaglehole 1961, pp. xix–xxiv; for his plans, Cook to Lord Sandwich, February 1772, Beaglehole 1961, pp. xx–xxi. **39. 'in the more Hospitable latitudes'**: Cook to Lord Sandwich, February 1772, Beaglehole 1961, p. xxi. **39. 'to observe the Genius'**: Admiralty, Secret Instructions for Capt Cook, Commander of His Majesty's Sloop Resolution, 25 June 1772, Beaglehole 1961, p. clxviii. **40. They stopped at Madeira**: from 28 July to 1 August 1772, Cook, 29 July 1772; see also 13 July 1772, Beaglehole 1961, pp. 15, 21. **40. birds which the Forsters dissected**: GF, 24 September 1772, GF Voyage 2000, p. 43. **40. hooked a shark . . . bonitos**: GF, 18 August 1772, GF Voyage 2000, p. 38. **40. dinghies . . . the Forsters could fish**: GF, 5, 27 September, 12 October 1772, GF Voyage 2000, pp. 40–2; JRF, 5 September 1772, JRF Journal 1982, p. 171 (for the exact method how to measure currents). **40. '*Experimental Gentlemen*'**: JRF, 25 June 1773, JRF Journal 1982, p. 310. **40. 'The sea appeared luminous'**: GF, 23 July 1772, GF Voyage 2000, p. 20. **40. 'whole ocean seem to be'**: GF, 29 October 1772, GF Voyage 2000, p. 43; see also JRF, 30 October 1772, JRF Journal 1982, p. 181. **40. 'alarming appearance'**: Elliott Journal, October 1772, Holmes 1984, p. 13. **40. 'Great bodies of light'**: GF, 29 October 1772, GF Voyage 2000, p. 43. **40. Banks' mistress in Madeira:** Cook to unknown, 1 August 1772, Beaglehole 1961, p. 685; Elliott Journal, July 1772, Holmes 1984, pp. 11–12. **41. minute creatures were awe-inspiring**: GF, 29 October 1772, GF Voyage 2000, p. 44. **41. everything became mouldy**: JRF, 8 August 1772, JRF Journal 1982, p. 149. **41. adapted to life on board**: GF, 'Cook, der Entdecker' (1787), AA 5, pp. 254–6. **41. 'waddling along like ducks'**: Ibid, p. 256. **41. meals on board.**: Ibid, p. 255; see also Cook, 13 July 1772, Beaglehole 1961, p. 14. **41. 'What empire is not like'**: GF, 5 August 1772, GF Voyage 2000, p. 32. **42. 'our swallow returned'**: GF, 21 August 1772, GF Voyage 2000, p. 39; JRF, 21 August 1772, JRF Journal 1982, p. 159. **42. Charles Clerke**: Elliott's Memoirs, Holmes 1984, p. xxx; McLynn 2011, pp. 174, 177; Cowley and Deacon 2002; Sides 2024, p. 31. **42. 'by God, I'll go'**: Clerke to Banks, 15 May 1772, Beaglehole 1961, p. 931. **42. giants . . . in Patagonia**: Clerke 1767, p. 77. **42. 'Clerke is a brave'**: GF to Spener, 30 January 1780. **42. Richard Pickersgill**: McLynn 2011, p. 177, Beaglehole 1961, p. xxxv. **42. 'a good officer'**: Elliott's Memoirs, Holmes 1984, p. xxx. **42. 'The glory inseparable'**: Pickersgill Journal, 23 November 1772, Holmes 1984, p. 61. **43. 'quite a great feather'**: Beaglehole 1961, p. xxxvi, see also p. 874. **43. Cook taught the young midshipmen**: Elliott Journal, April 1774, Holmes 1984, p. 30; GF, 'Cook, der Entdecker' (1787), AA 5, pp. 283–4. **43. William Hodges**: Beaglehole 1961, pp. xli–xlii. **43. James Cook**: McLynn 2011. **44. Cook's eyes and precision**: GF, 'Cook, der Entdecker' (1787), AA 5, pp. 242–3. **44. to prevent scurvy**: Cook, 13 July 1772, Beaglehole 1961, pp. 13–17, for carrot marmalade, 25 November 1771,

Admiralty Secretary to Secretary of Society for Encouragement of Arts, Manufactures; and Commerce and Sick and Hurt Board to Admiralty, 10 March 1772, Beaglehole 1961, pp. 900, 918; for cleanliness on board: GF, 'Cook, der Entdecker' (1787), AA 5, p. 271; for sauerkraut, pp. 272–3; see also Marra, May/June 1773, Marra 1775, p. 42; 'punished dirty hands,' Cook, 15 February 1773, Beaglehole 1961, p. 94. **45. Forsters met Anders Sparrman**: GF, November 1772, GF Voyage 2000, p. 51; Cook, 30 October and November 1772, Beaglehole 1961, pp. 47, 51. **45. Sparrman to steerage**: GF, 8 September 1774, GF Voyage 2000, p. 578. **45. departure from Cape Town**: GF, 22 November 1773, GF Voyage 2000, p. 61. **45. legs and sleeves too short**: GF, 29 November 1772, GF Voyage 2000, p. 62. **45. 'one might wring'**: Marra, February 1775, Marra 1775, p. 322. **45. his eighteenth birthday**: JRF, 27 November 1772, JRF Journal 1982, p. 184; for the exact position, Cook, 27 November 1772, Beaglehole 1961, p. 53. **45. 'a scene of desolation'**: JRF, 29 November 1772, JRF Journal 1982, p. 186; see also 27 November 1772, p. 184. **45. Chairs flew through cabins**: JRF, 30 November 1772, JRF Journal 1982, p. 186. **45. first iceberg**: GF, 10 December 1772, GF Voyage 2000, pp. 64–5; JRF, 11 December 1772, JRF Journal 1982, p. 193; Cook, 11 December 1772, Beaglehole 1961, p. 57; Elliott Journal, January 1773, Holmes 1984, p. 14. **45. waves breaking over ... icebergs**: JRF, 12 December 1772, JRF Journal 1982, p. 194; Cook, 11–14 December 1772, Beaglehole 1961, pp. 57–9. **46. 'entangled among the ice'**: Marra, 26 December 1772, Marra 1775, p. 7. **46. sleet, hail and snow**: GF, 26 December 1772, GF Voyage 2000, p. 70; see also Marra, January 1773, Marra 1775, pp. 10–11; for noise, GF, 29 November 1772, GF Voyage 2000, p. 62. **46. icebergs were anything but white**: GF, 18 and 26 December 1772, GF Voyage 2000, pp. 68–9. **46. southern lights**: GF, 17 February 1773, GF Voyage 2000, p. 76. **46. whales ... shearwaters**: JRF, 16 December 1772, 13, 14 and 20 February 1773, JRF Journal 1982, pp. 198–9, 226, 228. **46. Petrels ... albatrosses**: GF, 11 and 26 December 1772, 17 February 1773, GF Voyage 2000, pp. 66, 69, 75. **46. eighty-six penguins**: JRF, 30 December 1772, JRF Journal 1982, p. 209; Pickersgill in Beaglehole 1961, p. 69. **46. penguins ... overtook the ship**: JRF, 13 February 1773, JRF Journal 1982, p. 226. **46. William Wales**: Beaglehole 1961, pp. xl–xli. **46. 'preferring a Voyage'**: Wales at RS, 18 December 1767, CMRS, vol. v, f. 228. **46. at Hudson Bay**: Wales 1770, p. 124; Wales and Dymond 1770, p. 144. **47. JRF and Wales lost in fog**: GF, 15 December 1772, GF Voyage 2000, pp. 67–8; JRF 15 December 1772, JRF Journal 1982, p. 198. **47. their most likely death**: Sparrman, February 1773, Sparrman 1953, p. 9. **47. 'heavenly music to'**: GF, 15 December 1772, GF Voyage 2000, p. 67. **47. 'undoubtably the first'**: Cook, 17 January 1773, Beaglehole 1961, p. 80; see also JRF, 17 January 1773, JRF Journal 1982, p. 216. They reached 66°36' ½ S – five miles south of the Antarctic Circle. **47. 'compleat christal ropes'**: Elliott Journal, January 1773, Holmes 1984, p. 14; see also GF, 'Cook, der Entdecker' (1787), AA 5, p. 220, and Cook, 1 January 1773, Beaglehole 1961, p. 71; Marra, January 1773, Marra 1775, p. 21; for water freezing in a barrel, JRF, 14 March 1772, JRF Journal 1982, p. 233; for cracked hands: GF, 25 March 1773, GF Voyage 2000, p. 78. **48. 'candied cinnamon of'**: Sparrman, 1 January 1773, Sparrman 1953, p. 21. **48. numb ... fingers and limbs**: Marra, December 1772, Marra 1775, p. 8. **48. 'shit & pissed'**: JRF, 15 March 1773, JRF Journal 1982, p. 233. **48. *Adventure* ... vanished**: GF, 8 February 1773, GF Voyage 2000, p. 75; Cook, 8 and 9 February 1773, Beaglehole 1961, pp. 90–9. **48. 'they made a continual'**: Clerke Journal, 1 February 1773, Beaglehole 1961, p. 86. **48. symptoms of scurvy**: GF, 17 March 1773, GF Voyage 2000, p. 76. **48. 'he divided the prey'**: Sparrman, March/April 1773, Sparrman 1953, p. 42. **48. 'They had no inclination'**: Cook, 13 February 1773, Beaglehole 1961, p. 93. **48. needle and thread:** Clerke Journal, 6 March 1773, Beaglehole 1961, p. 102. **49. 'A clever, but'**: Elliott's Memoirs, Holmes 1984, p. xxx. **49. 'olde Mr Forster'**: Elliott Journal, March 1775, Holmes 1984, p. 44. **49. Reinhold had fights**: Ibid. **49. 'After having circumnavigated'**: JRF, 15 March 1773, JRF Journal 1982, p. 234. **49. Cook had him thrown out:** Elliott Journal, March 1775, Holmes 1984, p. 44. **49. JRF threatened to tell king:** Wales (1778) 2000, p. 701; for JRF's German accent, p. 723. **50. GF's appearance and personality**: GF Letters 1829, pp. 61–2; see also painting of Reinhold and George Forster by John Francis Rigaud, c. 1780; **50. 'a clever good'**: Elliott's Memoirs, Holmes 1984, p. xxx.

CHAPTER 4

51. north towards New Zealand: Cook, 17 March 1773, Beaglehole 1961, p. 106. **51. *Endeavour* at Dusky Sound**: Cook, 14 March 1770, Beaglehole 1968, p. 264. **51. 'The weather was'**: GF, 26 March 1773, GF Voyage 2000, p. 79. **52. 'the most delicious'**: Ibid. **52. anchorage at Dusky Sound**: The first night, they anchored at Anchor Island (hence the name), but Pickersgill found a snug harbour with a stream nearby (which Cook named Pickersgill Harbour) and where they moved the next day. Cook, 27 and 28 March 1773, Beaglehole 1961, pp. 111–12; Pickersgill Journal, March 1773, Holmes 1984, p. 68; see also Hodges' painting *View of Pickersgill Harbour* in the colour-plate inset; GF, 27 March 1773, GF Voyage 2000, p. 80. **52. beautiful Yellowhead**: *Mohoua ochrocephala*, JRF, 2 April 1773, JRF Journal 1982, p. 245; GF Zoological Drawing plate 156, NHM; for tame birds and cats, GF, 27 March 1773, GF Voyage 2000, p. 81. **52. South Island Fantail**: *Rhipidura fuliginosa*, JRF, 27 March 1773, JRF Journal 1982, p. 241; GF Zoological Drawing, plate 154, NHM. **52. flightless *weka***: *Gallirallus australis*, JRF, 27 March 1773, JRF Journal 1982, p. 240; GF Zoological Drawing, plate 123, NHM. **52. 'both new'**: JRF, 27 March 1773, JRF Journal 1982, p. 240. **52. the *kōtare*: Todiramphus sanctus**, GF Zoological Drawing, plate 59, NHM. **52. wood pigeon**: *Hemiphaga novaeseelandiae*, ibid, plate 134, NHM. **52. the *tūī***: *Prosthemadera novaeseelandiae*, ibid, plate 61, NHM. **53. 'made many delicious'**: Sparrman, March/April 1773, Sparrman 1953, p. 30. **53. canoe with ... Māori**: GF, 28 March 1773, GF Voyage 2000, p. 83; it is impossible to identify the Māori tribe at Dusky Sound with any certainty. Anne Salmond suggested that they were most likely Ngaati Mamoe, although Ngaai Tahu also went to Dusky Sound (Tamatea), Salmond 1997, p. 50. **53. 'It is an island'**: Salmond 2004, p. 113; for early encounters between Māori and Europeans, Salmond 1997, pp. 18–20. **53. 'When our old men'**: Salmond 1997, p. 19. **53. 'a brave, warlike people'**: Cook to J. Walker, 13 September 1771, Young 1836, p. 115; see also Cook, 15 November 1769, Beaglehole 1968, p. 203. **53. Māori cosmos**: Salmond 1997, pp. 32–3. **55. camp and repairs at Dusky Sound**: Sparrman, 1953, p. 27; GF, 27 March 1773, GF Voyage 2000, pp. 80–1; Hodges' painting *View of Pickersgill Harbour*. **55. They brewed beer**: From the tea tree (*Leptospermum scoparium*) and rimu (*Dacrydium cupressinum*), GF, 27 March 1773, GF Voyage 2000, pp. 81–2; for the recipe, Cook, 11 May 1773, Beaglehole 1961, pp. 137–8. **55. 'The superiority of'**: GF, 26 April 1773, GF Voyage 2000, pp. 105–6. **55. tried to find plants**: JRF, 28 March 1773, JRF Journal 1982, p. 241; Sparrman, March 1773, Sparrman 1953, p. 26. **55. 'We were . . . greatly tantalized'**: GF, 29 March 1773, GF Voyage 2000, p. 84. **56. 'The smoothness of the'**: GF, 1 April 1773, GF Voyage 2000, p. 84. **56. Old Māori on rocky outcrop**: GF, 6 April 1773, GF Voyage 2000, pp. 85–7; see also Cook, 7 April 1773, Beaglehole 1961, pp. 116–17, and Elliott Journal, April 1773, Holmes 1984, p. 17. **56. 'did not, however, stir'**: GF, 6 April 1773, GF Voyage 2000, pp. 85–6. **56. 'He was brave'**: Elliott Journal, March/April 1773, Holmes 1984, p. 17. **56. 'we spent about half'**: Cook, 7 April 1773, Beaglehole 1961, p. 116. **56. Māori name of South Island**: GF, 8 April 1773, GF Voyage 2000, p. 89. **57. William Hodges sketched**: GF, 6 April 1773, GF Voyage 2000, p. 86. **57. 'Their hair was combed'**: GF, 8 April 1773, GF Voyage 2000, p. 88. **57. 'which seemed to have'**: GF, 19 April 1773, GF Voyage 2000, p. 97; see also p. 438. **58. George continued sketching**: JRF, 5 and 26 April 1773, JRF Journal 1982, pp. 246, 267. **58. his cabin . . . was cramped**: JRF, 10 April 1773, JRF Journal 1982, p. 251; GF, 8 April 1773, GF Voyage 2000, p. 89. **58. food at Dusky Sound**: GF, 8 April 1773, GF Voyage 2000, p. 89. **58. Broad-billed Prions**: *Pachyptila vittata*, GF Zoological Drawing, plate 85, NHM. **58. They shot . . . seals**: JRF, 13 April 1773, JRF Journal 1982, p. 254; GF, 13 April 1773, GF Voyage 2000, p. 93. **58. 'The grandeur of'**: GF, 11 April 1773, GF Voyage 2000, p. 91. **59. 'One of the boat's'**: GF, 19 April 1773, GF Voyage 2000, p. 99. **59. 'intermixed with hearty'**: Ibid. **59. 'I could not help'**: GF, 20 April 1773, GF Voyage 2000, p. 100. **59. 'the courage of this'**: Ibid, p. 102. **59. George . . . went on an excursion**: GF, 6–8 May 1773, GF Voyage 2000, pp. 107–8 ; JRF, 6–8 May 1773, JRF Journal 1982, pp. 270–2. **60. 'by way of encouragement'**: GF, 6 May 1773, GF Voyage 2000, p. 107. **60. 'We saw the billows'**: GF, 7 May 1773, GF Voyage 2000, p. 108. **60. departure from Dusky Sound**: GF, 11 May 1773, GF Voyage 2000, p. 109. **60. 'we are now (thank God)'**: Wales, 10 May 1773, Beaglehole 1961, p. 784. **60. 'the Country a heap'**: Ibid, p. 785. **60. 'better flavoured than'**: Cook, 11 May 1773, Beaglehole 1961, p. 135; for Cook's instructions and descriptions, pp. 131–9. **61. information for future navigators**:

Ibid, p. 131. **61. mountains . . . covered in snow**: GF, 11 May 1773, GF Voyage 2000, p. 109. **61. *Adventure* in Tasmania for a few days**: Burney, 9–15 March 1773, Burney 1975, pp. 34–40. **61. *Adventure*'s arrival Queen Charlotte Sound**: Burney, 6 April 1773, Burney 1975, p. 47. **61. '*Tobia Tobia*'**: Burney, 9 April 1773, Burney 1975, p. 49; see also Cook, 24 May and 3 June 1773, Beaglehole 1961, pp. 167 and 171. **62. Raiatea . . . ancestral homeland**: Ihimaera 2022, vol. 1, p. 27. **62. Māori and Tupaia**: Salmond 1997, pp. 73–4; Druett 2011; Tupaia died in Batavia in December 1770. **62. waterspouts appeared**: GF, 17 May 1773, GF Voyage 2000, pp. 110–12. **62. 'A phænomenon which'**: Ibid, p. 111. **63. arrival Queen Charlotte Sound**: GF, 18 May 1773, GF Voyage 2000, p. 113. **63. celebrated their reunion**: JRF, 19 May 1773, JRF Journal 1982, p. 283. **63. to learn Māori names**: GF, 27 May and 1 June 1773, GF Voyage 2000, pp. 120 and 125. **63. 'strongly carved with'**: GF, 4 June 1773, GF Voyage 2000, p. 128. **63. Māori women appearance**: GF, 29 May 1774, GF Voyage 2000, p. 122; JRF, 5 June 1773, JRF Journal 1982, p. 292. **63. 'amazing bushy hair'**: GF, 29 May 1773, GF Voyage 2000, p. 122. **63. 'an apron, made'**: GF, 1 June 1773, GF Voyage 2000, p. 125; for canoes, p. 124. **64. 'alternately extending their'**: Ibid, p. 126. **64. birds at Queen Charlotte Sound**: For oystercatchers (*Haematopus unicolor*), JRF, 24 May 1773, JRF Journal 1982, p. 285; for shags (*Phalacrocorax punctatus*), JRF, 25 May 1773 and GF Zoological Drawing, plate 102, NHM; for falcons (*Falco novaeseelandiae*), JRF, 22 May 1773, and GF Zoological Drawing, plates 36, 37, 38, NHM; for Fluttering Shearwater (*Puffinus gavia*), JRF, 22 May 1773; for owl (*Ninox novaeseelandiae*), JRF, 28 May 1773, and GF Zoological Drawing, plate 39, NHM; for *kōkako* (*Callaeas cinereus*), JRF, 3 June 1773, and GF Zoological Drawing, plate 52, NHM. **64. trees and forests at Queen Charlotte Sound**: rimu (*Dacrydium cupressium*), pukatea (*Laurelia novae-zelandiae*); for ponga or silver-tree fern (*Alsophila tricolor*) and mamaku or black-tree fern (*Sphaeropteris medullaris*), GF, 23 November 1773, GF Voyage 2000, p. 277; for cabbage tree (*Cordyline australis*), GF Botanical Drawing, plates 147–9, NHM. **64. trading with Māori**: GF, 23 May 1773, GF Voyage 2000, p. 118. **64. 'they were not inclined'**: GF, 1 June 1773, GF Voyage 2000, p. 125. **65. 'ever debased themselves'**: GF, 29 May 1773, GF Voyage 2000, p. 121; for Cook's worries, Cook, 4 June 1773, Beaglehole 1961, p. 175. **65. fighting with Koa**: GF, 30 May 1773, GF Voyage 2000, p. 123; for Koa's name, Salmond 1997, p. 78. **65. 'I fear that hitherto'**: GF, 29 May 1773, GF Voyage 2000, p. 121. **65. 'ferocious Cannibals'**: Elliott Journal, May 1773, Holmes 1984, p. 18. **65. 'desire to tear their'**: Sparrman, May/June 1773, Sparrman 1953, p. 38. **65. definition 'barbarian'**: *Oxford English Dictionary*, entry for 'Barbarian.' **65. struck by their courage**: GF, 19 April 1773, GF Voyage 2000, p. 102. **65. 'the little progress'**: GF, 4 June 1773, GF Voyage 2000, p. 128. **66. 'banish all rash'**: GF, 'Brodbaum' (1784), AA 6. 1, p. 70. **66. 'aberrations of the mind'**: GF, 'Über lokale und allgemeine Bildung' (1791), AA 7, p. 51; see also GF to TF, 16 April 1794. **66. 'in the sharply defined'**: GF, 'Über lokale und allgemeine Bildung' (1791), AA 7, p. 50. **66. twenty-eight men arrived**: GF, 4 June 1773, GF Voyage 2000, p. 127ff. **66. 'from the various tones'**: Ibid, p. 127. **66. GF**

and Hume: Hume 1896, p. 415; Bödeker 1992, p. 108. **67. 'It must be evident'**: GF, 4 June 1773, GF Voyage 2000, pp. 131–2. **67. Māori leadership**: Salmond 1997, p. 83. **68. sailed out of Ship Cove**: GF, 7 June 1773, GF Voyage 2000, p. 132. **68. Cook's plans** : Cook, 4 June and 17 July 1773, Beaglehole 1961, pp. 173, 184. **68. average miles per day**: This is based on the mileage that Cook recorded every day in his logbook (but I've converted nautical miles to land miles); Cook, 9 June–15 August 1773, Beaglehole 1961, pp. 176–97. With thirteen miles in twenty-four hours, 26 June 1773 was particularly slow, whereas 21 July 1773 was their fastest on their run to Tahiti covering 180 miles. **68. 'May providence continue'**: JRF, 13 July 1773, JRF Journal 1982, p. 314; for comparing watches, Cook, 7 July 1773, and for a goat, Cook, 9 July 1773, Beaglehole 1961, p. 181. **68. 'to introduce any New'**: Cook, 29 July 1773, Beaglehole 1961, p. 187. **68. 'last night Mr Scott'**: Bayly, 11 July 1773, Beaglehole 1961, p. 182. **69. 'The spirits of all'**: GF, 17 July 1773, GF Voyage 2000, p. 137; this was also the day when they packed away their winter clothes. **69. 'the setting sun illumined'**: GF, 25 July 1773, GF Voyage 2000, p. 137. **69. 'The Trade wind'**: Clerke Journal, 7 August 1773, Beaglehole 1961, p. 191.

CHAPTER 5

70. 'It was one of those': GF, 16 August 1773, GF Voyage 2000, p. 143; The *Resolution* first anchored at Vaitepiha Bay (today Tautira Bay). **70. 'The east-wind which'**: Ibid. **70. trading through porthole**: Ibid, p. 144. **71. *Resolution* driven towards reef**: GF 15 August 1773, GF Voyage 2000, p. 147; Cook, 16 and 17 August 1773, Beaglehole 1961, pp. 197–9; Sparrman, August 1773, Sparrman 1953, pp. 51–2. **71. Maui had foreseen**: Henry 1928, pp. 430–1; Druett 2011, p. 11. **72. 'There will come'**: Henry 1928, p. 10. **72. 'The glorious offspring'**: Newell 2018, p. 95; some say that the tree was uprooted by a storm and not felled by invaders from Bora Bora. **73. *Dolphin* in Tahiti and battle:** Salmond 2009, pp. 46–56; Druett 2011, pp. 11–44. **73. women ... exposed their genitals**: Salmond 2011, p. 94. **73. 'Oro's signs of power**: Ibid. **73. explicit sexual gestures**: Douglas 2011, p. 88. **73. 'These people breathe'**: Salmond 2011, p. 99. **73. 'Eve before her sin'**: Tscherkézoff 2009, pp. 117–18. **74. JRF's Tahitian vocabulary**: Moser 1840, p. 34ff. **74. war had broken out**: GF, 21 August 1773, 6 May 1774, GF Voyage 2000, pp. 167, 372–3; Oliver 1974, p. 1225ff, Salmond 2009, p. 242ff. **74. 'being greatly enriched'**: GF, 6 May 1774, GF Voyage 2000, p. 372. **74. '*Te-tamai-i-te-tai-'ute 'ute*'**: Salmond 2009, p. 243; Oliver 1974, p. 1230. **74. 'I never could learn'**: Cook, 1 September 1773, Beaglehole 1961, p. 213. **74. Vehiatua II**: GF, 23 August 1773, GF Voyage 2000, pp. 169–71. **74. JRF and Bougainville's list**: Moser 1840, p. 35. **75. another European ship**: Cook, 23 August 1773, Beaglehole 1961, p. 204. **75. 'With a great deal'**: GF, 23 August 1773, GF Voyage 2000, p. 171. **75. pigs in Tahiti**: GF, 16, 18, 21 August 1773; for scarcity of food, 24 August 1773, GF Voyage 2000, pp. 145, 153, 160, 172. **75. to buy a**

breastplate: GF, 20 August 1773, GF Voyage 2000, p. 158. **76. 'I have been indefatigable'**: JRF, 21 August 1773, JRF Journal 1982, p. 331. **76. 'hurl hurriedly on'**: JRF Journal 1982, p. 81 (JRF's preface of *Enchiridion*, p. iii). **76. 'Experimental Men'**: Marra to Banks, 30 July 1775, Banks 2008, vol. 1, p. 186. **76. 'pick up various circumstances'**: GF, 19 August 1773, GF Voyage 2000, pp. 157–8. **76. plants in Tahiti**: breadfruit (*Artocarpus altilis*), plants from arum family (*Alocasia macrorrhizos*), paper mulberry (*Broussonetia papyrifera*) and purple yam (*Dioscorea alata*), JRF, 25 August 1773, JRF Journal 1982, p. 337. **76. *Gardenia taitensis***: GF, 18 August 1773, GF Voyage 2000, p. 151, and JRF, 25 August 1773, JRF Journal 1982, p. 337. Although the national flower of Tahiti today, it's not native to the island but originated from Western Polynesia. **76. ventured up a steep mountain**: This was at Matavai Bay, GF, 30 August 1773, GF Voyage 2000, pp. 190–1. **76. 'in miniature'**: Sparrman, April 1774, Sparrman 1953, p. 125. **77. 'It astonished us'**: Ibid, pp. 125–6. **77. 'infinitely superior'**: GF, 19 August 1773, GF Voyage 2000, p. 155. **77. 'beyond comparison'**: GF, 14 September 1773, GF Voyage 2000, p. 220. **77. 'as if to convince'**: GF, 16 August 1773, GF Voyage 2000, p. 145. **77. chief tied hair in ponytail**: Ibid, p. 146. **77. 'Teoree'**: and other Tahitian names for Europeans, GF, 21 August 1773, GF Voyage 2000, p. 162; for Cook as Toote, 1 September 1773, p. 196. **77. 'every harsh and'**: GF, 16 August 1773, GF Voyage 2000, p. 145. **78. 'Surely from all'**: GF, 25 August 1773, GF Voyage 2000, p. 177. **78. Tahitians were hesitant**: GF, 30 August 1773, GF Voyage 2000, p. 194. **78. 'that it was totally'**: Wales (1778) 2000, p. 711; for Wales' Yorkshire accent, GF, 'A Reply to Mr. Wales's Remarks' (1778), in GF Voyage 2000, p. 780. **78. Christopher Columbus**: Goldstein 2013, p. 43. **78. 'a high forehead'**: GF, 16 August 1773, GF Voyage 2000, p. 146. **78. 'The punctuation, which'**: GF, 8 September 1773, GF Voyage 2000, p. 211. **78. 'a fine white cloth'**: GF, 16 August 1773, GF Voyage 2000, p. 144. **78. 'a kind of turban'**: GF, 10 September 1773, GF Voyage 2000, p. 216. **78. 'had as elegant'**: Ibid. **79. 'the movement of their'**: Ibid. **79. 'Three men performed'**: GF, 14 September 1773, see also 26 May 1774; for wearing European clothes, 10 September 1773, GF Voyage 2000, pp. 216, 224, 393. **79. 'a kind of drowsy'**: GF, 21 August 1773, GF Voyage 2000, p. 162. **79. 'with a lively intelligent'**: and the following quote, GF, 9 and 10 September 1773, GF Voyage 2000, pp. 213 and 215. **80. 'On a kind of stage'**: GF, 21 August 1773, GF Voyage 2000, p. 164. **80. 'which is a mark'**: GF, 26 August 1773, GF Voyage 2000, p. 178. **80. 'the evening-sun illuminating'**: GF, 25 August 1773, GF Voyage 2000, p. 175. **80. 'silvered over the'**: Ibid, p. 176. **80. 'dead drunk'**: GF, 14 September 1773, GF Voyage 2000, pp. 220–1. **81. 'did not know how'**: GF, 2 May 1774, GF Voyage 2000, p. 370. **81. The Tahitians examined every**: For examining *Resolution* and *Adventure*, GF, 16 August 1773; for weapons and clothing, GF, 21 August 1773; for bagpipes, GF, 26 August and 5 September 1773; for opening shirts and asking after wives, GF, 16, 21, 23 August 1773, GF Voyage 2000, pp. 145–6, 161–2, 170–1, 181, 207. **81. 'when we told him'**: GF, 23 August 1773, GF

Voyage 2000, p. 170. **81. Tahitians … particular about cleanliness**: Meleisea and Schoeffel 1997, p. 128. **81. 'Knights of Otaheite'**: Elliott Journal, September 1773, Holmes 1984, p. 20; for method of tattooing, Banks, 5 July 1769, Beaglehole 1962, vol. 1, p. 309; Cook, 'Description of King Georges Island,' July 1769, Beaglehole 1768, p. 125. **81. 'as they lay contiguous'**: Cook, August 1769, Beaglehole 1968, p. 151. **82. At six foot three**: GF, 26 August 1773, GF Voyage 2000, p. 180. **82. When Tu visited**: GF, 27 August 1773, GF Voyage 2000, pp. 182–3. **82. *mana* as ceremonial gesture**: Newell 2010, p. 232. **82. 'now entirely deprived'**: GF, 1 September 1773, GF Voyage 2000, p. 195. **83. a corpulent chief**: GF, 8 September 1773, GF Voyage 2000, p. 212. **83. 'We were at a loss'**: Ibid, p. 213. **83. 'Therefore nothing but'**: Ibid. **83. Tahitian cosmos**: Newell 2010, pp. 80–1; Oliver 1974, pp. 56–62, 65–6; for specific examples see Henry 1928, pp. 382–95. **83. 'who held the sky'**: Henry 1928, p. 390; for spirits and gods manifested in plants, animals etc., pp. 329, 384–5. **84. 'shadows of the gods'**: Ibid, p. 384. **84. 'annexed an idea'**: GF, 3 September 1773, GF Voyage 2000, p. 206. **84. 'peculiar gentleness of'**: GF, 16 August 1773, GF Voyage 2000, p. 145. **84. Sparrman attacked**: GF, 5 September 1773, GF Voyage 2000, pp. 208–9; JRF, 6 September 1773, JRF Journal 1982, p. 353; Sparrman, September 1773, Sparrman 1953, pp. 78–9. **84. 'which made me see'**: Sparrman, September 1773, Sparrman 1953, p. 78. **84. 'Red with anger'**: Ibid, p. 79; for chief returning with items, p. 81. **84. Reinhold … shot at the man**: JRF, 13 September 1773, JRF Journal 1982, p. 363; for GF's testimony of the incident, pp. 363–4. **84. 'Mr Sparrmans robbery'**: JRF, 13 September 1773, JRF Journal 1982, p. 363. **85. 'my Independency of him'**: Ibid, p. 365. **85. JRF's fight with Cook**: JRF, 14 and 17 September 1773, JRF Journal 1982, pp. 365 and 369. **85. 'gentle, paternal discipline'**: GF, 'Cook der Entdecker,' (1787), AA 5, p. 285. **85. 'called Barbecuing'**: Elliott Journal, September 1773, Holmes 1984, p. 19. **85. Cook tried everything**: Ibid, p. 20. **85. islands … map drawn by Tupaia**: GF, 10 September 1773, GF Voyage 2000, p. 215. **85. stuck a blossom**: Wales (1778) 2000, p. 744. **85. Hitihiti … join the expedition**: GF, 14 September 1773, GF Voyage 2000, p. 222; for his height, Elliott Journal, September 1773, Holmes 1984, p. 21; related to Tupaia: Salmond 2009, p. 290. **86. 'forsake the easy way'**: GF, 14 September 1773, GF Voyage 2000, p. 222. **86. 'He may be of use'**: Cook, 17 September 1773, Beaglehole 1961, p. 230. **86. 'ought to make good'**: Dodds Pennock 2023, p. 33. **86. 'irrational animals'**: Berg 1982, p. 19. **87. 'altogether void of'**: This was Martin Frobisher's expedition, Dodds Pennock 2023, p. 232. **87. 'brute beasts'**: Ibid, p. 212. **87. 'as different from others'**: Aristotle, *Politics*, 1. 5 1254b, 16–17. **87. Quirós arrived in Vanuatu**: Jolly 2009, pp. 64–5. **87. strange and phantasmagorical**: Berg 1982, pp. 19–20. **87. 'a compilation, or particular'**: Bacon, *Novum Organum* (1620), Bacon 1902, p. 180. **88. 'I who had no intention'**: Cook, 4 October 1773, Beaglehole 1961, p. 251. **88. 'I was so exasperated'**: Cook, 18 August 1773, Beaglehole 1961, p. 201. **88. 'Virtue and vice'**: GF, 'O-Taheiti' (1779), AA 5, p. 64; see also GF, 'Cook, der

Entdecker' (1787), AA 5, p. 197. **88. Polynesian word *taio***: Oliver 1974, p. 845ff; Newell 2010, pp. 34–5; for the Tahitians saying *taio*, GF, 18 August 1773, GF Voyage 2000, p. 151. **88. 'the blame then lies'**: GF, 29 August 1773, GF Voyage 2000, p. 188. **88. 'encourage the Natives'**: JRF, 7 September 1773, JRF Journal 1982, p. 355. **88. 'too much lenity'**: Ibid. **89. 'We have met with the'**: GF, 5 September 1773, GF Voyage 2000, p. 210. **89. 'Vicious characters are'**: Ibid; for later comments about good and evil, GF, 'Über die Beziehung der Staatskunst auf das Glück der Menschheit' (1793), AA 10. 1, p. 578. **89. blamed it on human nature**: GF, 27 August 1773, GF Voyage 2000, p. 185. **89. 'as if we had lain at'**: Ibid, p. 184. **89. infections travelled with them**: GF, 2 September 1773, GF Voyage 2000, p. 201. **89. 'had been injured by their'**: Marra, 29 September 1773, Marra 1775, p. 56. **89. 'bred to the practice'**: Marra, August 1773, Marra 1775, p. 44. **89. 'the simplicity of their'**: GF, 1 September 1773, GF Voyage 2000, p. 199. **89. 'The lowest man'**: Ibid. **90. 'There is not'**: Ibid. **90. 'all the necessaries'**: Ibid. **90. 'here and in many'**: GF, 3 September 1773, GF Voyage 2000, p. 206. **90. George identified three classes**: GF, 1 September 1773, GF Voyage 2000, p. 199; see also Newell 2010, pp. 37, 267–70. **90. 'we saw a luxurious individual'**: GF, 21 August 1773, GF Voyage 2000, p. 165. **90. 'like in Europe'**: GF, 'Cook, der Entdecker' (1787), AA 5, p. 281. **90. Tahitian class system**: GF, 1 September 1773, GF Voyage 2000, pp. 199, 444, 494; Newell 2010, pp. 267–70. **91. revolution – even in Tahiti**: GF, 1 September 1773, GF Voyage 2000, p. 200.

CHAPTER 6

92. 'the Men being all': Elliott Journal, August 1773, Holmes 1984, p. 19. **92. *Resolution* left with 209 pigs**: GF, 5 and 18 September 1773, GF Voyage 2000, pp. 210, 227. **92. Mai's appearance and background**: GF, 5 September 1773, GF Voyage 2000, p. 211; see also Mai's portraits by Joshua Reynolds, William Perry and others; Burney, Journal, September 1773, pp. 70–1; for Mai's scar, Solander to Lind (?), 19 August 1774, Beaglehole 1961, p. 949. **93. Mai on *Adventure***: GF, 5 September 1773, GF Voyage 2000, p. 212; Cook, 7 September 1773, and 'The Ships' Companies,' Beaglehole 1961, pp. 221 and 892. **93. Mai nicknamed Jack**: Burney, Journal, September 1773, p. 70. **93. Mai's fishing skills**: William Anderson, 29 December 1776, Beaglehole 1961, p. 991. **93. George about Mai**: GF, 5 September 1773, GF Voyage 2000, p. 211; see also p. 11; for GF about Hitihiti: GF, 14 September 1773, p. 222. **93. 'in every respect'**: Elliott Journal, September 1773, Holmes 1984, p. 21; see also Wales, 2 June 1774, Beaglehole 1961, p. 845. **94. Hitihiti became seasick**: GF, 19 September 1773, GF Voyage 2000, p. 228; Bayly, 27 September 1773, Beaglehole 1961, p. 242. **94. Mai terrified by Sunday service**: Burney, September 1773, Burney 1975, p. 80. **94. 'he is a Small matter'**: Ibid, p. 81. **94. GF and Hitihiti taught each other**: GF, 12 December 1773, GF Voyage 2000, pp. 288–9. **94. Hitihiti traded and bartered**: for red feathers at Tonga: GF, 2–4 October

1773, GF Voyage 2000, p.244; for drums at Marquesas: GF, 9 April 1774, p. 339; for dogs at Takaroa: GF, 17 April 1774, p. 344. **94. 'takes great notice'**: Burney, September 1773, Burney 1975, p. 70. **95. Mai and Hitihiti's journals**: for Mai, Burney, September 1773, Burney 1975, p. 80; for Hitihiti, GF, 15 March 1774, GF Voyage 2000, p. 324. **95. averaging a swift 110 miles**: Cook, 18 September–2 October 1773, Beaglehole 1961, pp. 239–43. **95. To determine longitude**: Richardson 2005, pp. 34–5. **96. H4 . . . watchmaker Larcum Kendall**: Cook, 13 July 1772; see also Minutes of Bord of Longitude 1771–1772, Beaglehole 1961, pp. 16–17, 719ff. **96. 'Mr Kendalls Watch'**: Cook, 30 October 1772, Beaglehole 1961, p. 47; for Cook comparing watches, Cook, 27 September 1772 and 7 July 1773; see also Minutes of Bord of Longitude 1771–1772, pp. 18, 39, 726. **96. a library of travel accounts**: GF, early April 1774, GF Voyage 2000, p. 326. **96. 'Had all the former Navigators'**: JRF, 2 April 1774, JRF Journal 1982, p. 480. **97. 'the indigenous name of'**: GF, 5 August 1774, GF Voyage 2000, p. 510. **97. 'Ea-Oowhe' and 'Tonga-Tabboo'**: GF, 2 October 1773, GF Voyage 2000, p. 230. **97. 'Friendly Islands'**: GF, 2–4 October 1773, GF Voyage 2000, p. 256; Cook, July 1774, Beaglehole 1961, p. 449. **97. 'Though they are strangers'**: JRF, 7 October 1773, JRF Journal 1982, pp. 392–3. **97. 'best Spaniels'**: JRF, 7 October 1773, JRF Journal 1982, p. 395. **97. 'There is not a trace'**: GF to Jacobi, 10 October 1779. **97. 'neither attachment nor'**: GF Voyage 2000, p. 10. **97. Tongans' generosity**: GF, 2–4 October 1773, GF Voyage 2000, pp. 231 and 233. **97. 'they beat time to'**: Ibid, p. 232. **97. 'as if our best workmen'**: Ibid, p. 238; GF on Tongan gardens: GF, 2–4 October 1773, pp. 234, 245, 257; for trees JRF, 7 October 1773, JRF Journal 1982, p. 399. **97. islands in the Marquesas archipelago:** JRF, 7 April 1774, JRF Journal 1982, pp. 482–3. **98. 'that the customs'**: GF, 6 October 1773, GF Voyage 2000, p. 258; for Mai and Hitihiti's ability to communicate, 2–4 October 1773, p. 242. **98. 'must have had one common'**: GF, 6 October 1773, GF Voyage 2000, p. 260; see also p. 258. **98. 'from such little *data*'**: GF, 12 November 1773, GF Voyage 2000, p. 275. **98. an owl at Tongatapu**: This was a barn owl (*Tyto alba lulu*), Cook, 7 October 1773, Beaglehole 1961, p. 263. **98. 'was eaten by the'**: JRF, 7 October 1773, JRF Journal 1982, p. 393. **99. 'feathered-work':** GF, 2–4 October 1773, GF Voyage 2000, pp. 244 and 469. **99. attached some human faeces**: Cook, 5 October 1773, Beaglehole 1961, p. 255. **99. 'white and polished'**: GF, 2–4 October 1773, GF Voyage 2000, p. 249; this was probably from Fiji but had been traded or stolen by the Tongans, Kaeppler 1998, p. 210; for apron, GF, 2–4 October 1773, GF Voyage 2000, p. 248; see also Kaeppler 1978, pp. 213–15; Hauser-Schäublin and Krüger 1998, p. 114. **99. 'elegant in the highest'**: GF, 2–4 October 1773, GF Voyage 2000, p. 236. **99. 'which for workmanship'**: Ibid, p. 240. **99. woodworking skills**: Ibid, p. 251. **99. traded more in Tonga**: Kaeppler 1998, p. 196. **99. bought a parrot:** *Prosopeia tabuensis*, JRF, 3 October 1773, JRF Journal 1982, p. 382; GF Zoological Drawing, plate 42, NHM. **99. 'we immediately conjectured'**: GF, 2–4 October 1773, GF Voyage 2000, pp. 236, 246. **99. 'they will make better'**:

Ibid, p. 250. **99. 'though perhaps not perfectly'**: GF, 6 October 1773, GF Voyage 2000, p. 256, see also p. 260. **99. 'corresponded very ill with'**: GF, 2–4 October 1773, GF Voyage 2000, p. 239; for waging war, p. 240; for Tonga and war, Krüger 2011, p. 119; Taonui 2006, p. 39. **100. 'Savage man'**: Rousseau (1755) 1992, p. 22; for GF and Rousseau's 'Savage man,' GF, 25 December 1774, GF Voyage 2000, p. 631. **100. *Discourse on the Origin***: Rousseau had written the essay in 1754 and published in 1755. **100. 'that original condition'**: Rousseau (1755) 1992, p. 26. **100. 'nothing so gentle as'**: Ibid, p. 48. **100. 'toward the decrepitude'**: Ibid, p. 49. **100. 'a perpetual conflict'**: Ibid, p. 52. **101. 'The happiness of the'**: GF, 'Über die Beziehung der Staatskunst auf das Glück der Menschheit' (1793), AA 10. 1, p. 573. **101. 'the state of nature, as'**: Ibid, p. 569. **101. *Resolution* and *Adventure* in Tonga**: GF, 2–8 October 1773, GF Voyage 2000, pp. 229–61. **101. storm ... Cook Strait**: GF, 25 October–2 November 1773, GF Voyage 2000, pp. 266–8; JRF, 26 October–2 November 1773, JRF Journal 1982, pp. 411–16; Cook, 23 October–2 November 1773, Beaglehole 1961, pp. 280–4; for sailors in storm, GF, 'Cook, der Entdecker' (1787), AA 5, pp. 246–7. **101. 'The tremendous roar'**: GF, 25 October 1773, GF Voyage 2000, p. 267. **101. Mai was terrified**: Bayly, 25 October 1773, Beaglehole, p. 281; for JRF clinging to his cot, JRF, 26 October 1773, JRF Journal 1982, p. 411. **102. 'was at once magnificent'**: GF, 25 October 1773, GF Voyage 2000, pp. 266–7. **102. *Resolution* and *Adventure* separated**: GF, 29 October 1773, GF Voyage 2000, p. 267. **102. into Ship Cove**: GF, 3 November 1773, GF Voyage 2000, p. 269.

CHAPTER 7

103. dropped anchor in Ship Cove: GF, 3 November 1773, GF Voyage 2000, p. 269. **103. 'in short, from being'**: GF, 4 November 1773, GF Voyage 2000, p. 270. **103. preparations and repairs**: GF, 7 November 1773, GF Voyage 2000, p. 271. **104. Shining Cuckoo**: *Chalcites lucidus*, JRF, 5 November 1773, JRF Journal 1982, p. 419; GF Zoological Drawing, plate 57, NHM. **104. *Forsterygion varium***: Named after the Forsters in 1801; GF Zoological Drawing, plate 185, NHM. **104. 'croaking like frogs'**: GF, 12 November 1773, GF Voyage 2000, p. 274. **104. impressed by his friend's marksmanship**: GF, 4 November 1773, GF Voyage 2000, p. 270. **104. Hitihiti's language skills**: GF, 12 November 1773, GF Voyage 2000, pp. 274–5; see also Cook, 23 November 1773, Beaglehole 1961, p. 295. **105. 'He also frequently expressed'**: GF, 12 November 1773, GF Voyage 2000, p. 274. **105. scrambled up a high hill**: GF, 15 November 1773, GF Voyage 2000, p. 275. **105. Māori attack their enemies**: GF, 21 November 1773, GF Voyage 2000, p. 276. **105. 'I am much afraid'**: GF, 22 November 1773, GF Voyage 2000, p. 276. **106. sea celery, wild spinach**: GF, 23 November 1773, GF Voyage 2000, p. 277; for specific species, Sparrman, March/April 1773, Sparrman 1953, p. 43. **106. witness of cannibalism**: GF, 23 November 1773, GF Voyage 2000, pp.

278–9; Elliott Journal, November 1773, p. 22; Marra, November 1773, Marra 1775, pp. 102–3; JRF, 24 November 1773, JRF Journal 1982, pp. 426–7; Cook, 23 November 1773, Beaglehole 1961, pp. 291–4; Wales, 23 November 1773, Beaglehole 1961, pp. 818–19. **106. 'In accordance with human'**: Kant, 'Physical Geography', Kant 2012, p. 504. **106. 'shew us that they'**: Cook, 17 January 1770, Beaglehole 1968, pp. 236–7. **106. 'Barbarrous cruelty these'**: Pickersgill, January 1770, Beaglehole 1968, p. 236. **107. purchase the half-eaten head**: GF, 23 November 1773, GF Voyage 2000, p. 278. **107. 'a genal favorite'**: Elliott's Memoirs, Holmes 1984, p. xxx. **107. Clerke put the cheek**: Clerke, 24 November 1773, Beaglehole 1961, p. 293. **107. 'Being desireous of'**: Cook, 23 November 1773, Beaglehole 1961, p. 293. **107. 'that the New Zealanders'**: Ibid, p. 294. **107. 'Metamorphosed into the'**: Wales, 23 November 1773, Beaglehole 1961, p. 819; for GF consoling Hitihiti, GF, 23 November 1773, GF Voyage 2000, p. 279. **107. 'The New Zealanders never'**: Ibid, p. 281. **108. 'the action of eating'**: Ibid, p. 280. **108. 'was the liking'**: Wales, Journal, 23 November 1773, Beaglehole, p. 819. **108. 'we do not find'**: GF, 23 November 1773, GF Voyage 2000, p. 280. **108. 'exceed them in all'**: Montaigne, 'Of the Canniballes' (1580), Montaigne 2001, p. 292. **108. 'LOOK UNDERNEATH'**: Burney, November 1773, Burney 1975, p. 88; Marra, 24 and 25 November 1773, Marra 1775, p. 105; for Cook's message, Cook, 24 November 1773, Beaglehole 1961, p. 297. **108. *Adventure* after being separated**: Marra, November 1773, Marra 1775, pp. 90–1. **108. George owned Montaigne's**: Bödeker 1992, p. 111. **109. 'not the least hopes'**: and Mai finding the bottle, Burney, November 1773, Burney 1975, p. 88. **109. the Māori stole valuable instruments**: Marra, 13 December 1773, Marra 1775, pp. 91–2; Burney, December 1773, Burney 1975, pp. 90–1. **109. collect greens and wild celery**: Marra, 17 December 1773, Marra 1775, p. 92. **109. sent out a search party**: The following section is based on ibid, pp. 92–7; Burney, 'The Grass Cove Massacre', Burney 1975, pp. 95–7; GF, 25 October 1774, GF Voyage 2000, pp. 606–7. **110. 'The place was throngd'**: Burney, 'The Grass Cove Massacre', Burney 1975, p. 97. **110. 'such a shocking scene'**: Ibid. **110. *Adventure* ... Southern Continent**: Furneaux, December 1773–March 1774, Beaglehole 1961, pp. 744–5. **110. *Adventure* to Cape Town**: Furneaux, 3 March 1774, Beaglehole 1961, p. 745. **111. circuit around Antarctica**: During their first attempt, they had travelled from 18°E to 166°E; and during their second attempt they had travelled from New Zealand all the way to 44°W; Cook, 1 December 1772 and 25 March 1773, Beaglehole 1961, pp. 54 and 108. **111. 'chilling horrors'**: GF, 26 November 1773, GF Voyage 2000, p. 284. **111. 'My & my Sons'**: JRF, 10 April 1773, JRF Journal 1982, p. 251. **111. 'every thing I touch'**: JRF, 21 December 1773 JRF Journal 1982, p. 438. **111. 'my Cabin cold'**: Ibid. **111. 'Excessive cold and raw'**: and following quotes, Marra, 10–13, 22 December 1773, Marra 1775, pp. 110 and 115; snowflakes the size of goose feathers: 17 December 1773, p. 113. **111. 'grotesques forms of'**: Marra, 15 December 1773, Marra 1775, p.

111. **111. 'horror to the scene'**: Ibid. **111. *Resolution* scraped ice floes**: Cook, 15 December 1773, Beaglehole 1961, p. 305. **112. 'To describe the horror'**: Elliott Journal, mid-December 1773, Holmes 1984, p. 26. **112. icicles . . . from their noses**: Marra, 18 December 1773, Marra 1775, p. 113. **112. 'Our ropes were like'**: Cook, 24 December 1773, Beaglehole 1961, pp. 308–9. **112. two and a half degrees**: GF, 23 December 1773, GF Voyage 2000, p. 289. **112. walked the quarterdeck**: GF, 'Cook, der Entdecker' (1787), AA 5, pp. 255–6, and GF, 12 December 1773, GF Voyage 2000, p. 287. **112. in Cook's Great Cabin**: GF, 12 December 1773, GF Voyage 2000, p. 287; and JRF, 21 December 1773, JRF Journal 1982, p. 438. **112. language lessons . . . red feathers**: GF, 12 December 1773, GF Voyage 2000, pp. 287–8; Marra, 25 January 1774, Marra 1775, p. 123. **112. 'He is still indulged'**: Marra, 25 January 1774, Marra 1775, p. 123. **112. the birds . . . died**: GF, 12 December 1773, GF Voyage 2000, p. 288. **112. 300 icebergs**: Elliott Journal, 25 December 1773, Holmes 1984, p. 25. **112. 'whole scene looked'**: GF, 26 December 1773, GF Voyage 2000, p. 291. **112. 'the ocean about'**: GF, 16 January 1774, GF Voyage 2000, p. 293. **112. 'had no *pacific* aspect'**: JRF, 16 January 1773, JRF Journal 1982, p. 447. **113. 'white land, or *whennua*'**: GF, 12 December 1773, GF Voyage 2000, p. 287; Hitihiti felt cold more acutely, Marra, 22 December 1773, Marra 1775, p. 115. **113. 'white stones'**: GF, 12 December 1773, GF Voyage 2000, p. 287. **113. 'wonders of petrified'**: Ibid, p. 290. **113. 'as if the whole earth'**: Marra, 30 January 1774, Marra 1775, p. 125. **113. cold, hungry and bored**: GF, 'Cook, der Entdecker' (1787) AA 5, pp. 250–1. **113. a knife fight**: Marra, 1 January 1774, Marra 1775, p. 117; Clerke, January 1774, Beaglehole vol. 2, p. 313. **113. 'as if they had been'**: Sparrman, March 1775, Sparrman 1785, p. 108. **113. men dreaded mealtimes**: GF, 16 January 1774, GF Voyage 2000, p. 293. **113. 'for he was close'**: Elliott Journal, January 1774, Holmes 1984, p. 25. **113. 'Nothing . . . could be more'**: GF, 6 January 1774, GF Voyage 2000, p. 292. **113. 'drunken Sailors hollowing'**: JRF, 27 December 1773, JRF Journal 1982, p. 441; for JRF staying in his cabin, GF, 28 January 1774, GF Voyage 2000, p. 294. **114. water . . . ankle deep**: JRF, 16 January 1774; for JRF worrying about future and frustrations, JRF, 21 and 24 December 1773, 5 and 27 January 1774, JRF Journal 1982, pp. 439–40, 443, 447, 450. **114. a huge wave crashed**: GF, 15 January 1774, GF Voyage 2000, p. 292; JRF, 15 January 1774, JRF Journal 1982, pp. 446–7. **114. reached 71°10' south**: GF, 30 January 1774, GF Voyage 2000, p. 294; JRF, 30 January 1774, JRF Journal 1982, p. 451; Cook, 29 January 1774, Beaglehole 1961, p. 322. **114. 'we could not proceed'**: Ibid. **114. 'the situation of which'**: Cook, 6 February 1774, Beaglehole 1961, p. 326. **114. 'I think it a point'**: Ibid. **114. Walgreen Coast**: Beaglehole 1961, p. 322. **115. 'there remained nevertheless'**: Cook, 6 February 1774, Beaglehole 1961, p. 327. **115. GF had scurvy**: GF, 1 March 1774, GF Voyage 2000, p. 297. **115. 'my poor stomach'**: GF to Spener, 17 September 1776; see also GF to Soemmerring, 1 June 1784. **115. 'All things look gloomy'**: JRF, 17 January 1773 JRF Journal

1982, p. 447. **115. strict cleaning regime**: Marra, 13, 17, 19, 21 February 1774, Marra 1775, pp. 129–30, 133. **115. Cook was ill**: GF, 8 and 25 February 1774, GF Voyage 2000, pp. 296–7; JRF, 26 February 1774, JRF Journal 1982, pp. 456–7.

CHAPTER 8

116. first tropical birds: GF, 1 March 1774, GF Voyage 2000, p. 297. **116. sighted Easter Island**: GF, 11 March 1774, GF Voyage 2000, pp. 298–300 **116. 'The sudden emotions'**: GF, 13 March 1774, GF Voyage 2000, p. 300; for swollen legs, GF, 14 March 1774, p. 303; for burned skin: GF, 17 March 1774, p. 325. **117. 'and from what we ... or kings'**: GF, 14 March 1774, GF Voyage 2000, p. 309. **117. 'The workmanship of this'**: GF, 14 March 1774, GF Voyage 2000, p. 306. **117. 'the arts in their infancy'**: Ibid. **117. Easter Island statues**: Hunt 2006. **118. similar to Tahitians**: GF, 13 March 1774, GF Voyage 2000, p. 301. **118. 'in order to bring'**: GF, 14 March 1774, GF Voyage 2000, p. 304. **118. 'one common origin'**: GF, 15 March 1774, GF Voyage 2000, p. 322. **118. 'as large as the full'**: GF, 14 March 1774, GF Voyage 2000, p. 305. **118. 'indubitable testimonies of'**: Ibid, p. 303. **118. snatched Hitihiti's cap**: Ibid, p. 309; for headdresses being sacred, Salmond 2009, p. 297. **119. 'that Europeans too often'**: GF, 15 March 1774, GF Voyage 2000, p. 318. **119. islanders tricked them**: Ibid, p. 312; no interest in beads, GF, 14 March 1774, but keen on coconut shells and Tahitian barkcloth, GF, 15 March 1774, pp. 308 and 312. **119. Hitihiti's purchases**: GF, 15 March 1774, GF Voyage 2000, pp. 313–14. **119. 'remembered Easter Island'**: Ibid, pp. 324 and 465, 'Ta'ata maita'i, fenua 'ino.' **119. 2,500 miles**: based on Cook's mileage in his logbook, Cook, 18 March–6 April 1774, Beaglehole 1961, pp. 360–3; they averaged around 125 miles per day. **119. journey to Marquesas**: GF, 17–24 March and April 1774, GF Voyage 2000, pp. 325–6. **119. almost 900 miles**: based on Cook's mileage in his logbook, Cook, 12–22 April 1774, Beaglehole 1961, pp. 376–81. **119. 'I crawled on deck'**: GF, 21 April 1774, GF Voyage 2000, p. 348. **119. 'would give him weight'**: GF, 20 April 1774, GF Voyage 2000, p. 348. **119. arrival Tahiti's Matavai Bay**: GF, 22 April 1774, GF Voyage 2000, pp. 350–1. **120. 'He was courted'**: Ibid, p. 351. **120. 'te Tae-aï'**: GF, 28 April 1774, GF Voyage 2000, pp. 364 and 470. **120. 'His stories'**: Ibid, p. 364. **120. 'diamond of the Great'**: Ibid, p. 360. **120. pigsty at beach**: GF, 25 April 1774, GF Voyage 2000, p. 353. **120. warrior's breast ornament**: GF, 20 August 1773 and 26 April 1774, GF Voyage 2000, pp. 158, 357; for mourner's costume, GF, 28 April 1774, pp. 361–3. **121. 'one of the most magnificent'**: GF, 26 April 1774, GF Voyage 2000, p. 355; for full description of armada and warriors, pp. 355–8. **122. 'resembling that glory'**: Ibid, p. 357. **122. 'whose heart is at peace'**: Rousseau (1755) 1992, p. 34. **122. Hitihiti wanted to stay**: GF, 5 May 1774, GF Voyage 2000, p. 370; see also Wales, 13 May 1774, Beaglehole 1961, p. 838. **122. 'what great things he'**: Cook, 13 May 1774, Beaglehole 1961, p. 400; for JRF warning Hitihiti, JRF, 14 May 1774, JRF Journal 1982, p. 511. **122. chief**

Tu: and others who wanted to join, Cook, 13 May 1774, Beaglehole 1961, p. 400. **122. 'There is no arguing'**: JRF, 12 May 1774, JRF Journal 1982, p. 509; see also GF, 5 May 1774, GF Voyage 2000, p. 370. **122. Marra . . . tried to escape**: and GF's reasoning about it, GF, 14 May 1774, GF Voyage 2000, p. 379; JRF, 15 May 1774, JRF Journal 1982, p. 514; Marra, May 1774, Marra 1775, p. 236. **123. locals asked for a ride**: GF, 14 May 1774, GF Voyage 2000, p. 376. **123. 'Hurree-hurree'**: GF, 23 May 1774, GF Voyage 2000, p. 388; his name would have been Hurihuri, Salmond 2009, p. 314. **123. crew also found stowaway**: GF, 14 May 1774, GF Voyage 2000, p. 382. **123. George sat down with Tutavai**: GF, 3 June 1774, GF Voyage 2000, pp. 399–402; Salmond 2009, p. 317. **123. 'the sun, which was created'**: GF, 3 June 1774, GF Voyage 2000, p. 399; for Polynesian traditions of Maui, Oliver 1974, p. 730, and Henry, 1928, pp. 430–32. **123. Hitihiti often took Cook aside**: Cook, 4 June 1774, Beaglehole 1961, p. 428. **123. 'dark, ugly and a downright'**: Ibid. **124. 'keep him as a curiosity'**: Banks, 12 July 1769, Beaglehole 1962, vol. 1, pp. 312–13. **124. 'would have been [a] better'**: Cook, 4 June 1774, Beaglehole, 1961, p. 428. **124. Cook gave Hitihiti a letter**: Marra, 4 June 1774, Marra 1775, p. 246. **124. 'seemed torn to'**: and Hitihiti's reaction on *Resolution*'s departure, GF, 4 June 1774, GF Voyage 2000, p. 402. **124. 'Our civilized education'**: GF, 14 September 1773, GF Voyage 2000, p. 226. **124. Cook and Bligh met Hitihiti during later expeditions**: Cook, 24 August 1777, Beaglehole 1767, part 1, p. 195; for Bligh, p. 239. **125. 'The best method in'**: Cook, 22 November 1773, Beaglehole 1961, p. 292. **125. 'a detestable eagerness'**: GF, 21 May 1774, GF Voyage 2000, p. 388. **125. killed an islander for stealing**: GF, 8 April 1774, GF Voyage 2000, p. 330. **125. 'catching him under'**: GF, 6 October 1773, GF Voyage 2000, p. 254; Cook, 5 October 1773, Beaglehole 1961, p. 256. **125. 'Though they are members'**: GF, 25 December 1773, GF Voyage 2000, p. 290. **125. receive twelve lashes**: Cook, 22 November 1773, Beaglehole, 1961, p. 292. **125. 'It has ever been a maxim'**: Ibid. **125. In Tonga, JRF had hit islander**: JRF, 13 September and October 1773, JRF Journal 1982, pp. 364 and 392. **125. Quick to anger**: Elliott Journal, March 1775, Holmes 1984, p. 44; Wales (1772) 2000, p. 701; JRF, 13 and 14 September 1773, JRF Journal 1982, pp. 364–5; GF, *A Letter to the Right Honourable The Earl of Sandwich*, 1778, AA 4, p. 82. **126. JRF punished George**: and JRF's fight with Cossacks: GF Letters 1829, p. 7; TF to F. and J.G. Johann Reinhold, 6 and 8 May 1806; Report of Chancellery for the Guardianship of Foreigners, enclosed in a letter from Lord Cathcart to Earl of Halifax, 17/28 June 1771, Bartlett 1975, p. 495. **126. 'None is punished for'**: JRF, 19 May 1774, JRF Journal 1982, p. 517; see also 16 May 1774, p. 515. **126. 'In case one were shot'**: JRF, 19 May 1774, JRF Journal 1982, p. 517. **126. on Niue . . . armed warriors**: GF, 20 June 1774, GF Voyage 2000, pp. 406–8; Cook, 22 June 1774, Beaglehole, 1961, pp. 433–8; JRF, 22 June 1774, JRF Journal 1982, pp. 537–8. **126. 'The Conduct and aspect'**: Cook, 22 June 1774, Beaglehole 1961, p. 435. **127. 'the shot had torn'**: GF, 28 June 1774, GF Voyage 2000, p. 416. **127. New Hebrides**: The *Resolution* was in the

Vanuatu archipelago from 2 July to 31 August 1774; for Cook naming it, Cook, 31 August 1774, Beaglehole 1961, p. 521. **127. On Erromango**: GF, 4 August 1774, GF Voyage 2000, pp. 503–4; Cook, 4 August 1774, Beaglehole 1961, pp. 477–9; Sparrman, August 1774, Sparrman 1953, pp. 141–2. **127. 'For my own part'**: GF, 4 August 1774, GF Voyage 2000, p. 505.

CHAPTER 9

128. rumble of an active volcano: GF, 5 August 1774, GF Voyage 2000, pp. 506–7. **128. arrival in Tanna**: GF, 5 August 1774, GF Voyage 2000, pp. 508–11. **128. When two owls**: These were *Tyto alba* according to JRF, JRF, 6 August 1774, JRF Journal 1982 p. 587; for the meaning of owls in Tanna, Lindstrom 2020, p. 11. **128. were ghosts of their ancestors**: GF, 8 August 1774, GF Voyage 2000, p. 519; Marra, August 1774, Marra 1775, p. 261; Salmond 2004, p. 265; for Tanna cosmology, Bonnemaison 1994, p. 37. **129. 'be troublesome to us'**: JRF, 6 August 1774, JRF Journal 1982, p. 586; see also Cook, 5 and 6 August 1774, Beaglehole 1961, pp. 482–6. **129. volcano ... set the dark sky ablaze**: GF, 5 August 1774, GF Voyage 2000, p. 510. **129. account of second day and battle**: GF, 6 August 1774, GF Voyage 2000, pp. 511–13; Cook, 6 August 1774, Beaglehole 1961, pp. 483–6. **129. 'I had not forgot the trap'**: Cook, 6 August 1774, Beaglehole 1961, p. 485. **130. 'absurd and unjust that'**: GF, 6 August 1774, GF Voyage 2000, p. 512. **130. 'They looked upon us'**: GF, 5 August 1774, GF Voyage 2000, p. 510. **130. 'Pavegn'**: GF recorded his name as 'Paw-yangom', GF, 6 August 1774, GF Voyage 2000, pp. 513, 819. **130. 'It's a Man!'**: Wales, August 1774, Beaglehole 1961, p. 859; see also Lindstrom 2020, p. 25. **130. wrapped these gifts in leaves**: GF, 7 August, GF Voyage 2000, p. 519; for spiritual powers, Jolly 2009, p. 88. **130. 'owing to some superstitious'**: GF, 8 August 1774, GF Voyage 2000, p. 519. **131. 'intercourse with human'**: GF, 31 July 1774, GF Voyage 2000, p. 500. **131. naming of Tanna**: GF, 5 August 1774, GF Voyage 2000, p. 510; JRF, August 1774, JRF Journal 1982, p. 586. **131. They also looked very different**: GF, 21 July 1774, GF Voyage 2000, pp. 480–1, see also p. 491. **131. 'poor mean despicable'**: Marra, July 1774, Marra 1775, p. 261. **131. 'Monkey race'**: Cooper, 23 July 1774, Beaglehole 1961, p. 465. **131. 'grimace of an ape'**: Sparrman Journal, July 1774, Sparrman, 1953, p. 135. **131. 'ill-favoured set of'**: JRF, *Observations* (1778), JRF 1996, p. 164. **131. 'this Apish Nation'**: Cook, 23 July 1774, Beaglehole 1961, p. 466. **131. 'the most Ugly'**: Ibid, p. 464. **131. 'the features of these'**: GF, 22 July 1774, GF Voyage 2000, p. 491. **132. 'ill-natured comparisons'**: GF, 21 July 1774, GF Voyage 2000, p. 481. **132. 'We should be sorry'**: Ibid; for orangutans theory, Burnet 1774, vol. 1, p. 270; see also Uhlig 2010, pp. 142–3. **132. 'most intelligent people'**: GF, 21 July 1774, GF Voyage 2000, p. 481. **132. At Malakula ... their languages**: GF, 22 July 1774, GF Voyage 2000, p. 484; for faces painted black, 21 July 1774, p. 480. **132. 'we had reason to'**: GF, 22 July 1774, GF Voyage

2000, p. 484. **132. Lord Monboddo's theory**: Uhlig 2010, p. 143, Hoorn 2004, p. 70. **133. Fannòkko**: JRF, 10 August 1774, JRF Journal 1982, pp. 593–4; see also GF, 9 August 1774, GF Voyage 2000, p. 520. **133. the islanders stopped them**: GF, 9 August 1774, GF Voyage 2000, p. 521, see also p. 526; for volcano as a sacred place, Adams 1984; Bonnemaison 1994, p. 97. **133. 'they bit their own'**: GF, 10 August 1774, GF Voyage 2000, p. 526. **133. their artful deception**: Ibid, p. 530; see also pp. 539–40. **133. 'without bloodshed'**: GF, 14 August 1774, GF Voyage 2000, p. 540. **133. 'yawinatuan'**: This was *Ducula pacifica*, JRF, 15 August 1774, JRF Journal 1982, p. 605; Wales (1778) 2000, p. 746; JRF spelled 'yawinatuan' as 'Gvānättān'. **133. JRF's fight with Clerke and Cook**: JRF, 15 August 1774, JRF Journal 1982, p. 606. **134. 'never passed a week'**: Wales (1778) 2000, p. 701. **134. Cardinal Honeyeater**: *Myzomela cardinalis*, GF Zoological Drawing, plate 63, NHM. **134. Vanuatu White-eye**: *Zosterops flavifrons*, Ibid, plate 157, NHM. **134. they tried throwing stones**: JRF, 18 August 1774, JRF Journal 1982, p. 610. **134. sailors cut, salted and fried**: GF, 10 August 1774, GF Voyage 2000, p. 531. **134. 'Head dark pearly'**: *Thalassarche chlororhynchos*, GF Zoological Drawing, plate 99, NHM; for colouring a single leaf, e.g. *Fuchsia excorticata* and *Olearia aborescens*, GF, Botanical Drawings, plate 166 and 307, NHM. **135. significance of Māori carving:** : Kaeppler 2008, p. 64. **136. green stone blades ... show imperfections**: Thyng 2020, p. 161. **136. woven baskets in Tonga**: Kaeppler 1998, pp. 211–12; for Tongan mats, p. 202. **137. war and skirmishes**: GF, 13 August 1774, GF Voyage 2000, p. 535; see also p. 554. **137. 'We desired them'**: Ibid, p. 534. **137. Their music was ... superior**: GF, 13 August 1774, GF Voyage 2000, p. 535. **137. 'peeped at us'**: Ibid, p. 538. **138. murder of islander**: GF, 19 August 1774, GF Voyage 2000, pp. 549–50; Cook, 19 August 1774, Beaglehole 1961, pp. 498–500; Sparrman, August 1774, Sparrman 1953, pp. 150–1; Elliott Journal, August 1774, Holmes 1984, p. 34. **138. red uniforms, sailors in loose shirts**: See Hodges' paintings such as *The Landing at Tanna* and *The Landing at Mallicolo*. **138. 'I who was present'**: Cook, 19 August 1774, Beaglehole 1961, p. 498. **138. 'refused to be controuled'**: GF, 19 August 1774, GF Voyage 2000, p. 550. **138. 'to let us see'**: Cook, 19 August 1774, Beaglehole 1961, p. 499. **138. 'The question was'**: Elliott Journal, August 1774, Holmes 1984, p. 34. **139. 'I ask ... whether the world'**: Wales (1778) 2000, p. 740. **139. 'saw only a small part'**: John Whitehouse, quoted in ibid, p. 741. **139. 'The officer's right to'**: John Edgecumbe, quoted in Beaglehole 1961, p. 500. **139. 'that the man was entitled'**: John Edgecumbe, quoted in Sparrman Journal, 19 August 1774, Sparrman 1953, p. 151. **139. 'lost sight of both'**: Elliott Journal, August 1774, Holmes 1984, p. 34. **139. 'no person ... but the centinel'**: Wales (1778) 2000, p. 741. **139. twelve lashes ... to a sailor**: for Cook punishing sailor in New Zealand, Cook, 22 November 1773, Beaglehole 1961, p. 292; for butcher being flogged, Molyneux Journal, 29 April 1769, Beaglehole 1968, pp. 554–5. **139. Wedgeborough had to be punished**: Sparrman, August 1774, Sparrman 1953, p. 151. **139. 'was better fed and'**: Ibid, p. 152. **139. 'gently drove**

back by': JRF, 19 August 1775, JRF Journal 1982, p. 611. **139. 'He, to vindicate'**: GF, 19 August 1774, GF Voyage 2000, p. 550. **140. 'we had wantonly made'**: Ibid, p. 551. **140. Europeans brought death**: GF, 21 August 1773, GF Voyage 2000, p. 168.

CHAPTER 10

141. 'another Southern Cruse': Cook, 31 August 1774, Beaglehole 1961, p. 520. **141. named the island New Caledonia**: Cook, 1 October 1774, Beaglehole 1961, p. 562; for arrival in New Caledonia, GF, 4 September 1774, GF Voyage 2000, p. 563. **141. it looked rather barren**: GF, 5 September 1774, GF Voyage 2000, p. 564. **141. 'could not wait'**: GF, 4 September 1774, GF Voyage 2000, p. 563. **141. little produce** : GF, 5 and 13 September 1774, GF Voyage 2000, pp. 571 and 590. **141. 'When we consider how'**: GF, 13 September 1774, GF Voyage 2000, p. 592. **142. codpieces ... Europe**: GF, 5 September 1774, GF Voyage 2000, p. 568. **142. 'They were totally naked'**: Clerke, September 1774, Cowley and Deacon, 2002, p. 98. **143. passionflower**: *Passiflora aurantia*, GF, 8 September 1774, GF Voyage 2000, p. 576; GF Botanical Drawing, plate 349, NHM. **143. New Caledonian birds**: For New Caledonian Whistler (*Pachycephala caledonica*), JRF, 8 September 1774; for Grey-eared Honeyeater (*Lichmera incana*), JRF, 12 September 1774; for Horned Parakeet (*Eunymphicus cornutus*), GF, 11 September 1774, GF Voyage 2000, p. 583, JRF, 12 September 1774, and GF, Zoological Drawing, plate 43, NHM; for Red-throated Parrotfinch (*Erythrura psittacea*), JRF, 13 September 1774, and GF, Zoological Drawing, plate 151, NHM; JRF Journal 1982, pp. 648, 654–5. **143. 'entirely new to'**: GF, 11 September 1774, GF Voyage 2000, p. 583. **143. 'not bigger than a hummingbird'**: JRF, 13 September 1774, JRF Journal 1982, p. 655. **143. 'the character of the'**: GF, 4 September 1774, GF Voyage 2000, p. 573. **143. ship's butcher ... died**: JRF, 6 September 1774, JRF Journal 1982, p. 646; for poisonous fish, GF, 8 September 1774, GF Voyage 2000, p. 578; see also 13 September 1774, p. 587; Cook, 8 September 1774, Beaglehole 1961, p. 535. **143. 'I reeled like a drunken'**: JRF, 8 September 1774, JRF Journal 1982, p. 649. **144. *Lagocephalus sceleratus***: GF, Zoological Drawing, plate 244, NHM. **144. tried to collect plants**: GF, 10 September 1774, GF Voyage 2000, pp. 579–81. **144. 'spasmodic pains over'**: GF, 13 September 1774, GF Voyage 2000, p. 587. **144. 'His Britannick Majesties'**: JRF, 13 September 1774, JRF Journal 1982, p. 656. **144. sailed into ... Queen Charlotte Sound**: GF, 18 October 1774, GF Voyage 2000, p. 601. **144. 'to leave not the least room'**: Cook, 21 February 1775, Beaglehole, p. 643; for their circuit around Antarctica and Cook's plans, Cook, 1 December 1772, 25 March 1773, 5 February and 11 November 1774, pp. 54, 108, 324, 581. **144. trees had been felled ... bottle**: GF, 18 October 1774, GF Voyage 2000, p. 602; Cook, 18 and 19 October 1774, Beaglehole 1961, pp. 569–70. **144. They lit fires**: JRF, 23 October 1774; JRF Journal 1982, pp. 674–5. **144. 'came up & killed'**: JRF, 28 October 1774,

JRF Journal 1982, p. 676; see also Cook, 28 October 1774, Beaglehole 1961, p. 573. **144. piece of paper represented ship**: GF, 25 October 1774, GF Voyage 2000, p. 605; see also Cook, 6 November 1774, Beaglehole 1961, p. 577. **145.** ***Resolution*** **left three weeks later**: GF, 9 and 10 November 1774, GF Voyage 2000, pp. 616–17. **145. more miles in one day**: They sailed 183 nautical miles (210 land miles) according to Clerke's log, Clerke, 27 November 1774, Beaglehole 1961, p.583; GF, 27 November 1774, GF Voyage 2000, p. 619. **145. 'This is the most desolate'**: Cook, 19 December 1774, Beaglehole 1961, p. 590. **145. 'Coast of Desolation'**: GF, 20 December 1774, GF Voyage 2000, p. 621; Pedro Sarmiento de Gamboa had not called it 'Desolation Coast' but 'Desolation Island.' **145. 'Barren as these rocks'**: GF, 21 December 1774, GF Voyage 2000, p. 622. **145. large delicious mussels**: GF, 22 December 1774, GF Voyage 2000, p. 624. **145. sixty-three geese**: GF, 24 December 1774, GF Voyage 2000, p. 627; Cook recorded 62 geese plus 14 which the other party shot, Cook, 24 December 1774, Beaglehole 1961, p. 596; Sparrman, December 1774, Sparrman 1953, p. 192. **146. Christmas Sound**: Cook, 27 December 1774, Beaglehole 1961, p. 598. **146. 'a kind of bonnet'**: GF, 25 December 1774, GF Voyage 2000, p. 628. **146. 'I cannot figure'**: Ibid, pp. 630–1. **147. 'It was the most loathsome'**: Ibid, p. 628. **146. 'out-casts of some'**: Ibid, p. 632. **146. Rousseau's ... happy savage**: Ibid, p. 631. **147. 'it was incomparably better'**: GF, 'Ueber Leckereyen' (1788), AA 8, p. 166. **147. Wedgeborough ... fell overboard**: GF, 28 December 1774, GF Voyage 2000, p. 633. **147. to sober up**: GF, 26 December 1774, GF Voyage 2000, p. 632. **148.** ***Resolution*** **passed Cape Horn**: GF, 29 December 1774, GF Voyage 2000, p. 633. **148. the giant animals breached**: Ibid, p. 634. **148. they spotted an island**: GF, 16 January 1775, GF Voyage 2000, p. 644ff. **148. Emperor Penguin**: GF, 17 January 1775, GF Voyage 2000, p. 645; see also Wienecke 2010, p. 271. In 1844 George Gray at the British Museum compared a penguin brought back by James Ross from his expedition to Antarctica with GF's drawing, and named it *Aptenodytes forsteri*. Rosove 2018, pp. 43–5; GF, Zoological Drawing, plate 79, NHM. **148. 'to give greater weight'**: GF, 16 January 1775, GF Voyage 2000, p. 646. **149. His skills had sharpened**: these zoological drawings are today at the NHM; Bearded or Chinstrap Penguin (*Pygoscelis antarcticus*), plate 80; Spotted Eagle Ray (*Aetobatus narinari*), plate 250; South Island Robin (*Petroica australis*), plate 146; see also Rifleman (*Acanthisitta chloris*) and Bush Wren (*Xenicus longipes*), plates 163 and 164; Blue Petrel (*Halobaena caerulea*), plate 84; common dolphin (*Delphinus delphis*), plate 31; New Zealand kākā (*Nestor meridionalis*), plate 50; New Zealand Pipit (*Anthus novaeseelandiae*), plate 140; Red Shining Parrot (*Prosopeia tabuensis*), plate 42. **150. His botanical drawings**: these botanical drawings are today at the NHM; from New Zealand *Dichelachne crinite*, plate 19 (with note 'Queen Charlottes Sound, November 18th'); *Lachnagrotis filimormes*, plate 29 (with note '18 November 1773'); from Tanna *Rottboellia coelorachis*, plate 31; from Marquesas *Solanum ferox var. repandum*, plate 96. **150. 'one of the most beautiful'**: GF, 30 August 1773, GF Voyage 2000, p. 190; *Barringtonia speciosa*, GF,

Botanical Drawing, plate 267, NHM. **150. 60°04'S latitude**: Cook, 28 January 1775, Beaglehole 1961, p. 629. **150. 'I was now tired'**: Cook, 27 January 1775, Beaglehole 1961, p. 639. **150. until they crossed 19°E**: Cook, 21 February 1775, Beaglehole 1961, p. 642. **150. 'I had now made'**: Ibid, p. 643. **151. 'whoever has resolution'**: Ibid, p. 646. **151. ships on the horizon**: GF, 16–18 March 1775, GF Voyage 2000, pp. 653–4. **151. 'I am however every'**: JRF, 14 March 1775, JRF Journal 1982, p. 728. **151. 'I'm as great a stranger'**: Clerke to Banks, 30 July 1775, Banks 2008, vol. 1, p. 185. **151. 'delicate roast goose'**: Sparrman, March 1775, Sparrman 1953, p. 200. **152. 'Sweden delivered from'**: GF, 21/22 March 1775, GF Voyage 2000, p. 657. **152. 'a right kind of Liberty'**: Wolff 2016, p. 104. **152. 'resting from his triumphs'**: GF, 21/22 March 1775, GF Voyage 2000, p. 657. **152. 'promised general happiness'**: Ibid. **152. 300 chests of tea**: Roberts 2021, pp. 230–1. **153. 'but they are a people'**: Cook, 18 March 1775, Beaglehole 1961, p. 653. **153. 'been exceeding desirous'**: GF, 25 October 1774, GF Voyage 2000, p. 606. **153. 'The whole tenour'**: Ibid, p. 610. **153. set sail for Europe**: GF, 27 April 1775, GF Voyage 2000, p. 659. **153. 'I was very agreeably'**: GF, 18 and 19 May 1775, GF Voyage 2000, p. 666. **153. Ascension Island**: GF, 28 May 1775, GF Voyage 2000, p. 667. **153. 'our arrival put her'**: GF, 14 July 1775, GF Voyage 2000, p. 675. **153. 'how many mothers'**: Ibid. **153. *Resolution* left the Azores**: GF, 19 July 1775), GF Voyage 2000, p. 683.

CHAPTER 11

157. On 24 June 1775: Cook, 25 June 1775, Beaglehole 1961, p. 672; C.G. Woide Diary, 24 June 1775, Woide Papers, BM Add 48.702, f. 202, BL. **157. began house hunting**: C.G. Woide Diary, 28 June and 1 July 1775, Woide Papers, BM Add MS 48.702, f. 203, BL. **157. '260 New Plants'**: Solander to Banks, 28 June 1775, Banks 2008, vol. 1, p. 183. **157. 75,000 miles**: Cook 1777, vol. 2, pp. 265–6. **158. 'Thus, after escaping'**: GF, 30 July 1775, GF Voyage 2000, p. 684. **158. Stagecoach to London** : JRF, 30 July 1775, JRF Journal 1982, p. 769; Elliot, 30 July 1775, Beaglehole 1961, p. 682. **158. 'he rather looks better'**: Solander to Banks, 7 August 1775, Banks 2008, vol. 1, p. 186. **158. 'I assure you'**: Clerke to Banks, 30 July 1775, Banks 2008, vol. 1, p. 185. **158. 'Pickersgill made the'**: Solander to Banks, 14 August 1775, Banks 2008, vol. 1, p. 188. **158. On their arrival in London**: C.G. Woide Diary, 31 July 1775, Woide Papers, BM Add MS 48.702, f. 206, BL. **158. In the German edition:** AA 3, p. 451. **159. Banks and Linnaeus received specimens**: for Banks, JRF and GF, MSS Catalogue of a collection of plants presented to Joseph Banks Esq., NHM; for Linnaeus, GF to Linnaeus, 4 August 1775. **159. Solander held off**: C.G. Woide Diary, 2 August 1775, Woide Papers, BM Add MS 48.702, f. 206, BL. **159. Percy Street**: Hoare 1976, p. 153; Gordon 1975, p. 190ff; Survey of London 1949, vol. 21, https://www.british-history.ac.uk/survey-london/vol21/pt3/pp7-11. **159. hills of Hampstead and Highgate**: GF to Spener, 19 September

1775. **159. thieves broke into**: Hoare 1976, p. 153; JRF to T. Pennant, 11 August 1775; Lichtenberg to J.A. Schernhagen, 16 October 1776, Lichtenberg's Letters, vol. 1, p. 568; *Gentleman's Magazine*, 10 August 1775, vol. 45, p. 404; GF to F.A. Vollpracht, 1 September 1776; for JRF's finances, JRF to Banks, ca. May to July 1777, GF AA 13, p. 617. **159. Justina Elisabeth ... collapsed**: C.G. Woide Diary, 11 August 1775, Woide Papers, BM Add Ms 48.702 f. 208, BL. **159. 'great expectations are'**: *Gentleman's Magazine*, 10 August 1775, vol. 45, p. 404. **160. audience with King George III**: Audience on 16 August 1775 and at Kew on 19 and 21 August 1775. *Gentleman's Magazine*, 19 August 1775, vol. 45, p. 405; *London Chronicle*, 17–19 and 24–26 August 1775, pp. 175 and 194; GF to Spener, 19 September 1775; see also Hoare 1976, p. 154; Uhlig 2004, p. 75; AA1, p. 687. **160. South African animals**: GF, 11 June 1775, GF Voyage 2000, p. 672; Hoare 1976, pp. 128–9. **160. no RS summer meetings**: The last meeting was on 6 July 1775 and the next was on 9 November 1775, JBRS, vol. 28, pp. 630 and 637. **160. Royal Society Club**: RS, Minutes RS Club, 10 August 1775, vol. 6, no page number; for Mitre Tavern, Geikie 1917, p. 25. **161. reunion with Mai**: GF Voyage 2000, pp. 10–11, 364, 371, 391; Solander to Lind (?), 19 August 1774, Beaglehole 1961, p. 949; see also Fullagar 2020, p. 189ff; Mai at Royal Society Club: e.g. 20 July, 26 October, 9 November, 7 December 1775, 11 and 25 January 1776, RS Minutes RS Club, vol. 6, no page numbers. **161. 'Cold, cold'**: Lichtenberg Diary, 24 March 1775, Lichtenberg 1977, vol. 1, p. 79. **161. 'Omiah, the senseless'**: *London Magazine*, vol. 44, 1775, p. 441; see also *General Evening Post*, 25 August 1774, p. 3, reporting about his smallpox inoculation. **161. 'nymphs ... ripe for amorous'**: Anonymous 1775, p. 31. **161. Mai also collected 'curiosities'**: GF Voyage 2000, p. 11; National Library of Australia 2001, pp. 31–3; McCormick 1977, p. 180. **161. Prince of Anhalt-Dessau**: Geyer-Kordesch 2007, pp. 202–4. **162. Map with *Resolution*'s route**: Quilitzsch 2020, p. 60. **162. visitors at Percy Street**: Titius (1777) 1783, vol. 10, p. 151; Bahrdt 1791, vol. 3, p. 324; Gordon 1975, p. 283. **162. Lichtenberg went to Deptford**: Lichtenberg Diary, 30 November 1775, Lichtenberg 1967–1972, vol. 2, p. 693. **162. 'excellent draughtsman'**: Lichtenberg to A.G. Kästner, 16 October 1775, Lichtenberg 1983–2004, vol. 1, p. 562. **162. 'is a man of extraordinary'**: Ibid, p. 563. **163. 'we would now know three'**: Lichtenberg to J.A. Schernhagen, 16 October 1775, Lichtenberg 1983–2004, vol. 1, p. 567. **163. talked as casually about Tahiti**: Lichtenberg to H.C. Boie, 30 November 1775, Lichtenberg 1983–2004, vol. 1, p. 597. **163. enrol at Oxford University**: Sparrman to GF, 22 July 1776. **163. 'It was never my lot'**: GF to Banks, 1 September 1782; see also GF to TF, 22 May 1784. **163. theatre and new books**: GF to F.A. Vollpracht, 12 March 1776. **163. *Sorrows of Young Werther***: GF to Spener, 9 November 1775 and 12 September 1777. **163. 'Stop, that's not true'**: Ibid, 9 April 1776. **163. JRF and Pennant**: Pennant 1793, p. 36; see also JRF's long dedication to Pennant in Osbeck's *Voyage to China*. **164. JRF's problems with Admiralty**: JRF to Banks, mid-May/mid-July 1777, AA 13, pp. 611–18; GF, *A Letter to the Right Honourable The Earl of Sandwich*,

1778, AA 4, p. 74ff; Hoare 1976, p. 159; see also AA 1, pp. 688–94. **164. 'I think the public'**: Earl of Sandwich to JRF, 28 October 1775, Hoare 1976, p. 156. **164. 'philosophical remarks'**: 'Agreement between Admiralty, Cook and Reinhold Forster,' 13 April 1776, AA 4, p. 90; for editor to improve manuscript: GF, *A Letter to the Right Honourable The Earl of Sandwich*, 1778, AA 4, p. 75. **164. 'submit to that Indignity'**: JRF to Barrington, June 1776, Hoare 1976, p. 161. **164. 'every word he had'**: GF to Spener, 15 November 1781. **164. Benjamin White**: See *A Voyage Round the World* and *Characteres Genera Plantarum*. **164. writing ... *A Voyage Round the World***: GF first mentioned writing *Voyage* on 1 September 1776 and JRF told Boie on 8 August 1776, GF to F. A. Vollpracht, 1 September 1776; Gordon 1975, p. 225. Cook left England on his third voyage in July 1776, leaving his manuscript with the publisher, Uhlig 2004, pp. 80–1. **164. sold drawings for £420**: The agreed price was 400 guineas which was £420, JRF to Banks, 9 August 1776, AA 13, p. 621; they are today at the NHM, London. **164. His health deteriorated**: GF to Spener, 17 September and 22 October 1776; GF to F.A. Vollpracht, 31 December 1776. **165. 'Life! ... this is no life'**: GF to Spener, 17 September 1776. **165. 'what is written is written'**: GF, 'Georg Forsters Antwort an die Göttingischen Recensenten' (1778), AA 4, p. 53. **165. GF paced up and down**: GF to F.A. Vollpracht, 10 May 1776. **165. he sealed letters** : GF to Spener, 23 May 1777. **165. *Wortgemählden***: GF, 'Georg Forsters Antwort an die Göttingischen Recensenten' (1778), AA 4, p. 54. **165. Christopher Columbus**: Goldstein 2013, p. 45. **165. 'was as smooth as'**: GF, 18 August 1773, GF Voyage 2000, p. 150. **000. 'tall coco-palms nodded'**: Ibid, p. 151. **165. 'murmured over a bed'**: GF, 30 August 1773, GF Voyage 2000, p. 192. **165. 'no poet could paint it'**: GF, 21 August 1773, AA 2, p. 244; I used GF's German edition here as it captures his way of writing more evocatively. **165. 'The noise of the'**: GF, 11 April 1773, GF Voyage 2000, p. 91. **165. excellent memory ... imagination**: Aikin 1803, vol. 4, p. 171. **165. GF was a natural storyteller**: GF, 19 August 1774, GF Voyage 2000, pp. 548–50. **166. 'We found a most beautiful'**: GF, 22 December 1774, GF Voyage 2000, pp. 623–4. **166. 'because in the end'**: GF to Jacobi, 15 November 1789. **166. 'Two travellers'**: GF Voyage 2000, p. 9. **166. He followed his heart**: Ibid. **166. 'a mere compiler'**: GF to Spener, 14 January 1779. **167. 'had their wish'**: GF Voyage 2000, p. 9. **167. 'the first point from'**: GF, 'Vorlesungen über allgemeine Naturkenntnis,' AA 6. 2, p. 1758. **167. 'Never before has there'**: GF to Heyne, 30 August 1790. **167. To compose his narrative**: GF Voyage 2000, p. 7; for GF expanding JRF's journal, GF to Spener, 17 September 1776. **167. getting lost in the fog**: GF, 15 December 1772, GF Voyage 2000, pp. 67–8; JRF, 15 December 1772, JRF Journal 1982, p. 198. **167. Or a day on Tahiti**: JRF, 21 August 1773, 'Journal of a Voyage on board his Majesties Ship Resolution,' Ms.germ.qu. 224, 1773, f. 90–1, Stabi Berlin and GF, 21 August 1773, GF Voyage 2000, pp. 159–68. **167. GF rewrote JRF's journal entries**: JRF, 15 March 1774, JRF Journal 1982, pp. 468–74, and GF, 15 March 1774, GF Voyage 2000, pp. 316–20. **168. 'The forehead in general'**: GF, 5

September 1774, GF Voyage 2000, p. 571. **168. 'beard shaven or'**: GF, 2–4 October 1773, GF Voyage 2000, p. 234. **168. 'they have likewise arrows'**: GF, 5 August 1774, GF Voyage 2000, p. 515. **168. 'four feet long, strait'**: Ibid, p. 516. **168. 'they throw with great'**: Ibid. **168. 'made of coco-nut fibres'**: Ibid, p. 515. **168. 'these punctures were'**: GF, 8 April 1774, GF Voyage 2000, p. 332. **168. 'desirous to see their'**: GF, 5 September 1774, GF Voyage 2000, p. 577. **168. girl's dexterity . . . five gourds**: GF, 6 October 1773, GF Voyage 2000, p. 258; for woodworking in Tonga, GF, 2–4 October 1773, p. 238. **168. 'seemed ready to fall'**: GF, 2 October 1773, GF Voyage 2000, p. 240. **168. 'remarkably ugly, and'**: GF, 6 April 1773, GF Voyage 2000, p. 86. **168. 'prodigious thick legs'**: GF, 5 September 1774, GF Voyage 2000, p. 566; see also 11 September 1774, p. 583, where GF called it 'elephantiasis' – this was probably filariasis, also known as elephantiasis, a disease caused by parasitic worms. **168. 'foreseeing that it would'**: GF, 12 November 1773, GF Voyage 2000, p. 274. **169. 'admirable similarity in'**: GF, 5 October 1773, GF Voyage 2000, p. 253. **169. 'with all the art'**: GF, 2 June 1774, GF Voyage 2000, p. 398. **169. 'were to report to'**: GF, 22 April 1774, GF Voyage 2000, p. 351. **169. 'mere drudges'**: GF, 23 November 1773, GF Voyage 2000, p. 277. **169. 'By force of habit'**: GF, 25 December 1773, GF Voyage 2000, p. 290. **169. shot and killed islanders**: In Tonga, GF, 6 October 1773 and 28 June 1774, GF Voyage 2000, pp. 253–4, 415; on Niue, GF, 20 June 1774, p. 407; on Easter Island, GF, 15 March 1774, p. 318; on Malakula, GF, 22 July 1774, p. 482; on the Marquesas, GF, 8 April 1774, p. 330; on Erromango, GF, 4 August 1774, pp. 503–4; on Tanna, GF, 19 August 1774, pp. 549–50. **169. 'Europeans, above all'**: GF, 10 September 1774, GF Voyage 2000, p. 581. **170. 'the general rights of mankind'**: GF, 1 September 1773 and 13 August 1774, GF Voyage 2000, p. 200; for the German edition, AA 2, p. 300, and AA 3, p. 252. **170. 'By separating the animals'**: GF, 5 November 1773, GF Voyage 2000, p. 271; in the German edition GF replaced 'to civilize them' with 'to make them happier', AA 2, p. 392. **170. 'seemed to be well situated'**: GF, 26 July 1774, GF Voyage 2000, p. 498; this was the island Efate. **170. 'if it were ever possible'**: GF, 25 November 1773, GF Voyage 2000, p. 283. **171. Publication was eagerly awaited**: G. White to J. White, 30 January 1776, White 1901, p. 302. **171. begin the German translation**: GF to Spener, 22 October 1776. **171. Karl Spener**: GF to F.A. Vollpracht, 16 July and 1 September 1776; during Spener's previous visit, Reinhold had taken him to a Royal Society meeting in 1771, JBRS, vol. 27, 21 November 1771. **171. written German . . . erratic**: e.g. GF to Spener, 9 November and 22 December 1775; 2 April 1776. **171. 'I just have to'**: Ibid, 27 December 1776. **171. George was ill**: GF to F.A. Vollpracht, 31 December 1776. **171. Raspe . . . Royal Society**: Geikie 1917, p. 129. **171. *Baron Munchausen* tales**: Raspe 1785. **171. Raspe . . . German translation**: GF to Spener, 24 June 1777, 1 July 1777, 19 August 1777; for Raspe lying, 17 February 1778; for turning two translations into one, 29 July 1777. **172. GF's drawings in Cook's book**: e.g. *Prosthemadera novaeseelandiae*, GF, Zoological Drawings, plate 61, NHM, is plate lii in Cook 1777, vol. 1, and *Barringtonia asiatica*,

GF, Botanical Drawings, plate 266, NHM, is plate xxiv in Cook 1777, vol. 2. **172. GF delighted with reviews**: GF to Spener, 22 April 1777. **172. 'a great affection of fine'**: Boswell 1934, vol. 3, p. 180. **172. 'he carries you along'**: Ibid. **172. 'Captain Cook's own narrative'**: *The Town and Country Magazine*, vol. 9, 1777, AA 1, p. 706. **172. 'Every page of it'**: Ibid. **172. The German translation**: GF to Spener, 2 September 1777 and GF AA 4, p. 169. **172. 'ravishing' and 'admirable'**: *Erfurter Gelehrte Zeitung*, AA 4, pp. 172–3. **173. 'cruel and ambitious'**: AA 4, p. 173. **173. 'acerbic allusions to'**: *Göttingischen Anzeigen von gelehrten Sachen*, March 1778, AA 1, p. 707. **173. 'Why not deliver eulogies'**: GF, 'Georg Forsters Antwort an die Göttingischen Recensenten' (1778), AA 4, 53. **173. 'I therefore show real'**: Ibid, p. 54. **173. review ... *Teutsche Merkur***: Wieland, *Teutsche Merkur*, 1778, AA 4, p. 176ff. **173. 'I alone was his leader'**: JRF to Wieland, 9 January 1798, Wieland 1992–94, vol. 14, p. 151. **173. pirated ... translations**: AA 1, pp. 702–4. **173. the book ... a classic**: Archenholz 1785, vol. 1, pt. 2, p. 592. **173. *Voyage* and Cook's account**: GF to Spener, 22 April 1777; see also AA 13, p. 608.

CHAPTER 12

174. 'Supped gloriously, sumptuously': GF Diary, 5 October 1777, AA 12, p. 8. **174. 'uniformly clothed in'**: Ibid, p. 9. **174. 'one very pretty'**: GF Diary, 4 October 1777, AA 12, p. 8. **174. 'really a fine piece'**: Ibid, 6 October 1777, AA 12, p. 13; for GF's lodgings, p. 14. **174. The coachman drove**: Ibid, p. 14. **174. 'The cries of Paris'**: Ibid. **175. 'ugliest, beastly town'**: H. Walpole to T. Gray, 19 November 1765, Lewis 1937–61, vol. 14, p. 143. **175. 'a prodigious Mixture'**: Franklin to P. Stevenson, 14 September 1767, BF online. **175. 'I drove furiously'**: GF Diary, 9 October 1777, AA 12, p. 18. **175. Jean-Baptiste Le Roy**: Ibid, 7 and 9 October 1777, AA 12, pp. 14–15, 19. **175. 'he is old, and wrinkled'**: Ibid, 7 October 1777, AA 12, p. 15. **175. 'They have small feet'**: Ibid, p. 14. **175. 'large and beautiful Eyes'**: Ibid, 8 October 1777, AA 12, p. 18. **175. 'I fell into the snare'**: Ibid. **176. 'so that the impurities'**: and getting lost in Palais Royal, ibid, p. 16. **176. 'attended by welllooking'**: Ibid. **176. The hospital next door**: Ibid, p. 17. **176. he enjoyed nice clothes**: Ibid, p. 15 and GF Letters 1829, p. 62. **176. 'I value my feelings'**: GF Diary, 3 October 1777, AA 12, p. 5. **176. freemasons ... a Parisian lodge**: This was the *Les Neuf Soeurs* lodge, Steiner 1985a, pp. 235–6; for JRF and freemasons, Steiner 1985b, p. 21ff; see also Sahmland 1994. **177. 'to come rushing to'**: Steiner 1985b, p. 12. **177. Franklin ... Royal Society**: JBRS, vol. 27, 28 February 1771. **177. GF and Passy**: GF Diary, 9 October 1777, AA 12, p. 18–19; for Franklin at Passy, Issacson 2004, pp. 329–30. **177. Franklin's appearance**: GF Diary, 9 October 1777, AA 12, p. 19; Isaacson 2004, p. 328; McCullough 2001, p. 194. **177. 'coiffure à la Franklin'**: Isaacson 2004, p. 325. **178. Franklin famous in Paris**: McCullough 2001, p. 193. **178. Madame Brillon**: Ibid, p. 204. **178. GF's visit at Passy**: GF Diary, 9 October 1777, AA 12, p. 19, and GF, *Erinnerungen aus dem Jahr 1790* (1792), AA 8, pp. 309–13.

178. 'I was as happy': GF Diary, 9 October 1777, AA 12, p. 19. **178. 'Papa'**: Ibid. **178. 'who seem'd to be'**: Ibid. **178. 'Everything is allowed'**: Ibid. **178. 'the *venerable* philosopher'**: Ibid; for GF seeing Franklin several times in Paris, JRF to Franklin, 30 July 1778. **179. hung Franklin's portrait**: GF to J.E. Biester, 24 April 1783; GF left Paris on 24 November 1777, GF to J.J. Oberlin, 24 November 1777. **179. fellow of the Royal Society**: GF, Election Certificate, 9 January 1777, RS EC/1776/22. **179. he had criticized Rousseau**: GF, 'Des Schiffhauptmanns Forrest zertreute Nachrichten von der Insel Magindanao' (1782); 'Cook, der Entdecker' (1787); 'Geschichte des Schiffbruchs des Herrn von Brisson' (1790); 'Des Abbés Rochon Reise nach Madagaskar und Ostindien' (1792), AA 5, pp. 108–9, 193, 262, 373, 635; 'Ueber Leckereyen' (1788), AA 8, p. 166; 'Über die Beziehung der Staatskunst auf das Glück der Menschheit' (1793), AA 10. 1, p. 569; GF, 21 July and 25 December 1774, GF Voyage 2000, pp. 481 and 631. **179. 'The traveller wanders'**: GF, 'Cook, der Entdecker' (1787), AA 5, p. 262. **179. 'almost certain that humankind'**: TF to Georgine Heyne, 26 March 1786. **179. 'I wanted to put'**: GF, 'Antwort an die Göttingischen Recensenten' (1778), AA 4, pp. 53–4. **179. 'the time of their reproduction'**: GF, 'Leitfaden zu einer künftigen Geschichte der Menschheit' (1789), AA 8, p. 191. **180. 'Great imperfections cannot'**: GF, 8 September 1773, GF Voyage 2000, p. 213. **180. 'The bold attempt'**: GF, 'Leitfaden zu einer künftigen Geschichte der Menschheit' (1789), AA 8, p. 193. **180. 'all Negroes stink'**: Kant, 'Of the Different Human Races' (1777), Kant 2013, p. 67. **180. Linnaeus and human races**: Linnaeus 1758, vol. 1, pp. 20–2; see also https://www.linnean.org/learning/who-was-linnaeus/linnaeus-and-race. **180. 'the small size'**: JRF (1778) 1996, p. 153. **180. 'the most beautiful'**: Oehler-Klein 1988, p. 62; see also Roberts 2024, p. 186. **181. harsher ... climates made people stronger**: Fink 1998, pp. 45–7. **181. 'I believe ... that the nations'**: JRF (1778) 1996, p. 192. **181. 'causes sluggishness, indolence'**: Ibid, p. 195. **181. 'The philosophers who are'**: GF, 13 September 1774, GF Voyage 2000, p. 592; for harsh environment in New Caledonia, GF, 5 September 1774, pp. 564 and 571. **181. 'I am far from'**: GF, 22 July 1774, GF Voyage 2000, p. 491. **181. 'And so humans'**: GF, 'Über lokale und allgemeine Bildung' (1791), AA 7, p. 45. **181. GF's translations of *Observations***: JRF (1778) 1996, p. 195; JRF 1783 (trans. by GF), pp. 261–2; GF to Spener, 15 November 1781. **182. 'that men in a similar'**: GF, 14 May 1774, GF Voyage 2000, p. 378. **182. 'All the various tribes'**: GF Voyage 2000, p. 9. **182. 'the passions and'**: GF, 13 August 1774, GF Voyage 2000, p. 538. **182. 'philosophize in an unphilosophical'**: GF to Jacobi, 2 January 1789. **182. 'precisely this systematic'**: GF, 'Cook, der Entdecker' (1787), AA 5, p. 274. **182. Reinhold ... spending lavishly**: JRF to Spener, 2 April 1775, Hoare 1976, p. 159. **182. 'They have no manner'**: G. White to J. White, 30 January 1776, White 1901, p. 302. **182. 'my friend, look out'**: Sparrman to GF, 15 September 1776. **183. 'the man was *quarrelsome*'**: GF, *A Letter to the Right Honourable The Earl of Sandwich*, 1778, AA 4, p. 82. **183. 'horrors of a Jail'**: JRF to Banks, summer 1777, AA 13, p. 618. **183. 'our**

situation here': GF to Banks, 4 January 1778. **183. step onto some scales**: Banks, MS. Book of weights of friends and acquaintances, 1778–1814, NHM. **183. Banks lent JRF £250**: GF to T. Pennant, 5 March 1787. **183. 'unforgiving when he'**: Lichtenberg to J.A. Schernhagen, 16 October 1775, Lichtenberg 1983–2004, vol. 1, p. 566. **183. Always mistrusting**: GF to Jacobi, 17 December 1778. **183. 'tendency toward self-love'**: Ibid, 24 October 1779. **183. George described his father**: e.g. GF to T. Pennant, 5 March 1787; GF to Jacobi's sisters, 9 March 1784; GF to Jacobi, 17 December 1778; GF to Spener, 15 December 1779; GF to Zimmermann, 20 January 1788. **183. had to endure hardship**: GF to Soemmerring, 27 May 1784. **183. Reinhold even shouted at plays**: Lichtenberg to J.A. Schernhagen, 16 October 1775, Lichtenberg 1983–2004, vol. 1, p. 567. **183. Wales ... forty-page attack**: The exact publication date of Wales' *Remarks on Mr. Forster's Account of Captain Cook's last Voyage round the World, in the Years 1772, 1773, 1774, and 1775* is not known. It's usually given as early 1778 but sometimes late in 1777. It was reviewed in *The Gentleman's Magazine* in January 1778 (vol. 48). GF's *A Reply to Mr. Wales's Remarks* was dated 21 February 1778. **183. 'written with so much arrogance'**: Wales (1778) 2000, p. 699. **184. 'Dr Forster says'**: and other inaccurate locations, ibid, p. 733. **184. '*We* hoisted a boat'**: Ibid. **184. 'the Doctor is always'**: Ibid, p. 711. **184. Wales disputed that muskets**: Ibid, p. 713. **184. 'which every one knows'**: Ibid, p. 714. **184. the telling of the murder**: Ibid, pp. 739–40. **184. 'cut, slash, and hack'**: GF, *A Reply to Mr. Wales's Remarks* (1778), GF Voyage 2000, p. 777. **184. 'It is time'**: Ibid, p. 775; for Wales refusing to share calculations, p. 763. **185. 'their butcheries in America'**: Ibid, p. 780. **185. 'poor shortsighted youth'**: Ibid, p.779. **185. 'informe all England'**: JRF to Banks, October/November 1777, AA 13, p. 681. **185. 'unequal contest was evident'**: GF to T. Pennant, 5 March 1787. **185. 'your Lordship ventured'**: GF, *A Letter to the Right Honourable The Earl of Sandwich*, 1778, AA 4, p. 77; for JRF demanding another £4,000, p. 83. **185. 'I know a man'**: GF to Jacobi, 25 November 1780. **185. Spener suggested translation of Buffon**: GF to Spener, 7 August and mid-August 1778. **185. reluctant to leave his family**: Ibid, mid-August 1778. **186. 'that presents everything sweet'**: Ibid, mid-August 1778. **186. left London for Harwich**: GF to JRF, 22 October 1778. **186. 'Are you healthy, dear'**: GF to J.E. Forster, 29 October–3 November 1778. **186. shaking off fleas**: Ibid. **186. In Rotterdam, The Hague**: Ibid. **186. 'People are clamouring'**: GF to Spener, 13 November 1778. **186. 'young argonaut'**: Wieland to J. von Müller, 8 June 1781, Wieland 1992–94, vol. 7, p. 371; GF didn't go to Weimar; Lessing had met GF at J.J. Eschenberg's house in Braunschweig on 14 January 1779 and invited him for 20 January 1779, Lessing to Eschenberg, undated, Lessing 1907, vol. 18, p. 306. **187. 'Forster who travelled'**: GF to JRF, 24 November 1778. **187. 'A truly noble person'**: F. Münter, 31 August 1784, Münter 1937, vol. 2, p. 56. **187. 'Never was I enough'**: GF to Spener, 22 April 1777. **187. 'How can you sleep'**: C.W.C. Dohm to J. Mauvillion, Harpprecht 2007, p. 205. **187. 'He is a**

magnificent young': Jacobi to S. von La Roche, 15 November 1778; Jacobi noted the wrong date as GF was in Düsseldorf from 21 to 26 November 1778. This letter was written around 28 November 1778; Götz 2007, p. 1; Jacobi 1825–27, vol. 1, p. 281. **187. 'do not speak a word'**: Jacobi to GF, 24 November 1778. **187. 'it would be dangerous'**: GF to JRF, 24 November 1778. **188. 'What will become of them?'**: Ibid. **188. 'a youth with'**: H.C. Boie to L. Meyer, 24 May 1779, Schreiber 1980, p. 38. **188. questioned him ... about Tahitian dogs**: GF to JRF, 24 December 1778. **188. 'We had a great man'**: L. Jacobi to G. Jacobi, 5 January 1779, Götz 2007, p. 1. **188. He was celebrated**: GF to JRF, 24 November 1778. **188. 'en famille'**: GF to JRF, 21 March 1779. **188. garden pavilion Wörlitz**: The garden pavilion was completed in 1785 and the objects are still on display (but for conservation reasons now in the main house), Quilitzsch 2019, p. 66. **188. GF and Lichtenberg**: GF to JRF, 24 December 1778. Lichtenberg lived in an apartment in the house of the publisher Johann Christian Dieterich, in today's Prinzenstrasse; for dinner in GF's honour, Lichtenberg to C.F. Hindenburg, end December 1778, Lichtenberg 1983–2004, vol. 1, p. 927; GF to JRF, 24 December 1778. **189. 'The empty, insipid heads'**: GF to Jacobi, 23 April 1779; GF was in Berlin from 30 January to 5 March 1779. **189. 'I know my father'**: GF to Spener, mid-August 1778. **189. 'affairs are so entangled'**: Woide to J.D. Michaelis, 6 April 1779, Michaelis 1796, vol. 3, p. 152. **189. 'there is no business'**: JRF to Sandwich 18, 19, 20, 22, 25 February 1779; Lord Sandwich's reply is quoted in JRF to Sandwich, 22 February 1779, Gordon 1975, p. 314. **189. in the local newspaper**: This was *Casselische Policey- und Commercien Zeitung*, 7 December 1778, Merz-Horn 1990, p. 117. **190. professor of natural history**: GF to JRF, 8 and 14 December 1778; GF to Jacobi, 17 December 1778; GF moved to Kassel at the end of March 1779, GF to Spener, 31 March 1779. **190. 'no one has ever been treated'**: GF to Spener, 15 December 1779. **190. 'Without any ties'**: Ibid, 17 December 1778. **190. George continued to lobby**: GF to F.W. von Erdmannsdorf, early September 1779; GF to Spener, 14 January 1779.

CHAPTER 13

191. elephant in Kassel: Soemmerring to unknown, after 21 August 1780, and Soemmerring to P. Camper, September 1780, Soemmerring 1996–2001, vol. 18, pp. 292 and 308; see also Wenzel 1988b, p. 78. **191. the landgrave's menagerie**: GF to Banks, 26 November 1780; Soemmerring to J.T. Soemmerring, ca. June 1779, Soemmerring 1996–2001, vol. 18, p. 237. **191. perform at the opera**: Wenzel 1988b, p. 77. **191. the dead animal exploded**: GF to Banks, 26 November 1780; Soemmerring to unknown, after 21 August 1780, and Soemmerring to P. Camper, September 1780, Soemmerring 1996–2001, vol. 18, pp. 292 and 308. **192. 'I'm keeping it hidden'**: Goethe to Charlotte von Stein, 7 June 1784; see also Goethe to Soemmerring, 9 June 1784, Goethe 1887–1919, part IV, vol. 6, pp. 288, 292–4.

192. 'Much asked and chatted': Goethe Diary, 14 September 1779, Goethe 1887–1919, part III, vol. 1, p. 98. **192. 'young Forster'**: Goethe to F. von Stein, 15 September 1779, Goethe 1887–1919, part IV, vol. 4, p. 61. **192. 'You know him'**: GF to Jacobi, 10 October 1779. **192. descriptions of Kassel**: Hassencamp 1783, pp. 49–63; Apell 1801; Günderode 1781; for 20,000 inhabitants, Apell 1801, p. 5. **192. 'No one reads'**: GF to Jacobi, 8 August 1781; for library, GF to J.W. von Archenholz, 12 November 1783; see also AA 13, p. 914. **192. 'the most miserable weather'**: GF to Jacobi, 7 February 1781. **192. luggage . . . had been shipwrecked**: GF to F.A. Vollpracht, 27 June 1780; GF to Banks, 26 November 1780; GF to Jacobi, 22 July 1779; GF to Spener, 5 June 1779; GF to F.W. von Erdmannsdorf, late summer 1779. **193. 'A complete herbarium'**: GF to Spener, 5 June 1779; see also AA 13, p. 705. **193. Books could be bought again**: GF bought 1,100 books from 1779 to 1785, Mey 2000, p. 95. **193. mahogany desk**: TF to Heyne, 27 August 1794 and 14 July 1797. **193. Soemmerring and position in Kassel**: GF to Soemmerring, 4 May and 6 June 1779; Soemmerring to Landgrave Hesse-Kassel, 15 May 1779, Soemmerring 1996–2001, vol. 18, pp. 214–15. **194. Soemmerring and GF in London**: Soemmerring to P. Camper, October 1778, Soemmerring 1996–2001, vol. 18, p. 193; Dumont 1788, p. 70. **194. 'Forster is my most'**: Soemmerring to J.T. Soemmerring, 14 December 1780, Soemmerring 1996–2001, vol. 18, p. 308. **194. rumours of homosexuality**: C.F. Rinck, 9 March 1784, Rinck 1897, p. 215; see also Dumont 1988, p. 82. **194. George . . . to an apartment close by**: Soemmerring to P. Camper, September 1780 and 4 January 1781, Soemmerring 1996–2001, vol. 18, pp. 307 and 312; GF had lived in Königstrasse in the Oberneustadt. The anatomy theatre was at Leipziger Platz, today's Unterneustädter Kirchplatz, and George moved to the 'Ziegeserischen Hause' (no. 1008, Waisenhaus Straße) near Leipziger Platz, Merz-Horn 1990, pp. 11–13. **194. Orangerie**: Apell 1801, pp. 80–8; for GF's walks in the gardens, GF to Spener, 30 June 1779. **195. 'I need not tell'**: GF to Banks, 9 February 1779; see also 1 April 1779; for JRF having to sell his library, GF to Spener, 9 January 1780. **195. Reinhold was sued by**: The judgement was on 9 December 1779, Gordon 1975, p. 316; JRF's debts of £700–£800, GF to Banks, 9 February 1779; see also Hoare 1976, p. 194; for £250 loan, GF to Pennant, 5 March 1787. **195. 'I have written several'**: GF to Spener, 15 December 1779; see also 19 April 1779 and 9 January 1780; GF to Banks, 9 February and 1 April 1779. **196. 'Whether he will be happy'**: GF to Jacobi, 14 February 1780; for Duke of Braunschweig and position in Halle, 2 November 1779 and 30 January 1780; JRF to K.A. von Zedlitz, 26 February 1779, AA 13, p. 683. **196. GF at Collegium Carolinum**: and teaching younger boys at the military academy, GF to Spener, 19 April 1779; GF to F.A. Vollpracht, 18 July 1780; GF to J.W. von Archenholz, 12 November 1783; today the building houses the Natural History Museum. **196. Buffon's *Histoire naturelle***: GF translated volume 6 of Buffon's *Histoire naturelle* (published spring 1780). **196. 'I'm Buffon's translator'**: GF to Spener, 5 July 1779. **196. landgrave's natural-history collection**: GF to Jacobi, 17 March 1780; GF to F.A. Vollpracht,

18 July 1780. **196. 'you can never stuff'**: GF to Soemmerring, 4 May 1779. **196. 'my drunken predecessor'**: GF to Spener, 19 July 1781. **196. nothing to do with antiquity**: GF to JRF, 30 March 1782; for the lectures at the Société des Antiquités, see e.g. 'Du Phénix' (1780) and 'De la Félicité des Etres physiques' (1782). **196. 'To write learnedly'**: GF to Spener, 20 June 1781; this was JRF's *Observations Made During a Voyage Round the World, on Physical Geography, Natural History, and Ethic Philosophy*, 1778; for the book being a hydrocephalus, GF to Spener, 21 July 1782. **196. 'my son in Cassel'**: JRF to Lichtenberg, 10–11 May 1780, Lichtenberg 1983–2004, vol. 2, p. 50. **197. 'My dearest, I am'**: GF to Jacobi, 22 July 1799; for needing ten hands and three heads, GF to Spener, 30 September 1781. **197. elected him as a member**: For Göttingen Academy of Science, GF to Heyne, 25 November 1778; for Leopoldina in Halle, GF to F.J. von Baier, 13 August 1780. **197. 'who brings rain'**: GF to Spener, 15 August 1782. **197. Heyne asked him to review**: Ibid, 14 July 1779; GF began to review for Heyne's *Göttingischen Anzeigen* in 1781. By 1792 he had written 115 reviews for Heyne; see AA 11 for all of his reviews. **197. including one about Tahiti**: GF, 'O-Taheiti' (1779), AA 5, pp. 35–71. **197. 'everyone has had opportunities'**: GF, 'O-Taheiti' (1779), AA 5, p. 35. **198. Newfoundland dogs**: GF, 'Herrn von Büffons Naturgeschichte der vierfüßigen Thiere' (1780), AA 6. 1, p. 687. **198. 'one cannot possibly be'**: Ibid, p. 695. **198. *A View into the Whole of Nature***: GF gave this lecture several times between the winter semester 1781/82 and summer semester 1783, AA 8, p. 390. **198. 'The sciences have become'**: GF, 'Ein Blick in das Ganze der Natur,' AA 8, p. 78; parts of this lecture were directly quoted from Buffon's *Histoire naturelle* (vol. 13), but I'm referring here only to the sections that were not from Buffon. For a comparison between which parts were from Buffon and which were by GF, Uhlig 1965, p. 268. **198. 'has been turned into'**: GF, 'Ein Blick in das Ganze der Natur,' AA 8, p. 78. **199. 'minute enquirers, whose'**: GF Voyage 2000, p. 9. **199. 'to bring my concepts'**: GF, 'Vorlesungen über allgemeine Naturkenntnis' (1792), AA 6. 2, p. 1754. **199. 'the great connections'**: GF, 'Ein Blick in das Ganze der Natur,' AA 8, p. 92. **199. 'active living power'**: Ibid, p. 81. **199. 'magic net of countless'**: GF, *Der Brodbaum* (1784), AA 6. 1, p. 69. **199. GF's finances**: GF earned 450 taler at the Collegium Carolinum, 120 taler for teaching the cadets, and 100 taler for looking after the landgrave's natural-history collection; for the 2,000-taler debt, GF to F.A. Vollpracht, 18 July 1780; GF to Jacobi, 12 October 1781; GF to Spener, 15 August 1782 and 25 September 1783; GF to JRF, 14 December 1778. **200. 'I am far too restricted'**: GF to Jacobi, 22 July 1779. **200. 'monster ... who now engages'**: GF to F.A. Vollpracht, 1 September and 31 December 1776. **200. 17,000 Hessians**: AA 13, p. 570; Mollo 1975, p. 26. **200. 'I am a poor'**: C.F. Rinck, 9 March 1784, Rinck 1897, p. 217. **201. falling asleep on his horse**: GF to Lichtenberg, 20 October 1783. **201. the earth ramparts**: C.F. Rinck, 10 February 1784, Rinck 1897, p. 198; Rintel 1794, p. 4. **201. students, professors ... library**: Anonymous 1783, pp. 373–4; Rintel 1794, p. 6; Böhme und Vierhaus 2002, vol. 2, pp. 173–4, 176; for dogs, C.F.

Rinck, 10 February 1784, Rinck 1897, p. 205. **201. Lichtenberg's apartment**: GF to JRF, 24 December 1778, and Lichtenberg to J.A. Schernhagen, 29 September 1783, Lichtenberg 1983–2004, vol. 2, p. 708. **201. Lichtenberg's character**: C.F. Rinck, 19 February 1784, Rinck 1897, p. 208; as womaniser, L. Mejer to H.C. Boie, 12 and 27 August 1782; H.C. Boie to L. Mejer, 8 September 1783, Schreiber 1980, pp. 163, 241–2; as lecturer, Geyken 2019, p. 25. **202. 'wizard of prose'**: Lichtenberg to Soemmerring, 14 March 1791, Lichtenberg 1983–2004, vol. 3, p. 882. **202. one two-week visit**: and hot-air balloons, Lichtenberg to J.A. Schernhagen, 8, 20, 23 October and 27 November 1783; Lichtenberg to Soemmerring, 2 January 1784, Lichtenberg, 1983–2004, vol. 2, pp. 719, 722, 727, 810–14; GF to JRF, 12 October 1783; GF to Banks, 1 December 1783; Soemmerring to J.H. Merck, 8 May 1784, Soemmerring 1996–2001, vol. 18, p. 456; see also Wenzel 1988b. **202. 'I have never lived'**: GF to Lichtenberg, 20 October 1783. **202. 'university-mademoiselles'**: TF to H. von Reden, 30 March 1818. **202. 'It is the practice'**: GF, 13 August 1774, GF Voyage 2000, p. 537. **202. 'beasts of burden'**: Ibid; see also 23 November 1773 and 10 August 1774, pp. 277 and 522. **202. 'higher degree of culture'**: GF, 13 September 1774, GF Voyage 2000, p. 592; for women as drudges in New Caledonia, 11 September 1774, p. 583. **203. 'An extraordinary woman'**: GF to Heyne, 18 August 1781; see also CS to J. von Studnitz, 3 September 1781, Schlegel-Schelling 1913, vol. 1, pp. 48–9. **203. attracted to Philippine Gatterer**: GF to JRF, 24 December 1778; GF to P. Gatterer, 31 December 1778 and early January 1779. **203. white Tahitian cloth**: CS to J. von Studnitz, 31 January 1779. Schlegel-Schelling 1913, vol. 1, p. 9. **203. Therese Heyne's infatuation**: GF to Soemmerring, 17 June 1784. **203. 'I read, read, read'**: and TF's education, TF to C.A. Böttiger, 10 January 1816. **204. novels in a cupboard**: Geiger 1901, p. 9. **204. 'The loss of the library'**: TF to L. Mejer, 3 October 1782; for library, Anonymous 1783, p. 398, says 130,000 books; Schweigard 2005, p. 22, says 80,000–150,000 books. **204. 'a girl full of fire'**: F. Münter-Brun, 14–18 June 1782, TF Letters, vol. 6. 1, p. 1212. **204. 'a strange mixture'**: L. Mejer to H.C. Boie, 24 March 1783, Schreiber 1980, p. 208.' **204. 'strange, foreign quality'**: TF to Therese Forster (daughter), 17 July 1803; GF was TF's first love, L. Mejer to H.C. Boie, 5 October 1784, and H.C. Boie to L. Mejer, 13 October 1784, Schreiber 1980, pp. 383 and 387; GF to Soemmerring, 17 June 1784. **204. 'As soon as he was animated'**: TF about GF, GF Letters 1829, pp. 61–2. **204. 'my bride is certainly'**: GF to Jacobi, 24 September 1780; see also 11 December 1781. **204. GF and the Rosicrucians**: Ewert 2009; Sahmland 1994; Sahmland 1988; GF Letters 1829, p. 26ff; GF visited the lodge 'Zum gekrönten Löwen' in Kassel for the first time on 5 December 1778 and was a member by 18 December 1778 (the minutes of the meeting noted: 'famous Brother Forster from London was celebrated'). It is not clear when GF joined the Rosicrucians exactly but possibly as early as the end of 1779, see Lichtenberg to J.A. Schernhagen, 3 November 1779, Lichtenberg 1983–2004, vol. 1, p. 1016; GF was a very active member of the Rosicrucians between 1781 and 1783. **205. 'the omnipresent God is'**: GF to E.F.H.

Falcke, 14 October 1781, Ewert 2009, p. 56. **205. 'remains always the first'**: GF, 'Ein Blick in das Ganze der Natur,' AA 8, p. 81. **205. 'True religion'**: GF to Justina Forster, August/early September 1782; for closeness to God, 27 September 1782. **205. 'religious fervour'**: GF to TF, 22 May 1784. **205. 'nothing is more intoxicating'**: Ibid, 1 August 1784. **205. Rosicrucians' laboratory**: Steiner 1985b, pp. 87–9; Sahmland 1994, pp. 400–2. **206. so-called star jelly**: GF to Soemmerring, 5 September 1780; see also Sahmland 1994, p. 403. **206. had left the brotherhood**: Ewert 2009, p. 10. **206. escape the Rosicrucians' maw**: GF to Soemmerring, 22 May 1784; see also 14 May and 5 June 1784; for GF warning others, GF to J. von Müller, 20 December 1783. **206. 'What is left'**: GF to Soemmerring, 10 July 1784. **206. 'burning thirst for'**: Ibid, 5 June 1784. **206. 'Children learn to walk'**: GF to J. von Müller, 20 December 1783. **206. experimented with fireflies**: GF, 'Ein Versuch mit dephlogistisirter Luft' (1782), AA 6. 1, p. 832. **206. 'Let us seek the'**: GF to Jacobi, 8 August 1781. **206. 'I would be far more useful'**: GF to J.H. Merck, 13 November 1783. **207. not seen a single wild**: GF, *Der Brodbaum* (1784), AA 6. 1, p. 67. **207. where breadfruit trees originated**: and exported to South Pacific, GF, *Der Brodbaum* (1784), AA 6. 1, pp. 66–7, 81, 86–7; the botanical books were by German botanist Georg Eberhard Rumphius (1627–1702), French naturalist Pierre Sonnerat (1748–1814) and Swedish botanist Carl Per Thunberg (1743–1828). **207. bred ... the originally small fruit**: GF, *Der Brodbaum* (1784), pp. 73–4. **207. 'bit by bit'**: Ibid, p. 74. **207. naming of breadfruit**: GF, *Characteres generum plantarum*, 1776, plates 51 and 51a. **208. Polynesian migration**: GF, *Der Brodbaum* (1784), pp. 66–7. **208. 'The breadfruit tree'**: Ibid, p. 67. **208. 'Bread fruit is procurd'**: Banks, after 14 August 1769, Beaglehole 1962, vol. 1, p. 341. **208. languages in South Pacific**: GF, 4 and 6 October 1773 at Tonga, GF Voyage 2000, pp. 242, 258, 260; GF, 15 March 1774 at Easter Island, p. 322; GF, 9 and 11 April 1774 at Marquesas Islands, pp. 338 and 341; GF, 28 June 1774 at Tonga, p. 419; see also Rensch 1999; Uhlig 2010, p. 146. **208. languages in Vanuatu and New Caledonia**: GF, 21 and 22 July 1774 in Malakula; GF, 4 September 1774 in New Caledonia, GF Voyage 2000, pp. 480, 491, 566. **208. Bligh and mutiny on *Bounty***: Wulf 2008, pp. 211–16. **209. 'their language [was] much'**: GF, 7 April 1774, GF Voyage 2000, p. 329. **209. 'must have had one common'**: GF, 6 October 1773, GF Voyage 2000, p. 260. **209. 'This is a sufficient proff'**: Cook, March 1770, Beaglehole 1968, p. 288. **209. the presence of Malay words**: JRF 1778, p. 283, the table of words is after p. 284; see also Rensch 1999, p. 241; GF, *Dissertatio inauguralis botanicomedica*, 1786, trans. in Uhlig, 2010, pp. 152–3. **210. 'so correspondent to those'**: GF, 23 November 1773, GF Voyage 2000, p. 281. **210. two distinctive groups**: GF, 21 and 22 July 1774 in Malakula; GF, 4 September 1774 in New Caledonia, GF Voyage 2000, pp. 480, 491, 566. **210. 'They appear to be'**: GF, 22 July 1774; for New Caledonia, GF, 4 September 1774, GF Voyage 2000, pp. 491 and 566; GF, *Dissertatio inauguralis botanicomedica*, 1786, trans. in Uhlig 2010, pp. 152–3. **210. Polynesian migration**: Dates vary immensely between different studies; Christan 2022, vol. 1, pp. 56–8; Bedford 2022, vol. 1, pp.

440–56; Abulafia 2019, pp. 3–39; Thomas 2021, pp. 76–137; for Polynesian navigation: Finney and Low 2006, pp. 156–82. **211. 'oppression by their own'**: GF, *Der Brodbaum* (1784), p. 66. **212. 'I cast a glance'**: Ibid. **212. talked of 'Oceania'**: Hau'ofa 2008, p. 31.

CHAPTER 14

213. 'I expect nothing perfect': GF to Spener, 25 August 1783. **213. named his son after him**: Ibid, 15 May 1782; for paying his debts, see e.g. 5 December 1782. **213. 'You're a husband'**: Ibid, mid-November 1782; see also 25 August 1783. **213. letters shuttled back and forth**: Ibid, 25 August, 4 and 25 September, 23 October, 10 November 1783. **213. 'I've gone over'**: Ibid, 4 September 1783. **214. 'which my wife'**: Ibid, 3 March 1784. **214. 'I revere Heyne'**: GF to Jacobi, 12 October 1781. **214. TF's appearance and character**: Pohl 1884, vol. 1, p. 266. **214. 'I have never heard a woman'**: F. Münter-Brun, 14–18 June 1782, TF Letters, vol. 1, p. 485; for Caroline Michaelis, CS to L. Gotter, 12 January 1781, Schlegel-Schelling 1913, vol. 1, p. 36. **214. 'her paintbrush was'**: L. Mejer to H.C. Boie, 28 October 1783, Schreiber 1980, p. 253. **215. 'only of what they had eaten'**: TF to L. Mejer, before 15 November 1783; see also TF to Soemmerring, 6 June 1784. **215. 'in being the secret critic'**: TF to P. Usteri, 8 February 1825. **215. 'which is of no use'**: TF to Soemmerring, 26 July 1784. **215. heated discussions about religion**: TF to L. Mejer, 29 December 1782. **215. 'a spirit of independence'**: TF to H. von Reden, 30 March 1818. **215. TF about her parents**: TF, 26 October 1803, Geiger 1901, p. 2ff; TF to C.A. Böttiger, 10 August 1812, 1 September 1812 and 10 January 1816. **215. an unhappy childhood**: TF to H. von Reden, 30 March 1818; TF to C.A. Böttiger, 1 September 1812. **215. stepbrothers and sisters**: Wilhelmine in 1779, Jeanette in 1780, Eduard in 1782, Friederike in 1783, Laura in 1789 and Alfred in 1792. **215. played with her doll**: TF to C.A. Böttiger, 1 September 1812. **215. tried to control her emotions**: Ibid. **215. 'Since I see no soul'**: TF to L. Mejer, 21 February 1782; see also 6 February 1782. **215. TF's admirers**: TF to L. Mejer, 23 March, 5 September and 2 December 1782, 26 January and 1 February 1783; TF to E. von Struve, 28 December 1806; L. Mejer to H.C. Boie, 5 May 1782. **215. 'I weep for a man'**: TF to L. Mejer, 23 March 1782; see also 5 May 1782 and 9 February 1783; TF reminded people how much she had been admired in her youth, TF to F. and J.G. Reinhold, 15 August 1805, 24 February 1806; TF to Therese Forster (daughter), 17–25 July 1803. **216. 'She built castles'**: L. Mejer to H.C. Boie, 5 May 1782, Schreiber 1980, p. 144.' **216. 'a thousand follies'**: Ibid, 24 March 1784, Schreiber 1980, p. 209. **216. 'so easily interested'**: TF to L. Mejer, 22 February 1783. **216. as if she had two souls**: Ibid, 13 March 1783; for GF having two souls, GF to Jacobi, 24 May 1783. **216. long letter of advice**: Heyne to TF, 31 May 1783, Leitzmann 1908, vol. 121, p. 2. **216. 'I'm a terrible creature!'**: TF to L. Mejer, 25–26 August 1783. **216. 'why am I condemned'**: Ibid.

216. 'Luiße, don't ask': Ibid, 2 September 1783; for the other man, 28 September 1783; for Luise feeling sorry, L. Mejer to H.C. Boie, 7 October 1783, Schreiber 1980, p. 248. **216. 'People are saying'**: Lichtenberg to A.G. Kästner, 7 December 1783. **216. elderly widower**: and brother of her stepmother, TF to L. Mejer, 5 November 1783, this was Johann Heinrich Füssli and Ernst Brandes. **216. 'he was Therese's'**: L. Mejer to H.C. Boie, 5 October 1784; for TF and GF before their marriage, see also H.C. Boie to L. Mejer, 24 May 1779, and 13 October 1784; GF to Soemmerring, 17 June 1784; TF to Therese Forster (daughter), 17–25 July 1803. **216. 'desire for something extraordinary'**: TF to Heyne, 16 September 1784, Gutfleisch-Ziche 2001, p. 168. **217. 'about Forster, and Therese'**: F. Münter, 16 September 1784, Münter 1937, vol. 2, p. 70. **217. They became engaged**: GF to Heyne, 19 April 1784. **217. 'nation's favourite writer'**: Heyne to TF, 16 March 1794. **217. 'an extravagant demand'**: GF to Soemmerring, 1 June 1784; GF only told JRF more than a year later, GF to Soemmerring, 19 May 1785. **217. university of Vilnius**: GF to Spener, 23 October 1783; JRF to M. Poczobut, 3 November 1783, AA 13, pp. 923–7; GF to Heyne, 17 December 1783. **217. accepted George's requirements**: GF to Heyne, 16 February 1784 and 7 December 1786; GF to J.B. Czempiński, 24 December 1783; for salary in Kassel, GF to Jacobi, 17 December 1778; see also AA 13, p. 932. **217. GF consulted Heyne**: GF to Heyne, 17 December 1783 and 16 February 1784. **217. 'That cursed money!'**: GF to Soemmerring, 10 May 1784; GF ordered books, GF to Spener, end of March 1784; bought a carriage, GF to Soemmerring, 23 June 1784. **217. 'I am shattered beyond'**: GF to Spener, 19 April 1784. **217. emotional farewell to Soemmerring**: GF to Soemmerring, 24 April 1784. **218. Heyne wanted to be sure**: GF to Heyne, 18 May 1784. **218. 'I saw his light'**: GF to Soemmerring, 26 April 1784.' **219. in Göttingen with Lichtenberg**: Lichtenberg to Soemmerring, 25 April 1784, Lichtenberg 1983–2004, vol. 2, p. 845. **219. 'I am still dazed'**: GF to Soemmerring, 24 April 1784. **219. 'Unfortunately, my dear Forster'**: Soemmerring to J.H. Merck, 1 May 1784, Soemmerring 1996–2001, vol. 18, p. 446. **219. 'God save poor Forster'**: J.H. Merck to Soemmerring, 4 May 1784, Soemmerring 1996–2001, vol. 18, p. 450. **219. 'lost one of the most'**: *Hessische Beiträge zur Gelehrsamkeit und Kunst*, vol. 2, 1784, p. 371. **219. 'England lost this'**: Archenholz 1785, vol. 1, pt. 2, 1785, p. 592. **219. 'we weakened and paralyzed'**: GF to Soemmerring, 14 May 1784; see also 5–6 June 1784. **219. 'Scene with my father'**: GF Diary, 15 May 1784, AA 12, p. 48; see also GF to Soemmerring, 22 May 1784. **220. visit in Halle**: GF saw his family from 24 December 1781 to 8 January 1782 (his first visit since he had left London). The second time was on 23 May 1784 on his way to Vilnius, GF Diary, 23–31 May 1784, AA 12, pp. 50–1. **220. 'always completely satisfied'**: GF to Soemmerring, 27 May 1784. **220. 'I believe suffering has'**: GF to TF, 22 May 1784. **221. 'I wonder . . . what right'**: GF to Soemmerring, 5 June 1784. **221. engravings from Cook's third voyage**: GF to Spener, 31 December 1783; Banks to GF, 31 May 1785; GF to Banks, 11 December 1785; GF to Spener, 26 December 1785; see also Spener to Banks, 14 August and 14

October 1784, Banks 2008, vol. 2, pp. 68–9, 74. **221. 'His most unfortunate'**: GF to Banks, 20 January 1780. **222. 'to fire at them'**: GF to Lichtenberg, 19 January 1780. **222. 'Something so marvellous'**: Ibid, 4 January 1784. **222. 'I am very well here'**: GF to Soemmerring, 7 June 1784. **222. 'German Florence'**: Herder quoted in Alt 2004, vol. 1, p. 409; for Dresden under August the Strong, Blanning 2024. **222. George went sightseeing**: GF Diary, 4–12 June 1784, AA 12, pp. 54–7; GF to Soemmerring, 17 June 1784. **223. 'surpasses all the profusion'**: GF to Soemmerring, 17 June 1784. **223. 'Italian Venus by Titian!!'**: GF Diary, 12 June 1784, AA 12, pp. 57–8. **223. read from his *Voyage***: Ibid, 15 June 1784, AA 12, p. 59; GF was from 20–23 June and 5–14 July 1784 in Freiberg, AA 12, pp. 61–3, 71–85; GF to Soemmerring, 23 June and 3 July 1784. **223. diet of milk and strawberries**: GF to Soemmerring, 3 July 1784. **223. Spener had asked for portrait**: GF to Spener, 3 March 1784. **223. painter's eyesight . . . so bad**: Ibid, 3 March and end of March 1784; see also Bertschinger 1988, p. 21; Bertschinger, however, argues that the Tischbein portrait was actually by Graff. **223. 'Graff captured me perfectly'**: GF to Soemmerring, 7 June 1784. **224. 'the beautiful secluded'**: GF Diary, 18 July 1784, AA 12, p. 87. **224. 'took a bath'**: Ibid, 29 June 1784, AA 12, p. 69. **224. 'succumbed to *masturbation*'**: Ibid, 16 June 1784, AA 12, p. 59. **224. 'Read Büffon, and'**: Ibid, 2 July 1784, AA 12, pp. 69–70. **224. carved the letter T . . . tree**: Ibid, 27 May 1784, AA 12, p. 51. **224. 'O God, O God!'**: Ibid, 17 July 1784, AA 12, p. 85.

CHAPTER 15

225. GF to Vienna: GF left Dresden on 20 July 1784, was in Prague from 22 to 27 July, GF Diary, 20–27 July 1784, AA 12, pp. 88–102; for increased traffic near Vienna, 28 July 1784, p. 103. **225. White Swan**: GF Diary, 29 July 1784, AA 12, p. 104; GF to TF, 1 August 1784. **225. he went to the Prater**: GF Diary, 29 July 1784, AA 12, p. 104. **225. GF's daily life in Vienna**: Ibid, 29 July–15 September 1784, AA 12, pp. 104–41. **225. 'to give compliments'**: Ibid, 3 August 1784, AA 12, p. 110. **226. 'all interrogating me'**: Ibid, 8 August 1784, AA 12, p. 112. **226. 'Beautiful women and'**: GF to TF, 3 September 1784. **226. 'our seafarer'**: GF to M.W. von Thun, 12 October 1784. **226. 'has lovely eyes'**: GF Diary, 8 August 1784, AA 12, p. 112; for Laura and Jeannette, see also GF to Soemmerring, 14 August 1784. **227. 'the greatest woman in'**: GF to TF, 3 September 1784. **227. badminton and *boules***: GF Diary, 2 and 8 September 1784, AA 12, pp. 131 and 135; for poems, 24 August 1784, p. 123. **227. 'in my opinion'**: GF to Soemmerring, 26–28 August 1784. **227. 'beautiful dear Kitty'**: GF Diary, 19 August 1784, AA 12, p. 118. **227. 'I was overcome today'**: Ibid, 11 and 14 August 1784, AA 12, pp. 114–15. **227. 'Coquettish with Mimi'**: Ibid, 1 September 1784, AA 12, p. 130. **227. 'Dearest Vienna'**: Ibid, 22 August 1784, AA 12, p. 120. **227. 'I believe that Kitty'**: Ibid, 5 September 1784, AA 12, pp. 133–4. **227. 'be careful'**: Ibid, 21 August 1784, AA 12,

p. 119. **227. 'all buttons are'**: GF to Soemmerring, 20 October 1784. **227. 'Vienna is a paradise'**: Ibid, 26–28 August 1784, see also 14 August 1784. **228. 'Imagine your clumsy'**: GF to TF, 3 September 1794. **228. 'He's in love with Vienna'**: TF to Soemmerring, 29 September 1784. **228. 'all without consequences'**: CS to L. Gotter, 28 May 1784, Schlegel-Schelling 1913, vol. 1, p. 85; see also TF to Soemmerring, 28 June 1784; for TF's other admirers, GF to Soemmerring, 3 May 1784. **228. 'I don't fear Michaelis'**: GF to Soemmerring, 5 July 1784; see also 10 October 1784. **228. 'flirt with all the counts'**: TF to K.J.H. Blumenbach, 4 November 1784, Gutfleisch-Ziche 2001, p. 165. **228. 'his vehemence exalted'**: TF to E. Struve, 28 December 1806; this was Franz von Wrede. **228. 'Protect her from all'**: Georgine Heyne to A. Schneider, 4 September 1784, Huber 1999–2013, vol. 1, p. 557; see also L. Mejer to H.C. Boie, 22 October 1784, Scheiber 1980, p. 391. **228. Auguste's physician**: TF to C.A. Böttiger, 10 January 1816; this was Johann Friedrich Karl Grimm. **228. 'Therese will make me'**: GF to Soemmerring, 10 October 1784. **228. Ignaz von Born**: Ibid, 14 and 26–28 August 1784; GF had met Born in London, Uhlig, p. 168. **229. 'From the Emperor'**: GF to Heyne, 1 September 1784. **229. 'The best minds of Vienna'**: GF to Soemmerring, 14–16 August 1784. **229. 'for political reasons'**: GF to Soemmerring, 14–16 August 1784. **229. met Angelo Soliman**: GF Diary, 3 September 1784, AA 12, p. 131; for Soliman in general, Blom 2012; Bauer 1993; for Soliman reading Cicero, A. Soliman to F. Kazinczy, 16 November 1792, Firla 2003, p. 34. **229. Haydn and Mozart**: Schuler 1988, pp. 16, 35. **230. Jan Ingenhousz**: GF Diary, 2, 19, 21, 22, 24, 28 August and 2, 9, 14 September 1784, AA 12, pp. 108, 118, 119, 123, 126, 131, 137, 140. **231. Nikolaus Joseph Jacquin**: Ibid, 2, 3, 19, 21, 23, 24, 28 August and 2, 14 September, AA 12, pp. 108–9, 118–20, 123, 125, 131, 140; GF to Soemmerring, 14 August 1784. **230. Alessandro Volta**: GF Diary, 2 August 1784, AA 12, p. 108. **231. 'Oh, if only we had Forster'**: GF to TF, 3 September 1784. **231. 'How are you my dearest?'**: GF Diary, 22 August 1784, p. 120. **231. 'You went on'**: and following quotes from the audience, ibid, 24 August 1784, AA 12, p. 121–3. **231. 'I have seen five'**: AH, 'Meine Bekenntnisse. Autobiographische Skizze 1769–1805', Biermann 1987, p. 61. **232. the carousel turned**: for GF flirting in the opera, GF Diary, 27 April 1784, AA 12, p. 125; for GF and Casanova, 9, 17, 22 August 1784, pp. 112, 116, 120; for ice cream, 30 July, 21 August 1784, pp. 104 and 119; for masked ball, 10 August 1784, p. 113; for delivering forget-me-nots, 14 August and 11 September 1784, pp. 115 and 138; for Kitty Jacquet's performance, F. Münter, 2 September 1784, Münter 1937, vol. 2, p. 58. **232. carriages . . . attend parties**: GF Diary, 7 September 1784, AA 12, p. 134. **233. 'Good heavens'**: Ibid, 16 August 1784, AA 12, p. 116. **233. Schönbronn . . . Augarten . . . country estates**: Ibid, 12, 23, 28, 29 August and 3, 7 September 1784, AA 12, pp. 114, 121, 125ff, 131, 134–5. **233. natural-history collection**: GF to Soemmerring, 14–16 August 1784. **233. more concerts, plays, dinners**: GF Diary, 29 August 1784, AA 12, p. 127. **233. delicious picnics**: Ibid, p. 128. **233. champagne headaches**: Ibid, 9 September 1784, AA 12, p. 137.

233. few more parties: and went out again, ibid, 13 September 1784, AA 12, pp. 139–40. **233. silhouettes and wax portraits**: Ibid, 11 and 14 September 1784, AA 12, pp. 138 and 141. **233. bid his farewell**: GF Diary, 15 September 1784, AA 12, pp. 140–1; GF to Soemmerring, 10 October 1784. **233. 'At 9.30 a.m. bleary'**: GF Diary, 16 September 1784, AA 12, p. 141. **233. Warsaw and Grodno**: Ibid, 7–27 October and 2–16 November 1784, AA 12, pp. 157–66, 173–83. **234. Stanislaw II August**: GF to Heyne, 20 November 1784; GF bored telling the same stories again, GF to TF, 12 November 1784. **234. 'the girl from the Sandwich'**: GF to Spener, 12 February 1785. **234. 'A handsome man'**: GF Diary, 3 November 1784, AA 12, p. 175; see also GF to Heyne, 20 November 1784; GF to JRF, 22 November 1784. **234. 'my back, being unaccustomed'**: GF to M.W. von Thun, 12 October 1784. **234. 'Nobility is a mere'**: GF to JRF, 22 November 1784. **235. GF's arrival in Vilnius**: GF Diary, 18 November 1784, AA 12, p. 189. **235. ten major fires**: Kasperaviciene, no date; for Vilnius inhabitants, GF to Soemmerring, 12–13 December 1784. **236. University of Vilnius**: Briedis 2009, p. 66. **236. 'consists of various buildings'**: GF to Soemmerring, 12–13 December 1784; for GF's apartments see also GF to M. Poczobut, 24 April 1785; TF to Georgine Heyne, 10 November 1785. **237. 'barely big enough'**: GF to JRF, 27 December 1784. **237. 'once you can pronounce'**: GF to TF, 22–24 January 1785. **237. servants … craftsmen … aristocrats**: Ibid, 18 November 1784; GF to Spener, 7 December 1784; GF to Heyne, 16 December 1784; GF to Soemmerring, 12–13 December 1784; GF to TF, 22–24 January 1785. **237. 'one may kiss'**: GF to Soemmerring, 3 February 1785. **237. 'Oh, this wicked serfdom'**: GF to TF, 22–24 January 1785. **237. 'half-wildness and'**: GF to Jacobi, 17 December 1784; for Polish and Tahitian languages, GF to TF, 13 December 1784. **237. 'seems just a sweet'**: GF to M.W. von Thun, 12 October 1784. **237. 'my only, my most'**: GF to Soemmerring, 12–13 December 1784. **237. every day was the same**: GF to TF, 13 December 1784; only thirty students, GF to Heyne, 7 April 1785. **238. 'It's an insurmountable'**: GF to Heyne, 12 October 1786. **238. he couldn't bear the cold**: GF to TF, 3–5 March 1785. **238. 'if there was a wall'**: Ibid, 16 February 1785. **238. 'My head remains too'**: GF to Soemmerring, 1–4 April 1785. **238. 'a full firm bosom'**: Ibid. **238. ordered furniture … household items**: GF to Spener, 14 March 1787. **238. she called him Willie**: TF to K.J.F. Blumenbach, 16 November 1784, Gutfleisch-Ziche 2001, p. 167; sometimes also Willi or Willy; TF to Meyer, 5 October 1804. **238. Meyer's appearance and character**: Zimmermann 1890, pp. 11–12; Campe 1847, vol. 1, pp. 9–10; Meyer's silhouette at SUB Göttingen (8 Cod. Ms. hist. lit. 103 Cim., Nr. 120). **238. 'Zebra Coat'**: CS to L. Wiedemann, 4 September 1805, Schlegel-Schelling 1913, vol. 2, p. 415. **239. 'You break my heart'**: Meyer to TF, summer 1785, Leitzmann 1921, p. 60; there are several undated letters from Meyer to TF in summer 1785, Leitzmann 1921, pp. 51–62. **239. They met secretly**: Meyer to TF, summer 1785, Leitzmann 1921, p. 55. **239. 'purest, simplest creature'**: TF, *Mehr Glück als Verstand*, Huber 1803, p. 124. **239. 'Oh, that I were among'**:

Meyer to TF, summer 1785, Leitzmann 1921, p. 56. **239. Let me kiss your feet**: TF to F. and J.G. Reinhold, 24 February 1806. **239. 'Therese can't remain'**: L. Mejer to H.C. Boie, 22 October 1784 , Schreiber 1980, p. 391. **239. 'For the first time'**: TF to F. and J.G. Reinhold, 24 February 1806. **240. Meyer's career**: Zimmermann 1890, p. 11ff; Campe 1847, vol. 1, pp. 9–10. **240. 'unfaithful to the entire'**: Geiger 1897, vol. 81, p. 635; Meyer to G.A. Bürger, 14 April 1789, Siegel 2002, p. 84; see also TF, *Mehr Glück als Verstand*, Huber 1803, p. 158. **240. 'I regard gloom'**: GF to TF, 22 May 1784. **240. 'Forgive me for'**: Ibid, 1 August 1784; TF destroyed most of the letters she wrote to GF but her concerns can be gleaned from his replies to her. **240. 'blind love, foolish'**: Ibid, 23 June 1785; for Meyer's hypnotizing fire, TF to F. and J.G. Reinhold, 24 February 1806. **240. George arrived in Göttingen**: GF to Soemmerring, 22 August 1785; he had left Vilnius on 26 July 1785, GF Diary, 26 July 1785, AA 12, p. 190; for GF and TF's meeting in Göttingen, see TF's novel *Mehr Glück als Verstand*, Huber 1803, pp. 148, 152. **241. 'It never occurred to me'**: TF to F. and J.G. Reinhold, 24 February 1806. **241. 'my overly tender'**: GF to Meyer, 4 February 1788, Sangmeister 2018, pp. 297–8; for TF's face lighting up, TF, *Mehr Glück als Verstand*, Huber 1803, p. 154. **241. self-denial almost felt natural**: GF to Meyer, 4 February 1788, Sangmeister 2018, p. 297. **241. hoped ... extend her feelings**: Ibid. **241. 'equality is the inescapable'**: GF Ansichten 1791–92, p. 68; for equal rights, GF to TF, 25 July 1784. **241. 'I hate everything'**: GF to TF, 3 March 1785. **241. afternoons in the garden**: GF to Meyer, 1 November 1785; see also TF, *Mehr Glück als Verstand*, Huber 1803, p. 160. **241. 'those days of intoxication'**: GF to Meyer, 4 February 1788, Sangmeister 2018, p. 297. **241. 'I masked my bleeding'**: TF to F. and J.G. Reinhold, 24 February 1806. **242. of a romantic novel**: TF to Heyne, 22–28 February 1788. **242. 'drawn from nature'**: TF to F. and J.G. Reinhold, 12–13 October 1805; see also T.J. to C. Carus, 14 March 1803. **242. 'alliance of the trinity'**: GF to Herder, 27 November 1787; see also TF to F. and J.G. Reinhold, 24 February 1806; for oath initiated by GF, TF to Heyne, 22–28 February 1788. **242. 'is the link in'**: GF to Meyer, 14 September 1785. **000. 'let us love each'**: Ibid, 7 October 1785. **242. 'I imagined an equal'**: Ibid, 4 February 1788, Sangmeister 2018, p. 297. **242. Meyer as their witness**: Georg Forster and Therese Heyne's marriage contract, 4 September 1785, KSW, GSA 16/15; see also TF, *Mehr Glück als Verstand*, Huber 1803, p. 165.

CHAPTER 16

243. two days at Weimar: Goethe to C. von Stein, 16 September 1785, Goethe 1887–1919, part IV, vol. 7, p. 96; GF to Heyne, 19 September 1785. **243. 'Goethe was lively'**: GF to Meyer, 14 September 1785. **243. Herder ... *Ideas:*** *Ideas for the Philosophy of the History of Mankind* was published in four volumes between 1784 and 1791. By the time of George's visit to Weimar, two volumes were available. **243. 'The book has a'**: GF to TF, 25 July 1784. **243. 'what a boon for'**: Herder,

Ideas for the Philosophy of the History of Mankind, Herder 2024, p. 150; see also pp. 43, 150, 158, 163. **244. 'natural organ of the'**: Herder, *Treatise on the Origin of Language* (1772), Herder 2002, p. 97; for GF using similar arguments later, GF, 'Neuholland und die brittische Colonie in Botany-Bay' (1786), AA 5, p. 162; GF, 'Cook, der Entdecker' (1787), AA 5, pp. 195, 280; and GF, 'Geschichte der Reisen (1791), AA 5, p. 569. **244. 'I found in him a man'**: GF to Heyne, 19 September 1785. **244. 'for who can see'**: Ibid. **244. Halle . . . Berlin . . . Warsaw**: GF to Heyne, 19 September, 2 and 14 October 1785. **244. 'a mind and heart'**: GF to Jacobi, 10 October 1785; for TF as soul of gatherings, GF to Meyer, 14 September 1785; see also Herder to TF, after August 1787 and Karoline Herder to TF, 3 March 1788, Geiger 1901, p. 51. **244. 'kiss this image'**: GF to Meyer, 14 September 1785. **244. 'I also believe this'**: Lichtenberg to Soemmerring, 11 September 1785, Lichtenberg 1983–2004, vol. 2, p. 117. **245. 'I only became a wife'**: TF to CS, 25 February 1794. **245. 'I wept in his arms'**: Ibid; see also TF to F. and J.G. Reinhold, 24 February 1806. **245. 'Had I not a wife'**: GF to Lichtenberg, 10 April 1786; for GF teaching TF botany, GF to Heyne, 25 May 1786. **245. 'Försterchen'**: TF to Georgine Heyne, mid-May 1786. **245. 'Green wallpaper, very'**: Ibid, 10 November 1785. **245. 'I'm still so unfamiliar'**: Ibid; see also GF to Soemmerring, 12–13 December 1784 and GF to M. Poczobut, 24 April 1785. **246. daily life in Vilnius**: TF to Georgine Heyne, 10 November and 10 December 1785, 27 January and mid-May 1786; GF to Georgine Heyne, 12 December 1785; GF to Lichtenberg, 10 April 1786. **246. read scientific books**: TF to Soemmerring, 17–19 March 1786; see also TF to Georgine Heyne, 5 April 1786. **246. starved of literary sustenance**: GF to Spener, 10 April 1786; see also GF to Lichtenberg, 5 November 1786; TF to Georgine Heyne, 27 January 1786; GF to Georgine Heyne, 30 January 1786. **246. a marriage built on trust**: TF to Georgine Heyne, 10 November and 10 December 1785; GF to Soemmerring, 1–5 December 1785; GF to Georgine Heyne, 12 December 1785; TF to Soemmerring, 13 December 1785; GF to Heyne, 19 December 1785; GF to Soemmerring, 16 January 1786; TF to Spener, 19 February 1786; GF to Lichtenberg, 10 April 1786. **246. 'Forster is an angel'**: TF to Georgine Heyne, 10 December 1785; see also TF to Soemmerring, 14 August 1786. **246. 'so, I'm asking for'**: GF to TF, 3 March 1785; see also GF to TF, 25 July 1784. **246. 'I love you more'**: TF to GF, 8 November 1785, Gutfleisch-Ziche 2001, p. 169. **246. 'Forster and I are'**: TF to Georgine Heyne, 27 January 1786. **246. renovated . . . carriage, spending money**: TF to Georgine Heyne, mid-May 1786; TF to Soemmerring, 17 March 1786; for debts mounting, GF to Heyne, 28 December 1786; Soemmerring told GF and TF to be frugal, Soemmerring to Heyne, 18 December 1786, Soemmerring 1996–2001, vol. 19. 1, p. 467. **246. 'In just fifteen minutes'**: TF to Georgine Heyne, mid-May 1786. **246. 'which makes me as happy'**: Ibid, 5 April 1786. **247. 'How often must'**: Ibid, 17 April 1786. **247. 'it is not entirely'**: TF to Soemmerring, 20 February 1786; see also TF to Georgine Heyne, 7 January 1786. **247. 'I am fully persuaded'**: GF to Soemmerring, 1–5 December 1785. **247. 'her entire mode'**:

Ibid, 20 February 1786; see also GF to Spener, 26 December 1785. **247. 'sparkle of my ideas'**: TF to Georgine Heyne, 12 February and 26 March 1786. **247. 'was conceived during'**: GF to Lichtenberg, 5 November 1786. **247. 'your tenderly loving'**: GF to Meyer, 10 August 1786. **247. Röschen, Little Rose**: GF to Heyne, 10 August 1786; for TF breastfeeding, GF to Heyne, 17 August 1786; GF to Lichtenberg, 5 November 1786. **247. 'the little devil'**: Ibid, 5 November 1786. **247. inherited sensitivity**: GF to Herder, 21 January 1787. **247. 'I don't see'**: GF to TF, 3 March 1785; see also GF to Soemmerring, 14 August 1786. **248. family ... his greatest joy**: GF to Soemmerring, 8 October 1786. **248. 'tremendous number of'**: GF to Lichtenberg, 18 June 1786. **248. Kant's latest treatise**: Kant, 'Bestimmung des Begriffs einer Menschenrasse,' *Berliner* Monatschrift, 1785, vol. 6, pp. 390–417, and 1786, vol. 7, pp. 1–17 ('Determination of the Concept of a Human Race'); Kant had already published 'Von den verschiedenen Racen der Menschen' in 1775 ('On the Different Human Races'). **248. 'the *whites*, the *yellow*'**: Kant, 'Determination of the Concept of a Human Race' (1785), Mikkelsen 2013, p. 130. **248. 'incapable of any culture'**: Kant, 'On the Use of Teleological Principles in Philosophy' (1788), Mikkelsen 2013, pp. 186–7; see also Kant 1802, vol. 2, p. 10. **248. 'everything in creation'**: GF, 'Noch etwas über die Menschenraßen' (1786), AA 8, p. 141. **248. 'on the whole'**: Herder, *Ideas for the Philosophy of the History of Mankind,* Herder 2024, p. 169. **249. 'I am apt to suspect'**: Hume, 'Of National Characters' (1748). Hume 1875, vol. 3, p. 252. **249. 'turgid puffed-up'**: Winckelmann, *Geschichte der Kunst des Altertums* (1764), Oehler-Klein 1988, p. 61. **249. GF didn't like term 'race'**: GF to Soemmerring, 19 January 1787. **249. 'if the public'**: Ibid, 23 July 1786. **249. GF's reply to Kant**: GF, 'Noch etwas über die Menschenraßen' (1786), AA 8, pp. 130–56; in English, GF, 'Something More about the Human Races' (1786), Mikkelsen 2013, pp. 146–67. **249. work from observation**: GF, 'Noch etwas über die Menschenraßen' (1786), AA 8, p. 131. **249. 'armchair philosophy'**: GF, 'Cook, der Entdecker' (1787), AA 5, p. 235; for abstraction as the wrong path, GF, 'Noch etwas über die Menschenraßen' (1786), AA 8, p. 132. **250. 'a few circumstances as facts'**: GF Voyage 2000, p. 9. **250. pre-existing concepts**: GF, 'Noch etwas über die Menschenraßen' (1786), AA 8, p. 132; see also GF to Soemmerring, 8–12 June 1786. **250. 'nature's order doesn't'**: GF, 'Noch etwas über die Menschenraßen' (1786), AA 8, p. 146. **250. 'still far from believing**: GF to Herder, 21 January 1787. **250. 'to look at the issue'**: Ibid; see also GF to Heyne, 20 November 1786. **250. 'That all humans'**: GF, 'Menschen-Racen' (ca. November 1786), AA 8, p. 157; see also GF to Heyne, 20 November 1786. **250. 'an old book against'**: GF, 'Noch etwas über die Menschenraßen' (1786), AA 8, p. 156. **250. 'which contained within'**: Ibid, p. 151. **250. 'Let me rather ask'**: Ibid, p. 154. **251. Europe's many despots**: Ibid. **251. 'I desire your judgement'**: GF to Meyer, 10 August 1786. **251. 'your candid opinion'**: GF to J.H. Merck, 10 September 1786. **251. 'I beg you to'**: GF to Spener, 13 November 1786. **251. people waiting for another instalment**: GF to Soemmerring, 7 December 1786. **251. 'Adam ... creature of**

some': GF, 'Geschichte der Reisen' (1791), AA 5, p. 569. **251. 'because I consider it'**: GF to Soemmerring, 19 February 1787. **251. Kant's reply**: Kant, 'Über den Gebrauch teleologischer Prinzipien in der Philosophie', *Teutsche Merkur*, January and February 1788; in English, Kant, 'On the Use of Teleological Principles in Philosophy' (1788), Mikkelsen 2013, pp. 173–94; see also Ribeiro Sanches 2003; for language like hedgehog, GF to Jacobi, 19 November 1788. **251. 'purely empirical groping'**: Kant, 'On the Use of Teleological Principles in Philosophy' (1788), Mikkelsen 2013, p. 174. **251. 'Moor seems closer'**: Soemmerring 1785, §69, pp. xxiv–1; see also Soemmerring 1784, p. 5. **251. 'true humans, just like'**: Soemmerring 1785, p. xx. **251. humans and monkeys**: Fabricius 1781, p. 330. **252. ability to speak and think**: GF to Soemmerring, 5 March 1785. **252. 'I am far from'**: GF, 'Noch etwas über die Menschenraßen' (1786), AA 8, p. 141. **252. 'stand very close'**: Ibid, p. 142. 000. **GF's essay collection**: GF, *Kleine Schriften. Ein Beytrag zur Völker- und Länderkunde, Naturgeschichte und Philosophie des Lebens* (1789). **252. unity in human diversity**: GF, 'Cook, der Entdecker' (1787), AA 5, p. 280. **252. 'entirely in factory style'**: GF to Spener, 2 November 1786. **252. In 1786 he worked on**: Ibid, December 1786; article against Kant: GF, 'Noch etwas über die Menschenraßen' (1786), AA 8, pp. 130–56; botanical treatises in Latin: GF, *De plantis esculentis commentatio botanico* and *Florulae insularum australium prodromus*, AA 6. 1, pp. 93–195; lectures: AA 5, p. 721; essay about Botany Bay: GF, 'Neuholland und die britische Colonie in Botany-Bay' (1786), AA 5, pp. 161–80; translation of Cook's travel account: *Des Capitain Jacob Cook dritte Entdeckungs-Reise in die Südsee und nach dem Nordpol* (1789); see also GF to Banks, 27 October 1783; Spener to Banks, 14 August 1784, Banks 2008, vol. 2, p. 68; James Cook and James King, *A Voyage to the Pacific Ocean* (London: W. and A. Strahan, 1784). **252. Cook project**: GF to Soemmerring, 23 July 1786; GF to Heyne, 2 April 1787; GF to Jacobi, 2 January 1789; for TF editing, GF to Spener, 31 July 1786 and 15 March 1787; TF helped by translating parts of the book but her work was not good enough, GF to Spener, 8 April and 7 May 1787. **252. 'many castrated'**: GF to Lichtenberg, 5 November 1786; for deleted preface, GF, 'Cook, der Entdecker' (1787), AA 5, pp. 187–90. **252. 'I regard these smaller'**: GF to Lichtenberg, 10 April 1786; see also 5 November 1786. **253. 'It is true, this man'**: Lichtenberg to Soemmerring, 2 June 1786, Lichtenberg 1983–2004, vol. 3, p. 219. **253. 'vivid and beautiful'**: and following quotes, *Nürnbergische gelehrte Zeitung*, 26 June 1787, AA 5, p. 740, *Gothaische gelehrte Zeitung*, 20 June 1787, p. 738, *Oberdeutsche Allgemeine Zeitung*, 27 September 1790, p. 745; GF completed 'Cook, der Entdecker' on 31 March 1787 and the translation on 16 June 1787, GF to Soemmerring, 17 June 1787. Spener had already printed the first volume in May 1787, but the second volume was only published in May 1789 (there were four volumes in total); see also AA 5, pp. 723–6. **253. translation better than the original**: *Nürnbergische gelehrte Zeitung*, 26 June 1787, AA 5, p. 740. **253. as a masterpiece**: *Allgemeine deutsche Bibliothek*, 1790, AA 5, p. 762.

253. 'his regard for': GF, 'Cook, der Entdecker' (1787), AA 5, p. 261. **253. 'His active mind'**: Ibid, p. 299. **253. 'the nobles, whose'**: Ibid, p. 310. **253. 'There is indisputably'**: Ibid, p. 278. **254. 'awareness of an abstract'**: Ibid, p. 195; GF repeated this idea in other essays, see also GF, 'Neuholland und die brittische Colonie in Botany-Bay' (1786), AA 5, p. 162, and GF, 'Geschichte der Reisen' (1791), AA 5, p. 569. **254. human . . . animals**: GF, 'Cook, der Entdecker' (1787), AA 5, p. 280. **254. 'ocean of humankind'**: Ibid, p. 197. **254. 'countless shades'**: Ibid, p. 194. **254. 'nature of man may'**: Ibid, p. 280. **254. 'characters of every nation'**: GF, 'Versuch einer Naturgeschichte des Menschen' (1786), AA 8, p. 158. **254. 'arithmetical precision'**: GF, 'Cook, der Entdecker' (1787), AA 5, p. 198. **254. 'We're engaged in slavery'**: GF, 'Ueber Leckereyen' (1788), AA 8, p. 174. **254. Africans in the German territories**: Bono 2012, pp. 35–46; Diedrich 2013, p. 96; Bauer 1993, pp. 9–11; Buckley 2012, pp. 49–64. **254. Africans in Kassel**: Schäfer 1988, pp. 41–2, 48–55; Diedrich 2013, pp. 93–108; for Soemmerring's dissections, Soemmerring to P. Camper, September 1780; Soemmerring to J.H. Merck, 1 May 1784, Soemmerring 1996–2001, vol. 18, pp. 307 and 447; Soemmerring 1785, p. xvii; Oehler-Klein 1988, p. 58. **255. Anton Wilhelm Amo**: Ette 2020; Knauß et al. 2021, p. 11ff. **256. 'in order to find out'**: Wigger and Hadley 2020, p. 89. **256. Soliman . . . stuffed and exhibited**: Schuster 1996, p. 99; Blom 2012, pp. 114–19; Bauer 1993, p. 83ff; Soliman's exhibited body burned in October 1848 during the Vienna Uprising. **257. Ludwig Höpfner'sbook**: This was his *Theoretisch-practischer Commentar über die Heineccischen Institutionen*, 1783 (Theoretical-Practical Commentary on the Heineccian Institutions), Mallinckrodt 2021, p. 141. **257. 'The King of Prussia'**: Ibid, p. 143. **257. 'not regarded as persons'**: Ibid, p. 144. **257. 'degrades man to'**: GF to C.D. Schreber, 18 September 1781. **257. 'to contribute to the true'**: GF to Soemmerring, 19 February 1787. **257. 'for what do we fear?'**: Ibid.

CHAPTER 17

261. Mulovsky in Vilnius: GF to Soemmerring, 4 June 1787 and 17 June 1787; for Mulovsky being illegitimate, 22 July 1787. **261. lead a five-ship expedition**: I. Chernyshyov to Catherine the Great, before 17/28 April 1787; Catherine the Great to I. Chernyshyov, 17/28 April 1787; I. Chernyshyov to Mulovsky, 1/12 May 1787, BBAW VA32182. **261. details of Russian voyage**: GF to Heyne, 3–4 June 1787; GF to Spener, 6 August 1787. **261. 'sweet thrill of the'**: GF to Soemmerring, 17 June 1787. **261. GF negotiated the terms**: and financial arrangements, Russian Admiralty to Catherine the Great, before 17 June 1787, BBAW VA32182 and GF to Heyne, 19 July 1787; for 5,400 roubles, A.N. Senyavin to GF, 28 June/9 July 1787. **261. 'So be it'**: Catherine the Great to Russian Admiralty, 16/27 July 1787; see also Russian Admiralty to Catherine the Great, before 17 June 1787, BBAW VA32182. **262. All his conditions . . . accepted**: A.N. Senyavin to GF, 28 June/9 July 1787; GF to Heyne, 19 July 1787; O.C. von Stackelberg to GF, 28 July 1787. **262. chancellor of the Russian Empire**: Harpprecht 2007, p. 363. **262. daily life in Vilnius**: TF to Spener, 21 January 1787. **262. 'This wretched land'**: GF to Spener, 8 February 1787. **262. 'I saw Forster pacing'**: TF to Spener, 21 January 1787. **262. 'mirror in which everything'**: TF to C.A. Böttiger, 5 September 1806. **262. 'Now, my brother'**: GF to Soemmerring, 4 June 1787. **262. 'Without any question'**: Soemmerring to GF, 22 June 1787. **263. 'I am still intoxicated'**: Ibid. **263. Soemmerring's questions**: Ibid, 30 June, 7 July, 21 August 1787. **263. 'what do we need'**: GF to Soemmerring, 22 July 1787; for urging to pack shirts and socks, 16 August 1787. **263. '18 nightshirts, 18 with'**: TF to Soemmerring, 23 July 1787. **263. 'I hope your good'**: Heyne to GF, 24 June 1787. **263. to inform his father**: GF to JRF, 6 August 1787. **263. 'he knows that I cannot'**: GF to Spener, 28 May 1787. **263. Reinhold strongly advised against**: JRF to GF, 25 August 1787. **264. 'as to surgical Operations'**: Ibid, 10 October 1787. **264. position in Berlin . . . Marburg**: GF to Spener, 28–30 October 1786; GF to Heyne, 21 December 1786; GF to Soemmerring, 28 December 1786; see also JRF to Soemmerring, 2 December 1786, Soemmerring 1996–2001, vol. 19. 1, p. 452. **264. 'The man ruins'**: Heyne to Soemmerring, 19 December 1786, Soemmerring 1996–2001, vol. 19. 1, p. 469. **264. 'that I always and everywhere'**: GF to Soemmerring, 28 December 1786. **264. 'I'm dizzy from all'**: GF to Heyne, 19 July 1787; see also GF to Soemmerring, 22 July 1787; for Heyne like a father, GF to Heyne, 16 August 1787. **264. departure from Vilnius**: GF's last letter from Vilnius was dated 22 August 1787, and on 24 August he wrote a letter from Warsaw. **264. 'my forthcoming journey'**: GF to Herder, 1 September 1787. **264. 'I am turning over'**: Herder to TF, 14 September 1787; for Goethe, Goethe to Herder, 8 and 12 October 1787, Goethe 1887–1919, pt. IV, vol. 32, pp. 102 and 113. **264. They reached Göttingen**: GF to JRF, 19 September 1787. **264. Dorothea Schlözer**: Kern and Kern 1988, pp. 115–20. **265. Göttingen Academy . . . George III's sons**: GF to JRF, 19 September 1787. **265. no letters from Mulovsky**: and war with Turkey, GF to Soemmerring, 23 September 1787. **265. 'All trunks and chests'**: Soemmerring to GF, 18 September 1787; see also 22 September 1787. **265. 'I am eagerly awaiting'**: Ibid, 29 September 1787. **265. Trying to calm his friend**: GF to Soemmerring, 23 September 1787. **265. 'I am free!'**: GF to Spener, 23 September 1787; for GF feeling healthier, GF to JRF, 19 September 1787. **265. arrangements for the expedition**: GF to Soemmerring, 23 September and 4 November 1787; GF to Spener, 23 September 1787; GF to Herder, 21 October 1787. **265. 'Since all is uncertain'**: GF to Spener 21 October 1787. **265. rumours about war**: GF to Soemmerring, 12 and 17 October 1787. **265. they had rented rooms**: Ibid, 12 October 1787; the rooms were in the house of pastor L.G. Wagemann at An der Mühlenpforte, today Angerstraße 14; for GF not working much, GF to Soemmerring, 17 October 1787. **266. JRF's conditions for joining**: JRF to GF, 11 December 1787. **266. 'I foresee endless'**: GF to Herder, 27 November

1787. **266. expedition to the Philippines**: F. d'Elhuyar y de Suvisa to GF, 10 November 1787, and GF to F. d'Elhuyar y de Suvisa, 23 December 1787. **266. 'I am 33 years old'**: GF to F. d'Elhuyar y de Suvisa, December 1787 (draft) and 23 December 1787. **267. Johann Georg von Zimmermann**: GF to J.G. von Zimmermann, 25 December 1787; for letters to Catherine the Great, GF to Catherine the Great, 25 December 1787 (draft); GF to Heyne, 27 December 1787; GF to J.G. von Zimmermann, 30 December 1787; J.G. von Zimmermann to Catherine the Great, 1 January 1788, AA 15, pp. 415–16. **267. expedition had been cancelled**: Mulovsky to GF, 26 November/7 December 1787; Catherine cancelled the expedition on 8 November 1787, BBAW VA32182; see also GF to Soemmerring, 7 January 1788. **267. Therese ... Wilhelm Meyer**: GF to Meyer, 4 February 1788, Sangmeister 2018, pp. 295–301. **267. 'You lived in the rapture'**: Ibid, p. 298. **267. 'exorcise passion through'**: Ibid. **267. 19 and 20 January 1788, the couple fought**: GF to J.G. von Zimmermann, 20 January 1788; for GF forcing TF to have sex, TF to CS, 25 February 1794; TF to Heyne, 22–28 February 1788; TF to F. and J.G. Reinhold, 24 February 1806; for GF demanding TF end relationship with Meyer, GF to Meyer, 4 February 1788, Sangmeister 2018, p. 298. **268. he departed for Berlin**: GF to J.G. von Zimmermann, 20 January 1788; GF to Meyer, 4 February 1788, Sangmeister 2018, p. 297; GF to Soemmerring, 27 January and 22 February 1788. **268. 'the result of the vexation'**: GF to J.G. von Zimmermann, 16–19 February 1788; for the Speners nursing GF, GF to Spener, 5 March 1788. **268. 'Your mother finds it'**: JRF to GF, 2 February 1788. **268. 'cringing Toadeaters'**: Ibid, 5 February 1788. **268. 'I hope God will'**: Ibid, 2 February 1788. **268. 'My heart bleeds'**: TF to GF, 23 January 1788. **269. 'I have used none'**: Meyer to Heyne, 23 January 1788, Huber 1999–2013, vol. 1, p. 602. **269. 'It would be good'**: Heyne quoted in Harpprecht 1990, p. 471. **269. 'I have been wrong'**: TF to Heyne, 22–28 February 1788. **269. 'was a wicked man'**: Ibid, 22 March 1793. **269. He was like a comet**: TF, *Mehr Glück als Verstand*, Huber 1803, p. 158. **269. 'I love you with'**: GF to Meyer, 4 February 1788, Sangmeister 2018, p. 300. **269. 'My contentment as'**: Ibid, pp. 297–8. **269. 'What should have'**: Ibid, p. 297. **270. 'Your love must'**: Ibid, p. 299. **270. GF's journey from Berlin and accident**: GF to Spener, 29 February and 5 March 1788; GF arrived in Göttingen on 2 March 1788. **270. 'to be happy with'**: Ibid, 5 March 1788. **270. 'Spring infuses all'**: GF to Soemmerring, 18 May 1788; for being ill and depressed in Berlin, GF to J.G. von Zimmermann, 16–19 February 1788; GF to Soemmerring, 22 February and 16 March 1788; GF to Spener, 5 March 1788. **270. a few happy years**: GF to J.G. von Zimmermann, 10 March 1788. **270. 'Maybe life should'**: GF to S.H. Jacobi, 9 March 1784. **270. Therese was devastated**: TF to F. and J.G. Reinhold, 24 February 1806. **271. 'I had to grit my'**: TF to CS, 25 February 1794. **271. 'All love in her'**: GF to Meyer, 28 April 1788, Sangmeister 2018, p. 304. **271. 'so, I wait for better'**: GF to Meyer, 30 March 1788, Sangmeister 2018, p. 302.

CHAPTER 18

272. 4,000 roubles: A.N. Sanyavin to GF, 21 December 1787; GF to A.N. Sanyavin, 12 February 1788. **272. 'a quiet, freedom-loving'**: GF to J.G. von Zimmermann, 10 March 1788; see also GF to Spener, 12 March 1788. **272. 'my daughter in Petersburg'**: Heyne to J. von Müller, 12 March 1788, AA 15, p. 533. **272. Heyne suggested GF**: Ibid, 3 February and 9 March 1788, AA 15, pp. 531–2. **272. 'it is quite beyond doubt'**: J. von Müller to Elector of Mainz, 14 March 1788, AA 15, p. 534. **273. Forsters left Göttingen**: GF to J. von Müller, 7 October 1788; GF to Soemmerring, 24 August 1788; for the intensive three-month course, GF to Soemmerring, 18 May 1788, and GF to Elector of Mainz, 12 August 1788. **273. Mainz**: Schweigard 2005, p. 55ff; Harpprecht 2007, p. 383ff; Uhlig 2004, p. 232ff. **274. Protestants and Jewish students**: WH Diary, 7 October 1788, Humboldt 1922, vol. 14, p. 40; see also Schweigard 2005, p. 78. **274. library in Mainz**: GF to J.D. Reuß, 21 October 1788; GF to Jacobi, 10 November 1788; GF to Heyne, 9 January 1789. **275. house in Neue Universitätsstrasse**: and for renovations, TF to Soemmerring, 12 May 1788; GF to Soemmerring, 30 June, 9 July, 7 August 1788; GF to Heyne, 14 November 1788; for engravings of Tahiti, TF to A. Rengger, 18 April 1798. **275. Röschen**: GF to Spener, 25 March 1788; see also GF to F.J. Bertuch, 3 October 1787; GF to Heyne, 4 April 1788. **275. proposal for a book**: WH Diary, 9 October 1788, Humboldt 1922, vol. 14, p. 50; for details about the book GF to J.G. von Zimmermann, 17 January 1788. **275. 'it was very beautifully'**: WH Diary, 9 October 1788, Humboldt 1922, vol. 14, p. 50. **275. 'was certainly the only'**: Ibid, 27–30 October 1789, Humboldt 1922, vol. 14, p. 211. **275. 'he must indeed have'**: Ibid, 9 October 1788, Humboldt 1922, vol. 14, p. 50. **276. 'that seems, I think'**: Ibid, 7 October 1788, Humboldt 1922, vol. 14, p. 41. **276. 'completely self-sufficient being'**: Ibid, p. 42.' **276. a remarkable woman**: Ibid, p. 43; for flirting, p. 42. **276. walks ... meals ... stars**: WH Diary, 8 October 1788, Humboldt 1922, vol. 14, p. 49. **276. 'kind, gentle, clever'**: WH to H. Herz and B. Veit, 30 November 1788, Humboldt 2014–17, vol. 1, p. 135. **276. their portraits**: Painted in 1789 in Mainz by an unknown artist, Mainz Stadtarchiv, George Forster Portrait BPSG/00041 and Therese Forster Portrait BPSG/00040 (see colour plates inset) **276. 'most dreadful period'**: TF to F. and J.G. Reinhold, 24 February 1806. **276. 'My heart has suffered'**: GF to Heyne, 2 December 1788. **277. Heyne ... advised fresh air**: Heyne to GF, 8 April 1789. **277. company of a few friends**: GF to J.G. von Zimmermann, 4 May 1788; GF to C. Kestner, mid-June 1789; WH Diary, 8 October 1788, Humboldt 1922, vol. 14, p. 49. **277. 'to let myself be jolted'**: GF to Heyne, 1 March 1791. **277. 'With gravity on'**: Jens Baggesen in July 1789, Baggesen 1986, p. 291. **277. '*cosmopolitanism* personified'**: Ibid. **278. Huber's daily work**: L.F. Huber to G. Körner, 26 April, 7 and 24 May 1788, Huber 1806, vol. 1, pp. 50, 265, 270–2. **278. Huber ... first impression**: Huber 1806, vol. 1, p. 19. **278. quotations from poems ... Schiller**: Ibid, p. 48. **278. Huber ... awaited George Forster's arrival**: L.F. Huber to G. Körner,

25 April 1788; see also 11 August and 18 September 1788, Huber 1806, vol. 1, pp. 264, 291, 302. **278. Huber was shy and clumsy**: Ibid, 3 October 1788, Huber 1806, vol. 1, p. 308. **278. 'I have set a slow'**: Ibid, 11 November 1788, Huber 1806, vol. 1, p. 313. **278. 'Forster seems to'**: Ibid. **278. Huber ... in Neue Universitätsstrasse**: Ibid, 11 December 1788, Huber 1806, vol. 1, p. 323; for GF taking Huber under his wing, p.52 **278. 'Forster is one'**: L.F. Huber to Schiller, 20 December 1788, Schiller 1943–2003, vol. 32. p. 273. **278. 'she has an excellent'**: Ibid. **279. Palau islands**: GF began to translate George Keate's *An Account of the Palau Islands* at the end of 1788, he finished it in early 1789 and it was published in August 1789. **279. 'man is neither good'**: GF, 'Nachrichten von den Pelew-Inseln (1789), AA 5, p. 337; for virtue, p. 329. **279. 'The audience is'**: ALZ, July 1790, AA 5, p. 762. **279. 'great storyteller'**: *Neue Wöchentliche Nachrichten*, 1789, AA 5, p. 762. **279. 'glorious writer'**: *Allgemeine deutsche Bibliothek*, 1790, AA 5, p. 762. **279. 'special pleasure'**: Goethe to GF, 16 November 1789. **279. 'what I so greatly'**: Lichtenberg to GF, 16 May 1789. **279. 'Even his most untenable'**: Schiller to L.F. Huber, 13 January 1790, Schiller 1943–2003, vol. 25, p. 391. **279 began to write at 5 a.m.**: GF to Jacobi, 10 November 1788; pacing through room, 8 February 1789, and GF to TF, 10–11 August 1793. **279. 'shackled to the quill'**: GF to Jacobi, 18 September 1790. **279. hated the cold German winters**: Ibid, 12–21 February 1789; for heating study, 18 February 1790. **280. 'my head is empty'**: Ibid, 15 November 1789; for feeling like prisoner, 2 January 1789. **280. 'the paltry twenty-four'**: Ibid, 15 November 1789. **280. 'There are people'**: Ibid, 8 February 1789. **281. 'What do you think'**: GF to Heyne, 30 July 1789. **281. first German journal to report**: Dumont 1997, p. 127. **281. '36,000 citizens banded'**: *Privilegierte Mainzer Zeitung*, 22 July 1789. **281. 'every person'**: Louis-Sébastien Mercier in *Tableau de Paris* (1781), quoted in Darnton 2023, p. 391. **282. 'murmur'**: Louis-Sébastien Mercier in *Les Entretiens du Palais-Royal de Paris* (1788), quoted in ibid, p. 90. **282. *émotions populaires:*** Darnton 2023, p. 446. **282. –23° Celsius**: Ibid, p. 379 (–9.6 Fahrenheit). **283. 'Voilà, the word'**: Nicolas Ruault on 21 June 1789, quoted in ibid, p. 424. **283. 'never to be separated'**: Schama 1989, p. 359. **284. reports ... perplexing ... contradictory**: *Privilegierte Mainzer Zeitung* in July, August and September 1789; see also L. F. Huber to G. Körner, 23 July 1789, Huber 1806, vol. 1, p. 356. **284. 'the English have worked'**: *Privilegierte Mainzer Zeitung*, 29 July 1789; the beginning of a civil war was reported on 22 July 1789; report about the lynching of Joseph François Foulon was on 1 August 1789. **284. like a drama on stage**: L.F. Huber to G. Körner, 23 July 1789, Huber 1806, vol. 1, p. 356. **284. 'what a session'**: GF to Heyne, 15 August 1789; see also *Privilegierte Mainzer Zeitung*, 15 and 22 August 1789. **284. *Declaration ... Privilegierte Mainzer Zeitung***: Printed in *Privilegierte Mainzer Zeitung*, 12 August 1789. **284. 'Men are born'**: *Declaration of the Rights of Man and of the Citizen*, 1789. **285. 'no body, no individual'**: Ibid. **285. 'France is shaking off'**: GF, 'Über Proselytenmacherei' (1789), AA 8, p. 206. **285. Humboldt ... Campe**: They were

in Paris from 4 to 27 August 1789 and arrived in Mainz on 3 September. Humboldt stayed until 20 September; Humboldt 1922, vol. 14, p. 140; WH to GF, 19 August 1789; GF to Heyne, 7 September 1789; GF to Jacobi, 23 September 1789. **285. 'The Bastille lies'**: WH Diary, 9 August 1789, Humboldt 1922, vol. 14, p. 119. **285. 'bulwark of despotism'**: Ibid. **285. girls and boys in Paris**: Ibid, 16 August 1789, Humboldt 1922, vol. 14, p. 132; Campe, 4 August 1789, Campe 1790, p. 29. **285. 'even as a mere'**: Campe, 4 August 1789, Campe 1790, pp. 27–8. **285. 'one gets swept'**: WH to C. von Beulwitz, 4 August 1789, Humboldt and Humboldt, 1910–16, pp. 52–3. **285. 'When will other'**: WH to GF, 7 August 1789. **285. 'It's wonderful to see'**: GF to Heyne, 30 July 1789. **285. 'were perhaps the happiest'**: WH to GF, 28 September 1789. **286. 'Vive la liberté!'**: Fuhrmann 1962–75, vol. 1, p. 16; for poems see e.g. Klopstock's *Ode an die Französische Revolution*, and later William Wordsworth's *The French Revolution as It Appeared to Enthusiasts at Its Commencement*. **286. 'I have seen the glory'**: Kühn 2001, p. 342. **286. 'dawn of freedom'**: Vieweg 2020, pp. 67 and 71. **286. 'pulling down an edifice'**: Burke 1790, p. 90. **286. German settlers . . . tyrannized**: GF Letters 1829, p. 9. **286. 'natural circle of human'**: GF, 1 September 1773, GF Voyage 2000, p. 200; for overweight man in Tahiti, GF, 'Cook, der Entdecker' (1787), AA 5, p. 281. **286. 'proper sense of the'**: GF, 1 September 1773, GF Voyage 2000, p. 200. **287. George criticized the Landgrave**: GF to F.A. Vollpracht, 1 September and 31 December 1776. **287. Vilnius . . . feudal system**: GF to F.J. Bertuch, 23 December 1784; GF to TF, 22–24 January 1785. **287. 'then all free discussion'**: GF, 'Über Proselytenmacherei' (1789), AA 8, p. 201; GF wrote the essay in September 1789 and it was published in December 1789; for WH staying in Mainz while GF was writing, GF to Heyne, 3 October 1789. **287. 'To be free'**: GF, 'Über Proselytenmacherei' (1789), AA 8, p. 202. **287. 'Let everyone *believe*'**: GF to Jacobi, 8 February 1789. **287. a writer's impact**: GF to Heyne, 30 January 1790. **287. 'therefore let us not'**: GF to Jacobi, 8 February 1789. **287. 'A hundred thousand'**: GF to TF, 7 July 1784. **287. 'apart from its usefulness'**: GF to Jacobi, 16 January 1789. **288. 'I've never liked'**: Ibid, 1 November 1789. **288. Adam Smith**: GF to Heyne, 9 December 1790. **288. 'insipid, pedantic and'**: GF to Voß, 11 December 1790; see also GF to Heyne, 9 December 1790. **288. 'half-humans'**: Meiners, 'Historische Bemerkungen über die so genannten Wilden, oder über Jäger- und Fischer-Völker,' *Göttingisches Historisches Magazin*, 1790, vol. 6, p. 275, AA 11, p. 413; for GF's criticism, GF to Heyne, 19 January 1789, and GF's review of Meiners' contributions to *Göttingisches Historisches Magazin* in ALZ (1791), AA 11, p. 243. **288. 'natural inequality'**: Meiners, 'Ueber die Natur der Afrikanischen Neger, und die davon abhangende Befreyung, oder Einschränkung der Schwarzen,' *Göttingisches Historisches Magazin*, 1790, vol. 6, pp. 391–2, AA 11, p. 414. **288. 'For a long time'**: GF to Heyne, 7 September 1789. **288. 'morally and physically'**: GF to Jacobi, 1 November 1789; see also GF to Heyne, 3 October 1789. **288. 'if one were to collect'**: GF's review of Meiners' contributions to *Göttingisches Historisches*

Magazin in ALZ (1791), AA 11, p. 241. **289. 'white, black, yellow'**: GF, 'Leitfaden zu einer künftigen Geschichte der Menschheit' (1789), AA 8, p. 193. **289. 'Instead of merely'**: GF's review of Meiners' contributions to *Göttingisches Historisches Magazin* in ALZ (1791), AA 11, p. 245. **289. 'is not bound to'**: Ibid, p. 247. **289. books on slavery to review**: Those against slavery were e.g. S. Hollingsworth's *A dissertation on the manners, government and spirit of Africa* (1788), reviewed by GF in 1789; J.B. Moreton's *Manners and Customs in the West India Islands* (1790), reviewed by GF in 1791; *A short journey in the West Indies, in which are interspersed curious anecdotes and characters* (1790), reviewed by GF in 1791; R. Nisbet's *The capacity of negroes for religious and moral improvement considered* (1789), reviewed by GF in 1791; J.P. Brissot's *Nouveau Voyage dans les Etats-Unis de l'Amerique* (1788), reviewed by GF in 1791; AA 11, pp. 174–5, 282–3, 287–91, 312–36. **289. He reviewed *Africa***: GF, review of D.H. Lamiral's *L'Afrique et le people africain* (1789), AA 11, p. 338. **289. 'there is no difference'**: GF, review of J.P. Brissot's *Nouveau Voyage dans les Etats-unis de l'Amerique* (1792), AA, vol. 11, p. 321. **289. 'We have, after all'**: GF, 'Über die Beziehung der Staatskunst auf das Glück der Menschheit' (1793), AA 10. 1, p. 573. **289. 'hereditary differences'**: GF Speech 15 November 1792, AA 10. 1, p. 12. **289. 'the same instincts'**: GF, 6 May 1774, GF Voyage 2000, p. 374. **290. her reluctance to have another child**: TF to J.G. Reinhold, 12 February 1808. **290. 'a little blue-eyed'**: TF to F.J. Bertuch, 11 May 1790. **290. 'Röschen, the foot'**: WH to C. von Dacheröden, 1 May 1790, Humboldt 2014–17, p. 273. **290. his loved ones happy**: GF to Heyne, 12 January 1790. **290. stank the next morning**: Ibid, 13 December 1789. **290. 'this homeland of his'**: TF to J. von Müller, 11 May 1790. **290. renew old friendships**: GF to Heyne, 12 March 1790.

CHAPTER 19

291. Humboldt character and childhood: WH to C. von Dacheröden, April 1790, 6 November 1790 and 3 June 1791, Humboldt and Humboldt 1910–16, vol. 1, pp. 134, 270, 477; AH to W.G. Wegener, 24, 25 and 27 February 1789; AH to C. Freiesleben, 5 June 1792, Humboldt 1973, pp. 39ff and 191ff; AH, 'Meine Bekenntnisse, 1769–1805', Biermann 1987, p. 50ff; Bruhns 1872, vol. 1, p. 20. **291. dedicating his first book to GF**: This was Humboldt's *Mineralogische Beobachtungen über einige Basalte am Rhein*, 1790. **292. stayed with the Forsters in Mainz**: AH to W.G. Wegener, 10 January 1790, Humboldt 1973, p. 80. **292. GF influence on Humboldt**: AH, 'Ich über mich selbst (Mein Weg zum Naturwissenschaftler und Forschungsreisenden, 1769–1790)', Biermann 1987, pp. 36–8; AH, 'Aus meinem Leben, 1769–1850', Biermann 1987, p. 87. **292. George left Mainz**: GF to TF, 25 March 1790; for elector's permission, GF to Heyne, 20 March 1790. **292. Humboldt and GF on Rhine**: GF to TF, 27 and 29 March 1790; see also AH Diary, 19 June 1799, Nachl. Alexander von Humboldt (Tagebücher) I, 15v,

Stabi Berlin. **292. 'Dearest, most loving'**: GF to TF, 26 March 1790. **292. Bonn ... Düsseldorf**: GF to Soemmerring, 4 April 1790; GF Ansichten 1791–92, pp. 37–81. **292. 'When I carry a'**: GF to Jacobi, 2 April 1790. **292. chatting with their fellow passengers**: GF to TF, 6 April 1790. **292. 'about whom he had'**: Ibid. **292. 'Once Humboldt is'**: Ibid; see also 25–28 April 1790. **293. 'I dream myself'**: Ibid, 17 April 1790. **293. 'The multitude of ideas'**: Ibid, 4 April 1790; see also GF Ansichten 1791–92, p. 111. **293. 'we don't want to'**: GF Ansichten 1791–92, p. 162. **293. religion ... the driving force**: GF to TF, 21–22 April 1790. **293. 'We assured them that'**: GF Ansichten 1791–92, p. 229. **293. 'Good heavens!'**: GF to TF, 14 April 1790; for GF in Lille, GF Ansichten 1791–92, p. 230; GF Diary, 12 April 1790, AA 12, p. 242. **294. 'those three years'**: GF Ansichten 1791–92, p. 236. **294. 'while the whole continues'**: Ibid. **294. barges ... canals**: GF to TF, 14 and 17 April, 4 May 1790. **294. 'he would have described'**: Ibid, 29 April 1790. **294. 'we both looked'**: Ibid, 17 April 1790. **295. 'Forster's name, which'**: AH to W.G. Wegner, 20 June 1790, Humboldt 1973, p. 93; see also AH to Jacobi, 3 January 1791, p. 117. **295. paintings in Antwerp**: and dinner with English ambassador, GF to TF, 22 April 1790; for night on yacht, 27 April 1790. **295. 'that I'm much paraded'**: Ibid, 25 April 1790. **295. 'if the Dutch were'**: Ibid, 28 April 1790. **295. orangutan ... Leiden ... Harlem**: Ibid, 25 April and 2 May 1790; GF to Soemmerring, 4 May 1790. **295. 'I would trade'**: GF to TF, 25 April 1790. **295. 'the past, present'**: Ibid, 28 April 1790. **295. inoculated Röschen**: Ibid, 22 April 1790, and GF to Soemmerring, 4 May 1790. **295. an affair with ... Huber**: TF to CS, 25 February 1794; TF to E. von Herder, 15 August 1806. **296. 'and may you bring joy'**: GF to TF, 26 March 1790. **296. would swim in the Rhine**: F. Münter, Diary, 29, 31 July and 2 August 1791, Andreasen and Mathy 1967, vol. 62, pp. 63, 67, 69. **296. 'We shall be happy'**: GF to TF, 4 April 1790. **295. sailed to England**: GF to Heyne, 5 May 1790. **296. 'I wasted the first'**: GF to Jacobi, 4 August 1790; see also AH, 'Aus meinem Leben, 1769–1850', Biermann 1987, p. 36. **296. Forster family had been excited**: JRF and Justina Elisabeth to GF, 11 April 1790. **296. Hodges ... Bligh**: GF to Heyne, 24 May 1790; GF to TF, 1 June 1790; AH to P. Usteri, 27 June 1790, Humboldt 1973, pp. 96–8. **296. Herschel ... telescope**: GF Diary, May 1790, AA 12, pp. 312–14. **297. 'naturally You will do'**: JRF to GF, 11 April 1790. **297. 'our drawings'**: Ibid. **297. 'Be so kind'**: Ibid. **297. They saw Banks**: GF to Heyne, 24 May 1790 and 15 January 1791. **297. 'Fear of a man'**: GF to Jacobi, 6 November 1791; see also GF to Heyne, 24 May 1790. **297. 'for some of the odium'**: GF to Heyne, 24 May 1790. **297. 'May the good spirit'**: GF to L.F. Huber, 23–25 May 1790. **297. 'Your absence'**: Soemmerring to GF, 14 May 1790. **298. Bath, Bristol and Birmingham**: GF Diary, 7–28 June 1790, AA 12, pp. 316–62. **298. elegant lady ... farmer's wife**: GF Diary, 7–8 June 1790, AA 12, pp. 318 and 321. **298. 'Bath is the most boring'**: Ibid, p.321; for Gloucestershire cheese, p. 318.' **298. 'how much the labour'**: Ibid, 9–12 June 1790, AA 12, p. 325; for representatives in Parliament, p. 324. **298. visit ... popular**

gardens: This was The Leasowes and Hagley, GF Diary, 9–12 June 1790, AA 12, pp. 327–33. **299. George . . . outside the carriage**: GF Diary, 12–13 June 1790, AA 12, pp. 333–4. **299. magic in nature**: Ibid, 13–15 June 1790, AA 12, p. 344. **299. 'I've had the happiest'**: AH to P. Usteri, 27 June 1790, Humboldt 1973, p. 97. **300. 'Vive la Nation!'**: GF Diary, 30 June 1790, AA 12, p. 365. **300. Festivities at Champ de Mars**: GF, *Erinnerungen aus dem Jahr 1790* (1792), AA 8, pp. 286–8. **301. 'frenzy of freedom'**: Ibid, p. 287. **301. 'To be human'**: Ibid, p. 286. **301. 'Menschenrepublik'**: GF Speech 1 January 1793, AA 10. 1, p. 59. **301. enthusiasm . . . deeply moving**: GF to Heyne, 13 July 1790. **301. left the French capital . . . Mainz**: Chronology of GF's travels, AA 12, p. 460. **301. Therese had been dejected**: TF to F. and J.G. Reinhold, 24 February 1806. **301. George discovered Therese's affair**: TF to E. von Herder, 15 August 1806. **301. Therese was in love**: TF to R. Hottlinger, 16 November 1793. **301. Huber's character**: Huber 1806, p. 32. **302. 'a person who understood'**: TF to F. and J.G. Reinhold, 24 February 1806. **302. 'grievous domestic matter'**: GF to Jacobi, 18 September 1790; see also TF to CS, 25 February 1794. **302. There were fights and tears**: TF to E. von Herder, 15 August 1806; for Huber moving in, GF to Schiller, 6 November 1790; GF to Voß, 14 November 1790. **302. 'to accept things'**: GF to TF 14 April 1790. **302. Therese . . . was ill**: GF to Heyne, 23, 30 November and 7 December 1790; for salammoniac pills, GF to Jacobi, 2 November 1790. **302. 'consumes herself through'**: Heyne to GF, 8 December 1790. **302. GF offered *Views* to Spener**: GF to Spener, 23 July 1790; see also 4, 27 September, 11 October and 6 November 1790. **302. Christian Friedrich Voß**: GF to Voß, 4 September, 11 and 20 October 1790. **302. 'I honour, esteem'**: GF to Spener, 5 May 1791. **302. *Views of the Lower Rhine***: *Ansichten vom Niederhein, von Brabant, Flandern, Holland, England, und Frankreich, im April, Mai und Junius 1790*; GF delivered the first volume on 27 November 1790 and the second on 2 March 1792; GF to Voß, 27 November 1790 and 2 March 1792; Huber published the third volume posthumously in 1794. **303. people discussing their rights**: GF Ansichten 1791–92, p. 111. **303. 'any truth that'**: GF to J.H. Campe, 20 November 1786. **303. 'to be inconsequent'**: GF Ansichten 1791–1792, p. 116; for his willingness to change his thinking, see also GF, 'Noch etwas über die Menschenraßen' (1786), AA 8, p. 132. **303. 'The idealized gods'**: GF Ansichten 1791–92, p. 67. **303. 'stand like apparitions'**: Ibid, p. 24. **303. 'a book about humans'**: Lichtenberg to Soemmerring, 20 April 1791, Lichtenberg 1983–2004, p. 882. **303. Ehrenbreitstein fortress**: GF Ansichten 1791–92, pp. 7–9. **304. 'The freedom of'**: Ibid, p. 8. **304. 'The ferment is everywhere'**: JRF to GF, 12 September 1790. **304. to control the students**: GF to Heyne, 7 September 1790; GF to JRF, 18 September 1790. **304. 'So, you also had'**: Lichtenberg to GF, 30 September 1790. **304. 'and sow only the good'**: GF to Jacobi, 22 March 1791. **304. 'you're walking on'**: Heyne to GF, 22 August 1790. **305. 'Violence, then, not'**: GF Ansichten 1791–92, p. 118. **305. 'the systematic murder of'**: Ibid, p. 230. **305. 'consequences of anarchy'**: Ibid, p. 249. **305. 'will cause a stir'**: AH to W.G. Wegener, 15 June 1790. **305. influenced by his mentor's**: AH, *Ansichten der Natur*, 1808. **305. 'wishes to travel'**: Goethe to GF, 25 June 1792; Goethe had already thanked GF for the first volume at the end of August 1791. **305. 'one of the foremost works'**: Lichtenberg to GF, 1 July 1791. **305. 'We're not at a point'**: GF to C.W. von Dohm, 5 April 1791; for GF believing to improve, rather than replace, old constitutions in Germany, GF Ansichten 1791–92, pp. 85–6.

CHAPTER 20

306. parlour . . . centre of revolutionary ideas: F. Münter Diary, 25 July–5 August 1791, Andreasen and Mathy 1967, vol. 62, pp. 60–73; J.E. Bollmann to his father, 26 October 1791, Kapp 1880, pp. 25–6; TF to J.F. Cotta, 14 June 1818; visitors in autumn 1791 were: Alexander von Humboldt, Christoph Girtanner, Johann Benjamin Jachmann, Thomas Brand, Justus Erich Bollmann, Frederick Münter, Frederik Sneedorff, Friedrich Leopold Graf Stolberg, Johann Wilhelm von Archenholz, Meta Forkel, Uhlig 2004, pp. 272–3. **306. TF carried his name with pride**: CS to Meyer, 17 December 1792, Schlegel-Schelling 1913, vol. 1, p. 280. **306. Huber worked as little as possible**: GF to M. Forkel, 12 December 1791; for visitors not noticing the affair, F. Brun Diary, June 1791, Huber 1999–2013, vol. 6. 1, p. 1212; J.E. Bollmann to his father, 26 October 1791, Kapp 1880, p. 26. **306. 'You will believe me'**: J.E. Bollmann to his father, 26 October 1791, Kapp 1880, p. 26. **306. 'deceiving everyone, negotiating'**: GF to Jacobi, 5 February 1791; about elector, F. Münter Diary, 26 July 1791, Andreasen and Mathy 1967, vol. 62, p. 61. **306. 'In Germany, the princes'**: GF to C.W. von Dohm, 7 January 1792. **307. 'Letters are opened'**: J.E. Bollmann to his father, 6 September 1791, Kapp 1880, p. 23; for elector's prohibitions, Schweigerd 2005, pp. 126–32. **307. 'I'm familiar with'**: Heyne to GF, 16 February 1792; this was J.P. Brissot's *Nouveau voyage dans les Etats-Unis de l'Amerique septentrionale, fait en 1788*, Paris, 1791. **307. 'your own zeal'**: Heyne to GF, 16 February 1792. **307. 'I can remain silent'**: GF to Heyne, 21 February 1792. **307. Louis XVI had tried to flee**: *Privilegierte Mainzer Zeitung*, 27 and 29 June 1791. **308. 'The flight of the king'**: GF to Heyne, 9 July 1791. **308. 'This moment in which'**: Ibid, 25 July 1791; for GF being impressed by the French, 12 July 1791. **308. 'the situation in which'**: Declaration of Pillnitz, 27 August 1791, Clarke 2019, p.390 **308. a third daughter, Louise**: born 4 June 1791, GF to Heyne, 4 June 1791; for Louise being Huber's child, GF to L.F. Huber, 16 July 1793 and CS to M. Forkel (then Liebeskind), 19 August 1804, Schlegel-Schelling 1913, p.392. **308. 'You do not know'**: GF to Heyne, 19 November 1791; see also GF to Jacobi, 17 November 1791. **308. 'losing the elder one'**: GF to Heyne, 26 November 1791. **308. 'I'm not sure how'**: Ibid. **309. He suffered from fevers**: GF to Voß, 11 October 1791; GF to Heyne, 13 October and 5 November 1791. **309. 'a certain quiet sorrow'**: GF to Voß, 11 October 1791. **309. 'I have perhaps never'**: GF to Jacobi, 6 November 1791. **309. 'My strength is depleted'**: Ibid. **309. 'several**

painful experiences': GF to Heyne, 21 April 1792. **309. 'a wild untamed rascal'**: Ibid, 23 November 1790. **309. 'she's brunette like the mother'**: GF to Herder, 10 December 1791. **309. everybody was ill**: GF to Voß, 27 March 1792. **309. 'Today, I am as feeble'**: Ibid; for Röschen having pneumonia, GF to Heyne, 31 March 1792. **310. They named him Georg**: He was born on 21 April 1792, GF to Heyne, 24 April 1792. **310. 'Things that cannot'**: Ibid, 28 April 1792. **310. 'French lava would not'**: Jacobi to A. von Gallitzin, 30 April 1792, Götz 1995, p. 205. **310. in Mainz the old fortifications**: GF to Heyne, 5 May 1792. **310. 'Sometimes I think'**: Ibid, 1 May 1792. **310. 'empty as a hollowed-out pumpkin'**: GF to Lichtenberg, 10 May 1792. **311. 'Stand your ground'**: Heyne to GF, 30 May 1792. **311. Meta ... Mainz ... Caroline**: Meta was in Mainz in summer 1789, May–October 1791 and October 1792–March 1793; Siegel 2000, pp. 90, 96, 105, 108; Caroline moved to Mainz in February 1792, CS to L. Gotter, 20 April 1792, Schlegel-Schelling 1913, vol. 1, p. 249. **311. Caroline Michaelis-Böhmer**: Wulf 2022, pp. 6, 73–4. **311. 'I am definitely happier'**: CS to L. Gotter, 31 October 1791, Schlegel-Schelling 1913, vol. 1, p. 233. **311. 'she's a clever woman'**: GF to Lichtenberg, 8 December 1792. **311. 'most wonderful man'**: CS to Meyer, 17 December 1792, Schlegel-Schelling 1913, vol. 1, p. 279. **311. 'pines for love'**: Ibid. **311. Meta Wedekind-Forkel**: Siegel 2009, pp. 85–104; Meta's husband was Johann Nikolaus Forkel; for Forkel as possible lover of Therese's mother, Geiger 1901, p. 5; Siegel believes that Forkel had only been a good friend, Siegel 2000, pp. 41–2. **312. shared lodgings with Caroline**: CS to Meyer, 27 October 1792, Schlegel-Schelling 1913, vol. 1, p. 276. **312. 'She is certainly much'**: GF to Heyne, 6 October 1789. **312. 'you are a more forgiving'**: GF to M. Forkel, 12 December 1791. **312. Meta ... literary collaborator**: Siegel 2000, p. 91ff; Meta translated seven books for GF, p. 102; see also GF to Voß, 28 May 1791; for translation of *Rights of Man*, GF to Voß, 4 June 1791, and M. Forkel to Voß, 28 June 1791; Paine's *Die Rechte des Menschen* was published by Voß in 1792. **313. 'human rights'**: GF, 'Vorläufige Schilderung des Nordens von Amerika' (1791), AA 5, p. 569. **313. Caroline and Meta ... Forster house**: CS to Meyer, 29 July 1792, Schlegel-Schelling 1913, vol. 1, pp. 256–7; J.E. Bollmann to his father, 26 October 1791, Kapp 1880, p. 26. **313. speculating ... the war**: GF to Heyne, 15 and 26 May 1792. **313. rumours of a ceasefire**: Heyne to GF, 30 May 1792; for Prussians in Göttingen, 18 and 29 June 1792. **313. little hope for ... the French king**: GF to Heyne, 26 May 1792. **313. 'All government, to be good'**: Antoine Barnave in July 1792, Clarke 2019, p. 407. **313. 'Democratical licentiousness'**: JRF to GF, 29 April 1792. **313. 'are now governed'**: Ibid, 31 July 1792. **313. 'most despicable people'**: Heyne to GF, 30 May 1792. **314. 'I gladly confess'**: GF to Heyne, 5 June 1792. **314. last dance of the old order**: the festivities were from 19–22 July 1792; GF, 'Darstellung der Revolution in Mainz' (1793), AA 10. 1, pp. 511–17; Dumont et al. 1998, pp. 308–9. **315. 'as if all the democrats'**: Letter (from unknown), 8 August 1792, Dumont et al. 1998, p. 308. **315. 'barbaric finery'**: GF, 'Darstellung der Revolution in Mainz' (1793), AA 10. 1, pp. 511–12. **315. the baby was dead**: TF to E. von Herder, 24 July 1806 and 24 July 1810; see also GF to Jacobi, 26 July 1792. **315. 'until I am carried'**: TF to E. von Herder, 24 July 1810. **316. 25 July 1793**: This declaration was the Brunswick Manifesto, Clarke 2019, pp. 419–20. **316. Mainz also dispatched 2,000**: AA 17, p. 629, and Dumont 2012, p. 23. **316. Goethe ... to join the troops**: Boyle 2000, pp. 114–16. **316. 'Goethe with the army!'**: Heyne quoted in Boyle 2000, p. 114. **316. Goethe ... with the Forsters**: Goethe, 23 August 1792, *Campagne in Frankreich*, Goethe 1887–1919, part I, vol. 30, pp. 4–5; L.F. Huber to G. Körner, 24 August 1792, Huber 1806, vol. 1, p. 441; for Goethe and revolution, Goethe 1982–96, vol. 3, p. 323; see also Goethe 1994, pp. 26–9; GF to J.P. Eckermann, 4 January 1824. **316. 'I finally got to meet'**: L.F. Huber to G. Körner, 24 August 1792, Huber 1806, vol. 1, p. 441. **317. 'Let the blood'**: Marat quoted in Hibbert 1982, p. 169; for September Massacres in Paris, Hibbert 1982, pp. 170–6, and *Privilegierte Mainzer Zeitung*, 12 September 1792. **317. 'the strangling and'**: *Privilegierte Mainzer Zeitung*, 14 September 1792. **318. 'not yet ready for'**: Wieland, *Teutsche Merkur*, 6 June 1791, Uhlig 2004, p. 285. **318. George disapproved of the violence**: GF, 'Darstellung der Revolution in Mainz' (1793), AA 10. 1, p. 531. **318. 'The lava of revolution'**: GF to TF, 24 October 1793. **318. 'a state shaken'**: GF, 'Darstellung der Revolution in Mainz' (1793), AA 10. 1, p. 531.

CHAPTER 21

319. carriages ... tried to leave the city: GF, 'Darstellung der Revolution in Mainz' (1793), AA 10. 1, pp. 535–6; CS to Meyer, 6 October 1792, Schlegel-Schelling 1913, vol. 1, p. 269; GF to Heyne, 5 October 1792; GF to C.F. Voß, 5 October 1792. **319. French had taken Speyer**: GF to Heyne, 2 October 1792; for French army in Oppenheim, GF to Voß, 5 October 1792 – but this turned out to be false, GF to L.F. Huber, 6 October 1792; for confusing reports, GF to Soemmerring, 6 October 1792; L.F. Huber to GF, 7 October 1792; Heyne to GF, 12 October 1792. **319. strengthening ramparts and army**: GF to Heyne, 2 October 1792; for the Electorate's army, AA 17, p. 629, and Dumont 2012, p. 23; for one-third of inhabitants fleeing, Dumont et al. 1998, p. 322. **320. 'We're prepared'**: GF to Heyne, 2 October 1792; see also 5 October 1792. **320. 'last convulsion of dying'**: GF, 'Darstellung der Revolution in Mainz' (1793), AA 10. 1, p. 536. **320. 'No pen and no tongue'**: Goethe to K.E. Goethe, 16 October 1792, Goethe 1887–1919, part IV, vol. 10, p. 35. **320. one other house**: GF to Heyne, 9 October 1792. **320. 'I will not move'**: GF to Soemmerring, 6 October 1792; Soemmerring was travelling to Vienna and after his return he remained in Frankfurt, except for a short visit to Mainz on 26 November and 8–12 December 1792; AA 17, p. 633. **320. George climbed a church tower**: GF to Heyne, 20 October 1792; see also GF, 'Darstellung der Revolution in Mainz' (1793), AA 10. 1, p. 547. **321. Mainz had only 3,000 men**: Around 1,100 soldiers from the Electorate's army remained in Mainz, supported by some 800 men from the allied armies and 1,000 Austrian troops, AA 17, p. 629; GF, 'Darstellung der Revolution in Mainz' (1793), AA 10. 1, p. 533, and Dumont 2012, p. 23. **321. 'We're quite calm'**: GF to Heyne, 20 October 1792.' **321. water to the attic**: GF, 'Darstellung der Revolution in Mainz' (1793), AA 10. 1, p. 549. **321. 'Vive la république!'**: GF Letters 1829, p. 88. **321. and tried to work**: GF to Heyne, 20 October 1792. **321. the city surrendered**: Ibid, 21 October 1792 and GF to Voß, 21 October 1792; Custine moved into castle, CS to Meyer, 27 October 1792, Schlegel-Schelling 1913, vol. 1, p. 274. **321. 'Général Moustache'**: Harpprecht 1990, p. 512. **321. He gave a speech**: GF to L.F. Huber, 24 October 1792; see also GF, 'Darstellung der Revolution in Mainz' (1793), AA 10. 1, p. 556. **321. 'like brothers'**: GF to Heyne, 22 October 1792. **321. 'Vivre libre ou mourir'**: CS to Meyer, 27 October 1792, Schlegel-Schelling 1913, vol. 1, p. 274; for cockades, see also 6 October 1792, p. 269, and GF to Soemmerring, 6 October 1792. **321. 'Society of the Friends'**: This was the Gesellschaft der Freunde der Freiheit und Gleichheit, founded on 23 October 1792, GF to L.F. Huber, 24 October 1792, and GF to Heyne, 25 October 1792; see also GF, 'Darstellung der Revolution in Mainz' (1793), AA 10. 1, p. 552. **321. *Mainzer National-Zeitung***: From 1 November 1792 to 17 April 1793 the *Privilegierte Mainzer Zeitung* was the *Mainzer National-Zeitung*, AA 17, p. 639. **321. 'What I think'**: GF to Heyne, 1 May 1792. **322. '*Urkeim*'**: Schlegel, 'Georg Forster. Fragment einer Charakteristik der deutschen Klassiker' (1797), Schlegel 1958–2006, vol. 2, p. 82. **322. Louis XVI had carted . . . sand**: GF, *Erinnerungen aus dem Jahr 1790* (1792), AA 8, p. 287. **322. 'Since the beginning'**: GF to Voß, 21 November 1792. **322. 'feel human and'**: GF Speech 1 January 1793, AA 10. 1, p. 60. **322. 'For heaven's sake'**: Heyne to GF, 31 October 1792. **322. impossible to remain neutral**: GF to Heyne, 10 November 1792; for GF ready to be a French citizen, GF to Voß, 10 November 1792. **322. 'attaching Mr. Forster'**: Custine, 4 November 1792, quoted in Uhlig 2004, p. 384. **322. Heyne urged moderation**: Heyne to GF, 10 and 14 November 1792; TF to Heyne, 20 November 1792. **322. 'We live in strange times'**: GF to Voß, 10 November 1792. **322. A routine soon developed**: Scheel 1975–1989, vol. 1, pp. 5–6. **323. 'what is true'**: GF Speech 15 November 1792, AA 10. 1, p. 14. **323. 'ruin and poverty'**: Ibid, p. 27. **323. 'the scum of the'**: Ibid, p. 13. **323. 'into proud, outspoken'**: Ibid. **323. 'Be free, fellow'**: Ibid, p. 25. **324. 'we kindle the sacred'**: Ibid, p. 15. **324. GF as vice president**: and his responsibilities, GF to Heyne, 20 November 1792; GF to Voß, 21 November 1792; see also Uhlig 2004, p. 307. **324. 'nothing prospers for me'**: GF to Jacobi, 6 November 1791. **324. 'There is too much'**: Ibid, 2 January 1789. **324. 'It is downright'**: GF to Voß, 21 November 1792. **324. 'living organic whole'**: GF, 'Cook, der Entdecker' (1787), AA 5, p. 287; for parts rotting, p. 289. **324. 'a natural phenomenon'**: GF, 'Parisische Umrisse' (1793–94), AA 10. 1, p. 595. **324. 'All creation is chaotic'**: GF, 'Über lokale und allgemeine Bildung' (1791), AA 7, p. 48; for French Revolution like storm, GF to C.W. von Dohm, ca. 13–18 July 1790. **325. Was it . . . necessary to publish the speeches**: Heyne to TF, 1 December

1792. **325. 'My opinions are my'**: GF to JRF, 26 November 1792. **325. 'Do not fear'**: GF to Voß, 10 November 1792. **325. 'in this respect'**: Ibid, 21 November 1792. **325. '*live and die*'**: Ibid. **325. anarchy not democracy**: Soemmerring to M. von Birkenstock, 22 November 1792, Soemmerring 1996–2001, vol. 20, p. 62. **325. 'My friends are all'**: Ibid. **325. *Memories from the Year:*** *Erinnerungen aus dem Jahr 1790*. The manuscript was ready at end of September 1792 and published in October. **326. 'fashionable democratic drivel'**: *Neuesten Critischen Nachrichten*, 20 December 1792, AA 8, p. 465. **326. 'calm observer to wild'**: ALZ, 22 February 1794, AA 8, p. 466. **326. 'would find it hard'**: Ibid. **326. 'Freedom has always'**: GF to J. von Müller, 16 November 1792. **326. 'I feel that I cannot'**: GF to L.F. Huber, 4 December 1792; see also 5 December 1792. **326. Therese ... to Strasbourg**: Ibid, 15 December 1792. **326. 'bon jour, citoyens!'**: GF Letters 1829, p. 106. **326. Therese ... to Neuchâtel**: GF to TF, 31 December 1792; see also GF Letters 1829, pp. 110–11. **327. 'Many suspect separation plans'**: CS to Meyer, 17 December 1792, Schlegel-Schelling 1913, vol. 1, p. 279. **327. Caroline convinced Huber**: Ibid, 15 June 1793, Schlegel-Schelling 1913, vol. 1, p. 295; see also TF to E. von Herder, 15 August 1806. **327. 'what I always gladly'**: TH to Heyne, 22 March 1793; for GF as brother not as husband, TF to CS, 25 February 1794, Schlegel-Schelling 1913, vol. 1, pp. 324–35. **327. separation would make him happy**: D. Stock to C. Schiller, 18 March 1793, Jonas 1882, p. 148. **327. 'I may say'**: L.F. Huber to Heyne, 12 June 1793, Geiger 1903, p. 682. **327. 'A thousand virtuous'**: Heyne to TF, 11 April 1793, Geiger 1903, p. 680; for Heyne on role of wives, Heyne to L.F. Huber, 3 September 1793, Leitzmann 1908, p. 13. **327. 'nature did not intend'**: TF to Heyne, 22 March 1793. **327. 'what was his right'**: Ibid; see also TF to R. Hottinger, 16 November 1793; TF to CS, 25 February 1794; TF to K.A. Böttiger, 6 April 1829. **328. 'God, how I have'**: Heyne to TF, 11 April 1793, Geiger 1903, p. 681. **328. Caroline and Meta ... scandals**: for Meta, Siegel 2000, p. 108; for CS, CS to Meyer, 30 July 1793, Schlegel-Schelling 1913, vol. 1, pp. 302–3; TF to Therese Forster (daughter), 17–25 July, 16 August 1803 and 3 September 1803. **328. 'Tree of Liberty'**: and festivities, Dumont 2012, p. 84; GF, *Neue Mainzer Zeitung*, 15 January 1793, AA 10. 1, pp. 218–19; Damm 2005, p. 33. **328. 'Long live freedom!'**: GF, *Neue Mainzer Zeitung*, 15 January 1793, AA 10. 1, p. 219; for *Ça ira* and *Carmagnole*, Harpprecht, p. 519. **329. 'for my very life'**: CS to L. Gotter, 20 April 1792, Schlegel-Schelling 1913, vol. 1, p. 250. **329. breaking the iron chains**: GF Speech 21 March 1793, AA 10. 1, pp. 462–3; see also GF Speech 15 November 1792, AA 10. 1, p. 14. **329. 'burning desire to see'**: GF to J.F. Mieg, 7 January 1793. **329. 'into a blind, lifeless'**: GF Speech 21 March 1793, AA 10. 1, p. 463. **329. 'Vengeance! Vengeance'**: Ibid. **329. 'today people have finally'**: *Mainzer National-Zeitung*, 28 January 1793. **329. 'Peoples of Europe!'**: Ibid. **329. 'We hurl at their feet'**: Danton, quoted in Hibbert 1982, p. 193. **330. 'it even becomes a duty'**: GF to TF, 29 December 1792. **330. 'code of law'**: Ibid, 28

January 1793. **330. 'Weakling Franz'**: GF Speech 21 March 1793, AA 10. 1, p. 464. **330. 'torchbearer of discord'**: Ibid. **330. 'I'm predicting that'**: Schiller to G. Körner, 21 December 1792, Schiller 1943–2003, vol. 26, p. 171. **331. 'incomprehensible to me'**: WH to C.G. von Brinkman, 7 December 1792; see also WH to Schiller, 7 December 1792, Humboldt 2014–17, vol. 2, pp. 110 and 112. **331. see him on the gallows**: JRF to Wieland, before 10 January 1794, Wieland 1992–94, vol. 12, p. 125; see also Heyne to Soemmerring, 3 February 1794, AA 17, p. 796; TF to Heyne, 16–22 January 1794; for Jacobi, F.L. zu Stolberg-Stolberg to Jacobi, 13 January 1793, Jacobi 1825–1827, vol. 2, p. 120. **331. 'He can't be saved'**: Soemmerring to Heyne, 29 January 1793, see also 19 March and 2 July 1793, Soemmerring 1996–2001, vol. 20, pp. 81, 88, 116; for Soemmerring moving to Frankfurt, AA 17, p. 633, and Soemmerring to Mainz administration, 10 December 1792, Soemmerring 1996–2001, vol. 20, p. 67. **331. 'I would have to station'**: GF to Soemmerring, 6 January 1793. **331. 'if only you had been'**: Ibid. **331. 'what I have done'**: GF to Voß, 29 January 1793; for GF willing to sacrifice his life, GF to Soemmerring, 6 January 1793; for own conscience to be judge of his behaviour, GF to J.F. Mieg, 7 January 1793. **331. 'our children will thank'**: GF to Heyne, 13 July 1790. **332. 'Here is some hair'**: GF to TF, 25 December 1792. **332. 'businessman en miniature'**: GF to Voß, 10 November 1792; for GF's daily life, GF to TF, 31 December 1792 and 21 March 1793. **332. 'finally freedom of the press'**: GF, *Neue Mainzer Zeitung*, 1 January 1793, AA 10. 1, p. 173; see also GF to TF 31 December 1792. **332. 'most noble struggle'**: GF, *Neue Mainzer Zeitung*, 1 January 1793, AA 10. 1, p. 173. **332. first elections in Mainz**: Uhlig 2004, p. 321; Dumont et al. 1998, p. 332ff. **332. swear an oath to freedom**: Scheel 1975–1989, vol. 2, p. 231; GF, *Neue Mainzer Zeitung*, 19 February 1793, AA 10. 1, p. 331; the oath was 'Loyalty to the people, to the principles of liberty and equality.' **333. 'in the end, we'**: GF to TF, 8 December 1792; for GF travelling across the region, GF to TF, 27 February 1793; see also AA 17, p. 702. **333. 'most solemn act'**: GF, *Neue Mainzer Zeitung*, 26 February 1793, AA 10. 1, p. 349. **333. 'Such stupid, heartless'**: GF to TF, 14 March 1793; for election results, Dumont et al. 1998, p. 334; only 372 eligible men voted out of 4,626. **333. compared to an amputation**: GF, *Neue Mainzer Zeitung*, 8 March 1793, AA 10. 1, pp. 375–6. **333. Germany's first independent republic**: Protocol, National Convention Mainz, 18 March 1793, Scheel 1975–1989, vol. 2, pp. 433–4. **333. 'The final hour'**: GF Speech 21 March 1793, AA 10. 1, p. 463. **333. Elected as vice president**: GF to TF, 21 March 1793. **333. 'a mighty leader'**: M. Forkel to Voß, quoted in Happrecht, p. 478; for soul of Convention, GF to TF, 21 March 1793. **333. 'Oh rescue, rescue'**: GF Speech 21 March 1793, AA 10. 1, p. 465–66. **333. Andreas Joseph Hofmann**: Schweigard 2005, pp. 147–51. **334. 'I'll probably be back'**: GF to TF, 25 March 1793; for reason to travel to Paris, Protocol, National Convention, 17 March 1793, Scheel 1975–1989, vol. 2, p. 429.

CHAPTER 22

335. from Mainz to Paris: GF to TF, 31 March 1793. **336. to give his speech**: GF, 'Adresse an den Pariser Nationalkonvent,' signed 25 March 1793, and GF, Speech National Convention Paris, 30 March 1793, AA 10. 1, pp. 467–70, 477; GF to TF, 31 March 1793. **336. Caroline . . . Meta . . . arrested**: GF to TF, 16 May 1793; see also Wulf 2022, pp. 5–9. **336. Rue des Moulins**: P. Haupt to L.F. Huber, 10 January 1794; for six shirts and other clothes, GF to TF, 5 April 1793. **336. 'I'm starting all over'**: GF to TF, 27 April 1793. **336. 'From a distance'**: Ibid, 8 April 1793; see also 16 April 1793. **337. 'Citizens, we have reason'**: P. V. Vergniaud in March 1793, Mignet 1902, p. 350. **337. 'We live in uncertain'**: GF to TF, 5 April 1793. **337. 'whoever rises to the top'**: Ibid, 27 April 1793. **337. General Dumouriez**: Schama 1989, p. 689; GF to TF, 5 April 1793. **338. 'We will give death'**: Marat, 13 March 1793, Scurr 2006, p. 238. **338. 'I cannot do it'**: GF to TF, 16 April 1793. **338. 'how beautiful nature is'**: Ibid, 2 June 1793; for nature after his arrival, 8 April 1793. **338. he went to Versailles**: Ibid, 19 May 1793. **338. translated . . . French constitution**: Ibid, 8 July 1793; for stipend, GF to TF, 8 April 1793; for GF accepting constitution, GF to president of National Convention, 17 July 1793, AA 10. 1, pp. 479–80. **338. 'because until now'**: GF to TF, 27 April 1793. **339. 'calm sense of liberty'**: Ibid, 13 April 1793. **339. Thomas Christie**: Ibid, 13 April, 16–19 May and 23 June 1793; see also, Todd 2000, pp. 198 and 210. **339. Helen Maria Williams**: GF to TF, 13 April 1793; see also, Todd 2000, p. 213. **339. Mary Wollstonecraft**: GF to TF, 5 and 13 April 1793. **339. 'I shall first consider'**: Wollstonecraft 1793, p. 3. **339. George had bought the book**: *A Vindication of the Rights of Woman* was part of GF's book collection auctioned in Mainz in 1797, Auction catalogue 1797, p. 97, and Bödecker 1992, p. 108 **339. Théroigne de Méricourt**: GF to TF, 23 July 1793; Hamel 1911, pp. 337–42; Moore 2007, p. 47ff. **339. 'martyr of freedom'**: GF to TF, 23 July 1793. **339. 'Imagine a 25- or'**: Ibid. **340. 'God Paine'**: M. Forkel to Voß, 28 June 1791, AA 16, p. 538. **340. 'I found not much remarkable'**: GF to TF, 17 May 1793. **340. 'I don't want to return'**: TF to GF, ca. 20 June 1793. **340. Huber arrived in Neuchâtel**: Huber 1806, vol. 1, p. 105; TF to F. and J.G. Reinhold, 19 January 1806. **340. 'What has happened'**: GF to L.F. Huber, 16 July 1793. **340. 'brought a man'**: Ibid. **340. 'so you also inherit'**: Ibid. **340. 'Today, 21 years'**: GF to TF, 13 July 1793; see also, 11 May and 4 June 1793. **340. 'Since I can't be'**: Ibid, 23 June 1793. **340. 'I would so love'**: GF to Therese Forster (his daughter), 16 June 1793. **341. 'She was radiant'**: GF to TF, 19 July 1793; for Corday's execution, see also executioner Charles-Henri Sanson, 17 July 1793, Sanson 1879, vol. 2, pp. 37–41, and Schama 1989, p. 741. **341. Adam Lux**: GF to TF, 23 and 24 July, 9 and 27 November 1793; Lux's pamphlet 'Charlotte Corday' was published on 19 July 1793; his trial and execution was on 4 November, AA 17, p. 748; see also Uhlig 2004, p. 332, and Goldstein 2015, pp. 217–18. **341. 'His intention is noble'**: GF to TF, 23 July 1793, p. 402.' **341. 'Are my letters'**: Ibid. **341. 'I don't deserve'**: Ibid. **341. 'the good man has completely'**: and for Lux's arrest, GF to TF, 24 July

1793. **342. 'This court of blood'**: GF to TF, 23 June 1793. **342. 'he *jumped* onto'**: GF to TF and L.F. Huber, 27 November 1793. **342. '*importance* of the revolution'**: GF to TF, 10 June 1793; see also 6 September 1793. **342. 'tree of liberty must'**: T. Jefferson to W.S. Smith, 13 November 1787, Boyd 1950–2009, vol. 12, p. 356. **342. 'swim in blood'**: GF to TF, 27 April 1793. **342. The fire . . . ravaged the city**: Soemmerring to Heyne, 29 June 1793, Soemmerring 1996–2001, vol. 20, pp. 113–14. **342. Prussians . . . confiscated . . . papers**: Heyne to F.J.M. v. Albini, 9 August and 12 December 1793; Heyne to W.F. Hufnagel, 18 October 1793, JRF to Voß, 25 January 1794, JRF to Elector of Mainz, 2 February 1794, AA 17, pp. 754–60. **342. George to the northern front**: GF to TF, 24 July 1793; he arrived in Cambrai on 1 August 1793, GF to TF, 1 August 1793; for conditions in town, 7 August 1793; for Arras, 8 August 1793; for English refusing to negotiate, 16 August and 18 September 1793. **343. George picked up his pen**: Ibid, 21 August 1793; for GF's account of the Mainz revolution, GF, 'Darstellung der Revolution in Mainz,' AA 10. 1, pp. 511–64; see also GF to TF, 26 August, 18 and 30 September 1793. **343. 'I write what I no'**: GF to TF, 8 October 1793. **343. 'that coincidence, which forced'**: GF, 'Darstellung der Revolution in Mainz,' GF AA 10. 1, pp. 562–3. **343. 'Instead of promising'**: GF, 'Über die Beziehung der Staatskunst auf das Glück der Menschheit' (1793), AA 10. 1, p. 591; for despotism reducing people to automatons, pp. 576 and 568. **343. Imagining . . . the girls**: GF to TF, 10 September 1793. **343. 'Happy children make'**: Ibid, 21 August 1793. **343. 'Children cannot and'**: Ibid, 1 September 1793. **343. 'No opportunity that invites'**: Ibid, 26 August 1793. **344. hadn't heard anything from the English**: Ibid, 30 September 1793. **344. 'mad unruly caprice'**: Ibid, 25 September 1793; for no hope for peace, 12 September 1793. **344. 'either by their conduct'**: 'Law of Suspects,' quoted in Scurr 2006, p. 258. **345. British people arrested**: H. M. Williams e.g. was arrested on 12 October 1793 and Paine on 28 December 1793; 250 British nationals were arrested in the night of 9/10 October 1793, Gordon 2005, p. 214. **345. twenty-one Girondins guillotined**: Sanson 1876, p. 70. **345. guillotined during Reign of Terror**: The overall figure for those who died during the Reign of Terror is around 50,000, including those who died in prison or were executed by different methods, Croker 1857, pp. 384–5; Doyle 2002, p. 253. **345. GF in Pontarlier**: GF to TF, 1 November 1793; for divorce plans, 3 October 1793, GF to Ministry of Foreign Affairs, 3 October 1793, and TF to Heyne, 19 October 1793; the French had passed a law in September 1792 that allowed divorce and TF knew the mayor of Pontarlier, hoping that the matter would be solved easily. **346. country inn in Travers**: AA 17, p. 776; TF to Heyne, 21 November 1793; Zincke 1915, vol. 2, pp. 144–5; Uhlig 2004, p. 338. **346. 'Oh my children!'**: GF to TF, 6 November 1793. **346. *Parisian Sketches***: GF wrote *Parisian Sketches* between October and December 1793 – it was published in Huber's *Friedens-Präliminarien* in 1793/4; GF sent the first part of the manuscript to TF from Pontarlier, GF to TF, 16 November 1793; see also GF to TF and L.F. Huber, 19 December 1793. **346. 'our true martyrdom'**: GF, 'Parisische

Umrisse' (1793–94), AA 10. 1, p. 600. **346. 'all idols lie in'**: Ibid, p. 615; for greatest revolution, p. 601; for violence being the reason, not fruit of revolution, p. 607. **347. 'Welcome, Revolution, with'**: GF to TF, 9–10 November 1793. **347. 'Without the rivers'**: GF, 'Parisische Umrisse' (1793–94), AA 10. 1, p. 621; for not denying millions reason, p. 604. **347. 'raw power of'**: Ibid, p. 596, see also p. 600. **347. 'thus the individual little'**: Ibid, p. 617. **347. 'The ground still trembles'**: GF to TF and L.F. Huber, 2 December 1793. **347. 'do you hear anything'**: Goethe to Soemmerring, 5 December 1793, Goethe 1887–1919, part IV, vol. 10, p. 130; for Heyne's concerns, Heyne to TF, 22 December 1793, Leitzmann 1908, p. 15. **347. 'In any case, let'**: GF to TF and L.F. Huber, 11 December 1793. **347. 'I lie here like a fly'**: Ibid, 14 December 1793. **347. failed to find a carriage**: Ibid, 20 December 1793. **348. 'I'm completely exhausted'**: Ibid, 27 December 1793. **348. 'For what?'**: Ibid, 19 December 1793. **348. 'sickness of the mind'**: Ibid, 27 December 1793; for TF being annoyed, 22 and 28 December 1793. **348. he took opium**: GF to TF and L.F. Huber, 14 December 1793. **348. the executioner's tally**: Schama 1989, p. 782. **348. 'The Revolution is a hurricane'**: GF to TF and L.F. Huber, 28 December 1793. **348. 'I have no strength'**: Ibid, 4 January 1794. **348. on 10 January 1794 ... he died**: P. Haupt to L.F. Huber, 10 January 1794, AA 17, p. 792. **348. 'domestic sorrows'**: *Moniteur*, 18 January 1794, AA 17, p. 801. **348. 'some domestic uneasiness'**: Aikin 1803, vol. 4, p. 171. **348. 'I'd rather keep'**: Lichtenberg to J.W. von Archenholz, 16 April 1794, Lichtenberg 1983–2004, vol. 4, pp. 292. **348. 'Oh, how gladly'**: Lichtenberg to Soemmerring, 5 June 1795, Lichtenberg 1983–2004, vol. 4, p. 492. **349. 'raging fool'**: Schiller and Goethe's 'Xenien', *Musenalmanach* für das Jahr 1797, Xenien, Nr. 347. **349. 'Ah, how they shouted'**: Ibid, Nr. 337. **349. 'so, poor Forster'**: Goethe to Soemmerring, 17 February 1794, Goethe 1887–1919, part IV, vol. 10, p. 142. **349. obituary in *ALZ***: *Intelligenzblatt der ALZ*, 19 March and 6 April 1794; see also Uhlig 2004, p. 344; Unterberger 2002, p. 176. **349. 'Oh, he was so'**: TF to Heyne, 16–22 January 1794. **349. appalled by his daughter's**: Heyne to Soemmerring, 3 February 1794, AA 17, p. 796. **349. 'Since the news'**: Heyne to TF, 31 January 1794. **350. 'with all his faults'**: Ibid, 16 March 1794. **350. 'one of our best'**: Ibid. **350. 'is it true that our dear'**: S. von La Roche to Soemmerring, 29 January 1794, Soemmerring 1996–2001, vol. 20, p. 159. **350. 'and I shed'**: Ibid. **350. 'Oh, but our Forster'**: AH to Soemmerring, 6 February 1794, Soemmerring 1996–2001, vol. 20, p. 167.

EPILOGUE

351. 'He never possessed': TF to CS, 25 February 1794. **351. 'he was to us what God'**: Ibid. **351. 'I would have never'**: Ibid. **351. Reinhold wrote to ... Voß**: JRF to Voß, 25 January 1794, AA 17, p. 758. **351. 'the wicked snake'**: JRF to Elector of Mainz, 2 February 1794, AA 17, p. 759. **351. Soemmerring saved manuscripts**: Soemmerring to Heyne, 17 August 1793 and 21 February 1796; W. Heinse to

Soemmerring, 21 February 1796; Soemmerring to JRF, 21 February 1796, Soemmerring 1996–2001, vol. 20, pp. 127, 273, 274, 356; Heyne to L.F. Huber, 3 July 1797, Huber 1999–2013, vol. 1, p. 658. **351. 'I fear we have'**: TF to Therese Forster (daughter), 17–25 July 1803. **352. 'Therese has done me'**: CS to Meyer, 7 June 1794, Schlegel-Schelling 1913, vol. 1, p. 341. **352. Therese married Huber**: TF to Heyne, 16 April 1794. **352. Therese published Huber's correspondence**: *L.F. Huber's Sämtliche Werke seit dem Jahre 1802, nebst seiner Biographie*, ed. Therese Huber, 1806; for TF altering and editing letters, Zincke 1915, vol. 1, p. 132. **352. 'what does Therese'**: CS to M. Forkel (then Liebeskind), March 1805, Schlegel-Schelling 1913, vol. 2, p. 405. **352. 'bizarre work of art'**: CS to L. Wiedemann, 30 November 1806, Schlegel-Schelling 1913, vol. 2, p. 482. **352. 'I believe ... that one'**: Goethe to C.L. von Knebel, 3 January 1807, Goethe 1887–1919, part IV, vol. 19, pp. 258–9; for Goethe reading Huber's letters and biography, Goethe Diary, 15 and 20 December 1806, Goethe 1887–1919, part III, vol. 3, pp. 182–3. **352. *Elective Affinities***: Goethe jotted down the first ideas and notes for the novel in July 1807, began to write the first draft in April 1808, and published it in 1809, Boyle 2015, p. 96; for Goethe's inspiration for *Elective Affinities*, Rasmussen 1985, p. 88; François-Poncet 1910, pp. 24–5; see also WH to C. von Humboldt, 6 March 1810, Humboldt and Humboldt 1910–1916, vol. 3, p. 356; Goethe to C.L. von Knebel, 3 January 1807, Goethe 1887–1919, part IV, vol. 19, pp. 258–9. **352. 'Do you see in everything'**: TF to C. Forster (then von Greyerz), 25 November 1819; see also TF to F. von Breuning, 8 December 1819; TF to C. Pilcher, 26 March 1820. **352. 'I always only wanted'**: TF to F. von Breuning, 8 December 1819. **352. Therese ... began to write novels**: TF to V.A. Huber, 9 January 1817; see also Bergmann 2008, p. 274. **352. the editor of *Morgenblatt***: Geiger 1901, p. 282ff. **353. 'a large laundry basket'**: TF to E. von Reinbeck, May 1824, Geiger 1901, p. 379; for GF's published correspondence by TF, see *Johann Georg Forster's Briefwechsel nebst einigen Nachrichten von seinem Leben*, ed. Therese Huber, 1829. **353. 'I prune everything'**: TF to P. Usteri, 26 February 1827; see also TF to E. von Reinbeck, May 1824, Geiger 1901, pp. 379 and 386; for a detailed account of how radically TF changed, destroyed and edited letters, Zincke 1915, vol. 1. **353. 'It was Forster's greatest'**: Zinke, vol. 1, p. xii. **353. JRF published account**: JRF *Philosophischer Anzeiger*, 1795; for JRF wanting GF hanged, JRF to Wieland, before 10 January 1794, Wieland 1992–94, vol. 12, p. 125; see also Heyne to Soemmerring, 3 February 1794, AA 17, p. 796; TF to Heyne, 16–22 January 1794. **353. 'a propensity for self-love'**: GF to Jacobi, 2 November 1779. **353. 'trained him to'**: JRF to Wieland, 9 January 1798, Wieland 1992–94, vol. 14, p. 151. **353. 'How much have we'**: Herder 1796, p. 164. **354. GF and ... Coleridge's verses**: Bohm 1983; Smith 1956. **354. 'And now there came'**: Coleridge, *The Rime of the Ancient Mariner.* **354. Coleridge's maths teacher:** Smith 1956, p. 120. **355. 'they received a confused'**: GF Voyage 2000, p. 9. **355. 'Little-ists'**: Coleridge, quoted in Levere 1981, p. 61. **355. 'connective powers of'**: Coleridge, 'Science and System of Logic,' transcription of Coleridge's lectures of 1822,

Wiegand 2002, p. 106. **355. 'ingenious Georg Forster'**: Humboldt 1845–48, vol. 1, p. 317. **355. Humboldt inspired by GF**: AH to M.-A. Pictet, 24 January 1796, Humboldt 1973, p. 487; AH to F. Creuzer, 15 February 1846, BBAW AH Forschungsstelle Briefboxen; AH to H. König, 28 July 1758, Bruhns 1872, vol. 1, p. 104; see also AH's publications where he mentioned GF's influence: Humboldt 1849, vol. 2, p. 365; Humboldt 1845–47, vol. 1, p. 345, and vol. 2, pp. 5 and 72; Humboldt 1814–29, vol. 1, p. 4; Humboldt and Bonpland 1807, p. iii; AH Diary, 19 June 1799, Nachl. Alexander von Humboldt (Tagebücher) I, 15v, Stabi Berlin; AH Diary, 15 September 1802, Humboldt 2003, vol. 2, p. 162. **355. 'What I owe to'**: AH to JRF, 12 January 1797, Humboldt 1973, p. 564. **355. 'A world of memories'**: AH to F. Lampert, 12 December 1856, BBAW AH Forschungsstelle Briefboxen. **355. *Personal Narrative***: Humboldt 1814–29, vol. 1, p. 4. **355. inspiration for ... *Cosmos***: AH to W. Grimm, 15 September 1845, BBAW AH Forschungsstelle Briefboxen. **355. 'Through him has been'**: Humboldt 1845–48, vol. 2, p. 70. **356. 'Shackles, walls and'**: Schlegel, 'Georg Forster. Fragment einer Charakteristik der deutschen Klassiker' (1797), Schlegel 1958–2006, vol. 2, p. 81. **356. 'without feeling not'**: Ibid. **356. 'undoubtably Forster'**: Ibid, p. 97. **356. 'For me to feel'**: GF to Spener, 16 September 1782; for emphasis on feeling, GF Voyage 2000, p. 9, and GF to Heyne, 30 August 1790. **356. 'human shells'**: GF, 'Über lokale und allgemeine Bildung' (1791), AA 7, p. 52. **357. 'Don't forget that'**: GF, 'Vorlesungen über allgemeine Naturkenntnis' (1792), AA 6. 2. p. 1755; for the Young Romantics and world reduced to monotonous machine, see e.g. Novalis, *Lehrlinge zu Sais*, Novalis 1960–2006, vol. 1, p. 99, and Wulf 2022, pp. 12–13, 165–6. **357. 'The sciences must all'**: Novalis to A.W. Schlegel, 24 February 1798, Novalis 1960–2006, vol. 4, p. 252. **357. 'a licentious and'**: Samuel Johnson, *The Rambler*, quoted in Bate 1986, p. 10. **357. 'Reason, feeling and'**: GF, 'Über lokale und allgemeine Bildung' (1791), AA 7, p. 55. **357. Heinrich Heine**: Heine 1840, p. 319. **357. 'why not glorify'**: Engels, 'The State of Germany, Letter II,' *The Northern Star*, 8 November 1845. **357. 'the imperial ban'**: Kisch (1937) 1993, p. 139. **358. 'we should leave'**: Zincke 1915, vol. 1, p. xiv. **358. 'He forgot his fatherland'**: Menzel 1836, vol. 2, p. 185. **358. 'Georg Forster, Naturalist'**: Gottschall, 'Georg Forster, der Naturforscher und – Vaterlandsverräter,' *Die Gartenlaube*, 1904, pp. 870–4. **358. Walter Benjamin**: Benjamin 1936, p. 24; see also Benjamin 1972, vol. IV. 2, p. 945ff. **358. absence from literary canon**: Peitsch 2001; see also Scheuer 1997, pp. 1–18. **358. eighteen-volume edition**: This is *Georg Forsters Werke. Sämtliche Schriften, Tagebücher, Briefe*, published and edited by Akademie der Wissenschaften der DDR, Berlin: Akademie-Verlag, from 1958. The edition is incomplete (because the volumes with comments and notes for volumes 6 and 10 are missing), but the project has been stopped. **358. 'as a human, a citizen'**: GF to Voß, 8 November 1793. **359. 'Oh, if only one'**: GF Diary, 16 August 1784, AA, vol. 12, p. 116. **359. Humans are like harp strings**: GF, Über lokale und allgemeine Bildung, 1791, AA 7, p. 52. **359. 'Freedom and equality?'**: GF to TF, 16 April 1793.

Bibliography

In order to avoid confusion, I have spelled George Forster in the bibliography 'Georg' because most academic titles keep to the German spelling – but when his name was 'George' on the cover of his own books, I kept the English spelling.

Everything published by Therese Heyne-Forster-Huber can be found under 'Huber, Therese' as she only published after her marriage to Huber.

'A list of original pictures at the Royal Society House. Communicated by a Connoisseur,' *Gentleman's Magazine*, vol. 38, 1768

Abulafia, David, *The Boundless Sea: A Human History of the Oceans*, London: Allen Lane, 2019

Ackerknecht, Erwin H., 'George Forster, Alexander von Humboldt, and Ethnology,' *Isis*, vol. 42, no. 2, 1955

Adams, Ron, *In the Land of Strangers: A Century of European Contact with Tanna, 1774–1874*, Canberra and New York: The Australian National University, 1984

Aikin, John et al., *General Biography; or Lives, Critical and Historical, of the Most Eminent Persons of all Ages, Countries, Conditions, and Professions*, vol. 4, London: J. Johnson, 1803

Alt, Peter-André, *Schiller: Leben – Werk – Zeit: Eine Biographie*, Munich: C.H. Beck, 2004

Anderson, Atholl, 'Seafaring and Colonization in the Southern Ocean, 1000 CE–1850 CE', in *The Cambridge History of the Pacific Ocean*, ed. Ryan Tucker Jones and Matt K. Matsuda, vol. 1, Cambridge: Cambridge University Press, 2022

Andreasen, Øjvind and Helmut Mathy (eds), 'Frederik Münters Reise nach Mainz (1791),' *Mainzer Zeitschrift*, vol. 62, 1967

Anonymous, *An Historic Epistle from Omiah to the Queen of Otaheite; Being his Remarks on the English Nation*, London: T. Evans, 1775

Anonymous, 'Reise von Cassel und Göttingen durch Braunschweig und Lübeck nach Kiel, im Jahre 1782,' *Johann Bernoulli's Sammlung kurzer Reisebeschreibungen und anderer zur Erweiterung der Länder- und Menschenkenntniß dienender Nachrichten*, vol. 10, Berlin: Johann Bernoulli, 1783

Anonymous, 'Obituary Justina Elisabeth Forster,' *Hallisches Patriotisches Wochenblatt*, 15 December 1804

Apell, David, *Cassel und die umliegende Gegend. Eine Skizze für Reisende*, Kassel: J.H. Martin Aubel,1801

Appel, Sabine, *Caroline Schlegel-Schelling. Das Wagnis der Freiheit. Eine Biographie*, Munich: C.H. Beck, 2013

Archenholz, Johann Wilhelm von, *England und Italien*, Leipzig: Dykische Buchhandlung, 1785

Archenholz, Johann Wilhelm von, *A Picture of England, containing a description of the laws, customs and manners of England*, Dublin: P. Byrne, 1790

Auction catalogue, *Verzeichniß der hinterlassenen Bücher von Georg Forster welche den 4ten September 1797 zu Mainz auf der sogenannten Bursch versteigert werden sollen*, Mainz:no publisher, 1797

Bacon, Francis, *Novum Organum* (1620), ed. Joseph Devey, New York: P.F. Collier & Son, 1902

Baggesen, Jan, *Das Labyrinth oder Reise durch Deutschland und Schweiz 1789*, ed. Gisela Perlet, Munich: C.H. Beck, Munich, 1986

Bahrdt, Carl Friedrich, *Dr. Carl Friedrich Bahrdts Geschichte seines Lebens, seiner Meinungen und Schicksale*, Berlin: Friedrich Vieweg, 1791

Banks, Joseph, *The Scientific Correspondence of Sir Joseph Banks*, ed. Neil Chambers, London: Pickering & Chatto, 2007

Banks, Joseph, *The Indian and Pacific Correspondence of Sir Joseph Banks*, ed. Neil Chambers, London: Pickering & Chatto, 2008

Bartlett, Roger Paul, 'J.R. Forster's Stay in Russia 1765–1766: Diplomatic and Official Accounts', *Jahrbücher für die Geschichte Osteuropas*, vol. 23, 1975

Bate, Jonathan, *Shakespeare and the English Romantic Imagination*, Oxford: Clarendon Press, 1986

Bauer, Wilhelm A., *Angelo Soliman, der hochfürstliche Mohr. Ein exotisches Kapitel Alt-Wien*, ed. Monika Firla-Forkl, Berlin: Edition Ost, 1993

Beaglehole, J.C. (ed.), *The Journals of Captain James Cook on His Voyages of Discovery, vol. 2, The Voyage of the* Resolution *and* Adventure *1772–1775*, Cambridge: Cambridge University Press for the Hakluyt Society, 1961

Beaglehole, J.C. (ed.), *The* Endeavour *Journal of Joseph Banks, 1768–1771*, Sydney: Angus & Robertson, 1962

Beaglehole, J.C. (ed.), *The Journals of Captain James Cook on His Voyages of Discovery, vol. 3, The Voyage of the* Resolution *and* Discovery *1776–1780*, Cambridge: Cambridge University Press for the Hakluyt Society, 1967

Beaglehole, J.C. (ed.), *The Journals of Captain James Cook on His Voyages of Discovery, vol. 1, The Voyage of the* Endeavour *1768–1771*, Cambridge: Cambridge University Press for the Hakluyt Society, 1968

Bedford, Stuart, 'Austronesian Colonization of the Pacific Islands, 1200 BCE–1250 CE', in *The Cambridge History of the Pacific Ocean*, ed. Ryan Tucker Jones and Matt K. Matsuda, vol. 1, Cambridge: Cambridge University Press, 2022

Benjamin, Walter, *Deutsche Menschen. Eine Folge in Briefen*, Luzern: Vita Noval Verlag, 1936

Benjamin, Walter, *Gesammelte Werke*, ed. Tillman Rexroth, vol. IV, 2, Frankfurt: Suhrkamp, 1972

Beratz, Gottlieb, *Die deutsche Kolonien an der unteren Wolga in ihrer Entstehung und ersten Entwickelung*, Berlin: Verlag der wolgadeutschen Bauern, 1923

Berg, Eberhard, *Zwischen den Welten: über die Anthropologie der Aufklärung und ihr Verhältnis zu Entdeckungs-Reise und Welt-Erfahrung, mit besonderem Blick auf das Werk Georg Forsters*, Berlin: Dietrich Reimer Verlag, 1982

Bergmann, Ulrike, *Die Mesalliance. Georg Forster, Weltumsegler – Therese Forster, Schriftstellerin*, Frankfurt: Edition Büchergilde, 2008

Bertschinger, George M., *The Portraits of Johann Reinhold Forster and George Forster*, California: no publisher, 1988

Blanning, Tim, *Reform and Revolution in Mainz, 1743–1803*, Cambridge: Cambridge University Press, 1974

Blanning, Tim, *August the Strong: A Study in Artistic Greatness and Political Fiasco*, London: Allen Lane, 2024

Blom, Philipp, 'Von Mmadi Make zu Angelo Sollima – Eine Spurensuche', in *Angelo Soliman. Ein Afrikaner in Wien*, exhibition catalogue, ed. Philipp Blom and Wolfgang Kos, Wien: Christian Brandstätter Verlag, 2012

Blom, Philipp and Wolfgang Kos (eds), *Angelo Soliman. Ein Afrikaner in Wien*, exhibition catalogue, Wien: Christian Brandstätter Verlag, 2012

Bode, Christoph, 'Georg Forster in Paris (1793/94)', *Litteraria Pragensia. Studies in Literature and Culture*, vol. 29, issue 57, 2019

Bohm, Arnd, 'George Forster's *A Voyage Round the World* as a Source for *The Rime of the Ancient Mariner*: A Reconsideration', *English Literary History*, vol. 50, 1983

Bonnemaison, Joël, *The Tree and the Canoe: History and Ethnography of Tanna*, Honolulu: University of Hawai'i Press, 1994

Bono, Salvatore, 'Sklaven in der mediterranen Welt. Von der Ersten Türkenbelagerung bis zum Wiener Kongress (1529–1815)', in *Angelo Soliman. Ein Afrikaner in Wien*, exhibition catalogue, ed. Philipp Blom and Wolfgang Kos, Wien: Christian Brandstätter Verlag, 2012

Borofsky, Robert (ed.), *Remembrance of Pacific Pasts: An Invitation to Remake History*, Honolulu: University of Hawai'i Press, 2000

Boswell, James, *Boswell's Life of Johnson. Together with Boswell's Journal of a Tour to the Hebrides and Johnson's Diary of a Journey into North Wales*, ed. George Birbeck Hill, Oxford: Clarendon Press, 1934

Bott, Elizabeth, *Tongan Society at the Time of Captain Cook's Visits: Discussions with her Majesty Queen Sālote Tupou*, with the assistance of Tavi, Wellington: The Polynesian Society, 1982

Bougainville, Louis de, *A Voyage Round the World*, London: J. Nourse and T. Davies, 1772

Boyd, Julian P. (ed.) et al., *The Papers of Thomas Jefferson*, Princeton and Oxford: Princeton University Press, 1950–2009

Boyle, Nicholas, *Goethe: The Poet and the Age, vol. 1, The Poetry of Desire: 1749–1790*, Oxford: Clarendon Press, 1992

Boyle, Nicholas, *Goethe: The Poet and the Age, vol. 2, Revolution and Renunciation: 1790–1803*, Oxford: Clarendon Press, 2000

Boyle, Nicholas, 'The Composition of Die Wahlverwandschaften', *Publications of the English Goethe Society*, vol. 82, no. 2, 2015

Bödeker, Hans Erich, 'Die Bibliothek eines Aufklärers: Georg Forster', *Aufklärung*, vol. 6, no. 1, 1992

Böhme, Ernst and Rudolf Vierhaus (eds), *Göttingen. Geschichte einer Universitätsstadt*, vol. 2, Göttingen: Vandenhoeck & Ruprecht, 2002

Briedis, Laimonas, *Vilnius: City of Strangers*, Vilnius: Baltos Lankos, 2009

Bruhns, Karl, *Alexander von Humboldt. Eine wissenschaftliche Biographie*, Leipzig: Brockhaus, 1872

Buckley, Veronica, 'Afrikaner an den Höfen Europas: Biografien und Bilder', in *Angelo Soliman. Ein Afrikaner in Wien*, exhibition catalogue, ed. Philipp Blom and Wolfgang Kos, Wien: Christian Brandstätter Verlag, 2012

Burke, Edmund, *Reflections on the Revolution in France*, London: J. Dodsley, 1790

Burnet, James, *Of the Origin and Progress of Language*, Edinburgh and London: J. Balfour and T. Cadell, 1774

Burney, James, *With Captain James Cook in the Antarctic and Pacific. The private journal of James Burney, Second Lieutenant of the Adventure on Cook's Second Voyage, 1772–1773*, ed. Beverley Hooper, Canberra: National Library of Australia, 1975

Campe, Elisabeth, *Zur Erinnerung an F.L.W. Meyer, den Biographen Schröders*, Braunschweig: Friedrich Vielweg, 1847

Campe, Joachim Heinrich, *Briefe aus Paris zur Zeit der Revolution geschrieben*, Braunschweig: Schulbuchhandlung, 1790

Christan, David, 'The Pacific Region in Deep Time', in *The Cambridge History of the Pacific Ocean*, ed. Ryan Tucker Jones and Matt K. Matsuda, vol. 1, Cambridge: Cambridge University Press, 2022

Clarke, Stephen, *The French Revolution and What Went Wrong*, London: Arrow, 2019

Clerke, Charles (here spelled Clarke), 'An Account of the very tall Men, seen near the Streights of Magellan, in the Year 1764, by the Equipage of the Dolphin Man of War, 3 November 1766', *Philosophical Transactions of the Royal Society*, vol. 57, 1767

Combs Stuebe, Isabel, *The Life and Works of William Hodges*, New York and London: Garland Publishing, 1979

Connaughton, Richard, *Omai: The Prince Who Never Was*, London: Timewell Press, 2000

Cook, James, *A Voyage towards the South Pole, and Round the World, Performed on His Majesty's Ships the Resolution and Adventure, In the Years 1772, 1773, 1774, and 1775*, London: W. Strahan and T. Cadell, 1777

Cook, James, *Des Capitain Jacob Cook dritte Entdeckungs-Reise in die Südsee und nach dem Nordpol*, Berlin: Haude und Spener, 1789

Cook, James and James King, *A Voyage to the Pacific Ocean*, London: W. and A. Strahan, 1784

Cowley, Gordon and Les Deacon, *In the Wake of Captain Cook: The Life and Times of Captain Charles Clerke*, Boston: Richard Kay, 2002

Croker, J.W., *Essays on the Early Period of the French Revolution*, London: John Murray, 1857

Damm, Sigrid (ed.), *Caroline Schlegel-Schelling: Die Kunst zu leben*, Frankfurt and Leipzig: Insel Verlag, 2005

Darnton, Robert, *The Revolutionary Temper, Paris, 1748–1789*, London: Allen Lane, 2023

Décultot, Elisabeth and Janna Kittelmann, Andrea Thiele und Ingo Uhlig (eds), *Weltensammeln. Johann Reinhold und Georg Forster*, Göttingen: Wallstein Verlag, 2020

Dening, Greg, *Beach Crossings: Voyages Across Times, Cultures and Self*, Philadelphia: University of Pennsylvania Press, 2004

Diderot, Denis and Jean le Rond d'Alembert, *Encyclopédie ou Dictionnaire Raisonné des Sciences, des Arts et des Métiers*, vol. 12, Neufchastel: Samuel Faulche, 1765

Diedrich, Maria I., 'From American Slaves to Hessian Subjects: Silenced Black Narratives of the American Revolution,' in *Germany and the Black Diaspora: Points of Contact, 1250–1914*, ed. Mischa Honeck, Martin Klimke and Anne Kuhlmann, New York and Oxford: Berghahn, 2013, p. 96

Dippel, Horst, 'Georg Forster und England: Weltläufigkeit und Tradition im Denken des Forschers und Revolutionärs,' *Georg-Forster-Studien*, vol. 1, 1997

Dippel, Horst, 'Revolutionäre Anthropologie? Oder der Versuch, Georg Forster neu zu lesen,' *Historische Zeitschrift*, vol. 291, 2010

Dodds Pennock, Caroline, *On Savage Shores: How Indigenous Americans Discovered Europe*, New York: Alfred A. Knopf, 2023

Douglas, Bronwen, 'Encountering Agency: Islanders, European Voyagers, and the Production of Race in Oceania,' in *Changing Contexts, Shifting Meanings: Transformations of Cultural Traditions in Oceania*, ed. Elfriede Hermann, Honolulu: University of Hawai'i Press, 2011

Doyle, William, *The Oxford History of the French Revolution*, Oxford: Oxford University Press, 2002

Druett, Joan, *Tupaia: Captain Cook's Polynesian Navigator*, Santa Barbara, Denver and Oxford: Praeger, 2011

Dumont, Franz, 'Das "Seelenbündnis". Die Freundschaft zwischen Georg Forster und Samuel Thomas Soemmerring,' in *Der Weltumsegler und seine Freunde. Georg Forster als gesellschaftlicher Schriftsteller der Goethezeit*, ed. Detlef Rasmussen, Tübingen: Gunter Narr Verlag, 1988

Dumont, Franz, 'Georg Forster als Demokrat. Theorie und Praxis eines deutschen Revolutionärs,' *Georg-Forster-Studien*, vol. 1, 1997

Dumont, Franz, Scherf, Ferdinand and Friedrich Schütz, *Mainz. Die Geschichte der Stadt*, Mainz: Philipp von Zabern Verlag, 1998

Dumont, Franz, 'Die Mainzer Republik 1792/93. Französischer Revolutionsexport und deutscher Demokratieversuch,' *Schriftenreihe des Landtags Rheinland-Pfalz*, vol. 55, 2012

Earle, Peter, *Sailors: English Merchant Seamen, 1650–1775*, London: Methuen, 2007

Engels, Friedrich, 'The State of Germany, Letter II,' *The Northern Star*, vol. VIII, no. 417, 8 November 1845

Ette, Ottmar, *Anton Wilhelm Ano. Philosophieren ohne festen Wohnsitz. Eine Philosophie der Aufklärung zwischen Europa und Afrika*, Berlin: Kadmos, 2020

Ewert, Michael, '*Vernunft, Gefühl und Phantasie, im schönsten Tanze vereint*'. *Zur Essayistik Georg Forsters*, Würzburg: Königshausen & Neumann, 1993

Ewert, Michael and Hermann Schüttler (eds), 'Georg Forster. Briefe an Ernst Friedrich Hector Falcke,' *Georg-Forster-Studien*, Beihefte, vol. 4, 2009

Fabricius, Johann Christian, *Betrachtungen über die allgemeinen Einrichtungen der Natur*, Hamburg: Karl Ernst Bohn, 1781

Feest, Christian F., 'Tierra del Fuego,' in *James Cook: Gifts and Treasures from the South Seas. The Cook-Forster Collection, Göttingen*, ed. Brigitta Hauser-Schäublin and Gundolf Krüger, Munich and New York: Prestel, 1998

Fiedler, Horst, 'Über die Büchersammlung Georg Forsters und ihre Versteigerung,' in *Studien zur Neueren Deutschen Literatur*, ed. Hans Werner Seiffert, Berlin: Akademie-Verlag, 1964

Fiedler, Horst, 'Alexander von Humboldt and Georg Forster,' *HiN* XXI, vol. 41, 2020

Fink, Gonthier-Louis, 'Klima- und Kulturtheorien der Aufklärung,' *Georg-Forster-Studien*, vol. 2, 1998

Finney, Ben and Sam Low, 'Navigation,' in *Vaka moana: Voyages of the Ancestors. The Discovery and Settlement of the Pacific*, ed. K.R. Howe, Auckland: Auckland War Memorial Museum, 2006

Firla Monika, '*Segen, Segen, Segen auf Dich, guter Mann!' Angelo Soliman und seine Freunde Graf Franz Moritz von Lacy, Ignatz von Born, Johann Anton Mertens und Ferenc Kazinczy*, Wien: Tanz Hotel / ArtAct Kunstverein, 2003

Forster, George, *A Voyage Round the World in his Britannic Majesty's Sloop*, Resolution, *commanded by Capt. James Cook, during the Years 1772, 3, 4, and 5*, London: B. White, 1777

Forster, George, *A Letter to the Right Honourable The Earl of Sandwich* (1778), AA 4

Forster, Georg, 'Georg Forsters Antwort an die Göttingischen Recensenten' (1778), AA 4

Forster, Georg, *Reise um die Welt* (1778–1780), AA 2 and 3

Forster, Georg, 'O-Taheiti' (1779), AA 5

Forster, Georg, 'Herrn von Büffons Naturgeschichte der vierfüßigen Thiere' (1780), AA 6. 1

Forster, Georg, 'Des Schiffhauptmanns Forrest zertreute Nachrichten von der Insel Magindanao' (1782), AA 5

Forster, Georg, 'Ein Versuch mit dephlogistisirter Luft' (1782), AA 6. 1
Forster, Georg, *Der Brodbaum* (1784), AA 6. 1
Forster, Georg, 'Neuholland und die brittische Colonie in Botany-Bay' (1786), AA 5
Forster, Georg, 'Noch etwas über die Menschenraßen' (1786), AA 8
Forster, Georg, 'Versuch einer Naturgeschichte des Menschen' (1786), AA 8
Forster, Georg, 'Cook, der Entdecker' (1787), AA 5
Forster, Georg, 'Ueber Leckereyen' (1788), AA 8
Forster, Georg, 'Die Kunst und das Zeitalter' (1789), AA 7
Forster, Georg, 'Ein Blick in das Ganze der Natur', first published in *Kleine Schriften* (1789), AA 8
Forster, Georg, *Kleine Schriften. Ein Beytrag zur Völker- und Länderkunde, Naturgeschichte und Philosophie des Lebens*, Leipzig: Paul Gotthelf Kummer, 1789
Forster, Georg, 'Leitfaden zu einer künftigen Geschichte der Menschheit' (1789), AA 8
Forster, Georg, 'Nachrichten von den Pelew-Inseln' (1789), AA 5
Forster, Georg, 'Über Proselytenmacherei' (1789), AA 8
Forster, Georg, 'Geschichte des Schiffbruchs des Herrn von Brisson' (1790), AA 5
Forster, Georg, 'Geschichte der Reisen die seit Cook an der Nordwest- und Nordost-Küste von America und im nördlichen Amerika selbst von Meares, Dixon, Portlock, Coxe, Long u.a.m unternommen worden sind' (1791), AA 5
Forster, Georg, 'Über lokale und allgemeine Bildung' (1791), AA 7
Forster, Georg, 'Vorläufige Schilderung des Nordens von Amerika' (1791), AA 5
Forster, Georg, *Ansichten vom Niederrhein, von Brabant, Flandern, Holland, England und Frankreich im April, Mai und Junius* 1790, (1791–92), AA 9
Forster, Georg, 'Des Abbés Rochon Reise nach Madagaskar und Ostindien' (1792), AA 5
Forster, Georg, *Erinnerungen aus dem Jahr 1790* (1792), AA 8
Forster, Georg, 'Über das Verhältniß der Mainzer gegen die Franken', 15 November 1792, AA 10. 1
Forster, Georg, 'Vorlesungen über allgemeine Naturkenntnis' (1792), AA 6. 2
Forster, Georg, 'Anrede an die Gesellschaft der Freunde der Freiheit und Gleichheit am Neujahrstage', 1 January 1793, AA 10. 1
Forster, Georg, 'Rede über die Vereinigung des rheinisch-deutschen Freistaat mit der Frankenrepublik', 21 March 1793, AA 10. 1
Forster, Georg, 'Darstellung der Revolution in Mainz' (1793), AA 10. 1
Forster, Georg, 'Über die Beziehung der Staatskunst auf das Glück der Menschheit' (1793), AA 10. 1
Forster, Georg, 'Parisische Umrisse' (1793–94), AA 10. 1
Forster, Georg, *Johann Georg Forster's Briefwechsel, nebst einigen Nachrichten von seinem Leben*, ed. Therese Huber, Leipzig: F.A. Brockhaus, 1829
Forster, Georg, *Sämmtliche Schriften*, ed. Therese Forster, Leipzig: F.A. Brockhaus, 1843
Forster, Georg, *Briefe und Tagebücher Georg Forsters von seiner Reise am Niederrhein, in England und Frankreich im Frührjahr 1790*, ed. Albert Leitzmann, Halle: Max Niemeyer, 1893

Forster, George, *A Reply to Mr. Wales's Remarks* (1778), in George Forster, *A Voyage Round the World: George Forster*, ed. Nicholas Thomas and Oliver Berghof, Honolulu: University of Hawai'i Press, 2000

Forster, George, *A Voyage Round the World: George Forster*, ed. Nicholas Thomas and Oliver Berghof, Honolulu: University of Hawai'i Press, 2000

Forster, Georg, 'Something More about the Human Races,' in *Kant and the Concept of Race: Late Eighteenth-Century Writings*, trans. and ed. Jon M. Mikkelsen, Albany: Suny Press, 2013

Forster, Johann Reinhold, 'Specimen Historiae Naturalis Volgensis,' *Philosophical Transactions of the Royal Society*, vol. 57, 1767

Forster, Johann Reinhold, 'A treatise on the natural history of the river Volga,' 1767, RS, Letters & Papers, 4/394

Forster, Johann Reinhold, 'A Letter from Mr. J.R. Forster, F.A.S. to M. Maty, M.D. Sec.R.S. containing some Account of a new Map of the River Volga,' *Philosophical Transactions of the Royal Society*, vol. 58, 1768

Forster, Johann Reinhold, 'Observations on some Tartarian Antiquities, described in the preceding Article, read on 26 February 1767,' *Archaeologia*, vol. 2, 1773

Forster, Johann Reinhold, *Observations Made During a Voyage Round the World*, London: G. Robinson, 1778

Forster, Johann Reinhold, *Bemerkungen über die Gegenstände der physischen Erdbeschreibung, Naturgeschichte und sittlichen Philosophie auf seiner Reise um die Welt gesammlet*, Berlin: Haude und Spener, 1783

Forster, Johann Reinhold, 'Ueber Georg Forster,' *Philosophischer Anzeiger*, 1795

Forster, Johann Reinhold, *The* Resolution *Journal of Johann Reinhold Forster, 1772–1775*, ed. Michael E. Hoare, London: Hakluyt Society, 1982

Forster, Johann Reinhold, *Observations Made During a Voyage Round the World* (1778), ed. Nicholas Thomas, Harriet Guest and Michael Dettelback, Honolulu, University of Hawai'i Press, 1996

Forster, Johann Reinhold and George Forster, *Characteres Generum Plantarum*, London: B. White, T. Cadell and P. Emsly, 1776

François-Poncet, André, *Les Affinités Électives de Goethe*, Paris: Félix Alcan, 1910

Franke, Ernst August, 'Über Georg Forsters Krankheiten und Tod,' *Georg-Forster-Studien*, vol. 4, 2000

Fuhrman, Horst (ed.), *F.W.J. Schelling. Briefe und Dokumente*, Bonn: Bouvier Verlag, 1962–75

Fullagar, Kate, 'Envoys of Interest: A Cherokee, a Ra'iatean, and the Eighteenth-Century British Empire,' in *Facing Empire: Indigenous Experiences in a Revolutionary Age*, ed. Kate Fullagar and Michael A. McDonnell, Baltimore: Johns Hopkins University Press, 2018

Fullagar, Kate, *The Warrior, the Voyager, and the Artist: Three Lives in an Age of Empire*, New Haven: Yale University Press, 2020

Geiger, Ludwig, 'Aus Therese Hubers Herzensleben', *Westermanns Illustrierte Deutsche Monatshefte*, vol. 81, 1897

Geiger, Ludwig, *Therese Huber. 1764–1829, Leben und Briefe einer deutschen Frau*, Stuttgart: Cotta'sche Buchhandlung, 1901

Geiger, Ludwig, 'Aus Therese Hubers Herzensleben', *Westermanns Illustrierte Deutsche Monatshefte*, vol. 94, 1903

Geikie, Archibal, *Annals of the Royal Society Club. The Record of a London Dining-Club in the Eighteenth and Nineteenth Centuries*, London: Macmillan & Co, 1917

Geyer-Kordesch, Johanna, *Die Englandreise der Fürstin Louise von Anhalt-Dessau im Jahr 1775*, Berlin: Nicolai Verlag, 2007

Geyken, Frauke, *Zum Wohle aller. Geschichte der Georg-August-Universität Göttingen von ihrer Gründung 1737 bis 2019*, Göttingen: Steidl, 2019

Gifford, Edward Wilson, *Tongan Myths and Tales*, Honolulu: Bernice P. Bishop Museum, 1924

Gilli, Marita, 'Reform und Revolution bei George Forster', *Georg-Forster-Studien*, vol. 4, 2000

Gilli, Marita, 'Die Grenzen der Demokratie: Die Gewalt in den *Parisischen Umrissen*', *Georg-Forster-Studien*, vol. 8, 2003

Gilli, Marita, 'Das Politische in Forsters Rezensionen', *Georg-Forster-Studien*, vol. 9, 2004

Gilli, Marita, 'Die Flucht in die Politik als letzte Reise', *Georg-Forster-Studien*, vol. 15, 2010

Goethe, Johann Wolfgang von, *Tagebücher*, in *Goethes Werke*, Part III, published on behalf of Grand Duchess Sophie of Saxe-Weimar-Eisenach, Weimar: Herman Böhlau, 1887–1919

Goethe, Johann Wolfgang von, *Briefe*, in *Goethes Werke*, Part IV, published on behalf of Grand Duchess Sophie of Saxe-Weimar-Eisenach, Weimar: Herman Böhlau, 1887–1919

Goethe, Johann Wolfgang von, *Goethes Leben von Tag zu Tag: Eine dokumentarische Chronik*, ed. Robert Steiger, Zurich: Artemis Verlag, 1982–96

Goethe, Johann Wolfgang von, *Tag- und Jahreshefte*, ed. Irmtraut Schmid, Frankfurt: Deutscher Klassiker Verlag, 1994

Goldstein, Jürgen, *Die Entdeckung der Natur. Etappen einer Erfahrungsgeschichte*, Berlin: Matthes & Seitz, 2013

Goldstein, Jürgen, *Georg Forster. Zwischen Freiheit und Naturgewalt*, Berlin: Matthes & Seitz, 2015

Gordon, Joseph Stuart, *Reinhold and Georg Forster in England, 1766–1789*, PhD Thesis, Duke University, 1975

Gordon, Lyndall, *Mary Wollstonecraft: A New Genus*, London: Little Brown, 2005

Gottschall, Rudolf von, 'Georg Forster, der Naturforscher und – Vaterlandsverräter', *Die Gartenlaube*, 1904

Götz, Carmen, 'Friedrich Heinrich Jacobi und die Französische Revolution', *Düsseldorfer Jahrbuch*, vol. 66, 1995

Götz, Carmen, 'Der Stoff, aus dem die Netze sind. Einige Gewebeproben aus dem Briefwechsel zwischen Georg Forster und Friedrich Heinrich Jacobi', *Georg-Forster-Studien*, vol. 12, 2007

Günderode, Friedrich, *Briefe eines Reisenden über den gegenwärtigen Zustand von Cassel*, Frankfurt und Leipzig: Fleischerischen Buchhandlung, 1781

Gutfleisch-Ziche, Barbara, 'Unbekannte Briefe der Schriftstellerin Therese Huber in Jena', *EDITIO*, vol. 14, 2001

Hamel, Frank, *A Woman of the Revolution: Théroigne de Méricourt*, New York: Brentano's, 1911

Harpprecht, Klaus, *Georg Forster oder Die Liebe zur Welt. Eine Biographie*, Hamburg: Rowohlt, 2007

Hassencamp, Johann Matthäus, *Briefe eines Reisenden von Pyrmont, Cassel, Marburg, Würzburg und Wilhelmsbad*, Leipzig: no publisher, 1783

Hatch Gray, Sally, 'Kant's Race Theory, Forster's Counter, and the Metaphysics of Color', *The Eighteenth Century*, vol. 53, 2012

Hau'ofa, Epeli, *We Are the Ocean: Selected Works*, Honolulu: University of Hawai'i Press, 2008

Hauser-Schäublin, Brigitta and Gundolf Krüger (eds), *James Cook: Gifts and Treasures from the South Seas. The Cook-Forster Collection, Göttingen*, Munich and New York: Prestel, 1998

Hawkesworth, John, *An Account of the Voyages Undertaken by the Order of his Present Majesty for Making Discoveries in the Southern Hemisphere*, London: W. Strahan and T. Cadell, 1773

Heeren, Arnold Hermann Ludwig, *Christian Gottlieb Heyne. Biographisch dargestellt*, Göttingen: Johann Friedrich Röwer, 1813

Heine, Heinrich, *Über Ludwig Börne*, Hamburg: Hoffmann und Campe, 1840

Heintze, Dieter, 'Dem Ethnologischen bei Forster nachspürend', *Georg-Forster-Studien*, vol. 1, 1997

Heintze, Dieter, 'Unter Melanesiern', *Georg-Forster-Studien*, vol. 11, no. 1, 2006

Heintze, Dieter, 'Die Forsters und die Südsee-Sprachen', *Georg-Forster-Studien*, vol. 17, 2012

Henry, Teuira, *Ancient Tahiti*, Honolulu: Bernice P. Bishop Museum, 1928

Herder, Johann Gottfried von, *Ideen zur Philosophie der Geschichte der Menschheit*, in *Herder's Sämmtliche Werke*, ed. Bernhard Suphan, Berlin: Weidmannsche Buchhandlung, vol. 13, 1887

Herder, Johann Gottfried von, *Ideas for the Philosophy of the History of Mankind*, trans. and ed. Gregory Martin Moore, Princeton and Oxford: Princeton University Press, 2024

Herder, Johann Gottfried von, 'Treatise on the Origin of Language' (1772), in *Johann Gottfried von Herder: Philosophical Writings*, trans. and ed. Michael N. Forster, Cambridge: Cambridge University Press, 2002

Herder, Johann Gottfried von, *Briefe zur Beförderung der Humanität*. Achte Sammlung, Riga: J.F. Hartnoch, 1796

Hermann, Elfriede (ed.), *Changing Contexts, Shifting Meanings: Transformations of Cultural Traditions in Oceania*, Honolulu: University of Hawai'i Press, 2011

Heuser, Magdalene, 'Georg und Therese Forster – Aspekte einer gescheiterten Zusammenarbeit,' in *Literarische Zusammenarbeit*, ed. Bodo Plachta, Tübingen: Niemeyer, 2001

Hibbert, Christopher, *The French Revolution*, London: Penguin Books, 1982

Hinz, Berthold, 'Kunst-Ansichten vom Niederhein – insbesondere zum Kölner Dom und "flammändischen Machwerk"', *Georg-Forster-Studien*, vol. 5, 2000

Hoare, Michael E., *The Tactless Philosopher: Johann Reinhold Forster*, Melbourne: The Hawthorn Press, 1976

Holmes, Christine (ed.), *Captain Cook's Second Voyage: The Journals of Lieutenants Elliott and Pickersgill*, Dover: Caliban Books, 1984

Hoorn, Tanja van, *Dem Leibe abgelesen. Georg Forster im Kontext der physischen Anthropologie des 18. Jahrhunderts*, Tübingen: Max Niemeyer Verlag, 2004

Howe, K.R., *Where the Waves Fall: A New South Sea Islands History from First Settlement to Colonial Rule*, Honolulu: University of Hawai'i Press, 1984

Howe, K.R., *Vaka moana: Voyages of the Ancestors. The Discovery and Settlement of the Pacific*, Auckland: Auckland War Memorial Museum, 2006

Huber, Ludwig Ferdinand, *Sämtliche Werke seit dem Jahre 1802 nebst seiner Biographie*, ed. Therese Huber, Tübingen: Cotta'sche Buchhandlung, 1806

Huber, Therese, *Mehr Glück als Verstand. Eine Erzählung in Briefen*, Braunschweig: Friedrich Vieweg, 1803 (originally published under Ferdinand Ludwig Huber's name)

Huber, Therese, *Therese Huber. Briefe*, ed. Magdalene Heuser, Berlin: De Gruyter, 1999–2013

Humboldt, Alexander von, *Personal Narrative of Travels to the Equinoctial Regions of the New Continent during the years 1799–1804*, London: Longman, Hurst, Rees, Orme, Brown, and John Murray, 1814–29

Humboldt, Alexander von, *Cosmos: Sketch of a Physical Description of the Universe*, London: Longman, Brown, Green, Longmans, and John Murray, 1845–48 (vols 1–2)

Humboldt, Alexander von, *Kosmos. Entwurf einer physischen Weltbeschreibung*, Stuttgart and Tübingen: J.G. Cotta'scher Verlag, 1845–47 (vols 1–2)

Humboldt, Alexander von, *Ansichten der Natur mit wissenschaftlichen Erläuterungen*, Stuttgart and Tübingen: J.G. Cotta'scher Verlag, 1849

Humboldt, Alexander von, *Die Jugendbriefe Alexander von Humboldts 1787–1799*, ed. Ilse Jahn and Fritz G. Lange, Berlin: Akademie Verlag, 1973

Humboldt, Alexander von, *Lateinamerika am Vorabend der Unabhängigkeitsrevolution: eine Anthologie von Impressionen und Urteilen aus seinen Reisetagebüchern*, ed. Margot Faak, Berlin: Akademie-Verlag, 1982

Humboldt, Alexander von, 'Aus meinem Leben, 1769–1850', in *Alexander von Humboldt. Aus meinem Leben. Autobiographische Bekenntnisse*, ed. Kurt-R. Biermann, Munich: C.H. Beck, 1987

Humboldt, Alexander von, 'Ich über mich selbst (Mein Weg zum Naturwissenschaftler und Forschungsreisenden, 1769–1790)', in *Alexander von Humboldt. Aus meinem Leben. Autobiographische Bekenntnisse*, ed. Kurt-R. Biermann, Munich: C.H. Beck, 1987

Humboldt, Alexander von, 'Meine Bekenntnisse. Autobiographische Skizze 1769–1805', in *Alexander von Humboldt. Aus meinem Leben. Autobiographische Bekenntnisse*, ed. Kurt-R. Biermann, Munich: C.H. Beck, 1987

Humboldt, Alexander von, *Reise auf dem Río Magdalena, durch die Anden und Mexico*, ed. Margot Faak, Berlin: Akademie Verlag, 2003

Humboldt, Alexander von and Aimé Bonpland, *Ideen zu einer Geographie der Pflanzen nebst einem Naturgemälde der Tropenländer*, Tübingen: G. Cotta, and Paris: F. Schoell, 1807

Humboldt, Wilhelm von, *Gesammelte Schriften, Wilhelm von Humboldts Tagebücher*, ed. Albert Leitzmann, vol. 14, Berlin: B. Behr's Verlag, 1922

Humboldt, Wilhelm von, *Briefe*, ed. Philip Mattson, Berlin: De Gruyter, 2014–17

Humboldt, Wilhelm von and Caroline von Humboldt, *Wilhelm und Caroline von Humboldt in ihren Briefen*, ed. Anna von Sydow, Berlin: Mittler & Sohn, 1910–16

Hume, David, *A Treatise of Human Nature (1739)*, ed. L.A. Selby-Bigge, Oxford: Clarendon Press, 1896

Hume, David, *The Philosophical Works*, ed. Thomas Hill Green and Thomas Hodge Grose, London: Longmans, Green, and Co, 1875

Hunt, Terry L., 'Rethinking the Fall of Easter Island', *American Scientist*, vol. 94, no. 5, 2006

Ihimaera, Witi, 'Te Moana Nui a Kiwa: The Original Ocean', in *The Cambridge History of the Pacific Ocean*, ed. Ryan Tucker Jones and Matt K. Matsuda, Cambridge: Cambridge University Press, 2022

Isaacson, Walter. *Benjamin Franklin: An American Life*, New York: Simon & Schuster, 2004

Jacobi, Friedrich Heinrich, *Friedrich Heinrich Jacobi's auserlesener Briefwechsel*, ed. Friedrich Roth, Leipzig: Gerhard Fleischer, 1825–27

Jacobi, Friedrich Heinrich, *Briefwechsel: Gesamtausgabe*, ed. Michael Brüggen et al. , Stuttgart: Frommann-Holzboog, 1981–2017

Jolly, Margaret, '"Ill-natured comparisons": Racism and Relativism in European Representations of ni-Vanuatu from Cook's Second Voyage', in *Colonialism and Culture, History and Anthropology*, ed. Nicholas Thomas, vol. 5, 1992

Jolly, Margaret, 'The Sediment of Voyages: Remembering Quirós, Bougainville and Cook in Vanuatu', in *Oceanic Encounters: Exchange, Desire, Violence*, ed. Margaret Jolly, Serge Tcherkézoff and Darrell T. Tyron, Acton: Australian National University Press, 2009

Jolly, Margaret, Serge Tcherkézoff and Darrell T. Tyron (eds), *Oceanic Encounters: Exchange, Desire, Violence*, Acton: Australian National University Press, 2009

Jonas, Fritz, *Christian Gottfried Körner: Biographische Nachrichten über ihn und sein Haus*, Berlin: Weidmannsche Buchhandlung, 1882

Joppien, Rüdiger and Bernard Smith, *The Art of Captain Cook's Voyages*, New Haven: Yale University Press, 1985

Jordan, Sabine Dorothea, *Ludwig Ferdinand Huber (1764–1804): His Life and Works*, Stuttgart: Akademischer Verlag Hans-Dieter Heinz, 1978

Kaeppler, Adrienne L., *'Artificial Curiosities', being an exposition of native manufactures collected on the three Pacific voyages of Captain James Cook at the Bernice Pauahi Bishop Museum*, Honolulu: Bishop Museum Press, 1978

Kaeppler, Adrienne L., 'Tonga – Entry into Complex Hierarchies', in *James Cook: Gifts and Treasures from the South Seas. The Cook-Forster Collection, Göttingen*, ed. Brigitta Hauser-Schäublin and Gundolf Krüger, Munich and New York: Prestel, 1998

Kaeppler, Adrienne L., *Oxford History of Art: The Pacific Arts of Polynesia & Micronesia*, Oxford: Oxford University Press, 2008

Kaeppler, Adrienne L. (ed.), *James Cook and the Exploration of the Pacific*, exhibition catalogue, Kunst- und Ausstellungshalle der Bundesrepublik Deutschland, London: Thames & Hudson, 2009

Kalm, Per, *Travels into North America*, London: T. Lowndes, 1770–71

Kant, Immanuel, 'Bestimmung des Begriffs einer Menschenrasse', *Berliner Monatschrift*, vols 6 and 7, 1785–86

Kant, Immanuel, 'Über den Gebrauch teleologischer Prinzipien in der Philosophie', *Teutsche Merkur*, January and February 1788

Kant, Immanuel, *Immanuel Kant's Physische Geographie*, ed. Friedrich Theodor Rink, Königsberg: Göbbels und Unzer, 1802

Kant, Immanuel, *Observations on the Feeling of the Beautiful and Sublime and Other Writings*, ed. Patrick Frierson and Paul Guyer, Cambridge: Cambridge University Press, 2011

Kant, Immanuel, *Natural Science*, trans. Eric Watkins, Cambridge: Cambridge University Press, 2012

Kant, Immanuel, 'Determination of the Concept of a Human Race' (1785), in *Kant and the Concept of Race: Late Eighteenth-Century Writings*, trans. and ed. Jon M. Mikkelsen, Albany: Suny Press, 2013

Kant, Immanuel, 'Of the Different Human Races' (1777), in *Kant and the Concept of Race: Late Eighteenth-Century Writings*, trans. and ed. Jon M. Mikkelsen, Albany: Suny Press, 2013

Kant, Immanuel, 'On the Use of Teleological Principles in Philosophy' (1788), in *Kant and the Concept of Race: Late Eighteenth-Century Writings*, trans. and ed. Jon M. Mikkelsen, Albany: Suny Press, 2013

Kapp, Friedrich, *Justus Erich Bollmann. Ein Lebensbild aus zwei Welttheilen*, Berlin: Julius Springer, 1880

Kasperaviciene, Audrone, *Damages of Monuments by Fire in the History of Vilnius: Damages of Monuments and Current Prevention Strategies*, Vilnius: Vilnius Old Town Renewal Agency, ICOMOS-Lithuania, report, no date

Kern, Bärbel and Horst, *Madame Doctorin Schlözer. Ein Frauenleben in den Widersprüchen der Aufklärung*, Munich: C.H. Beck, 1988

Kisch, Egon Erwin, *Landung in Australien* (1937), Berlin: Aufbau Taschenbuch Verlag, 1993

Klenke, Claus-Volker, Jürgen Garber and Dieter Heintze (eds), *Georg Forster in interdisziplinärer Perspektive*, Berlin: Akademie Verlag, 1994

Knauß, Stefan, Louis Wolfradt, Tim Hofmann and Jens Eberhard (eds), *Auf den Spuren von Anton Wilhelm Amo. Philosophie und der Ruf nach Interkulturalität*, Berlin: Transcript Verlag, 2021

Knigge, Adolph Freiherr von, *Über den Umgang mit Menschen* (1788), Hanover: Christian Ritscher, 1790

Krüger, Gundolf, 'Reflexionen über Krieg und Gewalt in der Südsee', *Georg-Forster-Studien*, vol. 8, 2003

Krüger, Gundolf, 'An Encounter with Violence in Paradise: Georg Forster's Reflections on War in Aotearoa, Tahiti, and Tonga (1772–1775)', in *Changing Contexts, Shifting Meanings: Transformations of Cultural Traditions in Oceania*, ed. Elfriede Hermann, Honolulu: University of Hawai'i Press, 2011

Kühn, Manfred, *Kant: A Biography*, Cambridge: Cambridge University Press, 2001

Leitzmann, Albert, 'Aus Heynes Briefen an seine Tochter Therese und seine Schwiegersöhne Forster und Huber', *Archiv für das Studium der neueren Sprachen und Literaturen*, vol. 12, 1908

Leitzmann, Albert, 'Briefe F.L.W. Meyer an Therese Heyne', *Funde und Forschungen, Festschrift J. Wahle*, Leipzig: Insel Verlag, 1921

Lepenies, Wolf, 'Eine vergessene Tradition der deutschen Anthropologie', *Saeculum*, vol. 24, 1973

Lessing, Gotthold Ephraim, *Sämtliche Schriften*, ed. Karl Lachmann, Leipzig: Göschen'sche Verlagshandlung, 1907

Levere, Trevor H., *Poetry Realized in Nature: Samuel Taylor Coleridge and Early Nineteenth-Century Science*, Cambridge: Cambridge University Press, 1981

Lichtenberg, Georg Christoph, *Lichtenberg's Visits to England as described in his Letters and Diaries*, trans. Margaret Mare and W.H. Quarrell, Oxford: Clarendon Press, 1938

Lichtenberg, Georg Christoph, *Schriften und Briefe*, ed. Wolfgang Promies, Munich: Hanser, 1967–72

Lichtenberg, Georg Christoph, *Lichtenberg in England. Dokumente einer Begegnung*, ed. Hans Ludwig Gumbert, Wiesbaden: Otto Harrassowitz, 1977

Lichtenberg, Georg Christoph, *Briefwechsel*, ed. Ulrich von Joost und Albrecht Schöne, Munich: C.H. Beck, 1983–2004

Lindstrom, Lamont, *Tanna Times: Islanders in the World*, Honolulu: University of Hawai'i Press, 2020

Linnaeus, Carl, *Species Plantarum*, facsimile of the first edition 1753, London: Ray Society, 1957

Linnaeus, Carl, *Systema naturae*, tenth edition, Holmiae: Impensis Direct. Laurentii Salvii, 1758

Little, Stephen and Peter Ruthenberg (ed.), *Life in the Pacific of the 1700s: The Cook / Forster Collection of the Georg August University of Göttingen*, exhibition catalogue, Honolulu: Honolulu Academy of Arts, 2006

Livingstone Lowes, John, *The Road to Xanadu: A Study in the Ways of the Imagination*, Princeton: Princeton University Press, 1986

Locke, John, *An Essay Concerning Human Understanding*, Oxford: Clarendon Press, 1894

Mallinckrodt, Rebekka von, 'Slavery and the Law in Eighteenth-Century Germany', in *Beyond Exceptionalism: Traces of Slavery and the Slave Trade in Early Modern Germany, 1650–1850*, ed. Rebekka von Mallinckrodt, Josef Köstlbauer and Sarah Lentz, Berlin and Boston: De Gruyter Oldenbourg, 2021

Mariner, William, *An Account of the Natives of the Tonga Islands in the South Pacific Ocean, with an Original Grammar of their Language*, compiled by John Martin, London: John Murray, 1817

Marra, John, *Journal of the Resolution's Voyage in the Years 1772, 1773, 1774, and 1775, on Discovery of the Southern Hemisphere*, London: F. Newberry, 1775

McCormick, Eric Hall, *Omai: Pacific Envoy*, Auckland: Auckland University Press, 1977

McCullough, David, *John Adams*, New York: Simon & Schuster, 2001

McLynn, Frank, *Captain Cook: Master of the Seas*, New Haven and London: Yale University Press, 2011

Meleisea, Malama and Penelope Schoeffel, 'Discovering Outsiders', in *The Cambridge History of the Pacific Islanders*, ed. Donald Denoon, Cambridge: Cambridge University Press, 1997

Menn, Stephen and Justin E.H. Smith (eds), *Anton Wilhelm Amo's Philosophical Dissertations on Mind and Body*, Oxford: Oxford University Press, 2020

Menzel, Wolfgang, *Die deutsche Literatur*, Stuttgart: Hallberger'sche Verlagshandlung, 1836

Merck, Johann Heinrich, *Johann Heinrich Mercks Briefe an die Herzogin-Mutter Anna Amalia und den Herzog Carl August von Sachsen-Weimar*, ed. Hans Gerhard Gräf, Leipzig: Insel-Verlag, 1911

Merck, Johann Heinrich, *Briefe*, ed. Herbert Kraft, Frankfurt: Insel Verlag, 1968

Merz-Horn, Silvia, *Georg Forster (1754–1794). Die Kasseler Jahre. Texte – Materialien – Dokumente*, Kassel: Verlag Jenior & Preßler, 1990

Mey, Eberhard, 'Georg Forster und der Büchermarkt in der Residenzstadt Kassel in der Regierungszeit Landgraf Friedrichs II.', *Georg-Forster-Studien*, vol. 4, 2000

Michaelis, Johann David, *Literarischer Briefwechsel von Johann David Michaelis*, ed. Johann Gottlieb Buhle, Leipzig: Weidmannsche Buchhandlung, 1796

Mignet, F.A., *History of the French Revolution from 1789 to 1814*, London: George Bell & Sons, 1902

Molesky, Mark, *This Gulf of Fire: The Great Lisbon Earthquake, or Apocalypse in the Age of Science and Reason*, New York: Vintage Books, 2016

Mollo, John, *Uniforms of the American Revolution*, New York: Macmillan Publishing Co, 1975

Montaigne, Michel de, 'Of the Canniballes' (1580), in *Amazons, Savages & Machiavels: Travel & Colonial Writing in English, 1550–1630. An Anthology*, ed. Andrew Hadfield, Oxford: Oxford University Press, 2001

Moore, Lucy, *Liberty: The Lives and Times of Six Women in Revolutionary France*, New York: HarperCollins, 2007

Moritz, C.P., *Journeys of a German in England. Carl Philip Moritz. A walking-tour of England in 1782*, London: Eland, 1983

Moser, I.G., 'Nachschrift von einer Handschrift J.R. Forster's in der Kön. öffentlichen Bibliothek zu Stuttgart', *Serapeum. Zeitschrift für Bibliothekswissenschaft, Handschriftenkunde und ältere Literatur*, vol. 1, 1840

Münter, Friedrich, *Aus den Tagebüchern Friedrich Münters. Wander- und Lehrjahre eines dänischen Gelehrten*, ed. Øjvined Andreasen, Copenhagen and Leipzig: P. Haase & Sohn and Otto Harrassowitz, 1937

Mylius, Christlob, 'Christlob's Mylius Tagebuch seiner Reise von Berlin nach England, 1753', *Johann Bernoulli's Archiv zur neuern Geschichte, Geographie, Natur- und Menschenkenntnis*, vol. 7, Leipzig: Georg Emanuel Beer, 1787

National Library of Australia, *Cook & Omai: The Cult of the South Seas*, exhibition catalogue, Canberra: The Australian National University, 2001

Newell, Jennifer, *Trading Nature: Tahitians, Europeans and Ecological Exchange*, Honolulu: University of Hawai'i Press, 2010

Newell, Jennifer, 'New Ecologies: Pathways in the Pacific, 1760s–1840s', in *Facing Empire: Indigenous Experiences in a Revolutionary Age*, ed. Kate Fullagar and Michael A. McDonnell, Baltimore: Johns Hopkins University Press, 2018

Nicolson, Dan H. and F. Raymond Fosberg, *The Forsters and the Botany of the Second Cook Expedition (1772–1775)*, Ruggell: A.R.G. Gantar Verlag, 2004

Novalis, *Schriften. Die Werke Friedrich von Hardenbergs*, ed. Paul Kluckhohn and Richard Samuel, Stuttgart: Kohlhammer, 1960–2006

Nyree J.C. Zerega, Diane Ragone and Timothy J. Motley, 'Complex Origins of Breadfruit (Artocarpus altilis, Moraceae): Implications for Human Migrations in Oceania', *American Journal of Botany*, vol. 91, no. 5, 2004

Oehler-Klein, Sigrid, 'Soemmerrings Werk aus seiner Kasseler Zeit', in *Samuel Thomas Soemmerring. Naturforscher der Goethezeit in Kassel*, ed. Manfred Wenzel, Kassel: Stadtsparkasse Kassel, 1988

Oliver, Douglas L., *Ancient Tahitian Society*, Honolulu: University of Hawai'i Press, 1974

Osbeck, Peter, *A Voyage to China and the East Indies*, London: Benjamin White, 1771

Peitsch, Helmut, *Georg Forster: A History of his Critical Reception*, New York: Peter Lang, 2001

Pennant, Thomas, *The Literary Life of the late Thomas Pennant Esq., by Himself*, London: Benjamin and John White, and Robert Faulkner, 1793

Peschel, Emil and Eugen Wildenow, *Theodor Körner und die Seinen*, Leipzig: Seemann, 1898

Pickerodt, Gerhart, 'Georg Forster als politischer Schriftsteller,' *Georg-Forster-Studien*, vol. 4, 2000

Pohl, Pieter, *Bilder aus vergangener Zeit*, Hamburg: Agentur des Rauhen Hauses, 1884

Porter, Roy, *Enlightenment: Britain and the Creation of the Modern World*, London: Penguin Books, 2001

Quilitzsch, Uwe, 'Zur Geschichte der Forster-Sammlung in Wörlitz,' in *Georg Forster. Die Südsee in Wörlitz*, ed. Frank Vorpahl, Munich: Hirmer, 2019

Quilitzsch, Uwe, 'Zur Geschichte der Forster-Sammlung in Wörlitz. Georg Forster und das Gartenreich,' in *Weltensammeln. Johann Reinhold und Georg Forster*, ed. Elisabeth Décultot, Janna Kittelmann, Andrea Thiele und Ingo Uhlig, Göttingen: Wallstein Verlag, 2020

Rasmussen, Detlef (ed.), *Goethe und Forster. Studien zum gegenständlichen Dichten*, Bonn: Bouvier, 1985

Rasmussen, Detlef (ed.), *Der Weltumsegler und seine Freunde. Georg Forster als gesellschaftlicher Schriftsteller der Goethezeit*, Tübingen: Gunter Narr Verlag, 1988

Raspe, Rudolf Erich, *Baron Munchausen's Narrative of his Marvellous Travels and Campaigns in Russia* (published anonymously), Oxford, 1785

Reichardt, Rolf (ed.), *Weltbürger – Europäer – Deutscher – Franke: Georg Forster zum 200. Todestag*, exhibition catalogue, Mainz: Universitätsbibliothek, 1994

Rensch, Karl H., 'Wegbereiter der historisch-vergleichenden Sprachwissenschaft: Reinhold und Georg Forster als Erforscher der Sprachen des Pazifiks auf der zweiten Reise von Cook 1772–75,' *Georg-Forster-Studien*, vol. 3, 1999

Ribeiro Sanches, Manuela, 'Dunkelheit und Aufklärung – Rasse und Kultur. Erfahrung und Macht in Forsters Auseinandersetzung mit Kant und Meiners,' *Georg-Forster-Studien*, vol. 8, 2003

Richardson, Brian W., *Longitude and Empire: How Captain Cook's Voyages Changed the World*, Vancouver: University of British Columbia Press, 2005

Rinck, Christoph Friedrich, *Studienreise 1783/84*, ed. Mortiz Geyer, Altenburg: Stephan Seibel Verlagsbuchhandlung, 1897

Rintel, Moses, *Versuch einer skizzirten Beschreibung von Göttingen nach seiner gegenwärtigen Beschaffenheit*, Göttingen: Ruprechtische Buchhandlung, 1794

Roberts, Andrew, *George III: The Life and Reign of Britain's Most Misunderstood Monarch*, London: Allen Lane, 2021

Roberts, Jason, *Every Living Thing: The Great and Deadly Race to Know all Life*, London: Riverrun, 2024

Robertson, Ritchie, *The Enlightenment: The Pursuit of Happiness, 1680–1790*, London: Allen Lane, 2020

Rosove, Michael H., 'Who Discovered the Emperor Penguin? A Historical Survey from James Cook to Robert F. Scott', *Polar Record*, vol. 54, issue 1, 2018

Rousseau, Jean-Jacques, *Discourse on the Origin and the Foundations of Inequality among Men* (1755), in *Discourse on the Origins of Inequality (Second Discourse); Polemics; and Political Economy*, ed. Roger D. Masters and Christopher Kelly, Hanover and London: University of New England, 1992

Rödel, Wolfgang, *Forster und Lichtenberg. Ein Beitrag zum Problem deutsche Intelligenz und Französische Revolution*, Berlin: Rütten & Loening, 1960

Sahmland, Irmtraut, 'Auf der Suche nach dem Stein der Weisen – Samuel Thomas Soemmerring und Georg Forster als Rosenkreuzer', in *Samuel Thomas Soemmerring. Naturforscher der Goethezeit in Kassel*, ed. Manfred Wenzel, Kassel: Stadtsparkasse Kassel, 1988

Sahmland, Irmtraut, 'Georg Forsters Wirken als Freimaurer und Rosenkreuzer', in *Weltbürger – Europäer – Deutscher – Franke: Georg Forster zum 200. Todestag*, exhibition catalogue, ed. Rolf Reichardt, Mainz: Universitätsbibliothek, 1994

Sahmland, Irmtraut, 'Soemmerring als Freimaurer und Rosenkreuzer in Kassel', in *Samuel Thomas Soemmerring in Kassel (1779–1784)*, ed. Manfred Wenzel, Stuttgart, Jena and New York: Gustav Fischer Verlag, 1994

Salmond, Anne, *Two Worlds: First Meetings Between Maori and Europeans, 1642–1772*, Auckland and London: Viking, 1991

Salmond, Anne, *Between Worlds: Early Exchanges Between Maori and Europeans, 1773–1815*, Honolulu: University of Hawai'i Press, 1997

Salmond, Anne, *The Trial of the Cannibal Dog: Captain Cook in the South Seas*, London: Penguin, 2004

Salmond, Anne, *Aphrodite's Island: The European Discovery of Tahiti*, Berkeley, Los Angeles and London: University of California Press, 2009

Salmond, Anne, 'Aphrodite's Island: Sexual Mythologies in Early Contact Tahiti', in *Changing Contexts, Shifting Meanings: Transformations of Cultural Traditions in Oceania*, ed. Elfriede Hermann, Honolulu: University of Hawai'i Press, 2011

Sangmeister, Dirk, 'Der tiefe Zwiespalt zwischen Verlangen und Versagen. Unbekannte Briefe Georg Forsters an Wilhelm Meyer, den Dritten im Bunde', *Lichtenberg-Jahrbuch*, 2018

Sanson, Henry, *Memoirs of the Sansons from Private Notes and Documents, 1688–1847*, London: Chatto and Windus, 1876

Sauer, Walter, 'Angelo Soliman. Mythos und Wirklichkeit', in *Von Soliman zu*

Omofuma. Afrikanische Diaspora in Österreich – 17. bis 20. Jahrhundert, ed. Walter Sauer, Innsbruck, Wien und Bozen: Studien Verlag, 2007

Schama, Simon, *Citizens: A Chronicle of the French Revolution*, London: Penguin Books, 1989

Schäfer, Wolfram, 'Von "Kammermohren", "Mohren"-Tambouren und "Ost-Indianern". Anmerkungen zu Existenzbedingungen und Lebensformen einer Minderheit im 18. Jahrhundert unter besonderer Berücksichtigung der Residenzstadt Kassel', *Hessische Blätter für Volks- und Kulturforschung*, vol. 23, 1988

Scheel, Heinrich (ed.), *Die Mainzer Republik*, Berlin: Akademie-Verlag, 1975–89

Scheuer, Helmut, '"Apostel der Völkerfreiheit" oder "Vaterlandsverräter"? Georg Forster und die Nachwelt', *Georg-Forster-Studien*, vol. 1, 1997

Schiller, Friedrich, *Schillers Werke: Nationalausgabe. Briefwechsel*, ed. Julius Petersen and Gerhard Fricke, Weimar: Böhlaus, 1943–2003

Schiller, Friedrich, *Sämtliche Werke*, ed. Gerhard Fricke et al. , Munich: Hanser, 1962

Schlegel, Friedrich, 'Georg Forster. Fragment einer Charakteristik der deutschen Klassiker' (1797), in *Kritische Friedrich-Schlegel-Ausgabe*, ed. Ernst Behler, Munich: F. Schöningh, 1958–2006

Schlegel, Friedrich, *Kritische Friedrich-Schlegel-Ausgabe*, ed. Ernst Behler, Munich: F. Schöningh, 1958–2006

Schlegel-Schelling, Caroline, *Briefe aus der Frühromantik*, ed. Erich Schmidt, Leipzig: Insel Verlag, 1913

Schreiber, Ilse (ed.), *Ich war wohl klug, daß ich dich fand. Heinrich Christian Boies Briefwechsel mit Luise Mejer*, Munich: C.H. Beck, 1980

Schroeder, David P., *Haydn and the Enlightenment: The Late Symphonies and their Audience*, Oxford: Clarendon Press, 1990

Schuler, Heinz, '"Mozart von der Wohlthätigkeit" – die Mitglieder der gerechten und vollkommenen St.-Johannis-Freimaurer-Loge "Zur Wohltätigkeit" im Orient von Wien', *Mitteilungen der Internationalen Stiftung Mozarteum*, vol. 36, 1988

Schuster, Gabriele, 'Der "Mohr" als Schauobjekt im k.k. Naturalienkabinett Wien', in *Fremde Erfahrungen. Asiaten und Afrikaner in Deutschland, Österreich und in der Schweiz bis 1945*, ed. Gehard Höpp, Berlin: Das Arabische Buch, 1996

Schweigard, Jörg, *Die Liebe zur Freiheit ruft uns an den Rhein. Aufklärung, Reform und Revolution in Mainz*, Gernsbach: Casimir Katz Verlag, 2005

Scurr, Ruth, *Fatal Purity: Robespierre and the French Revolution*, London: Chatto & Windus, 2006

Seibt, Gustav, *Mit einer Art von Wut. Goethe in der Revolution*, Munich: C.H. Beck, 2014

Sides, Hampton, *The Wide Wide Sea: Imperial Ambition, First Contact and the Fateful Final Voyage of Captain James Cook*, New York: Doubleday, 2024

Siegel, Monika, '*Ich hatte einen Hang zur Schwärmerey …*'. *Das Leben der Schriftstellerin und Übersetzerin Meta Forkel-Liebeskind im Spiegel ihrer Zeit*, PhD Thesis, Technische Universität Darmstadt, 2000

Siegel, Monika, 'Meta Forkel-Liebeskind und Georg Forster: Nur eine Arbeitsbeziehung – oder auch Freundschaft?', *Georg-Forster-Studien*, vol. 14, 2009

Smith, Bernhard, 'Coleridge's Ancient Mariner and Cook's Second Voyage', *Journal of the Warburg and Courtauld Institutes*, vol. 19, 1956

Smith, James Edward (ed.), *A Selection of the Correspondence of Linnaeus and other Naturalists*, London: Longman, 1821

Smith, Linda Tuhiwai, *Decolonizing Methodologies: Research and Indigenous People*, London: Bloomsbury Academic, 2024

Smolianinov, M. (ed.), 'Correspondance diplomatique des Représentants de France à la cour de l'Impératrice Catherine II, 1766–1769', *Sbornik Imperatorskago Russkago istoričeskago obščestva* (SIRIO), vol. 141, 1913

Soemmerring, Samuel Thomas, *Ueber die körperliche Verschiedenheit des Negers vom Europäer*, Mainz: no publisher, 1784

Soemmerring, Samuel Thomas, *Ueber die körperliche Verschiedenheit des Negers vom Europäer*, Frankfurt: Barrentrapp Sohn und Wenner, 1785 (extended second edition)

Soemmerring, Samuel Thomas, *Briefwechsel*, ed. Franz Dumont, Stuttgart, Jena and New York: Gustav Fischer Verlag, 1996–2001

Sparrman, Anders, *A Voyage of the Cape of Good Hope, towards the Antarctic Polar Circle, and Round the World: but Chiefly into the Country of the Hottentots and Caffres, from the Year 1772 to 1776*, Dublin: White, Cash and Byrne, 1785

Sparrman, Anders, *A Voyage Round the World with Captain James Cook in H.M.S. Resolution*, ed. Owen Butter, London: Robert Hale, 1953

Steiner, Gerhard, 'Johann Reinhold Forsters und Georg Forsters Beziehungen zu Russland', in *Studien zur Geschichte der russischen Literatur des 18. Jahrhunderts*, ed. Helmut Grasshoff and Ulf Lehmann, Berlin: Akademie-Verlag, 1968

Steiner, Gerhard, 'Aspekte der Beziehungen Georg Forsters zu den Geheimbünden', in *Ethik in der Geschichte von Medizin und Naturwissenschaften*, ed. Wolfram Kaiser and Arina Völker, Halle-Wittenberg: Martin-Luther-Universität, 1985a

Steiner, Gerhard, *Freimaurer und Rosenkreuzer – Georg Forsters Weg durch Geheimbünde*, Berlin: Akademie-Verlag, 1985b

Survey of London, *The Parish of St Pancras Part 3: Tottenham Court Road and Neighbourhood*, vol. 21, London: London County Council, London, 1949

Taonui, Rawiri, 'Polynesian Oral Traditions', *Vaka moana: Voyages of the Ancestors. The Discovery and Settlement of the Pacific*, ed. K.R. Howe, Auckland: Auckland War Memorial Museum, 2006

Taylor, John Patrick, *The Other Side: Ways of Being and Place in Vanuatu*, Honolulu: University of Hawai'i Press, 2008

Thomas, Nicholas, *In Oceania: Visions, Artifacts, Histories*, Durham, NC: Duke University Press, 1997

Thomas, Nicholas, *Voyagers: The Settlement of the Pacific*, London: Apollo, 2021

Thyng, Alana, 'Maori Artifacts Cross Cultures: Johann Reinhold and Georg Forster's

Nephrite Objects at Wörlitz', in *Weltensammeln. Johann Reinhold und Georg Forster*, ed. Elisabeth Décultot, Janna Kittelmann, Andrea Thiele und Ingo Uhlig, Göttingen: Wallstein Verlag, 2020

Titius, D.C.H., 'Auszug aus dem Reisejournal Herrn D. Carl Heinrich Titius ... in dem Jahr 1777 durch Deutschland, nach Holland, Engeland und Frankreich angestellten Reise', *Johann Bernoulli's Sammlung kurzer Reisebeschreibungen und anderer zur Erweiterung der Länder- und Menschenkenntniß dienender Nachrichten*, vol. 10, Berlin: Johann Bernoulli, 1783

Todd, Janet, *Mary Wollstonecraft: A Revolutionary Life*, New York: Columbia University Press, 2000

Tcherkézoff, Serge, *'First Contacts' in Polynesia: The Samoan Case (1722–1848). Western Misunderstandings about Sexuality and Divinity*, Canberra: ANU Press, 2008

Tcherkézoff, Serge, 'A Reconsideration of the Role of Polynesian Women in Early Encounters with Europeans: Supplement to Marshall Sahlins' Voyage around the Islands of History', in *Oceanic Encounters: Exchange, Desire, Violence*, ed. Margaret Jolly, Serge Tcherkézoff and Darrell T. Tyron, Acton: Australian National University Press, 2009

Turner, Samuel Wilhelm, 'Kurze Nachrichten aus dem Leben verschiedener verstorbener Mitglieder', *Der Gesellschaft der naturforschenden Freunde zu Berlin Neue Schriften*, vol. 2, 1799

Uhlig, Ludwig, *Georg Forster: Einheit und Mannigfaltigkeit in seiner geistigen Welt*, Tübingen: Max Niemeyer Verlag, 1965

Uhlig, Ludwig, '*Instructio peregrinatoris*. Georg Forsters Lehrjahre im Schatten seines Vaters', *Euphorion*, vol. 94, 2000

Uhlig, Ludwig, *Georg Forster. Lebensabenteuer eines gelehrten Weltbürgers (1754–1794)*, Göttingen: Vandenhoeck & Ruprecht, 2004

Uhlig, Ludwig, 'Erkenntnisfortschritt und Traditionsbindung in Georg Forsters naturwissenschaftlichem Werk', *Georg-Forster-Studien*, vol. 15, 2010

Uhlig, Ludwig, 'Die Südseevölker und Georg Forsters Rassenbegriff', *Georg-Forster-Studien*, vol. 15, 2010

Uhlig, Ludwig, 'Herder und Georg Forster: Affinitäten und gegenseitige Anregungen', *Georg-Forster-Studien*, vol. 17, 2012

Unterberger, Rose, *Die Goethe-Chronik*, Frankfurt and Leipzig: Insel Verlag, 2002

Vennel, Robert, *The Meaning of Trees: The History and Use of New Zealand's Native Plants*, Auckland: HarperCollins, 2019

Vieweg, Klaus, *Hegel. Der Philosoph der Freiheit*, Munich: C.H. Beck, 2020

Voltaire, François-Marie Arouet, *Oeuvres complètes de Voltaire*, Paris: Garnier Frères, 1879

Vorpahl, Frank, *Der Welterkundler: Auf der Suche nach Georg Forster*, Berlin: Galiani, 2018

Vorpahl, Frank, 'Ulu im Umu: Von Forsters *Brodbaum* zu Global Breadfruit', *Georg-Forster-Studien*, vol. 21, 2018

Vorpahl, Frank (ed.), *Georg Forster. Die Südsee in Wörlitz*, Munich: Hirmer, 2019

Wahl, *Hans and Anton Kippenberg, Goethe und seine Welt*, Leipzig: Insel Verlag, 1932

Wales, William, 'Journal of a Voyage, Made by Order of the Royal Society, to Churchill River, on the North-West Coast of Hudson's Bay, of Thirteen Months Residence in That Country; and of the Voyage Back to England, in the Years 1768 and 1769', *Philosophical Transactions of the Royal Society*, vol. 60, 1770

Wales, William, *Remarks on Mr. Forster's Account of Captain Cook's last Voyage round the World, in the Years 1772, 1773, 1774, and 1775*, London, 1778, in *A Voyage Round the World: George Forster*, ed. Nicholas Thomas and Oliver Berghof, Honolulu: University of Hawai'i Press, 2000

Wales, William and Joseph Dymond, 'Observations on the State of the Air, Winds, Weather, &c. Made at Prince of Wales's Fort, on the North-West Coast of Hudson's Bay, in the Years 1768 and 1769', *Philosophical Transactions of the Royal Society*, vol. 60, 1770

Walpole, Horace, *Horace Walpole's Correspondence*, ed. W.S. Lewis, New Haven and London: Yale University Press, 1937–61

Wenzel, Manfred (ed.), *Samuel Thomas Soemmerring in Kassel (1779–1784)*, Stuttgart, Jena and New York: Gustav Fischer Verlag, 1994

Wenzel, Manfred, '"Der gute Mann half mir noch füllen ..." Soemmerrings Experimente aus der Frühzeit der Ballonfahrt', in *Samuel Thomas Soemmerring. Naturforscher der Goethezeit in Kassel*, ed. Manfred Wenzel, Kassel: Stadtsparkasse Kassel, 1988a

Wenzel, Manfred, '"Eine für die hiesige Gegend gar seltene Erscheinung . . ." Goethe, Soemmerring und der Elefant aus der Menagerie von Friedrich II. von Hessen-Kassel', in *Samuel Thomas Soemmerring. Naturforscher der Goethezeit in Kassel*, ed. Manfred Wenzel, Kassel: Stadtsparkasse Kassel, 1988b

White, Gilbert, *The Life and Letters of Gilbert White of Selborne*, ed. Rashleigh Holt-White, London: John Murray, 1901

Whitehead, P.J.P., 'The Forster Collection of Zoological Drawings in the British Museum (Natural History)', *Bulletin of the British Museum (Natural History)*, vol. 6, no. 2, 1978

Wiegand, Dometa, 'Alexander von Humboldt and Samuel Taylor Coleridge: The Intersection of Science and Poetry', *Coleridge Bulletin*, 2002

Wieland, Christoph Martin, *Wielands Briefwechsel*, ed. Siegried Scheibe and Annerose Schneider, Berlin: Akademie Verlag, 1992–94

Wienecke, Barbara, 'The History and the Discovery of Emperor Penguin Colonies', 1902–2004', *Polar Record*, vol. 46, issue 3, 2010

Wigger, Iris and Spencer Hadley, 'Angelo Soliman: Desecrated Bodies and the Spectre of Enlightenment Racism', *Race and Class*, vol. 62, issue 2, 2020

Wolff, Charlotta, *Noble Conceptions of Politics in Eighteenth-Century Sweden (ca. 1740–1790)*, Helsinki: Finnish Literature Society, 2016

Wollstonecraft, Mary, *Vindication of the Rights of Women with Strictures on Political and Moral Subjects* (1792), Dublin: James Moore, 1793

Wulf, Andrea, *Brother Gardeners: Botany, Empire and the Birth of an Obsession*, London: William Heinemann, 2008

Wulf, Andrea, *Magnificent Rebels: The First Romantics and the Invention of the Self*, London: John Murray, 2022

Young, George, *The Life and Voyages of Captain James Cook*, London: Whittaker, Treacher & Co, 1836

Zimmermann, Curt, *F.L.W. Meyer, sein Leben und seine schriftstellerische Wirksamkeit*, Halle: Ehrhardt Karras, 1890

Zincke, Paul, *Georg Forster nach seinen Originalbriefen*, Dortmund: F.W. Ruhfus, 1915

Züge, Christian Gottlob, *Der russische Colonist oder Christian Gottlob Züge's Leben in Rußland*, Webel: Zeitz und Naumberg, 1802

Acknowledgements

I'm a writer – a writer of stories, a writer of ideas, a writer of past lives. It's the best job ever – sometimes lonely (which I also like to a certain degree), mostly mind-expandingly wonderful. This is my eighth book – and I think it's time to start my acknowledgements with those people who allow me to be a writer. My readers. Thank you to each and every one of you. Thank you for reading my books – for enjoying them, for writing to me to share your thoughts, for giving them as presents to friends, family and colleagues, for believing that the past is still important, and for spending your precious time with my words. It is an honour and privilege to be read by you.

Following and unearthing George Forster's search for our shared humanity has allowed me to meet and work with a great many remarkable human beings over the past few years. This has been especially joyful after the solitude of writing during the pandemic. So, it's with the greatest pleasure and humble gratitude that I would like to thank the many wonderful individuals who have made the writing of *The Traveler* richer, better and rewarding.

Thank you for reading, commenting, helping, finding, sharing, shaping, listening, explaining, guiding, walking with me and so much more. Thank you (in alphabetical order) to Paul Atallah for a tour of Huahine; Volker Böge and all the organizers and contributors of the inspiring Pacific Islands workshop, 'Climate Loss, Conflict and Peace: Relational Responses to Existential Crisis'; Antje Boetius for introducing me to the Okeanos Foundation; Katharina Bott; Markley Boyer, tech extraordinaire, for converting eighteenth-century Latin botanical treatises into English; at the Brandenburgische Akademie der Wissenschaften I would like to thank Carmen Götz, Tobias Kraft and Ingo Schwarz for their steadfast support – and Christina Wilke at the archive; Jake Bransgrove for pointing me to Banks' eccentric 'Book of weights'; Hinanui Cauchois at the Museum of Tahiti and The Islands; Diane Coleman Brandt for a long walk through Göttingen and emergency scans of letters; Andreas Christoph at Thüringer Universitäts- und Landesbibliothek Jena for digitalizing obscure sources; Julia Donaldson at Harris Manchester College, Oxford; Michael Ewert at the Georg-Forster-Society for invaluable help throughout and for his generous comments on the manuscript; Christian Fieseler at Georg-August-Universität Göttingen for a fabulous tour through the historic buildings and collections; Anette Froesch at Kulturstiftung Dessau-Wörlitz; Ulrich Joost at TU Darmstadt for a wonderful tour of Göttingen and Lichtenberg's letters;

Moeata Galenon, the first female Polynesian navigator to be trained in the ancestral knowledge of wayfinding, for sharing her knowledge and showing me the traditional double-hulled canoe Fa'afeite in Tahiti; Christian Hain at the Goethe-Schiller-Archiv in Weimar; Andrea Hart at the Natural History Museum Library in London and the rest of the library team; Iris Hartmann at the Mainz Wissenschaftliche Stadtbibliothek; at Heritage Expedition I would like to thank Lyn Wade and Marcus Richards for being such knowledgeable guides in Dusky Sound; Julia Hoffmann for generously sharing her contacts in Kassel and Göttingen, and for showing me the water displays in Bergpark Kassel-Wilhelmshöhe; Matthias Claudius Hofmann at the Museum der Weltkulturen, Frankfurt; Beate Hofmann and Kai Jakob at Städtische Museen Hanau; Frank Holl; Simone Hübner at the Städtisches Museum Göttingen; Sandra Knapp at the Natural History Museum, London, for opening George Forster's herbarium and for looking through Reinhold Forster's Latin list of plants in the middle of the International Botanical Congress; Eliane Koller; Lasinga Koloamatangi for sharing his stories from Tonga; Laurie Launey; Bertram Lesser at Staatsbibliothek Berlin; everybody at the beloved London Library; Naïki Lutz for a tour of Raiatea and sharing the magic of Taputapuatea; Laura Metz and Bianca Slowik at the Germanisches Nationalmuseum Nürnberg; Keith Moore at the Royal Society London; Monika Müller at the Forschungsbibliothek Gotha der Universität Erfurt; Anna Naupa for contacts in Vanuatu; Ingo Pfeifer for a lovely tour of Wörlitz; Christina Reich at the Stadtmuseum Kassel; Lisa Marie Roemer at the Universitätsbibliothek Mainz; Victoria Rozemblum at Vilnius University Library; Andreas Schlüter at the Herzogin Anna Amalia Bibliothek in Weimar; Oliver Schröer at the Stadtarchiv Göttingen; Ruth Scurr; Marion Struck-Garbe for generously sharing her knowledge of Tonga; Susanne Speth and Regina Zölßmann at the Stadtarchiv Mainz; and a big thank you to Tahiti Tourism for organizing such a fabulous trip to French Polynesia; Rakeipoho Taiaroa from Tūwharetoa Māori Trust Board; Nicholas Thomas at the Museum of Archaeology and Anthropology, Cambridge, for discussing the Forsters with me (and his wonderful books); Teivo Vero, owner of *Moana Explorer* in Tahiti, for a thrilling sailing trip; Lyuba Vinogradova and Zhanna Beresneva for Russian research, and for thinking around corners in their effort to locate the long-lost report that Reinhold Forster wrote about the conditions of the Volga settlers – but sadly the report really seems to be lost; Karl-Hermann Wegner, former director of the Stadtmuseum Kassel and Andrea Linnebach for a magical tour of Kassel.

I always imagined this book filled with illustrations – engravings and paintings of all the places George Forster travelled to and lived in, portraits of him and his friends, and of course, his own drawings. This would not have been possible without the many museums, libraries and archives that have made their out-of-copyright collections freely available, as well as those which generously allowed me to reproduce their material at a significant discount. So, a huge thank you to: Deutsche Fotothek; Forschungsbibliothek Gotha der Universität Erfurt; Germanisches

Nationalmuseum, Nürnberg; Historische Museum der Pfalz; Metropolitan Museum of Art, New York; Mitchell Library, the State Library of New South Wales; Wien Museum; the National Library of Australia; Natural History Museum, London; Musée Carnavalet, Histoire de Paris; Museum of New Zealand Te Papa Tongarewa; Rijksmuseum, Amsterdam; SLUB Dresden; Stadtarchiv Mainz; Stadtmuseum Göttingen; Stadtmuseum Kassel; SUB Göttingen; Universitätsbibliothek Kassel; Universitätsbibliothek Leipzig; Vilnius University Library; Wellcome Collection, London; and Yale Center for British Art, Paul Mellon Collection.

And now some extra special thanks:

Thank you to Kirsty Lang – wise, insightful, funny, and the best title-finder ever, thank you so much for coming up *again* with the perfect title – first *Magnificent Rebels* and now *The Traveler*. And thank you to the big heart and smile that is my intrepid Kiwi friend Joanna Grochowicz, who turned my New Zealand trip into something truly special. She introduced me to Pania Tyson-Nathan at New Zealand Māori Tourism and her fabulous team Gail Parata and Lee Beazley, who pulled out all stops on the North Island in true Māori hospitality – with special thanks to Ceillhe Sperath from Time Unlimited Tours, who ensured that we wouldn't starve by dropping off six huge bags full of food for the journey. And thank you to Joanna's generous mother Honey Cunningham for letting us stay in her house to recover from jet lag. Best start to my Aotearoa adventure. Thank you!

I continue to be astonished that the Santa Fe Institute invites me back again and again – their very generous Miller Scholarship has allowed me to write and think in the glorious mountains of New Mexico. It has become something like a second home. *The Traveler* is the first book that has accompanied me to the SFI from its proposal stage to the very end. There are too many inspiring, fun and fabulous people in Santa Fe to list them all but my special thanks go to the brilliant and polymathic David Krakauer (although he teases me about my pathetically old-fashioned database), Kate Joyce, Cris Moore and Tracy Conrad (best cocktails and ribs in town), Chris Kempe, Caroline Seigel, Renee Tursi and Jen Leighton. Thank you for your generosity, creative minds and hospitality.

I've also been incredibly lucky to have received a very generous grant from the wonderful Okeanos Foundation – with particular thanks to marvellous whale whisperer Dieter Paulmann and wonderful Jana Steingässer – thank you, thank you! I don't know what I would have done without you.

I'm grateful to my wonderful publishers in the UK and US. This is my first book with Allen Lane and I have loved working with Stuart Proffitt – insightful, unbelievably knowledgeable, and *genau* as we say in German. And after many years, I finally got to work together with Annabel Huxley, who knows exactly what she's doing. And thank you to Vartika Rastogi, Richard Duguid, my copy-editor Richard Mason, and the rest of the Allen Lane team. Knopf has been the US home for my books for the past two decades – it's a privilege to be published by them. A very big thank you to my editor Edward Kastenmeier for believing in me and for the many wise comments and edits during those years. And thank you to Chris Howard-Woods, Margot Lee, Jess Purcell, Sara Eagle and the rest of the team.

And thank you to the fabulous PEW Literary Agency team: Alex Chernova, Dorcas Rogers, Cora MacGregor, and the remarkable Margaret Halton who spins the globe for us authors so that we are published across the world. I wouldn't be the writer I am without my friend and agent Patrick Walsh. In 2002 he plucked me from the darkness and has been my greatest supporter ever since – always present, always magnificent. With love, kindness, insightful advice, tough edits and roaring laughter, he has shaped and defined me as a writer. Patrick understands me so well that he knows exactly when to push me harder and when to comfort a panicking author. Thank you for everything.

A big fat thank you to my friends and family for supporting me in so many different ways. To my mother Brigitte Wulf for deciphering German letters and diary entries; to Linnéa – my Pippilotta – for being the best daughter on this planet and for making me a grandmother of two gorgeous boys; to Trixi Wulf for being part of the team; to Saskia Manners for being the mothership and those countless dinners you cook for me; to Katharina Kroll for a regular Berlin research base which included bed, delicious food, drinks and laughter; to Misha Glenny, who makes me think around corners; to Regan Ralph for support, words, and wisdom.

I will never take for granted the people in my life who spend a great many days reading and commenting on my writing when it's still a messy raw thing. Before anyone else sees the manuscript, they plough their way through it. So, thank you to my brilliant father Herbert Wulf for going through *The Traveler* in all its many versions and your comments; and thank you to my wonderful friend Victoria Johnson who dissects and suggests with love yet also with steely candour (and a hallelujah to technology that connects us across too many thousands of miles). And as always, a massive thank you to my oldest (of course not in age, just in friendship time) and wise friend Julia-Niharika Sen for working through *The Traveler* line by line – taking it apart, advising, suggesting, and always improving – thank you for somehow finding the hours and days, and for being there for me (sometimes even just across the courtyard) despite the difficult times.

And thank you to Reiner, the best of all men . . . where to begin? Thank you for feeding a perpetually hungry woman with the most delicious food, and battling slugs and deer to grow fresh vegetables. Thank you for letting me write at all hours, for your love and for coming along on the Forster ride with me – from Kassel and Mainz to Dusky Sound, from Santa Fe and Göttingen to Huahine and Taputapuatea, and then all the way back to the far north. And thank you for so much more (you know what it is).

Picture Credits

BLACK AND WHITE

Frontispiece: *George Forster*, unknown artist, Deutsche Fotothek

[p. 2] *View of the Island of Tanna*, W. Woollett after William Hodges, 1777, Wellcome Collection, London

[p. 10] *Le cours de la rivière de wolga anciennement appellée Rha*, Adam Olearius, 1659, Gallica – Bibliothèque nationale de France, Paris

[p. 11] *Detail of View of Burgfeld and Nassenhuben*, J. Wandelaar after J.B. Hoffmann, 1721, Rijksmuseum, Amsterdam

[p. 12] *Johann Reinhold Forster*, J.F. Brause after Anton Graff, 1781, 15/103, Universitätsbibliothek Leipzig, Porträtstichsammlung

[p. 23] *City of London from Somerset House*, unknown artist, ca. 1780, Yale Center for British Art, Paul Mellon Collection, New Haven, CT

[p. 29] *The Royal Society at Crane Court*, Wood after [W.H.], 1877, Wellcome Collection, London

[p. 43] *James Cook*, J.K. Sherwin, after N. Dance, 1779, Mitchell Library, State Library of New South Wales, Sydney

[p. 47] *The Ice Islands, seen the 9th of January 1773*, B.T. Pouncy after William Hodges, 1777, Mitchell Library, State Library of New South Wales, Sydney

[p. 49] *The German Doctor with his Family on his Travels to England*, unknown artist, ca. 1775, National Library of Australia, Canberra

[p. 57] *Family in Dusky Bay, New Zealand*, Lerperniere after William Hodges, 1777, Mitchell Library, State Library of New South Wales, Sydney

[p. 63] *Māori of New Zealand*, Michel after William Hodges, 1777, Mitchell Library, State Library of New South Wales, Sydney

[p. 67] *A New Zealand Warrior in his Proper Dress, & Completely Armed, according to their Manner*, T. Chambers after Sydney Parkinson, 1784, Mitchell Library, State Library of New South Wales, Sydney

[p. 71] *The Island of Otahiete bearing S.E.*, W. Watts after William Hodges, 1777, Mitchell Library, State Library of New South Wales, Sydney

[p. 79] *Heads of divers Nations of the Islands of Otaheite, Huaheine, & Oheiteroah*, T. Chambers after Sydney Parkinson, 1784, Wellcome Collection, London

[p. 80] *A Toupapow with a Corpse on it, Attended by the Chief Mourner in his Habit of Ceremony*, W. Woollett after William Hodges, 1777, Mitchell Library, State Library of New South Wales, Sydney

[p. 82] *View of Huaheine*, W. Byrne after J. Webber, 1784, Mitchell Library, State Library of New South Wales, Sydney

[p. 86] *O-Hedidee*, J. Caldwall after William Hodges, 1777, Mitchell Library, State Library of New South Wales, Sydney

[p. 93] *Omai* [sic], J. Caldwall after William Hodges, 1777, Mitchell Library, State Library of New South Wales, Sydney

[p. 98] *A View of the Island of Rotterdam*, W. Byrne after William Hodges, 1777, Mitchell Library, State Library of New South Wales, Sydney

[p. 104] *Chart of Cook Strait*, J. Ryland, 1773, Mitchell Library, State Library of New South Wales, Sydney

[p. 105] *The Infide of a Hippah, in New Zealand*, B.T. Pouncy after John Webber, 1784, Mitchell Library, State Library of New South Wales, Sydney

[p. 117] *Monuments in Easter Island*, W. Woollett after William Hodges, 1777, Mitchell Library, State Library of New South Wales, Sydney

[p. 118] *Man of Easter Island*, W. Woollett after William Hodges, 1777, Mitchell Library, State Library of New South Wales, Sydney

[p. 121] *The Fleet of Otaheite assembled at Oparee*, W. Woollett after William Hodges, 1777, Mitchell Library, State Library of New South Wales, Sydney

[p. 126] *The Landing at Erramanga one of the New Hebrides*, J.K. Sherwin after William Hodges, 1777, Mitchell Library, State Library of New South Wales, Sydney

[p. 129] *The Landing at Tanna, one of the New Hebrides*, J.K. Sherwin after William Hodges, 1777, Mitchell Library, State Library of New South Wales, Sydney

[p. 131] *Man of the Island of Tanna*, J. Basire after William Hodges, 1777, Mitchell Library, State Library of New South Wales, Sydney

[p. 131] *Woman of the Island of Tanna*, J. Basire after William Hodges, 1777, Mitchell Library, State Library of New South Wales, Sydney

[p. 135] *Specimens of New Zealand workmanship*, in Cook 1777, vol. 1, plate xix, Mitchell Library, State Library of New South Wales, Sydney

[p. 136] *Ornaments, utensils, and weapons at the Friendly Isles*, in Cook 1777, vol. 1, plate xxi, Mitchell Library, State Library of New South Wales, Sydney

[p. 142] *Sauvage de la Nouvelle-Calédonie lançant une zagaie*, Copia after Peron, 1800, Mitchell Library, State Library of New South Wales, Sydney

[p. 146] *Christmas Sound, Tierra del Fuego*, W. Watts after William Hodges, 1777, Mitchell Library, State Library of New South Wales, Sydney

[p. 147] *Man in Christmas Sound, Tierra del Fuego*, J. Basire after William Hodges, 1777, Mitchell Library, State Library of New South Wales, Sydney

[p. 149] *South Island Robin* (*Petroica australis*), George Forster, 1773, plate 146, Natural History Museum, London

[p. 150] *Delphinus delphis*, George Forster, 1774, plate 31, Natural History Museum, London

[p. 162] *Johann Reinhold Forster and George Forster*, Daniel Berger, 1782, Historisches Museum der Pfalz, Speyer

[p. 175] *Le Jardin du Roi de Tuileries, Paris*, Reinier Vinkeles, 1770, Rijksmuseum, Amsterdam

[p. 178] *Benjamin Franklin*, after C.N. Cochin, 1777, Wellcome Collection, London

[p. 187] *Friedrich Heinrich Jacobi*, C.G. Geyser after Johann Friedrich Eich, undated, Rijksmuseum, Amsterdam

[p. 189] *Georg Christoph Lichtenberg*, F.W. Bollinger after J.L. Strecker, undated, Wellcome Collection, London

[p. 193] Samuel Thomas Soemmerring, Ambroise Tardieu after Johann Valentin Bender, undated, 49/19, Universitätsbibliothek Leipzig, Porträtstichsammlung

[p. 195] *Das Orangerieschloss, Kassel*, Johann Heinrich Tischbein the Elder, 1783, SLo 0002, Stadtmuseum Kassel

[p. 201] *Universitäts Bibliothec*, Georg Daniel Heumann, 1748, SUB Göttingen

[p. 203] *Therese Heyne-Forster-Huber*, unknown artist, undated, Cod. Ms. Th. Huber 7, Nr. 7, SUB Göttingen

[p. 205] Vignette in *Freymäurische Versammlungsreden der Gold- und Rosenkreuzer des alten Systems*, 1779, Amsterdam

[p. 214] *Christian Gottlob Heyne*, E.L. Riepenhausen after Johann Heinrich Wilhelm Tischbein, undated, Rijksmuseum, Amsterdam

[p. 218] Detail of *Am Leinekanal, Blick nach Süden, Göttingen*, Friedrich Besemann, ca. 1820, Städtisches Museum Göttingen

[p. 222] *A Dance in Otaheite*, J.K. Sherwin after John Webber, 1784, Mitchell Library, State Library of New South Wales, Sydney

[p. 224] *George Forster*, after Anton Graff, 1784, Deutsche Fotothek

[p. 226] *Der Feuerwerksplatz im Prater, Vienna*, Johann Ziegler, 1783, Wien Museum, Vienna

[p. 232] *Ansicht vom Graben gegen den Kohlmarkt*, Carl Schütz, ca. 1792, Wien Museum, Vienna

[p. 234] *A young woman of the Sandwich Islands*, J.K. Sherwin after J. Webber, 1784, Wellcome Collection, London

[p. 235] *Vilnius*, Józef Peska, 1808, Vilnius University Library

[p. 236] *The Grand Courtyard of Vilnius University*, Pranciškus Smuglevičius, 1786, Vilnius University Library

[p. 239] *Friedrich Ludwig Wilhelm Meyer*, Silhouetten-Sammlung Carl Friedrich Schubert, 1777–79, 8 Cod. Ms. hist. lit. 103 Cim., Nr. 120, SUB Göttingen

[p. 255] *Hessen-Kasselischer Truppenbestand und Uniformtafeln*, 1785, 2° Ms. Hass. 267(1), Universitätsbibliothek Kassel, Landesbibliothek und Murhardsche Bibliothek der Stadt Kassel

[p. 256] *Angelo Soliman*, G. Haid after J.N. Steiner, ca. 1760–65, Wien Museum, Vienna

[p. 274] *Ansicht von Mainz*, before 1793, Kartensammlung, SLUB/KS B4247, Universitätsbibliothek Dresden

[p. 277] *Ludwig Ferdinand Huber*, Dora Stock, 1788, Peschel 1898

[p. 280] *Caricature George Forster*, unknown artist, 1785, Cod. Ms. Lichtenberg IV, 42 a: Bl. 1, SUB Göttingen

[p. 282] *Prise de la Bastille le 14 Juillet 1789*, Charles Thévenin, ca. 1793, Metropolitan Museum of Art, New York

[p. 291] *Alexander von Humboldt*, A.G.L. Desnoyers, 1805, private collection

[p. 294] *View of towpath and canal from The Hague to Delft*, Paulus Constantijn la Farque, 1764, Rijksmuseum, Amsterdam

[p. 299] *Matlock Tor*, Samuel Middiman, 1785, Yale Center for British Art, Paul Mellon Collection, New Haven, CT

[p. 300] *Aux bons citoyens travailleurs du Champ de Mars*, unknown artist, 1790, Paris Musées, Musée Carnavalet, Histoire de Paris, Paris

[p. 304] *Ansicht der Festung Ehrenbreitstein*, J. Ziegler after Laurenz Janscha, 1792, *Fünfzig malerische Ansichten Rhein-Stroms von Speyer bis Düsseldorf*, Vienna: Artaria, 1798

[p. 310] *Caroline Michaelis-Böhmer-Schlegel-Schelling*, after Johann Friedrich August Tischbein, 1798, Wahl 1932

[p. 312] *Meta Wedekind-Forkel*, in Gregorius Franz von Berceviczy's album, ca. 1784–86, in *Zeitschrift für Bücherfreunde*, 1921

[p. 314] *Ansicht der Orangerie des Schloss Favorite in Mainz*, J.A. Delsenbach after Salomon Kleiner, 1726, BPSP 01875. 9B, Stadtarchiv Mainz

[p. 317] *Massacre à la prison du Châtelet et à la maison de Bicêtre, les 2–3 septembre 1792*. Estampe en deux tableaux pp. 427 et 429 du Journal des Révolutions de Paris dès 1–8 septembre 1792, unknown artist, Paris Musées, Musée Carnavalet, Histoire de Paris, Paris

[p. 323] *Sitzung des Mainzer Jakobiner Klub*, Johann Jacob Hoch, 1792, BPSF 2778A, Stadtarchiv Mainz

[p. 328] *Baal der Freyheit und Gleichheit zu Mainz*, unknown artist, ca. 1793, Germanisches Nationalmuseum, Nürnberg

[p. 330] Detail of *Journée du 21 janvier 1793. La mort de Louis Capet sur la Place de la Révolution*, engraved by Isidore-Stanislas Helman after Charles Monnet, 1794, Paris Musées, Musée Carnavalet, Histoire de Paris, Paris

[p. 335] *National Assembly, Paris*, unknown artist, 1795, Yale Center for British Art, Paul Mellon Collection, New Havén, CT

[p. 345] *Rév. de Paris. Brissot et 20. de ses Complices à la Guillotine*, unknown artist, 1793, Paris Musées, Musée Carnavalet, Histoire de Paris, Paris

COLOUR PLATES

1. *HMS Resolution*, Henry Roberts, 1772–75, Mitchell Library, State Library of New South Wales, Sydney
2. *Reinhold and George Forster*, Jean-François Rigaud, ca. 1780, National Portrait Gallery, Parkes, Australia

3. *Ice Islands*, George Forster, ca. 1773, Mitchell Library, State Library of New South Wales, Sydney
4. *Dusky Sound*, William Hodges, 1772–75, Mitchell Library, State Library of New South Wales, Sydney
5. *Pickersgill Harbour, Dusky Bay, New Zealand*, William Hodges, c. 1776, National Maritime Museum, Greenwich, London
6. *Blue Petrel* (*Halobaena caerulea*), George Forster, Memb.I 131, Forschungsbibliothek Gotha der Universität Erfurt
7. *Tūī* (*Prosthemadera novaeseelandiae*), George Forster, Memb.I 131, Forschungsbibliothek Gotha der Universität Erfurt
8. *Cook's Scorpionfish* (*Scorpaena cardenalis*), George Forster, 1773, plate 190, Natural History Museum, London
9. *Ship Cove, Queen Charlotte Sound, New Zealand*, John Webber, ca. 1788, Museum of New Zealand Te Papa Tongarewa, Wellington
10. *Fantail* (*Rhipidura fuliginosa*), George Forster, Memb.I 131, Forschungsbibliothek Gotha der Universität Erfurt
11. *A View of Matavai Bay in the Island of Otaheite*, William Hodges, 1776, Yale Center of British Art, Paul Mellon Collection, New Haven, CT
12. *Breadfruit* (*Artocarpus communis* J.R. & G. Forst.), J. Pass after J. Ihle, ca. 1796, Wellcome Collection, London
13. *Red Shining Parrot* (*Prosopeia tabuensis*), George Forster, Memb.I 131, Forschungsbibliothek Gotha der Universität Erfurt

14 and 15. *Green kākā* (*Nestor meridionalis*), George Forster, 1773, plate 50, Natural History Museum, London

16. *Atlantic Yellow-nosed Aalbatross* (*Thalassarche chlororhynchos*), George Forster, 1772–75, plate 99, Natural History Museum, London
17. *Bearded Penguin* (*Pygoscelis antarcticus*), George Forster, 1773, plate 80, Natural History Museum, London
18. *Spotted Eagle Ray* (*Aetobatus narinari*), George Forster, 1774, plate 250, Natural History Museum, London
19. *Blue Morning Glory* (*Ipomoea indica*), George Forster, 1774, plate 70, Natural History Museum, London
20. *Passiflora aurantia* (G. Forst), George Forster, 1774, plate 349, Natural History Museum, London
21. *Barringtonia asiatica*, George Forster, 1773–74, plate 266, Natural History Museum, London
22. *George Forster*, attributed to Johann Heinrich Tischbein the Elder, ca. 1784, Museum der Weltkulturen, Frankfurt
23. *A View of Somerset House with St. Mary's Church in the Strand, London*, Thomas Bowles III, mid-eighteenth century, Yale Center of British Art, Paul Mellon Collection, New Haven, CT

24. *The Palais Royal Garden Walk*, L. Lecoeur after Claude Louis Desrais, 1787, Rijksmuseum, Amsterdam
25. *Friedrichsplatz, Kassel*, Werner Kobold, 1789, SL0 0104, Stadtmuseum Kassel
26. *Stadtansicht um 1790, Mainz*, BSP262B, Stadtarchiv Mainz
27. *George Forster*, unknown artist, 1789, BPSG/00041, Stadtarchiv Mainz
28. *Therese Forster*, unknown artist, 1789, BPSG/00040, Stadtarchiv Mainz

Index

Also by Andrea Wulf

This Other Eden: Seven Great Gardens and 300 Years of English History (with Emma Gieben-Gamal)

The Brother Gardeners: Botany, Empire and the Birth of an Obsession

The Founding Gardeners: How the Revolutionary Generation Created an American Eden

Chasing Venus: The Race to Measure the Heavens

The Invention of Nature: Alexander von Humboldt's New World

The Adventures of Alexander von Humboldt (with Lillian Melcher)

Magnificent Rebels: The First Romantics and the Invention of the Self